CW00538660

Studies in Church History

52

(2016)

DOUBTING CHRISTIANITY:
THE CHURCH AND DOUBT

DOUBTING CHRISTIANITY:
THE CHURCH AND DOUBT

EDITED BY

FRANCES ANDREWS

CHARLOTTE METHUEN

ANDREW SPICER

PUBLISHED FOR
THE ECCLESIASTICAL HISTORY SOCIETY
BY
CAMBRIDGE UNIVERSITY PRESS
2016

Published by Cambridge University Press
on behalf of the Ecclesiastical History Society
University Printing House, Cambridge CB2 8BS, United Kingdom

First published 2016

ISBN 978-1-107-18073-4

ISSN 0424–2084

Bible quotations are taken from the following versions:

Revised Standard Version, copyright © 1946, 1952 and 1971 the Division of
Christian Education of the National Council of the Churches of Christ in the
United States of America. Used by permission. All rights reserved.

The 21st Century King James Version, copyright © 1994 by Deuel Enterprises,
Inc., Gary, SD 57237, USA. All rights reserved.

New International Version®, NIV®, copyright © 1973, 1978, 1984, 2011 by
Biblica, Inc.® Used by permission. All rights reserved worldwide.

SUBSCRIPTIONS: *Studies in Church History* is an annual subscription journal
(ISSN 0424–2084). The 2016 subscription price (excluding VAT), which
includes print and electronic access, is £95 (US $152 in the USA, Canada and
Mexico) for institutions and £55 (US $88 in the USA, Canada and Mexico) for
individuals ordering direct from the Press and certifying that the volume is for
their personal use. An electronic-only subscription is also available to
institutions at £75 (US $120 in the USA, Canada and Mexico). Special
arrangements exist for members of the Ecclesiastical History Society.

Previous volumes are available online at www.journals.cambridge.org/StudCH

Printed in the United Kingdom by Bell & Bain Ltd
A catalogue record for this publication is available from the British Library

Contents

Contents

Contents

The fifty-second volume of Studies in Church History takes as its theme *Doubting Christianity: The Church and Doubt*. It presents the plenary papers and a selection of the communications delivered at the Summer Conference of the Ecclesiastical History Society held under the presidency of Frances Andrews at the University of Sheffield in July 2014 and the Winter Meeting hosted by Dr Williams's Library, London, in January 2015.

The theme of doubt has proved a very fruitful area of engagement, and we would like to thank Professor Andrews for her choice of this topic and for her focused leadership as President during a period of change for the Society. Thanks are due to the authors of the essays published here, to those who acted as peer reviewers, to those who chaired communications sessions, and to all those who attended and contributed to the discussion. We are particularly grateful to Dr Tim Grass for his continuing efficient and eagle-eyed work as Assistant Editor, and to the Ecclesiastical History Society for funding his post.

The success of the Summer Conference and Winter Meeting owed much to the Society's Conference Secretary, Professor Michael Walsh, supported by the conference team at the University of Sheffield and the staff of Dr Williams's Library. To them all, thanks are also due.

In 2014, Dr Stella Fletcher stood down as Secretary of the Ecclesiastical History Society, a post which she had taken up in 2005. On behalf of the Society, we would like to thank Stella for her long and dedicated work in this role.

This is the first volume of Studies in Church History to appear as a Cambridge University Press journal. We would like to express our gratitude to Peter Clifford, Michael Middeke and all at Boydell & Brewer for their support over the past nineteen years, and to them and to Daniel Pearce, Alison Fox, Corinna McCorristine and the rest of the team at CUP for helping us to achieve a smooth transition. We are delighted to announce that the whole run of SCH is now available digitally (at http://journals.cambridge.org/action/displayJournal?jid=stc) as well as in hard copy.

Charlotte Methuen
University of Glasgow

Andrew Spicer
Oxford Brookes University

Contributors

Frances Andrews (*President*)
  Professor in Mediaeval History, University of St Andrews

Gareth Atkins
  Postdoctoral Research Fellow, Centre for Research in Arts, Social Science and Humanities, University of Cambridge

Kirstie Blair
  Professor of English Studies, University of Stirling

Lucy Busfield
  Postgraduate student, St John's College, Oxford

Matteo Duni
  Professor of History, Syracuse University in Florence

Ian Forrest
  Associate Professor of Later Medieval History, University of Oxford

Emily E. Graham
  Assistant Professor, History Department, Oklahoma State University

Tim Grass
  Senior Research Fellow, Spurgeon's College, London

Colin Haydon
  Sometime Reader in Early Modern History, University of Winchester

Kimberley-Joy Knight
  Postdoctoral Research Fellow, University of Sydney

Anik Laferrière
  Postgraduate student, Keble College, Oxford

Philip Lockley
> Anglican ordinand, Cranmer Hall, Durham University

Patrick S. McGhee
> Postgraduate student, University of Cambridge

Charlotte Methuen
> Senior Lecturer in Church History, University of Glasgow

Jinty Nelson
> Emeritus Professor of Medieval History, King's College London

Greg Salazar
> Postgraduate student, Selwyn College, Cambridge

Charles M. Stang
> Professor of Early Christian Thought, Harvard Divinity School

Robert N. Swanson
> Professor of Medieval Ecclesiastical History, University of Birmingham

Jan Vandeburie
> Leverhulme Abroad Postdoctoral Research Fellow, Dipartimento di Studi Umanistici, Università degli Studi Roma Tre

Alexandra Walsham
> Professor of Modern History, University of Cambridge

Cordelia Warr
> Senior Lecturer in Art History, University of Manchester

Steven Watts
> Postgraduate student, University of St Andrews

Rowan Williams
> Master of Magdalene College, Cambridge

Kelly Diehl Yates
> Postgraduate student, University of Manchester

Abbreviations

ActaSS	*Acta sanctorum*, ed. J. Bolland and G. Henschen (Antwerp etc., 1643–)
AFH	*Archivum Franciscanum Historicum* (1908–)
AFP	*Archivum fratrum praedicatorum* (1931–)
ANF	Ante-Nicene Fathers, ed. A. Roberts and J. Donaldson, 10 vols (Buffalo, NY, 1885–96 and subsequent edns)
BL	British Library
BN	Bibliothèque nationale de France
Bodl.	Bodleian Library
CChr.CM	Corpus Christianorum, continuatio medievalis (Turnhout, 1966–)
CChr.SL	Corpus Christianorum, series Latina (Turnhout, 1953–)
CChr.T	Corpus Christianorum in Translation (Turnhout, 2010–)
CERS	Church of England Record Society
ChH	*Church History* (1932–)
CICan	*Corpus iuris canonici*, ed. E. Richter and E. Friedberg, 2 vols (Leipzig, 1879–81)
CYS	Canterbury and York Society
DBI	*Dizionario biografico degli italiani* (Rome, 1960–)
DNB	*Dictionary of National Biography*, 63 vols (London, 1885–1900)
EETS	Early English Text Society
EHR	*English Historical Review* (1886–)
EME	*Early Medieval Europe* (1992–)
ET	English translation
FOTC	The Fathers of the Church: A New Translation (Washington DC, 1947–)
FS	*Franciscan Studies* (1941–)
HistJ	*Historical Journal* (1958–)
HThR	*Harvard Theological Review* (1908–)
JAAR	*Journal of the American Academy of Religion* (1967–)
JECS	*Journal of Early Christian Studies* (1993–)
JEH	*Journal of Ecclesiastical History* (1950–)
JMedH	*Journal of Medieval History* (1975–)
JRH	*Journal of Religious History* (1960–)
LMA	London Metropolitan Archive

LPL	Lambeth Palace Library
MedS	*Mediaeval Studies* (1939–)
MGH	Monumenta Germaniae Historica inde ab a. c. 500 usque ad a. 1500, ed. G. H. Pertz et al. (Hanover, Berlin, etc., 1826–)
MGH Capit.	Monumenta Germaniae Historica, Capitularia regum Francorum (1883–)
MGH Conc.	Monumenta Germaniae Historica, Concilia (1893–)
MGH Epp.	Monumenta Germaniae Historica, Epistolae (1887–)
MGH Quellen	Monumenta Germaniae Historica, Quellen zur Geistesgeschichte des Mittelalters (1955–)
MGH S	Monumenta Germaniae Historica, Scriptores, 29 vols (1826–94)
MGH Schriften	Schriften der Monumenta Germaniae Historica (1938–)
MGH SRM	Monumenta Germaniae Historica, Scriptores rerum Merovingicarum (1884–1951)
MGH SS	Monumenta Germaniae Historica, Scriptores (in folio) (1826–)
n.d.	no date
n.pl.	no place
NPNF I	*A Select Library of Nicene and Post-Nicene Fathers of the Christian Church*, ed. P. Schaff, 14 vols (New York, 1887–92 and subsequent edns)
ODNB	*Oxford Dictionary of National Biography*, ed. H. C. G. Matthew and Brian Harrison (Oxford, 2004)
os	old series
P&P	*Past and Present* (1952–)
PBA	*Proceedings of the British Academy* (1904–)
PG	Patrologia Graeca, ed. J.-P. Migne, 161 vols (Paris, 1857–66)
PL	Patrologia Latina, ed. J.-P. Migne, 217 vols + 4 index vols (Paris, 1844–65)
SC	Sources Chrétiennes (Paris, 1941–)
SCH	Studies in Church History
s.n.	*sub nomine* ('under the name')
Speculum	*Speculum: A Journal of Medieval Studies* (1925–)
s.v.	*sub verbo* ('under the word')
TRHS	*Transactions of the Royal Historical Society* (1871–)
VC	*Vigiliae Christianae* (1947–)

Illustrations

Introduction

Doubt is a promising subject of inquiry for historians. Its initial definition in the *Oxford English Dictionary* reads '[t]he (subjective) state of uncertainty with regard to the truth or reality of anything; undecidedness of belief or opinion', which might be advocated as a necessary mindset for any historically inclined investigator embarking on research. Although not always articulated, historians constantly face the 'state of uncertainty' of knowledge of the past and the continuous need, therefore, to test the evidence. The compilers of the *OED* then, perhaps unwittingly, underscore the particular relevance of 'doubt' as a subject for ecclesiastical historians by further defining it as 'uncertainty as to the truth of Christianity or some other religious belief or doctrine'.[1] The prominent placing of this second definition acknowledges the reality that doubts about religious ideas and individual doctrines, if not faith itself, have long been conspicuous in human language, and not just when speaking about Christianity. Nonetheless, the means and the consequences of communicating doubt depend on, and are intensely revealing of, changing historical circumstance.

The potential for doubt as a barometer of historical change was central to the selection of the twin themes of 'Doubting Christianity: The Church and Doubt' for the Summer Conference and Winter Meeting of the Ecclesiastical History Society in 2014–15. Like all historical questions, doubt has moved in and out of fashion. In publishing terms the 1980s and early 1990s saw a creative and influential burst of work on pre-modern atheism and scepticism with broad implications for the study of doubt.[2] More recently, historians of religion have pushed harder on unbelief and incredulity, while

---

[1] See <www.oed.com>, *s.v.* 'doubt noun 1', last accessed 7 September 2015.
[2] For a few key English-language examples, see Michael Hunter, 'The Problem of "Atheism" in Early Modern England', *TRHS* 5th ser. 35 (1985), 135–57; David Wootton, 'Unbelief in Early Modern Europe', *History Workshop* 20 (1985), 82–100; Susan Reynolds, 'Social Mentalities and the Case of Medieval Scepticism', *TRHS* 6th ser. 1 (1991), 21–41 (much quoted by authors in this volume); Michael Hunter and David Wootton, eds, *Atheism from the Reformation to the Enlightenment* (Oxford, 1992). An influential earlier work was Keith Thomas, *Religion and the Decline of Magic: Studies in Popular Beliefs in Sixteenth- and Seventeenth-Century England* (London, 1971).

others have concentrated on epistemological (un)certainty.[3] There has been much imaginative exploration of how different societies have sought to cope with the limitations of knowledge, to construct proof and secure truth. Those working on trust or distrust, reputation, witnessing or false witness, memory and other features of human interaction have all come to deal, explicitly or not, with doubt.[4] It is a good moment for the Ecclesiastical History Society to tackle the subject.

To encourage cross-fertilization, the description of doubt in the call for papers which lies behind this volume was intentionally broad, from individual, existential doubts to epistemic uncertainty. The conferences in Sheffield and London that followed attracted an inspiring variety of papers, and generated lively discussion. Speakers reflected on historians' identification of particular periods as ages of doubt or faith, the interdependence of faith and doubt, the careers of doubters, the experience of doubt between private and public, individual and community, pastoral efforts to cohabit with, restrain or explain doubts, polemical attempts to silence them, textual and material means of articulating the nuance of uncertainties and their resolution, institutional and bureaucratic endeavours to cope with uncertainty, and the many individual and communal struggles to avoid doubt altogether, whether by alternative forms of argument or by changing behaviour and process. Doubt emerged as inevitable, as concomitant to faith, occasionally as a virtue, more often as a struggle, an ailment to be overcome. For many Christian theologians,

---

[3] See, to mention only some of those in my own field, John Arnold, *Belief and Unbelief in Medieval Europe* (London, 2005); Paolo Golinelli, *Il Medioevo degli increduli. Miscredenti, beffatori, anticlericali* (Milan, 2009); Peter Dinzelbacher, *Unglaube im 'Zeitalter des Glaubens'. Atheismus und Skeptizismus im Mittelalter* (Badenweiler, 2009); Dorothea Weltecke, *'Der Narr spricht: Es ist kein Gott'. Atheismus, Unglauben, und Glaubenszweifel vom 12. Jahrhundert bis zur Neuzeit* (Frankfurt, 2010); Alex Novikoff, *The Medieval Culture of Disputation: Pedagogy, Practice and Performance* (Philadelphia, PA, 2013); Dallas G. Denery II, Kantik Ghosh and Nicolette Zeeman, eds, *Uncertain Knowledge: Scepticism, Relativism and Doubt in the Middle Ages* (Turnhout, 2014); Dorothea Weltecke, 'Doubt', in John H. Arnold, ed., *The Oxford Handbook of Medieval Christianity* (Oxford, 2014), 357–74.

[4] For example, Geoffrey Hosking, *Trust: A History* (Oxford, 2014); Thelma Fentress and Daniel Lord Smail, eds, *Fama: The Politics of Talk and Reputation in Medieval Europe* (Ithaca, NY, 2003); Jamie K. Taylor, *Fictions of Evidence: Witnessing, Literature, and Community in the Late Middle Ages* (Columbus, OH, 2013); Nancy Caciola, *Discerning Spirits: Divine and Demonic Possession in the Middle Ages* (Ithaca, NY, 2003). On memory, a vast field, an interesting starting place is the philosophically based volume by Dmitri Nikulin, *Memory: A History* (Oxford, 2015).

after all, doubt is a consequence of the fall. Dialectically, the 'shadow of doubt' remains something to avoid.

Since the selection of essays that resulted is published here in chronological order and each has its own abstract, this introduction is limited to drawing attention to a few of the common questions which flicker across their pages, some of the many possible ways that links can be seen when reading between their multifaceted arguments. It is worth warning readers at the outset that relatively few writers deal in depth with what 'doubt' might be. Rather they offer insightful readings of how different actors described and dealt with doubt and uncertainty in themselves and in others, often, but not always, the clergy and ministers in relation to their flocks.

PERSISTENT DOUBTING?

In Western Europe, on which the writers in this volume have focused predominantly, post-Enlightenment expressions of fundamental doubts about matters of faith rarely have stark personal, social or political consequences. Yet it is so much easier to hear modern doubters that doubt itself is popularly assumed to be a feature of modernity, regularly contrasted with a credulous, undoubting Middle Ages. Recent work has dismantled some features of this picture, restoring to the late Middle Ages, for example, at least a 'sceptical undercurrent'.[5] Others have questioned the weight of doubt in more recent centuries, but the conventional picture remains powerful. Several of the essays here contribute further ways to deepen and widen the chronological depth of the challenge to its assumptions. Jinty Nelson's study of Carolingian doubt lays out a series of cases designed in the first instance to show that the early Middle Ages also knew doubt. Her evidence begins with a famous handbook written for a beloved absent son by a ninth-century Frankish noblewoman, Dhuoda. The mother warns her son of the suffering and spiritual sadness that may engender uncertainty about divine power and the need to resolve this by turning to prayer. The evidence of Dhuoda's or her son William's doubt requires careful extrapolation: she did not use the word. But this reading of personal struggle provides a backdrop for Nelson's delineation of high-level religious doubts and

---

[5] 'Introduction: The Varieties of Uncertainty', in Denery, Ghosh and Zeeman, eds, *Uncertain Knowledge*, 1–12, at 9.

doctrinal divergences set out in male-authored letters, learned commentary and hagiographical texts. These expose disagreements, shifting certainties and doubts. The monk Gottschalk thought doubt inevitable, beautifully pinpointing the difficulty of relying on the senses by evoking the way sight is misled by distortion when a stick is placed in water. He came to be convinced of double predestination – to heaven or to hell – contradicting contemporary orthodoxy, and ended his days in monastic prison. These and other cases in Nelson's analysis point to how doubt moved between private and public and also the importance of particulars of place. Different contexts, from Carolingian court circles to frontier zones between Christian and pagan, or areas under Muslim rule, generated different responses from Christian leaders and scholars who were often themselves unsure.

Whereas Nelson reinstates doubt as a feature of the early medieval Christian experience, both lay and clerical, Charles Stang adds to the bonfire of 'doubt' as a feature of modernity by taking us back to the New Testament. Challenging Lawrence of Arabia's epigram of doubt as 'our modern crown of thorns', he traces how the writers of the four canonical gospels variously built tension and sought to diffuse it, alternately opening up doubts and plugging gaps, reacting to doubt's 'persistent purchase'. He proposes distinct understandings of doubt in each gospel: as a threat to which we are vulnerable; a shadow without obvious origin or purpose but which may provide relief (shade); as something rooted in human desires; or as a 'defiant conditional' between humans and faith. While the different gospel writers may have set out to quicken faith, he argues, the cumulative effect of the gospels is that doubt 'cannot be fully dispelled'. Faith and doubt appear coincident, questions abound.

One of the many gospel questions is also a starting point for my own contribution, focused on the figure of 'doubting John' detectable in Matthew 11: 2–3, the moment when John the Baptist sent his disciples to ask Christ whether he was 'the one who is to come'. The essay first seeks to fathom late antique and late medieval currents of doubt by tracing how biblical exegetes handled the uncertainties John's question raised, constructing arguments to distance him from doubt and driving polemical texts seeking a solution to those doubts. Drawing on late medieval anti-heretical dispute literature and feast-day sermons produced in Italy, where John was a popular patron saint, it then illustrates how place, audience and genre determined when doubt was more likely to be stemmed, or where it might be energetically debated. Doubt emerges as a powerful current that often surfaced and may have had a visual echo in representations of John debating with his anxious disciples.

The power of doubt in the late Middle Ages also flows indirectly from Anik Laferrière's examination of its strategic excision from accounts of the life of their alleged founder, Augustine of Hippo, by five fourteenth-century Augustinian hermit friars. Augustine's own *Confessions* attributed to his mother Monica a central role in helping him overcome his doubts about Christianity. Such doubts were inconvenient, Laferrière argues, not because their resolution was bound up in female authority, but because they did not fit the hermit friars' vision of Augustine as the direct source of their own form of life, itself still apparently vulnerable to a curb on new religious orders reiterated by the Council of Lyons in 1274. In building certainty about their claims to be his longstanding and true sons, and therefore exempt from the 1274 restrictions, Augustine's wavering must be set aside. Monica therefore disappeared, along with her son's doubts.

An alternative approach to the examination of doubt in the late Middle Ages is explored in Robert Swanson's essay, which sets out to revise conceptions of doubt and uncertainty on a broad scale. Explaining the sophisticated interpretations of numerous thinkers, he demonstrates both that doubt and insecurity about belief were much more accepted than most historians recognize and that uncertainty was an inevitable feature of the late medieval Church, a congregation of humans of diverse beliefs and practices in which the boundaries between acceptable and unacceptable, orthodox and heretic were unstable. Like Nelson's early medieval clerics, Swanson's late medieval churchmen were not inexorably sure of their ground. Challenging any crude portrayal of belief and unbelief as binaries, he shows how theologians and canonists acknowledged a spectrum, understanding belief as a movement from suspicion, doubt, opinion to conviction, with the danger at any moment of making the wrong choice and ending up heading in a different direction, towards a different place, still unsure whether heaven or hell. Acquiring faith may be helped by reason, but knowledge is beyond belief; true knowledge is not for this world. How the boundaries depended on rival intellectual worlds, how they were to be drawn in the living Church, and how scrupulosity drove uncertainty and reformation are questions which tie together the dual themes of doubt and doubting, in Christianity and in the Church.

Kirstie Blair's essay also tests traditional chronologies in the historical discussion of doubt, this time by moving the focus to nineteenth- and twentieth-century poetry. She argues that the work of modern poets such as Carol Ann Duffy, creating a poetry of doubt which often rejects churchgoing and the function of Christianity, remains haunted all the same by Victorian religious literature, with its poetics of faith and doubt. Focusing on the sonnet form, she observes how structures, rhythms and language echo the writing of Victorians such as Matthew Arnold, Christina Rossetti or Alfred Tennyson. In Blair's analysis, continuity undermines the conception of the nineteenth century as the eponymous 'age of doubt': what we tend to think of as Victorian anxieties about faith and doubt still resonate.

LIVING WITH DOUBT

Modern historians have gradually been coming to terms with the reality that doubts and uncertainty (like belief and faith) flow through Christian experience in all periods, if unevenly. This is a faint shadow of the many struggles of the historical actors they study to live with the limits of human knowledge and the inevitability of doubt. As Tim Grass observes in his reading of the newly accessible correspondence of Samuel Rawson Gardiner and his family, this Victorian historian came to the belief that 'all apprehension of truth in this life [is] partial at best: no ideology or system of religious dogma could fully encapsulate it'. Many of those studied here might have agreed with both sentiments, but in Gardiner's case he was able to act upon his doubts about a particular 'system of religious dogma' with relative impunity. He had been brought up in the Catholic Apostolic Church, but new scientific understandings of geological time had kindled his doubts about the dogmatic certainty of his Church's leaders. Their failure to adapt was one reason which led Gardiner to move to the Church of England around 1870, an uncomfortable break from the circle of people among whom he had grown up, as his wife's letters reveal. A further reason for his doubts, Grass suggests, may have been his work as a historian, so that he was no longer able to accept something as true simply on the authority of another. The essay thus neatly illustrates another way in which doubt as a subject and history as a discipline coincide.

The relationship of doubt to commitment and coercion implicit in Grass's study of Gardiner is a more central theme in Rowan Williams's reconsideration of how certainty and uncertainty, personal conviction and public adherence were handled in the writings of the Elizabethan theologian Richard Hooker (d. 1600). At various different moments Hooker sought to distinguish between what he understood to be certain in itself – the revealed character of God – and issues where doubt would be wise, such as the much debated definition of Christ's presence in the sacrament, the God-given character of any specific Church order, or assumptions about the spiritual state of any other baptized person. But for Hooker, living in the decades when the Church of England was painfully taking shape, doubt about the Church to which allegiance was commanded by law was not wise: legal enforcement of conformity was a pastoral good which allowed the uncertain some stability in the midst of their fluctuating convictions and emotions. It seems unlikely that Gardiner would have agreed (though other Victorians might well have done).

Three other writers demonstrate the longevity of doubts generated by the difficulty of discerning the true from the untrue, the holy from the demonic. Charlotte Methuen reflects on how two third-century churchmen, Firmilian, bishop of Caesarea, and Cyprian, bishop of Carthage, debated the validity of the sacraments. Her account of Firmilian's letter describing his doubts about the eucharist administered by a woman who was later deemed to be demonically possessed first suggests that such discussions helped determine the identity and practices of the early Church. Placing the letter in its original context indicates that gender was not the original issue for Firmilian, but Methuen shows how the modern Roman Catholic Church has taken up his lines in rejecting women priests. The study thus links the selective continuity of institutional memory and the persistence of specific doubts and debates (on which more below).

Doubts about identifying the demonic also surface in the work of the early Dominican master-general, Jordan of Saxony (d. 1237), who included them in his account of the beginnings of his order, studied here by Steven Watts. A hybrid text, Jordan's *Libellus* combines history, hagiography and self-writing, this last including a lengthy account of Jordan's doubts on being faced with an apparently virtuous brother's demonic possession. At first this tale seems incongruous, as most critics have suggested. But drawing attention to evidence for the text's pedagogical purpose and use with Dominican novices,

Watts argues that Jordan's account of his own attempts to pin down the demon's wiles turns doubt into a teaching tool. The original demonic possession was divinely granted to test the brothers' tenacity, Jordan's own behaviour providing a model of how to cope in the face of doubt. Later versions of his life, keen to promote Jordan's holiness, nonetheless deleted the doubts as inappropriate to the certainty expected of a saint.

Distinct perspectives on how to distinguish the holy and the demonic emerge more fully in Matteo Duni's contribution, an analysis of a number of secular writers' doubts about the reality of witchcraft and therefore the validity of witch-hunts in the fifteenth and sixteenth-centuries. Whereas inquisitors – including the author of the *Malleus maleficarum* – now lived with the idea that God permitted demons to carry out malevolent acts in the physical sphere, such as witches' flight or procreation with the Devil, several lay practitioners of law argued that it was extremely unlikely, preferring to restrict demonic action to the spiritual world. These doubters expressed their concerns in ways that variously exploited the arguments of their own discipline and those of medicine and biblical criticism. Their ideas were influential, eventually perhaps feeding into changes in inquisitorial practice, but also to at least one threat to burn the incriminating volume. Alongside science-based reasoning about the inability of demonic spirits to have physical children, comparisons with biblical figures who could fly (as had Christ in the gospel account of his temptations), were rejected as a legal precedent because of the exceptionality of this sort of event; real-life repetition would require too many divine 'special permissions'. These lawyers also identified a fundamental weakness in the assessment of witnesses. They voiced serious doubts about the legality of acting upon witches' testimony or their accusations against supposed accomplices, adopting a stance more in line with the early medieval canon *Episcopi*, which had defined witches' visions as delusional, created by the Devil. Had God wanted to punish humans in this way, they argued, he would have chosen a different kind of witness, not women or 'uncouth country folk', since neither would be widely believed.

The question of trustworthy witnesses is also one of the central elements in the essay by Ian Forrest, who explores one way in which living with doubt impinges on the history of the social and institutional Church. Working from cases in late medieval English episcopal registers, Forrest concentrates on the risks involved in assessing truth and trustworthiness at a distance and how bishops sought to reduce these 'costs of doubt'. One way they did so was by relying on local knowledge and on the testimony available during visitations and before tribunals from trustworthy men – frequently the sort of country folk whose witness would not otherwise be admitted – with the result that canon law boundaries between opinion and legally accepted fact were elided. Doubts were ignored in the construction of an acceptable, liveable truth. Forrest also reminds historians to keep in mind the sometimes subtle and often varying differences in attitudes to certainty, doubt, or reason underlying the assumptions of writers even when they agreed with one another, let alone when they did not.

THE NEED FOR DOUBT

Faith as a virtue is logically dependent on the possibility of doubt and unbelief. While doubt is often described as a wound, a sometimes incapacitating struggle, the positive connotations occasionally trickle through to pastoral writing. A version of this is evident in the guidance for puritans studied by Lucy Busfield. Focusing on letters written to counsel the faithful, she observes how the personal battles with doubt and despair of a London puritan, Nehemiah Wallington (d. 1658), could be recognized as 'particularly fitting', equipping this layman to assist others in the same predicament. For the individual struggling with the insecurity born of pious self-scrutiny, doubt was a sign of belief (as Hooker would have agreed), one which enabled mutual spiritual growth towards faith. It is this sort of insight that has driven previous historians to assign to Wallington an exemplary role as a Calvinist doubter, expressing individual conscience, part of the narrative of the emergence of the modern individual. In keeping with recent, less optimistic assessments of the autonomy of spiritual memoirs, and recognition of the communal dimensions to religious culture, Busfield disrupts the conventional narrative by showing how Wallington's efforts continue to rely on clerical mediation. He carefully copied out an extensive collection of the published letters of puritan ministers which record the laity turning to them for expert diagnosis of their spiritual health. Doubts may be kept at bay by 'fraternal counselling' in Wallington's own letters, but this differed entirely from the 'paternal', pastoral mode of ministers dealing with doubts and complex cases of conscience.

Doubt is again present as both necessity and virtue – though with broader, social implications – in Kelly Yates's elucidation of the idea of the 'catholic spirit' promoted by the Methodist leader John Wesley (d. 1791). The essay clarifies how Wesley, thinking in tune with contemporary philosophers, including Locke, developed a case for ecumenism through insisting on doubt. As Yates quotes Locke, 'doubt of one's own opinions leads to humility, which leads in turn to tolerance'. The limits of human capacity to know require acceptance that another's opinions may be right. In this case doubt becomes a way for Wesley to argue for liberty of conscience (within Trinitarian limits). It is also an important part of the conceptual work necessary to enable different denominations to tolerate and live alongside each other.

FLICKERING DOUBTS

As Robert Swanson writes of the late Middle Ages – a point with wider application – faith is 'not a monolith of clarity, but an amalgam of opportunities for uncertainty and disagreement'. The means to salvation were always unsure, and often hotly debated. In these disagreements, some issues emerge as the staple content of doubts about Christianity and its Churches; what changes is the manner of their articulation and the consequences.

Unsurprisingly, doubts about the eucharist shine brightly. Where Rowan Williams notes Hooker's lack of investment in a precise definition of Christ's presence in the eucharist, Alexandra Walsham hints at a possible reason for Hooker's reserve by setting out how, among other sixteenth-century Protestants, fierce disagreement over interpretations of the Last Supper animated emerging denominational and confessional identities. Her essay also reminds us of the importance of objects, beginning as it does with the Bosworth Hall burse, a remarkable embroidered case for carrying the liturgical corporal. The embroidery commemorates a vision of the crucified Christ seen during the first mass of a friend by the English Catholic missionary priest John Payne in 1575, just seven years before his death as a martyr in 1582. The record of Payne's vision, which came as he was doubting the real presence in the consecrated eucharist, resonates closely with accounts of medieval miracles such as the miracle of Bolsena in 1263, when blood dripping from the host in his hands convinced a doubting priest of the truth of transubstantiation. At the same time as marking continuities in the content of doubts, Walsham draws out how the burse came to be read as a symbol of the dogmatic certainties that drove institutional divisions, the conflicts over transubstantiation and the real presence that 'divided Wittenberg, Geneva, Rome and Lambeth'.

A doctrine which has prompted similar recurring doubts is that of the three persons of the Trinity, the nature and meaning of the relationship between Father, Son and Holy Spirit. It is one of several doctrinal difficulties raised by Colin Haydon's account of the career of Francis Stone, an Anglican rector, who nearly three centuries after the English Reformation voiced his doubts about Anglican teaching and the Thirty-Nine Articles. Stone preached publicly that Christ was merely human and that the virgin birth was a myth. He doubted the doctrine of the atonement and advocated Unitarian thinking, questioning the Trinitarianism of the Athanasian Creed on the grounds that it could not be 'proved by the Scripture'. Drawing on the biblical texts as proof is an essential tool in debates about belief, but an Anglican clergyman doing so in this radical form in the early 1800s provoked a storm, as Stone must surely have expected. It led to the loss of his living and disaster for his large family, rescued only by Unitarian generosity to a member of the Church of England.

Another staple to which several essays make more or less extensive reference is the story of doubting Thomas, an accustomed biblical witness in pre- and early modern accounts of doubt and sensory belief. Patrick McGhee makes this story the heart of his contribution, probing its extensive explication in the early seventeenth-century work of another Protestant clergyman, Nicholas Bownde (d. 1613). In keeping with much of the pastoral literature of his time (some of it discussed by Busfield, Williams and Walsham), Bownde wrote to offer comfort to those experiencing unbelief and criticized sight and touch as a means to access the spiritual – as we would expect of a post-Reformation Protestant. McGhee explores how Bownde nonetheless acknowledged the place of the senses, materiality and the body in the individual's struggle for faith and in his approach to doubt. In his attempt to explain the relation of faith and believing, Bownde compared belief in Christ with a pregnant woman's ongoing belief in the living presence of an unborn child even in the moments when she cannot feel it stirring. For Bownde, unbelief was akin to a physical affliction that required pastoral comfort, characterized by the search for sensory confirmation of God, a product of a misunderstanding, but one that Christ is nonetheless able to remedy among the apostles through Thomas. In highlighting the connections Bownde made between doubt, unbelief, the senses and the body, McGhee demonstrates that physicality had not been entirely excluded from the logic of faith by early modern religious writers.

A final commonplace of doubt rekindled here several times is that of the role of women in the social body of the Church, all too often a smoky grey area on the edges of a male-dominated space. Can women administer sacraments? Yes, it seems, in third-century Caesarea, as long as they are not then found to be demonically possessed. Should women be seen to weep profusely in Church? Once again, as we shall see in Kimberley-Joy Knight's essay, the answer is a conditional yes, but it is preferable if this can be explained as a test of sanctity. Can women's words be accepted as proof of miracles? Yes, according to Cordelia Warr's study of one use of the sermons of the Spanish Franciscan mystic, Juana de la Cruz (d. 1524). In the writings of Antonio Daza (d. 1640), another Spanish Franciscan, Juana's words became an important witness to the miraculous truth of Francis of Assisi's unique stigmata. But once again, there is a condition: for Daza, Juana's witness was reliable because God had spoken through her, a woman who herself had received stigmata, a logical challenge to the singularity of Francis's gift that Daza chose to ignore.

CATCHING FIRE

If living with doubt is a feature of Christian experience in all periods, and doubts about particular features of belief and the Church regularly recur, several writers ask what it is that causes these flickering doubts to catch fire and with what effects. Emily Graham takes up these questions in the context of Franciscan lay communities in fourteenth-century Aragon, suspended in the troubled air trailing the condemnation of reformist Franciscan 'Spirituals'. She suggests that in this delicately poised situation, where heretical texts and preaching were recent memory, the provocative actions of an individual were enough to cause waning doubts to fire up once more, generating a pervasive atmosphere of doubt and suspicion. Accusation and counter-accusation about a community's orthodoxy triggered official inquests and destroyed the equilibrium, forcing the community to disperse, even though almost no one was condemned and the provocateur seems to have been expelled, only to wreak havoc elsewhere.

Greg Salazar explores the triggers in another context, demonstrating how changing political plans might stir up anxiety and doubts about adherence to a particular confessional identity in post-Reformation London. He does so by using Protestant accounts of a debate with Catholics in Sheer Lane, in June 1623. The debate was staged against the background of government relaxation of anti-Catholic legislation preparatory to a proposed marriage alliance with the Spanish crown, known to the English as the 'Spanish Match'. Salazar shows how the Protestant controversialists were keen to prevent a Catholic revival, anxious that doubt about the nature of the true Church was prompting undesirable conversion among the laity. In their attempts to prove that Protestantism was the genuine expression of Christianity, they organized a crowded and quasi-public meeting, risking royal displeasure to further their aims, but were rescued by the change of policy accompanying the demise of the Spanish Match.

Like the early modern era, the nineteenth century is another moment when historians have traditionally recognized newly expressed Christian encounters with doubt. Since these took place against a long backdrop of doubt, they do not make the nineteenth century, as Kirstie Blair might observe, an 'age of doubt'. Nonetheless, industrial change and scientific discovery did lead to new modes and reasons for articulating uncertainties and doubts. This is evident in the contributions of Tim Grass and Colin Haydon already discussed and comes to the fore once more in Philip Lockley's study of the early history of socialism, before the rise of the Christian Socialist movement. The New Lanark entrepreneur Robert Owen (d. 1858) gradually developed into a 'classic enlightenment deist, dismissing all beliefs contrary to reason'. Driven by his perception of the effect of industrial working conditions on individual lives, and how circumstances form human behaviour, Owen objected to Christianity's teachings on sin and eventually came to condemn its divisive nature and role in hindering the coming of socialism. His public campaign was followed by men and women on both sides of the Atlantic, including Charles Newman, the forgotten younger brother of John Henry, and Frances Wright, who set up the first secularist Hall of Science in New York City in 1829 and advocated free rational enquiry against the truth claims of revealed religion. Despite many Christians' deep hostility, Lockley shows how each of the issues exercising Owenite doubters also generated alternative Christian answers. The Anglican philanthropist, John Minter Morgan, praised Owen's plans for housing the poor and argued that such social projects offered 'a better system' which would help remove circumstances conducive to sin. Other writers claimed the idea of cooperation as essentially Christian and capable of realizing the Christian millennium, restoring the early Church's 'pure and perfect communities'. Socialist doubts about Christianity, Lockley concludes, were accompanied by hope about the future in forms that were 'open to recognition and reclamation by Christians'. Whether Owen would have approved is less clear.

DOUBT LINES

A final subject which emerges again and again in these essays is the utility of doubt as a tool in producing texts and in moving ideas beyond the text. Several of the contributions already discussed demonstrate how writers deployed or excised doubt as a rhetorical feature of their writing. Kimberley-Joy Knight's essay offers a case study of this process based on hagiographic composition, a *locus classicus* of clerical attempts to overcome doubts. She begins with Jacques de Vitry's *Life of Marie d'Oignies*, written *c.*1215, in which male clerical doubts about the spiritual validity of copious, public, female tears are framed as part of the testing a saint must endure if she is to be proven right beyond all doubt, a topos exploited to promote sanctity. Despite this positive message, and the vast success of Jacques's work, Knight goes on to observe how holy women's tears in later saints' lives are more often described as internalized, invisible weeping. One reason for this change, she proposes, may be both a textual and a real-life reaction to persistent doubts about bodily spirituality and displays of tears.

Jan Vandeburie's essay also starts from the cult of Marie d'Oignies. In a supplement to Jacques de Vitry's life of Marie, Thomas of Cantimpré describes Vitry's gift of a reliquary containing her finger to Cardinal Hugolino of Ostia, later pope as Gregory IX (1227–41). Gregory is described as plagued by the *spiritus blasphemiae*, an allegorical personification of doubt and distrust in God. Jacques also urged Hugolino to read the *Vita* to help him deal with his uncertainties. A simultaneous gift of a silver cup was, however, refused. Confirming Knight's assessment of Vitry's purpose, Vandeburie points out that Marie's reputation in dealing with doubt was well established, but also takes his exploration of the reasons for Gregory's doubts beyond hagiographical writing, identifying his standing in the curia as one of several possible causes for anxiety, doubts which were only to become louder once he became pope and found himself without time for spiritual contemplation. But Vandeburie's careful reading also identifies other reasons for the account of the exchange between Jacques and Hugolino and the refusal of the silver cup: Thomas was disappointed that a man he greatly admired had risen in power and wealth, betraying Marie d'Oignies's ideals of poverty and humility. Whether or not Thomas's readers caught the criticism of Vitry, doubt in this essay is once more about self and community, individual ways to God and community expectations.

As several writers in this volume underscore, an essential tool in discussions of doubt among Christians is critical analysis of the text of the Bible, itself much contested by the different confessional and denominational groups studied here. Biblical criticism aimed at establishing the integrity of the text plays a prominent role in Gareth Atkins's work on the changing use of prophetic passages in nineteenth-century Britain, an essay which brings us full circle, back to the years when Samuel Rawson Gardiner's doubts were gradually taking him away from his adherence to the Catholic Apostolic Church and into the Church of England.

In the early 1800s demonstrations of the prophetic precision of the Bible might still be used to protect believers against doubt, or to celebrate the success of British naval endeavours by metaphorically comparing them to the 'ships of Tarshish' mentioned in Isaiah, as did the Bolton clergyman Walter Chamberlain in a volume published in 1860. Atkins shows that by 1860 this sort of literal reading was becoming old-fashioned, rejected not only by liberal thinkers – who prized the moral value of the Bible, not its historicity – but also by clerical scholars. New discoveries in geography and natural sciences persuaded Bible students to investigate its account of the lands of the Middle East, confirming the text's historical integrity to their own satisfaction, but in the process undermining its prophetic qualities. As Atkins shows, however, doubts about prophecy did not mean that providential language disappeared. Different approaches persisted: for scholars, the Bible prophecies demonstrated the veracity of the Bible as a set of Near Eastern texts. For poets the text offered a store of powerful language. But Atkins also points to a third group, a 'subculture' that read prophetic passages as a very different kind of protection against doubt, 'as a code waiting to be unscrambled by faithful exegetes alert to the unfolding of events'.

* * *

This introduction has pointed out only some of the many ways into this collection: very different routes could have been chosen. The essays open up numerous fascinating trails barely mentioned here and point to still others waiting to be investigated. It is hoped that together they may inspire other historians to delight in the rich potential of investigating the history of doubt.

Frances Andrews

Doubting John?

Frances Andrews*

University of St Andrews

This essay focuses on the figure of John the Baptist in prison and the question he sent his disciples to ask Christ: was he 'the one who is to come' (Matthew 11: 2–3)? Having observed how the Fathers strove to distance John from the perils of doubt in their readings of this passage, it traces the way their arguments were picked up by twelfth- and thirteenth-century biblical exegetes and then by authors of anti-heretical dispute texts in urban Italy, where the Baptist was a popular patron saint. So as to give force to their own counter-arguments, learned polemicists, clerical and lay, made much of heretics' hostility to John, powerfully ventriloquizing a doubting, sceptical standpoint. One counter-argument was to assign any doubts to John's disciples, for whose benefit he therefore sent to ask for confirmation of the means of Christ's return, neatly moving doubt from questions of faith to epistemology. Such ideas may have seeped beyond the bounds of a university-trained elite, as is perhaps visible in a fourteenth-century fresco representing John in prison engaging with anxious disciples. But place, audience and genre determined where doubt was energetically debated and where it was more usually avoided, as in sermons for the laity on the feast of a popular saint.

In the realm of faith, doubt is an elusive concept. A modern working definition might sit in a tight circle with uncertainty, scepticism and unbelief, the non-existence of faith. Yet doubt can also be a result of deep engagement with belief. The combination is one reason why in recent years doubt and its close neighbour 'unbelief' have been the subject of lively discussion among medieval historians.[1] This essay

* Department of Mediaeval History, University of St Andrews, 71 South St, St Andrews, KY16 9QW. E-mail: fea@st-andrews.ac.uk.
 I am very grateful to John Arnold and Mark Elliott, who kindly read and commented on earlier drafts, as also to my co-editors and the anonymous reviewers.
[1] Some of the most recent contributions include Dallas G. Denery II, Kantik Ghosh and Nicolette Zeeman, eds, *Uncertain Knowledge: Scepticism, Relativism, and Doubt in the Middle Ages* (Turnhout, 2014), which deals with doubt in epistemological, not faith terms; Paolo Golinelli, *Il Medioevo degli increduli. Miscredenti, beffatori, anticlericali* (Milan, 2009), who writes of mental reserve within popular mentality ('grande chiacchieria'); Peter Dinzelbacher, *Unglaube im Zeitalter des Glaubens. Atheismus und Skeptizismus im Mittelalter* (Badenweiler, 2009) who narrows the focus to nonbelief in a God active in the world or in the soul's im-

Studies in Church History 52 (2016) 17–48   © Ecclesiastical History Society 2016
doi: 10.1017/stc.2015.2

is intended as a further contribution to that discussion, pursuing the location and treatment of doubt in a new context.

Among the many stimulating approaches to belief and doubt, three works in particular triggered this essay. At the beginning of the 1990s, in a lecture to the Royal Historical Society, Susan Reynolds further undermined the already ailing 'Age of Faith', with its assumption of credulity and the 'incapacity for atheism, of the medieval mentality'. She warned against the homogenizing tendencies of scholars who, in seeking to understand the past, took the existence of different but all-encompassing 'social mentalities' not as a potential deduction emerging from their research but as an unargued premise.[2] To this she objected that 'even in the most untouched and traditional societies', anthropologists have found that '[s]ome people … seem, even if only privately, to doubt or question practices which reflect generally accepted beliefs and do so in a way that implies some kind of common-sense rationalism'.[3] Applied to the Middle Ages, this led her to argue that, although 'most people probably accepted the Church's teachings without agonizing over them', it would be difficult to maintain rationally 'that [theologians] were unaware of the possibility of unbelief or unworried about it. They clearly knew about unbelief and regarded it as dangerous.'[4] In place of an 'Age of Faith' Reynolds offered different degrees of faith, with people of all social classes making the choices Christianity requires, some believing, others doubting, yet others hardly believing at all. She recognized that all three choices might entail hardship: faith could be difficult, piety ebbed and flowed, unbelief was sometimes dangerous.[5]

---

mortality, thereby avoiding most heresy but finding nonbelief everywhere; Sabina Flanagan, *Doubt in an Age of Faith: Uncertainty in the Long Twelfth Century*, Disputatio 17 (Turnhout, 2008), who discusses doubt and uncertainty in the widest sense; and Steven Justice, 'Did the Middle Ages Believe in their Miracles?', *Representations* 103 (2008), 1–29, who shows how writers of miracle stories risk scepticism to reinvigorate belief. On a later period, see also Stefania Tutino, *Shadows of Doubt. Language and Truth in Post-Reformation Catholic Culture* (Oxford, 2014); Susan Schreiner, *Are You Alone Wise? The Search for Certainty in the Early Modern Era* (Oxford, 2011).

[2] Susan Reynolds, 'Social Mentalities and the Case of Medieval Scepticism', *TRHS* 6th ser. 1 (1991), 21–41, at 25, 40, 41.

[3] Ibid. 24.

[4] Ibid. 38, 35.

[5] Ibid. 37, 39.

The astuteness of Reynolds's approach was acknowledged fifteen years later by John Arnold in an extended examination of belief and unbelief among the late medieval laity.[6] Using a wide spectrum of evidence, Arnold explored levels of belief through the lenses of acculturation, community, selfhood and dissent, concluding that 'there was no one medieval lay faith, but a spectrum of faith, belief and unbelief'. He proposed, furthermore, that 'quite a bit of disbelief existed'.[7] Like Reynolds, in using 'unbelief', Arnold had in mind both complete disbelief and those practices which diverged from official norms and might be deemed superstitious or heretical by Church leaders, but which we might now interpret as expressions of belief.[8]

The combined impact of the insights of Reynolds and Arnold and those on whose research they were building has, I believe, been very fruitful and it is one reason for the focus on doubt in this volume.[9] A third historian, Dorothea Weltecke, illustrates how the discussion has been taken further. Weltecke has regretted the use of the English word 'unbelief' as a poor translation of *infidelis*, with connotations of individualism and emancipation inappropriate to the Middle Ages. For Weltecke, like Reynolds and Arnold, there is no question of reinstating any idea of religious unity, which 'was and is a fiction'.[10] But the way historians have categorized 'unbelief' is unconvincing, a 'soft conceptual substitute to designate "atheist" phenomena'.[11] 'Atheism', as she observes, is an early modern concept, though its precise historical contours are not yet agreed.[12] She takes as her core evidence scholastic debates about whether God existed, arguing – surely

---

[6] John Arnold, *Belief and Unbelief in Medieval Europe* (London, 2005), 217.

[7] Ibid. 217, 230.

[8] Ibid. 217, quoting Reynolds, 'Social Mentalities', 29.

[9] In anglophone scholarship a key voice behind both Reynolds and Arnold is that of Alexander Murray: see his 'Piety and Impiety in Thirteenth-Century Italy', in G. J. Cuming and Derek Baker, eds, *Popular Belief and Practice*, SCH 8 (Cambridge, 1972), 83–106; idem, 'The Epicureans', in Piero Boitani and Anna Torti, eds, *Intellectuals and Writers in Fourteenth-Century Europe: The J. A. W. Bennett Memorial Lectures* (Tübingen, 1986), 138–63.

[10] Dorothea Weltecke, *'Der Narr spricht: Es ist kein Gott.' Atheismus, Unglauben und Glaubenszweifel vom 12. Jahrhundert bis zur Neuzeit* (Frankfurt, 2010), 99 (translations are my own unless otherwise indicated).

[11] Dorothea Weltecke, 'Beyond Religion: On the Lack of Belief during the Central and Late Middle Ages', in Heike Bock, Jörg Feuchter and Michi Knecht, eds, *Religion and its Other: Secular and Sacral Concepts and Practices in Interaction* (Frankfurt, 2008), 101–14, at 101; see also eadem, *Der Narr spricht*, 456.

[12] Weltecke, *Der Narr spricht*, 450–2.

rightly – that when medieval scholars used proofs of the existence of a God they did not do this to oppose God-deniers, but rather to prove 'the truth of Christianity in dispute with other religions' (and, I might add, to win arguments with their academic peers).[13] So, she concludes, 'we learn nothing of the reality of thinking about the non-existence of God from this sort of text'.[14]

Weltecke's target is the historical anachronism of arguing for a modern category of God-deniers in the Middle Ages. Her twin purposes seem to have been to challenge historians of the inquisition who do not distinguish sin from justiciable crime, and to propose a distinction between courtly, learned and other uses of the language of belief and doubt. As well as objecting to the use of learned texts as sources for modes of thinking outside the schools, she thus suggests that the vernaculars for 'doubt' – the medieval forerunners of the modern German *Zweifel* – are still more unsuitable than 'unbelief' as a category of analysis. The meanings of *Zweifel* encompassed secular as well as spiritual, intellectual or emotional modes and might be used in very different circumstances to render ideas such as fickleness, suspicion, unreliability and conflict.[15]

There is a disciplinary divergence in the purposes and approaches of these three writers. Reynolds was exploring social relations and the gap between *mentalité* and the individual. Arnold was testing, and seeking to establish, the agency of the laity. Both argued for the feasibility and indeed the inevitability of doubts and unbelief. Weltecke's interest lay in the intellectual history of concepts used in the Middle Ages, which is one reason why she found modern uses of 'unbelief' or the umbrella term 'doubt' problematic. In their place, she has sought to distinguish emotional uncertainty and intellectual doubt and to underline the differences of treatment in diverse textual genres.[16] Thus she too has sought to offer new strategies for critiquing constructions of a 'believing Middle Ages'.[17] As she put it in a recent handbook essay, *pace* the continuing objections of many scholars, the idea is gaining ground that it makes sense to approach our sources

---

[13] Ibid. 229.
[14] Ibid. 230.
[15] Ibid. 457.
[16] Ibid. 460.
[17] Ibid. 467.

with the existence of religious doubt, indifference or absence of faith in mind.[18]

Continuing attention needs nonetheless to be paid to the language used to express doubt and the distinctions intended. In the Latin texts discussed below, both epistemological doubt (uncertainty about means of knowing), and doubt about matters of faith are conveyed using verbs, adverbs and adjectives such as *dubito* and *haesito*, *dubius*, *incertus* and their opposite *certus sum* or the judicious use of a negative (*non certus*). The meaning is communicated (and analysed) through syntax, not just technical terminology. The extent to which historians can contextualize the use of this sort of language to grasp the reality of ideas about doubt or unbelief is one aspect of what will be tested here.

* * *

My title, 'Doubting John', is not a mistake. It is intended to conjure up Doubting Thomas, a familiar figure in biblical ideas on this theme, who, according to John 20: 24–31, declared that he needed to see and poke his finger into Christ's wounds and side in order to believe. But I will argue that John the Baptist is another, fundamentally more important, biblical doubter. Doubting Thomas appears in a single, short biblical text and his lack of conviction is quickly resolved. The proofs – sight and touch – are clear, and so the textual (and visual) echo is relatively focused, generating thought-provoking but relatively unproblematic resonances.[19] Indeed the exemplary potential of Thomas's swift realization of the truth made excellent material for sermons. John the Baptist, by contrast, is a protagonist of the gospels, a harbinger of Christ himself, making a 'doubting John' a much more challenging figure. Any resolution of his doubt is also much less clear. The Baptist's status as a doubter thus features prominently in so-called dispute texts, directed by twelfth- and thirteenth-century Catholic polemicists against the teachings of heretics, real or imagined. Reading these texts is what awoke my interest in 'Doubting John', and discussion of some of the ideas they tackle will form the end point of what follows. Two ways of understanding my title should thereby emerge into view: on one hand, John himself as a doubter; on

---

[18] Dorothea Weltecke, 'Doubt', in John H. Arnold, ed., *The Oxford Handbook of Medieval Christianity* (Oxford, 2014), 357–74, at 362.

[19] See Alexander Murray, *Doubting Thomas in Medieval Exegesis and Art* (Rome, 2006).

the other, those who for this reason, amongst others, doubted John's virtue.

* * *

The medieval reception of John the Baptist was many-headed. After sketching his gospel story and its visual echoes, the discussion will concentrate on the episode where John might be deemed to be doubting, examining first the late antique biblical exegetes whose writings framed later thinking. It will then fix the focus on the years around 1200 in northern Italy, where John was both politically and visually significant. As Véronique Rouchon Mouilleron has noted, the Baptist was omnipresent in the visual repertoire of the peninsula, a reflection of his integration into both the political and the religious self-image of the Italy of the communes.[20]

THE BIBLICAL BAPTIST AND VISUAL REPRESENTATIONS

The Baptist appears prominently in three clustered episodes all mentioned in more than one Gospel. The first of these clusters treats his preaching, prophesying and the baptism of Jesus (Mark 1: 2–11; Matt. 3: 1–17; Luke 3: 1–22; John 1: 26–40). The second is his question from prison about Jesus, with Jesus's reply and praise of John (Matt. 11: 2–15; Luke 7: 18–30), and the third is his death (Mark 6: 14–29; Matt. 14: 1–12). Luke does not include John's execution, but does refer to Herod's perplexity when he hears about Jesus, wondering whether he is John risen from the dead (Luke 9: 7–9). The narrative of John's conception and birth, on the other hand, appears only in Luke 1, while the Gospel of John offers further details not found elsewhere, such as John's denial that he is either Christ or Elijah (John 1: 19–27). The biblical John is a precursor of Christ, a prophet who knows the Messiah even in the womb, and later becomes a locust-eating, camel-hair wearing ascetic, a light burning in the desert. He is a preacher of repentance and baptizer at the river Jordan who again recognizes Christ, calls him the Lamb of God, and

[20] Véronique Rouchon Mouilleron, 'Saint Jean le Baptiste dans les chapelles peintes du Palais des Papes d'Avignon et de la Chartreuse de Villeneuve (1347 et 1355)', in *L'Église et la vie religieuse des pays Bourguignons à l'ancien royaume d'Arles (XIVᵉ–XVᵉ siècle). Rencontres d'Avignon (17 au 20 septembre 2009)*, Publication du Centre Européen d'Études Bourguignonnes (XIVᵉ–XVIᵉ s.) 50 (Neuchâtel, 2010), 279–302, at 279.

hears the voice of the Father: 'This is my beloved son, in whom I am well pleased' (Matt. 3: 17; cf. Luke 3: 22; Mark 1: 11).[21] There is some confusion of the Baptist with Christ and a question as to whether he can be identified with the Old Testament prophet Elijah. But the key passage for our purpose is the description of the Baptist in prison, before being executed by Herod, posing a question about Jesus.

The visual representation of John the Baptist reflects this written version, with added details stemming from the New Testament Apocrypha. Until the twelfth century it was the Byzantines who produced most images of the Baptist, but already by the eleventh century he had become a common figure in Italian painting and sculpture.[22] In non-narrative images he appears in one of three guises: as a priest; as a shepherd wearing a camel- or other animal-hair coat, sometimes with a red cloak to symbolize his martyrdom; and, increasingly from the eleventh century, as an ascetic, naked, with long, unkempt hair, an image which may be associated with the new religious movements of the central Middle Ages. When portrayed as a prophet, he carries a banderole with the words *Ecce agnus dei*, 'Behold the Lamb of God' (John 1: 29, 36), one of the most familiar prophetic exclamations of the Bible and not only because of its resonance with the *Agnus Dei* of the liturgy. In the late twelfth and above all the thirteenth century, narrative cycles developed in the West in which the two most frequently repeated scenes link John directly to Christ: the Baptism in the river Jordan and the Visitation of Mary and Elizabeth, when John leaps in the womb, recognizing the Messiah. Rouchon Mouilleron points out that these narratives became increasingly prominent on the facades of cathedrals or (particularly in Italy) on baptisteries, 'monumental symbols of city cohesion'.[23] She also reminds us of the link with the emergence of the mendicants, both in the way that Francis of Assisi was equated not only to Christ but also to John and in the growing visual stress on John's preaching role, a defining activity of the friars.[24] The Baptist was, furthermore, one of only three biblical figures celebrated with a feast for his nativity, the others being Mary

---

[21] The Bible is quoted throughout from *Biblia Sacra iuxta vulgatam versionem* (1994), online at: <https://www.biblegateway.com/versions/Biblia-Sacra-Vulgata-VULGATE/#copy>, and The 21st Century King James Version.

[22] See Louis Réau, *Iconographie de l'art chrétien*, 2: *Iconographie de la Bible* (Paris, 1956), 431–63.

[23] Rouchon Mouilleron, 'Saint Jean le Baptiste', 39–40, 43–4.

[24] Ibid. 41–2, 44.

and Jesus. Moreover, in thirteenth-century Florence, he was claimed as a figure under whose name the city was governed, his image impressed on the reverse of coins, though he became an episcopal patron only in the 1300s.[25] In brief, by the thirteenth century, John the Baptist was a prominent urban image. His reputation and status were entwined with the world of the Italian communes and with the new religious orders associated with them.

Whereas a common element in narrative cycles is the decapitation of John, his head often extended through the window of Herod's prison, the earlier episode of John in prison talking with his disciples appears less prominently in the iconography than it does in the Bible. A striking exception is the fresco painted by Giusto de' Menabuoi in the baptistery of Padua, *c.*1378 (Fig. 1). One of the biblical texts which this scene evokes is Matthew 11: 2–3, known by the operative phrase, *Cum audisset [Johannes]*: 'Now when John had heard in prison of the works of Christ, he sent two of his disciples, And they said unto him, Art thou he that should come, or do we look for another?' To this question Matthew has Jesus answer (verses 4–6): 'Go and show John again (*euntes renuntiate Iohanni*) those things which you see and hear: the blind receive their sight, and the lame walk, the lepers are cleansed and the deaf hear, the dead are raised up and the poor have the gospel preached to them. And blessed is he, whosoever shall not be offended in me.' Once the messengers have gone, Jesus turns to the crowd and praises John, explaining that he is greater than the other prophets, greater than any other man born of woman, but that the least in the kingdom of God is greater than he. The same episode is narrated in Luke 7: 18–28 with slight variations, one of which underlines that John is the source of the question, since his disciples specifically inform Jesus that John had sent them to ask.

EARLY EXEGESIS

In the historical, literal method of reading the Bible – the starting point for biblical exegesis – the episode of John's question from prison poses a problem. Why did the prophet need to ask whether Jesus was the one? Had he forgotten his own earlier teaching and actions? Was he doubting Christ's role as the Messiah? And why, in

---

[25] On the later date for episcopal patronage, see Richard C. Trexler, *Public Life in Renaissance Florence* (New York, 1980), 1–2 n. 2.

Figure 1. Giusto de' Menabuoi, *The Baptist in prison debates with his disciples*, Padua, Cathedral Baptistery. Reproduced by courtesy of the Museo Diocesano Padua.

Giusto de' Menabuoi's image – in so far as it portrays this moment – is it the disciples who are looking uncertain, if not doubtful, facing a finger-pointing, masterful Baptist behind bars?

To begin to answer these questions and understand what approaches to John the Baptist can tell us about doubt in central and late medieval Italy, we need first to probe the writings of the patristic exegetes whose ideas so often worked their way into medieval texts, whether or not they were explicitly acknowledged. For all of them, the suggestion that John doubted was troubling, but Tertullian (d. 220) appears to be the only one who took the *Cum audisset* passage in Matthew to mean that John doubted Jesus's messianic status.[26] For Tertullian, in a treatise composed against the teachings of Marcion of Pontus (whose ideas are known only through the writings of opponents), John's change of mind followed the transition to Jesus of that part of the Holy Spirit (*portionem spiritus sancti*) which had animated him as a prophet. Jesus needed it while preaching on earth. So the Baptist, now a common man of the crowd, became a doubter – up to a point: 'No-one will have doubts (*haesitabit*) about someone he knows not to exist and of whom he has neither hopes nor understanding. … Plainly it is easier for him to have doubts about one whom, though he knows he exists, yet he does not know whether this is the man himself'.[27] Jesus's ensuing reference to those offended in him therefore applies to John but, by reminding the Baptist of his miracles, Jesus proves that he has really come, rescuing the prophet from his uncertainty.

Tertullian uses both *haesito* and *dubito* to describe John's predicament, but confines its scope by emphasizing what the Baptist did know: 'he was certain (*certus erat*) that no one was God except the Creator'. Any doubt is tightly circumscribed. Even in this restricted form, however, Tertullian's interpretation appears to be an outlier. Whether or not they were writing to counter heretical views, the patristic exegetes whose ideas were picked up later narrow the implications of John's question, not accepting that John himself doubted, but at most arguing that he may have sent the question because he lacked information about the details of Christ's advent.

The teacher and ascetic, Origen of Alexandria, writing in the 240s, was the first to suggest that John's question perhaps had something to do with the descent into hell: John recognizes Jesus as the Messiah, but is asking if he is to go down into the underworld.[28] The belief that Christ spent the time between his death and resurrection

---

[26] See Josef Ernst, *Johannes der Täufer. Interpretation – Geschichte – Wirkungsgeschichte* (Berlin, 1989), 249.

[27] 'Nemo haesitabit de aliquo, quem dum scit non esse nec sperat nec intellegit … Plane facilius quis haesitabit de eo quem cum sciat esse an ipse sit nesciat': Tertullian, *Adversus Marcionem* 4.18.4–6 (CChr.SL 1, 478).

[28] Origen, *Homilies on Jeremiah and 1 Kings 28, 3–25* 7 (FOTC 97, 329). The relevant passage of Origen's commentary on Matthew does not survive.

in the underworld was a regular feature of early Christian teaching.[29] Linking it to John's question was an idea with a long future, as was another, more obvious theme picked up by Origen: the didactic role of the Baptist. In a homily on Luke, Origen described John having a conversation with his disciples during which a question arose, so he sent his disciples to ask because he could not go himself.[30]

A century later, Hilary, earliest recorded bishop of Poitiers (d. 367/8), who spent much of his career opposing Arianism, again portrayed John as a teacher and explicitly located the difficulty in the minds of his disciples.[31] In his first work to circulate, a commentary on Matthew, Hilary wrote:

> Accordingly John asked (*consulit*, literally, 'took counsel') not for his own example but because of the ignorance of the disciples; since he had preached that [Christ] was to come in remission of sins. But he sent his disciples so that they would know that he had not preached another [and] so that [Christ's] works would be understood, would confirm the authority of his [the Baptist's] words and no other Christ would be expected than the one whose works bore witness.[32]

Here John is certain; it is his disciples who need reassurance.

Two generations or so later, in 390 or 391, Ambrose, bishop of Milan (d. 397) completed his *Exposition on the Gospel according to Luke*, which – as his near contemporary Jerome was only too keen to point out – depended heavily on Origen.[33] For Ambrose, a literal reading of the passage would appear to suggest that John, who had previously known Christ, no longer recognized him. But he dismissed this reading: 'So great a prophet as John cannot be suspected of such an error'. The bishop of Milan thereby introduced a core concept, 'error', which underlines the weight of the problem of a doubting

---

[29] J. N. D. Kelly, *Early Christian Creeds*, 3rd edn (London, 1972), 378–83.

[30] Origen, *Homilies on Luke* 27 (FOTC 94, 113).

[31] For Hilary's use of Tertullian, Cyprian and classical writers, see David G. Hunter, 'Fourth-Century Latin Writers: Hilary, Victorinus, Ambrosiaster, Ambrose', in Frances Young, Lewis Ayres and Andrew Young, eds, *The Cambridge History of Early Christian Literature* (Cambridge, 2004), 302–17, at 303.

[32] Hilary of Poitiers, *Commentarius in Matthaeum* 11 (PL 9, col. 978). A less direct translation is provided by *Commentary on Matthew*, FOTC 125, 130.

[33] For the date, see Origen, *Homilies on Luke and Fragments on Luke*, FOTC 94, xxxiv.

John.[34] But having established that a simple interpretation is contradictory (*conpugnat*), Ambrose took refuge in the spiritual meaning, suggesting that by sending his disciples to ask the question, the Baptist, earlier identified as himself representing the Law, was now ensuring that in Christ his disciples received the fullness of that Law. The bishop added that John had sent them because deeds are more effective than words, and drew similarly on the image of Thomas's fingers, introduced as a form of proof: 'But we too have seen in John, with our eyes we have seen the Apostles, and we have examined with our hands in the fingers of Thomas'.[35] For Ambrose, John's doubt that the one who was to come was to die arose not from want of faith, but out of love or devotion (*pietate dubitavit*). Thus he was like Peter, who doubted when he protested the suffering of Christ (Matt. 16: 22).

Ambrose's critic, Jerome, likewise offered an explanation of John's question, including it in a commentary on Matthew completed in just two weeks in 398, an effort of speed-writing which – like the works of Hilary and Ambrose – was to give rise to a standard reference work for the Middle Ages and beyond.[36] Jerome, too, used Origen as a major source, pointing out that when John put his question, 'he did not say "Art thou he who *has* come", but "Art thou he who *is* to come?"' For Jerome, the meaning of this is: 'Command me, since I am about to descend to the lower world, whether I should announce you there … Or does it not befit the Son of God that he should taste death? Are you to send another to carry out these mysteries?'[37]

Jerome again explained away any possibility that John was doubting Christ. At most the Baptist was uncertain about how the mystery of salvation was to be completed. Nonetheless the presence of doubt about Christ did not entirely dissolve. Having begun by affirming that John did not ask his question out of ignorance, Jerome explained that the Baptist 'sends his disciples to Christ, so that on

---

[34] '[N]on cadit igitur in talem prophetam tanti erroris suspicio': Ambrose, *Expositio euangelii secundum Lucam* 5.93–8, Centre 'Traditio Litterarum Occidentalium' 14 (Turnhout, 2010; based on the text of CChrSL 14).

[35] 'Sed etiam nos uidimus in Iohanne, oculis nostris perspeximus in apostolis et manibus nostris perscrutati sumus in Thomae digitis': ibid.

[36] On the significance of Jerome among the patristic writers, see Peter Widdicombe, 'The Patristic Reception of the Gospel of Matthew: The Commentary of Jerome and the Sermons of John Chrysostom', in Eve-Marie Becker and Anders Runesson, eds, *Mark and Matthew II. Comparative Readings: Reception History, Cultural Hermeneutics, and Theology* (Tübingen, 2013), 105–19.

[37] Jerome, *Commentary on Matthew* 11.2 (FOTC 117, 129, adapted).

this occasion, when they see the signs and miracles, they may believe in [Christ] and, with their teacher asking, learn for themselves'. Signs and miracles would resolve any outstanding questions. Moreover, for Jerome, the crowd around Jesus was explicitly struggling to understand: they were 'not aware of the mystery of [John's] question' and 'thought that John was in doubt about Christ, whom he himself had presented (*demonstraverat*)'.[38] Doubt moved from John to the crowd. Jesus's subsequent sermon was therefore understood as a means to correct their misunderstanding.

Three other patristic exegetes require mention before turning to how these ideas were picked up in the central and late Middle Ages. John Chrysostom, preaching at the end of the fourth century, almost certainly in Antioch, attacked Origen's interpretation head-on.[39] He used a form of language which underlines epistemological rather than faith-based grounds for the doubt expressed. First Chrysostom affirmed that '[John] did not send because himself disputing (ἀμφιβάλλων), nor did he ask in ignorance.'[40] 'For it does not belong to John to dispute this, nor to any ordinary person, nor even to one extremely foolish and frenzied'. So why did John send his disciples to ask? Chrysostom's answer drew on analysis of other elements in the biblical context: John's disciples were jealous of Jesus, who was baptizing and attracting crowds, 'and wanted to find some handle against him'. They did not yet know who Christ was, imagining Jesus to be a mere man, and John greater than man, so they were 'vexed at seeing the former held in estimation' while 'their own master was now diminishing'. Their jealousy was 'blocking access' to Christ. As long as John was with them, he had been trying to persuade them, without success. Now on the point of dying, he feared that they would remain apart from Christ. According to Chrysostom, if John had said, 'Go to Him, He is better than I', he would still not have persuaded them,

as he would have been thought to be saying this out of modesty, and they would have been all the more attached to him; or if he had said

---

[38] Ibid. (FOTC 117, 130).

[39] See Wendy Mayer, *The Homilies of St John Chrysostom: Provenance, Reshaping the Foundations* (Rome, 2005), for the debates about the date and place of delivery.

[40] John Chrysostom, *Homilies on the Gospel of Matthew* 36 (PG 57, cols 414–15). My translation is a modernized and adapted version of that of G. Prevost, revised by M. B. Riddle: NPNF I 10, 424–32, online in the Christian Classics Ethereal Library, at: <http://www.ccel.org/ccel/schaff/npnf110.pdf>, last accessed 31 July 2014.

nothing, again nothing would have been gained. … Accordingly he waits to hear from them that Christ is working miracles, and sends two (whom he perhaps knew to be more teachable than the rest), so that the inquiry could be made without suspicion, in order that from Jesus's acts they might learn the difference between Jesus and himself. Thus he says, Go, and say, 'Art thou he who should come, or do we look for another?' Christ, knowing John's purpose, did not say, I am He; for this would again have offended the hearers, though it is what it would have been natural for him to say; instead he leaves them to learn it from his acts … when they were come to him, then 'He cured many'.[41]

Having set out his own extended interpretation, Chrysostom summarily rejected the views of those who suggested that John asked his question because he was in ignorance, that he knew that Jesus was the Christ, but not whether he was also to die for humankind. For Chrysostom this was 'not tenable; for John was not ignorant of this'; after all, he had preached: 'Behold the Lamb of God who takes away the sins of the world'. So Chrysostom dismissed as unsustainable the idea that John's question related to the descent into hell, and scorned its implications for sin as the doctrine of 'old wives tales' and 'Jewish fables'. Chrysostom's John is psychologically acute, as a prophet needs to be. He does not experience doubt, but recognizes it in his disciples and acts to ensure that they follow Christ.

A generation later, Augustine (d. 430), incidentally the first witness to a feast of John the Baptist, celebrated on 24 June, again built on the pattern of interpretation of his predecessors. In his *De consensu evangelistarum* (*Harmony on the Gospels*), Augustine's main concern was to show that there was no real contradiction in the different gospel accounts of John, although he admitted that he could not reconcile the precise sequence of events in relation to John sending his disciples to ask Jesus a question.[42] In a sermon on the *Cum audisset* passage, however, Augustine began by observing that '[the Gospel] has set before us a question touching John the Baptist'. He then adopted the by now traditional view that John sent his disciples to resolve their uncertainties, not his own. First he described the virtues and

---

[41] Chrysostom, *Homilies on Matthew* 36.

[42] '[S]ed quis eorum recordationis suae, quis rerum ipsarum hic ordinem teneat, non apparet' ('but it is not clear which of them gives the order of his own memories, and which keeps to the [historical] order of the things themselves'): Augustine, *De consensu evangelistarum* 2.31.78.

actions of John and observed that 'when he [John] saw the Lord, he … pointed his finger toward him and said, "Behold the Lamb of God, who takes away the sins of the world", "behold, here he is"'.[43] We will return to the significance of the pointing finger, an image also used by Jerome. What is more, Augustine imagined the words John used, having John himself deny his doubting:

> Go then, ask him: not because I doubt, but that you may be instructed (*non quia ego dubito, sed ut uos instruamini*). Go, ask him, hear from him himself what I am in the habit of telling you; you have heard the herald, be confirmed by the judge. Go, ask Him, 'Art thou he who should come, or do we look for another?' So they went and asked; for their own sake, not for John (*propter se, non propter Ioannem*).[44]

Finally, Gregory the Great (d. 604) touched on the subject of John's question in his sixth Homily on Ezekiel, and expanded his interpretation in a Homily on the Gospels.[45] In the latter, Gregory began, like Augustine, by drawing attention to the question raised by a literal reading: 'It must be asked, dear brethren, why John asked … as if he did not know whom he had prophesied and baptized'.[46] For Gregory, following Origen and Jerome, John did not ask because he doubted that Jesus was the Redeemer of the world, but so as to know whether the one who had come into the world would descend into hell and, as the one who had announced Jesus in this world, he should do the same in hell. But Gregory also invited his listeners to think about the change of location, observing:

> the question can be quickly resolved if we think about the order of events: on the river Jordan, John had stated that [Jesus] was the Redeemer of the world, but now in prison, he poses the question – not because he doubted that this was the Redeemer of the world (*non quia ipsum esse mundi Redemptorem dubitat*), instead, he asks that he may know whether he who, in his own person had come into the world, would in his own person descend also to the world below.[47]

---

[43] Augustine, *Sermo* 66, line 49 (CChr.SL 41Aa). For Jerome, see *Commentary on Matthew* 11.9 (transl. Scheck, 130).

[44] Augustine, *Sermo* 66, lines 49–53.

[45] Gregory the Great, *Homiliae in Hiezechihelem prophetam* 1.1, line 95 (CChr.SL 142).

[46] Gregory the Great, *Homiliae in Euangelia* 1.6.1, line 1 (CChr.SL 141).

[47] Ibid., line 11.

For Gregory, location and context modified John's thinking, which was focused on Christ's actions.

In sum, these Church Fathers, Latin and Greek, acknowledged that a literal reading raised the possibility that John was a doubter, for why else did he ask a question? The extent of many of their responses – barely hinted at here – indicates that the question was troubling. It is not surprising that they minimized the possibility that this was doubt in faith, arguing that the Baptist was either requesting information about his own future role or asking so as to instruct his jealous disciples. They imagined the encounter and, in the case of Augustine, enlivened the exchange by putting words into John's mouth. Doubt on the part of the Baptist himself, if acknowledged at all, was about means. Apart from Tertullian, doubting John was acknowledged only as a phantom to be argued away, usually by assigning the doubt or uncertainty to his disciples, or, less often, to the crowd listening to Jesus. The means to dissolving these doubts were then supplied: seeing and hearing, signs and wonders, as well as, in Ambrose, the virtual touching experienced through Thomas.

MEDIEVAL ECHOES 1: BIBLICAL EXEGESIS

The Ordinary Gloss (*Glossa Ordinaria*) as developed in the central Middle Ages relied heavily on patristic scholarship as well as on early medieval exegetes, particularly Bede, for whose contribution there is insufficient space here. Begun in the late eleventh century as a teaching tool at the school of Anselm in Laon, the gloss was completed in Paris by *c.*1175, taking a more or less stable, though never entirely fixed, form.[48] The treatment of Matthew's Gospel was among the earliest, produced in Laon. As Lesley Smith has recently reminded us, the gloss was the work which in the late Middle Ages 'gave the simple [Bible] text its voice'.[49] It was the key most scholars would have encountered. On John's question it offered a series of familiar points: John, who was to be killed by Herod, asked the question, but not because he doubted or disputed (*non quia dubitet*) what he himself had said and heard elsewhere (with a reference to 'Behold the Lamb of God' [John 1: 29], and 'This is my beloved son' [Mark 1: 11; Matt.

---

[48] Lesley Smith, *The* Glossa Ordinaria: *The Making of a Medieval Bible Commentary* (Leiden, 2009).

[49] Ibid. 1.

3: 17; Luke 3: 22]). Rather, John asked his question 'so that the messengers seeing the signs should believe in the miracles of Christ, lest another Christ be expected'. This was needed because John's disciples had shown pride against, and envy of, Christ. Again echoing earlier commentators, the glossator explained the grammatical nuance to be understood in the question, 'Art thou he who is to come?', pointing out that John did not use 'who came'. John was therefore to be understood as asking whether, as the one who announced Christ on this earth and was about to descend to hell, he should announce Christ below. In short, 'is it appropriate for the son of God to die, or are you to send another to this sacred [task]?'[50]

In summing up earlier learning, the Ordinary Gloss was by no means an end point: scholars continued to produce commentaries which drew on, clarified and added to its content. In the 1230s and early 1240s, for example, the earliest major mendicant commentator, the Dominican Hugh of Saint-Cher (d. 1263), completed a commentary based on his teaching in Paris, the *Postilla in totam bibliam*. It was intended as a supplement to the Ordinary Gloss and some 420 manuscripts have so far been located, with the peak of circulation in the two decades to *c*.1260.[51] In the longer gloss on Matthew, completed *c*.1239, the *Postilla* made explicit use of earlier writers, including Gregory and Hilary. It introduced no new arguments: once more the disciples doubted, not John. The structure of the gloss may nonetheless reflect what was uppermost in the writer's mind: it opened by asserting that John, knowing he was about to die, asked his question because he wished 'to remove from the hearts of his disciples all doubt about Christ (*omnem dubitationem amovere … de Christo*)'.[52]

The other thirteenth-century commentary which cannot be passed over in silence is the *Catena Aurea* of a still more famous Dominican, Thomas Aquinas (d. 1274). A compilation of the writings of the Fathers arranged around gospel passages, the *Catena* was

[50] *Biblia Latina cum Glossa ordinaria*, ed. Karlfried Froehlich and Margaret T. Gibson, 4 vols (facsimile reprint of the *editio princeps* of Adolph Rusch of Strassburg, 1480/81; Turnhout, 1992), vol. 4, on Matthew 11.
[51] See Patricia Stirnemann, 'Les manuscrits de la *Postille*', in L.-J. Bataillon, G. Dahan and P.-M. Gy, eds, *Hugues de Saint-Cher (†1263). Bibliste et théologien* (Turnhout, 2004), 31–42, at 31, 37, 42 (table).
[52] Hugh of Saint-Cher, *In Evangelia secundum Matthaeum, Lucam, Marcum & Ioannem*, in *Hugonis de sancto Charo, Opera Omnia in Universum Vetus & Novum Testamentum*, vol. 8, ed. Armand Benjamin Caillau and B. Saint-Yves (Venice, 1703), 42va.

composed in 1263.[53] On Matthew 11: 2–5 Aquinas drew the Fathers into a virtual conversation, in a format designed to be memorable. Thus he quoted Gregory's emphasis on the need to investigate the passage and establish whether John knew Christ, and answered this with Ambrose's argument that John doubted, though not in faith. To Ambrose, Chrysostom was made to respond critically: to think that John could have doubted seemed hardly reasonable, since John was not in ignorance of Christ's death, having been the first to preach it. The conversation continued with further passages from Gregory, Ambrose and Chrysostom and from Hilary, Jerome and the Ordinary Gloss. It concluded with mystical interpretations which go beyond the historical, literal reading which is of concern here.

A primary purpose of works such as the Ordinary Gloss, Hugh's *Postilla* and Aquinas's *Catena* was to guide students. The Dominican Aquinas presumably had in mind the preaching friars of his own order, but many other university students would have been heading towards careers in the Church outside the religious orders and were increasingly anticipating that they would preach. So we might expect to find echoes of the biblical commentaries in sermons produced in this period. The pericope including Matthew 11: 2, *Cum audisset Iohannes*, was, conveniently for our purposes, the gospel reading for the second or third Sunday of Advent. A quick exploration of the Biblioteca Nazionale in Florence for manuscript collections containing sermons on this pericope or for the feast of the Baptist that were produced or widely circulated in thirteenth- and early fourteenth-century northern Italy turned up eight: those of the Franciscans Luca de Bitonto (*fl.* before 1255) and Bonaventure (d. 1274), the Dominicans Aldobrandinus de Toscanella (*fl.* 1287–92), Giordano da Pisa (d. 1311), Hugo da Prato florido (d. 1322) and Giovanni da San Gimignano (*c.*1260–*c.*1333), a Servite, Luca da Prato, and an eighth which remains anonymous.[54] Like biblical commentaries, these sermons made use

---

[53] Thomas Aquinas, *Catena aurea in quatuor Evangelia*, 1: *Expositio in Matthaeum*, ed. A. Guarenti, 2nd edn (Turin, 1953). For the date, see Michael Arges, 'New Evidence concerning the Date of Thomas Aquinas's *Lectura* on Matthew', *MedS* 49 (1987), 517–23, at 519–20. On the text more generally, see Thomas Weinandy, Daniel A. Keating and John Yocum, eds, *Aquinas on Scripture: An Introduction to his Biblical Commentaries* (London, 2005).

[54] Florence, Biblioteca Nazionale Centrale [hereafter: BNCF], Conventi soppressi (CS) D 7 2710, Luca da Bitonto, *Sermonario festivo et dominicales*, fol. 13ᵛ (*Cum audisset*); CS E 6 1017, Bonaventure, Sermons, in the index to the manuscript, on fol. 130ᵛ, has: 'In sancto iohanne baptista. Ille erat lucerna ardens [John 5: 35]', but the relevant pages of the manuscript are now missing; CS B 2 1026, Aldobrandinus de Toscanella, Sermon

of patristic writers. Of the latter, as we have seen, Augustine, Gregory the Great and John Chrysostom, whose sermons or homilies were widely copied, had all preached on the Matthew passage and the question it raised. Moreover, as in the late antique period, so in thirteenth-century Italy, heresy was a key concern in the extant writings of learned believers, both clerical and lay. Three of this small sample of thirteenth- or early fourteenth-century sermons on the Baptist used the pericope *Cum audisset*. Yet doubt seems to have made its way into only one, that of Aldobrandino da Toscanella, who spent most of his career as a *lector* in Dominican *studia*, communicating Thomist teachings to younger friars.[55]

The holdings of the Florentine Biblioteca Nazionale are by no means a complete guide to Italian sermon collections. There may well be a bundle of thirteenth-century sermons on the Baptist and doubt in another library. It would probably be possible to expand this brief list by looking at published editions. But it would remain risky to push this sort of argument any harder, given the fragmentary evidence we have for mostly oral events. If most of the preachers identified knew at least the *Glossa Ordinaria* on *Cum audisset*, with its implications of a doubting or at least uncertain prophet, why did this quality not make it into their sermons on the Baptist?

One immediate explanation for the silence on doubting John lies in the purpose of sermons, and in particular of the sermon collections consulted. They were intended to assist other preachers, perhaps to demonstrate the learning of the writer, but above all to promote firm belief, in the wake of the Fourth Lateran Council of 1215 and its

---

for the nativity of John the Baptist, fols 43^r–45^v ('[H]ic e[st] d[e] quo scriptum est ecce m[it]to angelum meum qui preparabit uiam ante faciem tuam' [Matt. 11: 10]), and another sermon for his feast day, fols 58^v–60^r ('[P]osuisti de super caput eius co[ronam] de la[pi]', Ps. 20: 4, a common usage for feasts of saints); II iv 145, Giordano da Pisa, *Le prediche*, fol. 35^v, Sermon preached in the bishop's palace on the feast of the Baptist, 24 June 1303 ('Exultauit infans in utero eius' [Luke 1: 41]); CS I ii 33, Hugo da Prato florido, *Sermones Dominicales, de sanctis, de gratia*, fols 119^v–120^r ('[E]rat etiam magnus coram domino' [Luke 1: 15]); I II 40, Giovanni da San Gimignano, *Sermones de festis per totum annum*, fol. 17^v (*Cum audisset*); CS C 4 1668, Luca da Prato, *Sermones*, fol. 9^r (*Cum audisset*); CS I VIII 39, *Sermones sacri incerti auctoris* (a manuscript once owned by San Marco, Florence), fol. 20^v (*Cum audisset*), fols 21^r–22^r ('Quid existis in desertum uidere arundinem?').

[55] For the date, see T. Kaeppeli, 'La tradizione manoscritta delle opere di Aldobrandino da Toscanella', *AFP* 8 (1938), 163–92. On Aldobrandino as a Thomist, see Carlo Delcorno, *La predicazione nell'età comunale* (Florence, 1974), 29; also Anna Pecorini Cignoni, 'Un sermone latino *Francisci confessoris* di Albrandino da Toscanella', *Studi Francescani* 98 (2001), 285–99, at 286.

opening constitution, *Firmiter credimus*.[56] As numerous modern writers have made plain, however, not all Christians were required to perform or demonstrate the same level of firm belief.[57] For Aquinas, full understanding of faith, *cognitio*, was expected of the *maiores*, the clergy, responsible for teaching the *minores*, the laity.[58] Was there any benefit in raising the problematic question of his doubt or uncertainty when preaching to the laity about the Baptist? As the list in note 55 illustrates, there were after all, other useful pericopes to which a preacher could turn.

MEDIEVAL ECHOES 2: DISPUTE LITERATURE

Arguments from silence are never very convincing, so let us move to firmer ground, and texts where we do find an emphasis on doubting John: the dispute literature. A genre which returned to prominence in the central Middle Ages, in part as a result of disputation in the Schools, these texts engaged directly with the teaching of various groups, including dualists whom modern historians tend to call Cathars but whose followers called them 'good men' or 'good women'.[59] Eckbert von Schönau (d. 1184) and Alain de Lille (d. 1202) produced two of the early classics. The patristic dialogue form also continued: Gerhard Rottenwöhrer has catalogued a large number of anti-heretical polemics constructed in the form of debates with heretics which were not infrequently written by

---

[56] 'Constitutiones', Lateran IV, in J. Alberigo et al., eds, *Conciliorum Oecumenicorum Decreta* (Bologna, 1973), 230–71, at 230.

[57] See, for example, J.-C. Schmitt, 'Du bon usage du "Credo"', in *Faire croire: Modalités de la diffusion et de la réception des messages religieux du XII* au XV* siècle. Table ronde organisée par l'École française de Rome, en collaboration avec l'Institut d'histoire médiévale de l'Université de Padoue* (Rome, 1981), 337–61; Norman Tanner and Sethina Watson, 'Least of the Laity: The Minimum Requirements for a Medieval Christian', *JMedH* 32 (2006), 395–423; Peter Biller, 'Intellectuals and the Masses: Oxen and She-asses in the Medieval Church', in Arnold, ed., *Oxford Handbook of Medieval Christianity*, 323–39.

[58] 'Sed contra, maiores debent docere fidem minoribus. Sed qui docet, debet plenius scire. Ergo tenentur magis explicite scire quam minores. Praeterea, ei cui plus est commissum, plus exigetur ab eo. Sed maioribus plus commissum est quam minoribus. Ergo plus ab eis exigetur de fidei cognitione': Aquinas, *Scriptum super Libros Sententiarum magistri Petri Lombardi*, III dist 25 q.2, a. 1 quaestiuncula 3.

[59] For an illuminating introduction to these writings, see Lucy Sackville, *Heresy and Heretics in the Thirteenth Century: The Textual Representations* (York, 2011). On dialogue and dialectic as 'the science of doubt,' see Giles Constable, *The Reformation of the Twelfth Century* (Cambridge, 1996), 130.

converts to orthodoxy.[60] Of the dispute texts probably produced in Italy, one of the earliest to refer to John the Baptist as a doubter was the *Summa contra haereticos* of Pseudo-Prepositinus of Cremona, written in the late twelfth century and extant in ten thirteenth- or fourteenth-century manuscripts.[61] The structure of the text as a dispute allowed the anonymous writer to distinguish clearly between the arguments attributed to the voice of the *Catholicus* and to the *Cathari*. For Cathars, who denied the humanity of Christ, John's role as a prophet had to be refuted because it formed part of the narrative of the redemption of humanity through Christ's birth, death and resurrection.[62]

Pseudo-Prepositinus is one of just two writers who did more than briefly assert the heretical view of John as a doubter:

Again, in the same gospel of Matthew it is said (11: 2–3): 'Now when John had heard in the prison the works of Christ, he sent two of his disciples, And said unto him, Art thou he that is to come, or should we look for another?' See, here it is held that John had doubts about Christ (*dubitavit de Christo*); therefore he did not believe he exists; therefore he did not have his faith; therefore he did not please God; because (cf. Hebrews 11: 6): 'without faith it is impossible to please God'; thus therefore he was evil, and consequently to be damned.[63]

---

[60] Gerhard Rottenwöhrer, *Der Katharismus*, 5 vols (Bad Honnef, 1982–90), especially vol. 1/i–ii, *Quellen zum Katharismus*.

[61] *The* Summa contra haereticos *ascribed to Praepositinus of Cremona*, ed. Joseph N. Garvin and James A. Corbett (Notre Dame, IN, 1958).

[62] For a brief list of Cathar teachings on the Baptist, but without reference to doubt, see Arno Borst, *Die Katharer*, MGH Schriften 12, 160, 314. Confessions describing Cathar teachings occasionally confirm the idea that the Baptist was damned: see, for example, Toulouse, Bibliothèque publique, MS 609, fol. 142ᵛ (1245), Confession of Na Gauzio, widow of Raymund Sans of Cumiers (Aude): 'et beatus Joannes Baptista erat diabolus', in 'Interrogatoires subis par des hérétiques albigeois par-devant frère Bernard de Caux, inquisiteur, de 1245 à 1253', typescript, 5 vols, 5: 935, online at: <http://babel.hathitrust.org/cgi/pt?id=nnc1.0047197366;view=1up;seq=331>,   last accessed 24 March 2015. See also a much later example from Turin: Confession of Jacobus Bech of Chieri, 21 August 1388: 'quod prophete, patriarce ac eciam beatus Iohannes Batista, quos ecclesia romana tenet sanctos seu veneratur, sunt dampnati', in G. Amati, ed., 'Processus contra Valdenses in Lombardia superiori anno 1387', *Archivio storico italiano* 3rd ser. 1/ii (1865), 3–52; 2/i (1865), 3–61, at 52.

[63] Summa contra haereticos *ascribed to Praepositinus of Cremona*, ed. Garvin and Corbett, 32.

Doubt here is immediately equated to lack of belief and to absence of faith, indeed to a failure to believe that Christ exists at all. Lack of faith justifies damnation.

Pseudo-Prepositinus's counter-arguments derived from texts or ideas that we have already come across, placing doubt in the heads of John's disciples, and insisting on the need to learn in faith:

> To the first [point], let us reply by interemption [i.e. by total destruc-
> tion of the argument], saying that John did not doubt, but rather, since
> his disciples were doubting, he sent them to Christ, wishing to teach
> them in faith, so that hearing and considering his words and miracles,
> they would be instructed and believe. For how could doubts about
> Christ have been held by the man who not long before had pointed
> him out with his finger (*digito demonstraverat*), saying (John 1: 29):
> 'Behold the Lamb of God, Behold he who takes away the sins of the
> world?'[64]

Like Augustine and Jerome, when Pseudo-Prepositinus referred to a standard proof that John knew who Christ was, in the phrase 'Behold the Lamb of God', he used a visual, gestural image, a pointing finger. This language did not derive from the biblical account of the Baptist. Instead, in imagining John pointing, it both stemmed from the commentary tradition and matched contemporary iconography, where John was often shown pointing, a mark of certainty and of knowledge, with a strongly epideictic function.

The interplay between written and visual modes of argument is no surprise. In a sermon on the resurrection for the first Sunday after Easter, Pope Innocent III (1198–1216) drew on visual evidence, for example, when considering the various questions that might be asked about Christ's resurrection. The questions included why Jesus appeared to women first rather than to men, why he appeared ten times and whether his resurrected body was clothed. To answer the last of these queries, the pope supplied passages from the New Testament to demonstrate that the resurrected Christ was dressed and then added: 'and this is proven not just from new paintings in churches but also from old ones, which claim their origin from the primitive Church'.[65] There can be no certainty about which images Innocent

---

[64] Ibid.

[65] '[H]oc ipsum non solum novae, sed veteres ecclesiarum picturae testantur, quae ab ipsa primitiva Ecclesia causae primordium asserunt': PL 217, cols 403–4.

had in mind, although there are many candidates: perhaps a scene of Christ's life in the nave of Old St Peter's;[66] or the resurrected Christ in the Christological cycle in the eighth-century oratory of John VII in the same basilica, which housed the Veronica, an icon dear to his heart;[67] or perhaps something heard about or remembered from earlier travels, such as the mosaic of Christ appearing to the Apostles, at Sant'Apollinare Nuovo in Ravenna (*c*.520). Innocent was happy to exploit the power of both text and image as proof. The same sermon also introduced another allusion to the power of the visual: 'Indeed, lest anyone could doubt this (*ne quis posset super hoc aliquatenus dubitare*), [Christ] kept the signs of the wounds on his body, one reason for which was to confirm the faith of the apostles more strongly'.[68] For Innocent, as for his contemporaries, visual evidence could be a powerful tool.

Another dispute text produced in Italy in the late twelfth century originated as the confession of Bonacursus, a convert from the Cathars, to whose words were later added materials intended for the rebuttal of unorthodox doctrines. On John, the resulting composite text stated simply that the Cathars

> … condemn John himself, than whom none is greater, according to the word of the Lord. Why? Because the Lord says in the Gospel, 'He that is the lesser in the kingdom of God is greater than he' and because he had doubts about Christ (*dubitavit de Christo*) by saying 'Art thou he who is to come, or do we look for another?'[69]

The response was furnished later in the text and gathered together biblical texts explaining John's virtues without directly tackling the question of doubt.[70]

---

[66] Giacomo Grimaldi produced a very incomplete image of the cycle, so it is impossible to ascertain whether it included a clothed resurrected Christ.

[67] Drawing in Vatican City, BAV, Barb. lat. 2732, Grimaldi, 'Instrumenta Autentica' 1612, for which see Ann Van Dijk, 'Jerusalem, Antioch, Rome and Constantinople: The Peter Cycle in the Oratory of Pope John VII (705–707)', *Dumbarton Oaks Papers* 55 (2001), 305–28, fig. 3.

[68] PL 217, col. 401.

[69] *Manifestatio haeresis catharorum quam fecit Bonacursus*, transl. in Walter L. Wakefield and Austin P. Evans, *Heresies of the High Middle Ages* (New York, 1969), 170–3, at 172; for the Latin, see PL 204, col. 776. See also Ilarino da Milano, 'La "Manifestatio heresis catarorum"', *Aevum* 12 (1938), 281–333; Raoul Manselli, 'Per la storia dell'eresia', *Bullettino dell'Istituto Storico Italiano per il Medioevo e Archivio Muratoriano* 67 (1955), 189–211, which includes an edition of a different version, Paris, BN, MS lat. 14927.

[70] PL 204, col. 780.

Judging from the numbers extant, the production of dispute texts in northern Italy seems to have grown in the early thirteenth century. The *Disputatio inter Catholicum et Paterinum haereticorum* written by an otherwise unidentified layman called Georgius has been dated to *c*.1210–34 by its recent editor, Carola Hoécker. It was among the most successful northern Italian texts against heresy, surviving in more than fifty manuscripts and widely copied. This time the text attributed to the *Manicheus* (by this date a generic term) links John's doubt with the timing of his death. John doubted when he sent two of his disciples to ask Jesus, "'Art thou he who is to come or do we look for another?' Moreover on their return he had [already] been seized by death and died in doubt and thus he is damned.'[71] In constructing his response, Georgius adopted multiple approaches, turning first to the words of Jesus, with a summary of his sermon to the crowds after John's disciples had left. He also offered a clue to his tactic of reading verse-by-verse down the page of a biblical text so as to construct his argument:

> *Catholicus* [addressing the *Manicheus*]: Jesus Christ gives much better witness of [John] after the departure of these disciples than you suggest, saying of him to the crowds 'What went ye out into the wilderness to see? A reed tossed by the wind?' As though he were saying 'No', to which he adds, 'A man clothed in soft raiment?' No, [Matt. 11: 7–8]. … *And below (Et infra)*[72] he calls him 'More than a prophet' [Matt. 11: 9]. … Because [John] had been his angel on earth, he wanted to be his angel in hell. In fact therefore [John] doubted the passage of Christ to hell and asked him about it. 'Art thou he who should come …'

Having explained John's question, Georgius then addresses the 'most wicked ones' with a fuller discussion of doubt itself:

> Not every doubt is damning and deadly … And even if this doubt of John's were damaging, you do not have it from the Gospel that he died in doubt. More correctly: his messengers could have returned and reported to him. For if, as you say, he had already been seized by death, then Jesus instructed them poorly when he said: *Ite, renunciate Iohanni* [Matt. 11: 4], because he ordered something impossible; and his yoke there would not be easy [Matt. 11: 30], but 'grievous to be

---

[71] Georgius, *Disputatio inter Catholicum et Paterinum haereticum. Untersuchungen zum Text, Handschriften und Edition*, ed. Carola Hoécker (Florence, 2001), 37.

[72] Emphasis mine.

borne' [Matt. 23: 4] because he died before he could renounce. It is evident, therefore, that your teaching is false, because you condemn one praised by the Lord, and turn the teaching of Christ into the vice of impossibility.[73]

For Georgius – like the Fathers – the type of doubt was to be differentiated. Doubt about Christ as the Messiah would surely have been 'damning and deadly'. Georgius acknowledged that John's doubt might have been damaging, but did not accept that he died in doubt.

In case his first arguments did not convince, Georgius went on to introduce the familiar idea that it was John's disciples who doubted Christ and did not believe John: 'Therefore, lest they should remain in this doubt, he sent them to Jesus, so that Jesus himself should proffer witness of himself as a good prophet.' In conclusion, Georgius again tried to downplay the significance of John's question. To prove that putting a question need not imply that the one asking did not know the answer, he referred to Christ's exchange with the Pharisees about paying tribute to Caesar: 'Nor does it follow [that "because] he asked, therefore he doubted." Take for example (*instantia*): Christ [who] asked, saying, "Whose is this coin?" [cf. Matt. 22: 29]. "Therefore, he doubted", is not true'.[74]

Whoever Georgius was, his is a sophisticated, multi-layered reply: grammatically aware, deploying the language of scholastic disputation, careful about the potentially diverse meanings of doubt and drawn from biblical commentary, but also based on direct perusal of the relevant gospel passages. Hoécker convincingly concludes, nonetheless, that he was a layman, and probably a notary.

Another work which originated in a lay context was the *Liber Suprastella* (Book of the Higher Star) by Salvus Burci, a notary in Piacenza, on the river Po south of Milan. Burci wrote his treatise in 1235 and chose the title, he explained, to differentiate it from a book by heretics entitled 'Star'. His other reason for the title was that, 'just as the stars show the way to those travelling at sea and bring them to harbour, so this book shows the way of the true faith and leads to the port of salvation'.[75] The modern editor of the *Liber*, Caterina Bruschi, proposes that Burci had probably been involved as a notary in

---

[73] Ibid.

[74] 'Nec sequitur, *interrogavit*, ergo dubitavit. Instantia: Christus *interrogavit dicens: Cuius est hoc numisma* (cf. Matt 22: 29)? "Ergo dubitavit", non est verum': ibid. 37–8.

[75] Salvus Burci, *Liber Suprastella*, ed. Caterina Bruschi (Rome, 2002), 3.

episcopal inquisitions which had been taking place in Piacenza. Part at least of his reason for taking up his pen may have been to prove the innocence of the patrons in whose house he was writing, a family linked to some of those accused of heretical beliefs in the preceding years.[76]

Burci's text is less orderly than some of the other dispute texts and his method – like that of Georgius – stems as much from his training as a notary and the *ars dictaminis* as from biblical commentary. In the same manner as other writers of dispute texts, he first sets out the arguments of the heretics, often quoting biblical passages, and then gives his answer, the Catholic viewpoint, again using biblical passages and arguments drawn from them. The *Liber* dedicates a whole chapter to John the Baptist, including the assertion that heretics believe that John is 'most false, because he was a liar and doubted the advent of Christ' and, if he was not actually a demon, he at least came from the devil.[77] The case for John the doubter is further tied to particular groups among contemporary heretics. According to Burci, the Concorezzenses – one of the Cathar groups identified by inquisitors in northern Italy – argued that John doubted Christ on the simple grounds that he sent his disciples to put the question, 'Are you the one?' 'So, he doubted the advent of Christ, therefore he is evil'. So far, so familiar. But Burci then puts the following words in the mouths of the heretics: 'Oh Church of the devil which is called Roman, be still! Why? Because you believe John to be a member of Christ, but he is a member of the devil'.[78]

Demonizing heretics as the body of the devil, contrasted to Catholic Christians as the body of Christ, is a topos in anti-heretical polemics.[79] It therefore might seem appropriate to set aside the heat of Burci's imaginative ventriloquizing as the rhetorical flourish of a writer seeking to underline his own and his patrons' orthodoxy by denigrating his opponents' extreme tone. But the pitch is equalled by the voice Burci adopted to explain his own, orthodox viewpoint: 'I respond, "Oh, hopeless heretics not understanding Scripture, when

[76] Ibid. xii–xiii.
[77] Ibid. 85.
[78] Ibid.
[79] See, for example, the Cistercian Caesarius of Heisterbach's *Dialogus miraculorum*, ed. N. Nösges and H. Schneider, Fontes Christiani 86/1–5 (Turnhout, 2009), distinctio 5, 'De daemonibus', written in the early thirteenth century and discussed in Grado Giovanni Merlo, '"Membra Diaboli". Demoni ed eretici medievali', *Nuova rivista storica* 72 (1988), 583–98.

will you sustain the punishment for such great blasphemy … ?'"[80] Heat is matched by heat.

Among the further arguments listed, Burci then analyses the syntax of John's words in a manner which echoes his training as a notary as much as it does earlier biblical commentary. He separates the sentence into two halves, the first of which, in his view, is not to be read as a question (*non legatur interrogative*):

> And note that John did not say, 'Are you (*es tu*), the one who is to come?' Rather he said, 'You are (*tu es*) the one who is to come'. That is, to judge (*ad judicandum*) … But then what follows is to be read as a question, 'Or do we expect another?' That is, to judge? As though he were saying we are not 'expecting another'. The heretics would perhaps say, 'Why did he send his disciples to Jesus if he did not doubt?' I reply: 'note that John sent them at a time when Christ was doing miracles, therefore he sent them because John wanted [to ensure that] his disciples would believe firmly (*crederent firmiter*) in Jesus Christ, without any doubt, as he foresaw that he would have to be separated from them because he was to be decapitated.[81]

Addressing the 'snake-like heretics', Burci asks whether they wish to see openly (*videre aperte*) that John did not doubt, noting as his evidence that when John sent his disciples, Jesus started praising him immediately, 'which he would not have done so quickly had John doubted, instead he would have censured, not praised [him]'. This opens the path to a discussion of the *similitudines* which Christ used in praising John, who was *not* like 'a reed, moved by the wind' (cf. Matt. 11: 7–8). Rather, it is as though Jesus was saying that John was 'certain about Christ, without any doubt' (*firmus de Christo sine dubitatione aliqua*). Earlier in this passage Burci focused on the phrase 'more than a prophet', observing: 'The prophets, in truth, prophesied Christ's advent, this [prophet] however pointed with his finger, saying "Behold the Lamb of God", etc.' Burci then explained the meaning of the pointing finger: 'If he pointed with his finger then he was not doubting (*Si digitto ostendit ergo non fuit dubius*), as the ignorant heretics say, therefore in consequence [he was] good.'[82]

---

[80] Burci, *Liber Suprastella*, 85.

[81] Ibid. 87.

[82] 'Prophete vero prophetiçaverunt de adventu Christi, iste vero digitto ostendit, dicens: "ecce Agnus Dei", et cetera. Si digitto ostendit ergo non fuit dubius, sicut dicunt erretici idiote, ergo per consequenciam bonus': ibid. 88.

As with the biblical commentaries and the sermons, there are too many details in the argument and too many dispute texts to do them justice here. A few final works cannot, however, be ignored. The first is a *Summa contra haereticos* dated to *c*.1235 and attributed to the Dominican Peter of Verona (d. 1252), who had grown up among heretics.[83] In Peter's *Summa*, as in Burci's *Liber Suprastella*, a whole chapter is dedicated to John the Baptist (Fig. 2). As proof that John was a doubter, the heretic proffers the *timing* of Christ's reply to the disciples: he tells them to go and tell John what they had seen, but John was dead before they got back to him, so could not have known the truth. Moreover Christ's reference to the blessed who are not scandalized is to be understood as an explicit allusion to John, who was. To this, the Catholic answers that the doubt was not John's but that of his disciples, and he sent them so that *oculata fide* ('with the confidence of eye-witnesses'), they could see what they were doubting. John acts in the manner of a good schoolmaster (*more boni magistri*). The Catholic also adds that for Christ to send the disciples back would have been otiose had the Baptist been already dead, and that thinking such a thing of Christ is wicked.[84]

Another work attributed to a friar, the *Summa contra hereticos* written by a Franciscan, Pseudo-James of Capelli *c*.1240–60, provides an almost identical statement: it was John's disciples who doubted, not John himself.[85] The more famous writings of Moneta of Cremona, a Dominican (d. after 1238) who again dedicated a chapter to John the Baptist in his *Adversus Catharos et Valdenses*, or Andreas Florentinus, who wrote another *Summa* between 1270/80 and 1300, add refinements to these dispute texts.[86] Moneta elegantly reworks existing arguments, asserting that John 'never doubted of Christ' (*nunquam dubitavit de Christo*) and instead that '[his] disciples doubted and were even unbelieving' (*Constat ergo Johannis discipulos dubitasse de Christo &*

---

[83] For medieval hagiographers' insistence that 'nearly all his kinsmen were heretics', see Donald Prudlo, *The Martyred Inquisitor: The Life and Cult of Peter of Verona (†1252)* (Aldershot, 2008), 19–21.

[84] BNCF, CS, A 9 1738, fol. 40ʳ.

[85] 'Ad predicta igitur respondemus dicentes, quoniam beatus Iohannes numquam de christo dubitavit, quin crederet eum filium dei et pro salute hominum in mundo venisse, sed discipulis eius dubitaverunt': Pseudo-James of Capelli, *Summa contra hereticos*, in *L'Eresia catara. Saggio storico filosofico con in appendice* Disputationes nonnullae adversus haereticos, *codice inedito del secolo xiii della biblioteca Malatestiana di Cesena*, ed. Dino Bazzocchi (Bologna, 1920), cvii.

[86] Andreas Florentinus, *Summa contra hereticos* (MGH Quellen 23).

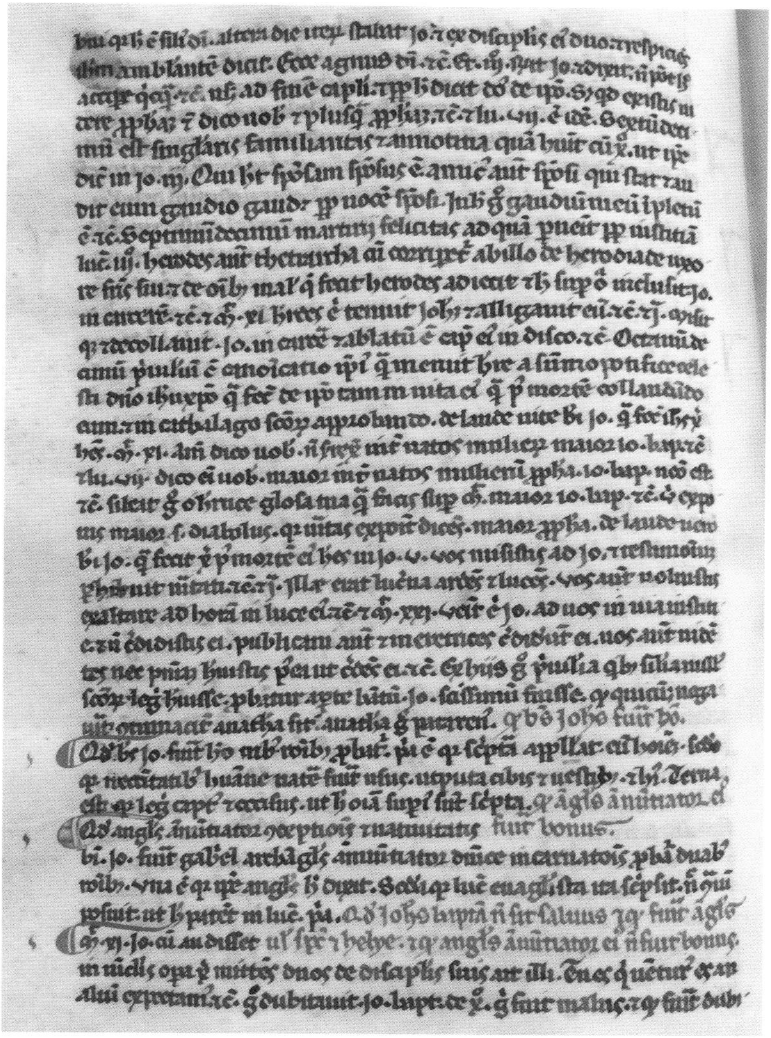

Figure 2. BNCF *conventi soppressi* A 9 1738, fol. 39ᵛ, an elegant, rubricated example of the format of these dispute texts, allowing the reader to track and easily separate arguments and counter-arguments. Note the final rubric: 'Quod Iohannes Baptista non sit saluus …'

etiam fuisse incredulos). So, once again, 'John asked on behalf of his disciples' (*Licet ergo quaesiverit Johannes per discipulos, non tamen dubitavit*).[87] Andreas, on the other hand, pointing out how to read the passage and explaining the correct understanding of the punctuation, suggests that John 'wanted to make his disciples certain about Christ, because he recognized that they were doubting' (*de Christo certificare discipulos voluit, quia sensit eos dubitare*).[88] Other texts could be added, but they would not change the figure of a doubting John.

DEFENDING JOHN FROM DOUBT

In her 1991 Royal Historical Society lecture, Susan Reynolds observed that '[r]ecent work by medievalists suggests that differences in the content and processes of thought can better be approached through seeing how particular groups of people develop quite specific elements of thought and considering the methods of transmission both within the group and from it to society at large.'[89] This essay has sought to illustrate some of the content of thought about John the Baptist and how it was transmitted. It has shown how the figure of a 'doubting John', perceptible in a biblical story, was acknowledged, perpetuated, reinterpreted or denied. For the early exegetes, other than Tertullian, John's question revealed uncertainty about the means of salvation, but not about Christ's message. Yet even this uncertainty was distanced from John, and located instead in his disciples or the crowd listening to Jesus. The Fathers wrote about this in both commentary and sermon and did so in a context of often heated discussion, both with heretics such as Marcion of Pontus and with each other. For Ambrose, that John might have doubted acquired the connotations of an impossible 'error'. In twelfth- and thirteenth-century northern and central Italy, where the Baptist enjoyed particular prestige, the contours of the discussion relied heavily on the teachings of the Fathers. As Aquinas's *Catena Aurea* neatly reminds us, these were sufficiently familiar among the learned that they might even be read in a decontextualized, sequential mode similar to the scheme necessarily adopted here. But the dispute texts suggest more direct wrestling with the problem of unbelief. Learned

---

[87] Moneta of Cremona, *Adversus catharos et valdenses libri quinque* 3.1 (ed. Thomas Augustinus Ricchini [Rome, 1743], 229–30).

[88] Andreas Florentinus, *Summa* (MGH Quellen 23, 31).

[89] Reynolds, 'Social Mentalities', 40.

polemicists, both clerical and lay, portrayed heretics as constructing a doubting John on biblical grounds: heretics doubted his virtue and his status as a prophet. One of the means used to articulate the case was the literal, historical reading of the gospel account of John sending a question, a reading which would have been familiar to Jerome, Augustine or Gregory. Sometimes the heretics were ventriloquized into pushing this further, suggesting that John was a demon, beyond redemption because he died in doubt. In response, Catholic polemicists again drew on a repertoire of longstanding arguments, underlining the distinction between uncertainty and doubt. 'Not all doubt is damning and deadly', was how Georgius put it. Dorothea Weltecke is right to emphasize that different genres determined where different sorts of discussion could and did take place – in this case dispute literature – and others where it was more often avoided – in this instance, perhaps, sermons to the laity on the subject of John the Baptist. The figure of a doubting John was acknowledged in dispute texts in order to allow the counter-argument full play. The extent to which it was avoided in sermons on the Baptist deserves further investigation.

As Reynolds also argued, theologians considered a failure to believe to be dangerous.[90] Learned lay writers such as Georgius and Salvus Burci articulated the same view. The numbers of extant manuscripts show that a few of the dispute texts discussed here circulated widely. It would be hard to prove that they had an extensive lay audience, but some of the concern they evinced was surely prompted by anxiety about the possibility that Cathars were preaching and by the debates with heretics that we know took place, such as that between Bartolomeo da Breganza, bishop of Vicenza, and Petrus Gallus, a Cathar bishop, in the 1260s.[91] On the other hand, the biblical story of John the Baptist encompassed an element which, as Aquinas might have put it, made it simpler to restrict the discussion to the *maiores*.

Visual representations are not straightforward as evidence for doubt, though the use of gestures – particularly prominent in the visual representation of John – offer one technique for constructing a clear message.[92] Whether or not Giusto de' Menabuoi or his patrons

---

[90] Ibid. 35.

[91] See Lorenzo Paolini, 'Italian Catharism and Written Culture', in Peter Biller and Anne Hudson, eds, *Heresy and Literacy 1000–1530* (Cambridge, 1994), 83–103, at 90 n. 30.

[92] One reason Golinelli explicitly omitted them from his study was the possibility of alternative readings: Golinelli, *Il Medioevo degli increduli*, 15.

were aware of the debates about doubting John when planning his fresco for the baptistery in Padua, or were even paying attention to its likely viewers, I hope it is now evident why the disciples, not John, were the ones who needed to be portrayed looking uncertain. It is also, I hope, evident that the debates which took place in the Schools resonated in very particular ways beyond their benches.

'The very deceitfulness of devils': Firmilian and the Doubtful Baptisms of a Woman possessed by Demons

Charlotte Methuen*

University of Glasgow

In the mid-third century, a controversy relating to the validity of baptism by the lapsed broke out between Cyprian, bishop of Carthage, and Stephen, bishop of Rome. The former maintained that baptisms carried out by those who later lapsed had no validity, but must be repeated by a priest of whose behaviour there could be no doubt. Stephen maintained that baptisms carried out in the name of the Father, the Son and the Holy Spirit were to be viewed as valid, whoever had carried them out. Cyprian appealed to his fellow bishops for support. In 256, Firmilian, bishop of Caesarea, wrote to him outlining the case of a woman who had for some time baptized and celebrated the eucharist, but who had then been identified as being possessed by demons, casting her earlier actions into question. This essay will analyse the grounds for Firmilian's doubts about the validity of the woman's actions, his proposed response, and the way in which this episode has been used in modern debates about the ordination of women.

In the year 256, Firmilian, bishop of Caesarea, wrote to Cyprian, bishop of Carthage, about baptism. Firmilian's letter was a contribution to a heated debate about baptism which had been initiated by Cyprian. In the midst of a period of persecution, first under Decius and then under Valerian, Cyprian was seeking to establish a consensus amongst Christians concerning how baptisms by heretics should be regarded. He held that the validity of baptisms by any priest or bishop who was not recognizably a part of 'the Catholic church' was doubtful, and argued that in his own diocese candidates should only be baptized by a minister whose claim to authority had been confirmed by him as bishop. Stephen, bishop of Rome, did not agree, arguing that anyone who had been baptized in the name of the Father, the Son and the Holy Spirit should be regarded as properly baptized. Firmilian wrote in support of Cyprian, rejecting Stephen's position.[1]

* Theology and Religious Studies, No. 4 The Square, Glasgow, G41 2NW. E-mail: charlotte.methuen@glasgow.ac.uk.

[1] For a summary of the dispute between Cyprian and Stephen over rebaptism, see Maureen A. Tilley, 'When Schism becomes Heresy in Late Antiquity: Developing Doctrinal

Cyprian's substantial surviving correspondence about the status of those baptized by heretics or schismatics illustrates the significant anxieties experienced by third-century Christians in relation to the status of the sacraments they had received. In Cyprian's context, this question was related to the status of the lapsed. Could the authority of someone who had not stood firm under persecution be trusted, and with it the sacraments they offered? Or did confessors – those who had held to their faith under cross-examination – have an intrinsic and superior spiritual authority which trumped that of those who had lapsed or fled? This was a particular issue for Cyprian, who had himself fled Carthage when persecution broke out, much to the detriment of his own standing amongst the confessors.[2] Tensions around these questions were not yet as high in North Africa as they would become during the Diocletian persecution (303–5), which would see the rise of Donatism and its denial of the effectiveness of sacraments administered by those who had lapsed: Cyprian's discussion of the validity of baptism by heretics or schismatics laid the foundation for the position that the Donatists would later adopt. Firmilian's concerns, however, were somewhat different. Although his community too knew persecution, the role of the lapsed was not his main focus. Rather, Firmilian was engaged with a different question: how is it possible to be sure that someone's actions are inspired by the Holy Spirit? Unlike Cyprian, whose primary concern was the fallout after a period of persecution, Firmilian was confronted with a number of prophets, all of whom claimed to preach Christ, and was anxious

---

Deviance in the wounded Body of Christ', *JECS* 15 (2007), 1–21, at 7–10. For the controversy and its consequences, see also S. G. Hall, 'Stephen I of Rome and the Baptismal Controversy of 256', *Bibliothèque de la Revue d'histoire ecclésiastique* 8 (1987), 78–82; Hubert Kirchner, 'Der Ketzertaufstreit zwischen Karthago und Rom und seine Konsequenzen für die Frage nach den Grenzen der Kirche', *Zeitschrift für Kirchengeschichte* 81 (1970), 290–307. A good overview of Cyprian's writings on the question of rebaptism can be found in J. Jayakiran Sebastian, ' … *baptisma unum in ecclesia sancta* …': *A Theological Appraisal of the Baptismal Controversy in the Work and the Writings of Cyprian of Carthage*, Wissenschaftliche Beiträge aus Europäischen Hochschulen Reihe 1, Theologie Band 7 (Ammerbek bei Hamburg, 1997). Recent debate about the dating of some of Cyprian's key writings is not of relevance here: see Karl Shuve, 'Cyprian of Carthage's Writings from the Rebaptism Controversy: Two Revisionary Proposals reconsidered', *Journal of Theological Studies* 61 (2010), 627–43.

[2] Joseph M. Bryant, 'The Sect-Church Dynamic and Christian Expansion in the Roman Empire: Persecution, Penitential Discipline, and Schism in Sociological Perspective', *British Journal of Sociology* 44 (1993), 303–39, especially 324–7. For Cyprian's motivation for his behaviour, see Hugo Montgomery, 'Saint Cyprian's postponed Martyrdom', *Symbolae Osloenses* 63 (1988), 123–32.

to differentiate between the influence of the true Spirit and that of demons.

This essay explores the ways in which Firmilian sought to discern true from doubtful inspiration, focusing on the example which he himself offered: that of a woman who was discovered to be possessed by a demon. The historiographical discussion of this text is particularly interesting because Firmilian's account was adduced in the twentieth century as patristic evidence against the ordination of women. Written as a contribution to one debate about doubtful ministries, Firmilian's letter has come to be seen as a witness in another. It will be argued here, however, that Firmilian's letter is not articulated in explicitly gendered terms. Nonetheless, it points towards the problems which would later be faced by women who sought to convince the doubtful of the divine nature of their inspiration.

For Firmilian, the authority of the Church was essential to the removal of doubt. At a synod at which 'very many of us' met in Iconium, he reported, 'we' – by which he seems to mean the 'elders and prelates' (*seniores et praepositi*), or elsewhere the 'senators' (*majores natu*) of the Church – 'decided that every baptism arranged for without the Church was altogether to be rejected'.[3] A heretic, Firmilian thought, 'may not lawfully ordain nor lay on hands, so neither may he baptize, nor do anything in a holy or spiritual way, since he is a stranger to spiritual and deifying sanctity' (*ita nec baptizare nec quicquam sancte nec spiritaliter gerere, quando alienus sit a spiritali et deifica sanctitate*).[4] Rather, 'all power and grace are established in the Church where the elders preside, who possess the power both of baptizing, and of imposition of hands, and of ordaining'.[5] Because 'they who maintain their false prophesying against the faith of Christ cannot have Christ',[6] and because 'spiritual birth cannot be without the Spirit', Paul himself, Firmilian believed, had 'baptized anew with a spiritual baptism those who had already been baptized by John before the

---

[3] Cyprian, Epistle 75.4, 7, 19 (PL 3, cols 1153–78); an English translation is available in ANF 5, numbered as Epistle 74, online at: <http://www.ccel.org/ccel/schaff/anf05.iv.iv.lxxiv.html>, accessed 16 July 2014. Translations are given according to ANF, modified where appropriate by the author. Firmilian presumably conducted his church life in Greek, although we only have a Latin version of his letter.

[4] Cyprian, Ep. 75.7.

[5] Ibid.

[6] Ibid.

Holy Spirit had been sent by the Lord'.[7] However, he also observed that the distinction between the heretics and those of the true faith could be difficult: 'some had doubts about the baptism of those who, although they receive the new prophets, yet appear to recognize the same Father and Son with us'.[8]

Key amongst the problematic groups known to Firmilian were the followers of Montanism or the 'New Prophecy': 'if we ask what Christ they announce, they will reply that they preach him who sent the Spirit that speaks by Montanus and Prisca'.[9] Such false prophets were not easy to identify. In particular, Firmilian recorded that he had been unsettled by the case of a woman who, in a period of local persecution and great confusion twenty-two years earlier, 'in a state of ecstasy presented herself as a prophet (*prophetens se praeferret*), and acted as if filled with the Holy Ghost'.[10] Moreover, 'for a long time she made the brotherhood anxious and deceived them, accomplishing certain wonderful and portentous things, and promised that she would cause the earth to be shaken'.[11] This woman showed marks of authority: she was able to walk 'with bare feet over frozen snow, and not to be troubled or hurt in any degree by that walking'; she said that she had come from Judea and Jerusalem. She sanctified the bread and celebrated the eucharist 'with an invocation not to be condemned' (*invocatione non contemptibili sanctificare se panem et eucharistiam facere simularet*), offered 'sacrifice to the Lord, not without the sacrament of the accustomed utterance' (*sacrificium Domino [non] sine sacramento solitae praedicationis offerret*: probably the sermon[12]), and she baptized many people, 'laying claim to the usual and lawful words of interrogation, that nothing might seem to be different from the ecclesiastical rule' (*baptizaret quoque multos usitata et legitima verba interrogationis usurpans, ut nil discrepare ab ecclesiastica regula videretur*).[13] In

---

[7] Ibid. 8.

[8] Ibid. 19. These 'new prophets' were presumably followers of Montanus and Prisca, that is, of the New Prophecy.

[9] Ibid. 7.

[10] Ibid. 10; cf. Ute E. Eisen, *Amtsträgerinnen im frühen Christentum. Epigraphische und literarische Studien* (Göttingen, 1996), 84–5; ET *Women Officeholders in Early Christianity: Epigraphical and Literary Studies* (Collegeville, MN, 2000), 72.

[11] Cyprian, Ep. 75.10.

[12] R. P. C. Hanson, 'The Liberty of the Bishop to improvise Prayer in the Eucharist', *VC* 15 (1961), 173–6, at 175. The 'non' is missing from the Latin in PL, but commentators are agreed that it is implied by the sense.

[13] Cyprian, Ep. 75.10.

short, she looked and behaved like a person who had been moved by the Holy Spirit to prophesy, perform miraculous deeds and celebrate the legitimate sacraments of the Church. Such was her apparent authority, Firmilian reports, that 'one of the presbyters … and another, a deacon' were convinced by her teachings, and 'associated with' her (*ut eidem mulieri commiscerentur*).[14]

So what was the problem? Why was doubt suddenly cast on this woman's use of the 'invocation not to be condemned', 'the sacrament of the accustomed utterance' and the 'usual and lawful words of interrogation' at baptism? Firmilian recounts that a local exorcist, 'a man approved and always of good conversation in respect of religious discipline', supported by 'very many brethren who were themselves strong and praiseworthy in the faith', observed that this woman was in fact possessed by a demon, and, 'inspired by God's grace, … showed that that which was before thought holy, was indeed a most wicked spirit'.[15] He does not offer any further explanation: we are given no sense of the process of discernment which led to the revelation of demonic possession. But he is clear that this leaves the Church with a problem:

> What, then, shall we say about the baptism carried out by this woman, by which a most wicked demon baptized through means of a woman? Do Stephen and they who agree with him approve of this also, especially when neither the symbol of the Trinity nor the legitimate and ecclesiastical words of interrogation were wanting in her? Can it be believed that remission of sins was given, or that the regeneration of this saving bath [i.e. baptism] was properly completed, when all these things, although they had the image of truth, were done by a demon?[16]

This episode, Firmilian concludes, demonstrates 'the very deceitfulness of devils, since the Holy Spirit is in no way amongst them'.[17] And yet these demons have masqueraded as the Holy Spirit, causing

---

[14] Ibid. The meaning of the verb is ambiguous, and could mean either 'had contact with' or 'slept with': see Christine Trevett, 'Spiritual Authority and the "Heretical" Woman: Firmilian's Word to the Church in Carthage', in Jan Willem Drijvers and John W. Watt, eds, *Portraits of Spiritual Authority: Religious Power in Early Christianity, Byzantium and the Christian Orient* (Leiden, 1999), 45–62, at 57–8.

[15] Cyprian, Ep. 75.10.

[16] Ibid. 11.

[17] Ibid.

considerable confusion and uncertainty amongst the faithful. Firmilian appears not a little dismayed that so many had been taken in by their deceitfulness.

Firmilian's account of the ministry of this unnamed woman in the period before she was discerned to be possessed by a devil raises interesting questions about the validity of her ministry, about her ecclesiastical allegiance and about the significance of her gender. The most obvious interpretation is that she was a follower of Montanism.[18] Andrzej Wypustek points out that until the early twentieth century 'most scholars connected this female miracle-worker with Montanism'; a rare exception was Pierre Labriolle, who argued that her association with Jerusalem and Judea was not consistent with Montanism's focus on Pepuza.[19] Anne Jensen has followed Labriolle, taking this 'baptizing, eucharist making, prophesying, sign-performing, perhaps ascetic female leader' to be catholic.[20] However, more recent interpreters have returned to the hypothesis that she was a Montanist. Hanson sees the woman as 'under the influence of Montanism'.[21] Trevett concludes that – if the woman existed at all (for, she suggests, the woman 'may even have been a composite of various stereotypes and projected fears with regard to the kinds of teachers and teaching she was used to represent') – then she was 'one of those "who are called Cataphrygians and attempt to employ new prophecies," i.e. a Montanist'.[22]

In this reading, the doubtful nature of the baptisms this woman had administered is attributable to the fact that she is associated with a heretical group in which female prophets were known to be active. Trevett argues that Firmilian, writing from Asian Cappadocia, wishes to emphasize to Cyprian, based in North Africa, the real danger of the New Prophecy.[23] If this is the case, then by implication Firmilian is also highlighting the real difficulty of distinguishing a Montanist prophet from a member of the 'Great Church'. Wy-

---

[18] For an introduction to Montanism, see Christine Trevett, *Montanism: Gender, Authority and the New Prophecy* (Cambridge, 1996).
[19] Andrzej Wypustek, 'Magic, Montanism, Perpetua, and the Severan Persecution', *VC* 51 (1997), 276–97, at 279; cf. P. de Labriolle, *La Crise montaniste* (Paris, 1913), 487.
[20] Anne Jensen, *Gottes selbstbewußte Töchter. Frauenemanzipation im frühen Christentum?* (Freiburg, Basel and Vienna, 1992), 352–8, especially 357 (ET *God's Self-Confident Daughters?: Early Christianity and the Liberation of Women* [Louisville, KY, 1996], 182–6).
[21] Hanson, 'Liberty of the Bishop', 175.
[22] Trevett, 'Spiritual Authority', 45, 50.
[23] Ibid. 51–5.

pustek has argued, following Eusebius of Caesarea, that Montanism 'resembled madness' and that it was associated with 'superstition … the sign of *delirium*, *deliramentum* … [which] to some extent means *insanus*, *insaniens*'.[24] However, Montanism was not easy for its contemporaries – including members of the ecclesiastical hierarchy – to identify or to categorize: Tertullian (probably himself by then a sympathizer) asserts that *c*.200, having 'acknowledged the prophetic gifts of Montanus, Prisca and Maximilla', the bishop of Rome wrote a 'letter of peace' to the churches in Asia and Phrygia. A certain Praxeas, however, 'importunately urging false accusations against the prophets themselves and their churches, and insisting on the authority of the bishop's predecessors in the see', persuaded him to recall the letter.[25] As Nancy Caciola observes: 'There seems to have been little dispute over the fact that Montanus and his followers were possessed by a spirit. Rather, the central issue was the character of that spirit: Holy or demonic?'[26] This is precisely the dilemma that exercises Firmilian. Despite his explicit mention of Montanus and Prisca elsewhere in his letter, Firmilian himself does not make a connection between them and this woman; rather he affirms that she had ministered in accordance with the expected rites of the Church – and yet she had been possessed.

Whether or not she was a Montanist, the unmasked prophetess was certainly a woman. Of what significance was her gender? In Christine Trevett's view, Firmilian's letter provides

a pointer to the developing Christian definition of propriety and impropriety in female behaviour. … She had been, according to Firmil-

[24] Wypustek, 'Magic, Montanism', 277; cf. Eusebius: '[Montanus] became beside himself, and … raged in a frenzy and ecstasy, and began to babble and utter strange things': *Church History* 5.16, as cited by Nancy Caciola, *Discerning Spirits: Divine and Demonic Possession in the Middle Ages* (New York, 2003), 6–7.

[25] Tertullian, *Ad Praxean* 1.5; cf. Frederick C. Klawiter, 'The Role of Martyrdom and Persecution in Developing the Priestly Authority of Women in Early Christianity: A Case Study of Montanism', *ChH* 49 (1980), 251–61, at 252. Klawiter sees the authority of the Montanist prophets as arising primarily from their experience as confessors or martyrs, but, as noted above, in Firmilian's context response to persecution does not seem to be the main concern.

[26] Caciola, *Discerning Spirits*, 7. Karen L. King makes a similar point: 'For Christians, the rhetoric was clear: true prophets were inspired by divine agency; false prophets were inspired by the devil and his demons. In practice, however, distinguishing the two was trickier': 'Prophetic Power and Authority: The Case of the *Gospel of Mary* [Magdalene]', in Beverly Mayne Kienzle and Pamela J. Walker, eds, *Women Preachers and Prophets through Two Millennia of Christianity* (Berkeley, CA, 1998), 21–41, at 29.

ian, in the public and not the private sphere, behaving [in a] disorderly [way] and disrupting ordered community, demonically wily and deceitful, usurping the rites of men, and sexually predatory.[27]

Eisen, in contrast, observes: 'Firmilian accuses [the woman] of sexual immorality and of being possessed by a demon, but he does not support his argument by saying that as a woman she has illegitimately laid claim to the charism and the right to celebrate the sacraments', concluding (with Reinhold Seeberg over a century ago) that the fact that Firmilian does not condemn the ministry of this woman because of her sex 'indicates, as does the long prophetic and priestly career of this woman, that women who had a prophetic, liturgical or sacramental function were accepted in Cappadocia in the third century'.[28] Similarly, Klaus Thraede and Anne Jensen argue that Firmilian's account of the affair implies that before the suspicion of possession arose, her ministry had been accepted, and that initially there had been no doubt whatsoever about the validity and effectiveness of her celebrations of the eucharist and her administration of baptism.[29] Hanson observes that she had 'made herself a church leader' (without reflecting that she could not have done this without the support, or at least the acceptance, of the people to whom she ministered), but concedes that 'this woman could compose a prayer whose style and content were not discreditable'.[30] The implication is that her gender was not initially a decisive factor.

Looking back in this episode with the benefit of hindsight, and knowing that she had been discredited, Firmilian is concerned to define the status of those who had been baptized by someone possessed by a demon, and to resolve the doubts about the validity of these baptisms, but he does not seem at all exercised by the fact that the minister of these baptisms had been a woman. Rather, as David Frankfurter observes, '[t]he possessed woman functioned with

---

[27]   Trevett, 'Spiritual Authority', 58–9.

[28]   Eisen, *Amtsträgerinnen im frühen Christentum*, 85 (*Women Officeholders in Early Christianity*, 72, amended).   Eisen cites Reinhold Seeberg, 'Über das Reden der Frauen in den apostolischen Gemeinden', *Deutsch-Evangelisches Jahrbuch* 2 (1899), 19–43.

[29]   Klaus Thraede, 'Ärger mit der Freiheit, Die Bedeutung von Frauen in Theorie und Praxis der alten Kirche', in Gerta Scharffenorth and Klaus Thraede, eds, *'Freunde in Christus werden …'. Die Beziehung von Mann und Frau als Frage an Theologie und Kirche*, Kennzeichen 1 (Gelnhausen and Berlin, 1977), 31–182, at 136; Jensen, *Gottes selbstbewußte Töchter*, 355 (*God's Self-Confident Daughters?*, 184); cf. Charlotte Methuen, 'Widows, Bishops and the Struggle for Authority in the *Didascalia Apostolorum*', *JEH* 46 (1995), 197–213, at 212.

[30]   Hanson, 'Liberty of the Bishop', 175.

considerable authority for some time as the vehicle of a prophetic spirit.' Indeed, Frankfurter suggests that in his letter 'Firmilian tries to balance the spirit's *appearance* of holiness (i.e., its behavior within the roles expected for holy spirits) with his *subsequent* recognition of its demonic identity.'[31] In other words, and as Joseph Wright concludes, 'the heart of Firmilian's objection is that the person baptizing is the instrument of a demon, not that she is a woman'.[32] Trevett also concedes that 'not many decades previously, and still doing the same things, she might simply have been a prophet'.[33] In Trevett's reading, Firmilian's account of this woman is located in a Church poised on the cusp between accepting that women might exercise a legitimate ministry,[34] and doubting that this was possible.

This conclusion is consistent with the findings of scholars, including Ute Eisen, Rebecca Lyman, Gary Macy, Kevin Madigan, Carolyn Osiek, Ilaria Ramelli, Karen Jo Torjesen and myself,[35] that well into the third century, and even into the fourth, women were accepted – at least in some parts of the Church – as ministers at the eucharist

---

[31] David Frankfurter, 'Where the Spirits Dwell: Possession, Christianization, and Saints' Shrines in Late Antiquity', *HThR* 103 (2010), 27–46, at 30.

[32] John H. Wright, 'Patristic Testimony on Women's Ordination in *Inter Insigniores*', *Theological Studies* 58 (1997), 516–26, at 519.

[33] Trevett, 'Spiritual Authority', 59.

[34] King argues that 'women's prophetic speech was highly valued in early Christian movements and contributed to the construction of early Christian teaching and practice': 'Prophetic Power and Authority', 32. Karen Jo Torjesen concurs: 'Prophecy was considered a natural role for women in antiquity. … Second-century Christians familiar with the spirit-inspired worship of churches like that of Corinth would have associated the *orans* [praying and prophesying with outstretched arms] with women's "liturgical" prophecy': 'The Early Christian *Orans*: An Artistic Representation of Women's Liturgical Prayer and Prophecy', in Kienzle and Walker, eds, *Women Preachers and Prophets*, 42–56, at 47.

[35] See Eisen, *Amtsträgerinnen im frühen Christentum* (*Women Officeholders in Early Christianity*); Rebecca Lyman, 'Women Bishops in Antiquity: Apostolicity and Ministry', in Harriet Harris and Jane Shaw, eds, *The Call for Women Bishops* (London, 2004), 37–50; Kevin Madigan and Carolyn Osiek, eds, *Ordained Women in the Early Church: A Documentary History* (Baltimore, MD, 2011); Charlotte Methuen, '*Vidua – Presbytera – Episcopa*: Women with Oversight in the Early Church', *Theology* 108 (2005), 163–77; eadem, 'Die Autorität von Frauen in der Alten Kirche am Beispiel der Syrischen *Didascalia*', in Leonore Siegele-Wenschkewitz, Gury Schneider-Ludorff and Beate-Irene Hämel, eds, *Frauen Gestalten Geschichte. Im Spannungsfeld zwischen Religion und Geschlecht* (Wiesbaden, 1998), 9–32; Karen Jo Torjesen, *When Women were Priests: Women's Leadership in the Early Church and the Scandal of their Subordination in the Rise of Christianity* (San Francisco, CA, 1993); Ilaria Ramelli, 'Theosebia: A Presbyter of the Catholic Church', *Journal of Feminist Studies in Religion* 26 (2010), 79–102. For subsequent developments, see Gary Macy, *The Hidden History of Women's Ordination: Female Clergy in the Medieval West* (Oxford, 2008).

and at baptism, as attested by sources including the writings of Tertullian (*c.*150–220) and Origen (*c.*185–254), the *Didascalia Apostolorum*, a Church order composed in Greek probably around 230, and, later, the Council of Laodicea (*c.*363–4), and supported by inscriptional evidence.[36] That the ministry of women was not uncontested in this period is also clear, but, as Virginia Burrus has argued, 'the common association of women with heresy that emerges in fourth-century texts is not somehow "found" in the historical context but is rather a symbolic creation'.[37] Firmilian's account can, therefore, be read as offering evidence that the ministry of women was not viewed as necessarily doubtful in this period, but that women (unless they were possessed by demons) were – at least in some contexts – accepted as presidents at the eucharist and ministers of baptism.

Trevett, Frankfurter and Wright nonetheless suggest that the woman's gender was, at least to some extent, an issue for Firmilian. As we have seen, Trevett (with the benefit of hindsight) suggests that Firmilian defines the woman 'in categories which would in due course come to be markers of the heretical woman proper'.[38] Wright suggests that the fact '[t]hat she is a woman may aggravate the matter in Firmilian's view', although he maintains that her gender 'is not the point of [Firmilian's] objection'.[39] Frankfurter argues that the 'oscillating perspectives' offered by Firmilian 'were made all the more acute given that the woman was performing sacraments'.[40] It is not entirely clear on what basis these claims are made, for although Firmilian mentions the fact that the case concerns a woman, he does not comment further on her gender.[41] Frankfurter is surely right to conclude that 'of most historical significance in this letter is Firmilian's depiction of the real ambiguity of possessing spirits and the imprecision of people's attempts to classify spirits as either "holy" or "demonic / wicked"'.[42] His suggestion that 'even after the exorcist's

---

[36] For a useful summary of the evidence, see Ramelli, 'Theosebia', 87–9; for more detail, Eisen, *Amtsträgerinnen im frühen Christentum* (*Women Officeholders in Early Christianity*); Madigan and Osiek, eds, *Ordained Women*.

[37] Virginia Burrus, 'The Heretical Woman as Symbol in Alexander, Athanasius, Epiphanius, and Jerome', *HThR* 84 (1991), 229–48, at 248.

[38] Trevett, 'Spiritual Authority', 58.

[39] Wright, 'Patristic Testimony', 519.

[40] Frankfurter, 'Where the Spirits Dwell', 30.

[41] Since no other writings by Firmilian are extant, we do not know whether he discussed these questions elsewhere.

[42] Frankfurter, 'Where the Spirits Dwell', 30.

pronouncement there was probably some conflict over the definition of the spirit, reflected in Firmilian's own ambivalent tone' also seems convincing.[43]

The ambiguity about the significance of the woman's gender might be a pointer to a further level of complexity. If such an ambiguity existed after the condemnation – and Frankfurter's reading of Firmilian seems plausible – then it probably existed before, and may well have contributed to the unease about the woman's ministry felt by the exorcist who denounced her. If that is the case, then the original doubts about her ministry may indeed – implicitly, if not explicitly – have been associated with her gender. The accusations of demonic possession could then represent an expression of uncertainty about the holiness of these activities when carried out by a woman. That such uncertainty did exist in this period, and that it could be specifically and explicitly related to the ministry of women, can be seen from advice given in the *Didascalia Apostolorum*:

> that a woman should baptize, or that one should be baptized by a woman, we do not counsel, for it is a transgression of the commandment, and a great peril to her who baptizes and to him who is baptized. For if it were lawful to be baptized by a woman, our Lord and Teacher Himself would have been baptized by Mary His mother, whereas He was baptized by John, like others of the people. Do not therefore imperil yourselves, brothers and sisters, by acting beyond the law of the Gospel.[44]

When compared with the *Didascalia*, it is clear that Firmilian does not condemn the actions of the woman *qua* woman in the same unequivocal terms. This might, however, imply that in the context in which Firmilian is writing, doubts about the sacramental ministry of a woman *qua* woman seemed more properly expressed in terms of demonic possession rather than (as in the *Didascalia*) in terms of her gender. In Firmilian's narrative, the accusation of demonic possession placed the woman at odds with the structures of the Church in a way that her being a woman had not, apparently, initially done. This could well bring us back to Montanism, for it is clear that women were accepted as leaders within that movement,[45] and Firmilian's letter testifies to

---

[43] Ibid.

[44] *Didascalia Apostolorum*, transl. and ed. by R. Hugh Connolly (Oxford, 1929), 142.

[45] Jensen, *Gottes selbstbewußte Töchter?*, 279 (*God's Self-Confident Daughters?*, 139).

the difficulties of distinguishing between it and the catholic Church. He was writing in a context in which the authority of women could be accepted.

As noted at the outset, Firmilian's letter was written as a contribution to a debate about doubt and certainty relating to the sacraments, and particularly to baptism. It is clear that Firmilian's reasons for raising doubts about the baptisms administered by this woman – certainly demonic possession, perhaps her affiliation to the New Prophecy and possibly her gender – are rather different from those raised by Cyprian in the North African context, which centre on behaviour under persecution. In both contexts, however, such doubts seem to have been a factor in the way in which the third-century Church sought better to define itself and its structures and processes.

Firmilian's letter, however, does not merely contribute to our understanding of the role of doubt in the third century. It can also act as a case study illustrating the role of doubt in modern scholarly discourse, and in particular in the expansion of research into the role of women in the early Church. For Firmilian's female prophetess was granted a bit-part in the 1976 encyclical *Inter Insigniores*, a papal 'declaration on the question of admission of women to the ministerial priesthood', which categorically rejected the possibility of ordaining women to the priesthood on a number of grounds, including that of tradition. In a paragraph which continues to represent the official teaching of the Roman Catholic Church, *Inter Insigniores* states:

> The Catholic Church has never felt that priestly or episcopal ordination can be validly conferred on women. A few heretical sects in the first centuries, especially Gnostic ones, entrusted the exercise of the priestly ministry to women. This innovation was immediately noted and condemned by the Fathers, who considered it as unacceptable in the Church.[46]

Five Fathers are cited as evidence for this 'immediate' condemnation: Irenaeus (*Adversus haereses* 1.13.2), Tertullian (*De praescriptione haereticorum* 41.5), Firmilian of Caesarea (Cyprian, *Epistola* 75), Origen (*Fragmentum in 1 Cor.* 74) and Epiphanius (*Panarion* 49.2–3, 78.23;

---

[46] *Inter Insigniores*, §1 n. 7, online at: <http://www.papalencyclicals.net/Paul06/p6interi.htm>, accessed 28 August 2014.

79.2–4). In this way, *Inter Insigniores* applies Firmilian's doubts about the ministry of the prophetess to an argument about doubt in quite another context: the twentieth-century debate on the ordination of women. Firmilian's uncertainty about the woman's ministry is taken to relate only to her gender, and his letter is read as implying the intrinsic doubtfulness of the ordained ministry, not just of this, but of any woman.

Wright's exploration of Firmilian's attitude towards the woman, discussed above, was written in direct engagement with *Inter Insigniores*. His article considers the eight patristic passages cited by *Inter Insigniores* in their context, seeking to reveal the underlying assumptions both of the patristic authors and of *Inter Insigniores*. He concludes that none of the texts cited in *Inter Insigniores* is directly relevant to the debate about the ordination of women. Instead, what he found were assumptions about the nature of women which, he claimed (in my view somewhat over-optimistically) had since been rejected by the Church: 'the conviction that women by nature, temperament, and social status are inferior to men'.[47] He concludes:

> It seems to me that if the examples cited by the CDF [Congregation for the Doctrine of the Faith] as the testimony of the Church Fathers are at all representative of what tradition has to offer, we must acknowledge that their testimony offers meager support for the claim that the tradition of not ordaining women was motivated primarily by the Church's intention to remain faithful to the will of Christ.[48]

Wright thus cast doubt upon the interpretation offered by *Inter Insigniores*. He was not the only scholar to be inspired by the official statements of the Church to examine the sources more closely. Anne

---

[47] Wright, 'Patristic Testimony', 526. As most recently articulated in *Mulieris Dignitatem* (1988), Roman Catholic teaching holds, not that women are inferior, but that men and women are complementary: 'The personal resources of femininity are certainly no less than the resources of masculinity: they are merely different.' However, the presentation of women as receptive could very easily shade into suggesting that they are inferior: 'the woman is the one who receives love in order to love in return … This "*prophetic*" *character of women in their femininity* finds its highest expression in the Virgin Mother of God. … the "perfect woman" (cf. *Prov* 31:10) becomes an irreplaceable support and source of spiritual strength for other people, who perceive the great energies of her spirit': *Mulieris Dignitatem*, §§10, 29, 30, online at: <http://www.vatican.va/holy_father/john_paul_ii/apost_letters/documents/hf_jp-ii_apl_15081988_mulieris-dignitatem_en.html>, accessed 28 August 2014.
[48] Wright, 'Patristic Testimony', 526.

Jensen observed that studies of the role of women in the early Church proliferated as the debate about the ordination of women gained momentum in many denominations during the 1960s and 1970s. Arguments like that presented in *Inter Insigniores*, that the Church Fathers had acted immediately to suppress the ministry of women, began to be questioned by the findings of new research, more attentive both to the complexities of defining heresy and orthodoxy[49] and to the assumptions about women which had shaped much (although by no means all) earlier scholarship.[50] Nonetheless, the Vatican's most recent statement about women and ordination, *Ordinatio Sacerdotalis* (1994), reaffirms its earlier reading, citing 'the constant practice of the Church, which has imitated Christ in choosing only men', and referring to *Inter Insigniores* as the definitive presentation of the arguments for its position.[51] This contrasts with references to women's role in the early Church (though not to Firmilian) in Anglican debates, which show some evidence of engagement with recent scholarship.[52] Such debates offer an example of the way in which a change of assumptions in society can give rise to new questions.[53] They also suggest that such a historiographical reorientation might be trig-

---

[49] See, for instance, Walter Bauer, *Orthodoxy and Heresy in Early Christianity* (Philadelphia, PA, 1971); Henry Chadwick, *Heresy and Orthodoxy in the Early Church* (Aldershot, 1991); Rebecca Lyman, 'Hellenism and Heresy', *JECS* 11 (2003), 209–22.

[50] Hans Achelis, for instance, one of the translators and editors of a German translation of the *Didascalia Apostolorum* published in 1904, had no doubt that its author was seeking to suppress the ministry of 'prophetesses empowered by the Spirit' (*geistesmächtige Prophetinnen*), known as widows, and witnessed to by other early sources: 'The widows, whom the author has in mind, are not weak women but prophetesses empowered by the Sprit.' He comments further: 'Should anyone be surprised by this conclusion, I would point initially to the Apostolic Church Order [a third-century church order] 21 (24): "Three widows are to be appointed, two to devote themselves to prayer on behalf of all those who are tempted and to revelations about whatever is necessary, and one to sit with the women who are sick".' Hans Achelis and Johannes Fleming, *Die syrische Didaskalie*, Texte und Untersuchungen 25, Neue Folge 10 (Leipzig, 1904), 275 and n. 2. For the widows in the Apostolic Church Order, see also Gillian Cloke, *This Female Man of God: Women and Spiritual Power in the Patristic Age, AD 350–450* (London, 1995), 90.

[51] *Ordinatio Sacerdotalis*, online at: <http://www.vatican.va/holy_father/john_paul_ii/apost_letters/1994/documents/hf_jp-ii_apl_19940522_ordinatio-sacerdotalis_en.html>, accessed 28 August 2014.

[52] See, for instance, *Women Bishops in the Church of England? A Report of the House of Bishops' Working Party on Women in the Episcopate* (London, 2004), 167–8, albeit for a very brief discussion.

[53] Macy, for instance, notes 'how concern over the ordination of women in the present has driven the historical question of whether women had ever been ordained in the past': *Hidden History*, 21. He also highlights the danger of uncritical assumptions that the term

gered by growing awareness of – and doubt about – the assumptions which underlie earlier results. Thomas Kuhn posited that the acceptance of scientific 'truth' depends upon the narrative accepted by the scientific community which generates that truth, and that a shift in the interpretative paradigm results from the recognition of anomalies which raise doubts about the underlying assumptions of the existing paradigm. However, he observed, not all interpreters will accept the revised paradigm.[54] Despite its historiographical shortcomings, Kuhn's model still offers useful insights both into developments in gender history, and into the Churches' various responses to it.

Firmilian was writing at a time in which Church structures, and with them greater clarity – but also greater concern – about who was within and who 'without the Church',[55] were emerging. He appeals to a synod of the Church, but he was puzzled by how to deal with this case of a woman who had appeared to fulfil all the criteria for belonging to, and indeed being authorized by, the Church – the use of the correct words and forms, the respect of some of the clergy – but who seemingly turned out to be possessed. The Christian Church of the third century was witnessing a shift from the New Testament dependence on charismatic or spiritual power to a more institutional understanding of power, and Firmilian's letter offers evidence that this development was in part driven by the challenge of resolving doubts about the authenticity of spirits. Introducing a concept of institutional authority into the Church (at least in theory) made it possible to discern where God's grace was truly at work.[56]

'ordination' as it was used in Late Antiquity or the early medieval period can be taken to be congruent with its meaning today: ibid. 15–17, 23–48.

[54] Thomas S. Kuhn, *The Structure of Scientific Revolutions*, 2nd enlarged edn (Chicago, IL, 1970). Kuhn's thesis is, however, based upon a reading of the history of science which has not gone unchallenged: see, for example, J. V. Field, 'On the Revolutions: Copernicus (1543) and Kuhn (1957, 1962, 1987)', *Bulletin of the Society for Renaissance Studies* 5 (1988), 2–6.

[55] Cyprian, Ep. 75.19.

[56] For a North African case study examining similar questions in relation to Perpetua, Felicitas and Cyprian, see Charlotte Methuen, '"I, who knew that I was privileged to converse with the Lord …": Christian Women and Religious Authority in Third-Century North Africa', *Modern Believing* 54 (2013), 23–33. Caciola identifies in the high Middle Ages 'a practice of institutionalised mistrust regarding individual claims to visionary or prophetic authority' and traces the ongoing difficulty that this process of discernment caused for the medieval Western Church, exploring 'how the testing of spirits was coded and recoded in response to changing social, cultural and religious currents of the late twelfth through fifteenth centuries': *Discerning Spirits*, quotations at 1–2. For this process

In general, women were excluded by these developments from exercising a recognized ministry within the Church, and ever greater doubts were expressed about their capability of experiencing God in any way other than through direct revelation.[57] Consequently, in the medieval Western Church, such spiritual authority as women were able to exercise – with the occasional exception of those who held high office in a convent – was of necessity charismatic authority. Women received visions, the nature of which was always doubtful, so that the visions, together with the women who experienced them, were rigorously tested by the hierarchy of the Church in order to discern whether they were of the Spirit or the result of possession. Firmilian's uncertainty about the status of the spirits was shared by the later hierarchy. His initial acceptance of the authenticity of this woman's ministry was not. It would be more than sixteen hundred years before any Western Christian author could report as matter-of-factly as Firmilian that a woman had celebrated the eucharist, preached and administered baptism; the Church of England's decision to admit women to the episcopate (with continuing provisos for the minority who have doubts about the legitimacy of this decision) was made while this essay was being written. And the Roman Catholic Church continues to hold that the validity of the ordained ministry of women is inherently doubtful – citing Firmilian to sustain a position with which he might well have profoundly disagreed.

---

and its historiographical repercussions for interpreting the contribution of women, see Anke E. Passenier, 'Der Lustgarten des Leibes und die Freiheit der Seele. Wege der Mittelalterlichen Frauenspiritualität', in: Elisabeth Hartlieb and Charlotte Methuen, eds, *Sources and Resources of Feminist Theologies*, European Society for Women in Theological Research Yearbook 5 (Mainz, 1997), 244–65; Charlotte Methuen, 'Mystikerinnen im Mittelalter: Theologie einer weiblichen Gotteserfahrung?', in Elzbieta Adamiak and Marie-Theres Wacker, eds, *Feministische Theologie in Europa – Mehr als ein Halbes Leben. Ein Lesebuch für Hedwig Meyer-Wilmes*, Theologische Frauenforschung in Europa 25 (Munster, 2013), 126–41.

[57] For evidence that some women continued nonetheless to exercise ministries of leadership, cf. Eisen, *Amtsträgerinnen im frühen Christentum* (*Women Officeholders in Early Christianity*); Methuen, '*Vidua – Presbytera – Episcopa*'; Macy, *Hidden History*; Joan Morris, *Against Nature and God: The History of Women with Clerical Ordination and the Jurisdiction of Bishops* (London and Oxford, 1973), also published as *The Lady was a Bishop: The Hidden History of Women with Clerical Ordination and the Jurisdiction of Bishops* (New York and London, 1973).

Carolingian Doubt?

Jinty Nelson[*]
King's College London

This essay seeks to refute the idea that doubt is an essentially modern phenomenon and to show that doubt was also a feature of earlier medieval existence. It argues that in the Carolingian period, for both individuals and groups, debate, disturbance and religious doubt coexisted uneasily with religious faith and cultic community. Religious experience is examined at the level of individuals, groups, and larger social organizations. Three case studies focus on the noblewoman Dhuoda, unique in having left a detailed record of a spiritual life lived out within a family and in social and political relationships at once collaborative and conflictual; the heretic Gottschalk, whose voluminous works reveal something of his spirituality and much about the religious and political pressures that taxed his faith; and Archbishop Elipand of Toledo, a Church leader living under Muslim rule, and accused of heresy by Christian scholars themselves uncertain of their ground. Two further sections discuss particular contexts in which doubts were harboured: conversion from paganism, in a world of Christian mission; and local cults of relics which depended on the establishing of authenticity where there had been doubt, and then the forming of believer-solidarities. Finally the figure of Doubting Thomas is considered in a period when faith and cult sustained individual identities in dyadic relationships founded on oaths of fidelity and mutual trust but also on collective solidarities.

Frances Andrews chose a presidential theme that might have been thought ever timely for ecclesiastical historians, yet only now has the Ecclesiastical History Society tackled it squarely. True, a few volumes of Studies in Church History, for instance *Popular Belief and Practice*, *Religious Motivation* and *Elite and Popular Religion*, gave doubt some coverage.[1] But in the present volume doubt is the focus of attention. Frances Andrews is a later medieval historian, with a special interest in southern Europe. She is one of a distinguished band: John Edwards thought doubt 'an intrinsic part of faith'; Sandy Murray

* Kings College London, Strand, London, WC2R 2LS. E-mail: jinty.nelson23@gmail.com.

[1] G. J. Cuming and Derek Baker, eds, *Popular Belief and Practice*, SCH 8 (Cambridge, 1972); Derek Baker, ed., *Religious Motivation: Biographical and Sociological Problems for the Church Historian*, SCH 15 (Oxford, 1978); Kate Cooper and Jeremy Gregory, eds, *Elite and Popular Religion*, SCH 42 (Woodbridge, 2006).

Studies in Church History 52 (2016) 65–86   © Ecclesiastical History Society 2016
doi: 10.1017/stc.2015.4

identified *pia dubitatio* as an element in thirteenth-century Italian piety; more recently John Arnold has found in 'some beliefs, or rather unbeliefs, … evidence for doubts as much as conscious dissent'.[2] In an illuminating paper to the Royal Historical Society on medieval scepticism, Susan Reynolds pointed out that 'Christianity, even medieval Christianity, tends to invite a modicum of personal commitment, and therefore lays itself open to conscious, if often unacknowledged, doubt'.[3] Bob Moore has come close to contemplating the thing itself in the eleventh and twelfth centuries, and John Arnold in considering unbelief addresses what he explicitly calls doubt expressed by numerous later medieval people. It is perhaps surprising, then, that neither Moore's book nor Arnold's has an index entry for doubt.

Doubt has long been considered a symptom of modernity par excellence. Historians of doubt have preferred to focus on early modern and modern periods. Medievalists used to skip from the thrills of Christian Late Antiquity to the spills of the later Middle Ages. The present volume's span is part of a step-change, already signalled by the work of Moore and Arnold. Dorothea Weltecke's excellent contribution to Arnold's recent *Oxford Handbook of Medieval Christianity* starts with the twelfth century. *Pace* the assumptions of many later medievalists and early modernists, the early Middle Ages were not doubt-free either; and in this essay, I treat them as part of a continuum of pre-modern Christianity.[4] Taking 'Carolingian' as a chronological marker covering roughly the mid-eighth to the later ninth centuries, I look at some early medieval Christians who seem to be

---

[2] John Edwards, 'Religious Faith and Doubt in Late Medieval Spain', *P&P* 120 (1988), 3–25, at 3; Alexander Murray, 'Piety and Impiety in Thirteenth-Century Italy', in Cuming and Baker, eds, *Popular Belief and Practice*, 83–106. See further R. I. Moore, 'Popular Heresy and Popular Violence, 1022–1179', in W. J. Sheils, ed., *Persecution and Toleration*, SCH 21 (Oxford, 1984), 43–50; idem, *The First European Revolution* c.*970–1215* (Oxford, 2000), 23–9, 55–64; cf. John Arnold, *Belief and Disbelief* (London, 2005), 3.

[3] Susan Reynolds, 'Social Mentalities and the Case of Medieval Scepticism', *TRHS* 6th ser. 1 (1991), 21–41, at 32–3.

[4] Dorothea Weltecke, 'Doubts and the Absence of Faith', in John H. Arnold, ed., *The Oxford Handbook of Medieval Christianity* (Oxford, 2014), 357–74, introduces her excellent article by starting with the twelfth century. For some unfortunate consequences of conventional periodizations splitting the earlier from the high Middle Ages, see Janet L. Nelson, 'Liturgy or Law: Misconceived Alternatives', in *Early Medieval Studies in Memory of Patrick Wormald*, ed. Stephen Baxter et al. (Farnham, 2009), 433–47, at 442. See further the recent notable contributions of Janneke Raaijmakers, *Mind over Matter: Debates about Relic Veneration in Late Antiquity and the Early Middle Ages* (Utrecht, 2012); and her website at: <http://www.uu.nl/hum/staff/JERaaijmakers/0>.

grappling with varieties of doubt: tormented by the problem of theodicy, anxiously pondering biblical paradoxes, uncertain of the fate of the individual soul and body after death, passionately engaged in big doctrinal debates over Christology and predestination, and questioning the authenticity and meaning of relics. Material is much scantier and more refractory than for earlier and later times. *Pauperes*, less powerful and illiterate people, are seldom documented directly. Nevertheless, in the belief that there is enough evidence even in this source-poor period, this essay aims to expose and de-pathologize Carolingian religious doubt and, positively, to take seriously doubters among high and low.

TRIBULATION AND DOUBT

Opening up doubt historically means choosing instances to examine in particular contexts of time and place. Frances Andrews has asked when doubt might be a necessary corollary to achieving certainty.[5] Christians have often doubted when afflicted by unforeseen sufferings or misfortunes, for which a generic term in the Carolingian period was *tribulationes*. The term was biblical. It was in the Psalms, especially, that an individual believer could be found begging for divine help in times of tribulation. In the early 840s, particularly fraught years of civil war, a Frankish noblewoman called Dhuoda wrote a handbook offering moral guidance to her son William.[6] She gives the reader some precise dates – something seldom encountered in an earlier medieval author – which could be said to peg the personal to the public. William, she said, was born on 29 November 826, and she began writing the handbook on 30 November 841, 'on the Feast

---

[5] See, in this volume, Frances Andrews, 'Doubting John?', 17–49.

[6] *Manuel pour mon fils*, edited with a still invaluable introduction, notes, and indices of Scripture references, ancient authors and rare words (but no index of names or themes), by Pierre Riché, with French translation by Bernard de Vregille and Claude Mondésert (Paris, 1975), is the edition from which I cite (giving page references for clarity); English translations are my own. Marcelle Thiébaux's edition, *Dhuoda: Handbook for her Warrior Son* (Cambridge, 1998), has a good English translation, as does Carol Neel, *Dhuoda. Handbook for William: A Carolingian Woman's Counsel for her Son* (Lincoln, NE, 1991; repr. with 'Addendum on Historiography', 1999). Dhuoda herself called the book *Liber Manualis* (hereafter: *LM*), literally 'a book that can be held in the hand', as explained by Augustine, *Enchiridion* (PL 40, col. 951). For further bibliography, see Janet L. Nelson, 'Dhuoda', in Patrick Wormald and Janet L. Nelson eds, *Lay Intellectuals in the Carolingian World* (Cambridge, 2007), 106–20; eadem, 'Dhuoda on Dreams', in *Motherhood, Religion and Society: Essays presented to Henrietta Leyser*, ed. Conrad Leyser and Lesley Smith (Farnham, 2011), 41–54.

of St Andrew and at the beginning of Advent'. William, already at the Carolingian court of King Charles the Bald serving in the royal retinue of *comilitones*, had come of age at fifteen the day before, five months after an exceptionally bloody battle between Franks on 22 June 841.[7] She finished writing 'on the feast of the Purification of the Holy and Ever-Virgin Mary', 2 February 843, when preparations were already being made for the Treaty of Verdun which in July 843 divided the Carolingian empire effectively for good.[8]

Dhuoda never mentioned doubt directly, but she offered indirect reflections on it. They cluster in Book 5,[9] which consists of eight chapters about *tribulationes*, *tristitiae* and *angustiae temptationum*, 'tribulations', 'sadnesses' and the 'problems of temptations', followed by a ninth on 'giving glory to God in all things'. The third longest chapter in the book's 72 chapters (5.1) is a series of indirect reflections on doubt. Here Dhuoda sees the tribulations of this life as trials, *temperamenta*, that test faith, and from which faith emerges strengthened.[10]

---

[7] *LM*, bk 11, ch. 2 (ed. Riché, 368); for Fontenoy, its context, and its repercussions in texts, see Nelson, 'The Search for Peace in a Time of War: The Carolingian Brüderkrieg, 840–843', in Johannes Fried, ed., *Träger und Instrumentarien des Friedens im Hohen und Späten Mittelalter*, Vorträge und Forschungen vom Konstanzer Arbeitskreis für mittelalterliche Geschichte 43 (Sigmaringen, 1996), 87–114.

[8] For the Feast of the Purification (2 February), see Michael Sierck, *Festtag und Politik: Studien zur Tagewahl karolingischer Herrscher* (Cologne, 1995), 282–4; for Verdun, see Janet L. Nelson, 'Le partage de Verdun', in Michèle Gaillard et al., eds, *De la Mer du Nord à la Méditerranée. Francia Media: Une region au cœur de l'Europe* (Luxembourg, 2011), 241–54.

[9] *LM*, bk 5, chs 1–9 (ed. Riché, 260–85). In 'Dhuoda', 112, I suggested that this was a halfway point in the work. *LM* is divided into chapters in all three manuscripts, but the divisions and numberings do not fully coincide; the books have been created by Riché to aid modern readers: Introduction, 53–4. Going by chapters, *LM*, bk 5, ch. 1 is 31 in the Nîmes and Barcelona manuscripts, 32 in the Paris copy, and this can in no way be said to be halfway in terms of chapters overall: there are 72 in the Barcelona manuscript. I would still want to argue that the chapter marked a thematic dividing point in the work as a whole, but I ought certainly to have noted the artificiality of Riché's 'Books'. I also want to correct here a mistranslation which I carelessly copied from Thiébaux (*Dhuoda*, 218), of *LM*, bk 10, ch. 1, line 21 (ed. Riché, 340), which does not allude to chapters at all (nor indeed *paragraphes*, as in the translation of Riché's collaborators), but to the first letters in the *versus*, 'lines', of the acrostic poem that follows.

[10] Nearly all the relevant passages of bk 5, ch. 1 survive uniquely in MS Barcelona Biblioteca Central 569, a fourteenth-century copy recently rehabilitated as exceptionally valuable because of its Catalan origin and its inclusion of other Carolingian works: see Cullen J. Chandler, 'Barcelona BC 569 and a Carolingian Programme on the Virtues', *EME* 18 (2010), 265–91. The chapter's 160 lines are headed in the Barcelona MS *tribulationibus temperamenta*, but in the seventeenth-century paper copy in Paris, BN, no. 12.293, fol. 260, *De diversarum tribulationum temperamentis*; in Riché's translation, 'Les diverses formes d'épreuves', 261 (cf. Riché's comments on the manuscript in Introduction,

She treats *tribulatione*s and *tristitiae* as more or less synonymous, but distinguishes lower and higher forms of *tristitiae*, one carnal and this-worldly, leading to death, the other, spiritual and nobler, drawing to eternal life. No time or place could ever be called free of tribulations, of course, but in the Carolingian period, tribulations appeared more often than before under that name, partly because rulers and their advisers took cognizance of famines and extreme climatic events in terms of divine punishment, partly because, at the same time, rulers and their agents were making strenuous efforts to cope with their effects by creating their own version of a welfare state.[11] In Book 5, Dhuoda approached tribulations through the Bible. In chapter 1, following St Paul (2 Cor. 7: 10), *Tristitia saeculi mortem operatur*, 'The sadness of this world wreaks death', Dhuoda distinguishes carnal *tristitia* from 'the more noble spiritual kind that promotes the soul's utility'. She comments that 'though that sadness assails the human heart for all kinds of reasons, the wisest men say that thinking critically [about it] is preferable to forgetting about it'.[12] She then cites Job 14: 1, 'man that is born of woman …', and 7: 5–6: 'My skin is parched and withered … My days have passed more quickly than the weaver cuts his cloth'. Dhuoda comments with a characteristic expansion of the simile and a personalized touch: 'The felicity of the human condition is fragile to such a great extent, and so brief is its duration, according to the wise, that even for someone who lived for a thousand years, his last day would be counted as having been as lasting as a spider's web'.[13] Later in the chapter, after a string of citations from Job and

---

45–6); in Thiébaux, *Dhuoda*, 165, 'On observing self-control under various hardships'; and in Neel, *Handbook*, 65, 'On being tested in various troubles'. See Nelson, 'Dhuoda on Dreams', 44, where I thought Thiébaux's reading 'attractive', but I now consider 'tests' or 'trials' nearer the mark. Cf. Alcuin, *De virtutibus et vitiis* 33 (PL 101, col. 635): 'Tristitia salutaris est, quando de peccatis suis animus contristatur peccatoris … ut confessionem et paenitentiam quaerat … Alia est tristitia huius saeculi … Ex ipsa nascitur malitia, rancor, animi pusillanimitas, amaritudo, desperatio'.

[11] Janet L. Nelson, 'Making Ends Meet: Wealth and Poverty in the Carolingian Church', in W. J. Sheils and Diana Wood, eds, *The Church and Wealth*, SCH 24 (Oxford, 1987), 25–36, repr. in eadem, *The Frankish World* (London, 1996), 145–54; eadem, 'Religion in the Reign of Charlemagne', in Arnold, ed, *Oxford History of Medieval Christianity*, 497–8.

[12] 'Tristitia namque quae impeditur resecanda est; illa vero quae ad utilitatem proficit animae adhibenda est et firmiter tenenda. Nobilior tamen est spiritalis quam carnalis, et, licet pro aliquibus certis ex causa tristitia in corde accedat humano, oblivioni censura peritissimi praeponenda esse fatentur': *LM*, bk 5, ch. 1, lines 17–22 (ed. Riché, 260).

[13] 'Cutis namque aruit mea et contracta est. … dies mei velocius transierunt quam a texente tela succiditur, et consumpti sunt absque ullo termino spei' (citing Job 7: 5–6) and

Ecclesiastes, Dhuoda cites Psalm 1: 3: 'For those that can see [Christ, the true vine], and have sure faith in him, can be compared to the lovely tree planted by the banks of the running waters'.[14] Dhuoda, after thus indirectly reflecting on the possibility that spiritual sadness can engender doubt about the power of God, sees *fiducia certa* as the antidote to the withering that results from carnal *tristitia*.

In chapter 4, titled 'Si tribulatio fuerit', Dhuoda cites a little string of Psalm passages: 'I cried to the Lord when I was afflicted' (*Ad Dominum cum tribularer clamavi*, Ps. 119: 1); 'In my affliction you have called to me, "I have delivered you and heard you"' (*In tribulatione invocasti me, liberavi et exaudivi te*, Ps. 80: 8); then, with a special comment for her son's benefit: 'You, my son, when you come into tribulation, cry out so that you are worthy to be heard. And having been heard, you will be able to praise [him] in faith (*fiducialiter*) and to say: "I called upon the Lord in my tribulation and he heard me in a large way"'.[15] The Christian's trajectory, for Dhuoda, is through trials and tribulations and unarticulated doubt to God through faith.

A final point about Dhuoda's understanding of doubt as a result of suffering is that she does not mention penance as a remedy, nor indeed is she acquainted with the penitential psalms as such (though Cassiodorus's list had existed since the sixth century). She seldom mentions priests; and on the subject of confession she says only: 'make your confession to them [*sacerdotes*] secretly, as far as you can, with a sigh and with tears'.[16] To her son, she commends prayer, not just in church but wherever an opportunity is offered him, and still

---

Dhuoda's comment: 'In tantum est felicitas humanae conditionis fragilis et a peritissimis in brevi usque perducta, ut etiam mille annorum tempora volvens, extrema illius dies ad instar telae computatur araneae': *LM*, bk 5, ch. 1, lines 68–71 (ed. Riché, 264).

[14] 'Videntes enim et in illo fiduciam habentes certam, conparantur ligno almifico, quod transplantatur iuxta decursus aquarum. Qui cum ad humorem alte et profunde fixerunt radices, non arescent tempore aestatis. Eruntque folia eorum semper virida et fecunda, nec aliquando desinent facere fructum.' Here Dhuoda draws on Ps. 1: 3 and also Jer. 17: 8: *LM*, bk 5, ch. 1, line 141 (ed. Riché, 270).

[15] 'Tu ergo, fili, cum in tribulationem veneris, clama ut merearis audiri. Exauditus autem valeas fiducialiter laudare et dicere: "In tribulatione invocavi Dominum et exaudivit me in latitudine"' (Ps. 117: 5): *LM*, bk 5, ch. 4 (ed. Riché, 276). Riché points out (ibid. n. 5) that none of these citations occurs in a work which Dhuoda certainly knew, Defensor of Ligugé, *Liber scintillarum* 50 (SC 86, 114), 'De tribulatione'. She commented on Scripture directly, then, not via Defensor.

[16] *LM*, bk 3, ch. 11 (ed. Riché, 196); cf. Riché, Introduction, 30. In discussing 'the Manual and Carolingian spirituality', Riché makes no reference to Book 5's lengthy treatment of tribulations: ibid. 27–32.

more strongly does she commend direct appeal to God through the self-help of daily private prayer. This strikes me as a distinctively lay form of piety. William must pray in these words: 'O Merciful One, … give me memory and sensitivity, so that I can understand how to believe in you, love, fear, praise and thank you, and accomplish [this] in every good work through right faith and good will, O Lord my God'. She strongly recommends to William that the best way to protect himself against the Devil is prayer at bedtime, and specifically to 'make the sign of the cross on your forehead and over your bed … like this +, and say: "I worship your cross, Lord, and I believe in your holy resurrection … The cross is my salvation, the cross my defence, … The cross is life to me, but to you, Devil, death, you enemy of truth and bringer-forth of what is vain!"'[17] This is a layperson's do-it-yourself exorcism.

DOUBTS ABOUT DOCTRINE: GOTTSCHALK ON PREDESTINATION

It is often assumed, wrongly, that there was little if any doctrinal doubt in this period. In the case of predestination, for instance, intellectual historians tend to skip from Augustine to Calvin. But predestination was a burning question in the Carolingian period also. I want to focus in this section on Gottschalk (*c*.805–*c*.870). He was a child-oblate who grew to be an unwilling monk (that unwillingness tells us a lot about the man). He was a passionate student of Augustine, from the *Confessions* to *The City of God*. In the course of a lengthy visit/journey south of the Alps, where he was sheltered at the courts of Marquis Eberhard of Friuli and then of King Tripimer of Croatia, for whom he apparently fought, Gottschalk became convinced that predestination was double: the elect were predestined to heaven, the damned to hell.[18] The teachings of this *sciolus* (a dilettante, one with a

---

[17] *LM*, bk 2, ch. 3 (ed. Riché, 126, 128–30, 126).

[18] Still fundamental are Klaus Vielhaber, *Gottschalk der Sachse* (Bonn, 1956); David Ganz, 'The Debate on Predestination', in Margaret T. Gibson and J. L. Nelson, eds, *Charles the Bald: Court and Kingdom*, 2nd edn (London, 1990), 283–302; see also idem, 'Theology and the Organisation of Thought', in Rosamond McKitterick, ed., *The New Cambridge Medieval History*, 2: *c.700–c.900* (Cambridge, 1995), 758–85, at 767–73; D. E. Nineham, 'Gottschalk of Orbais: Reactionary or Precursor of the Reformation?', *JEH* 40 (1989), 1–18; Paul Kershaw, 'Eberhard of Friuli, a Carolingian Lay Intellectual', in Wormald and Nelson, eds, *Lay Intellectuals*, 77–105, especially 91–7. For Gottschalk's service in Croatia,

smattering of knowledge) were summarized by Archbishop Hrabanus of Mainz, writing to Marquis Eberhard of Friuli:

[Gottschalk] dogmatized that God's predestination constrained every human being, so that if anyone wanted to be saved and strove for this with a righteous faith and good works so that he would come to eternal life through God's grace, that person would be toiling in vain and pointlessly if he was not predestined to life, as if God by his predestination – he who is the author of our salvation, not our perdition – compelled a person to die. And through this he, and that sect (*haec secta*) that was with him, led many into despair, so that they said, 'Why should I have to toil for my salvation and eternal life, because if I do good and I am not predestined to life, nothing can help me, but if I do evil, that is no obstacle to me for God's predestination will make me reach life eternal'.[19]

Three of Gottschalk's crucial insights were Augustinian. One was his citing of Augustine on love:

A body by its weight tends to move upward to its proper place. Oil poured under water is drawn to the surface on top of water ... My weight is my love. Wherever I am carried my love carries me. By your gift we are set on fire and carried upwards: we grow red-hot and ascend.[20]

The second insight was that things were not as they seemed. Gottschalk gave an example of his own: 'just as a bough in a stream looks broken, and your fingers look shorter seen in water – something people who have not experienced can try out in the bath (*quod inexpertes experiri possunt in balneo*) – so verisimilitude deceives those who do not look with care'.[21] As David Ganz put it, grace was 'the

---

see Cyrille Lambot, ed., *Œuvres théologiques et grammaticales de Godescalc d'Orbais* (Louvain, 1945), 169, 325.

[19] Archbishop Hrabanus Maurus of Mainz to Marquis Eberhard, MGH Epp. 5, 481–2 (no. 42); cf. also Hrabanus to Noting, bishop-elect of Verona, ibid. 428 (no. 22).

[20] Augustine, *Confessions* 8.9.10, ed. with commentary James J. O'Donnell, 3 vols (Oxford, 1992), 1: 187: 'ponderibus suis aguntur, loca sua petunt. oleam infra aquam fusum super aquam attollitur, aqua supra oleum fusa infra oleum demergitur: ... . pondus meum amor meus; eo feror, quocumque feror. dono tuo accendimur et sursum ferimur; inardescimus et imus'; for commentary, ibid. 3: 356–9. The English translation is from *St Augustine: Confessions*, transl. Henry Chadwick (Oxford, 1991), 278. This passage is quoted by Gottschalk: Lambot, ed., *Œuvres théologiques*, 156.

[21] Lambot, ed., *Œuvres théologiques*, 375.

fragile link between the elect and the salvation of which they could never be sure. Gottschalk's writings record his doubt.'[22] Gottschalk's third insight was that doubt was inevitable: he cited and labelled Augustine's *laudabilis dubitatio* over 'why the innocent new-born needs the grace of baptism'.[23] Gottschalk's was the doubt of the justified sinner.

Archbishop Hincmar of Reims wrote a treatise 'to those who have withdrawn from the world (monks, nuns, hermits) and to his beloved children, the simple believers of his see', warning them against Gottschalk and assuring them that 'there is but one predestination to redemption through Christ's sacrifice and through the grace of God almighty'.[24] It was an episcopal view, a professional's view. It prevailed. The king of the West Franks, who already had imperial pretensions, assumed what he viewed as his God-given role as summoner of theologians' opinions and arbiter of them. Ten more or less lengthy written submissions were the result. Though some came near to predestinarian readings of relevant works of Augustine, none fully endorsed Gottschalk. Indeed, in 849 Gottschalk was locked up in a monastic prison at Hautvilliers near Rheims, where he died in 868.[25]

Archbishop Elipand of Toledo on Adoptionism

A second high-level doctrinal dispute with cross-border dimensions related to Adoptionism.[26] On this subject, conflicting positions had hardened and left little room for doubt on the part of any participant on either side. Even when Pope Hadrian I mentioned Thomas's 'exploration' of Christ's wounds, it was because he wished to affirm the argument that no evangelist or apostle ever called Christ a

---

[22] Ganz, 'Predestination', 288.

[23] Lambot, ed., *Œuvres théologiques*, 284.

[24] Hincmar, *Ad simplices*, ed. Wilhelm Gundlach, 'Zwei Schriften des Erzbischofs Hinkmar von Reims', *Zeitschrift für Kirchengeschichte* 10 (1889), 92–145, 258–309, at 92–3, 269–70.

[25] Whether Gottschalk's teachings persisted in Croatia is an interesting but unanswerable question. On Gottschalk and his teachings, see now M. B. Gillis, 'Heresy in the Flesh: Gottschalk of Orbais and the Predestination Controversy in the Archdiocese of Rheims', in Rachel Stone and Charles West, eds, *Hincmar of Rheims: Life and Work* (Manchester, 2015), 247–67.

[26] John C. Cavadini, *The Last Christology of the West: Adoptionism in Spain and Gaul, 785–820* (Philadelphia, PA, 1993); David Ganz, 'Theology and the Organisation of Thought', 762–6.

'servant' or 'slave' but only 'Lord' or 'God'.[27] Archbishop Elipand of Toledo (c.716–805) knew how to fight *ad hominem* in a way calculated to raise doubts; he addressed his chief opponent, the Anglo-Saxon Alcuin, Charlemagne's theological adviser, thus: 'Beware of becoming another Arius, who turned the Christian emperor Constantine into a heretic, so that Isidore said of him, Alas, the beginning was good, the end was bad'. The warning was repeated at the end of his diatribe.[28] Elipand's case was thoroughly orthodox; but doubts arose because Alcuin did not understand (any more than Pope Hadrian did) the concept of Christ's self-emptying, as in Philippians 2: 6–7: 'Who being in the form of God, thought it not robbery to be equal with God: But emptied himself, taking the form of a servant, being made in the likeness of men, and in habit found as a man.'[29] This, as John Cavadini pointed out, was 'the fundamental parameter of [Adoptionist] reflection'.[30] From this came a creed: 'that He [Christ] was made of a woman, under the law, Son of God not by generation but by adoption, and not by nature but by grace, as the same Lord testifies, saying, "The Father is greater than I" [Joh. 14: 28]'.[31]

Two contextual features created further and particular possibilities of doubt. One was that if you lived in late eighth-century Toledo, you coexisted perforce with Islam, and various types of accommodation ensued. It has been argued that some Spanish Adoptionists chose to 'sound Nestorian' in order to make concessions to Muslims. Cavadini convincingly rebuts this. But debates between different peoples of the book happened in this period, with the effect that doubts sometimes turned into apostasy, as in the case of the Frankish Christian Bodo, who converted to Judaism in Spain.[32] The other contextual feature was the suggestion by Alcuin and others that heresy

[27] Pope Hadrian I to the bishops of Spain, MGH Conc. 1, 127 (no. 19C, Concilium Francofurtense),

[28] Elipand to Alcuin, MGH Epp. Karolini Aevi 2, 300–7, at 303, 307 (no. 182).

[29] The Vulgate reads: 'qui cum in forma Dei esset, non rapinam arbitratus est esse se aequalem Deo; sed semetipsum exinanivit, formam servi accipiens'. The English translation is taken from the Douai-Rheims version.

[30] Cavadini, *Last Christology*, 88.

[31] 'Credimus eum factum ex muliere, factum sub lege, non genere esse filium Dei set adobtione [*sic*] neque natura set gratia': Letter from the bishops of Spain to the bishops of Francia (MGH Conc. Aevi Karolini 1, 112).

[32] Frank Riess, 'From Aachen to Al-Andalus: The Journey of the Deacon Bodo (823–76)', *EME* 13 (2005), 131–57. Alcuin, writing to Charlemagne in 799, reported his efforts to acquire the text of a disputation between the Adoptionist Felix, bishop of Urgel, and a 'Saracen', and also recalled that when he was young, he had heard at Pavia a disputation

had become rife in south-western parts of the Carolingian empire, that is, Septimania (southern Gaul) and Catalonia. Was Adoptionism changing from an elite to a popular heresy, and did that raise political concerns at the court of Charlemagne?[33] On that toxic combination scholarly debates are still rumbling audibly enough to indicate that religious doubts and high-powered doctrinal discussions were live in this part of Charlemagne's world.

DOUBTS ABOUT CONVERSION

I want now to discuss in more detail three kinds of doubt, along with some aptly dubious documentation. The first is doubt about conversion. My text is the *Life* of an eighth-century missionary saint, Wulfram, who spent years trying and failing to convert the Frisian chief Radbod (d. 718). The author of the *Life* gave himself a false identity, and claimed to have been writing early in the eighth century, but he was actually a monk from the royally patronized monastery of St-Wandrille, near Rouen, writing between 796 and 807.[34] Fortunately Radbod is documented in a number of strictly contemporary works of history and hagiography.[35] The details of the encounters between Radbod and Wulfram are unique to the *Life*, but the Frisian setting and Wulfram's interest in Frisia are corroborated by the contemporary evidence. The *Life* is not what it seems, then. Yet it does throw light on doubt by giving a plausible account of why the Frisian chief in the early eighth century, despite the fact that some of his own people converted, had doubts about doing so himself. The cult of the ancestors was a central feature of Frisian religion. If the

---

between a Jew named Lull and Peter of Pisa 'who was famed for teaching grammar in your palace': MGH Epp. Karolini Aevi 2, 285 (Ep. 172).

[33] See Cullen C. Chandler, 'Heresy and Empire: The Role of the Adoptionist Controversy in Charlemagne's Conquest of the Spanish March', *International History Review* 24 (2002), 505–27, raising interesting questions; cf. Yitzhak Hen, 'Charlemagne's *Jihad*', *Viator* 37 (2006), 33–51; the online response of Jonathan Jarrett at: <https://tenthmedieval.wordpress.com/2007/01/14/charlemagnes-jihad>, last accessed 26 February 2016; and the reservations of Janet L. Nelson, 'Religion and Politics in the Reign of Charlemagne', in Ludger Körntgen and Dominik Waßenhoven, eds, *Religion and Politics in the Middle Ages* (Berlin, 2013), 17–30, at 22.

[34] See *Vita Vulframni* (MGH SRM 5, 657–73); and, for excellent comment, Ian N. Wood, *The Missionary Life: Saints and the Evangelisation of Europe 400–1050* (London, 2001), 92–4.

[35] See Wood, *Missionary Life*, 92–4.

Franks wanted to ease the transition to Christianity they had to allay Frisian doubts about the posthumous fate of the ancestors.[36]

The key passage is as follows:

> The above-mentioned *princeps* Radbod, when he was being imbued (*imbueretur,* 'dampened' or 'being instructed') to receive baptism, and was being earnestly questioned by the holy Bishop Vulfram, binding himself with oaths by the name of God [asked]: 'could the bishop promise where would be the greater number of kings and princes and nobles of the people of the Frisians, whether in that heavenly region which he would reach if he were to be baptized, or in that hellish damnation which he, the bishop, was speaking about?'

> Then the blessed Wulfram [replied]: 'Make no mistake about it, O famous *princeps*, with God the number of the elect is certain. As for your predecessors it is certain that the *principes* of the people of the Frisians who died without the sacrament of baptism have received the judgement of damnation.'

> The chief (*dux*), hearing this, no longer wished to believe (*incredulus* [*erat*]) – he had already reached the font – and, so it is reported, he withdrew his foot from the font, saying that he could not be without the companionship of his predecessors the *principes* of the Frisians, and instead reside in that heavenly kingdom with only a small number of poor people. No! he would not find it easy to give his assent to new instructions – rather than that, he would stay among those whom he had for a long time served with the whole people of the Frisians …

At this point, some Frisians converted, but Radbod still refused. Wulfram asked another bishop to help him but they were unable to persuade Radbod. 'But because he was saying that he was doubting the Catholic Faith and tempting the bishops through all sorts of [lies?] (*quia dubitando in fide catholica et temptando per omnia sanctos antistes loquebatur*), he was found unworthy to gain what he had sought under false pretences.'[37]

The author of the *Vita Wulframni* was writing in the final phase of the Franks' conquest of pagan Saxony. There, difficulties similar

---

[36] The problem was set in a wider context by Aaron Gurevič, 'Au Moyen Âge: Conscience individuelle et image de l'au-delà', *Annales. Économies, Sociétés, Civilisations* 37 (1982), 265–72.

[37] *Vita Vulframni* 9 (MGH SRM 5, 668).

to those with the Frisians were encountered on a much larger scale with the expansion of Frankish power and Frankish Christianity into Saxony. Saxons cremated their dead, and buried the ashes in burial mounds;[38] these mortuary rites were a stumbling block, and this suggests Radbod's doubts could have become topical again in the context of missions to late eighth-century Saxony. Was Charlemagne's law commanding that Saxons should be buried in Christian cemeteries a 'generous gesture', or only the appearance of one?[39] Was it, indeed, aimed at suppressing Saxon identity? If so, it was not a success. But I think what the Franks aimed at was co-existence and Saxon participation in the Frankish realm, on condition that they became Christians. Some aristocrats did so, rapidly; others more slowly. The upshot was never in doubt: it was a form of subsidiarity. Charlemagne's uncle married a Saxon, presumably a converted one; one of Charlemagne's concubines was a Saxon, likewise a convert. These women did not lose their Saxon identities, for their descendants recorded them. The pagan Saxon leader Widukind converted in 785, and no further hostility to the Franks is recorded for him: in the mid-ninth century his descendants were devoutly cultivating his memory and importing relics from Rome to reinforce the family's standing: there is no doubt about any of that.[40]

Radbod's was literally a marginal case, the doubter on the margin of Christendom and pagandom. This is part of a pattern in which doubts arise on frontiers. Here at the very time scholars in Charlemagne's circle were engaging in hagiographical battles, pitting one missionary saint (and his local Church) against another in Frisia and Saxony, in the frontier zone between Francia and Spain, nearly all of which had been for eighty years under Muslim rule, Adoptionism rumbled on; and there is intermittent but telling evidence of interfaith dialogue, even if it was often a dialogue of the deaf.[41]

---

[38] See MGH Capit. 1, 69 (no. 26, chs 7, 22).

[39] See Bonnie Effros, '*De partibus Saxoniae* and the Regulation of Mortuary Custom: A Carolingian Campaign of Christianization or the Suppression of Saxon Identity?', *Revue Belge de Philologie et d'Histoire* 75 (1997), 270–85.

[40] *Translatio sancti Alexandri* 4 (MGH SS 2, 676–8); see K. Schmid, 'Die Nachfahren Widukinds', *Deutsches Archiv* 20 (1964), 1–47.

[41] Celia Chazelle, *The Crucified God in the Carolingian Era: Theology and Art of Christ's Passion* (Cambridge, 2001), 52–74, with comment on the doubting St Thomas at 58–9.

The Relics of Saint Helena

The second case study concerns doubt about relics. My text is the *Translatio Sanctae Helenae*, written between 845/6 and 853 by Almannus, a monk of Hautvilliers in the province of Reims.[42] The removal of the relics from Rome to Francia is said to have occurred in 840/842, the procedures of authentication in 846. The story will remind a medievalist of Einhard's account of how relics of two saints were brought back for him and Abbot Hilduin of St-Denys from Rome in 828.[43] 'At night' is a key phrase in Almannus's as in Einhard's account: that is, these were *furta sacra* – holy thefts – and there were some shady characters in Rome who engaged in this lucrative trade. Almannus's story rings true because doubts were rife. By the eighth and ninth centuries, the little silk-wrapped bundles of bone or hair or cloth were often authenticated by tiny labels: 'from the cloth with which he wiped the feet of the disciples'; 'from the finger of St Denis'; 'from the beard of St Boniface' – to mention just three of those recently discovered in a reliquary at the convent of Chelles whose contents were collected by Charlemagne's sister abbess Gisela and labelled in a hand of *c.*800 – although more often the label read simply *reliquias sancti* … .[44] In the minds of the patrons who commissioned *furta sacra*, and the communities who received God-given gifts of egregious robbery (*egregiae dona rapinae*), belief and doubt coexisted. Cognitive dissonance is not necessarily experienced nowadays as discomfort and apparently was not in the Carolingian context either. What Almannus records is a series of more complicated responses than those in Einhard's equivalent account:

---

[42] Almannus of Hautvillers, *Historia translationis sanctae Helenae* (*ActaSS* Aug. 3, 668–9). See Patrick Geary, Furta Sacra: *Thefts of Relics* (Princeton, NJ, 1978), 54, 152; Hans A. Pohlsander, *Helena: Empress and Saint* (Chicago, IL, 1995), 157–9; Almannus of Hautvilliers, *Lebensbeschreibung oder eher Predigt von der heiligen Helena*, ed. Paul Dräger (Trier, 2007), 260–1; Flodoard, *Historia Remensis ecclesiae* 2.8 (MGH SS 46, 150–2, with n. 2, 'in ziemlich freier Bearbeitung' / 'rather free reworking' of Almannus's text). See more generally, Julia M. H. Smith, 'Portable Christianity: Relics in the Medieval West, *c.*700–1200', *PBA* 181 (2012), 143–67.

[43] Einhard, *Translatio et miracula sanctorum Marcellini et Petri auctore Einhardo* (MGH SS 15/1, 239–64); ET in Paul Edward Dutton, *Charlemagne's Courtier: The Complete Einhard* (Peterborough, ON, 1998), 69–130.

[44] Hartmut Atsma et al., eds, *Authentiques de Chelles et Faremoutiers*, Chartae Latinae Antiquiores 18 (Dietikon, 1985), 84–108 (no. 669); Jean-Pierre Laporte, *Le trésor des saints de Chelles* (Chelles, 1988), especially 124–30.

Theutgisus, a priest of the province of Reims, was ill for five years. Trusting St Helena would help him, and telling no-one but God of his vow he went to Rome. … God gave him the gifts of an exceptional theft (*egregia rapina*): he managed to remove [parts of] Helena's body at dead of night, and take them back to his homeland (*patria*). As he approached its border, the utility of doubt was born in the breasts of many people: how could it be that a woman of such great holiness in God that she was even worthy to find the wood of the Holy Cross and of such highness and nobility in this life that she became the mother of the empire and mistress of the world, could be in the hands of such a humble priest? And so as many people were continuing in this sort of struggle of doubt and dispute, because of the great need for the people not to be deluded by the dark cloud of error, a meeting was held at the church of Reims, and the histories were searched through and a map of the city of Rome was brought out and they discussed with each other, and asked and sought and took counsel and were led by the help of truth to a general certitude. They took the relics to Hautvilliers … but there envy was easily brought into being because so great a relic ought to be in a very excellent city rather than in a little monastery, so they said … and there was an unfaithful contention.

The monks fasted, performed litanies and masses, then sought a judicial inquiry to reveal the truth. But lest this inquiry be insufficient to win the certitude of the people, two priests and a monk were sent to Rome so that this word should stand firm in the mouths of two or three witnesses. They returned from Rome and brought back with them to Hautvilliers not only the [result of] the enquiry into the truth (*veritatis indaginem*) but also a double joy for they also brought the body of St Polycarp, relics of St Sebastian and Saints Urban and Quirinus … After all this some people still had doubts (*quibusdam dubitantibus*). Christ deigned to show them that a three-day fast and a judgement by water would be the judgement that gave proof (*iudicium probabile*). This is how it happened. King Charles who had heard about what had been brought to Hautvillers refused to believe it (*nullo modo credere volebat*). So he summoned Archbishop Hincmar of Reims along with many abbots to Hautvilliers, and wanted a public judgement to be held … And they judged that this would not be thought believable (*non aliter credendum*) unless the same monk who had brought her [Helena] back to us, as a testimony of the truth, were to go naked into the hot water and immerse his whole body, which he did. And in the eyes of all present,

God kept him unharmed amidst the heaving waters (*inter fervidas aquas*). Once this testimony had been seen, the faith of the king and his leading men was strongly towards believing (*fides … ad credulitatem invaluit*) and the king thereafter revered this place with the greatest devotion …[45]

Almannus not only acknowledged varieties of doubt, but saw how doubt could be thought useful: *utilitas dubietatis innascitur pectoribus plurimorum*. At one level, cognitive dissonance on the part of the *populus* is explicit, unabashed. The certitude of the people was something the monastery needed to gain, which was why further attempts were made to verify the authenticity of the original acquisition by sending men to Rome. They returned with yet more relics, presumably signifying clear support from papal officials. It was at this point that Christ put the idea of a judgement of God, that is, an ordeal, into the mind of the king, and the king mobilized the archbishop of Reims, who helpfully suggested that the ordeal be undertaken by the very man who had first brought the relics from Rome. On the part of the king and his entourage, 'faith strengthened into belief' (*fides … ad credulitatem invaluit*, *invaluit* being an intensive form of the verb *valere*). This was an ordeal that worked, uniting great church and monastery, king and *populus* in recognition of a *iudicium probabile*, meaning proven, commanding assent. There was no room left for doubt.

DOUBTING THOMAS

The doubter everyone knows is Thomas, whose response to Christ's resurrection is uniquely recorded in the Gospel of John (20: 24–9):

> Thomas autem unus ex duodecim, qui dicitur Didymus, non erat cum eis quando venit Jesus. Dixerunt ergo ei alii discipuli: Vidimus Dominum. Ille autem dixit eis: Nisi videro in manibus ejus fixuram

---

[45] '[U]tilitas dubietatis innascitur pectoribus plurimorum; quomodo posset fieri in femina tantae sanctitatis in Deo, ut etiam lignum sanctae crucis meruerit invenire, et tam magnae altitudinis et nobilitatis in saeculo ut fieret mater imperii et domina orbis, tam exigui presbyteri manibus tractaretur? Ergo in huismodi dubitationis altercationisque conflictu persistentibus multis, causa multae necessitatis, ne populus hujus erroris naevo deluderetur, fit conventus Remensis ecclesiae, revolvuntur historiae, profertur in medium mappa Romanae Urbis, sciscitantur ad invicem, interrogant, quaerunt, consulunt et veritatis auxilio perducuntur ad certitudinem omnimodam'. [They took the relics to Hautvilliers where] … nascebatur inde facilis invidentia quod debebatur tantum pignus potius urbi excellentissimae quam monasterio, ut dicebant, parvulo: … infidelis contentio': Almannus, *Historia translationis* (*Acta SS* Aug. 3, 668–9). The English translation is mine.

clavorum et mittam digitum meum in locum clavorum, et mittam manus meam in latus ejus, non credam.

Et post dies octo, iterum erant discipuli ejus intus, et Thomas cum eis. Venit Jesus, januis clausis, et stetit in medio et dixit: Pax vobix. Deinde dicit Thomae: Infer digitum tuum huc, et vide manus meas, et affer manum tuam, et mitte in latus meum; et noli esse incredulus, sed fidelis. Respondit Thomas, et dixit ei: Dominus meus et Deus meus. Dixit ei Jesus: Quia vidisti me, Thoma, credidisti; beati qui non viderunt et crediderunt'.

The word 'doubt' does not appear in this passage. Thomas told the other disciples there was no believing without seeing. The risen Christ himself then told Thomas: 'because you have seen you have believed', but 'blessed are those have *not* seen and [yet] believed'. 'Do not be *incredulus* – unbelieving – but be *fidelis* – one that has faith / is faithful'. John's Gospel was often thought difficult in the earlier Middle Ages. That was the view shared by Charlemagne's sister Gisela, the abbess of Chelles, and her niece Rotrud, who, when not residing at court, was a nun at Chelles. In the spring of 800, Gisela wrote to Alcuin for help:

We have come late to this study, and you are far away. … Please send us a commentary on St John, and give us also the interpretations of the Fathers. We have got Augustine's sermon on St John [i.e. John's Gospel] but it is in many places too obscure and in too elaborate language for the small intelligence of our littleness to penetrate. All we want is a small stream of pure water to drink, we do not want to launch our prows on deep waters with whirlpools. It is not for us to climb to the top of tall cedars, we just want, because we are not tall, like Zacchaeus to position ourselves in a sycamore, to watch Christ go by …[46]

Alcuin eventually produced a partial commentary, making plentiful use of Augustine and specifically in the section related to the Thomas passage, Gregory the Great's *Gospel Homily* 26.[47]

[46] Gisela and Rotrud to Alcuin (MGH Epp. Karolini Aevi 2, 323–5, at 324 [no. 196]).
[47] 'Venit iterum Dominus, et non credenti … discipulo latus palpandum praebuit, manus ostendit, et ostensa suorum vulnerum cicatrice, infidelitatis illius vulnus sanavit. … Numquid casu gestum creditis ut electus ille discipulus tunc deesset, post haec venit ut audiret, audiens dubitaret, dubitans palparet, palpans crederet? Non hoc casu, sed divina dispensatione gestum est. Egit namque miro modo superna clementia, ut discipulus du-

> The Lord returned again and offered his side to the disbelieving disciple to feel about in it, and when he showed the open incision of his wounds, he healed Thomas's wound. … Did it happen by chance, do you think, that that chosen disciple was absent, and then came and heard, and hearing doubted, doubting felt about, and feeling about believed? No! this happened not by chance but by divine dispensation … so that the doubting disciple when he felt about in the wounds in the flesh of his master healed the wounds of unbelief in us all. Thomas's unbelief did us more good for our belief than the belief of the believing disciples did for them: for since [Thomas] was led back to faith by feeling about, so our mind was made firm in belief once all doubt had been put aside. Thus [Christ] after his resurrection allowed his disciple to doubt, but he did not abandon him in doubt. For thus that disciple in doubting and feeling about was made a witness of the true resurrection.[48]

Via Alcuin's and especially Gregory's exegesis, this interpretation became widely influential throughout the Middle Ages.[49] In Gregory's lexicon, doubt was a wound, and doubts were wounds. Yet through doubt, and metaphorically feeling about, the wounds of unbelief were healed and faith made firm. Acquiring belief was a sensory as well as an intellectual process: though hearing, he doubted, through doubting he felt about, and through feeling about he believed.

It is apropos to add a near-final word on the expanded dimensions of faith – *fides* – as a corollary of concern about Carolingian doubt. *Fides*, in addition to the heavy load of overlapping, connecting meanings it already carried, gained (or regained) an additional political one.

---

bitans, dum in magistro suo vulnera palparet carnis, in nobis vulnera sanaret infidelitatis. Plus enim nobis Thomae infidelitas ad fidem, quam fides credentium discipulorum profuit: quia dum ille ad fidem palpando reducitur, nostra mens omni dubitatione postposita in fide solidatur. Sic quippe discipulum post resurrectionem suam dubitare permisit, nec tamen in dubitatione deseruit. … Nam ita factus est discipulus dubitans et palpans testis verae resurrectionis': Alcuin, *Commentary on John* 20: 24 (PL 100, cols 993–4), drawing on Gregory the Great, *Homiliae in Evangelia* 26.7–9 (CChr.SL 141, 224–5).

[48] In his polemic against the Adoptionist Felix of about the same time, Alcuin, *Adversus Felicem* (PL 101, col. 144), cited John 20: 28–9 as elaborated by Cassian, *De incarnatione Domini*: 'God is the Jesus whom I touched, God whose limbs I felt … I touch my Lord's body, I felt flesh and bones, I put my fingers in the wound'.

[49] Jean-Paul Bouhot, 'Les homélies de Saint Grégoire le Grand. Histoire des textes et chronologie', *RB* 117 (2007), 211–60, at 254–6, a sermon preached on the Saturday after Easter, 21 April 591.

Adult males all had to swear to the king an oath of fidelity on holy relics. They were addressed collectively by Charlemagne as the *fideles Dei et regis*. As well as Christian belief, *fides* was loyalty, trust, trustworthiness, credence, good faith. The centrality of the oath was underlined by old tales where men had been duped into swearing loyalty on empty relic-boxes: infamous betrayals on the part of the powerful which raised doubt in the hearts of *fideles*. In a recently published sermon, one of eight written early in the ninth century in northern Francia for a local priest or priests to convey to a lay audience in the *lingua romana* (Latin shifting into a vernacular Romance language), the preacher identifies twelve sins.

> Sin number 11. A person (*homo*) who perjures himself and breaks his faith (*fides*) is like a body without a soul. A person without faith is like a blown-up bag. What great works it is (sic) for a person to have good faith! for this is what the faith of men (*fides virorum*) is made for, just as the chastity of women adorns them and keeps them safe, and leads them to glory.[50]

The *fidelis* was exactly that: a man of good faith, who could be trusted to swear a truthful oath not just to the king but as a witness in all contexts connected with the law. The bits of evidence are linked by a recurrent connection. Doubt starts as personal, as in Dhuoda's struggle to makes sense of suffering, or, differently, in Radbod's determination not to lose contact with the ancestors. Like faith, its obverse, doubt or unbelief, can become public and collective, as (at several levels) in the case of St Helena's relics, and finally when doubt is resolved, and dissolved, by a judgement of God, discerned by all those present, from king and archbishop to *fideles* in general. The Carolingian preacher presents good faith as constituting a man's social identity just as chastity constitutes a woman's. These are categorical words of reassurance keeping doubt at bay. But the preacher ends his sermon with an awful warning: 'Woe to an unbelieving people (*Vae populi increduli*), because you have not believed, on that Day [of Judgement] which is to come.'[51] The religious dimension stretched into the eschatological, not in the way imagined by Gottschalk, but in Hrabanus's conception of universally available grace. That dimension

---

[50] James McCune, 'The Sermon Collection in the Carolingian Clerical Handbook, Paris, Bibliothèque nationale de France lat. 1012', *MedS* 75 (2013), 35–92, at 88–9, 91.
[51] Ibid. 91.

Figure 1. (Colour online) Ivory panel, Aachen, early ninth century, Domschatzkammer, Inv.-Nr. G 8, reproduced in Frank Pohle and Peter van den Brink,
eds, *Karl Charlemagne der Grosse*, Kurzführer (Dresden, 2014), 106, panel top left. I am
very grateful indeed to Frank Pohle for help in enabling me to use this image, and
to Gertraut Sofia Mockel on behalf of the Director of the Domschatzkammer, Dr
Georg Minkenberg, for kindly supplying me with a CD scan and granting permission
to reproduce it.

also connected the original Israel with the new Israel, Charlemagne's
fideles Dei et regis: the old law with the new law of the gospel.

Alcuin (with some help from Augustine and Gregory) helped
Gisela and Rotrud to understand the incarnation. Thomas signified everyman, Christ's beneficiary, just as Moses received God's law

Figure 2. Ivory Diptych, probably Trier, late tenth century, Bode Museum, Berlin, on Wikimedia Commons, online at: <http://commons.wikimedia.org/wiki/File:Trier_10_Jh_Diptychon_Moses_Thomas.jpg>, last accessed 29 May 2015.

for the people of Israel. A poem by the theologian Johannes Scotus Eriugena, whose commentary on the Gospel of John alas survives only in fragments, describes 'the peak of Mount Sinai shrouded in mist: then God taught Moses the ancient law' (lines 6–7), and near the poem's close (lines 71–2) alludes to a new law: 'You Christ, redeemer, cleanse the wounds of believers with the fount from your side' ('*tu Christe, redemptor,* | *fonte tui lateris credentum vulnera tergis*').[52]

I end with two images. The first is an ivory panel made at Charlemagne's court workshop early in the ninth century, showing the risen Christ who appears to the disciples, and shows his wound to Thomas, as in John 20: 26–9 (Fig. 1). The second is an ivory diptych made nearly two hundred years after Charlemagne's death, but inspired by a thoroughly Carolingian concept, double and connective, of old law, handed down vertically by God's hand to Moses from heaven, and new law made accessible laterally by Christ to Thomas who simply has to stretch a little to reach and feel about in the wound that heals and cleanses and brings salvation through Christ made flesh and blood (Fig. 2). For people in the Carolingian world – and I end where I began, but I hope having made clearer why – 'doubt was an intrinsic part of faith'.

---

[52] Johannes Scotus Eriugena, *Carmina* 8, ed. Michael W. Herren (Dublin, 1993), 84, 88.

'Sancte fidei omnino deiciar': Ugolino dei Conti di Segni's Doubts and Jacques de Vitry's Intervention

Jan Vandeburie*

Università degli Studi Roma Tre

Thomas de Cantimpré, in his Supplementum *to Jacques de Vitry's* Vita *of Marie d'Oignies, provides us with an account of how Cardinal Ugolino dei Conti di Segni, the future Pope Gregory IX, was struggling with his faith. At this decisive moment in Ugolino's career, the illustrious preacher and bishop of Acre, Jacques de Vitry, made an appearance at the curia. To combat Ugolino's doubt with a saintly intercession, Jacques presented him with the relic of Marie d'Oignies's finger, which he kept around his neck and which had protected him on several occasions. This well-known anecdote has not yet received any comprehensive attention and this essay seeks to analyse as well as contextualize the account of Jacques's intervention. By shedding light on the role of Marie d'Oignies and her finger relic and on the meaning of the 'spirit of blasphemy' plaguing Ugolino, I argue that the anecdote not only gives us a glimpse of the nature of the cardinal's spiritual concerns but also reflects Thomas's efforts to promote both Jacques de Vitry's influence on Gregory IX and the reputation of Marie d'Oignies.*

In Gregory IX's decretals we find the well-known dictum *dubius in fide infidelis est*.[1] Interestingly, in a contemporary gloss by the Dominican Guillaume de Rennes (*c*.1240/5) in the *Summa de Poenitentia* of Raymundus de Peñafort (d. 1275), that same dictum was nuanced.[2] Guillaume argued that if a person's faith is tempted by the 'spirit of blasphemy' with sorrow and anxiety, and that person eventually succumbs to the growing temptation despite fighting against

* Piazza Capri 20, 00141 Rome, Italy. E-mail: j.r.m.vandeburie@gmail.com.
 I wish to thank Brenda Bolton, Barbara Bombi, Frances Andrews and Anne-Laure Méril-Bellini delle Stelle for their kind help and invaluable suggestions. I also wish to thank the anonymous reviewers for their insightful comments.

[1] *Decretales Gregorii IX* 5.7, 'De Haereticis', ch. 1 (*CICan.* 2: 749).
[2] Guillaume de Rennes was a Dominican canonist whose apparatus was copied with Peñafort's *Summa* in most manuscripts and considered to be of almost equal importance: see Stephan Kuttner, 'Zur Entstehungsgeschichte der *Summa de casibus poenitentiae* des hl. Raymund von Penyafort', *Zeitschrift der Savigny-Stiftung für Rechtsgeschichte. Kanonistische Abteilung* 39 (1953), 419–34.

Studies in Church History 52 (2016) 87–101   © Ecclesiastical History Society 2016
doi: 10.1017/stc.2015.5

it, then such doubt is not to be considered a sin.[3] According to the Dominican preacher Thomas de Cantimpré (d. 1272), Ugolino dei Conti di Segni, soon to become Pope Gregory IX (1227–41), was confronted with this particular spirit. In his *Supplementum* to the *Vita* of Marie d'Oignies (d. 1213), Thomas described how Jacques de Vitry (d. 1240) gave Ugolino, then cardinal-bishop of Ostia, the finger-relic of Marie to help him in his fight against the *spiritus blasphemiae* and the doubts he was facing regarding his faith.[4]

The anecdote has often been mentioned by scholars, but has not yet received any comprehensive attention. This essay seeks to contextualize the account of Jacques de Vitry's intervention, which is found only in Thomas de Cantimpré's writings and which raises a number of questions: What is the role of Marie d'Oignies and her finger relic? What did Thomas mean by the 'spirit of blasphemy' that plagued Ugolino, and can we find traces of the origins of Ugolino's doubts in other source material? And finally, what was Thomas's intention behind the story? I will show that doubt is the *Leitmotiv* connecting the stories of Jacques, Ugolino and Thomas, and argue that the anecdote not only gives us a glimpse of the nature of Ugolino's spiritual concerns but also reflects Thomas's efforts to promote both Jacques's influence on Gregory IX and the reputation of Marie d'Oignies. This contribution serves as a case study for the nature of the doubts faced by medieval churchmen as well as for the role of doubt in the hagiographical rhetoric surrounding the movement of the *mulieres sanctae* in the southern Low Countries in the thirteenth century.[5]

Before looking into Ugolino's doubts, let me shed some light on the relation between Jacques de Vitry and Marie d'Oignies, specif-

---

[3] '[Q]ui per spiritum blasphemiae temptatur de fide cum dolore cordis et anxietate; cui, si bene pugnaverit, cedit ad profectum huius temptationis; cum nulla ei sit libido, id est, improba voluntas delectandi in creatura, sine qua nullum est actuale peccatum': Jena, Thüringer Universitäts- und Landesbibliothek, MS El. f. 59, Raymundus de Peñafort, 'Summa de Poenitentia et Matrimonio', fol. 36[r].

[4] I use the Latin text of the most recent edition of the *Vita* of Marie d'Oignies: *Iacobus de Vitriaco, Vita Marie de Oegnies & Thomas Cantipratensis, Supplementum*, ed. R. B. C. Huygens, CChr.CM 252; for the meeting between Jacques and Ugolino, see ibid. 186–9. Translations of the *Vita* and the *Supplementum* by Margot H. King and Hugh B. Feiss respectively were published in Anneke B. Mulder-Bakker, ed., *Mary of Oignies: Mother of Salvation* (Turnhout, 2006), 39–165. In 2014 a German translation of the *Vita* and the *Supplementum* was published: *Das Leben der Maria von Oignies*, transl. Iris Geyer, CChr.T 18.

[5] See Brenda M. Bolton, 'Mulieres Sanctae', in Derek Baker, ed., *Sanctity and Secularity: The Church and the World*, SCH 10 (Oxford, 1973), 77–93.

ically with regard to the relic finger.[6] Jacques's admiration for this *mulier sancta* and the spiritual influence they had on each other are unquestionable. Their close friendship and Jacques's role as her confessor ensured his lasting ties to the diocese of Liège and to the community of canons regular of St Nicholas at Oignies in particular. After a decade in the Holy Land as bishop of Acre (1216–26), Jacques returned to Oignies on several occasions and acted as a patron to the community, bestowing on the canons relics and gifts from the East. Through his *Vita* of Marie (*c.*1215), Jacques contributed greatly to the spread of Marie's reputation as well as to the development of the early Beguine movement.[7] In the *Vita* Jacques emphasized Marie's devoutness, contrition and spiritual strength, but also the extreme asceticism that would eventually lead to her death. As much as the sanctity of her body was central during Marie's lifetime, so her relics continued to play a crucial role after her death, further contributing to the construction of her memory and cult.[8] Marie had firmly rebuked Gilles d'Oignies, prior and founder of the community, for mutilating corpses in order to obtain relics, and had forbidden him to do any such thing to her body after her death.[9] Nonetheless, several of Marie's body parts were kept as separate relics. Aside from the seven teeth which her dead body miraculously spat out into the hands of prior Gilles,[10] it appears that at least one finger was removed shortly

---

[6] Some of the most significant recent contributions that deal with Jacques de Vitry and (the *Vita* of) Marie d'Oignies are Monica Sandor, 'Jacques de Vitry and the Spirituality of the "Mulieres sanctae"', *Vox Benedictina* 5 (1988), 289–312; Maria Grazia Calzà, *Die Begine Maria von Oignies (†1213) in der hagiographischen Darstellung Jakobs von Vitry (†1240)* (Würzburg, 2000); Brenda M. Bolton, 'Mary of Oignies: A Friend to the Saints', in Mulder-Bakker, ed., *Mary of Oignies*, 199–220; Jean Donnadieu, 'Entre Sentiment et ambition. Les Réseaux de Jacques de Vitry au miroir du *Supplementum ad Vitam Mariae Oignacensis* de Thomas de Cantimpré', in C. Carozzi et al., eds, *Vivre en société au Moyen Âge* (Aix-en-Provence, 2008), 133–50; Vera von der Osten-Sacken, *Jakob von Vitrys 'Vita Mariae Oigniacensis'. Zu Herkunft und Eigenart der ersten Beginen* (Göttingen, 2010); Anne-Laure Méril-Bellini delle Stelle, 'L'Ecriture de l'amitié spirituelle dans l'œuvre hagiographique de Thomas de Cantimpré (1200–*ca.*1265/1270)', *Médiévales* 64 (2013), 135–51. See also Ernest W. McDonnell's seminal *The Beguines and Beghards in Medieval Culture, with special emphasis on the Belgian Scene* (New York, 1969), at 20–39.
[7] Michel Lauwers, 'Expérience béguinale et récit hagiographique: À Propos de la *Vita Mariae Oigniacensis* de Jacques de Vitry (vers 1215)', *Journal des savants* (1989), 61–104.
[8] Bolton, 'Mary of Oignies', 203; see also Jennifer N. Brown, 'The Chaste Erotics of Marie d'Oignies and Jacques de Vitry', *Journal of the History of Sexuality* 19 (2010), 74–93.
[9] Thomas de Cantimpré, *Supplementum* 13 (CChr.CM 252, 184).
[10] Ibid. 185–6.

after 1213.[11] Both Thomas de Cantimpré and Jacques de Vitry tell us that the latter wore a silver reliquary case containing one of Marie's fingers as a pendant. In a letter of 1216, Jacques recounted the miraculous rescue of his books and belongings from a turbulent river in Lombardy, as the basket in which he had stored the relic of Marie kept his mule afloat.[12] Thomas wrote that during the journey from Acre to Rome, Jacques's ship was caught in a storm and, while the rest of the crew prayed to their respective saints, Jacques invoked the help of Marie through his reliquary pendant. In a vision, Marie promised she would pray for his salvation, showed her friend five new altars in the church of Oignies and told him to consecrate them. After the vision, the sea became calm.[13]

It is shortly after this miraculous rescue that one must date the meeting between Jacques and Ugolino, in the early months of 1226, upon Jacques's second and final return to Europe. Thomas, however, implied that the friendship between Ugolino and Jacques originated earlier.[14] Indeed, both Jacques's first encounter with the Franciscans and Ugolino's first encounter with the reputation of Marie and the early Beguines seem to have taken place around the same time, when Jacques, as bishop-elect of Acre, was received by Honorius III (1216–27) at Perugia in 1216.[15] Ugolino, who would be appointed cardinal-protector of the Franciscans at some point during 1217 or 1218, was a strong supporter of female (semi-)religious[16] communities and certainly sympathetic to Jacques's emphasis on

[11] The only extant finger relic of Marie d'Oignies is held in a phylactery crafted by Hugo d'Oignies's workshop (*c*.1230): Brussels, Musées royaux d'art et d'histoire, inv. no. 3673; Robert Didier and Jacques Toussaint, 'Le Trésor des soeurs de Notre-Dame à Namur', in eidem, eds, *Autour de Hugo d'Oignies* (Namur, 2003), 191–304, at 295–6.

[12] Jacques de Vitry, *Epistolae* 1 (CChr.CM 171, 550).

[13] Thomas de Cantimpré, *Supplementum* 18 (CChr.CM 252, 191–3).

[14] Ibid. 15 (186).

[15] McDonnell, *Beguines*, 34–6, 313–14; Herbert Grundmann, *Religiöse Bewegungen im Mittelalter* (Berlin, 1935), 172. See also Alcantara Mens, 'L'Ombrie italienne et l'Ombrie brabançonne. Deux courants religieux parallèles d'inspiration commune', *Études Franciscaines* 17 (1968), 44–7.

[16] Since Kaspar Elm coined the term 'semi-religious', the debate regarding the terminology for lay religious movements has been ongoing: Kaspar Elm, '*Vita regularis sine regula*. Bedeutung, Rechtsstellung und Selbstverständnis des mittelalterlichen und frühneuzeitlichen Semireligiosentums', in František Šmahel, ed., *Häresie und vorzeitige Reformation im Spätmittelalter*, Schriften des Historischen Kollegs Kolloquien 39 (Munich, 1998), 239–73. For the *status quaestionis* of the debate with regard to Marie d'Oignies and the Beguines, see Mulder-Bakker, 'General Introduction', in eadem, ed., *Mary of Oignies*, 18–24.

preaching, pastoral care and voluntary poverty, and to his efforts for the early Beguines.[17] Moreover, like Jacques, Ugolino was heavily involved in the preaching of the Fifth Crusade.[18] At the time of the meeting between Ugolino and Jacques in Rome in 1226, the latter was struggling with his own doubts regarding his mission in the East. After the failure of the Fifth Crusade, Jacques realized that neither the reform of the Christian communities in the Holy Land nor the fight against Islam was the easy undertaking that he had anticipated.[19] Seeking spiritual support and guidance, he appears to have visited Oignies to pray at Marie's tomb, before relinquishing his episcopal duties in Acre.[20] Jacques's definitive return to Europe may have indeed prompted him to give the relic of Marie to his good friend, who seemed to need it more than he did. In Thomas's *Supplementum* we read that Jacques presented Ugolino with a heavy silver cup filled with nutmeg. Ugolino accepted the nutmeg as it was the 'fruit of the East', but turned down the cup, saying that it was 'the fruit of the city of Rome'. Instead, the cardinal asked for Jacques's help as he was facing a spiritual crisis.[21] Jacques told Ugolino to read his *Vita* of Marie d'Oignies and, upon Ugolino's request, gave him her finger-relic.

In what seems to have been a very personal and private conversation between Jacques and Ugolino, or at least in what Thomas claimed he knew of this encounter, the cardinal confessed that his soul was troubled by a 'spirit of blasphemy' and overwhelmed by

---

[17] Rosalind B. Brooke, *Early Franciscan Government: Elias to Bonaventure* (Cambridge, 1959), 59–76; see also Pia Gemelli, 'Giacomo da Vitry e le origini del movimento francescano', *Aevum* 39 (1965), 474–95; Kurt Victor Selge, 'Franz von Assisi und Hugolino von Ostia', in *San Francesco nella ricerca storica degli ultimi ottanta anni. Convegno del Centro di studi sulla spiritualità medievale, 13–16 ottobre 1968* (Todi, 1971), 157–222.

[18] P. Pressutti, ed., *Regesta Honorii Papae III*, 2 vols (Rome, 1888–95), 1, no. 272.

[19] Honorius III addressed a letter to Jacques on 6 March 1224, encouraging him not to give up the battle against Christ's enemies and to keep on preaching: Vatican City, Archivio Segreto Vaticano, Vat. Reg. 12, vol. 8, no. 322, fols 168^r–^{v}. On Jacques's doubts, see Jan Vandeburie, 'The Preacher and the Pope: Jacques de Vitry and Honorius III', in J. Bird, ed., *The Papacy, Religious Life, and the Crusade in the Early Thirteenth Century* (Farnham, forthcoming 2016).

[20] Jacques did not resign as bishop of Acre in 1226, but only seems to have asked Honorius III to be released from his episcopal duties in the Holy Land, as he acted as auxiliary bishop in Liège (1226–9) and continued to be referred to as *episcopo acconensis* until he became cardinal-bishop of Tusculum in 1229: see Vandeburie, 'The Preacher and the Pope'.

[21] Thomas de Cantimpré, *Supplementum* 15 (CChr.CM 252, 186–9).

waves of temptation, driving him to desperation.[22] Ugolino noted how his suffering was eased when he was sitting with his brothers the cardinals, assembled in consistory, but succumbed to despair again as soon as he was alone. He feared that his worn spirit and exhausted body would not be able to bear the burden and was afraid that he would be cast out from the holy faith (*sancte fidei omnino deiciar*).[23] Likewise, in his *Vita* of St Lutgard (Lutgard of Aywières, d. 1246), Thomas noted that Ugolino was savagely tempted (*atrociter tentabatur*) by the 'spirit of blasphemy'.[24]

Arguably, Thomas de Cantimpré's accounts merely sketch a vague idea of the nature of Ugolino's predicament. The notion of the *spiritus blasphemiae* is, however, rather interesting. Although *blasphemia* was generally understood as saying things unworthy of God, Alexander Murray has pointed out that 'there is a specifically monastic tradition, going back to the *Vitae patrum*, of understanding the term to indicate mere wrong *thinking* about God'. Murray added that 'when so used it is often in compounds like *blasphemia cordis* or *spiritus blasphemiae*'.[25] The notion of the 'spirit of blasphemy' as an evil entity which tempts its victim into sin, as suggested in Guillaume de Rennes's gloss mentioned above, is shown more imaginatively in the *Vita* of the Dominican friar Henry Suso (d. 1366). In his chapter on 'interior sufferings', Suso told the story of his encounter with the 'spirit of blasphemy' and described it as a 'hideous Moor, with eyes of fire and a terrific hellish look' who tried to shoot fiery arrows through his heart.[26] Upon invoking the help of the Virgin, the devil vanished.[27] The encounter between Henry and the evil spirit is similar to the account of Thomas de Cantimpré in which he reported the effect of Marie's finger. Thomas wrote that one night, when Ugolino was secretly praying before his altar, a lethargy (*torpor*) began to flood his mind. The cardinal stood

---

[22] 'Spiritus blasphemie adeo animam meam vexat et variis temptationum fluctibus obruit, et usque in desperationem cotidie fere detrudor': ibid. 187.

[23] Ibid. 187–9.

[24] Thomas de Cantimpré, *Vita Lutgardis*, in Barbara Newman, ed., *Thomas of Cantimpré: The Collected Saints' Lives*, Medieval Women, Texts and Contexts 19 (Turnhout, 2008), 211–96, at 291.

[25] Alexander C. Murray, 'The Temptation of St Hugh of Grenoble', in *Intellectual Life in the Middle Ages: Essays presented to Margaret Gibson*, ed. L. J. Smith and B. Ward (London, 1991), 81–101, at 97.

[26] Such imagery is found, for instance, in: Strasbourg, Bibliothèque nationale et universitaire, MS 2929, fol. 119^r, which shows the 'spirit of blasphemy' shooting a fiery arrow at Henry Suso.

[27] Thomas F. Knox, ed., *The Life of Blessed Henry Suso by Himself* (London, 1865), 214–15.

up and clasped Marie's finger tightly against his chest while asking for her intercession. Without delay, the 'spirit of blasphemy' was put to flight and the numbness of the mind disappeared.[28]

Thomas's use of the word *torpor* seems to identify further the nature of Ugolino's struggles. Ugolino's symptoms, a state of lethargy, despair, blasphemy in the form of distrusting God, and an impending dejection in his faith, point towards *acedia*, a spiritual depression.[29] When relating Ugolino's predicament to *acedia*, the *spiritus blasphemiae* can be identified with the *daemonium meridianum*,[30] the noonday demon, the personification of depression.[31] The use of Marie's finger relic to deal with this 'possession', or to ward off an evil spirit or demon, is evident.[32] With his story of the successful repelling of the evil spirit or demon, Thomas thus provided evidence for the authenticity of the relic and for the sanctity of Marie d'Oignies.[33]

Marie's reputation in dealing with doubt was well established by this time. Doubt features often in her *Vita* and Jacques noted that after her death Marie did not abandon those she loved and continued to guide and protect them from danger by providing secret

---

[28] Thomas de Cantimpré, *Supplementum* 15 (CChr.CM 252, 188–9).

[29] Jeffery J. Tyler, 'The Misery of Monks and the Laziness of the Laity: Overcoming the Sin of Acedia', in *Frömmigkeit – Theologie – Frömmigkeitstheologie: Contributions to European Church History. Festschrift für Berndt Hamm zum 60. Geburtstag*, ed. Gudrun Litz, Heidrun Munzert and Rland Liebenberg (Leiden, 2005), 119–30; Rubén A. Peretó Rivas, 'Acedia y depresion. Entre pecado capital y desorden psiquiatrico', in *In umbra intelligentiae. Estudios en homenaje al Prof. Juan Cruz Cruz*, ed. Ángel Luis González and María Idoya Zorroza (Pamplona, 2011), 655–66. Ineke van 't Spijker, 'Saints and Despair: Twelfth-Century Hagiography as "Intimate Biography"', in Anneke B. Mulder-Bakker, ed., *The Invention of Saintliness* (London, 2002), 185–205, at 198–9, discusses the idea of blasphemy against the Holy Spirit (Matt. 12: 31), a concept distinctly different from the 'spirit of blasphemy'. Twelfth-century theologians saw blasphemy against the Holy Spirit as impenitence leading to despair: see Odo of Tournai, *De blasphemia in Spiritum Sanctum* (PL 160, cols 1111–18); Richard of St Victor, *De Spiritu blasphemie* (PL 196, cols 1185–92).

[30] Ps. 90: 6 (Vulgate).

[31] See also Barbara Newman, 'Possessed by the Spirit: Devout Women, Demoniacs, and the Apostolic Life in the Thirteenth Century', *Speculum* 73 (1998), 733–70, at 740–1.

[32] Ibid. 752. The shape of some reliquary pendants suggests they were 'designed for intimate inspection in the palm of the hand and required the physical interaction of the owner to release [their] spiritual value': James Robinson, 'From Altar to Amulet: Relics, Portability, and Devotion', in Martina Bagnoli et al., eds, *Treasures of Heaven: Saints, Relics, and Devotion in Medieval Europe* (Baltimore, MD, 2011), 111–16, at 114–15.

[33] On the notion of Marie's sanctity and the canonization processes of the *mulieres sanctae*, see Michel Lauwers, 'Entre béguinisme et mysticisme. La *Vie de Marie d'Oignies* (†1213) de Jacques de Vitry, ou la définition d'une sainteté féminine au XIIIᵉ siècle', *Ons geestelijk erf* 66 (1992), 46–70.

signs that removed any doubt from the heart (*a cordibus eorum dubitationem removens*).[34]   In the *Supplementum*, Thomas emphasized that Marie never doubted Christ, and was 'never once deceived by the enemy of man'.[35]   Moreover, he described how Jacques told Ugolino that God had granted Marie a 'special grace of expelling blasphemous spirits' (*in effugandis blasphemie spiritibus*).   In the *Vita*, Jacques often portrayed Marie as the ideal intercessor when confronted with the 'spirit of blasphemy', which he saw as the most evil spirit of all temptations (*contra spiritum blasphemie et desperationis preminebat*).[36]   Jacques recorded how Marie helped a young Cistercian nun whom the devil attacked with 'blasphemies and unclean thoughts'.[37]   Similarly, Thomas included the story of a pilgrim who, after joining the Cistercian order, was 'troubled and stung by the spirit of blasphemy'.[38]

The hagiographical character of the source material relating the predicament of Ugolino demands a search for corroborating evidence.   Aside from Thomas's account, are there any traces of the origins and nature of Ugolino's doubts in other documents? Ugolino had been a member of the College of Cardinals for almost three decades before ascending the papal throne in March 1227.[39]   Between 1207 and 1209, he was in charge of the crucial legation to protect the papacy's interests in the conflict between Otto IV and Philip of Swabia.[40]   The murder of Philip on 21 June 1208, and the consequent setback for the papal legation, seems to have coincided with the death of Ugolino's mentor and spiritual father Raniero da Ponza, a monk at the Cistercian abbey of Fossanova who was himself involved in papal diplomacy with Germany.[41]   A letter from Ugolino to the Cistercians of the abbeys of Fossanova, Casamari and Salem, written sometime between 1207 and 1209, testified to Ugolino's profound grief at Raniero's death. The cardinal referred to the monk as

---

[34] Jacques de Vitry, *Vita* 2.13 (CChr.CM 252, 163).

[35] Thomas de Cantimpré, *Supplementum* 10 (CChr.CM 252, 180).

[36] Jacques de Vitry, *Vita* 2.3 (CChr.CM 252, 113–14).

[37] Ibid. 1.9 (CChr.CM 252, 76–9).

[38] Thomas de Cantimpré, *Supplementum* 16 (CChr.CM 252, 189–90).

[39] See also Maria Pia Alberzoni, 'Dalla domus del cardinale d'Ostia alla curia di Gregorio IX', in *Gregorio IX e gli ordini mendicanti (Assisi, 7–9 ottobre 2010)*, Fondazione Centro italiano di studi sull'alto medioevo (Spoleto, 2011), 73–122; Ovidio Capitani, 'Gregorio IX', in *Enciclopedia dei Papi*, 3 vols (Rome, 2000), 2: 363–80.

[40] Friedrich Kempf, *Regestum Innocentii III papae super negotio Romani imperii* (Rome, 1947), no. 141, at 334–5; Werner Maleczek, *Papst und Kardinalskolleg von 1191 bis 1216. Die Kardinäle unter Coelestin III. und Innocenz III* (Vienna, 1984), 129–30.

[41] Maria Pia Alberzoni, 'Raniero da Ponza e la curia romana', *Florensia* 11 (1997), 83–112.

his spiritual father and doubted whether he was worthy of his father's virtue because of the multitude of sins piled up over his own head. At the end of the letter, Ugolino noted that his many worries and difficulties, especially regarding his spirit, were hindering his activities in Germany.[42] Nevertheless, Ugolino's doubts do not seem to have affected his reputation. In March 1221 Honorius III appointed him as legate to the court of Frederick II and both the pope and the emperor were full of praise for the cardinal. Honorius praised Ugolino for his zeal and virtuous life, calling him incorruptible and a pillar and ornament of the Church.[43] Frederick II, in turn, rejoiced at Ugolino's appointment and described the cardinal as honest, clear-sighted in religion, pure in life, resourceful, eloquent, knowledgeable and cautious.[44]

After the legation of 1221, Ugolino seems to have been less active, and Guido Levi has suggested that the cardinal was gathering strength for his expected pontificate. Since the cardinals had chosen Honorius over Ugolino in 1216, the latter may have been anticipating the papal throne in the next papal election. Levi also alludes to a conflict between the pope and Ugolino's nephew, Riccardo Conti, over control of the city of Ostia. Levi suggests that there may have been a cooling on the pope's part towards his cardinal because of this.[45] Ernst Brem, however, is not convinced that the actions of members of the Conti family would have impinged on Ugolino.[46] Nonetheless, tensions between the cardinal's family and Pope Honorius may indeed have contributed to the doubts Ugolino was facing.

Ugolino's wish for Marie's support in 1226 was not his first invocation of a religious woman to provide spiritual help. In 1220, in a letter to Clare of Assisi, Ugolino wrote that he was weighed down by so many sins, that he had offended the Lord, and would no longer be

---

[42] '[C]onsolationes invenire non possum. … nisi quia ex multitudine iniquitatum mearum, que supergresse sunt caput meum': Eduard Winkelmann, 'Analecta Heidelbergensia', *Archivio della Società Romana di storia patria* 2 (1879), 361–7, at 363, 367. Maleczek also linked the spirituality of Ugolino to the influence of Raniero: *Papst und Kardinalskolleg*, 128.

[43] Heinrich Zimmermann, *Die päpstliche Legation in der ersten Hälfte des 13. Jahrhunderts* (Paderborn, 1913), 230.

[44] Guido Levi, *Registri dei cardinali Ugolino d'Ostia e Ottaviani degli Ubaldini* (Rome, 1890), 150–2.

[45] Ibid. xvii, 126–7, 141.

[46] Ernst Brem, *Papst Gregor IX bis zum Beginn seines Pontifikats* (Heidelberg, 1911), 60; Salvatore Sibilia, *Gregorio IX* (Milan, 1961), 51.

worthy to be among his elect unless Clare's tears and prayers were to obtain him mercy.[47]

The cardinal's letter to Clare is reminiscent of his earlier letter mourning the death of Raniero da Ponza. Furthermore, Maria Pia Alberzoni, discussing Gregory IX's involvement in the new female religious movements, points to a later letter from July 1227 that Ugolino, by then Gregory IX, addressed to the Poor Clares of Sant'Apollinare at Milan.[48] In this letter, too, Ugolino expressed his fear that he was not worthy to be among the elect of the Lord, for his many temporal concerns, especially since he had become pope, had kept him from spiritual contemplation. Ugolino's words in these letters leave little doubt regarding his uncertainties about his faith.[49]

While the source material may support Thomas de Cantimpré's account of Ugolino's crisis, we must also, however, consider that Ugolino was elected pope only a year later, and the assessment of the severity of the cardinal's doubts must therefore be nuanced. Neither his plea for spiritual support from Clare of Assisi and for her special prayers nor the emphasis on his sins was unusual: indeed, such language was common in the writings of the faithful concerned about their souls. Given Ugolino's support for the Franciscans and the Poor Clares, his letter to Clare perhaps testifies more to the cardinal's admiration for her devotion and religious life. The admiration Ugolino showed for Clare was part of a wider appreciation of the new order in the curia. Similarly, in a letter of 1216, Jacques de Vitry had observed that Honorius III and the cardinals greatly admired the Franciscans and the Poor Clares.[50]

Besides the perspective of Ugolino, Thomas's intentions in reporting the anecdote and (perhaps more importantly) the genre-specific characteristics of these hagiographic accounts also need to be

---

[47] '[Q]uod tot peccatorum sum sarcina praegravatus et in tantum universae terrae Dominatorem offendi, quod non sum dignus electorum eius consortio aggregari et ab occupationibus terrenis avelli, nisi lacrymae et orationes tuae mihi veniam impetrent pro peccatis': *Analecta Franciscana*, 3: *Chronica XXIV generalium Ordinis Minorum cum pluribus appendicibus inter quas excellit hucusque ineditus Liber de laudibus S. Francisci Fr. Bernardi a Bessa* (Quaracchi, 1897), 183; see also Kajetan Esser, 'Die Briefe Gregors IX. an die hl. Klara von Assisi', *Franziskanische Studien* 35 (1953), 274–95, at 274.

[48] Maria Pia Alberzoni, *Francescanesimo a Milano nel duecento* (Milan, 1991), 209.

[49] Maria Pia Alberzoni also noted that the letters reveal that the cardinal was often plagued by a profound spiritual despair: '*Servus vestrum et ancillarum Christi omnium. Gregorio IX e la vita religiosa femminile*', *FS* 64 (2006), 145–78, at 164–5.

[50] Jacques de Vitry, *Epistolae* 1 (CChr.CM 171, 553).

considered. Thomas, born in 1201, grew up in Brabant and Liège. As a young boy, he heard Jacques preaching and was so impressed that he vowed to love and venerate the preacher.[51] Like Jacques, Thomas studied theology and became a successful preacher and a prolific writer. Inspired by Jacques's *Vita* of Marie d'Oignies, Thomas not only added a supplement to it, but also wrote hagiographies of other *mulieres sanctae* from Liège and Brabant, showing his admiration for these holy women.[52] And just as Jacques's *Vita* of Marie d'Oignies, dedicated to the ardent anti-Cathar bishop Foulques of Toulouse (d. 1231), was also intended to provide an alternative to Cathar women in the south of France,[53] so too Thomas's *Supplementum* was more than a biographical account.

A first and rather subtle message in the *Supplementum* is Thomas's disappointment with Jacques's rise in the ecclesiastical hierarchy. This moralizing character is evident in Ugolino's refusal to accept Jacques's gift of a silver cup mentioned above. Saying it was not a gift from the East, but from Rome, the cardinal implied that the cup represented temporal wealth. Through this anecdote, Thomas criticized Jacques's rise to power and wealth, accusing him of betraying the ideals of poverty and humility propagated by Marie d'Oignies. While it is clear, considering other parts of the *Supplementum*, that Thomas was trying to convince Jacques that his rightful place was with the community of Oignies rather than at the curia, these comments also reflect a broader contemporary criticism of the Roman prelates. Elsewhere in the *Supplementum*, Thomas claimed that 'all of France with its abundance scarcely suffices for the annual taxes of cardinals'.[54] Indeed, in the spirit of the reforms of the Fourth Lateran Council (1215), and before his rise through the ranks of the Roman hierarchy, Jacques himself had expressed his dismay at the cardinals' temporal concerns. Just as Ugolino lamented his lack of time for spiritual contemplation, so Jacques noted that '[at the curia] they are really absorbed by concerns for secular or temporal matters, … so much that it is hardly

---

[51] Thomas de Cantimpré, *Supplementum* 23 (CChr.CM 252, 201).

[52] See also Barbara Newman, 'Devout Women and Demoniacs in the World of Thomas of Cantimpré', in Juliet Dor, Lesley P. Johnson and Jocelyn Wogan-Browne, eds, *New Trends in Feminine Spirituality: The Holy Women of Liège and their Impact*, Medieval Women, Texts and Contexts 2 (Turnhout, 1999), 35–60.

[53] André Vauchez, 'Prosélytisme et action antihérétique en milieu féminin au XIIIᵉ siècle. La "Vie de Marie d'Oignies" (†1213) par Jacques de Vitry', *Problèmes d'histoire du christianisme* 17 (1987), 95–110.

[54] Thomas de Cantimpré, *Supplementum* 22 (CChr.CM 252, 197).

permitted to speak about spiritual matters'.[55] Ironically, when Jacques
became cardinal, he was accused of the same temporal concerns.

Moreover, the fact that in Thomas's account we encounter the
'spirit of blasphemy' predominantly in a Dominican context is surely
no coincidence, and the story of Ugolino's triumph over his doubts
should also be regarded as an *exemplum*.[56] Thomas presented the
story of Ugolino as a lesson for readers who found themselves in
a similar predicament: as Pope Gregory IX, Ugolino could be compassionate about their weaknesses because he had been tempted as
they were.[57] The more important message, however, was Marie's
exemplary devout life. Thomas noted that Jacques not only gave
Ugolino Marie's finger to help him combat his doubts, but above all
urged him to read the *Vita* to help him deal with his uncertainties.
Elsewhere, Jacques referred to his books as the means by which he
was able to subdue the devil;[58] here he recommended that Ugolino
read Marie's *Vita* to bring him back onto the right path. Similarly,
through his *Supplementum*, Thomas also advertised the use of the *Vita*
of Marie d'Oignies as an example for a devotional life.[59] Marie
was the paradigm of a *mulier sancta* and the embodiment of the *vita
apostolica*: living a poor, humble, penitential and deeply spiritual life,
concerned with the *cura animarum* of the faithful.[60] Thomas's emphasis on the power of Marie's relics emulated Jacques's efforts to advance the reputation of his spiritual mother.[61] Jacques's *Vita* of Marie

[55] Jacques de Vitry, *Epistolae* 1 (CChr.CM 171, 553).
[56] Thomas himself noted that he had selected some *exempla* among many cases of encounters with the *spiritus blasphemiae*: Thomas de Cantimpré, *Supplementum* 16 (CChr.CM
252, 190).
[57] Ibid. Thomas paraphrases Heb. 4: 15. A few lines earlier, he compared Ugolino to St
Peter, who also wrestled with doubts and temptation.
[58] Jacques de Vitry, *Epistolae* 1 (CChr.CM 171, 550).
[59] Jacques urged the reader to imitate the virtues of Marie, but did not commend her
physical excesses. It is important to note that while Jacques used the subjunctive '*eius virtutes imitemur*' ('we should imitate'), his subsequent use of the infinitive '*imitari non possumus*'
('we cannot / are unable to imitate') is in line with his emphasis on her special fervour:
'Nec hoc dixerim ut excessum commendem, sed ut fervorem ostendam. … eius virtutes
imitemur, opera vero virtutum eius sine privato privilegio imitari non possumus': Jacques
de Vitry, *Vita* 1.2 (CChr.CM 252, 58).
[60] Some iconography depicts Marie as *magistra*, seemingly teaching the *vita apostolica*: e.g.
Turin, Biblioteca Statale Universitaria, MS D.II.21, fol. 3^r; Leuven, Maurits Sabbebiblio-
theek, Coll. Mechelen, Bibliotheek van het Grootseminarie, MS 20, fol. 72^r.
[61] On the relics of Marie, see also Brenda M. Bolton, 'Spiegels van vroomheid: Relieken
van Maria van Oignies', in M. Monteiro et al., eds, *De Dynamiek van Religie en Cultuur.
Geschiedenis van het Nederlands Katholicisme* (Kampen, 1993), 124–37.

included most characteristics of a typical saint's life: her virtuous childhood, the renunciation of temporal possessions, persecution, and testimonies of her devotion and asceticism. However, he did not include the necessary *miracula* that would help to promote Marie to sainthood. Rather, the *Vita* echoed the focus on practical theology amongst his fellow preachers and theologians in the circle of Paris masters around Peter the Chanter. In the *Vita* Jacques emphasized the concern for pastoral care and the apostolic lifestyle demonstrated by Marie, and by extension other *mulieres sanctae*, providing his readers with an example to imitate. While he showed some appreciation for the burgeoning lay religious movements, he seems to have been reluctant to go too far in endorsing asceticism and devotion outside the walls of the cloister. In contrast, Thomas de Cantimpré, writing in the context of the rise of the friars, was more eager to elevate the *mulieres sanctae* to sainthood and added a number of *miracula* to Marie's *Vita*.

A final element to consider is Thomas's own doubt. Jacques only mentioned the silver reliquary pendant with Marie's finger once and did not claim explicitly that it was Marie who had saved his mule from drowning. Thomas, on the other hand, attributed two more miracles to Marie's finger-relic. These specific instances, however, need to be seen in the context of the author's love and admiration for another *mulier sancta*, St Lutgard of Aywières, and the *Vita* he wrote in her memory.[62] It is known that Thomas tried to convince the abbess of Aywières to give him Lutgard's hand after her death. We read in the *Vita Lutgardis* that, when she found out about his intentions, Lutgard asked her friend what he planned to do with her hand. Thomas replied that he believed her hand would be good for his body and soul. When Lutgard told him that one of her fingers would suffice, he answered that no part of her body would be enough for him, unless he had her hand or head to comfort him when she was gone.[63] In his *Vita Lutgardis* Thomas revealed the intention behind his emphasis on Marie's relic, for he told those who berated him for venerating Lutgard's finger that Jacques had cut off Marie's finger even though she was not yet canonized.[64]

---

[62] Thomas Merton, 'Saint Lutgarde: Nun of Aywières, Belgium', *Cistercian Studies Quarterly* 35 (2000), 219–30.
[63] 'Nihil inquam, mihi ex tuo, Mater, corpore sufficere poterit, nisi manum aut caput habeam, quo tunc relevere toto orbatus': Thomas de Cantimpré, *Vita Lutgardis*, 290.
[64] Ibid. 291.

Faced with the thought of losing Lutgard, Thomas seems to have used the account of the miracles attributed to the finger of Marie d'Oignies as a justification for his obsession with obtaining a relic of his own spiritual mother. As Marie's finger had protected and consoled Jacques and Ugolino, Thomas hoped that Lutgard's relic would not only protect his body and soul but would also help to console him.

Jacques's assistance in overcoming Ugolino's doubts provided the foundation for a lifelong friendship between the two prelates. Alberic de Trois-Fontaines noted that upon the election of Ugolino as the new pope in 1227 Jacques was called to travel to the papal see 'with haste' (*cum festinatione*); the new Pope Gregory IX appointed him as cardinal-bishop of Tusculum, a high-ranking position in the Roman Church.[65] In so far as we can reconstruct these events from hagiographical texts, and taking into account Thomas's agenda in the *Supplementum*, it would seem that Jacques and Ugolino had earlier encountered each other at a crossroads, at a time when both were struggling with doubts about their careers. Jacques's intervention seems to have given Ugolino the strength to overcome his doubts and move on to become pope. Ugolino, in turn, helped Jacques to continue his reform and his crusade efforts as his close advisor in the curia.[66]

Thomas de Cantimpré's description of the temptation of Ugolino by the 'spirit of blasphemy' might be taken as a rhetorical device employed by the preacher to make his account of the cardinal's tribulations more dramatic. As in Jacques de Vitry's writings, the *spiritus blasphemiae* is used as an allegorical personification of doubt, much as it is in the story of Henry Suso mentioned above. Doubt in the form of an evil spirit also ties in with the seven gifts Marie receives from the Holy Spirit: she is given seven virtues which Jacques presents as seven spirits.[67] Nonetheless, while Thomas may have exaggerated the severity of the cardinal's crisis in order to emphasize the intercessory role and power of Marie, Ugolino's own writings do seem to testify to his doubts regarding his worthiness for his office. For the reader today, therefore, the story of Ugolino provides a glimpse

[65] Albrici monachi Triumfontium, *Chronicon* (MGH S 23, 919).
[66] The influence of Jacques on Gregory IX's decision-making certainly deserves further research. To date, the main research into Jacques's role as cardinal is a brief chapter in Philipp Funk, *Jakob von Vitry. Leben und Werke* (Leipzig, 1909), 60–7.
[67] Jacques de Vitry, *Vita* 2.2–8 (CChr.CM 252, 94–145).

of the doubts of a medieval prelate: his suffering upon the death of his mentor and his uncertainty about his worthiness for the office of cardinal, and later that of pope, would eventually lead him to the brink of *acedia*. The value of Thomas's account, however, transcends its anecdotal biographical information. The story of Ugolino serves as an *exemplum* and has a clear didactic value. Through it, and despite the subtle criticism of Jacques's temporal concerns, Thomas had a chance to ascribe to two of the people he most admired, Jacques and Marie, a crucial role in Ugolino's ascent to the throne of St Peter. The *Vita* of Marie was portrayed as a model life for the reader to imitate and as the perfect tool for the overcoming of doubt. The intercessory powers of Marie d'Oignies against the temptations of doubt, despair and blasphemy were made clear. Through the relic of her finger, Marie's intercessory powers triumphed against Jacques de Vitry's doubts, repelled the 'spirit of blasphemy' vexing Ugolino, and alleviated Thomas de Cantimpré's despair when faced with the loss of his own personal saint, Lutgard.

Diabolical Doubt: The Peculiar Account of Brother Bernard's Demonic Possession in Jordan of Saxony's *Libellus*

Steven Watts*

University of St Andrews

Jordan of Saxony's Libellus, *first produced in 1233, has struck scholars as an unwieldy combination of hagiography and early Dominican history. Compounding its somewhat awkward nature are its various jumps in chronology and idiosyncratic biographical asides. Perhaps the most idiosyncratic of them all is Jordan's lengthy account of Brother Bernard's demonic possession. While this account provides the setting for the institution of the Dominican custom of chanting the* Salve Regina *after compline, it is difficult to see at first glance what benefit the story as told would have had for Jordan's audience. Upon closer inspection, however, some method appears in the madness. From a pedagogical point of view – the* Libellus *is described in the mid-thirteenth-century* Vitas fratrum *as a journal Jordan read to novices in Paris – the revelation of Jordan's various attempts at identifying the demon's wiles suggests a master willing to allow his students to witness his own doubts about how to proceed. Furthermore, the possessed brother shows a remarkable capacity to imitate ideals central to Dominican identity, in so far as Jordan reveals such ideals in his* Libellus: *a master of theology, a charismatic preacher and a prospective saint. This essay offers a close analysis of this perplexing narrative, describing the significance of the various demonic phenomena and Jordan's reactions to them, and reflecting on the pedagogical implications of the portrayal of Jordan's uncertainty.*

In Sabina Flanagan's recent study on doubt in 'the Long Twelfth Century', she reflects on the paradoxical capacity of uncertainty to engender confidence.[1] While medieval authors generally sought to eliminate doubt from their texts, Flanagan highlights the 'Doubting Thomas' episode in the Gospel of John (20: 24–31) as a rare example in which doubt is praised in medieval sources for its positive

* Department of Mediaeval History, University of St Andrews, 71 South St, St Andrews, KY16 9QW. E-mail: sew8@st-andrews.ac.uk.

[1] Sabina Flanagan, *Doubt in an Age of Faith: Uncertainty in the Long Twelfth Century* (Turnhout, 2008), 12–13, 143–4.

Studies in Church History 52 (2016) 102–117
doi: 10.1017/stc.2015.6

contribution to belief.[2] Thomas's unbelief is interpreted as a providential opportunity to demonstrate certainty. In this case, potential doubts about the resurrection are pre-emptively answered for the gospel's audience. Doubt – albeit in a controlled environment – is employed for the sake of greater certitude. Here I shall discuss how Jordan of Saxony (d. 1237), master general of the Order of Preachers, uses uncertainty in a similar capacity in the concluding narrative of his *Libellus*. This otherwise peculiar account of Brother Bernard's demonic possession provides a setting in which doubt is employed pedagogically to engender confidence in the order's mission.

Jordan probably produced the first redaction of the *Libellus* in the spring of 1233.[3] In the prologue (§§1–3), he explains that it was written to satisfy the many brothers who desired an account of the origins of the order's institutions and its first friars. The *Libellus* appeared amid a surge of devotion to the cult of Dominic of Caleruega (d. 1221) that would lead to the translation of his bones within the church of St Nicholas of the Vineyards, Bologna, in May 1233 and his canonization in August 1234. Taking this context into account, scholars have been perplexed by the text's peculiar combination of early Dominican history, hagiographical tropes and biographical asides.[4] Most peculiar of all is Jordan's decision to conclude the *Libellus*, not with a laudatory passage on Dominic's great example for the brothers, but with an episode centred on Jordan's encounter with another brother, Bernard, and the demon that possessed him (§§110–20).

---

[2] Ibid. 13.

[3] The standard edition is *Libellus de principiis Ordinis Praedicatorum*, ed. Heribert Christian Scheeben, Monumenta Ordinis Fratrum Praedicatorum Historica [hereafter: MOPH] 16 (Rome, 1935), 1–88. Translations of this text, and all others, are my own. For recent discussions relating to the date of the production of the *Libellus*, see Simon Tugwell, 'Notes on the Life of St Dominic', *AFP* 68 (1998), 1–116, at 5–33; Giulia Barone, 'Il *Libellus* de initio Ordinis fratrum Predicatorum e lo sviluppo dell'Ordine nel primo cinquantennio', in *Domenico de Caleruega e la nascita dell'Ordine dei frati Predicatori. Atti del XLI convegno storico internazionale, Todi, 10–12 ottobre 2004* (Spoleto, 2005), 431–40; Luigi Canetti, 'La Datazione del *Libellus* di Giordano di Sassonia', in Giovanni Bertuzzi, ed., *L'origine dell'Ordine dei predicatori e l'Università di Bologna* (Bologna, 2006), 176–93; Achim Wesjohann, *Mendikantische Gründungserzählungen im 13. und 14. Jahrhundert. Mythen als Element institutioneller Eigengeschichtsschreibung der mittelalterlichen Franziskaner, Dominikaner und Augustiner-Eremiten*, Vita regularis 49 (Berlin, 2012), 372–84.

[4] Most notably Heribert Christian Scheeben, 'Der literarische Nachlass Jordans von Sachsen', *Historisches Jahrbuch im Auftrag der Görres-Gesellschaft* 52 (1932), 56–71, at 61–2; C. N. L. Brooke, 'St Dominic and his First Biographer', *TRHS* 5th ser. 17 (1967), 23–40, at 24–6; Tugwell, 'Notes', 11.

Simon Tugwell has suggested that the odd conclusion to the text is indicative of the rushed and unfinished nature of its composition.[5] With the important exception of Jordan's encomium to his deceased friend Henry of Cologne (d. *c.*1225–9?), the majority of the events mentioned in the *Libellus* occurred no later than 1221.[6] This gives the impression that the text was initially something akin to a journal, in which Jordan recorded some of the order's earliest memories.[7]   He seems, however, to have been motivated as much by pedagogy as by posterity.[8]   In the *Vitas fratrum*, a mid-thirteenth-century collection of Dominican stories, Gerald de Frachet (d. 1271) recalls that he had been present when Jordan read from his *Libellus* to Dominican novices in Paris.[9]   As the overarching purpose of the *Libellus* was – at least in part – to benefit recent entrants into the order through a recollection of its past (§§2–3, 109), it is reasonable to conclude that Jordan was employing the story to teach the novices about what he thought it meant to be a member of the Order of Preachers.

Most helpfully for present purposes, what Jordan read on that occasion was none other than the culminating sequence of the Brother Bernard narrative (§§116–18), in which the demon's deceits are finally overthrown by means of divine intervention.

Gerald must have gone back to the official rendering of the *Libellus* to recollect the story, as much of his account follows the text verbatim. However, it is striking that all references in the original

---

[5] Tugwell, 'Notes', 19.

[6] Ibid. 18–23. See Canetti, 'La Datazione', 178–9; Simon Tugwell, *Pelagius Parvus and his 'Summa': A Preliminary Enquiry and a Sample of Texts*, Dissertationes historicae 34 (Rome, 2012), 172–3. As Tugwell has pointed out, the account of the translation of Dominic's bones in 1233 that Scheeben appends to his edition of the *Libellus* (§§121–30) is not part of the original text: 'Notes', 8 n. 9.

[7] Barone, 'Il *Libellus*', 439.

[8] John Van Engen, 'Dominic and the Brothers: *Vitae* as life-forming *Exempla* in the Order of Preachers', in Kent Emery Jr and Joseph Wawrykow, eds, *Christ among the Medieval Dominicans: Representations of Christ in the Texts and Images of the Order of Preachers* (Notre Dame, IN, 1998), 7–25, at 13.

[9] *Vitas fratrum* 3.33 (B.-M. Reichert, ed., *Vitae Fratrum Ordinis Praedicatorum necnon Cronica Fratrum Ordinis ab anno MCCIII usque MCCLIV*, ed. B.-M. Reichert, MOPH 1 [Rome, 1896], 1–320, at 126). Despite Reichert's use of the title *Vitae fratrum*, this collection originally circulated as *Vitas fratrum*. For a brief reconstruction of its convoluted manuscript tradition, see Simon Tugwell, 'L'évolution des *vitae fratrum*. Résumé des conclusions provisoires', *Cahiers de Fanjeaux* 36 (2001), 415–18; idem, ed., *Miracula sancti Dominici mandato magistri Berengarii collecta. Petri Calo legendae sancti Dominici*, MOPH 26 (Rome, 1997), 32–9. On the basis of his ongoing reconstruction, Tugwell identifies Gerald as being responsible for this particular story: personal communication, 19 November 2014.

text to Jordan's self-doubt are conspicuously absent from Gerald's account. For instance, Gerald's recollection jumps from Jordan's description of a sweetness that seemed to permeate the latter's bones to a request that God would reveal its origins, entirely bypassing Jordan's original admission that he had been stupefied (*stupefactus*) and dismayed (*perculsus*) by the phenomenon (§118). By omitting Jordan's uncertainty in the face of demonic falsehood, Gerald's rendition becomes but one of many stories, repeated with verve by a number of mid-thirteenth-century Dominican authors, which display Jordan's confident engagement in spiritual warfare.[10] For our purposes, however, Gerald's narrative provides two important insights: Jordan had used the original story to instruct novices and Gerald appears to have omitted all reference to Jordan's doubt in his revision of the story.

The story of Brother Bernard's possession is set shortly after Jordan's account of Dominic's death in early August 1221. We find Jordan on the road to Bologna in order to fulfil his newly appointed role as prior provincial of Lombardy. Upon arriving at the convent, Jordan discovers Brother Bernard. Possessed and tormented by the fiercest demon, the friar was being harassed by horrible frenzies and disturbing his brothers beyond all measure. Jordan explains that God, 'in his divine mercy, had undoubtedly provided that trouble to produce endurance in his servants'.[11]

Jordan's explanation, with its allusion to Romans 5: 3 ('but we also boast in our tribulations, knowing that trouble produces endurance'), informs his text's audience that no matter what takes place in the narrative, they may be certain not only of its divine sanction but also of its providential purpose. This explanation also makes clear that Jordan himself had no doubt about how to interpret the narrative. This helps to enforce an important distinction in the episode between Jordan-as-narrator, who in an assured manner interprets the events as they are happening, and Jordan-as-protagonist, who grows increasingly uncertain as the demon's machinations become more

---

[10] See *Vitas fratrum* 3.28–34 (ed. Reichert, 122–8); Thomas de Cantimpré, *Bonum universale de apibus* 2.19.2, 2.57.46 (ed. George Colvener, 2 vols in 1 [Chantilly, 1627], 569–70, 572–80); Étienne de Bourbon, *Tractatus de diversis materiis praedicabilibus* §§188, 189, 229 (*Anecdotes historiques. Légendes et apologues tirés du recueil inédit d'Etienne de Bourbon*, ed. A. Lecoy de la Marche [Paris, 1872], 101–2, 164–5, 197).

[11] '[Q]uam tribulationem haud dubium operande patientie servorum suorum misericordia divina providerat': *Libellus* §110.

sophisticated. Doubt in this text is employed within a controlled environment.

Jordan continues the story with an explanation of how the possession came to be (§111). He relates that Bernard told him that he had been so tormented by the sorrow of his sins that it was suggested to his heart that, as a form of purgation, he should seek demonic possession. Although Bernard's mind was initially revolted by the proposition, he finally gave his assent, and with God's permission he was immediately assailed by a demonic spirit. The demon began a series of trials, but not initially by means of the frenzies Jordan first described. Instead, the narrative reveals a strategy in which the demon fabricates ideals central to the identity of the order – the theologian, the preacher and even the prospective saint – in order to lead the community into falsehood.

Jordan recounts that, through the brother's mouth, the demon 'vomited out ... many marvellous things, including such profound opinions concerning the Holy Scriptures that they might deservedly be considered utterances praiseworthy enough to rival those of Augustine'.[12] Moreover, Bernard uttered these even though he was unskilled in theology and ignorant of the Bible. In effect, the possessed brother played the part of a *magister theologiae*.

The demon's eloquence was not exceptional. Barbara Newman has drawn attention to a variety of thirteenth-century *exempla* that record demoniacs expounding upon theological subjects despite their lack of learning.[13] For instance, in the *Dialogus miraculorum* of Caesarius of Heisterbach (d. *c.*1240), there is a story of a possessed woman who, despite being illiterate, pointed out the phrase in the missal that bound 'her master' in hell.[14] Caesarius reports that this miraculous event was a source of great edification to the woman's audience.[15] In Jordan's account, however, the demon plays a more devious role – one characteristic of an ancient Christian tradition, in which demons seek to undermine the devotion of the holy by means of pretended

---

[12] 'Multa miranda per os eiusdem demon euomuit. Interdum quoque, licet obsessus ille non foret in theologia peritus et sanctarum velut inscius scripturarum, adeo tamen per os eius profundas de scripturis sanctis eliciebat sententias ut huiusmodi etiam per Augustinum edita laudabilia merito censerentur': *Libellus* §112.

[13] Barbara Newman, 'Possessed by the Spirit: Devout Women, Demoniacs, and the Apostolic Life in the Thirteenth Century', *Speculum* 73 (1998), 733–70, at 749–53.

[14] Caesarius of Heisterbach, *Dialogus miraculorum* 1.5.13 (ed. Josephus Strange, 2 vols [Cologne, 1851], 292).

[15] Ibid.

holiness.[16] In this case the demon's false 'holiness' has a distinctly Dominican resonance, playing upon theology's central role within the order.

By 1221, the order had already established a theological presence within the university milieu in Bologna.[17] By 1231, they would have two chairs of theology in Paris and one in Oxford. Jordan himself had been a bachelor of theology at Paris and had received many students into the order as a result of his recruiting efforts at the university.[18] In fact, we can claim with some confidence that the majority of the novices to whom Jordan read his story in Gerald's account were, or had been, arts students, probably still in their teens, who were now being directed toward theological studies.[19] Brother Bernard, however, was unskilled in such matters (§112), which is what made his behaviour so striking. The demon made it appear as if Bernard had fulfilled the highest calling a friar could accomplish through study: to become a master of theology. It would have been a master's prerogative, beyond even that of the convent's doctor of theology, to give an authoritative theological opinion (*sententia*) and to ascertain a truth not open to all, but hidden below the surface of a text *(profunda)*.[20] That the possessed did this in a manner consonant with Augustine is particularly worthy of note, for Augustine was not only the authority behind the Dominicans' rule, but also the foremost patristic authority in Latin theology.

Jordan-as-protagonist, however, is not fooled by this first trial. He sees through the falsehood by drawing attention to the brother's pride. Jordan-as-narrator explains that Bernard gloried greatly in himself whenever anyone lent an ear, which incidentally reveals that some did listen. Indeed, he records that on one occasion the possessed

---

[16] Nancy Caciola, *Discerning Spirits: Divine and Demonic Possession in the Middle Ages* (New York, 2003), 12–14. For an early example, see, in this volume, Charlotte Methuen, '"The very deceitfulness of devils": Firmilian and the Doubtful Baptisms of a Woman possessed by Demons', 50–66.

[17] M. Michèle Mulcahey, 'The Dominicans' Studium at Bologna and its Relationship with the University in the Thirteenth Century', *Memorie Domenicane* 39 (2008), 17–30, at 23–4.

[18] *Vitas fratrum* 3.11–13 (ed. Reichert, 108–10).

[19] Ibid. 3.42 (ed. Reichert, 141). See M. Michèle Mulcahey, *'First the Bow is Bent in Study …': Dominican Education before 1350* (Toronto, ON, 1998), 54–9; William A. Hinnebusch, *The Early English Friars Preachers* (Rome, 1951), 266.

[20] See Monika Asztalos, 'The Faculty of Theology', in Hilde de Ridder-Symoens, ed., *A History of the University in Europe*, 1: *Universities in the Middle Ages* (Cambridge, 2003), 409–41, at 410–11; Mulcahey, *'First the Bow'*, 39–40.

offered him a contract: if Jordan were to stop preaching, he would cease being a trial to the brothers (§113).[21] Jordan recounts his own self-assured response: 'God forbid that I would enter into a pact with death or make a treaty with hell! Despite your intent, the brothers will benefit from your trials and will grow strong toward a life of grace, because trial is the life of men upon the earth.'[22] Jordan's retort appears to draw from Gregory the Great's tropological interpretation of Job 7: 1 ('[Trial] is the life of man upon the earth'), where 'trial' (*tentatio*) is understood to refer to spiritual warfare.[23] But while the reply is ostensibly directed toward the demon, it is clearly intended for the benefit of the text's audience. It demonstrates the master's confidence in the face of demonic attack and his intent to reinforce the spiritual significance of the order's mission. The message appears to have been well received. We find it repeated in Étienne de Bourbon's *Tractatus de diversis materiis predicabilibus* (1250–61) and in the *Vitas fratrum*, albeit without any mention of the demon's mimesis or of Jordan's later doubts.[24]

Despite Jordan's confidence, the demon continued to spread his wickedness in the brothers' hearts (*in cordibus nostris*, lit. 'our hearts') by means of his false words (§114). Here too the demon struck at something integral to the Dominican community: the rule's apostolic exhortation for the brothers 'to live in perfect unity in one heart'.[25] And so Jordan confronts the demon a second time, demanding to know why the demon had redoubled his efforts even though the brothers were aware of his intentions. The demon offers a spirited rejoinder: 'It is I who am aware of your falsehood! For the moment you reject and condemn what I offer you, but after a while, my wicked devices will trip you up so easily that you will receive it

[21] I have chosen to translate *tentatio* as 'trial', but its other meaning, 'temptation', is equally valid in this setting, i.e. a temptation to depart from the right path. For the use of *tentatio* in the second sense see the Vulgate of Matt. 6: 13; 1 Tim. 6: 9.

[22] 'Absit ut fedus cum morte ineam aut pactum faciam cum inferno. Tuis temptationibus te nolente fratres proficient et ad uitam gratie conualescent, quia tentatio est uita hominis super terram': *Libellus* §113.

[23] Gregory the Great, *Moralia in Iob* 8.6 (CChr.SL 143, 385). Note that the usual reading of the biblical text is *militia*, not *tentatio*. Gregory explicitly prioritizes the older reading *tentatio* in his moral interpretation of the text.

[24] Étienne de Bourbon, *Tractatus* §118 (ed. de la Marche, 101–2); *Vitas fratrum*, 3.30 (ed. Reichert, 124).

[25] 'Primum, propter quod in unum estis congregati, ut unanimes habitetis in domo et sit vobis anima una et cor unum in Deum': *Regula sancti Augustini* 1.2 (L. Verheijen, *La Règle de Saint Augustin*, 1: *Tradition manuscrite* [Paris, 1967], 417).

with joy!'[26] Jordan now breaks from the narrative to address his text's audience. With an allusion to Ephesians 6: 10–17, he instructs 'soldiers in Christ' to take heed, as they are not fighting against flesh and blood but against the spirits of wickedness. They should learn from the unflagging assiduity of their enemies to continue in their fervour and to avoid any inclination to laziness.[27]

The exhortation to learn and to persevere would have resonated powerfully with an audience of novices, seated before their master. They had just been told of the demon's strategy and its effects. They had observed Jordan's steadfast confidence in the face of demonic opposition and the demon's equally steadfast determination to continue until even the master was led into falsehood. The novices are challenged to learn from the master's story. Will they persevere on the path they have chosen, or will they grow lazy and prove vulnerable to the demon's deceits?

Thus far, Jordan-as-narrator has described a demon capable of imitating a master of theology. Next, we find the demon adding to his repertoire by playing the part of a gifted preacher (§115). It sometimes occurred, Jordan relates, that the possessed friar 'used such effective language as if in the manner of preaching'.[28] By means of his way of speaking and his piety, he 'drew abundant tears from the hearts of those who heard him'.[29] Moreover, and to add a further dimension to the deceit, Jordan says that sometimes the sweetest aromas, beyond all human invention, would imbue the possessed.

Once again, the demon's behaviour is not exceptional. Other thirteenth-century *exempla* also describe demoniacs preaching sermons of impeccable orthodoxy.[30] Whatever the origins of these stories, Newman notes that they function primarily as a form of clerical self-criticism, which acts to reinforce the pastoral and homiletic expectations emerging in the wake of the Fourth Lateran Council.[31] A

---

[26] 'Et ego cognoui figmentum tuum. Quod semel oblatum tibi respuis et contempnis tandem mea supplantatus improbitate facile et gratanter admittes': *Libellus* §114.

[27] '[D]iscant ex ipsorum hostium sedulitate continua, suum e contra continuare fervorem et vitare spiritus in se torpentis ignaviam': ibid.

[28] '[T]am efficacibus utebatur velut in modum predicationis sermonibus': *Libellus* §115.

[29] '[U]beres elicuerit lacrimas de cordibus auditorum': ibid.

[30] Newman, 'Possessed', 753–62; cf. Aviad M. Kleinberg, 'The Possession of Blessed Jordan of Saxony', in Miri Rubin, ed., *Medieval Christianity in Practice* (Oxford, 2009), 265–73, at 271.

[31] Newman, 'Possessed', 755, 768.

representative example is found in Jacques de Vitry's *Historia occidentalis*, where a German demoniac preaches the truth of the gospel in order to demonstrate the local clergy's incompetence.[32] The point of Jacques's story is clear: it is to chasten inept ecclesiastics so that they might better fulfil their pastoral role. Jordan's purpose, in contrast, is more to exhort than to criticize.

For a Dominican, preaching was not simply a function, but a gift of special grace that had to be identified by the superiors of any prospective preacher.[33] The portrait of Henry of Cologne, found earlier in Jordan's *Libellus*, powerfully illustrates its significance: 'This is brother Henry on whom the Lord lavished a great and wonderful grace in regard to his preaching to the clerics of Paris, whose living and effective speech most violently penetrated the hearts of those who heard it.'[34] Henry's abilities as a preacher were consonant with his holy behaviour. Jordan recounts his manifold virtues: obedience, patience, meekness and charity, amongst others (§78). In fact, Jordan's laudatory exposition of Henry's word and example, and the substantial attention he devotes to him in the *Libellus*, suggests that Henry is being held up as an exemplar.[35] It is all the more remarkable, then, that the example of this 'angel' – as Jordan refers to Henry – is so successfully imitated by the demon that possesses Brother Bernard.[36] Indeed, the false preacher appears to mislead at least a portion of his audience. Jordan recounts that those who heard him were brought to tears, an expression of devotion that the *Libellus* otherwise associates with Dominic (§§12, 105), Henry (§74) or the brothers' response to the antiphon *Salve Regina* (§120). But it is not only profound theology and pious preaching – and the genuine devotion that they produce – that are within the demon's grasp; so too is the appearance of sanctity.

---

[32] Jacques de Vitry, *Historia occidentalis* 5 (*The* Historia occidentalis *of Jacques de Vitry: A Critical Edition*, ed. John F. Hinnebusch [Fribourg, 1972], 86–7).

[33] Simon Tugwell, 'The Evolution of Dominican Structures of Government III: The Early Development of the Second Distinction of the Constitutions', *AFP* 71 (2001), 5–182, at 107–9.

[34] 'Hic est frater Henricus, cui multam atque mirabilem in verbo suo ad clerum Parisiensem dominus largitus est gratiam, cuius sermo vivus et efficax audientium corda violentissime penetrabat': *Libellus* §77.

[35] *Libellus* §§66–85; see Grado Giovanni Merlo, 'Gli inizi dell'Ordine dei Predicatori. Spunti per una riconsiderazione', *Rivista di storia e letteratura religiosa* 31 (1995), 415–41, at 438–9.

[36] *Libellus* §§67, 74, 78.

Up to this point, Jordan-as-protagonist has remained unconvinced. He has confronted the demon, even if he has not been able to repel him. Indeed, he does not seem formally to have tried, as there is no description of an exorcism in his account. However, in the second part of the episode (§116, which Gerald later revised for the *Vitas fratrum*) the demon's plan to undermine Jordan's confidence finally succeeds, and it is here that the full depth of the protagonist's uncertainty is revealed.

Jordan-as-narrator explains to his audience that the demon covered the possessed brother with a sweet fragrance so that it seemed as if an angel – and not a demon – was responsible. When the fragrance then surrounded Jordan, the demon intended him to mistake it as a sign of his own sanctity rather than a diabolical concoction. And so, just as planned, when the sweetness appeared, Jordan was at a loss: 'Confused, and in great uncertainty, I was distrustful of its merits. Yet still I was hesitating, unsure of how I should proceed. Surrounded by the wonderful fragrance, I scarcely dared to extract my hands [from my sleeves], afraid to lose that sweetness, which I did not yet understand.'[37] Jordan-as-narrator goes on to explain that one day, when he was carrying the chalice in preparation for the mass, this same sweetness so enveloped him that he felt overwhelmed by its power. But, he explains, the 'spirit of truth' soon put a stop to the 'spirit of malice' (§118).

Jordan recalls that he began reading Psalm 34, which, he notes instructively, is effective for repelling trials.[38] He was ruminating on the line (v. 10), 'All my bones will declare, Lord, who is like you?', when suddenly such a sweetness enveloped him that it appeared to permeate through to the marrow of his bones. Jordan was initially uncertain (*incertus*), then stupefied (*stupefactus*) and dismayed (*perculsus*). He prayed that the Lord would come to his aid and show him whether this was the demon's work, for like the poor man (quoting

---

[37] '[E]go multa perplexus ambiguitate diffidebam quidem de meritis, sed tamen hesitabam incertus quocumque pergerem mira circumfusus fragrantia uix ipsas manus audebam extrahere ueritus eam de qua nondum conscius eram mihi perdere suavitatem': *Libellus* §117. In Gerald's rendering, Jordan hides his hands (*ipse manus suas absconderet*), presumably in his sleeves, which helps to clarify what Jordan means when he recalls that he 'scarcely dared to uncover (his) hands': *Vitas fratrum* 3.33 (ed. Reichert, 126). I have rendered *qua nondum conscius eram* as 'which I did not yet understand', rather than the more literal 'of which I was not yet aware', as it reflects the sense of Jordan's explanation better.

[38] 'Iudica domine nocentes me': Ps. 34: 1 (references to the Psalms follow the Vulgate numbering); see John Cassian, *Conferences* 7.21 (SC 42, 264).

Ps. 71: 12) he had no other helper.[39] However, Jordan informs his audience, as soon as he finished praying, '[i]nwardly I received such a great enlightenment of spirit and, through an infusion of truth, such indisputable proof that I was completely secure, that I had no doubt (*nihil ambigerem*) whatsoever that all these things were the fabrications of the deceitful enemy.'[40] Jordan then informed (*certum fecissem*, lit. 'made him certain') the possessed brother about this diabolical trial.[41] Immediately, the aromas ceased, and so too did the demon's mellifluous words. In their place, Brother Bernard began saying evil and shameful things and, when asked why, responded that there was no longer any point in pretending. Thus ends the peculiar account of the possession of Brother Bernard.

We have observed a demon capable of manifesting Dominican ideals by offering profound theological exposition and inspiring sermons. We have also seen how some of his audience – probably Bernard's brother friars – were unaware of the falsehood. What is the implication? Is Jordan suggesting that the fulfilment of these Dominican ideals does not necessarily provide a reliable indication of a good and faithful friar, let alone of God's inspiration and blessing? How would a novice be able to discern the falsehood of a theologian or preacher? What if even the manifestation of sanctity – otherwise held to be a sure indication of God's blessing on the order – was a diabolic ruse?

Jordan-as-narrator had explained to his audience that the demon had intended Jordan-as-protagonist to presume his own sanctity. A friar familiar with Cassian's *Conferences* would know that a monk could often be tempted to cultivate a misguided belief in his own holiness.[42] Presumption, then, is certainly a concern. But, as with the demon's other strategies, it appears that something more directly relevant to the order is also intended. Within the opening paragraphs of the *Libellus*, Jordan describes Dominic as having been pervaded since his childhood by an odour of sanctity (§5). Indeed, amongst Dominic's

---

[39] '[Q]uia eruet pauperem a potente et inopem cui non est adiutor': Ps. 71: 12.

[40] '[T]antam recepi spiritus illustrationem intrinsecus et tam indubitatum per infusam veritatem plene securitatis indicium, ut iam omnino nihil ambigerem cuncta haec fraudulentis hostis extitisse figmenta': *Libellus* §118.

[41] '[F]ratrem illum certum de diabolica tentatione fecissem': *Libellus* §119.

[42] Jordan refers to Cassian's *Conferences* as a book Dominic valued highly: *Libellus* §13. For examples detailing the dangers of presumptive holiness, see Cassian, *Conferences* 2.2, 2.5 (SC 42, 112–14, 116–17).

fellow canons in Osma, his manner of life was held to be like 'sweet-smelling frankincense in the days of summer' (§12).[43] As it stands in the text, the parallel between Dominic's odour and the demon's fragrance is strongly suggestive, but this power of association could veer toward provocation when we consider that the *Libellus* was probably issued during the General Chapter in 1233, when Dominic's tomb was opened and the witnesses described their wonder – and their relief – when Dominic's corpse was found to emit a marvellous fragrance.[44]

Luigi Canetti has suggested that the episode of Brother Bernard's possession was told with Dominic's cult in mind.[45] But if Jordan were attempting to vouch for the authenticity of Dominic's sanctity on the basis of the sweet fragrance at his tomb, demonstrating that a demon was capable of fabricating such aromas would seem a strange way to do it. Rather than being directed toward the cult of Dominic, then, we might better understand the quandary if we continue to follow the logic of Jordan's narrative. To the false theologian and false preacher, we may add, finally, the false saint.

In Jordan's account it is his own sanctity, not Dominic's, which is being doubted. Indeed, it is Jordan who is doing the doubting. The candid evocation of his own uncertainty is remarkable. One wonders how his audience of novices might have responded. The *Vitas fratrum* includes a variety of stories, many of which involve Jordan, in which novices experience significant opposition, both spiritual and temporal, upon entering the Order of Preachers.[46] The *Libellus*, too, describes the initial consternation of the devout man and his two friends who had trained Henry of Cologne when they learned he had entered an order about which they knew nothing (§76). Had it not been for a divine word, spoken to them while they prayed, one of them would have gone to Paris in order to bring Henry back and divert him from his indiscretion.[47] Many Dominican novices, especially those drawn

---

[43] '[Q]uasi thus redolens in diebus estatis' : *Libellus* §12.

[44] *Litterae Enyclicae 1234*, §§8–10 (*B. Iordanis de Saxonia, Litterae encyclicae annis 1233 et 1234 datae*, ed. Elio Montanari [Spoleto, 1993], 259–60); Angelus Walz, ed., *Acta canonizationis S. Dominici*, MOPH 16 (Rome, 1935), 89–194, at 130–2, 135–6. On the probable confirmation of the *Libellus* by the General Chapter in 1233, see Tugwell, 'Notes', 12–13.

[45] Luigi Canetti, *L'invenzione della memoria. Il culto e l'immagine di Domenico nella storia dei primi frati Predicatori* (Spoleto, 1996), 309–20.

[46] *Vitas fratrum* 2.21, 3.18, 3.42, 4.7, 5.17 (ed. Reichert, 81, 114–15, 143–4, 168, 201–5).

[47] '[V]adens Parisius ipsum ad hac indiscretione, ut videbatur, averteret atque retraheret': *Libellus* §76.

from the universities, would have found themselves in a similar position: their parents or benefactors would have had higher hopes for them than their entry into a recently founded religious order devoted to poverty and preaching.[48] It was in this uncertain environment that questions of doubt and certainty would have been felt most acutely.

In the concluding narrative of the *Libellus*, doubt is diabolical in origin. This is made emphatic by way of contrast. In the culminating sequence, God is the source for Jordan's indisputable proof, while the demon's aromas are the cause of Jordan's uncertainty. Throughout the narrative, what ought to be certain is made uncertain through demonic deceit. The demon systematically fabricates the ideals in which a Dominican might find his identity: the theologian, the preacher, and even the prospective saint, all for the sake of leading the brothers into falsehood. Even Jordan-as-protagonist, after an assured beginning, is at a loss. And yet, this all takes place within a controlled environment. The master, vindicated, is telling the story and a broader pedagogical strategy is at work. From the beginning, Jordan explains that the demonic possession was granted by divine mercy to prove the brothers' endurance. It is a point he reiterates, both in his rejoinder to the demon and in his exhortation that the brothers not slacken in their fervour against the attacks of the enemy. Indeed, Jordan tells them that they must learn from these attacks. But what are they to learn?

The short answer is that they must endure, even in the midst of uncertainty. If they fail to do so their demonic opponents will take advantage of their spiritual torpor and lead them into falsehood. If they continue faithfully and pray for assistance, as Jordan does in the narrative, even the most convincing deceit will be overcome by divine intervention. But beyond this lesson there is yet a further point being made, and here it is worth returning once more to those novices in Paris. Perhaps they were unsure of their choice; perhaps they were facing opposition from their parents and benefactors. In this uncertain setting, the master suffuses their decision to enter the order with profound spiritual significance. Demons are determined to undermine it. God is determined to uphold it. If they fail to continue with

---

[48] See *Vitas fratrum* 3.14 (ed. Reichert, 110–11); C. H. Lawrence, *The Friars: The Impact of the Early Mendicant Movement on Western Society* (London, 2013), 127. The opposition of Thomas Aquinas's parents to their son's choice of vocation is perhaps the most famous example of this phenomenon: see Guillelmo de Tocco, *Vita s. Thomae Aquinatis* 7–9, in D. Prümmer, ed., *Fontes vitae S. Thomae Aquinatis notis historicis et criticis illustrati*, fasc. 2 (Toulouse, 1911), 71–3.

total commitment, they will prove susceptible to diabolic machinations. If they endure, God will be their security. It is no wonder then that the account of Brother Bernard concludes with the chant, at compline, of the *Salve Regina*, an antiphon designed to stir up fervour among the brethren and to ensure divine favour (§120).

In the last analysis, the episode is perhaps not quite so peculiar after all. Jordan told the story to novices in Paris, and so it is clear that he intended it to contribute to their vocational formation. In this respect it is consistent with the intent of the *Libellus* to benefit recent entrants into the order through a recollection of its past. Jordan assured the brothers that God intended the episode to produce endurance, but what proves remarkably germane to his pedagogical purposes is the role of doubt. The demon's partially effective fabrication of Dominican ideals and Jordan's candid admission of uncertainty are employed, however paradoxically, to engender confidence in the Dominican vocation. Indeed, Jordan's divine deliverance at the narrative's height provides the surety. In this respect then, the master's account of the demoniac, like others found in contemporary *exempla*, has essentially 'dramatized the eternal warfare between God and Satan … and provided reassuring proof that God was winning'.[49] Newman has interpreted many of these demoniac accounts, especially those dealing with preaching, confession and the eucharist, as serving ultimately to confirm the pastoral agenda of the Fourth Lateran Council.[50] Jordan, it would seem, is more interested in securing the brothers' total commitment to the Dominican order. The episode illustrates that they can be certain that the order is doing God's work, that it is a 'secure path of salvation' (§69). Doubt may ultimately be the work of the devil, but it has its uses.

Gerald de Frachet, in contrast, seems to have had little use for doubt in his rendition of Jordan's narrative in the *Vitas fratrum*.[51] As noted above, he removes from the *Libellus* all traces of Jordan's uncertainty, and also passes over the demon's initial success. Perhaps Gerald, or Master General Humbert of Romans (d. 1277), who oversaw the creation of the *Vitas fratrum*, was embarrassed by Jordan's admission of doubt.[52] It is more probable, however, that Gerald omitted

---

[49] Newman, 'Possession', 768.

[50] Ibid.

[51] *Vitas fratrum* 3.33 (ed. Reichert, 126).

[52] Humbert, in particular, seems to have supressed names and edited stories in the work because they could have proved controversial or embarrassing: see Tugwell, 'L'Évolution',

uncertainty from the narrative because his version of the story was intended to contribute to a portrait of Jordan's sanctity and thus served a rather different purpose.

On the whole, the *Vitas fratrum* was designed to function in a similar manner to the *Libellus*. Humbert explains in his prologue that the stories of past friars compiled and edited therein were offered for the consolation and spiritual progress of present and future brethren.[53] That having been said, however, the portrait of Jordan that emerges in the *Vitas fratrum* is tantamount to that of a prospective saint. Jordan receives substantially more attention than either Dominic or Peter of Verona (d. 1252), who at the time of the text's composition and and its subsequent revisions (1255–60) were the order's only saints.[54] In the third part of the *Vitas fratrum*, which is devoted entirely to Jordan, he is introduced as a 'holy and remarkable father', a 'mirror of all religious observances and an example of every virtue'.[55] Various and lively accounts of Jordan's virtues, visions and miracles populate the work as a whole.[56] Gerald's portrait of Jordan's sanctity is consistent with the notion that the order had once considered initiating a canonization process for the late master.[57] Jordan could well have been the order's second saint, had Peter of Verona not been martyred in 1252 and swiftly canonized by Pope Innocent IV the fol-

---

417; idem, ed., *Humberti de Romanis Legendae sancti Dominici*, MOPH 30 (Rome, 2008), 53–5, 316–18.

[53] 'Sane multimoda fratrum de diversis nacionibus relacione frequenter ad nos pervenit, quod multa contigerunt in ordine et ordinis occasione, que si scripto commendata fuissent, multum valere possent in perpetuum ad fratum [*sic*] consolacionem et spiritualem profectum': *Vitas fratrum* (ed. Reichert, 4).

[54] Tugwell, 'L'Évolution', 414–17. Van Engen notes the textual imbalance between Jordan and Dominic: 'Dominic and the Brothers', 16. For a reappraisal of Peter of Verona's life and cult, see Donald Prudlo, *The Martyred Inquisitor: The Life and Cult of Peter of Verona (†1252)* (Aldershot, 2008).

[55] 'De sancto ac memorabili patre nostro fratre Iordane … dicimus eum tamquam speculum tocius religionis et virtutum exemplar': *Vitas fratrum* 3.1 (ed. Reichert, 100–1).

[56] Ibid., 1.7, 3.1–42, 4.10, 4.12, 4.13, 4.14, 4.15, 4.24, 5.2, 5.4 (ed. Reichert, 60, 100–46, 173–7, 179–80, 187–8, 192–3, 195–6, 216, 253–4, 270–1).

[57] The Dominican General Chapter in 1245 sought stories of any miracles attributed to either Dominic or Jordan, which has been interpreted to mean that the order was preparing to seek Jordan's canonization: see B.-M. Reichert, ed., *Acta capitulorum generalium Ordinis Praedicatorum,* 1: *Ab anno 1220 usque ad annum 1303*, MOPH 3 (Rome, 1898), 33; Tugwell, ed., *Miracula*, 29–30; Viktória Hedvig Deák, 'The Birth of a Legend: The so-called *Legenda Maior* of Saint Margaret of Hungary and Dominican Hagiography', *Revue Mabillon* 20 (2009), 87–112, at 98.

lowing year.[58] Perhaps the stories Gerald originally collected were intended to contribute to the late master's canonization process. In any case, Gerald's revision of Jordan's narrative must be interpreted within this hagiographical setting, in which the protagonist's doubt was probably inadmissible.

Jordan's engagement with the false aromas is but one of six stories in the *Vitas fratrum* in which the late master overcomes demonic opposition,[59] proving himself to be a worthy successor to Dominic. In the second book of the *Vitas fratrum*, the order's saintly founder assuredly dismantles diabolical falsehoods and sends his demonic opponents into confusion.[60] Jordan's uncertainties would have proved anomalous in comparison, for following Dominic's example, it was the demons who should have suffered confusion. Gerald's revision of Jordan's story is in keeping with the hagiographical norms of the *Vitas fratrum*. In conclusion, then, we may make a final observation about the nature of doubt in the two narratives. In the *Libellus*, the demon's deception and Jordan's self-doubt both hinge on Jordan's presumption of sanctity. In Gerald's rendering, however, it is the absence of doubt that proves the saint.

---

[58] For Pope Innocent IV's eagerness to promote an anti-heretical saint, see Prudlo, *Martyred Inquisitor*, 77–9. Interestingly, Prudlo notes that the initial steps for Peter's canonization were 'entirely non-Dominican': ibid. 77.

[59] *Vitas fratrum* 3.25–33 (ed. Reichert, 120–6).

[60] Ibid. 2.14–17 (ed. Reichert, 77–9).

Lachrymose Holiness and the Problem of Doubt in Thirteenth- and Fourteenth-Century Hagiographies

Kimberley-Joy Knight*

University of Sydney

By the thirteenth century, tears were a ubiquitous feature of accounts of saints' lives. Despite the widespread acceptance of tears as an expression of holiness, they could, however, present a special challenge for interpretation and female tears were often the subject of doubt. Divinely bestowed tears might be subject to criticism and uncertainty over whether they could be read as an authentic sign of devotion and the presence of God. This essay argues that doubt over the sincerity of tears was a topos in the narrative of saintly struggle – something a saint must endure as a test of faith and sanctity – and was a corollary to achieving certainty in thirteenth-century female saints' lives. As the century came to a close, however, tears began to be more openly questioned. The essay assesses the evolving doubt surrounding lachrymose expressions of devotion in the fourteenth century and accounts for changing attitudes by drawing on both saints' lives and theological sources. It is argued that this doubt was a reflection of broader changes in the acceptance of physical and emotional expressions of sanctity and was part of the 'gradual criminalization' of the female body in the fourteenth century.

In the fourth beatitude of his Sermon on the Plain (Luke 6: 21), Jesus assured his followers: 'Blessed are those who weep' (*beati qui nunc fletis*). From this statement, tears became an integral part of Christian spirituality and were associated with redemption, salvation and beatitude. As Christianity became entrenched in Western Europe, the meaning of tears as a medium of exchange between earthly and

* Room N346, John Woolley Building A20, Science Road, The University of Sydney, Sydney, 2006 NSW, Australia. E-mail: kimberley.knight@sydney.edu.au.

I am the recipient of an Australian Research Council Post-Doctoral Fellowship (project number CE110001011). I wish to acknowledge the kindness of the late Philippa Maddern, who generously shared with me her unpublished work on tears; I am grateful to her executors for allowing me to cite this research here. I also wish to thank Frances Andrews for taking the time to provide valuable feedback on this essay. Any infelicities that might remain are, of course, entirely my own.

Studies in Church History 52 (2016) 118–134
doi: 10.1017/stc.2015.7

divine evolved and expanded.[1] By the thirteenth century, hagiographies were awash with tears. The lachrymosity of saints streams across the pages of their *vitae* and flows through the testimonies of deponents at their canonization proceedings.[2] However, tears present a special challenge for interpretation and were often the subject of doubt.

Despite the widespread acceptance of tears as an expression of holiness, divinely bestowed tears might be subject to criticism and doubt as to whether they could be read as an authentic sign of devotion and the presence of God. Using a selection of thirteenth-century female saints' lives, in which scepticism about tears is often prominent, it will be seen that doubt over the legitimacy of tears was nonetheless a corollary to achieving certainty. Doubting the veracity of tears is a topos in the narrative of saintly struggle: something a saint must endure as a test of faith and sanctity. In the later fourteenth century, however, a subtle shift may be detected in the way in which tears were described in some hagiographic texts. The external manifestation of tears becomes less prominent in certain female hagiographic texts and was sometimes supplemented by internal lacrimation. This, it will be suggested, was a reaction to doubts surrounding the reliability of the body as a witness, coupled with growing scepticism about visions and revelations. This essay will therefore assess the doubt surrounding lachrymose expressions of devotion and account for changing attitudes by drawing on both saints' lives and theological sources. It will show how this doubt was a reflection of wider changes in the acceptance of emotional and physical expressions of sanctity during the course of the fourteenth century and, by doing so, contribute to the history of tears, doubt and devotional piety in the high Middle Ages.

THE STATE OF SCHOLARSHIP

In recent years, there has been a dramatic change in the landscape of scholarly output on both tears and the subject of doubt, yet few scholars have considered the nexus between the two, even though tears

---

[1] For a history of Christian tears until the central Middle Ages, see Piroska Nagy, *Le Don des larmes au Moyen Âge. Un Instrument spirituel en quête d'institution (V^e–XIIIe siècle)* (Paris, 2000).

[2] See Kimberley-Joy Knight, 'Blessed are those who weep: *Gratia lacrymarum* in Thirteenth-Century Hagiographies' (PhD thesis, University of St Andrews, 2014).

present a special challenge for interpretation and have always been subject to doubt.[3] In the Prolegomenon to the edited volume *Crying in the Middle Ages*, Lyn A. Blanchfield explores the connection between sincerity and tears as a way of demonstrating some of the problems inherent in studying weeping in the medieval period.[4] She suggests that weeping represents a 'challenging intersection between emotion and behaviour', and points out that in many medieval sources 'tears – which result from a complex physiological process that involves the body, mind, and the emotions – are often described as objects that can be manipulated'.[5] In this reading, weeping was a performative act that was open to manipulation and could be deceptive.[6] Blanchfield also notes that the relationship between weeping and deception was widely acknowledged in the ancient, medieval and early modern world.[7] Similarly, in his study of provoked religious weeping in early modern Spain, W. A. Christian Jr showed both how weeping was a behaviour that could be learnt for the purposes of a ritual and that tears were part of an 'economy of sentiment that could influence God'.[8] Collective weeping worked to achieve a particular goal such as the end of a plague, drought or famine.[9] Nevertheless, Christian was careful to point out that weeping still had to be provoked and was neither spontaneous nor entirely 'put on'. Emotion was consciously manipulated for religious purposes yet the consequences were effective and real.[10] Both scholars have demonstrated that weeping could be manipulated; it thus follows that tears could be the subject of doubt. It is apparent that this doubt came, not from a lack of faith, but from a desire to uphold the order of the Church and to protect it from false

---

[3] The increased interest in tears has, in part, been sparked by the buoyant interest in the history of the body and the history of emotions. Important studies of tears include Myrrha Lot-Borodine, 'La Mystère du don des larmes dans l'Orient chrétien', *Vie Spirituelle* 48 (1936), 65–116; Irénée Hausherr, *Penthos. La Doctrine de la componction dans l'Orient Chrétien* (Rome, 1944); Nagy, *Don des larmes*; Elina Gertsman, ed., *Crying in the Middle Ages: Tears of History* (New York, 2012). For recent studies on doubt see, in this volume, Frances Andrews, 'Doubting John?', 17–49.

[4] Lyn A. Blanchfield, 'Considerations of Weeping and Sincerity in the Middle Ages', in eadem, *Crying in the Middle Ages*, xxi–xxx.

[5] Ibid. xxi.

[6] Ibid. xxii.

[7] Ibid.

[8] W. A. Christian Jr, 'Provoked Religious Weeping in Early Modern Spain', in J. Davis, ed., *Religious Organisation and Religious Experience* (London, 1982), 97–114, at 98.

[9] Ibid. 98–9.

[10] Ibid. 111.

prophets.[11] Doubt surrounding tears stemmed from a concern as to whether they could be read as a true sign of piety or divine inspiration or whether they had been consciously or unconsciously manipulated. This essay will look to hagiographies to provide an insight into the doubt that was expressed surrounding the tears of holy women. First, however, it will consider the foundation of such doubt: the problem of interpreting tears.

Many scholars, of history, anthropology and sociology, have suggested that the body is a potentially problematic source of meaning, both for individuals and for wider society.[12] One of the most opaque bodily and emotional expressions is a tear. The sociologist Jack Katz recognized that what crying 'says' may be inherently mysterious and thus it presents a special challenge for interpretation.[13] Medieval authors struggled to describe tears, as do modern writers. Philippa Maddern's research highlights some of the major difficulties when analysing medieval descriptions of tears. In her examination of late medieval English sources, she notes that diverse meanings are attributed to lachrymose behaviour and suggests that 'medieval authors were unconvinced of any stable or uncontroversial relationship between tears and what they signified'.[14] Contemporaries were faced with problems of sincerity and classification. Examining the swell of tears in thirteenth-century hagiographic texts is no straightforward task, and such problems are often apparent in, and arise from, the *Vitae*.[15] Tears were the carriers of spiritual emotions but also had meaning in themselves. They could indicate excruciating pain or ecstatic joy; they were imitable and contagious, yet also rarefied, finite and sought after. Tears could carry a simple message of holiness, yet were also incomprehensible and recondite. They were part of the pathway to redemption and beatitude, and were received as a gift

---

[11] See Michael Goodich, *Miracles and Wonders: The Development of the Concept of Miracle, 1150–1350* (Aldershot, 2007), 47–68.

[12] See Blanchfield, 'Considerations of Weeping', xxi. Bodily and facial gestures have been explored by Elina Gertsman, 'The Facial Gesture: (Mis)Reading Emotion in Later Medieval Art', *Journal of Medieval Religious Cultures* 36 (2010), 28–46; Jean-Claude Schmitt, *La Raison des gestes dans l'Occident médiéval* (Paris, 1990); Moshe Barasch, *Gestures of Despair in Medieval and Early Renaissance Art* (New York, 1976).

[13] Jack Katz, *How Emotions Work* (London, 1999), 180.

[14] Philippa Maddern, 'The Meaning of Tears, or, Reading and Writing Tears in Late Medieval English Texts', paper given at the 'Languages of Emotion: Concepts, Codes, Communities' conference, University of Western Australia, 25 August 2012.

[15] See Knight, 'Blessed are those who weep', 6.

from God in the form of the divine grace, known as *gratia lacrymarum*. This multivalence could lead to doubt as to whether holy women's tears could or should be read as an authentic sign of devotion and the presence of God.

THE FEMALE BODY IN CHRISTIAN THOUGHT

Whilst much early Christian thought perceived the body and all bodily activity with profound suspicion, by around 1200 learned Christian discourse had re-evaluated the human body, becoming more open to its use in the expression of piety.[16] Regulation, restraint and modesty remained important hallmarks of saintly behaviour but there was place for somatic piety in which the body was used in the physical pursuit of God through excessive fasting, flagellation and genuflexion. This physical drive towards God was in turn rewarded with bodily imprints and rapturous excesses, which attested to contact with the divine. Beguine and mendicant spirituality was thus intensely physical and the female body was an important vehicle for conveying messages about sanctity as well as religious concepts and feelings.[17] Moreover, the female body was a privileged site of reception for divine graces.[18] Tears were intimately connected with the rise in physical piety, and conveyed meaning to those who witnessed or read about them. Nonetheless, even though the female body might be used to express religious sentiment, this did not mean that it was necessarily accepted or trusted.[19]

---

[16] Walter Simons, 'Reading a Saint's Body: Rapture and Bodily Movement in the *Vitae* of Thirteenth-Century Beguines', in Sarah Kay and Miri Rubin, ed., *Framing Medieval Bodies* (Manchester, 1994), 10–23, at 12–13. The ascent of bodily piety in the thirteenth century was also connected to changes in penitential practices. By the high Middle Ages exterior aspects of penitence were globally favoured: see Nagy, *Don des larmes*, 268. For the Early Church, see Peter Brown, *The Body and Society: Men and Women, and Sexual Renunciation in Early Christianity* (New York, 1998).

[17] Simons, 'Reading a Saint's Body', 12; see also Caroline Walker Bynum, 'The Female Body and Religious Practice in the Later Middle Ages', in Michel Feher, Ramona Naddaff and Nadia Tazi, eds, *Fragments for a History of the Human Body*, 3 vols (New York, 1989), 2: 160–219.

[18] See Dyan Elliott, 'The Physiology of Rapture and Female Spirituality', in Peter Biller and A. J. Minnis, eds, *Medieval Theology and the Natural Body* (York, 1997), 141–73, at 161.

[19] On fraudulent female saints and deceitful bodily piety, see Dyan Elliott, *Proving Woman: Female Spirituality and Inquisitional Culture in the Later Middle Ages* (Princeton, NJ, 2004), 193–203.

THE NATURE OF HOLY LACRIMATION

Many thirteenth-century hagiographies recount that those who shed tears were often unable to control either the tears or their efficacy. Divinely given tears were often violent in nature, seizing the whole body and rendering the recipient rapt in a moment of union with God. The anonymous hagiographer of the Cistercian nun Beatrice of Nazareth (d. 1268) describes how she struggled to stem the flow of her tears when she thought of her heavenly bridegroom: 'The witnesses of this event were tears dripping in abundance from her eyes, full of sweetness and devotion. And if she had wanted, no insistence would have been strong enough to hold back [the assault of tears] before the Bridegroom's face, whenever he returned to [her] mind.'[20] A lack of control when participating in devotional activities was a central theme in texts pertaining to women. Some churchmen, friars and onlookers saw tears as troublesome, as they challenged traditional modes of expressing devotion. Rather than meekly receiving the host, many holy women subverted the liturgy, erupting with flowing tears, groans and sighs. These tears were an instrument of separation from the ordinary confines of female devotion and the silence of the cloister.[21] Elizabeth Petroff argues that for a woman to become a saint she had to transgress in order to become visible.[22] However, this transgression had to be carefully undertaken; it had to be seen to be divinely sanctioned if the woman were not to be in danger of being branded a heretic. As Simons has observed, it was extremely difficult, if not impossible, to ascertain whether divine intervention or demonic possession had produced their behaviour.[23] The Franciscan tertiary Angela of Foligno (d. 1309) screamed because of the fire of love that she experienced. Although people accused her of being demonically possessed, she described through her *Memoriale* how she could not have stopped herself even had

---

[20] 'Huius rei testes fuerunt ille, plene dulcedinis et deuotionis, ex oculis eius distillantes in habundantia lacrime, quarum impetum ante sponsi faciem, quotiens ad mentem illi redijt: et-si voluisset, nulla tamen valuisset cohibere instantia': *Vita Beatricis* 1.17 (*The Life of Beatrice of Nazareth (1200–1268)*, ed. and transl. Roger de Ganck, Cistercian Fathers 50 [Kalamazoo, MI, 1991], 100–1). All translations are my own unless otherwise stated.
[21] Dhira B. Mahoney, 'Margery Kempe's Tears and the Power over Language', in Sandra J. McEntire, ed., *Margery Kempe: A Book of Essays* (London, 1992), 37–50, at 39.
[22] Elizabeth Alvida Petroff, *Body and Soul: Essays on Medieval Women and Mysticism* (Oxford, 1994), 166.
[23] Simons, 'Reading a Saint's Body', 19.

someone stood over her with an axe and threatened to kill her.[24] The Viennese beguine Agnes Blannbekin (d. 1315) found that she could barely speak because of her tears (*vix prae lachrymis loqui potuit*) and because of the desire that burned in her chest; she pleaded with the Lord that he would not let it be known what he was doing to her (*sed rogavit dominum, ne permitteret eam sic divulgari, quod dominus fecit*).[25] It is no coincidence that these instances occur in female *Vitae*. The attempt to limit or restrain certain forms of devotion is characteristic of the opposition faced by thirteenth-century religious women. The founder of the Damianites, Clare of Assisi (d. 1253), was known for her excessive fasting, and was restrained from carrying out the extremes of her ascetic wishes by her brother St Francis (d. 1226) and by the bishop of Assisi, who made her consume a minimum amount of bread.[26] The confessor of the Italian Franciscan tertiary Margaret of Cortona (d. 1297) was only allowed to visit her once a week because some of the friars at the provincial chapter considered that her consolations were delusions and that she was feigning her devotions in order to gain a reputation for holiness.[27] Restricting certain elements of female devotional practice may have acted as a shield against potential disbelievers. However, restraining tears was much more difficult. In one episode in the *Vita* of Ida of Louvain (d. 1261), a Beguine and then a Cistercian nun from Liège, her sisters mock her for weeping.[28] In the *Vita* of Margaret of Cortona, her hagiographer Giunta Bevegnati records that she tried to remain silent because others attributed her weeping to vainglory.[29] By contrast, religious men were not criticized for their tears, although these are

---

[24] Angela of Foligno, *Memoriale*, Library of Latin Texts Series A (Turnhout, 2010), 153; ET *Angela of Foligno's Memorial*, ed. Cristina Mazzoni, transl. John Cirignano (Woodbridge, 1999), 32.

[25] *Leben und Offenbarungen der Wiener Begine Agnes Blannbekin*, ed. and transl. Peter Dinzelbacher and Renate Vogeler, Göppinger Arbeiten zur Germanistik 419 (Göppingen, 1994), 349–50; ET *Agnes Blannbekin, Viennese Beguine: Life and Revelations*, transl. Ulrike Wiethaus (Bury St Edmunds, 2002), 112 (ch. 167).

[26] *Sanctae Clarae virginis assisiensis. Legenda latina*, ed. Giovanni Boccali, Italian transl. Marino Bigaroni (Perugia, 2001), 134.

[27] Giunta Bevegnati, *Legenda de vita et miraculis beatae Margaritae de Cortona* 5 (ed. Fortunato Iozzelli [Rome, 1997], 249); ET *Life and Revelations of Saint Margaret of Cortona*, transl. F. M'Donogh Mahony (London, 1883), 84–5.

[28] See 'Vita beatae Idae Lovaniensis' 1.15.37, *ActaSS* April. 2, 157–89, at 168.

[29] In this episode Christ rebukes Margaret for trying to stay quiet: Bevegnati, *Legenda de vita et miraculis beatae Margaritae* 5 (ed. Iozzelli, 254: 'qui tui fletum doloris temere pro uana gloria fieri extimant, silentium tibi penitus indidisti').

documented as being equally irrepressible. For example, the first deponent in the canonization enquiry of the founder of a congregation of Augustinian hermits, Giovanni Bono (d. 1249), a fellow hermit named Salveto, recalled how the holy man was unable to hold back his tears (*nulla ratione poterat ipse lacrimas continere*).[30] Where women could be ridiculed, degraded and doubted for their devotional practices, holy men who wept were more likely to be trusted and held up as models of perfection.

Tears, however, could not be modified or muted to suit the wishes of others. When the heart was pricked by compunction it was difficult to withhold the flow of tears. Moreover, *gratia lacrymarum*, by its very nature, was God-given and no man could stand in its way. Nonetheless, this did not stop churchmen from being irked and trying to subdue and control tears. One episode, from the life of the so-called 'first beguine', Marie d'Oignies (d. 1213), written *c.*1215 by her confessor Jacques de Vitry (d. 1240), is worth examining in detail, as it demonstrates the doubts that women often faced.[31] On a certain day, before Good Friday, Jacques records how Marie had begun to sacrifice (*mactare*) herself to the Lord with a great shower of tears, sighs and sobbing. One of the priests of the church rebuked her and urged her to pray in silence and hold back her tears. Modest and in dove-like simplicity, Marie tried to obey him but was conscious of how impossible this would be. The holy woman therefore left the church and hid herself in a place that was removed from everyone. Here, with tearful intercession, she obtained reassurance from the

---

[30] 'Processus canonizationis' 1.6, *ActaSS* Oct. 9, 771–814, at 772; see also Bonaventure of Bagnoregio, 'Legenda maior S. Francisci', *Analecta Franciscana*, 10: *Legendae S. Francisci Assisiensis saec. XIII et XIV conscriptae* (Quaracchi, 1941), 555–652, at 603.

[31] *Iacobus de Vitriaco, Vita Marie de Oegnies & Thomas Cantipratensis, Supplementum*, ed. R. B. C. Huygens, CChr.CM 252, 43–164. Huygens's 2012 edition of the *Vita* is used here rather than the Bollandists' *Acta sanctorum*. The *Acta* version has been shown by Huygens to be exceptionally unreliable as it omits entire sections or presents readings which do not exist in a single manuscript. Using sixteen manuscripts from the thirteenth century, and many others from the fourteenth and fifteenth centuries as part of the extensive critical apparatus, Huygens redresses this misrepresentation and presents a much more realistic picture of the *life* that circulated during the thirteenth century. For a translation of the *Acta* version, see *Mary of Oignies: Mother of Salvation*, ed. Anneke B. Mulder-Bakker (Turnhout, 2006), 33–127. On this *Vita*, see also, in this volume, Jan Vandeburie, "'*Sancte fidei omnino deiciar*'": Ugolino dei Conti di Segni's Doubts and Jacques de Vitry's Intervention', 89–104.

Lord that he would reveal to this priest that it was not within a man's power to hold back such an impetus of tears.[32]

In this episode the priest encourages Marie to pray in silence, viewed as a more fitting state, rather than with tears and sighs. He appears to doubt the validity of her tears, and to believe them to be under her control. Indeed, the witnesses to the tears portrayed in the hagiographies are generally themselves religious: men and women who knew, or who lived near, the saint in question. Although the nature of mendicancy made saints more visible during the thirteenth century, witnesses to female lacrimation would have been fewer than for their male counterparts. Any doubts conveyed through the pen of the hagiographer thus probably reflect the concerns of priests or religious rather than of lay people, and members of the Church's hierarchy often became deeply suspicious of forms of devotion that did not fit custom.[33] The incident described by Jacques again illustrates that tears were not always associated with divine grace; some doubted them, seeing them as a loss of self-control and seeking to restrict and even prevent them. Moreover, divinely given tears challenged the priest's authority as they could not be controlled or formalized. Marie removed herself to an isolated location and petitioned God with tears to show the priest that her action could not be repressed and was a legitimate expression of his presence. Throughout her holy life, Marie was ridiculed (*irridebat*) and characterized as downcast (*abiectus*),[34] hinting at the way in which religious women might be derided for their revelations and accused of being fantasists or insane. However, as Jacques asserts: 'Those who look down on any spiritual persons (*spirituales*) as insane or idiots and consider the prophecies or the revelations of saints as phantasms or illusions of dreamers, destroy much of the spirit in themselves and scorn the prophets.'[35]

---

[32] 'Quadam autem die ante parasceven, cum iam imminente Christi passione maiori lacrimarum imbre cum suspiriis et singultibus se domino mactare inchoasset, quidam de sacerdotibus ecclesie ut oraret cum silentio et lacrimas cohiberet quasi blande increpando hortabatur. Illa vero, sicut verecunda semper erat et omnibus columbina simplicitate obedire satagebat, impossibilitatis sue conscia egressa clam ab ecclesia in loco secreto et ab omnibus remoto se abscondit, impetravitque a domino cum lacrimis ut predicto sacerdoti ostenderet quod non est in homine lacrimarum impetum retinere, quando flante spiritu vehementi fluunt aque': Jacques de Vitry, *Vita Marie de Oegnies* 1.5 (CChr.CM 252, 61–2).

[33] See Beryl Smalley, 'Ecclesiastical Attitudes to Novelty *c.*1100–*c.*1250', in Derek Baker, ed., *Church, Society and Politics*, SCH 12 (Oxford, 1975), 113–31.

[34] Jacques de Vitry, *Vita* 1.4 (CChr.CM 252, 60).

[35] 'Ipsi vero spiritum quantum in se extingunt et prophetias spernunt, qui spirituales quosque quasi insanos vel ydiotas despiciunt et prophetias sive sanctorum revelationes

Nonetheless, women were not only mocked and degraded for their devotional practices but often found themselves criticized and rebuked for excessive weeping.[36] In order to redress the priest's admonition, Jacques alludes to a passage from Judith that sanctions the place of tears in otherwise silent prayer: 'praying with tears and moving her lips silently'.[37] Yet Marie's situation is only resolved when the priest himself is overcome by tears and realizes how his doubt has been misplaced:

Therefore, on the same day when that priest celebrated mass, 'the Lord opened and none shall shut' (Isa. 22: 22), 'he sent forth waters and they overturned the earth' (Job 12: 15): for the soul [of the priest] was submerged with such an inundation of tears that he almost suffocated, and however much he tried to hold back their vigour, the more not just he but also the book and the linen cloths of the altar were wetted by a greater shower of tears. What could he do, he who [had been] thoughtless, he who had rebuked the handmaid of Christ? He learned through experience [and] with shame what he had previously not wanted to learn through humility and compassion. After much sobbing and with much faltering and disorderly stammering, finally, he barely escaped from the wreckage. Someone who saw this and who knew the priest bears witness to this. A long time after mass had ended, the handmaid of Christ, returning in a wondrous manner as if she had been present, met the priest [and] entering hastily she said, 'Now you have learned through experience that it is not in a man's [power] to hold back the force of the spirit [when] the south wind is blowing.'[38]

---

tamquam fantasmata vel somniorum illusiones reputant': Jacques de Vitry, *Vita*, prologue (CChr.CM 252, 54).

[36] For other instances of a confessor encouraging a holy woman to moderate her tears, see Jordan of Saxony's letters to the Bolognese holy woman Diana d'Andalo (d. 1236): *Die Briefe Jordans von Sachsen, des zweiten Dominikanergenerals (1222–37)*, ed. Berthold Altaner, Quellen und Forschungen zur Geschichte des Dominikanerordens in Deutschland 20 (Leipzig, 1925), 7, 15, 34, 41 (letters 1, 11, 30, 39).

[37] '[S]tetitque Iudith ante lectum orans cum lacrimis et labiorum motu in silentio': Jud. 13: 6.

[38] 'Cum igitur sacerdos ille die eodem missam celebraret, aperuit dominus et non fuit qui clauderet, emisit aquas et subverterunt terram: tanto enim lacrimarum diluvio submersus est spiritus eius, quod fere suffocatus est, quantoque reprimere impetum conabatur, tanto magis lacrimarum imbre non solum ipse, sed et liber et altaris linteamina rigabantur. Quid ageret ille improvidus, ille ancille Christi increpator? Per experientiam cum rubore didicit quod prius per humilitatem et compassionem cognoscere non voluit. Post singultus multos, multa inordinate et cum interruptione pronuntians a naufragio tandem vix evasit, et qui vidit et cognovit testimonium perhibuit. Tunc vero longo tempore post misse comple-

This episode is important for several reasons. Primarily, it underlines that tears can be given by God and that the grace is arbitrary. Divine graces are more powerful than any priest and tears cannot be subdued to suit the requirements of others or of the recipient. Although no 'doubt words' are used in this episode, doubt of or at least scepticism about Marie's tears is implied by the priest's behaviour: he is quick to dismiss the sincerity and validity of her tears through his thoughtless (*improvidus*) response.[39] The soul of the priest is then submerged in tears and it is only through this experience that he gains the necessary knowledge that he had not previously wanted (*cognoscere non voluit*). The soul of the priest is overcome by tears granted to him by God, in a process akin to baptismal cleansing. Through this experience of tears he is given knowledge as a way of making him believe. The message is also critical in terms of legitimization and agency. When Marie is reproached for her tears she is characterized by Jacques as a meek woman who endeavours to obey the wishes of the priest: 'In truth, she was always modest and, in dove-like simplicity, she tried to obey in all things'.[40] However, when the priest is himself overwhelmed by divine tears, Marie becomes a powerful character who is able to teach him that tears should not be doubted. The relationship is inverted.

This event is pregnant with meaning. It affords Jacques the opportunity to discuss the importance of tears as a manifestation of grace and piety whilst also working as a wider commentary on bad priests. However, his decision to include this episode suggests that Jacques was dealing with wider incipient doubt surrounding tears and that he was trying to neutralize any scepticism that his intended audience may have had towards this form of female devotion. By addressing and quashing incredulity in a *Vita*, the hagiographer can try to diffuse criticism and doubt. Jacques's authority and success

---

tionem ancilla Christi revertens, miro modo acsi presens affuisset quecumque acciderunt sacerdoti improperando retulit: "Nunc", inquit, "per experientiam didicistis quod non est in homine impetum spiritus Austro flante retinere'": Jacques de Vitry, *Vita* 1.5 (CChr.CM 252, 62–3).

[39] For a discussion of the lexicography of doubt, see Sabina Flanagan, 'Lexicographic and Syntactic Explorations of Doubt in Twelfth-Century Latin Texts', *JMedH* 27 (2001), 219–40.

[40] 'Illa vero, sicut verecunda semper erat, et omnibus columbina simplicitate obedire satagebat': Jacques de Vitry, *Vita* 1.5 (CChr.CM 252, 62).

in this matter is revealed in the way that this episode became a touchstone for legitimizing female tears, retold in Margery Kempe's *Book* (*c*.1430).[41]

Despite the criticisms and doubt a saint must endure as a test of their faith and holiness, tears were a positive marker of sanctity in hagiographies. The hagiographers tell us that, try as they might, churchmen could not restrain the tears of others. Thirteenth-century female saints' *Vitae* always redress criticism of tears. For example, in one episode, reminiscent of John 20: 15, in which the resurrected Christ asks Mary Magdalene why she is weeping, the Lord asks Margaret of Cortona: 'Why are you weeping (*Cur fles*)?'[42] Margaret responds that she is battling against those who do not believe her. The Lord strengthens her with the knowledge that he too was doubted as the Son of God.[43] In another incident, Margaret goes out onto the balcony of her house in the middle of the night and begins to pray with loud tears. Her devotions wake those in her neighbourhood and, rather than being annoyed at the disruption, her hagiographer records how they were touched with compassion, edified and themselves moved to pity and tears.[44] It is evident from these and other accounts that doubting tears was corollary to achieving certainty and assisted in rebuffing further potential scepticism.

Fourteenth-Century Doubt and Distrust

Tears remained an important aspect of sanctity in the fourteenth century, but by the later part of the century some subtle shifts can be detected in the way in which they were being written about.[45] Whilst an external manifestation of tears persisted in most *Vitae*, some hagiographical texts point towards an internalization of weeping, perhaps reflecting a certain discomfort with and doubt about somatic lachrymosity. In one instance in the *Revelations of Divine Love* (*c*.1373) by the

---

[41] *The Book of Margery Kempe*, ed. Barry A. Windeatt (Harlow, 2000), 291–4 (ch. 62).

[42] Bevegnati, *Legenda* 5 (ed. Iozzelli, 249).

[43] Ibid. 5 (ed. Iozzelli, 250).

[44] Ibid. 2 (ed. Iozzelli, 190–4).

[45] For tears in the lives of fourteenth-century holy women, see, for example, Margaret of Faenza (d. 1320): *Vita* 2 (*ActaSS* Aug. 5, 847–51, at 849–50); Michelina of Pisaro (d. 1356): *Mariano of Florence, Vita*, lect. 5, and *Alia vita* 1–2 (*ActaSS* Jun. 3, 927–36, at 928, 930, 932–3); Dauphine of Puimichel (d. 1360): *Les Vies occitanes de Saint Auzias et de Sainte Dauphine*, ed. and French transl. Jacques Cambell (Rome, 1963), 138, 142, 148, 150, 180, 186, 200, 202, 226.

English anchoress and mystic Julian of Norwich (d. 1416), tears are mostly internal rather than being produced by the eyes:

> This weping meneth not al in poring out of teares by our bodily eye, but also to more gostly vnderstanding; for the kindly desire of our soule is so gret and so onmesurable that if it were goven us to our solice in erth, and we saw not the fair blisfull chere of hymselfe, yet we shuld not stynten of moning ne of gostly weping, that is to sey, peynfull longing, till whan we sen verily the faire blisfull chere of our maker.[46]

Similarly, in her Dialogue (*Dialogo*), the Dominican tertiary Catherine of Siena (d. 1380) suggests that once the soul has been enflamed with holy desire tears are no longer necessary for a personal transition from one state to another, and that the Holy Spirit is able to transform the desire of the individual into active work on behalf of those in need of salvation.

> It now remains to tell you, to satisfy your wish, of those who would like the perfection of tears but do not seem to be able to have it; is there another way than by means of the tears of the eye? Yes, it is a weeping of flame, that is of real and holy desire, consumed by the affection of love. She would like to dissolve her life in weeping for the hatred of herself and the salvation of souls, and it seems that she cannot. I say that these souls have tears of flame, in that the Holy Spirit weeps before me for them and for their neighbours.[47]

---

[46] Julian of Norwich, *A Revelation of Love*, ed. Marion Glasscoe (Exeter, 1976), 87 (ch. 72). It should be noted that Julian mentions tears at other points in the text.

[47] 'Restoti ora a dire, a satisfare del desiderio tuo che m'ài adimandato, d'alcuni che vorrebbono la perfezione delle lagrime e non pare che la possino avere: acci altro modo che lagrima d'occhio? Sí: ècci uno pianto di fuoco, cioè di vero e santo desiderio, il quale si consuma per affetto d'amore. Vorrebbe dissolvere la vita sua in pianto per odio di sè e salute dell'anime, e non pare che possa. Dico che costoro ànno lagrima di fuoco, in cui piagne lo Spirito santo dinanzi a me per loro e per lo prossimo loro': Catherine of Siena, *Il Dialogo della divina provvidenza ovvero libro della divina dottrina*, ed. Giuliana Cavallini (Rome, 1968), 211. See Heather Webb, '"Lacrime cordiali": Catherine of Siena and the Value of Tears', in George Ferzoco, Beverly Kienzle and Carolyn Muessig, eds, *A Companion to Catherine of Siena* (Leiden, 2011), 99–112. By contrast, during the thirteenth century the loss of tears was particularly disturbing: see Kimberley-Joy Knight, 'Si puose calcina a' propi occhi: The Importance of the Gift of Tears for Thirteenth-Century Religious Women and their Hagiographers', in Gertsman, ed., *Crying in the Middle Ages*, 136–55.

These nuanced descriptions of tears are a reflection of wider changes in the acceptance of emotional and physical expressions of sanctity in the early fourteenth century. Although thirteenth-century hagiographers dwelt on somatic lachrymose displays of piety, writers of theological treatises, including Aquinas, downplayed such physically rapturous responses.[48] As Dyan Elliott has suggested, this could be construed as a tacit assertion of how unreliable a witness the body was.[49] The enrapt female body was becoming a site of ambiguity, and its ability to be a conduit for holy messages doubted. In her study of the physiology of rapture and female spirituality, Elliott traced the 'gradual criminalization' of female bodily mysticism in the later Middle Ages.[50] In the late fourteenth century, the body's untrustworthy evidentiary status was probed by scholars. The German-born Parisian master of theology Henry of Langenstein (d. 1397) described how passions and melancholia could affect an individual's receptivity and perceptions and that excessive austerities could lead to stupefaction and madness.[51] In addition, he explained how some individuals, because of their vainglory, would be sent delusory visions by God.[52] Doubt over the legitimacy of the body and its expressions was also suggested by the scholar and reformer Jean Gerson (d. 1429) who in 1415 produced an influential treatise entitled *De probatione spiritum* (*On the Discernment of Spirits*) in which he summarized his doubts as to the veracity of the revelations of the Swedish holy woman and founder of the Bridgettines, Bridget of Sweden (d. 1373).[53] He explained that the visions and revelations experienced by women were connected to brain damage, melancholia and epilepsy, not to the presence of the divine.[54] In an earlier treatise, *De distinctione verarum revelationum a*

---

[48] See Elliott, 'Physiology of Rapture', 152.

[49] Ibid.

[50] Ibid. 142.

[51] Ibid. 152.

[52] Henry of Langenstein, *De discretione spirituum* 2, 4 (*Heinrichs von 'Langenstein Unterscheidung der Geister'*, ed. and German transl. Thomas Hohmann, Münchener Texte und Untersuchungen zur deutschen Literatur des Mittelalters 63 [Munich, 1977], 56–8, 70–1).

[53] It should be noted that Gerson's concerns about the legitimacy of the body, visions and revelations were not always directed exclusively against women. Some scholars have now begun to revise the view that Gerson had a misogynistic distrust of women: see Wendy Love Anderson, 'Gerson's Stance on Women', in Brian Patrick McGuire, ed., *A Companion to Jean Gerson* (Leiden, 2006), 293–315.

[54] Jean Gerson, *De probatione spirituum* 448 (*Oeuvres complètes*, ed. [Palémon] Glorieux, 10 vols [Paris, 1960–73], 9: 177–85, at 180); for ET and commentary, see Paschal Boland, *The*

falsis (*c*.1401), Gerson had already warned that shedding excessive tears could damage and disturb the brain.[55] Furthermore, in a long letter-treatise known as *De religionis perfectione et moderamine* (*On the Perfection and Moderation of the Religious Life*) written in 1422 for William Minaud, a medical doctor who had recently entered La Grande Chartreuse, Gerson expressed his doubts concerning tears: 'There is, I confess, in tears, something sweet and agreeable'. However, in such sweetness could be danger: 'flee as much as you can from such tears', advised Gerson, for 'the snake hides in the grass'.[56] In this reading, tears had the power to deceive and should not be encouraged. Gerson reiterated his concerns about the authenticity of revelations and false prophets in several treatises, and in *De examinatione doctrinarum* (*c*.1423) he suggested that potential candidates should be examined by six degrees of *examinatores* – council, pope, prelate, doctor, educated person and a discerner of spirits – before any official pronouncements about their suitability were made.[57]

However, the best insight into why tears may in some instances have become internalized can be gleaned from the writings of the Franciscan preacher Bernardino of Siena (d. 1444), who warned against 'the deception of artificial transformation' (*deceptionum et artificiosae transformationis*): 'For there are many who violate themselves for tears or fervours, and through certain outer acts they elaborate supernatural sentiments'.[58] Once again, the problem of

---

Concept of Discretio spiritum *in John Gerson's* 'De probatione spirituum' *and* 'De distinctione verarum visionum a falsis' (Washington DC, 1959).

[55] Gerson, *De distinctione verarum revelationum a falsis* 90 (*Oeuvres complètes*, ed. Glorieux, 3: 36–56, at 42).

[56] 'Est fateor in lacrimis aliquid dulce et mulcebre … Propterea fuge quantum poteris interim tales lacrimas, quoniam latet anguis in herba': Gerson, *De religionis perfectione et moderamine*, letter 49 (*Oeuvres complètes*, ed. Glorieux, 2: 232–45, at 243); see also Brian Patrick McGuire, *Jean Gerson and the Last Medieval Reformation* (University Park, PA, 2005), 312–13.

[57] Gerson, *De examinatione doctrinarum* 456 (*Oeuvres complètes*, ed. Glorieux, 9: 458–75, at 458); see also idem, *De distinctione verarum revelationum a falsis*; *De probatione spiritum*. For a full discussion of the discernment of spirits, see Nancy Caciola, *Discerning Spirits: Divine and Demonic Possession in the Middle Ages* (Ithaca, NY, 2003), especially 215–315.

[58] '[D]eceptionum et artificiosae transformationis. Sunt namque plerique qui seipsos violentant ad lacrimas et fervores, et per quosdam exteriores actus ad sentimenta supernaturalia elaborant': Bernardino of Siena, *De inspirationum discretione* (*Opera omnia*, ed. Fathers of the College of St Bonaventure, 7 vols [Florence, 1950–9], 6: 243–90, at 270).

interpretation is crucial. Bernardino's concern here is with an external act (*exteriores actus*), but other scholars, including the theologian and mystic Dionysius the Carthusian (d. 1471), also followed Gerson's lead and explained how bodily and rapturous experiences should be proven by a qualified judge.[59] Nonetheless, no evidence remains to suggest that any such judges were called upon when it came to tears. The arbitrary nature of a divine grace of tears would make the summoning of a suitable judge at the moment of reception challenging, if not impossible. Theologians and churchmen may have reached an impasse with such a complex and transient expression.

CONCLUSIONS

In the thirteenth century, tears were a fully, externally manifested expression of piety that reflected internal transformation and spiritual progress. Any doubt was neutralized 'at source', and the episodes in hagiographies are used to establish the sanctity of a holy woman beyond doubt by rebuffing the accusations of potential detractors. Tears are thereby rendered *ipso facto* a proof of sanctity. A selection of late fourteenth-century female texts, however, provides evidence that a state of emotional transformation was possible without external tears. In some cases, tears seem to have been driven inside as a consequence of doubt. The emergence of doubt relating to lachrymose expressions of devotion stemmed from a growing distrust of the body, visions and revelations and the wider theological preoccupation with the discerning of spirits. The parameters of accepted behaviour and expressions were changing, and these changes were further articulated in treatises written over the course of the fifteenth century. By internalizing tears, doubt over the veracity of external bodily displays of piety is removed. Yet, the reader or listener of the devotional text could still identify elements of spiritual progression, such as contrition and spiritual cleansing, that were demarcated with internal tears.

This essay has suggested that the internalization of tears may be one facet of what Elliott has called the 'gradual criminalization' of female bodily mysticism in the later Middle Ages.[60] The female body

---

[59] Dionysius the Carthusian, *De discretione et examinatione spiritum* (*Dionysii Carhusiensis Opera selecta*, 2 vols, CChr.CM 121, 121a, 2: 268, 270–2); see also Elliott, 'Physiology of Rapture', 153 n. 60.

[60] Elliott, 'Physiology of Rapture', 142.

was a place of potential divine dispensation, yet also held within it the power of deception: ascertaining the veracity of female tears was a challenging, if not impossible, task. Doubts as to whether a woman's body could be the trusted vessel for God's message could not be dispelled easily, but internalizing women's tears may have neutralized some of their observers' scepticism.

Heresy, Doubt and Identity: Late Medieval Friars in the Kingdom of Aragon

Emily E. Graham*

Oklahoma State University

The fourteenth-century Kingdom of Aragon enjoyed a reputation as a haven for religious dissidents, doubters, heretical refugees and malcontents. This is particularly true of those fleeing the upheaval that the Franciscan Order experienced early in the century, as debates over the nature of poverty within the order created serious conflicts within communities, between friars and superiors, and between the order and the papacy. These visitors operated at the highest levels of the royal court, as has been well documented in the recent surge of interest in figures such as Ramon Llull and Arnald of Villanova. But the effects were also felt in rural communities, arousing suspicion among local bishops. Court proceedings and other documents reveal the pervasive atmosphere of doubt and suspicion that focused on several Franciscan houses in the diocese of Barcelona as late as the middle of the fourteenth century.

In the twilight of an October evening in 1345, a group of Franciscan tertiaries stood arguing in the garden of their small house. A newcomer to the community, Francesc Joan, had reported to the local Franciscan lector that the group had heretical leanings. That evening two of the tertiaries, Domènec and Bartomeu, confronted him. The exchange became heated: soon each was accusing the other of heresy: 'You're a heretic' – 'No indeed, you're a heretic!' A fourth brother stepped in and suggested that each of the accused's rooms be searched for 'the writings of brother Peter John', to settle the matter.[1] Two months of brawling, extortion and accusation followed, during which the entire group was imprisoned awaiting trial before the bishop. Despite their innocence of heretical leanings, the

* 101 S Murray Hall, Stillwater, OK 74078, USA. E-mail: Emily.E.Graham@okstate.edu.

[1] Josep Perarnau i Espelt, *Beguins de Vilafranca del Penedès davant el Tribunal d'Inquisició (1345–1346). De captaires a banquers?*, Istituto Storico Italiano per il Medio Evo, Nuovi studi storici 85 (Rome, 2010), 49, lines 269–75. The manuscript of the depositions that are the focus of Perarnau's excellent critical edition is Barcelona, Arxiu Diocesà, Processo 3.

Studies in Church History 52 (2016) 135–149   © Ecclesiastical History Society 2016
doi: 10.1017/stc.2015.8

controversy broke the little community, which had lived in relative peace for decades prior to Francesc Joan's advent. Such was the power of doubt and the suspicion to which it led. Even far distant in time and place from the Franciscan poverty controversy and the related heresies of Peter John Olivi (1248–98), the mere raising of doubts about heterodoxy could destroy the fabric of a community's life in rural Catalonia.[2]

Much of the literature on the Spiritual Franciscans has focused on the Italian groups of these rigorist and schismatic friars, or on the Provençal beguins. These beguins were the followers of Peter John Olivi, and not the loosely organized houses of penitential women known as beguines, whose communities were widespread in northern France, the northern German lands and the Low Countries. But for the purposes of this essay we turn further south and westward to another centre of beguinism and the cult of Olivi: the Crown of Aragon, straddling the Pyrenees to control both Catalonia and Montpellier. By the fourteenth century, the kingdom already had a reputation as a haven for religious dissidents, doubters, heretical refugees and malcontents. The mountainous region in the northern part of the kingdom bordered Languedoc, a hotbed of heretical activity most famous for the Cathars active there in the thirteenth century. In both Languedoc and northern Aragon, refugees and sympathizers might move freely among small communities, circulating texts and ideas over several generations. Amongst those seeking refuge in the rural mountain communities or safe passage to quieter situations in Sicily or the Kingdom of Naples were those fleeing the upheaval that the Franciscan Order had experienced in the early part of the century. The consequences of that conflict continued to affect Franciscan communities in the region for decades.[3] Debates over the nature of poverty within the Order created serious conflicts within

---

[2] There is a vast and expanding bibliography on Olivi. Among others, see David Burr, *The Persecution of Peter John Olivi* (Philadelphia, PA, 1970); Alain Boureau and Sylvain Piron, eds, *Pierre de Jean Olivi (1248–1298)* (Paris, 1999); and the online resource 'Oliviana: Mouvements et dissidences spirituels XIIIe–XIVe siècles', at: <http://oliviana.revues.org>.

[3] In the late twelfth and early thirteenth centuries, until the advent of the Inquisition, Languedoc and possibly Catalonia served as a Cathar refuge: Edward Peters, *Inquisition* (Oakland, CA, 1989), 76. In the fourteenth century, the area became a way-station for Franciscans fleeing the fallout of the poverty controversy: Thomas N. Bisson, *The Medieval Crown of Aragon: A Short History* (Oxford, 1991), 96; Jill Webster, *Els Menorets: The Franciscans in the Realms of Aragon from St Francis to the Black Death* (Toronto, ON, 1993). Further works on the Franciscans in Catalonia include Pedro Sanahuja, *História de la será-*

communities, between friars and superiors, and between the Order and the papacy. The effects of this conflict at the curia were keenly felt even in rural areas, arousing the reservations of local bishops and distrust among small communities.

Catalonia experienced an elevated level of wariness and suspicion in the first half of the fourteenth century regarding these issues, as is made clear by the ambiguity about 'beguins', tertiaries and penitential groups in the sources; the persecution of poverty rigorists, and even of those commenting on the poverty debates; and the increased anxiety caused by proximity to heretical preaching and writings. Court proceedings and other documents surrounding two inquests in Girona (1325) and an inquest twenty years later in Vilafranca del Penedès (1345–6) reveal the long reach of the poverty controversy, as it contributed to a pervasive atmosphere of doubt and suspicion that affected laity and friars alike. The spectre of suppressed heresies continued to haunt the order a generation later, driving friars and tertiaries in the diocese of Barcelona to legal and physical extremes. This essay will explore several views in the Aragonese experience of the Franciscan poverty controversy. Firstly, it will provide some context for the larger controversy, and simultaneously explicate the ambiguity that surrounds the Franciscan Third Order in this region's sources and in the minds of their contemporaries. Secondly, it will explore the consequences of papal prosecution and persecution of poverty rigorists. Friars, tertiaries and laymen alike were acutely aware of the poverty debates taking place across the Pyrenees at Avignon, held strong opinions on them, and even hosted heretical penitents from time to time. And thirdly, it will demonstrate that even for relatively orthodox communities, proximity to heretical preaching itineraries and larger heretical communities created the opportunity for bursts of accusatory hysteria. Years later, the reverberations of the poverty controversy had the power to tear apart sleepy, stable groups in the mountain towns around Barcelona. Although poverty debates at Avignon lasted only a generation, ending bloodily and swiftly, the inquests, anxieties and above all doubts which they set in motion continued to inflict collateral damage at the fringes of the Order for decades.

---

fica provincial de Cataluña (Barcelona, 1959); José Pou y Martí, *Visionarios, beguinos y fraticelos catalanes (siglos xiii–xv)* (Alicante, 1996).

While doubt may be a positive agent of change, as the first step towards faith, or even towards conversion, it is the negative qualities of doubt which will be explored here. Doubt is inherent in the study of heretical groups: by their very nature, heretical beliefs often consist of the doubting, refusal or misbelieving of Church doctrine. But the mechanisms established by the Church to pursue and correct such errors, doubts and 'stubborn' heresies, also produced new forms of doubt within accused or suspect communities such as the tertiaries of Vilafranca del Penedès. To be tainted even by association with suspected heretics was cause for distrust, reservations, misgivings and suspicion. The Crown of Aragon is uniquely situated for an exploration of the effect of wider heretical movements and persecutions on local communities. Its rich archival holdings, close ties to the papal court and proximity to hotbeds of heresy in southern France and the western Mediterranean provide ample room for studying 'doubt' in the context of heretical activity. It was a major site for circulation of the works of Arnald of Vilanova, whose views have often been affiliated with the Spiritual Franciscans and beguin circles in Barcelona.[4] Aragon's geographical and political position put many levels of society – laymen, tertiaries, friars and the intellectual elite – in sometimes contentious opposition to the papacy and its policies. Much of this centred on the reception of the poverty controversy initiated by Peter John Olivi.

Although he died in 1298, Peter John Olivi cast a long shadow over tertiaries and beguins in the early fourteenth century. A Franciscan theologian and enthusiast for the apocalyptic writings of Abbot Joachim of Fiore, his doctrine of *usus pauper* strongly influenced the Spiritual Franciscans in the poverty debates of the early fourteenth century, despite the fact that many of his teachings had by that time been condemned. This doctrine was developed during the 1280s, and advocated a restricted use of goods without ownership: that is, even if a friar did not own the items he was using (such as food-stuffs, books, clothing) his vow of poverty should prevent him from using them more than strictly necessary. The Franciscan hierarchy, in Olivi's first censure in 1283, argued that going beyond this and embracing an unrestricted use of goods owned by non-Franciscans

---

[4] Clifford Backman, 'Arnau de Vilanova and the Franciscan Spirituals in Sicily', *FS* 50 (1990), 3–29; Joseph Ziegler, *Medicine and Religion* c.*1300: The Case of Arnau de Vilanova* (Oxford, 1998).

was not breaking the vow of poverty.[5] Rehabilitated, Olivi continued to write and expound his theories on the Book of Revelation and on Franciscan poverty, but after his death in 1298 the Franciscan General Chapter of 1299 condemned several of his teachings and burned his writings.[6] Olivi's tomb in Narbonne nonetheless became the centre of an active regional cult.[7] The following developed quickly: in 1299, only a year after his death, the provincial council at Béziers that condemned his writings also expressed suspicion of 'beguins', described in its acts as persons who wore distinctive clothing, practised penitence and preached on the coming apocalypse, all of which were resonant with both the tertiary movement (members of which were known as brothers and sisters of penitence) and Olivi's writings.[8]

The terms 'beguin' and 'Spiritual Franciscan' each present their own difficulties of interpretation and layered meanings. Historians have retroactively applied the term 'Spiritual Franciscan' to a hotchpotch of reformers and schismatics whose own self-description was '*fratres spirituales*'. These Spiritual Franciscans, both friars and tertiaries, sought more stringent observation of poverty as part of the *vita apostolica*, but they did so in ways that were broadly divergent from each other. It is clear from many sources, including the Girona inquests of 1325 (see below), that the Franciscan friars in Aragon were no strangers to the poverty controversy unfolding across the Pyrenees, and even educated laymen show awareness of the issues it raised.[9]

The issue of Franciscan poverty first became prominent in the 1280s, when several Franciscan theologians had called for more rigorous observance of poverty in the Order. During the short-lived pontificate of Celestine V in 1294, a group of friars in the March of Ancona briefly formed their own schismatic order. When this

---

[5] David Burr, *The Spiritual Franciscans: From Protest to Persecution in the Century after Saint Francis* (University Park, PA, 2001), 53–4.

[6] Ibid. 88; David Flood, 'Pierre Jean-Olivi et la règle franciscaine', in *Franciscains d'Oc. Les Spirituels (ca 1280–1324)*, Cahiers de Fanjeaux 10 (Fanjeaux, 1977), 139–54; Yves Congar, 'Les positions ecclésiologiques de Pierre Jean-Olivi', ibid. 155–64.

[7] Louisa A. Burnham, *So Great a Light, So Great a Smoke: The Beguin Heretics of Languedoc* (Ithaca, NY, 2008), 20–23.

[8] Malcolm Lambert, *Franciscan Poverty* (London, 1961), 155–6; Burr, *Spiritual Franciscans*, 51, 58, 62–5.

[9] Josep Perarnau i Espelt, 'Noves dades sobre beguins de Girona', *Annals de l'Institut d'Estudis Gironins* 25 (1979), 237–48; idem, 'Una altra carta de Guiu Terrena sobre el procés inquisitorial contra el franciscá fra Bernat Fuster', *Estudis Franciscans* 82 (1981), 383–92.

was dissolved on Celestine's abdication, the friars were returned to their former communities, where they were harshly treated by their superiors. The reformist and schismatic friars continued to press for reform, and hopes of a final settlement with the Order were raised by Clement V and the Council of Vienne *c.*1311–13, only to be dashed following his death in 1314. Events for the Spirituals unravelled rapidly thereafter: disobedient friars in Provence ejected their superiors by force, they were summoned before the new pope, John XXII, for trial, and those few who refused to obey their superiors and papal pronouncements on their poverty were burned in the spring of 1318.[10]

At the same time, from 1317 to 1323 John XXII was issuing decisive bulls in favour of the Franciscan hierarchy's position on *usus pauper*, which effectively ended the Spirituals' hopes of achieving reform through official channels. Many of them, already elderly, left the papal sphere and lived quietly in hermitages and refuges in the Kingdom of Naples or elsewhere. Among the papal bulls was *Sancta romana* (30 December 1317), condemning those identified as '*fraticelli*, *bizzochi* or beguins' found in Narbonne, Toulouse, Provence, Sicily and parts of Italy.[11] Interestingly, John XXII does not mention Aragon, though we know beguins to have been active in Catalonia from the early 1300s. Nevertheless, those possessing, preaching on or otherwise involving themselves in rigorist poverty views came under scrutiny from Catalonian bishops and inquisitors for many decades after *Sancta romana.* The poverty controversy and its aftermath created, sustained and gave force to effective and punitive expressions of doubt and suspicion within Franciscan communities throughout the first half of the fourteenth century.

The problem of defining these groups of pious laypersons living in common was a source of confusion for their contemporaries and for the inquisitors, and has also long been one among scholars. This is due in part to some confusion of terms, but more problematically to

---

[10] Burr, *Spiritual Franciscans*, 196–206.

[11] Conrad Eubel, ed., *Bullarium Franciscanum Romanorum Pontificium*, 5 (Rome, 1898), 134–5. All three terms were used to refer to errant Franciscans or poverty rigorists who opposed the papal position on Franciscan poverty. *Fraticelli* is now commonly used to refer to the Franciscans who opposed later papal proclamations on the nature of Christ's poverty: in the past they were often and confusingly conflated with the Spiritual Franciscans. *Bizzoche* was one of the terms used to describe beguin-like persons in regions of Italy.

the fluid nature of their own identities. One group might be referred to by many terms, some of which could be pejorative. For example, many of the Spiritual Franciscans and beguins who were tried and even executed in the early fourteenth century were found guilty of holding 'Olivian' heretical views or possessing his banned writings. When used as a pejorative, the term 'beguin' therefore carried the stigma of association with his suppressed cult, and the taint of heresy, but it could also be used simply to refer to penitential groups without heretical leanings. The problem of terminology is exacerbated when different sources use different terms for the same group: for instance, when founding a hospital to be run by tertiaries in Valencia in 1346, the king of Aragon and other donors referred to the hospital community variously as the women of the Third Order of St Francis, as brothers and sisters of penitence, and as beguins.[12] These terms were frequently used interchangeably, sometimes in the same document, and the different emphases of these identifications overlap and blur, even in the minds of those who had contact with these groups and their individual members.

Franciscan affiliation, intense penitential asceticism, devotion to the heretical doctrines of Peter John Olivi and lay apocalypticism were common to some but not all these groups, and even to a few members of otherwise unconnected communities. In some cases these were well-organized groups, such as tertiaries who were closely supervised and joined to local Franciscan houses. Others had a looser affiliation to the Franciscan Order, with little or no oversight and ad hoc local support.[13] Not all houses of penitents adhered either to Franciscan devotions or to heretical Olivian views. Some beguins were followers of Olivi's cult, but did not practise the penitential lifestyle. But often these identities overlapped, and orthodox tertiaries were brought under suspicion of heretical beguinism by

---

[12] Burr, *Spiritual Franciscans*, 91 and n. 66. The term *beguin* or *beguinos* as used in Aragon was certainly blurred between tertiaries, female beguines of the kind also found in the Low Countries or referred to elsewhere as *pinzocchere* or *bizzoche*, and followers of Olivi: it was used both to identify heretical Olivians at Vilafranca and elsewhere, and in the same period to describe an apparently perfectly legitimate hospital '*dels beguins*' established in Valencia for male and female penitents (though admittedly the hospital was also connected with the circle of Arnald of Villanova, himself connected with Olivians): Webster, *Els Menorets*, 247.

[13] Webster, *Els Menorets*, 241–59; Clément Schmitt, 'La position du Tiers-ordre dans le conflit des Spirituels et de Fraticelles en Italie', in Mariano d'Alatri, ed., *I frati penitenti di S Francesco nella società del due e trecento* (Rome, 1977), 179–90, at 180–1.

association, or penitential houses confused with tertiaries. Uncertainty and the doubt it could foster were thus inherent in the blended identities of loosely defined lay pious. These uncertain identities could generate doubt about their orthodoxy which presented an implicit danger to the group. Indeed, in northern Europe the prohibition against heretical beguins was also used by opportunistic guilds and clerics to rid themselves of houses of beguines, penitential women wholly unaffiliated with the beguin heresy, who happened to share their name with Olivi's followers.[14] And at the same time that the king was founding a hospital for 'good' beguins south of Barcelona, to the north of the city his bishop was investigating the Franciscan tertiaries of Vilafranca del Penedès on suspicion of their being 'beguinized tertiaries', Olivian heretics.

The poverty controversy was followed with interest by the members of Catalonian intellectual circles, friars and laity alike. As the debate evolved, twin enquiries in the cities of Girona and Mallorca illustrate clearly the scepticism with which the papal 'solution' to Franciscan poverty rigorists was viewed. In 1325, the secretary of the town of Girona and a Franciscan friar in Mallorca were the subject of linked inquests.[15] The subjects of the inquest were Fra Bernat Fuster, descended from several generations of heretical beguins, and the notary Guillem des Quer. They were regular correspondents, and exchanged at least sixteen letters of pointed commentary and critique on Franciscan poverty theology, including critiques of papal bulls by Nicholas IV and John XXII.

These letters express their authors' close attention to a fresh and vital issue: the poverty debate constantly evolving in the heyday of the controversy, the late 1310s and early 1320s. The rich letter collections at the Archive of the Crown of Aragon make it clear that the Aragonese court was uniquely well situated to gather detailed intelligence on public and private information at the papal court.[16] This

---

[14] Mario Sensi, *Storie di bizzoche tra Umbria e Marche* (Rome, 1995); Walter Simons, *Cities of Ladies: Beguine Communities in the medieval Low Countries (1200–1565)* (Philadelphia, PA, 2003); Elizabeth Makowski, *'A Pernicious Sort of Woman': Quasi-Religious Women and Canon Lawyers in the Later Middle Ages* (Washington DC, 2005), 44–9. While John XXII clarified his position in *Ratio recta* (1318), this clarification did not circulate widely.

[15] Josep Perarnau i Espelt, 'Opere di Fr Petrus Johannis in processi catalani d'inquisizione della prima metà del xiv secolo', *AFH* 91 (1998), 505–16, at 506–7; idem, 'Noves dades'; idem, 'Una altra carta'.

[16] Much of the correspondence is published in Heinrich Finke, *Acta Aragonensia*, 3 vols (Berlin and Leipzig, 1908–23).

included almost daily reports from their envoy and spymaster, from friendly cardinals, and from other well-placed agents, often Franciscans and local ecclesiastics.[17] Friars are not infrequently identified as messengers, bearing written and verbal communications. Add this to the region's relatively active beguin communities, with networks stretching to Languedoc, and it is apparent that the Catalan tertiaries, friars and laymen had access, interest and means to closely follow and develop strong opinions on the poverty debate.

The twin inquests situated in this information-rich sphere present a clear picture of the role of doubt among close observers of the debate. In a period of deeply imperfect communication, when doubt and confusion arose often from too little or imprecise information, this is a situation in which the intellectual middle strata of society – its educated laymen and friars outside the royal orbit – were led into more doubt, not less, by the regular availability of detailed information. And when that privately expressed doubt regarding papal pronouncements was identified by the authorities, it in turn caused them to doubt the orthodoxy of the correspondents' beliefs and teachings.

This informed epistolary discourse had grave consequences for its authors. The notary Guillem des Quer's case was prolonged for most of a year, and eventually referred to the papal court for further action if the pope so wished. To the best of my current knowledge, no documentation in the Vatican archives confirms that it was taken up at Avignon, although further work is needed to confirm this. The Franciscan friar, Bernat Fuster, was condemned by the papal court and imprisoned there for more than two years.[18]

Misgivings and suspicion surrounding Olivian heresy and the poverty issue affected not just individuals such as Bernat and Guillem, but also whole communities. Doubts might lie dormant for decades before an agitating factor brought underlying insecurities to the surface. The second example of the long reach of the poverty debate took place twenty years after the Girona inquests, in the neighbouring diocese of Barcelona. As observed at the beginning of this essay, in the autumn and winter of 1345–6 a tertiary known as Francesc Joan took less than a year to fragment the Franciscan tertiaries of Vilafranca del Penedès, with disastrous consequences for

---

[17] Stéphane Péquignot, *Au Nom du roi. Pratique diplomatique et pouvoir durant le règne de Jacques II d'Aragon (1291–1327)* (Madrid, 2009).

[18] Webster, *Els Menorets*, 250–1; Perarnau i Espelt, 'Una altra carta'.

tertiaries throughout the diocese of Barcelona. While the case of the twin inquests of 1325 illustrates the doubt and suspicion easily fostered in the immediate aftermath of new definitions of 'acceptable' beliefs and practices, the Vilafranca case deals with an entirely different, later generation, and clearly illustrates that the social and legal anxieties associated with these ideas had a long afterlife, which far outlived the viability of the ideas themselves.

In a detailed inquest on this controversy, carried out by the local bishop and an inquisitor, Vilafrancan tertiaries testified to heretical activities and strong suspicions of Olivian beliefs circulating in the community. While awaiting trial they were imprisoned for six months, along with a local priest who died in gaol. Unlike the tertiaries, who were eventually found innocent and returned, albeit to shattered lives, the priest was posthumously condemned and his goods confiscated. The inquest testimony is littered with references to the doubts, misgivings and distrust sown by the community members' ongoing relationships with those who continued to spread or embrace condemned texts, and is evidence of the atmosphere of Olivian views that still lingered in the region.

The protocols of the inquest of the Vilafranca tertiaries, which took place from October 1345 to January 1346, bring to life the prolonged impact of the diaspora of interested parties from the poverty debates: ageing friars with small collections of banned Olivian books, and preachers seizing on local alms-related disputes to hark back to John XXII's bulls on Franciscan poverty. The passage of these figures, or the slight interest stirred by their teachings, had occasioned no comment for several decades. It was only in the presence of official accusations and inquest, infused with new suspicion about the community's orthodoxy, that these began to be woven into a tapestry of doubt. The Vilafranca trial presaged a resurgence of attention and subsequent beguin trials and burnings in Barcelona, Carcassonne and Toulouse in 1347, and in Avignon as late as 1354.[19] It can thus be placed within the larger context of renewed suspicion and doubt which fuelled interest in stamping out a second generation, or ageing first generation, of Olivian followers throughout the region.

The extant record of the inquest is almost certainly incomplete, but includes the testimony of some nine witnesses, most of them women, and nearly all tertiaries. Several were close relatives of the

---

[19] Burnham, *So Great a Light*, 82 n. 94.

Franciscan friar Bernat Fuster, who had been condemned in the 1325 process in Mallorca. The community was, by its members' own account, host to a variety of beguinized travellers from southern France and as far distant as Naples, but there are no records to indicate that officials had previously suspected them of heretical leanings.[20] The depositions communicate a clear sense of the community's internally heightened sensitivity, if not paranoia, regarding the possibility of heresy among them and its potential consequences for the group. The argument in the garden with its aspersions and mutual accusations, the immediate suggestion that any heresy must involve the possession of Olivian writings, and the detailed retellings of decade-old events including the offer of hospitality to beguinized figures such as Fra Guillem Escriba, a known disciple of Olivi, represent minor, or long past, occurrences infused with sinister new meaning by the doubt and suspicion engendered in an inquisitorial context. Despite very occasional contacts with slightly heterodox figures, the tertiaries appear to have been a relatively peaceful small community, well integrated into the social strata of Vilafranca, with a strong relationship with the local friars, who are frequently mentioned in roles overseeing, preaching to and caring for the community.[21] The town was not entirely without religious conflict: the Franciscan friars themselves had a contentious relationship with the local parish clergy, and the bishop's register records recurring clashes with the parish clergy over burial rights and other sinecures as early as 1306.[22] There is also evidence that they had some connections with travelling friars with Olivian leanings (see below). However, there is no evidence to suggest that the tertiaries were under suspicion of heresy, or had any reason to anticipate an inquest. But then, in the spring of 1345, the

---

[20] The Kingdom of Naples was then under the rule of Robert of Anjou and his wife Sancha, a Mallorcan princess related to the Aragonese royal family. Like Aragon, it has been identified as a destination for religious dissidents and refugees: Ronald Musto, 'Franciscan Joachimism at the Court of Naples, 1309–1345: A New Appraisal', *AFH* 90 (1997), 419–86, at 422, 483.

[21] Perarnau i Espelt, *Beguins de Vilafranca*, 27–41.

[22] The incident is recorded in the episcopal register for the diocese of Barcelona: Barcelona, Arxiu Diocesà, Register Communium VI, fols 122^r–^{v}, 140^r–^{v}. For details of the heretical preaching of local Franciscan Pere Mercer, see ibid., fol. 122^v. On conflict between Catalonian parish clergy and Franciscan houses, including those of Vilafranca, see Jill Webster, 'Unlocking Lost Archives: Medieval Franciscan Catalan Communities', *Catholic Historical Review* 66 (1980), 537–50, at 540–3.

Italian tertiary Francesc Joan arrived at the house, and within a year, everything had changed.

On 13 June 1345, the bishop of Barcelona prohibited the community from receiving pecuniary alms.[23] That same year, on the feast days of St Louis of Toulouse (19 August) and St Francis of Assisi (8 October), a Franciscan friar addressed this pressing issue of the right to collect alms, referring to one of the final papal bulls of the poverty controversy, *Cum inter nonnullos*.[24] A week after the October sermon, the newest member of the group, Francesc Joan, approached the lector of the Franciscan convent, who supervised the tertiaries. At the inquest, the lector testified that Francesc Joan had expressed concern over what he perceived to be an Olivian tone in the two sermons' treatment of the topic of alms and poverty, raising the spectre of heretical teaching. The day after Francesc Joan's complaint, the lector gathered the tertiaries to warn them regarding the heresy of Olivian teachings: the aftermath of that meeting was the explosive brawl in the community garden with which this essay began. In his testimony Brother Raymond Cuch provided a vivid description of the conflict, and also described how afterwards Francesc Joan demanded money in exchange for leaving the tertiaries' house.[25]

Clearly fed up with the entire affair, the brawling brother Domènec denounced Francesc Joan to the local authorities for robbery.[26] Not one to back down from a fight, Francesc Joan in turn denounced the entire community, and the case was forwarded to the bishop. Moving the conflict into the legal realm does not appear to have cooled tempers – or perhaps this community, like the local friars and parish clergy, was particularly given to outbreaks of violence. During the first week of depositions, at the beginning of December, Sister Francesca was charged with physically assaulting Francesc Joan: the

---

[23] Perarnau i Espelt, *Beguins de Vilafranca*, 149–52, contains an excellent chronological summary of events, with corresponding document references.

[24] Ibid. 28–30, 44, 149. Louis of Toulouse, a relative by marriage of the Aragonese royal family, spent part of his youth as a hostage at the Aragonese court. He subsequently renounced the throne of Naples and became a Franciscan, and his family made him a bishop and later promoted his rapid canonization. Despite his royal connections, his ascetic lifestyle was reminiscent of the goals of the Spiritual Franciscans: Margaret Toynbee, *S. Louis of Toulouse* (Manchester, 1929); Edith Pasztor, *Per la storia di S. Ludovico d'Angio* (Rome, 1955); Jacques Paul, 'Saint-Louis d'Anjou, franciscain et évêque de Toulouse (1274–1297)', in *Les Évêques, les clercs et le roi (1250–1300)*, Cahiers de Fanjeaux 7 (Fanjeaux, 1972), 59–90.

[25] Perarnau i Espelt, *Beguins de Vilafranca*, 49–50.

[26] Ibid. 44.

charges were serious enough that she was imprisoned for some days, bailed in mid-December, and only cleared after the end of the proceedings in March.[27] Over the course of the depositions, details from previous decades emerged that show the tertiaries were not entirely without interest in the poverty controversy, or Olivi's teachings. A sibling pair from the community testified that they had intended to travel to Naples and seek more 'free and intensely Franciscan' communities, almost certainly a reference to the same hermitages and refuges to which the defeated Spiritual Franciscans had fled in the 1320s. Together with their apparent knowledge of the writings of Olivi, this suggests an interest in heretical beguin circles at least on the part of a few members of the community, but no concerted effort to learn or teach his doctrines.[28]

Even though the majority of the community were cleared of the charges, and Francesc Joan was presumably expelled from the community, the exposure of their internal convulsions and doubts regarding each other's orthodoxy had major consequences. The bishop of Barcelona issued a ruling, couched in strong language, that from Passion Sunday, 2 April 1346, male and female beguins or tertiaries within the diocese were no longer to hold houses in common, gather in private or beg.[29] The decision broke the little community: several of the female tertiaries are soon afterwards found entering local convents.[30]

It is clear from the testimonies that, despite the eventual verdict of innocence, there was cause to believe that some in the community

---

[27] Ibid. 128, referring now to Barcelona, Arxiu Diocesà, NC 14, fol. 14ᵛ (16 December 1345): 'Petrus de Pocha sanch, civis Barchinone, manulevavit a reverendo in Christo patre, domino episcopo … sororem Franciscam, de tercia regula, que capta detinebatur pretextu cuiusdam violencie, quam, uti dicitur, intulit fratri Francisco Iohannis, de dicta regula' ('Peter of Pocha sanch, citizen of Barcelona, frees by surety from the reverend in Christ father, the lord bishop … sister Francesca of the Third Order, who was held on the pretext of some sort of violence which, it is said, she inflicted upon Francesc Joan, of the said Order'); ibid. (4 March 1346): 'Fuit cancellata predicta manleuta de mandato dicti domini episcopi, de voluntate predicti fratris Francisci Iohannis' ('The aforementioned surety was ended by the order of the said lord bishop, by the wish of the aforementioned brother Francesc Joan').

[28] Perarnau i Espelt, *Beguins de Vilafranca*, 93–103, 115–17, 154–5, 160. On Naples, see n. 22 above.

[29] Ibid. 135–6.

[30] Josep Perarnau i Espelt, 'El bisbe de Barcelona fra Bernat Oliver (1345–1346) i els framenors de Vilafranca del Penedès. Un episodi de la "Qüestió franciscana" a Catalunya', *Estudios Franciscanos* 83 (1982), 277–306.

held Olivian views, an example of how blurred the lines could be between beguins, tertiaries and penitents. But the circumstances of the inquest also illustrate how larger events might encourage lingering doubts, providing ground for fear of heretical identification to be fertilized by common conflict. Here heated words, spat out in the course of more mundane events and then taken too far, were more the result of pervasive doubt that took easy hold than of deep-rooted heretical beliefs.

The story could conclude here, and one would be forgiven for chalking up Francesc Joan's accusations and his extortion demands to the actions of an overzealous and greedy troublemaker, or a dedicated and orthodox tertiary troubled by his new surroundings. But other sources present a different possible reading. Only a few short months after the Vilafranca inquest concluded, the episcopal register in the neighbouring diocese of Girona recorded an accusation of heresy made against that city's tertiaries, by a newcomer named Francesc Joan.[31] Girona was a known site of beguin activity, and the town where one of the twinned inquests into the correspondents Bernat and Guillem had been held in 1325. Together with the more complete records of Vilafranca, this evidence throws the use and abuse of doubt in the poverty controversy aftermath into even starker relief.

The source from Girona is very brief, only a dozen lines of text, but it presents a rough version of events eerily similar to those that had occurred in Vilafranca the previous winter. A tertiary and priest named Francesc Joan entered the local group and was soon refusing them the sacraments, accusing them of heresy. The similarities are striking: an accuser with the same name, making the same accusations against two identical groups in relatively close proximity, within the space of only a few months. It could very well be a coincidence: after all, Francesc Joan is not an uncommon name, and Girona was a known site of beguin activity. But I suggest an alternative reading: Francesc Joan found it either ideologically or financially profitable to exploit anxieties left over from the poverty controversy. He was able to manipulate events by joining vulnerable tertiary groups, ratcheting up internal tensions by pointing out possible heresies, and then threatening to expose them for prosecution unless they paid him off. The more detailed inquest records in Vilafranca lay out his scheme in full, including his demands for bribery, and the fact that he made

---

[31] Girona, Arxiu Diocesà, Lletres Episcopals, U–10, fols 69^r–^{v} (26 June 1346).

himself so abhorrent to his fellow tertiaries that several physically assaulted him on more than one occasion: recall the unlucky Sister Francesca.

The interloper who accused the Girona and Vilafranca tertiaries of heresy may have been one and the same person, or two persons with a rather common name. But it is the reverberations of the reactions of both the tertiaries and the bishops which tell us most about the potency of doubt in the long aftermath of a heretical movement. With the memories of beguin trials and burnings still fresh, it is no wonder that the Vilafrancan tertiaries were determined to fight to defend their reputation. Even twenty-five years after *Sancta Romana* had blackened the reputation of beguins and pious penitents, tertiaries were willing to sue, to pay, or even to commit acts of physical violence to rid themselves of the taint of doubt.

The Doubting Augustine: The Deletion of Monica from Fourteenth-Century *Vitae Augustini* in the Augustinian Order of Hermits

Anik Laferrière*

Keble College, Oxford

This study examines the erasure of Monica in five hagiographies of Augustine written by the Order of Hermits of St Augustine in the fourteenth century. It investigates how the character of Monica functions as a foil to Augustine's religious doubt in his Confessions *and why that emphasis was problematic for the Augustinian Hermits. The essay will demonstrate that the presence of Monica was incompatible with the hermits' desire to showcase Augustine's eremitism as the cornerstone of his religious practice. In order to emphasize Augustine's devotion to the eremitical life, the hermits denied any substantial presence to Monica, who was a problematic reminder both of Augustine's doubt about monasticism and of the hermits' doubts about the legitimacy of their parentage. This study explores the hermits' doubt about the role of Monica in Augustine's religious formation, and how that doubt was indicative of their institutionalized way of looking at their faith.*

During a span of twenty years in the early fourteenth century, five hermits of the *Ordo Eremitarum Sancti Augustini* [hereafter: OESA] produced five hagiographical texts detailing the life of their putative founder, St Augustine of Hippo, in order to demonstrate their order's foundation by the North African Church Father. While these texts display familiarity with Augustine's *Confessions*, his own autobiographical reflection on his life, they present a character strikingly different in religious expression from Augustine's portrayal of himself. In particular, the hermits' utter disregard for the presence and significance of his mother Monica in the tale of his life is conspicuous, flattening the story and removing the gendered complexity found in Augustine's original words. Monica, the only woman to be referred to by name in the *Confessions*, appears in Augustine's own account at every important stage in his life, featuring as a constant source of

*Keble College, Parks Rd, Oxford, OX1 3PG. E-mail: anik.laferriere@keble.ox.ac.uk.

Studies in Church History 52 (2016) 150–163   © Ecclesiastical History Society 2016
doi: 10.1017/stc.2015.9

spiritual guidance. Although her portrayal in the *Confessions* is fraught with ambiguity and her actions have often been interpreted as intrusive, his acclamation of her religious goodness, equated with virtue, paints a complex image of a woman who held a significant role in his religious formation.

This essay will argue that the Augustinian Hermits eliminated Monica from their depictions of the life of Augustine because they viewed her as a problematic reminder not only of Augustine's religious doubt but also of their own doubt regarding the validity of their Augustinian parentage. The fourteenth-century texts were created at a time when the OESA's own connection to Augustine was in question, and thus represented Augustine as the perfect example of the monastic life to which the hermits aspired, legitimizing their claims to be the *true* and *only* sons of Augustine.[1]

The hermits' deletion of Monica reflects a concern about the presence of Augustine's religious doubt within the narrative of the *Confessions* and stresses the importance of constancy in commitment to the eremitical life. Whereas in the *Confessions* Monica offers spiritual guidance to Augustine when he finds himself lacking faith, in the late medieval texts her absence is accompanied by the absence of his doubt. Instead, the constancy of his monastic vocation is asserted. I argue that the possibility that Augustine doubted his religious and monastic vocation carried with it implications for the hermits' own religious lineage, for it would implicitly have cast doubt upon their interpretation of the Augustinian lifestyle. It was in an effort to depict Augustine as the archetypal hermit that these hermit writers extinguished the colourful, enigmatic, but always supportive character of Monica. While she appears in texts written by other members of the order and in works of art painted for their churches in this period, in this series of texts, designed for the purpose of explicating the life of Augustine, she disappears, suggesting that this omission was a conscious choice.

---

[1] An example of this kind of language can be found in Verdun, Bibliothèque publique, MS 41, Henry of Friemar, 'Tractatus de origine et progressu Ordinis Fratrum Eremitarum S. Augustini', saec. XIV, fols 144^r–150^r. This text is also found in an edition by Rudolph Arbesmann: Henricus de Frimaria, *Tractatus de origine et progressu Ordinis Fratrum Heremitarum Sancti Augustini*, ed. Rudolph Arbesmann as 'Henry of Friemar's *Treatise on the Origin and Development of the Order of the Hermit Friars and its True and Real Title*', *Augustiniana* 6 (1956), 37–145.

PREVIOUS SCHOLARSHIP AND THE AUGUSTINIAN ORDER

The Augustinian Hermits found prominence in the late Middle Ages, transforming themselves from an eremitical to a mendicant order,[2] achieving distinction in the universities and maintaining involvement in active preaching in the cities.[3] While they were to maintain that their order was descended from eremitical communities founded directly by Augustine of Hippo, they were institutionalized as a single order only in 1256 by a papal fiat of Alexander IV, who united several eremitical groups under the Ordo Eremitarum Sancti Augustini.[4] Since the creation of any new religious orders had been restricted by the Fourth Lateran Council in 1215, Alexander's fiat, *Licet ecclesiae catholicae*, authenticated their origins as predating the council, which would prove useful again when the Second Council of Lyon (1274) sought to minimize further the proliferation of religious orders.

Recent work by Eric Saak has reinvigorated study of the OESA by examining the Augustinian myth characterized by the five hagiographical texts which form the basis for this essay.[5] Saak has focused primarily on the religio-political context in which the hermits developed their concept of Augustinianism, arguing that the order was modelled on a newly developed hagiographical image of Augustine, but otherwise neglecting the devotional and religious importance of the saint for the OESA. This essay's focus on the exemplarity of Augustine and on the hermits' seeming reluctance to associate doubt with Augustine goes some way towards redressing this balance.

---

[2] Frances Andrews, *The Other Friars: The Carmelites, Augustinians, Sack and Pied Friars in the Middle Ages* (Cambridge, 2006), 69.

[3] William J. Courtenay, *Schools and Scholars in Fourteenth-Century England* (Princeton, NJ, 1987), 72.

[4] Eric L. Saak, *High Way to Heaven: The Augustinian Platform between Reform and Reformation, 1292–1524*, Studies in Medieval and Reformation Thought 89 (Leiden, 2002), 5.

[5] See E[ric]. L. Saak, *Creating Augustine: Interpreting Augustine and Augustinianism in the Later Middle Ages* (Oxford, 2012); idem, 'Religio Augustini: Jordan of Quedlinburg and the Augustinian Tradition in Late Medieval Germany' (PhD dissertation, University of Arizona, 1993); idem, 'Quilibet Christianus: Saints in Society in the Sermons of Jordan of Quedlinburg, OESA', in Beverly Mayne Kienzle et al., eds, *Models of Holiness in Medieval Sermons: Proceedings of the International Symposium, Kalamazoo, 4–7 May 1995*, Textes et études du Moyen Âge 5 (Louvain-la-Neuve, 1996), 317–38; idem, 'The Reception of Augustine in the Later Middle Ages', in Irena Backus, ed., *The Reception of the Church Fathers in the West: From the Carolingians to the Maurists*, 2 vols (Leiden, 1997), 1: 367–404; idem, 'The Creation of an Augustinian Identity in the Later Middle Ages', *Augustiniana* 49 (1999), 109–64, 251–86; idem, 'Milleloquium Sancti Augustini', in Allan D. Fitzgerald, ed., *Augustine through the Ages: An Encyclopedia* (Grand Rapids, MI: 1999), 563; idem, *High Way to Heaven*.

Apart from Saak's seminal studies, the five hagiographical texts considered here have not received extensive analysis. Articles by Rudolph Arbesmann and Balbino Rano remain, to date, the authoritative studies of these fourteenth-century texts,[6] along with scanty references in the work of Winfridus Hümpfner, Marjorie Reeves and Katherine Walsh.[7] However, while these texts have received little theological or literary examination, they have found prominence in art historical studies,[8] particularly those of Louise Bourdua and Diane Cole Ahl,[9] which have remarked upon the hermits' depiction of Augustine in eremitical garb and the scenes describing his composition of the monastic rule. While this scholarship has fruitfully examined

[6] Arbesmann, ed., 'Henry of Friemar's *Treatise*'; idem, 'Jordanus of Saxony's *Vita S. Augustini*: The Source for John Capgrave's *Life of St Augustine*', *Traditio* 1 (1943), 341–53; idem, 'A Legendary of Early Augustinian Saints', *Analecta Augustiniana* 29 (1966), 5–58; idem, 'The *Vita Aurelii Augustini Hipponensis episcopi* in Cod. Laurent. Plut. 90 Sup. 48', *Traditio* 18 (1962), 319–55; Balbino Rano, 'Las dos primeras obras conocidas sobre el origen de la Orden Augustiniana', *Analecta Augustiniana* 45 (1982), 331–76; idem, 'San Agustín y los orígenes de su orden. Reglo, monasterio de Tagaste y *Sermones ad fratres in eremo*', *La Ciudad de Dios* 200 (1987), 649–727.]

[7] Winfridus Hümpfner, 'Introduction' to *Jordani de Saxonia Liber vitasfratrum*, ed. idem and Rudolph Arbesmann, Cassiciacum 1 (New York, 1943), lxxvi–lxxviii; Marjorie Reeves, *The Influence of Prophecy in the Later Middle Ages: A Study in Joachimism* (Oxford, 1969); Katherine J. Walsh, 'Wie ein Bettelorden zu (s)einem Gründer kam. Fingierte Traditionen um die Entstehung der Augustiner-Eremiten', in *Fälschungen im Mittelalter. Internationaler Kongreß der Monumenta Germaniae Historica München, 16.–19. September 1986*, MGH Schriften 33/v, 585–610.

[8] Examples include J. Courcelle and P. Courcelle, *Iconographie de Saint Augustin. Les Cycles du XIV* siècle* (Paris, 1965); eidem, *Iconographie de Saint Augustin. Les Cycles du XV* siècle* (Paris, 1969); S. Bettini and L. Puppi, *La chiesa degli Eremitani di Padova* (Vicenza, 1970); D. Blume and D. Hansen, 'Agostino pater e praeceptor di un nuovo ordine religioso (considerazioni sulla propaganda illustrata degli eremiti agostiniani)', in *Arte e spiritualità negli ordini mendicanti. Gli Agostiniani e il cappellone di S. Nicola a Tolentino* (Rome, 1992), 79–91; Cordelia Warr, 'Hermits, Habits and History: The Dress of the Augustinian Hermits', Janis Elliott, 'Augustine and the New Augustinianism in the Choir Frescoes of the Eremitani, Padua', Donal Cooper, 'St Augustine's Ecstasy before the Trinity in the Art of the Hermits, *c*.1360–1440', in Louise Bourdua and Anne Dunlop, eds, *Art and the Augustinian Order in Early Renaissance Italy* (Aldershot, 2007), 17–28, 99–126, 183–204 respectively. Important works of Augustinian iconography have been published by the contemporary Augustinian Order, notably in the volumes *Per corporalia ad incorporalia. Spiritualità, agiografia, iconografia e architettura nel medioevo agostiniano* (Tolentino, 2000); *Arte e spiritualità negli ordini mendicanti.*

[9] Louise Bourdua, '*De origine et progressu ordinis fratrum heremitarum*: Guariento and the Eremitani in Padua', *Papers of the British School at Rome* 66 (1998), 177–92; eadem, 'Entombing the Founder St Augustine of Hippo', in eadem and Dunlop, eds, *Art and the Augustinian Order*, 29–50; D. Cole Ahl, 'Benozzo Gozzoli's Frescoes of the Life of Saint Augustine in San Gimignano: Their Meaning in Context', *Artibus et Historiae* 7 (1986), 35–53.

the visual depiction of the origins of the OESA, there has been no discussion of the use of Augustine as a religious exemplar. Specifically, the absence of Monica within these late medieval accounts of Augustine's life has hitherto gone unnoticed.

The Augustinian Hermits' claim to descend from Augustine was challenged publicly in a conflict triggered by John XXII's bull *Veneranda Sanctorum* of 1327.[10] John had granted the hermits privileges, allowing them to share the Pavian church of San Pietro Ciel d'Oro, the home of Augustine's alleged relics, with the Augustinian Canons Regular, who had previously held exclusive rights to it.[11] In the ensuing conflict, both orders petitioned the pope directly, denigrating the other's Augustinianism in the process. In 1331 Cardinal Bertrand del Poggetto, who had been appointed by the pope to execute the bull, formally gave custody of Augustine's relics to the hermits, who had successfully defended their claim to unique and exclusive Augustinianism.[12]

The hermits who wrote these five hagiographies of Augustine each sought to establish Augustine's foundation of the OESA and thus, according to Louise Bourdua, 'gradually intensified their order's corporate identity as the "true" descendants of St Augustine'.[13] This reveals both the wider intention and the anticipated readership of these hagiographies: against the backdrop of the conflict surrounding the legitimacy of their descent from Augustine, the motivation for writing can only have been to demonstrate their Augustinianism. The texts display antagonism to other Augustinian orders, specifically the canons, casting doubts on the latter's claim to the legacy of Augustine and exalting the status of the hermits as unique and privileged. They were intended to demonstrate that Augustine had observed a pattern of the monastic life which the hermits had precisely and accurately maintained.

[10] This conflict is examined thoroughly in Kaspar Elm, 'Augustinus canonicus – Augustinus Eremita. A Quattrocento cause célèbre', in Timothy Verdon and John Henderson, eds, *Christianity and the Renaissance: Image and Religious Imagination in the Quattrocento* (Syracuse, NY, 1990), 84–107. See also Sharon Dale, 'A House Divided: San Pietro in Ciel d'Oro in Pavia and the Politics of Pope John XXII', *JMedH* 27 (2001), 55–77, at 56; Saak, *High Way to Heaven*, 164.

[11] John XXII's grants to the OESA are documented in *Codex Diplomaticus Ordinis Eremitarum Sancti Augustini Papiae*, ed. Rodolfo Maiocchi and Naz Casacca, 3 vols (Pavia, 1905–7), especially 1: 15. See also Saak, *High Way to Heaven*, 160.

[12] *Codex Diplomaticus*, ed. Maiocchi and Casacca, 1: 14.

[13] Bourdua, '*De origine et progressu ordinis fratrum heremitarum*', 178.

This polemical purpose excludes one possibility for the hermits' deletion of Monica, namely, that she might have been removed out of a concern for female spirituality and that her erasure served to discourage those who sought a female exemplar in her. The intended readership of these texts is implied by this function: the texts were directed to the hermits themselves, to help in defending the legitimacy of their order, or to the Canons Regular, in order to attack the canons' claims that they, and not the hermits, were the order genuinely founded by Augustine. While the removal of Monica may indicate some degree of dismissal of the validity of female spirituality, the readership was exclusively male and the texts were not aimed at female monastics. Monica's exclusion is much more convincingly read as buttressing the hermits' narrowed definition of Augustine's religious experiences, excluding doubt.

Monica and Augustine's Doubt in the *Confessions*

Earlier interpreters of the *Confessions* generally adopted an unflattering view of Monica, taking their cues from the passages in which Augustine finds her to have been interfering and overbearing.[14]   Recently, however, scholars including Rosemary Radford Ruether, Anne-Marie Bowery, Leo Ferrari, Elizabeth Clark, Virginia Burrus, Catherine Keller, Rosemary Rader and Silvia Benso have sought to rehabilitate Monica and imbue her character with religious significance.[15] In response to their work, there have been discussions of the analogy made by Augustine between his mother Monica and

[14] Examples include Robert Ottley, *Studies in the Confessions of St Augustine* (London, 1919), 5; Muriel Spark, 'St Monica', *The Month* 17 (1957), 309–20, at 310; Carl Levenson, 'Distance and Presence in Augustine's Confessions', *Journal of Religion* 65 (1985), 500–12, at 505; Eric J. Ziolkowski, 'St Augustine: Aeneas' Antitype, Monica's Boy', *Literature and Theology* 9 (1995), 1–23, at 3.

[15] Rosemary Radford Ruether, 'Augustine: Sexuality, Gender and Women', Anne-Marie Bowery, 'Monica: The Feminine Face of Christ', Virginia Burrus and Catherine Keller, 'Confessing Monica', in Judith Chelius Stark, ed., *Feminist Interpretations of Augustine* (University Park, PA, 2007), 47–67, 69–95, 119–45 respectively; Leo Ferrari, 'Monica on the Wooden Ruler', *Augustinian Studies* 6 (1975), 193–205; Elizabeth A. Clark, 'Holy Women, Holy Words: Early Christian Women, Social History, and the "Linguistic Turn"', *JECS* 6 (1998), 413–30; Rosemary Rader, *Breaking Boundaries: Male/Female Friendship in Early Christian Communities* (New York, 1983); Silvia Benso, 'Monica's Grin of Tension', in Carl G. Vaught, ed., *Contemporary Themes in Augustine's Confessions: Part II, Contemporary Philosophy* 15/2 (1993), 5–10.

the Mother Church,[16] the redemptive powers associated with Monica's tears,[17] and her mediating function, as she becomes Christlike in her faith.[18]

The wealth of discussion surrounding the religious function of Monica has alerted readers to the significance of her presence in Augustine's religious journey. Anne-Marie Bowery reads Augustine's portrayal of his passage to Christianity as one in which he becomes increasingly like Monica,[19] while Monica symbolically becomes male, 'in the clothing of a woman but with a virile faith' (*Matre adhaerente nobis mulieris habitu, virile fide*).[20] Her role as Augustine's biological mother is overtaken by her role as his spiritual mother: she remains the constant force exhorting him to place his faith in God. As Colin Starnes observes, 'Augustine always speaks of his baptism as a rebirth and … refers to Ambrose and Monica, respectively, as the father and mother of his second birth.'[21]

Having acknowledged the importance of Monica in Augustine's religious journey, it is possible to trace parallels between his physical distance from Monica and his spiritual distance from, and doubt of, God. In Book 1 of the *Confessions*, it is Monica who insists that God is Augustine's true father, and who is the first means by which he is introduced to God.[22] She is aware of the temptations that await him,[23] and banishes him from her home when he becomes a Manichee.[24] In Book 5, when Augustine becomes disillusioned with Faustus, he attributes this change not only to God but also to the blood of Monica's heart, recalling the redemptive power of the blood of Christ.[25] When he abandons his mother for Rome, he realizes retrospectively that he experienced there a false felicity.[26] After the miraculous conversion in Valerius's garden and his entrance into the

---

[16] Bowery, 'Monica: The Feminine Face of Christ', 75.
[17] Ferrari, 'Monica on the Wooden Ruler'; see also, in this volume, Kimberley-Joy Knight, 'Lachrymose Holiness and the Problem of Doubt in Thirteenth- and Fourteenth-Century Hagiographies', 122–38.
[18] Benso, 'Monica's Grin of Tension', 8.
[19] Bowery, 'Monica: The Feminine Face of Christ', 80.
[20] Augustine, *Confessions* 9.4.8 (ed. and transl. by Henry Chadwick [Oxford, 1991], 160).
[21] Colin Starnes, *Augustine's Conversion: A Guide to the Argument of Confessions I–IX* (Kitchener, ON, 1990), 129.
[22] Augustine, *Confessions* 1.11.17.
[23] Ibid. 1.11.18.
[24] Ibid. 3.11.19.
[25] Ibid. 5.7.13.
[26] Ibid. 5.8.14–15.

house of God, Augustine physically enters a house that he connects only to Monica. Overlooking the garden, she has symbolically overseen the entire event.[27] Augustine's description of Lady Continence in Book 8 as a serene, cheerful and fruitful mother, with the Lord as her husband, also bears noteworthy similarity to his descriptions of Monica.[28] His account of his grief at her death is perhaps the most striking, as he weeps uncontrollably once he finds some solitude.[29]

Monica features as a figure of spiritual guidance and reassurance for Augustine. She is a woman who experiences holiness without the philosophical education enjoyed by her son. Thus, as Kim Power argues, Monica represents an alternative model of spirituality that causes Augustine to reconsider the place and value of philosophy.[30] In Valerius's garden, Augustine laments to Alypius that 'uneducated people are rising up and capturing heaven and we with our high culture without any heart – see where we roll in the mud of flesh and blood!'[31] The unlettered form a counterpoint to Augustine's intellectualization of God, demonstrating to the reader that the way to God is one of faith, and not necessarily one of understanding. Monica is the best exemplar of this, remaining faithful in her devotion to God throughout her life, even though she does not understand the philosophical difficulties Augustine encounters on his road to conversion. Ultimately, it is an emotional and mystical religious experience that converts him and not a rational argument, and this culminates at Ostia, where Augustine and Monica share a vision of God.[32]

While Monica differs starkly from the well-educated Augustine, she also offers an example of constancy, never doubting her faith in God. She is essential to Augustine's account of his spiritual peregrinations, as it is through her censures and lamentations that the reader becomes acquainted with Augustine's distance from God. When Augustine steals fruit as a child, maintains inappropriate sexual relationships, finds spiritual solace in classical philosophy or Manichaeism, leaves for Rome in search of temporal success, and is unable to overcome his difficulties in accepting Christianity, it is Monica who

---

[27] Bowery, 'Monica: The Feminine Face of Christ', 85; cf. Augustine, *Confessions* 8.12.30.

[28] Bowery, 'Monica: The Feminine Face of Christ', 85; cf. Augustine, *Confessions* 8.11.27.

[29] Augustine, *Confessions* 9.12.30.

[30] Kim Power, *Veiled Desire: Augustine's Writing on Women* (London, 1995), 71–93.

[31] 'Surgunt indocti et caelum rapiunt, et nos cum doctrinis nostris sine corde, ecce ubi voluntamur in carne et sanguine!': Augustine, *Confessions* 8.8.19.

[32] Ibid. 9.10.23–6.

reproaches him for his doubt and sinful behaviour.[33] When he embraces faith, it is Monica whom he tells of his conversion and she with whom he experiences a vision of God at Ostia.[34] Through her example, Augustine is led to Christ and overcomes his doubt.

MONICA AND THE AUGUSTINIAN HERMITS

Augustine's depiction of Monica is all the more noteworthy when compared to her treatment (or the lack of it) in the five medieval texts written by Augustinian Hermits. In the first, the anonymous *Vita Aurelii Augustini Hipponensis episcopi* written between 1322 and 1331,[35] Monica is conspicuously absent from the narrative. The *Vita*'s only reference to her is to affirm that many religious men and women gathered to mourn her at her death.[36]

The second text, the *Initium sive processus Ordinis heremitarum sancti Augustini* (1330),[37] contains the same observation – that many

---

[33] For the theft of the pears, see ibid. 2.4.9. This is contrasted with Augustine's many references to Monica in the section on his infancy and youth as having already found God, such as when he describes his mother as having nourished him in the womb when he was sinful (1.7.12), or his comparison of the piety of his mother to the Church, which he describes as the mother of us all: 2.11.17. Monica fears for Augustine when he reaches sexual maturity and implores him not to act upon that maturity; Augustine dismisses her concerns as 'womanish counsels' and endeavours to keep up with the sexual exploits of his adolescent friends: 2.3.6–7. Augustine discusses his concubine and initially unwanted son with her at the beginning of Book 4, and sends her away in order to prepare for marriage to a Roman girl: 6.15.25. This follows a discussion about the lengths to which Monica went in order to arrange his marriage, so as to offer him a legitimate place to express his sexuality: 6.13.23. Augustine recalls how he was attracted to the philosophy of Cicero, particularly in the *Hortensius*, in spite of his mother's attempts to nourish him with the love of Christ: 3.4.8. He becomes a Manichee in Book 4, and describes his mother's weeping for his soul at length: 3.11.19–20. Monica begs Augustine not to go to Rome, or at least to allow her to accompany him; he deceives her and leaves in the night while she is asleep: 5.8.15. For examples of Augustine struggling to accept Christianity in his heart even though he had already rationally accepted the truth of Christ, see 8.11.25–7. In particular, he has difficulty letting go of his lustful desires, in spite of Monica's continued counsels on the subject.

[34] Augustine experiences a mystical conversion under the fig tree in Valerius's garden in Book 8. He tells his mother of his '*tolle lege*' experience and she rejoices: 8.12.30. For Augustine's vision at Ostia with Monica, the experience which marks his full acceptance of Christ and commitment to his faith, see note 32 above.

[35] Florence, Biblioteca Laurenziana, MS Plut. 90. Sup. 48, fols 1ʳ–13ʳ; see Arbesmann, 'The *Vita*', 320.

[36] MS Plut. 90. Sup. 48, fol. 7ʳ.

[37] Rano, 'Las dos primeras obras', 337. This work appears in the same manuscript as the *Vita Aurelii Augustini Hipponensis episcopi*, MS Plut. 90, Sup. 48.

religious men came to Monica's funeral[38] – but the author also comments that Evodius, one of Augustine's companions, sang at her death.[39] Moreover, the author remarks that '[Augustine's] mother rejoiced with him before the time of calm, because she saw him not only as a faithful Christian but even as a servant of God'.[40] In this use of the term *servus Dei*, generally adopted by Augustine to signify a monk,[41] the author seems to emphasize that Augustine converted not just to Christianity, but more specifically to a monastic – and by implication ascetic – form of Christianity, making a direct connection between Monica's rejoicing and Augustine's monasticism.

The third text, the *Sermo de beato Augustino* by Nicholas of Alessandria, from the mid-1330s,[42] was based upon the *Initium* and includes exactly the same references to Monica, supplemented by an additional reference to her as '[Augustine's] pious mother' (*pia matre*).[43] Nicholas gives no description or account of Monica's death except to say that Augustine was thirty-three at the time and that many hermits came to her funeral.[44] Similarly, Henry of Friemar, in his *Tractatus de origine et progressu Ordinis fratrum heremitarum sancti Augustini et vero ac proprio titulo eiusdem*, written in 1334 at the end of his career,[45] notes only the

---

[38] Ibid., fol. 38ᵛ.

[39] Ibid.

[40] 'Mater sua ante tempus quietationis eidem congratulabatur, quod non tantum fidelem christianum eum videbat, sed etiam Dei servum': ibid., fol. 58ᵛ.

[41] Van der Lof remarks that there were three ways in which Augustine used the term *servus Dei*, the development of which mirrors ecclesiastical developments in Augustine's time. Initially, Augustine appears to have used the term simply to mean any member of Christendom. As the concept of eremitism and monasticism grew, it evolved to signify a brotherhood of a special few, who practised a genre of asceticism in the search of religious perfection. Finally, after having founded a monastery in Hippo, he used the term to mean specifically those living a monastic life: L. J. van der Lof, 'The Threefold Meaning of *Servi Dei* in the Writings of Saint Augustine', *Augustinian Studies* 12 (1981), 43–59, at 56. Zumkeller also argues that Augustine's usage of the words *servire Deo* implied the goals of the monastic life and that *servus Dei* was increasingly used to mean 'monk' over any previous connotations. He found over seventy-five instances in Augustine's writings of *servus Dei* or *servire Deo* being so used: Adolar Zumkeller, *Das Mönchtum des heiligen Augustinus*, Cassiciacum 11, 2nd edn (Würzburg, 1968), 158.

[42] Prague, Clementum, Metropolitan Chapter Library, MS Metr. Kap. 812, fols 35ᵛ–40ʳ. This tentative dating is supplied by Saak (*High Way to Heaven*, 201), who uses Nicholas of Alessandria's involvement in the proceedings between the canons and the hermits as the motivation behind his authorship. An edition of this text appeared in Rano, 'Las dos primeras obras', 352–76.

[43] MS Metr. Kap. 812, fol. 38ʳ.

[44] Ibid.

[45] Saak, *High Way to Heaven*, 209.

death – and nothing of the life – of Monica, and does so almost as an afterthought, not as an event integral to Augustine's story. The first mention of her by name states that she was buried in Ostia, rather than with her husband in Africa. Augustine's grief is not described, and Henry attributes no significance to her death except to say that thereafter Augustine went to live in Tuscany with the hermits of Simplicianus for two years.

Jordan of Quedlinburg's text, the *Vita sancti Augustini*, from the late 1330s,[46] treats Monica in a rather different way. Using the *Confessions* and the pseudo-Augustinian *Sermones ad fratres suos in heremo* as direct sources,[47] Jordan includes much more of Augustine's account of his mother's influence. Jordan's first reference to Monica is as 'the most Christian woman' (*christianissima*),[48] and he notes Monica's admonitions of Augustine for his behaviour, but also that Augustine did not obey her counsels. He includes many of the instances of Monica's appearances in the *Confessions*, such as the episode of the wooden ruler, in which Monica is told by a mysterious figure that wherever she is, so too will Augustine be. Jordan also includes her lament at her son's perdition, such as when he leaves for Rome without her; and the circumstances surrounding her death.[49] However, whilst Jordan portrays her positively overall, his characterization of Monica lacks the complexity of the woman described in the *Confessions*, not least because he does not reproduce Augustine's long reflections on her piety and goodness. His is a superficial depiction, exploring little of her emotional impact on Augustine and lacking the imagery associated with the Church, Christ or a model Christian.

With the reduction of the role of Monica within these texts, Augustine's early experiences with sin and doubt are also significantly diminished. What had been an essential part of Augustine's own narrative, namely, his struggle with sin before his conversion, replete with theft, heresy and lust, is ignored in all five fourteenth-century texts.

---

[46] Paris, Biblothèque de l'Arsenal, MS 251, fols 1rb–104^{v}; cf. Arbesmann, 'Jordanus of Saxony's *Vita S. Augustini*'. There has been some debate regarding the date of authorship of this text, with Hümpfner assigning it a date of 1319–22: 'Introduction', xxiv; whereas Walsh has argued for the late 1330s, as it was at that time that Jordan was working with Henry of Friemar: 'Wie ein Bettelorden zu (s)einem Gründer kam', 593. The latter dating has generally found more acceptance.

[47] MS 251, fol. 54rb.

[48] Ibid.

[49] Ibid., fol. 54vb. For Augustine's departure for Rome and Monica's death, see ibid., fols 56ra, 61rb respectively.

Moreover, only one – Jordan of Quedlinburg's *Vita sancti Augustini* – even mentions Augustine's miraculous conversion, the event that forms the apex of the *Confessions*. These hermits portrayed Augustine's life as one of religious constancy by eliminating those problematic episodes, which took place primarily in his younger years, and in which Monica was a prominent feature. Monica's absence is a corollary of their desire to contain Augustine's spiritual peregrinations and doubt about the ascetic life.

THE IMPLICATIONS OF DOUBTING MONICA

It is possible that the lack of emphasis on Monica in these five texts is a result of reliance upon other medieval *Lives* of Augustine (Possidius, Philip of Harvengt or Jacobus of Voragine) which similarly mention Monica infrequently, rather than upon Augustine's *Confessions*. Several of the hermits' texts cite repeatedly from Possidius and Philip of Harvengt, whose work Jordan refers to as the *legenda famosa*.[50] Knowledge of these other *Lives* does not, however, preclude knowledge of the *Confessions*, which was widely available in late medieval Europe and is cited at length by all five authors.[51] Yet even Jordan of Quedlinburg, the most familiar of the five with the *Confessions*, still passes over Monica's part in the story.

The key to understanding the motivations behind this downplaying of Monica's role lies in the context of the composition of these texts. Given their polemical and apologetic nature – both as a defence of the heritage of the OESA as directly founded by Augustine

---

[50] Ibid., fol. 64[rb]. A phrase from Possidius's *Vita Augustini*, claiming that Augustine had lived in an eremitical way when overseas (i.e. when he was Italy) is used in the first four texts to prove that Augustine founded a monastic community while living in Italy: Possidius, *Vita Augustini* 5.52.7–8 (PL 32, 37). For the use made of this, see MS Plut. 90. Sup. 48, fol. 8[r] (*Vita Augustini*); Rano, 'Las dos primeras obras', 339–40 (*Initium*), 368 (Nicholas of Alessandria, *Sermo de beato Augustino*); Arbesmann, ed., 'Henry of Friemar's *Treatise*', 97, 121–7.

[51] For example, Petrarch possessed a small copy of Augustine's *Confessions*, which he claimed to carry everywhere with him, specifically on his famous climb of Mont Ventoux; he was given it by his friend Dionigi da Borgo San Sepolcro, an Italian Augustinian Hermit: *The Essential Petrarch*, ed. and transl. Peter Hainsworth (Indianapolis, IN, 2010), 220–6, especially 224–5. Jordan of Quedlinburg stated explicitly at the beginning of his text that he was using the *Confessions*, along with the *Sermones ad fratres in heremo*, as his primary source material: MS 251, fol. 54[rb]. Saak refers to the anonymous *Vita* as 'strung together portions of texts from Augustine's *Confessions*', and to the *Initium* as being based primarily on the *Confessions* and Possidius: *High Way to Heaven*, 190, 196.

and as a means of showing the exclusivity of the Augustinian rule, which (at least in their own view) was exemplified in its entirety only by the Augustinian Hermits – these texts strive to portray Augustine's religious example as synonymous with the eremitical lifestyle of the OESA. The authors define Augustine's life according to their own understanding of their order as the fulfilment of his example, and their characterization of Augustine in this sense reflects their own religious practice.

In the *Confessions,* however, the presence of Monica makes Augustine's religious experiences decidedly different from the daily practice of the OESA. Monica witnesses to a non-intellectual and non-clerical path to God that ultimately proved more successful than that initially taken by Augustine. When a mystical, emotional connection with God eventually leads Augustine to the religious path, the reader of the *Confessions* is reminded of Monica's example. While a portrayal of Augustine overcoming doubt could have been a useful hagiographical topos, any notion that Augustine doubted the eremitical path, and the discipline and rule of life associated with that path, would weaken the OESA's claims to Augustinian parentage and the exclusivity of their Augustinian religious practice. For the hermits to prove their claims over those of the canons, they needed eremitism to be at the centre of Augustine's religious practice, favouring rational enquiry of God over an emotional faith such as Monica's. The presence of Monica would have made that emphasis impossible, since it was her genre of devotion that Augustine utilized once his rational and austere religious life had failed to overcome his doubt. Augustine's doubt in the *Confessions*, ultimately, was a painful reminder to the hermits of contemporary doubt regarding their Augustinian parentage and the similarity of their own religion to that of their putative founder. The only substantial references to Monica in these texts – to her death and her funeral – serve to contain her guidance of Augustine; by mentioning her only in the context of her death, they controlled her influence by metaphorically silencing her and rejecting her religious excellence.

As a regular order under attack not only from the Augustinian Canons but also from ecclesiastical councils, which sought to minimize monastic diversity, it was only natural that the OESA would seek to promote its own religious rule and discipline above all others. By mentioning Monica only in conjunction with the hermit Simplicianus or with praise of the eremitical life, these hermit authors discarded an element of Augustine's life-story which did not lend itself to championing the eremitical life to the exclusion of all else. For these hermits, Monica was a representation of Augustine's problematic doubt about the intellectual and regular path and of the ultimate failure of that path in his religious experience. In order to overcome their own self-doubt about their heritage and foundation and to connect their order unequivocally to the legacy of Augustine, the hermits sought to minimize Augustine's own doubt and, with that, wrote the complex character of Monica out of the story.

Trust and Doubt: The Late Medieval Bishop and Local Knowledge

Ian Forrest[*]

Oriel College, Oxford

In governing their dioceses late medieval bishops faced significant epistemological challenges: how was it possible to determine the truth in disputes over local customs, patronage, the conduct of divine service and the provision of pastoral care? All such problems demanded an adjudication between competing stories about rights, history and usage, and while canon law provided a framework of principles, it did not provide the answers bishops needed. Increasingly from the thirteenth century the answers came from panels of local 'trustworthy men'. Bishops had to trust – to have 'faith' or belief in – informants who were often peasants. In the church courts and before visitation tribunals lay litigants, witnesses and parish representatives also used the language of faith and belief to characterize their knowledge of events and people: they had faith in their own perceptions. The role of faith in the knowledge that bishops and lay people claimed to have of the material and social world had much in common with the faith that brought Christians closer to having knowledge of God, but there were also important differences in the operation of faith in these three contexts. This essay describes and compares the epistemologies of late medieval bishops, lay people and theologians, paying particular attention to the relationship between trust and doubt in each instance.

At best, the old habit of referring to the Middle Ages as an 'age of faith' could be seen as historical shorthand for two interpretative positions. First, and most charitably, it might be seen as explaining a supposedly unified medieval culture to a modernizing world, conveying the integral position of religion within medieval society to an age when separation of the spheres was becoming instinctive. Second, and more realistically, the idea of an age of faith can be seen as an attempt to draw a line between the epistemologies of the medieval world (credulous, uncurious, accepting of authority) and those of modernity (rationalist, scientific, critical).[1] The omnipresence of

[*] Oriel College, Oxford, OX1 4EW. E-mail: ian.forrest@oriel.ox.ac.uk.

[1] Jaroslav Pelikan, *The Christian Tradition: A History of the Development of Doctrine*, 3: *The Growth of Medieval Theology 600–1300* (Chicago, IL, 1978), 1–8; Susan Reynolds, 'Social

Studies in Church History 52 (2016) 164–185   © Ecclesiastical History Society 2016
doi: 10.1017/stc.2015.10

religion and the fact that it cannot be treated as a separate sphere has been accepted by most medievalists.[2] Medieval epistemology, meanwhile, has been subjected to a great deal of powerful study. The centrality of rationalism, scientific modes of enquiry, criticism, scepticism and doubt to the fields of philosophy, theology and natural science (including medicine) is well known.[3] Epistemologies in the field of law have been less actively interrogated, but John Arnold's observation, that inquisitors approached problems of evidence and doubt with an awareness of the limitations of their knowledge, has proved influential.[4]

My primary aim in this essay, however, is to move the question of doubt in medieval culture away from the study of academic disciplines and into the realm of action. The particular field of action that I am interested in is the administrative and legal work undertaken by the medieval Church, for the most part overseen by bishops. The evidence comes largely from the bishops' registers, visitations and Church court records of late medieval England. Similar enquiries into other bodies of evidence would certainly yield some of the same results, but there would also be differences in the precise modalities of the relevant terminology, and in the political, economic and social contexts.[5] Using the English episcopal material, I will explore issues of trust and doubt in the language, assumptions, strategies and actions of bishops as they attempted to govern their dioceses, and in

---

Mentalities and the Case of Medieval Scepticism', *TRHS* 6th ser. 1 (1991), 21–41, at 25–6.

[2] Michael Prestwich, *Plantagenet England 1225–1360* (Oxford, 2005), ix, to take a recent notable example, offers a history of England that only refers to the Church 'where relevant'.

[3] Recent landmarks in this wide field include Katherine Tachau, *Vision and Certitude in the Age of Ockham: Optics, Epistemology and the Foundations of Semantics 1250–1345* (Leiden, 1988); Dallas G. Denery II, *Seeing and Being Seen in the Later Medieval World: Optics, Theology, and Religious Life* (Cambridge, 2005); Christophe Grellard, *Croire et savoir. Les Principes de la connaissance selon Nicolas d'Autrécourt* (Paris, 2005); Dominik Perler, *Zweifel und Gewissheit. Skeptische Debatten im Mittelalter* (Frankfurt, 2006); Alex Novikoff, *The Medieval Culture of Disputation: Pedagogy, Practice and Performance* (Philadelphia, PA, 2013).

[4] John Arnold, *Inquisition and Power: Catharism and the Confessing Subject in Medieval Languedoc* (Philadelphia, PA, 2001), 78.

[5] A particularly fertile recent study – Jan K. Bulman, *The Court Book of Mende and the Secular Lordship of the Bishop: Recollecting the Past in Thirteenth-Century Gévaudan* (Toronto, ON, 2008) – discusses the relationships between writing, memory, truth and proof in another specific context.

lay people's responses to episcopal action. This will illuminate some pragmatic attitudes towards doubt and faith which can then be compared to the epistemologies of the learned disciplines.[6]

Some of my questions concern institutional habits of thought and utterances made within asymmetrical relations of power. As such they could easily be applied to other periods and belief-systems as well. For this reason my approach has been informed by related work on these subjects in the social sciences and in histories of other periods. This, I hope to show, can take us further in understanding the medieval Church than if we analyse it purely on its own terms. Such intellectual borrowing must, nevertheless, be matched with due attention to the particularities of doubt and trust in later medieval Western Europe. In particular, it is impossible to understand how epistemology and practice accommodated doubt unless one grapples with late medieval ideas about God and belief. Although I am not going to say anything new about how Christians faced their God, the parallels and divergences between ideas about doubt in different areas of late medieval life mean that this is a sensible place to start.

I will begin by briefly outlining some of the psychological work that doubt and faith were thought to perform in the sphere of religious belief, before comparing this with the two spheres of action: first, the pragmatic epistemologies of bishops as they faced the inscrutability of the social world that they governed, and second, the epistemologies of lay people giving testimony as witnesses in the church courts. What were the valences of doubt, faith and knowledge in these three areas? How closely was trust in a human being related to trust in God?

RELIGIOUS BELIEF

Between the year 1000 and the Reformation, the relationship between faith and doubt was configured in many different ways. The particular positions of certainty, doubt, reason, emotion, grace, intention, authority, perception, love and virtue in the constellation of faith were subtly different, even amongst authors who agreed with one another, and sometimes radically different where there was substantial theological or philosophical disagreement. There were, nonetheless, a

---

[6] Sabina Flanagan, *Doubt in an Age of Faith: Uncertainty in the Long Twelfth Century* (Turnhout, 2008), 113–15, examines the differences between doubt in secular and sacred learning.

number of ideas about faith and doubt that were common enough that we can call them shared assumptions. Since my purpose is to compare the assumptions about faith and doubt underlying the actions and utterances of bishops and lay witnesses, it is pointless to ask whether any one of these was more of a realist or nominalist, more an intellectualist or a mystic. There is, of course, a great deal to say about changing conceptions of faith and doubt among learned writers.[7]

The common position from which all medieval theologians began their discussions of faith was that God is fixed and certain.[8] Human knowledge and perception were another matter. The fall from grace had had two effects. The first was to cloud human cognitive abilities, so that God could not be seen directly. Individuals destined for salvation would, in time, come to see God 'as if face to face' once again, but for now they had to settle for seeing 'through a glass darkly'.[9] The second effect was to cause the will to falter and doubt to creep into thought about God. While for some authors in natural science and philosophy doubt was seen as a productive foundation for knowledge, in theology it was generally thought of as a human deficiency.[10] To avoid doubt it was necessary to assent – through faith – to those things that were unseen or that lay beyond human reason.[11] Even Abelard, regarded by many of his contemporaries and successors as an arch-rationalist, cautioned that knowledge arrived at through reason fell short of 'the knowledge of the blessed in heaven', while for late medieval nominalists like William Ockham and Gabriel

---

[7] There are valuable introductory surveys of medieval theological positions on doubt and faith in Pelikan, *Growth of Medieval Theology*, 9–34; Avery Dulles, *The Assurance of Things Hoped For: A Theology of Christian Faith* (Oxford, 1994), 25–38; Rik Van Nieuwenhove, *An Introduction to Medieval Theology* (Cambridge, 2012), 62–3, 105–18, 191–4, 260–1.

[8] Mishtooni Bose, 'Vernacular Opinions', in Dallas G. Denery II, Kantik Ghosh and Nicolette Zeeman, eds, *Uncertain Knowledge: Scepticism, Relativism, and Doubt in the Middle Ages* (Turnhout, 2014), 239–59, at 252–3.

[9] 1 Cor. 13: 12; Hugh of St Victor, *De sacramentis Christianae fidei* 1.10.9 (*Hugh of Saint Victor on the Sacraments of the Christian Faith*, transl. Roy J. Deferrari [Cambridge, MA, 1951], 180–2); Flanagan, *Doubt in an Age of Faith*, 99–103.

[10] Kantik Ghosh, 'Logic, Scepticism, and "Heresy" in early Fifteenth-Century Europe: Oxford, Vienna, Constance', in Denery, Ghosh and Zeeman, eds, *Uncertain Knowledge*, 261–83; Dulles, *Assurance of Things Hoped For*, 32–4; *Quinque verba*, in John Shinners and William J. Dohar, eds, *Pastors and the Care of Souls in Medieval England* (Notre Dame, IN, 1998), 134.

[11] Augustine, *De fide rerum invisibilium* 1–8 (*The Works of Saint Augustine*, I/8: *On Christian Belief*, ed. Boniface Ramsey, transl. Edmund Hill [Hyde Park, NY, 2005], 183–91).

Biel, whatever faith could be acquired by reason fell short of the full specifically Christian faith that rested upon God's grace infusing the believer.[12] Augustine's aphorism that belief 'is nothing else than to think with assent' was interpreted variously as a cognitive acceptance of God's certainty and as an emotional receptiveness to the grace that would bring faith to the individual.[13]

Having faith, then, meant exercising human perception, cognition and reason while recognizing their limits. It also meant – for the vast majority of people – accepting a great deal on authority. Augustine called on Christians to have faith in the witnesses sent by God.[14] Hugh of St Victor responded to this in general terms by arguing that the 'simple minded in Holy Church' should believe those whose belief was more perfect (in language that would later be echoed in inquisitorial attempts to understand heretical belief).[15] In Bishop Peter Quinel's 1287 pastoral *Summula* for the diocese of Exeter, the laity were urged to 'believe what the church believes'.[16] Faith was a remarkably compulsory form of voluntary certainty. Commentators frequently explained this in contrast to the uncertainty that permeated the Christian's hope in her or his own individual salvation. They could trust in God's truth, goodness and existence, but not in their own justification. For ordinary Christians faith was therefore also an admission of their own inferior position within a hierarchy of knowing.[17] There might be greater merit in simple faith, believing

---

[12] Dulles, *Assurance of Things Hoped For*, 29, 36–8; Heiko A. Oberman, *The Harvest of Medieval Theology: Gabriel Biel and Late Medieval Nominalism* (Durham, NC, 1963), 68–88; Flanagan, *Doubt in an Age of Faith*, 105.

[13] Augustine, *De praedestinatione sanctorum* 5 (*Four Anti-Pelagian Writings*, transl. John A. Mourant, FOTC 86 [Baltimore, MD, 1992], 222); for discussion of the influence of this aphorism, see Flanagan, *Doubt in an Age of Faith*, 98–111.

[14] Augustine, *De Trinitate* 13.1 (*The Trinity*, FOTC 45, 369–71).

[15] Hugh of St Victor, *De sacramentis* 1.10.2–3, 6 (*On the Sacraments*, transl. Deferrari, 168–70, 173–4); cf. Vincent of Spain, *Apparatus in concilium quartum Lateranense*, c. 3, ad v. *Excommunicamus* (*Constitutiones Concilii quarti Lateranensis una cum Commentariis glossatorum*, ed. A. García y García, Monumenta Iuris Canonici Series A: Corpus Glossatorum 2 [Vatican City, 1981], 291: 'Credimus quod homines secte illius boni sunt'); Lucy Sackville, *Heresy and Heretics in the Thirteenth Century: The Textual Representations* (Woodbridge, 2011), 97–8, 117–21, 129.

[16] F. M. Powicke and C. R. Cheney, eds, *Councils and Synods with other Documents relating to the English Church, 2: A.D. 1205–1313* (Oxford, 1964), 1063.

[17] Berndt Hamm, *The Reformation of Faith in the Context of Late Medieval Theology and Piety* (Leiden, 2004), 159–62; Michel de Certeau, 'Une pratique sociale de la différence: croire', in *Faire croire: Modalités de la diffusion et de la réception des messages religieux du XIIᵉ au XVᵉ siècle.*

that which could not be understood, but it was clear who should be listening to whom.

The remainder of this essay is not an explication of a discrete body of thought or writing about truth and doubt in the worlds of episcopal administration and canon law. It is an extrapolation of the attitudes embodied in actions and rhetorical statements. Some of these actions and statements reflect habits of thought that may never have been the subject of much reflection. Some, by contrast, are likely to have been intentional and crafted to suit particular purposes. We are dealing with two main types of language: written instructions sent by bishops to their subordinates and the written records of oral testimony that had been given in the Church courts and before visitation tribunals. The actions under consideration are the social consequences of this language. Both varieties of language worked to their own norms and rules, and we must be mindful of these when using them as historical evidence. Bishops' letters were highly stylized; they were often based upon formularies which meant there were standard ways of writing about recognizable issues. But this still left room for intention and consideration. More importantly, there was as much meaning in formulae as there was in studied originality.[18] Written records of oral testimony have generated a huge volume of historiographical reflection and disagreement. Witness statements may not be the 'language of everyday life', but they were often faithful inscriptions of what people said in court. They are, as John Arnold has said of inquisition records, utterances produced by the encounter with power, but this is nonetheless a historically interesting interaction. We just need to be mindful that Church courts, visitations and inquisition tribunals were not Mass Observation.[19] We can use

---

Table ronde organisée par l'École française de Rome, en collaboration avec l'Institut d'histoire médiévale de l'Université de Padoue (Rome, 1981), 363–83, at 364–5, 373–5.

[18] See particularly here the work of Michael Burger: 'Sending, Joining, Writing and Speaking in the Diocesan Administration of Thirteenth-Century Lincoln', *MedS* 55 (1983), 151–82; idem, 'Bishops, Archdeacons and Communication between Centre and Locality in the Diocese of Lincoln, *c*.1214–1299', in *Thirteenth Century England*, 5: *Proceedings of the Newcastle upon Tyne Conference 1993*, ed. Peter Coss and S. D. Lloyd (Woodbridge, 1995), 195–206; idem, *Bishops, Clerks, and Diocesan Governance in Thirteenth-Century England: Reward and Punishment* (Cambridge, 2012).

[19] John Arnold, 'Inquisition, Texts, and Discourse', in Caterina Bruschi and Peter Biller, eds, *Texts and the Repression of Medieval Heresy* (Woodbridge, 2003), 63–80, penetrates a dense and interesting debate.

bishops' letters and recorded oral testimony to find out about attitudes to doubt held by an individual or agreed among a wider group.

THE COSTS OF LOCAL KNOWLEDGE

One element in the bureaucratization of the Church between 1100 and 1300 was a changing attitude towards local knowledge. As diocesan government intensified and disputes over rights and judgements became more frequent, bishops put more and more of a premium upon the acquisition of reliable local knowledge. Who was the rightful patron of this living? To which parish should tithes be paid from that piece of land? What would the repairs to this or that rectory cost and who was going to pay? Was the nominee for some benefice or other a person of good character? Had this man and that woman known how closely they were related at the time of their marriage? Were the clergy here and there performing the tasks that were expected of them? Bishops acquired their practical knowledge of such people and things in their dioceses by asking the locals.

But finding things out by asking the locals came at a cost. In fact, much of what we think of as the institutional Church was shaped by a never-ending dialectic of the 'costs' incurred by information problems and the costs of their solutions.[20] These costs were not necessarily monetary. They could involve the loss of certainty and the acceptance of doubt. In a hypothetical situation of perfect ignorance about the condition of his parishes, a bishop might possess absolute certainty as to what had to be done. This may be one reason why episcopal registers so often record a flurry of activity in the first few months of an episcopate. But as soon as he began to make himself better acquainted with local conditions, he paid for knowledge with the loss of certainty. All information had to be taken on trust. From the mid-thirteenth century onwards, bishops began referring to their local informants as 'trustworthy men' (*viri fidedigni*).[21] Taking things on trust meant living with doubt. Had the locals told the truth? Would their testimony stand the test of time? Had the inquest been rigged by some powerful family? In facing such doubts, bishops were no different from the personnel of all historic and contemporary

[20] Ian Forrest, 'Continuity and Change in the Institutional Church', in John H. Arnold, ed., *The Oxford Handbook of Medieval Christianity* (Oxford, 2014), 185–200.
[21] These themes will be fully explored in my forthcoming book, *Trustworthy Men: How Inequality and Faith made the Medieval Church*.

governing organizations, although the precise nature of the information problems they faced was, of course, particular to their situation.

Bishops had to live with doubt, but they were content to do so. This had much to do with their concept of trustworthiness. Before examining how trustworthiness figured in the solutions and the problems of the informational Church, it is worthwhile pausing to reflect on the nature of those problems. What were the costs of information?

In the *Critique of the Philosophy of Right*, Marx wrote that bureaucracy is 'a circle from which no-one can escape. Its hierarchy is a hierarchy of knowledge. The apex entrusts the lower circles with insight into the individual while the lower circles leave insight into the universal to the apex, so they deceive each other reciprocally.'[22] This mutual deception need not be intentional. It could, and often did, easily arise from the difference in culture between the top and the bottom of a hierarchy of knowledge. It is evident that the medieval Church is amenable to analysis in these terms. Bishops had to cross an enormous cultural divide in order to trust the laity to provide useful information. Sometimes the chasm was unbridgeable and the locals just did not understand what really mattered in the world of canon law and government. To give just one example, in 1346 the bishop of Hereford ordered an inquest into the patronage of Sibdon Chapel in Shropshire. He gathered information from local 'trustworthy men'. But they failed to understand the specifics of what they were being asked to do. They reported that the chaplain had a customary duty to celebrate mass twice a day and bemoaned the fact that the chapel could only be served three days a week; they identified the current chaplain; they described how a previous lord of Sibdon had endowed the chapel. But they did not say who had last presented to the chapel. Because of this the inquest was deemed to have 'failed' and the bishop's official, a university graduate and experienced administrator, was sent to repeat the exercise.[23] The men on the spot knew how to acquire local knowledge, but either they were so far removed from the culture of episcopal administration that they missed the point of the inquest, or they set out intentionally to deceive the

---

[22] Karl Marx, *Selected Writings*, ed. David McLellan, 2nd edn (Oxford, 2000), 37.
[23] *Registrum Johannis de Trillek, Episcopi Herefordensis, A.D. MCCCXLIV–MCCCLXI*, ed. J. H. Parry, CYS 8 (London, 1907), 39.

bishop. They provided lots of pertinent information, but failed on a technical point: actually spelling out who the patron was.[24]

There were many asymmetries of knowledge and information in the medieval Church, and so perhaps the Shropshire case should not surprise us. The clergy were a group marked out by specialist knowledge and the skills of reading and writing, as well as by the ritual of ordination; graduates and the higher clergy practised a literacy that was much more sophisticated than the pragmatic reading and documentary awareness of the average parish priest; legal rules of evidence were far narrower than everyday concepts of knowledge, and required a learned, or practised, precision. In Marx's terms, knowledge of the individual and knowledge of the universal could be mutually unintelligible. But in fact failed inquests were rare, or at least were not often recorded in bishops' registers. So we should perhaps imagine that it was normal for these things to proceed relatively smoothly. Most reports of inquests are careful itemizations of the facts adhering closely to the wording of the bishop's original instructions. Clearly a great deal depended upon the agents chosen by the bishop. If they were inexperienced or unversed in the cultures of law and administration, they might perform their tasks diligently, but in vain. Most of the time, however, this problem was limited by the ability of the bishop's agents to translate the universal into the local and vice versa. Many episcopal letters commissioned a local cleric and a member of the bishop's household to act together. Many parish priests were graduates themselves, or had built up a wealth of experience dealing with the business letters of their superiors. For the most part, then, bishops assumed that the recipients of their letters would know what to do. What remained problematic was the almost complete inability of the bishop to know how much was being kept from him and not communicated at all.

The concentration of power in the hands of the bishop (exemplified by the phenomenon of 'reserved cases' that only he could judge) and his reliance upon good information meant that his capacity for action could be severely hampered if he were starved of information. Bottlenecks of information could be created by the failure of officials

---

[24] The need for technical knowledge and precise adherence to rules figured as part of Weber's ideal type of bureaucratic administration, particularly associated with officials appointed by superior powers: Max Weber, 'Bureaucracy', in Hans H. Gerth and C. Wright Mills, eds, *From Max Weber: Essays in Sociology* (London, 1991), 196–244, at 201.

at different levels to pass material either upwards or downwards.[25] However, even the supposedly characteristically modern condition of 'information overload' also affected medieval administrators. The most studied examples are the Domesday Book of 1086 and Edward I's Hundred Rolls of 1279–80, both of which produced so much information that they were not put to much use, but many Church visitation records could be considered in the same light.[26] A great deal of information was merely recorded and never followed up.

Geography could also throw up significant barriers to the effective retrieval of information. The documentation surrounding visitations demonstrates this very well. Multiple groups of parish representatives had to be organized to appear at a particular time and place, each having submitted written reports in advance. Frequently these groups did not appear, or the information was not available all in one place, and so cases trailed along in the visitor's wake, dragging parishioners and litigants, letters and reports from place to place. This may not have made for efficient decision-making. But it did bring bishops closer to localities. They toured the parishes of their dioceses in order to collapse the geographical distance that separated them from their flocks; they travelled their estates in order to be a visible presence among the gentry and nobility living far from cathedral cities. They were aware of the information cost imposed by distance and they tried to do something about it.

This worked pretty well when something had happened that affected a single place and the bishop or his commissioner arrived in person to supervise an inquest. But when the information needed to resolve some issue was harder to locate, the costs of retrieving it could escalate, both in the sense of being more expensive and in the degree of faith one could place in the truth or stability of the information. For example, when in 1320 Andrew le Boteler claimed benefit of clergy after being charged with murder, the archbishop of York ordered an inquest into his life and character, his 'name and opinion', in his home region. Was either his guilt or any previous crime he might have committed well known there? The problem was that he had moved around a great deal and there was no question of sending

---

[25] Barry Barnes, *The Elements of Social Theory* (London, 1995), 204.

[26] There is no consensus on the much-studied Domesday Book, but the case for its utility over its symbolism has not been proven: David Roffe, 'Domesday Now', *Anglo-Norman Studies* 28 (2006), 168–87; Sandra Raban, *A Second Domesday? The Hundred Rolls of 1279–80* (Oxford, 2004).

a commissioner to empanel the trustworthy men of a single parish. Instead Archbishop Melton called for 'trustworthy clerics and laymen … from the places where he is most well known', and these were scattered across Nottinghamshire and the East Riding. Somewhat unsurprisingly, nothing definitive emerged from these attenuated efforts, and the only option after six months was to advertise Andrew le Boteler's desire to undergo purgation and see if 'objectors' came forward.[27] This was an unsatisfactory and inferior means of testing for truth. The verdict would come from the suspect's friends and supporters rather than a group of well-informed trustworthy men.

The most significant cost attached to information, in terms of the effort that could potentially be expended, was the difficulty involved in assessing trustworthiness.[28] So what did medieval bishops mean when they referred to 'trustworthy men'? The *fidedignus* had for centuries been a reasonably common way of describing the apostles, saints and martyrs of the church who were direct witnesses to God's truth.[29] They had not merely believed; they had seen the Lord in one way or another. Such trustworthy witnesses to God's truth were precisely the kind of authorities that the 'simple minded in Holy Church' were enjoined to believe.[30] They possessed knowledge and understanding that could not be attained by ordinary people. To apply such a term to laypeople – peasants – in the parishes was therefore something of a departure from the language and the epistemology of the Church in the first millennium. If faith should only be placed in that which was certain, like God, or in those who had been granted a privileged vision of divinity – the saints – how was it that bishops could place their trust – their *fides* (faith) – in peasants?

The answer is that the need for such local knowledge as would support the governance of the Church created an imperative for a

---

[27] *The Register of William Melton Archbishop of York 1317–1340*, ed. Rosalind M. T. Hill et al., 5 vols, CYS, 70, 71, 76, 85, 93 (Torquay, 1977–8; York, 1988; Woodbridge, 1997–2002), 4: 35–6, 42–3, 63–5.

[28] David Good, 'Individuals, Interpersonal Relations and Trust', in Diego Gambetta, ed., *Trust: Making and Breaking Cooperative Relations* (Oxford, 1988), 31–48, at 42.

[29] For example Theodoret of Cyrus (393–466) and Bede (672/3–735) praised the gospel authors as 'trustworthy': Theodoretus Cyrensis, *Philotheus* (PL 74, col. 797); Bede, *Super acta apostolorum expositio* (PL 92, col. 939). This usage was current in twelfth-century theological commentaries: *Biblia Latina cum Glossa ordinaria*, ed. Karlfried Froelich and Margaret T. Gibson, 4 vols (facsimile reprint of the *editio princeps* of Adolph Rusch of Strassburg, 1480/81; Turnhout, 1992), commentary on Acts 6: 5; 11: 24; 1 Tim. 1: 11; Peter Lombard, *The Sentences*, transl. Giulio Silano, 4 vols (Toronto, ON, 2008), 3: 101.

[30] Hugh of St Victor, *De sacramentis* 1.10.2 (*On the Sacraments*, transl. Deferrari, 168).

new epistemology and a new attitude to faith and doubt. The act of trust was no longer determined by the fixity of the object (God) or by the virtues of the witnesses, but by the bishop's attitude to risk. Let us consider for a moment the interplay of knowledge and trust in the cases we have been examining. Bishops did not, nor could they ever hope to, know the laymen in their dioceses in a meaningful way that would enable them to choose only the most honest and truthful individuals to be their informants. Moreover, it would have been prohibitively costly, in terms of time and effort, to attempt such a calculation. The economic sociologist Douglass North has made the general point that the people one deals with in any given situation might possess desirable attributes to varying levels, but '[t]he measurement of these levels is too costly to be comprehensive or fully accurate'.[31] So what is to be done? Since uncertainty and risk add costs to all transactions, it is necessary to find a way of reducing these costs.[32] How did bishops reduce the cost of doubt?

German sociologist Niklas Luhmann observed that 'the complexity of the future world is reduced by the act of trust'.[33] Economists often say that trust is a means of reducing transaction costs.[34] Notwithstanding the differences of language and purpose, this seems to be precisely the attitude to doubt, risk and the future adopted by medieval bishops. In 1309 Walter Reynolds, bishop of Worcester, called for an inquest of trustworthy men to find out which rectors of parish churches in the deanery of Warwick had failed to be ordained priest within a year of their appointment. It was commonplace for men not yet ordained priest to be put in charge of churches. Six rectors were reported, of whom three went on to be ordained even though they did not have their papers in order. They merely had to swear that they had not been in their churches more than a year and this allowed them to be ordained 'at their own risk'. That is, they had to accept that if their ordination was proved illegal in future it

---

[31] Douglass C. North, *Institutions, Institutional Change and Economic Performance* (Cambridge, 1990), 29.

[32] John Dunn, 'Trust and Political Agency', in Gambetta, ed., *Trust*, 73–93, at 73; Oliver Williamson, 'The New Institutional Economics: Taking Stock, Looking Ahead', *Journal of Economic Literature* 38 (2000), 595–613; idem, 'Calculativeness, Trust, and Economic Organization', *Journal of Law and Economics* 36 (1993), 453–86.

[33] Niklas Luhmann, *Trust and Power* (Chichester, 1979), 20, 24–30.

[34] Partha Dasgupta, 'Trust as a Commodity', in Gambetta, ed., *Trust*, 49–72, at 64; Williamson, 'Calculativeness, Trust, and Economic Organization'.

would be their problem and not the bishop's.[35] There must have been reasonable doubt. In this case and many others like it we do not know whether the inquiry exposed all offenders or merely those who were unpopular with some portion of their parish community. But we should not be too dismayed, since we share our ignorance with the bishops who commissioned such inquiries. The trust necessary to secure information was paid for with the shrugging acceptance that it might be incomplete or misleading. Reduced costs were accompanied by sub-optimal, but acceptable, outcomes.

Two years later Reynolds processed the case of John Mauduyt, a cleric who had received minor orders without a hitch, but had then been ordained a priest without having a 'title', that is a benefice in which to serve. Mauduyt's mistake 'was revealed to him through the prudence of another' and he went to Avignon to seek papal dispensation. The pope wrote to the bishop that since Mauduyt had actively sought to correct the fault he could be forgiven so long as the facts were as reported and there was no lingering sentence of excommunication. The bishop forced Mauduyt to abstain from all meat, eggs and dairy foods for a month, in the meantime launching an inquiry through trustworthy clerics and laymen. The inquiry was satisfactory and Mauduyt was recognized as a priest. The key fact that needed local verification was whether Mauduyt had 'knowingly' obtained false documentation. It is hard to imagine how this could be corroborated except by his own testimony, or perhaps from highly subjective and retrospective inferences drawn from his behaviour and bearing, but the bishop and the pope seemed happy with this degree of doubt.[36] As in the previous case, subsequent conflicting information might have changed matters. The authorities were trusting in the absence of knowledge. As Diego Gambetta wrote in 1988, trust 'is a peculiar belief predicated not on evidence but on the lack of *contrary* evidence'.[37]

In these and many hundreds of similar cases it may look as though bishops and popes were acting irrationally. They had no idea whether their trust had been misplaced or not. Were they not making a

---

[35] *The Register of Walter Reynolds Bishop of Worcester 1308–1313*, ed. Rowland Alwyn Wilson, Dugdale Society Publications 9 (London, 1928), 4–5, 9, 32–3. Diego Gambetta, 'Can we Trust Trust?', in idem, ed., *Trust*, 213–37, at 218–19, argues that trust always implies a degree of ignorance and the potential for being deceived or disappointed.

[36] *Register of Walter Reynolds*, ed. Wilson, 83.

[37] Gambetta, 'Can we Trust Trust?', 234.

mockery of the language of faith? Was it making a mockery of them? If we were to measure their faith in fallible parishioners against the explanations of faith given by later medieval theologians, this might seem to be the case. Whereas the object of faith – God – was certain, the object of a bishop's trust – the 'trustworthy man' – was not. Placing faith in local laymen attributed to them similar qualities to those embodied in God, such as stability and constancy. But the doubt involved in these contrasting attributions of faith was on a different plane. Doubt about God was a personal psychological defect, a product of man's fallen state, whereas doubt about local testimony was a product of a more politic circumspection.

There was a strong instrumental rationality about a bishop's trust in local testimony. When Bishop Reynolds trusted the locals despite the impossibility of knowing whether he had been fully informed, and when he accepted the word of delinquent priests despite a lack of strong evidence to exonerate them, he was acting rationally. Rationally, that is, in so far as he had a sound understanding of the benefits that trusting would bring to him and to the Church. Reynolds had decided that to trust and accept doubt was better than to attempt a precise calculation of probabilities.[38] He was working within tolerable levels of uncertainty, knowing that to have pursued the truth remorselessly would have been both costly and counterproductive. A degraded priest would have been a scandal. The prohibitive cost of perfect information meant that institutions had to find ways of living with incomplete information. 'Perfection' is of course impossible in the acquisition of knowledge about the social world and so this cost should be imagined as infinite. This could have presented a huge problem if churchmen had not had a pragmatic attitude towards truth. By trusting, and by accepting doubt, bishops could 'shift the problem into a realm where it [could] be mastered more effectively'.[39] Accepting incomplete information did not make the Church less powerful. It was done in the pursuit of power. Tolerating doubt

---

[38] Luhmann, *Trust and Power*, 26, 88. The instrumental rationality on display here is consonant with the ends-means reasoning described by David D'Avray, *Rationalities in History: A Weberian Essay in Comparison* (Cambridge, 2010), 59–65. D'Avray argues that institutions frequently work to a hierarchy of values in which the overt value rationality (in this case the value placed upon trust) can seem to be contradicted by instrumental reasoning; yet if one attends to the ends that the instrumental actions are serving, a higher set of values can be discerned. In this case the 'ends' served by lip-service to trustworthy testimony were the dignity of the clerical estate and the smooth functioning of Church administration.

[39] Luhmann, *Trust and Power*, 37.

made local society more 'legible', not less. Local knowledge accepted with judicious doubt brought power, whereas perfect knowledge of the social world would have overwhelmed the institution with its unbounded variety, its illegibility, unconformity and strangeness.[40]

Although acknowledged as being imperfect, episcopal information about the social world was idealized as a form of truth. Indeed, this was the stated object of all Church inquiries in our period. However, truth, like trust, was not something thought only to exist in some utopian place where all doubt had been extinguished. Not having certain knowledge of God or any sense-evidence of his existence or goodness, medieval Christians were expected nonetheless to place their trust in him and find certainty in assenting rather than knowing. God could not be separated from truth, and neither he nor it could be known by human faculties alone. Truth, like God, was something in which one had to have faith, confident of its existence in some rather unlikely places. Truth might be obscured, but it was still there.

Trustworthy men were expected to tell the truth. This was often spelt out in the instructions for visitation that bishops sent to their officers locally. In 1283 Archbishop Pecham wanted trustworthy men through whom he could 'best inquire into the truth'; in 1324 Bishop Orleton of Hereford wanted trustworthy men who would tell the truth 'in the proper way ... about those things asked of them that demand to be caught in the net of correction'; also in 1324 Archbishop Melton of York asked for parishioners who would say 'what they know to be true concerning those things required of them'.[41] Upon receiving information they regarded as meeting these requirements bishops might claim that their evidence was based upon the 'testimony of trustworthy jurors [which] we fully accept to be true'.[42] Truth, in these formulations, was something to be accepted rather

[40] James Scott, *The Art of Not Being Governed: an Anarchist History of Upland South East Asia* (New Haven, CT, 2009); idem, *Seeing Like a State: How Certain Schemes to Improve the Human Condition have Failed* (New Haven, CT, 1998), 64–73; John Law, 'Power/Knowledge and the Dissolution of the Sociology of Knowledge', in idem, ed., *Power, Action and Belief: A New Sociology of Knowledge?* (London, 1986), 1–19, at 10.

[41] *Registrum Johannis de Pontissara Episcopi Wyntoniensis A.D. MCCLXXXII–MCCCIV*, ed. C. Deedes, 2 vols, CYS 19, 30 (London, 1915–24), 1: 278–9; *Registrum Ade de Orleton, Episcopi Herefordensis, A.D. MCCCXVII–MCCCXXVII*, ed. A. T. Bannister, CYS 5 (London, 1908), 287; *Register of William Melton*, ed. Hill et al., 1: 134–5. For other examples, see *The Register of John de Grandisson, Bishop of Exeter (A.D. 1327–1369)*, ed. F. C. Hingeston-Randolph, 3 vols (London, 1894–9), 639, 1021, 1215.

[42] *Registrum Hamonis Hethe, diocesis Roffensis, A.D. 1319–1352*, ed. C. Johnson, 2 vols, CYS 48–9 (London, 1948), 1: 173–4, cf. 174–5.

than known beyond doubt. Bishops seem to have admitted the possibility of disagreement. As the twentieth-century liberal philosopher Michael Polanyi succinctly put it, the 'attribution of truth … is a fiduciary act'.[43] That is to say, in order to mitigate the costs of knowledge, truth must be taken on trust.

BELIEF AND LEGAL TESTIMONY

When bishops placed faith in lay parishioners, their trust was insured against the impossibility of objectivity by the weight of institutional power. They could operate effectively if they received reliable information most – and not necessarily all – of the time. Their expression of faith in local men was tinged with doubt about what they said. And when lay people in turn provided information to churchmen, they also had to navigate the bounds of human rationality and perception, and they likewise did so in words that borrowed from the language of religious belief.

The interplay between faith and doubt was most commonly enunciated in the language of belief. The constitutions of reforming councils and synods from the thirteenth century onwards encouraged Christians to learn the *credo* and the articles of faith. The submission of the will, the cognitive assent to authorized teaching and the attitude of receptiveness to God's grace were – idealistically – encapsulated in the moment when the Christian uttered the words 'I believe'. But there were other things in which people could believe. I do not mean alternative systems of religious belief, but belief as a commonplace epistemological act. One such act that affected the Church and other Christians in important ways was the assertion of belief made by witnesses in the Church courts, at visitation and before inquisition tribunals.

There was substantial common ground between theology and practical epistemology, especially the fact that faith or belief denoted a notion held on trust; that is, trust in an authority, in received wisdom, in natural principles or in one's own assumptions. But while trusting delineated common ground, trusting in what was an important point of difference. The 'I believe' of the creed had a very different meaning from the 'I believe' of the courts. Whereas the believer

---

[43] Michael Polanyi, *Personal Knowledge: Towards a Post-Critical Philosophy* (London, 1958), 294.

reciting the creed was meant to resign their doubts and submit to the certainty of God and the authority of the Church, the witness in court who said 'I believe' was placing trust in her or his own suppositions. But even this was a highly conditional kind of trust.

Assertions of belief were especially common in witness statements made for the church courts, and in the reports that trustworthy men submitted to visitations. For example, the deposition book of the bishop of London's consistory court between 1467 and 1476 is littered with the phrase 'as he or she believes' (*ut credit*).[44] This short but ubiquitous and meaningful phrase could be thought of as a firm assertion of knowledge, but it also contained the grounds for its own cautious qualification. The deponent may well have felt their evidence to be true so far as they were concerned. They had confidence in their own judgement and perception.[45] At the same time, this was a way of admitting the possibility of error and protecting oneself against the consequences of being proved wrong. In this, at least, the cautious witness was following closely Hugh of St Victor's aphorism that belief is 'a kind of certainty of the mind in things absent, established beyond opinion and short of knowledge'.[46] The witness was in a position that was at once privileged (telling the court what he or she knew) and subordinate (restricted to speaking about the facts of the case), which made cautious assertions of certainty the most appropriate form of utterance.

It is hard to discern exactly where along the spectrum between opinion and knowledge belief was thought to exist in any given instance. Statements of the type 'I believe' and 'I know' may well, in fact, do more to describe the feelings of the witness than the status of the evidence. Moreover, 'I believe' could be uttered with any inflection, steering it more towards doubt in one situation, more towards certainty in another. This is just one of the elements of speech that we cannot access as historians. Needless to say, such ambiguities must have given lawyers many opportunities to challenge witnesses' statements.

The trustworthy men reporting to several late medieval visitations adopted the language of belief with regard to everything from

---

[44] London, LMA, DL/C/0205.

[45] Polanyi, *Personal Knowledge*, 267, argued that all claims to knowledge must rest on certain unexamined assumptions, whether they concern God or an individual's belief about himself or herself.

[46] Hugh of St Victor, *De sacramentis* 1.10.2 (*On the Sacraments*, transl. Deferrari, 168).

commonplace sexual offences to politically tricky issues of authority. In Hereford diocese in 1397 the parish representatives of Norton had said that Sybil Gyfker fornicated with a clergyman called John Matthew or John Smith, 'or so they believed'. They did not know his name for certain, although he did live in Norton. Meanwhile the parishioners of Weobley said that Katherine Ondys was pregnant and it was not known (*nescitur*) by whom, but it was believed (*creditur*) to be the rector of Sarnesfield; the parishioners of Culmington in Shropshire reported two couples – Jankyn Tasger and Katherine 'whom he keeps as his wife', and Matthew Tailor and Philippa Bakon – for fornication because they believed both pairs were unmarried. They also reported Isabelle of Wales for fornicating with a Welshman whose name was not known, though they believed him to be Jankyn Tailor.[47] In Lichfield sometime in the 1460s the lay representatives of Stow Street and Tamworth Street said that they did not 'know' who had made Margaret Seyne pregnant, but they 'believed' that it had been William Harper; at Saddler Street they reported that the priest William Heyth had suspiciously gone to the house of Emmota Garnet with a woman called Helena Puella ('the girl'?). There, so they believed, he 'knew' her (*cognovit eam*). They were heard carousing and drinking later than was decent (*extra tempus honestum*).[48] In this carefully constructed report the closing of the brothel door set a seal upon the boundary between knowing and believing, but the level of detail suggests they were in no doubt themselves as to what had occurred.

Sometimes more subtle judgements were wrapped in the guarded language of belief. At Ruardean in Gloucestershire in 1397, it was said that Nicholas Cutler had told people how the spirit of his dead father went about the parish at night while Nicholas kept watch at the tomb. The trustworthy men said that this was to the great scandal of the Christian faith, 'as they believed'. Their final words were both an assertion of their firm views on Christian propriety, and an acknowledgement that the bishop was the only person with the authority to decide whether this was really orthodox or not. They were not qualified to judge, only to believe. Another matter of authority troubled the parish representatives of Waterdine, Shropshire, in the same year. They claimed that they were customarily served by

---

[47] Hereford, Hereford Cathedral Archives, 1779, fols 2ᵛ, 3ᵛ, 22ʳ.
[48] Lichfield, Lichfield Record Office, D 30/9/3/1, fols 23ʳ, 26ʳ.

a secular priest although their church was appropriated to Wenlock Priory. But the prior had foisted a parish chaplain upon them, taking away their vicar and his income 'without sufficient authority, as they believe'. They wanted the visiting bishop to demand that the prior show his authority. This was caution in the face of possible future documentary proof. The parishioners knew that documents were what secured rights, and that there should have been an episcopal 'ordination' made for the vicarage at the time when it was first appropriated to Wenlock. Without a copy of the document, and recognizing that this was an area where custom and memory alone would not do, all they could do was assert their cautious belief.[49] In the North Riding in 1428 the parish representatives of Farnham took a slightly different approach, but it amounted to the same thing. They said that William Smyth and Alice Verte had married and then separated because of his impotence, but they 'doubted' whether the separation was canonically sanctioned.[50] Canonical sanction was something that only a bishop or the pope could grant, and so the parishioners were right to express caution.

The men who represented parishes at visitation were thus aware of the huge power imbalances between them and their visitors. In this context belief was the perfect vehicle for expressing opinions and doubtful information. Belief brought with it huge implications of trust in authority and strength of judgement derived from faith in God. These men knew how to couch complaints so as to demand a bishop's attention. But assertions of belief also played mischievously on the weaknesses of human perception which, when coupled with the bishop's superior legal standing and the parishioners' subaltern status, became a way for a line to be drawn between what the locals were qualified to say and the establishment of fact and law by proper authorities.

In treading this line the representatives of both the parish and the institutional Church were aware of a rule to which most visitation proceedings conformed. In so far as canon law commentators wrote anything about visitation – and it was not much – they were clear that the reports of the laity constituted *fama*, that is, opinion or belief, and that only a judge could establish facts. In spite of this it was widely accepted that the articulation of *fama* as a form of provisional

---

[49] Hereford Cathedral Archives, 1779, fols 6[v], 24[v].
[50] York, Borthwick Institute for Archives, Register 19 (John Kempe), fols 211[v]–213[r].

knowledge set in train a process whereby report became fact.[51] With certain types of 'continuous fact' – things within the competency of collective remembrance, such as boundaries or ownership – *fama* had long been admissible. Gradually, between 1100 and 1250, *fama* was also allowed to play a part in establishing more transient facts such as whether a marriage had taken place.[52] In cases of this sort, where bishops were dependent upon local knowledge, the boundary between *fama* and fact was impossible to maintain. Local knowledge was not only valuable to bishops; they would have been unwise to reject it. For the most part bishops accepted the reports of trustworthy men and so, for all that they constituted 'mere' *fama* or belief, they arrived on the bishop's desk with the weight of local knowledge behind them, pushing them inexorably down the path towards accepted facts, alleged certainty and acknowledged truth.[53]

CONCLUSIONS

Across the learned disciplines of theology, philosophy, medicine and law, the twelfth and thirteenth centuries saw new distinctions being drawn between what was, and what was not, knowable by human faculties. Faith, belief, trust and doubt were coming to describe the liminal spaces within hierarchies of knowledge. In law *fama* was being distinguished from fact; in philosophy doubt was seen as an impetus for continuing enquiry; in medicine the limits of observation and experiment were being explored; while amongst theologians discussion of belief focused upon the limits of reason and its differentiation from faith.

---

[51] Thelma S. Fenster and Daniel Lord Smail, eds, Fama: *the Politics of Talk and Reputation in Medieval Europe* (Ithaca, NY, 2003); Charles Donahue, 'Proof by Witness in the Church Courts of Medieval England: An Imperfect Reception of the Learned Law', in *On the Laws and Customs of England: Essays in Honor of Samuel E. Thorne*, ed. M. S. Arnold et al. (Chapel Hill, NC, 1981), 127–58, at 131.

[52] Ian Forrest, 'The Transformation of Visitation in Thirteenth-Century England', *P&P* 221 (2013), 3–38, at 23–7; Donahue, 'Proof by Witness', 136–40.

[53] The tendency for opinion to be converted into fact, and for judges to play only a minimal role, has also been noted by historians of the English common law juries of presentment and trial: John H. Langbein, 'Jury Influence on Conceptions of the Judiciary', in Paul Brand and Joshua Getzler, eds, *Judges and Judging in the History of the Common Law and Civil Law: From Antiquity to Modern Times* (Cambridge, 2012), 67–82, at 69–72; Mike Macnair, 'Vicinage and the Antecedents of the Jury', *Law and History Review* 17 (1999), 537–90, at 547, 589–90; Morris S. Arnold, 'Law and Fact in the Medieval Jury Trial: Out of Sight, Out of Mind', *American Journal of Legal History* 18 (1974), 267–80, at 278.

In the two spheres of action that have been the subject of this essay – episcopal governance and lay assertions of local knowledge – this concern with the limits of certainty and the ubiquity of doubt were also of fundamental importance. I have tried to extrapolate assumptions about trust and doubt from the language and the actions of bishops and lay people within these frameworks. When we compare their assumptions with the conventional ideas about faith common to most theological writers there are some important similarities, but also some equally important points of difference. The similarities are most apparent at the level of language, with bishops placing faith in local men worthy of their trust and lay witnesses asserting the difference between what they believed and what they knew. In both spheres the language of faith, trust or belief pertained to that which lay beyond immediate comprehension: this was as true of events not witnessed in person and of the mysteries of local custom as it was of God. Furthermore, just as God was certain, bishops and lay witnesses tended to think of the objects of their trust as certain, if only for pragmatic reasons arising from the need for action.

But the differences are arguably more striking. The explicit placement of faith in lay – frequently peasant – informants in order to gain knowledge about the transient material and social world would have shocked earlier generations for whom faith was only worthy of being placed in God, Christ and the exceptional men and women who had been permitted direct knowledge of the divine. What is more, while bishops clearly thought reports from 'trustworthy men' were better than mere opinion, it is far less clear whether they also thought – as did Hugh of St Victor about religious faith – that those reports fell short of 'knowledge'. They treated them as knowledge; they had to. Moreover, lay expressions of belief made in witness depositions and visitation reports may have traced the boundary between the seen and the unseen in a way that was compatible with the epistemology of faith, but their faith was not being placed in God. Witnesses trusted their own suppositions. This is not how the 'simple minded' of the Church were urged to think about God.

These convergences and divergences in attitudes towards doubt and uncertain knowledge bring us back to one of the outstanding questions about medieval culture: how should we conceptualize the relationship between religion and everything else? Of course the Middle Ages were not an 'age of faith' in the sense that everyone shared an equal and unquestioning belief. We know too much to fall into that fallacy. But can everything be reduced to Christianity in the way that Richard Southern arguably did in treating Christendom as a 'compulsory society' (and in the way that some students new to medieval history, sensing the importance of religion in the period, can sometimes do as well)?[54]

There is no doubt that religious modes of thought permeated all others. But this is not the same as everything being reduced to the religious. Famously, Augustine had explained faith in God by a series of analogies with human belief in other unseen things, such as our own minds and the feelings of friends.[55] We cannot perfectly know the intentions of another person towards us, but we trust that our trust in them is reciprocated: without this, Augustine wrote, human society would fail. But these analogies can also serve to remind us that the patterns of thought necessary for belief in God were never confined to that objective. Religious faith was explained in terms that acknowledged the importance of doubt, belief and trust in other spheres of life; spheres that had their own imperatives. The need for doubt and the need for trust in knowing the social world were, in the later Middle Ages, being reframed in the language of religious faith. But they were not subsumed by it. Practices of faith, belief, trust and doubt were therefore connected at the epistemological level, but separated by their theologies. Whether or not, in the face of doubt, to trust God, trust the people or trust oneself were questions whose answers could be incompatible.

---

[54] Richard W. Southern, *Western Society and the Church in the Middle Ages* (Harmondsworth, 1970), 17.

[55] Augustine, *De fide rerum invisibilium* 2–4 (*On Christian Belief*, ed. Ramsey, transl. Hill, 184–6).

Dubius in fide fidelis est? Doubt and Assurance in Late Medieval Catholicism

Robert N. Swanson*

University of Birmingham

The canon law dictum that 'dubius in fide infidelis est' *offers a seemingly definitive statement on the place of doubt and uncertainty in medieval Catholicism. Yet where Catholic teaching was open to question, doubt was inseparable from faith, not merely as its obverse but as part of the process of achieving faithfulness – the trajectory outlined by Abelard in the twelfth century. The challenge for the Church was not that doubters lacked faith, but that having tested their doubts they might end up with the wrong faith: doubt preceded assurance, one way or the other. That problem is addressed in this essay by a broad examination of the ties between faith and doubt across the late Middle Ages (from the twelfth to the sixteenth centuries), arguing that uncertainty and doubt were almost unavoidable in medieval Catholicism. As the starting points in a process which could lead to heresy and despair, they also had a positive role in developing and securing orthodox faith.*

Many of this volume's essays offer specific instances and analyses of doubt in assorted contexts; several home in on individuals. This essay looks more broadly at the concept of doubt, and how it fits into medieval Catholicism between *c*.1100 and the Reformation. It suggests that doubt and insecurity were much more accepted among the faithful than is usually recognized, and were actually acknowledged as part of the process of attaining faith.

The originating stimulus is indicated by the question in the title: the possibility that doubt – whatever that may be – is the prelude to faith, or even that only someone experiencing and coping with doubt can be said to be faithful. The questioning Latin is a deliberate misquotation. The *Decretales* of Pope Gregory IX, issued in 1234, contained a blunt statement which remained part of Catholic canon law until 1918: 'Dubius in fide infidelis est'.[1] An obvious – but

* History Department, University of Birmingham, Edgbaston, Birmingham, B15 2TT. E-mail: r.n.swanson@bham.ac.uk.
[1] *CICan.* 2: 778.

Studies in Church History 52 (2016) 186–202   © Ecclesiastical History Society 2016
doi: 10.1017/stc.2015.11

potentially questionable – translation would be: 'Someone of doubt-ful faith is an infidel'. The text appears among statements about heresy; it became something of a tag in subsequent discussions of the distinctions between truth and falsehood, heresy and orthodoxy.

Dubius in fide appears a straightforward foundational text to jus-tify disciplinary action in place of debate, reconciliation and accep-tance, but becomes problematic when set in the fuller context of the pre-Reformation Western Church. Even on a superficial reading it challenges interpretation. What is this 'doubt', or this 'faith' being doubted? How much doubting of how much of the faith constitutes infidelity? And then questions begin to spiral: who (or what) has (or is) the authority by which faith is defined and doubt contested – or vice versa? Ultimately, where does truth lie, and with it the determina-tion of faith and faithlessness: who are sheep and who are goats? The traditional caricature of the medieval Church and Catholicism oblit-erates much of the uncertainty: this was a Church in which doubt was not allowed or acceptable; it was a case of believe or burn, with offi-cial indifference epitomized in the massacre at Béziers in 1209: 'Kill them! Truly God will know his own!'[2] In recent, and more subtle, scholarly formulations, fear of the challenge of doubt, and concern to protect their own authority among those commissioned to defend the faith, lay at the root of a persecuting society; while similar fears created or allowed the invention of heresy.[3]

The over-simplification of the traditional caricature does the me-dieval Church a massive disservice. Doubt, and the response to it, was no simple matter, nor was it necessarily a burning issue (in either sense).

The problem of doubt is inherently part of the problem of belief and credibility. Within Christianity, it has obvious biblical origins in the case of doubting Thomas, and the need for his doubt to be re-solved by personal experience (even if Christ's response stresses the

---

[2] Mark G. Pegg, *A Most Holy War: The Albigensian Crusade and the Battle for Christendom* (Oxford, 2008), 77.

[3] Mark G. Pegg, *The Corruption of Angels: The Great Inquisition of 1245–1246* (Princeton, NJ, 2001); idem, 'On Cathars, Albigenses, and Good Men of Languedoc', *JMedH* 27 (2001), 181–95; idem, '"Catharism" and the Study of Medieval Heresy', *New Medieval Literatures* 6 (2003), 249–69; Robert I. Moore, *The Formation of a Persecuting Society: Power and Deviance in Western Europe, 950–1250*, 2nd edn (Oxford, 2006); idem, *The War on Heresy: Faith and Power in Medieval Europe* (London, 2012).

greater merit of those who believe without experience).[4] More subtly, there is the uncertain doubting ascribed to John the Baptist,[5] and
the more radical potential for doubt in Christ's own self-questioning,
specifically in the agony in the Garden of Gethsemane: a fundamental anxiety about his own place in salvation history and his relationship to divinity which, without a resolution that necessarily had to
be based on conviction or resignation, could have become despair.
In Trinitarian terms, this becomes the question of whether divinity
could doubt itself, something best left to the scholastics.[6] A crucial
point is that the ambiguity inherent in doubt leads in different directions, evident in the dual thrust of the title for this volume. 'Doubting
Christianity' makes doubt a verb, in active engagement with the noun
and seemingly presupposing questioning and rejection. 'The Church
and Doubt' makes doubt a noun, implicitly requiring reaction from
a monolithic Church; yet how it reacts – positively or negatively, to
resolve or dissolve, or to reject by ejecting and contesting – is left an
open issue.

The openness of the questions which circulate around doubt and
doubting precludes easy answers. An avowedly tentative exploration
of the period between *c*.1100 and the onset of the Reformation reveals the potential for doubt, and locates it not as a fixed state of
mind, but within the process of attaining conviction and certainty by
achieving faith.

LOCATING DOUBT

Within modern mindsets, religious doubt largely invites attention as
rejection, challenging; it actively opposes certitude and belief. A pre-
supposition that doubt resists and rejects, and so leads to 'unbelief'
and 'scepticism', is seemingly wired into modern readings of religious

---

[4] John 20: 24–9. The medieval tradition of St Thomas is obscure, and seemingly little
studied. In Glenn W. Most, *Doubting Thomas* (Cambridge, MA, and London, 2005), the
survey of exegetical analysis 'from the church fathers to the Counter-Reformation' leaps
from *c*.1000 to the Reformation without comment: ibid. 122–54, at 145.

[5] See, in this volume, Frances Andrews, 'Doubting John?', 17–49.

[6] Kevin Madigan, 'Ancient and High-Medieval Interpretations of Jesus in Gethsemane:
Some Reflections on Tradition and Continuity in Christian Thought', *HThR* 88 (1995),
158–71; see also Sarah Covington, 'The Garden of Anguish: Gethsemane in Early Modern England', *JEH* 65 (2014), 280–308.

doubt.[7] It has produced at least one index entry, 'doubt: see scepticism', where the text treats 'the nature of doubt' accordingly.[8]

Here, though, there are two significant traps. The first is a linguistic problem: when using medieval texts, how do we get from the Latin of *dubietas* and its variants to the English 'doubt'? While medieval authors clearly understood the *dubius in fide* tag as referring to challenge and doubt, the nature of the dubiety can be nuanced (and, indeed, the application of the tag to actual doubt be questioned).[9] In their specific contexts, translation of the Latin lexicon around *dubius* to the equivalent vocabulary rooted in English 'doubt' often seems inappropriate: nuancing makes it more fitting to read 'uncertain', 'questionable', 'imprecise', and so on. This clearly affects meanings: 'Anyone who doubts the faith is an infidel' carries very different connotations from 'Someone of uncertain faith lacks faith'; yet both are valid translations of the *dubius in fide* tag. The real challenge is to select the most appropriate meaning for the specific context.

The second trap lies in assuming that along the broad spectrum of possible modes of believing or accepting Christianity – from utter rejection to absolute acceptance of its claims – there is a fixed tipping point into doubt and doubting; a movement away from rather than towards 'faith'. Doubt undercuts certitude; but the blunt bipolarity of belief and unbelief (the former as required certitude, the latter as a manifestation of doubt) can be challenged. Both states – belief and doubt – are best seen as medial. Medieval writers often adopt this stance when discussing a spectrum of attitudes to the faith and doubt. This spectrum does not require movement, yet does imply a latent trajectory of movement, an increasing commitment to Christianity or truth.

---

[7] Robert N. Swanson, '"Lollardy", "Orthodoxy", and "Resistance" in Pre-Reformation England', *Usuteaduslik Ajakiri* 64 (2013), 12–26; Susan Reynolds, 'Social Mentalities and the Case of Medieval Scepticism', *TRHS* 6th ser. 1 (1991), 21–41; John H. Arnold, *Belief and Unbelief in Medieval Europe* (London, 2005).

[8] Robert N. Swanson, *Religion and Devotion in Europe* c.*1215*–c.*1515* (Cambridge, 1995), 364, 333–6. Against medievalists' concern with scepticism, see Dorothea Weltecke, 'The Medieval Period', in Stephen Bullivant and Michael Ruse, eds, *The Oxford Handbook of Atheism* (Oxford, 2013), 164–78, at 169. Eadem, 'Doubts and the Absence of Faith', in John H. Arnold, ed., *The Oxford Handbook of Medieval Christianity* (Oxford, 2014), 357–74, addresses the issues from a different angle to the present essay, but complements it at several points.

[9] Weltecke, 'Medieval Period', 169.

An early but imperfect theological statement of that trajectory appears in the *De sacramentis* of Hugh of St Victor, written in the early twelfth century. He incorporates doubters into his spectrum, but omits a crucial part of the argument. His list works from deniers at one extreme through 'second the doubters, third the conjecturers, fourth the believers, [and] fifth the knowers'. His more detailed analysis bypasses the doubters: they must fit between those who 'straightway repel with the mind what is heard and contradict those things which are said' (the deniers) and those who, when presented with opposing claims, 'believe one of the two as more probable, yet they do not presume to assert whether it itself is still true. These are the conjecturers' (perhaps better labelled as 'the unconvinced').[10] Presumably the doubters cannot decide either way – as they cannot in Aquinas's echo of Hugh's scheme.[11]

An equivalent and clearer spectrum appears in some canonistic works. While canonists' concerns technically differed from those of theologians, dealing with absolute legal proof rather than the indubitability of concepts, their basic goal and sense of a trajectory towards knowledge of the truth was essentially identical.[12]

For William Lyndwood in fifteenth-century England, perhaps reflecting a common canonistic view, doubt is the first stage on the route to certainty. Things which are indubitable have the highest level, that is, faith. 'Doubt', as the departure point, has the mind wandering between possibilities, without inclining more fiercely to one than the other. As it advances, the mind veers to one side more than the other – this is 'suspicion': it starts to balance evidence and argument. Then comes 'opinion', an inclination to one side, but not without doubts (matching Hugh of St Victor's 'conjecture'). The final level is 'credibility', which is faith and firm belief – presumably equivalent to 'beyond reasonable doubt'.[13] Lyndwood's concern is with judicial proof, his stages those by which a judge reaches a decision.

---

[10] *Hugh of Saint Victor on the Sacraments of the Christian Faith*, transl. Roy J. Deferrari (Cambridge, MA, 1951), 168; for the Latin original, see PL 176, col. 330. There the third group are *opinantes*, perhaps making the third stage 'opinion' or 'inclination' rather than the 'conjecture' of the translation.

[11] Rik van Nieuwenhout, *An Introduction to Medieval Theology* (Cambridge, 2012), 192.

[12] For reference *c.*1395 to their agreement on the basic interpretation of *dubius in fide*, see Robert N. Swanson, 'A Survey of Views on the Great Schism, *c.*1395', *Archivum historiae pontificiae* 21 (1983), 79–103, at 102.

[13] William Lyndwood, *Provinciale, seu constitutiones Angliae … cui adjiciuntur Constitutiones Legatinae D. Othonis, et D. Othoboni … cum profundissimis annotationibus Johannis de Athona …*

The stages can, however, be transferred beyond the legal arena, to apply to almost any evolution towards intellectual conviction, apart from immediate inspiration or revelation.

In lived Catholicism, the trajectory becomes a journey, a pilgrim's progress, whose goal lies in the afterlife. The journey requires choices, decisions and commitments to select the appropriate route. These may well entail uncertainty and insecurity – doubt – which prevents further movement until those doubts are alleviated, even if not resolved. True or false guides and guidance will offer ways to resolve those doubts, and will help to determine choices, to consolidate, corrupt or corrode faith. Whether the final state is one of sufficient faith, specifically correct faith, will only become known at death, the final opportunity to choose and declare commitment.[14]

FINDING FAITH

The uncertainty of the route to salvation is the basic problem. As a process of enquiry and transformation, an intellectual endeavour, the journey to faith requires choice along the way, decisions and commitments which declare allegiance and accept or reject the alternatives on offer. Usually (in this medieval context) the alternatives are proffered by different purportedly authoritative institutions or individuals, ultimately by 'the Church' and those whom it conceives or perceives as its rivals or rebels. At any point the pilgrim may encounter questions, decisions and choices, which shape understanding without necessarily providing the understanding which the authorities would consider correct. After all, heresy is, etymologically, a faulty exercise of choice, and for the authorities which championed and defended orthodoxy, it was the determined choice of a false faith.

However, a simple spectrum from doubt to certainty is inadequate. Hugh of St Victor indicates the problem with his 'deniers'. He places them before doubt, as first in his sequence; but realistically they are on the other side of doubt, at the first stage in a sequence which he does not detail, going in the opposite direction. From them the spectrum can be traced, in reverse, to an alternative faith which can also inspire certitude. In a process of movement away from faith,

---

(Oxford, 1679), 323 ('Delicto notorio'); hereafter: 'Lyndwood' or 'Athona', depending on the part cited, as they are separately paginated; cf. Athona, 78 ('Ignorantia').

[14] See, for instance, Johannes de Bromyard, *Summa predicantium* (Nuremburg, 1518), fols 21^v–22^v [A.19], 26rb [A.21.27], 381^r–382^r [V.3].

at some point the havering of doubt becomes the starting point for alternative conviction, but still a journey towards faith. Where there are actively competing religions or denominations / confessions, that becomes a process of conversion, and the doubt-defying (maybe self-doubt-defying) assertiveness and conviction of the converted. Where there are variants within one broad tradition, the journey may lead to heresy, with authoritarian resistance and repression as its punishment.

The transition and evolution through to faith is therefore critical. Essential is the move beyond doubt, beyond the total uncertainty between two equally viable alternatives into a decision-making process in which doubts about one alternative increase commensurately with a sense of assurance about the other. That process – undergone by individuals or by the Church – may not reach a firm conclusion, leaving the individual still undecided and the Church still debating, and anxious.

'Belief' could be equated with faith, but neither of them was absolute knowledge: each remained open to question. Even though writing as a canonist rather than a theologian, John Acton (d. 1349) was perhaps thinking theologically and doctrinally when he commented that 'to believe is midway between two extremes, that is to know and to be ignorant, which pushes towards one side by fear of the other'. Knowledge, as an absolute, is positively beyond belief: 'To know truly is to have knowledge of something as indubitable.'[15] Implicitly, therefore, belief is always to some degree insecure, perhaps because it is there to be argued over, and dissected. Hugh of St Victor shares elements of that view, but not all of it. For him, as for St Paul (Heb. 11: 1), 'Faith is the substance … of things to be hoped for'; but its objects are terrestrially unknowable.[16] It cannot be proved by reason.[17] For Hugh, faith is

> … a kind of certainty of the mind in things absent, established beyond opinion and short of knowledge. … [W]e have called faith certainty, since when there is still doubt, there is no faith. … [T]hat certainty … which we call faith was established beyond opinion or conjecture and

[15] 'Sed *credere* est medium inter duo extrema, sc[ilicet] inter scire & ignorare: q[uo]d inclinat uni parti cum formidine alterius. … *Scire* vero est indubitanter aliquid noscere': Athona, 78 ('Ignorantiae'); cf. ibid. 3 ('In fide'), locating faith midway between knowledge and uncertainty, 'inter scientiam et dubitationem'.

[16] PL 176, cols 327–9 (*On the Sacraments*, transl. Deferrari, 166).

[17] PL 176, col. 329 (*On the Sacraments*, transl. Deferrari, 167).

short of knowledge. Since without doubt to believe something is less than to know, so also is to think more than [to] conjecture.[18]

Yet, if faith is imperfect knowledge (as Hugh concedes),[19] the possibility of doubt must exist.

Here, reason must be brought into the conjectures; for just as reason resolves doubt and uncertainty to build faith, so it also undermines faith by raising questions and challenging conviction. Unquestioning acceptance within a consensual or default faith community was not universal; questioning, reasoned doubting, could lead to firmer acceptance or equally firm rejection. Polarization between faith and reason – which, if faith is reasoned, clearly is not a polarization – is often represented by contrasting two twelfth-century intellectuals, Abelard and Anselm. Anselm – monk, mystic and saint – stands as the advocate of faith: 'I do not seek to understand so that I may believe, but I believe so that I may understand; and what is more, I believe that unless I do believe I shall not understand.'[20] For him faith is the starting point for understanding, which allows everything to fall into place. Meanwhile Abelard – the argumentative academic, flaunting his intellectual daring – revels in argument almost for its own sake, but as a rational balancing of propositions which lead from uncertainty to enlightenment: 'By doubting we come to enquiry; and by enquiry we perceive the truth.'[21] Yet, despite the apparent contrasts, their contradiction may be exaggerated by scholarly tradition. Regardless of methodological differences, both accept the power of argument. Abelard clearly advocates a version of the trajectory from uncertainty to knowledge (possibly even to theological

---

[18] PL 176, cols 330–1 (*On the Sacraments*, transl. Deferrari, 168).

[19] See n. 26 below.

[20] Anselm *Proslogion* 1 (*L'œuvre de S. Anselme de Cantorbéry*, 1: *Monologion, Proslogion*, ed. Michel Corbin [Paris, 1986], 242; *The Prayers and Meditations of Saint Anselm*, transl. Benedicta Ward (Harmondsworth, 1973), 244). The statement derives from Augustine, the pronouns changed to make it a first-person declaration: *Sancti Aurelii Augustini in Iohannis evangelium tractatus CXXIV* (CChr.SL 36, 287).

[21] Abelard, 'Prelude to the Yes and No', transl. A. Brian Scott, in Alastair J. Minnis, A. Brian Scott and David Wallace, eds, *Medieval Literary Theory and Criticism c.1100–c.1375: The Commentary Tradition* (Oxford, 1988), 87–100, at 99. For the Latin, see *Peter Abailard, Sic et non: A Critical Edition*, ed. Blanche B. Boyer and Richard McKeon (Chicago, IL, and London, 1977), 103.

truth, if the truth he seeks is the Truth which is Christ).[22] Moreover, his *Sic et non*, which provides his comment on doubt, includes the patristic quotation on which Anselm based his statement.[23] Anselm's writings show that his faith left room for questions (not least *Why did God become Man? – Cur Deus homo?*).[24] Anselm's understanding may build from faith, but it provides answers which presume questions, which must presume the questionable, and so the dubitable.

Anselm, moreover, stops short at understanding, before that true *scientia* of the wisdom which passes all understanding. Nevertheless, the search for understanding reinforces a sense of medieval Catholicism as a conscious attempt to comprehend the incomprehensible, the inconceivable. Seekers had to rationalize, argue, question and doubt, as they sought salvation and proximity to God. Yet, as Alan of Lille (d. 1202) recognized in his *Anticlaudianus*, that was not enough to achieve the goal. Reason, theology and questions had to yield place to a faith beyond reason (and so beyond reasonable doubt) in the progress towards God.[25] The desired state passed beyond the doubts and uncertainties which always darkened St Paul's glass, to the point where the truths of the faith were not merely indubitable, but beyond question, because no valid questions remained to be asked. For Hugh of St Victor, accordingly, faith remained only an image in a darkened mirror, because it was not true knowledge.[26] That true knowledge, though, was for another world: the Church militant had to accept doubt and uncertainty, and trust in the assertion of its own divinely authorized authority, with its members wandering pilgrims in an uncertain world.

[22] His next sentence in *Sic et Non* quotes Christ speaking as anthropomorphized Truth: *Abailard*, Sic et non, ed. Boyet and McKeon, 103–4; Minnis, Scott and Wallace, eds, *Medieval Literary Theory and Criticism*, 100.

[23] *Abailard*, Sic et non, ed. Boyet and McKeon, 115.

[24] *L'œuvre de S. Anselme de Cantorbéry*, 3: *Lettre sur l'incarnation du verbe; Pourquoi un dieu-homme*, ed. Michel Corbin (Paris, 1988), 300–473, the question posed at 300–3; Anselm of Canterbury, *The Major Works*, ed. Brian Davies and Gillian R. Evans (Oxford, 1998), 260–356, the question posed at 265.

[25] Alan of Lille, *Alain de Lille, Anticlaudianus, texte critique avec une introduction et des tables*, ed. R. Bossuat, Textes philosophiques du Môyen Âge 1 (Paris, 1955), bk 5, lines 69–543; bk 6, lines 1–197, online at: <http://www.hs-augsburg.de/~harsch/Chronologia/Lspost12/Alanus>, accessed 14 July 2015 (Alan of Lille, *Anticlaudianus, or the Good and Perfect Man*, transl. James J. Sheridan [Toronto, ON, 1973], 26, 139–63).

[26] PL 176, cols 341–2 (*On the Sacraments*, transl. Deferrari, 180–1).

DOUBTFUL CHURCH; DOUBTFUL CHRISTIANS?

Much of the preceding comment has been at an abstract level. However, correct Christian faith had to be not only in God, but in the Church and its claims to authority in matters of faith, and so in the definitions of faith which it provided. That generated its own problems. In the abstract, 'faith' is a state of mind, something equally attributable to those 'outside the faith'; but 'the faith' is a set of precepts and points to be believed.[27] The negativity of doubting presupposes dogmas and practices which can be doubted.

The myth of medieval Catholicism obviously provides the demanded uniformity for those who wish to promulgate it. It was indeed promulgated among contemporaries, as in Boniface VIII's *Unam sanctam* of 1302, asserting 'That there is one, holy, catholic and apostolic church ... and outside this church there is no salvation or remission of sins.'[28] Generally, however, the Church failed to provide a fixed standard. It provided creeds, sometimes in detail; but the most widely distributed, those that people were expected to know (especially the Apostles' Creed), were mere lists of unexplained statements. These needed interpretation to clarify their meaning, and so were open to question. While built on the Bible and authorized by the Church, the faith was not a monolith of clarity, but an amalgam of opportunities for uncertainty and disagreement – opportunities without which there would have been no need for scientific theology.

Accordingly, consideration of 'the Church and doubt' raises the question of the character of that Church, as structured institution, and as a congregation of the faithful who could be labelled as Catholics (whatever they actually believed). No matter how impersonally 'the Church' is conceived, it was run by and consisted of people. That alone was enough to make the mythic monolith unachievable; the practicalities of contemporary society made it even more so. The reality of late medieval Catholicism is best conveyed by the twelfth-century idea of 'diversity without adversity',[29] envisaging a unity which could accommodate seemingly incompatible differences. That need to accommodate did, however, necessitate a

---

[27] See comments at PL 176, cols 333–4 (*On the Sacraments*, transl. Deferrari, 171–2): infidels have faith, but not the right faith.

[28] *CICan.* 2: 1245–6 (Brian Tierney, ed., *The Crisis of Church and State, 1050–1300* [Englewood Cliffs, NJ, 1964], 188).

[29] Julian Haseldine, 'Friendship and Rivalry: The Role of *amicitia* in Twelfth-Century Monastic Relations', *JEH* 44 (1993), 390–414, at 390–1.

blurring of definitions, an uncertainty over boundaries, over what could and could not be accommodated. This is perhaps most striking at the boundary of heresy, in thirteenth-century references to 'Waldensians or heretics', and fifteenth-century ones to 'Lollards or heretics': the 'or' can amalgamate or differentiate, an interpretative conundrum which bedevils modern scholarship.[30] The overall imprecision – which made the Church an amalgam of local or communal certainties – could produce and reflect doubts and uncertainties at almost any level. Some might be on specific doctrinal issues, like the long-running debate over the Immaculate Conception.[31] Some were highly localized, in challenges to the sainthood of specific individuals and their alleged miracles (as voiced over some of Thomas Cantilupe's pre-canonization miracles).[32] Especially at local levels, official doubts were raised about unauthorized activities of questionable standing. Officials tried to quash cults and practices; but the inertia or determination of devotees could offer effective resistance.[33]

Considerable complexities arise here, as doubt and uncertainty creep in through the cracks. The faith had to be not only declared, but taught; and that required interpretation, maybe the resolution of doubts by resolving discordances. Interpretation brought questions, their answers meant to give security and knowledge – provided they could be answered. Theology itself was predicated on questions and interpretation, with academic disputations designed to force thought but channel it towards the right conclusions. Heresy among

---

[30] Peter Biller, 'Goodbye to Waldensianism?', *P&P* 192 (2006), 3–33; Anne Hudson, *The Premature Reformation: Wycliffite Texts and Lollard History* (Oxford, 1988); Richard Rex, *The Lollards* (Basingstoke, 2002); J. Patrick Hornbeck II, *What is a Lollard? Dissent and Belief in Late Medieval England* (Oxford, 2010); Andrew E. Larsen, 'Are all Lollards Lollards?', in Fiona Somerset, Jill C. Havens and Derrick G. Pitard, eds, *Lollards and their Influence in Late Medieval England* (Woodbridge, 2003), 59–72.

[31] The basic narrative is traceable through Hilda Graef, *Mary: A History of Doctrine and Devotion*, combined edn (London, 1984); see contents list and index to Part I, xix–xxi, 363.

[32] *ActaSS* Oct. 1, 698 (for offerings to this miracle's suggested alternative performer, see Hereford, Cathedral Archives, 2412–13, 2437); André Vauchez, *Sainthood in the Later Middle Ages* (Cambridge, 1997), 492, 547–8.

[33] Jean C. Schmitt, *The Holy Greyhound: Guinefort, Healer of Children since the Thirteenth Century*, Cambridge Studies in Oral and Literate Culture 6 (Cambridge, 1983); Dorothy M. Owen, 'Bacon and Eggs: Bishop Buckingham and Superstition in Lincolnshire', in G. J. Cuming and Derek Baker, eds, *Popular Belief and Practice*, SCH 8 (Cambridge, 1972), 139–42, at 141; Bernard Montagnes, 'La Repression des sacralités populaires en Languedoc au XVe siècle', *AFP* 52 (1982), 155–85; Nicholas Orme, 'Bishop Grandisson and Popular Religion', *Devonshire Association Transactions* 124 (1992), 107–18.

academics reflected that uncertainty; yet, as rival intellectual systems produced incompatible understandings with partisan adherents, the ground was laid for fundamental challenges which eventually produced reformation.[34]

The propositions within the formulations of the faith, and the theologizing which validated practices, invited – or received – responses across the spectrum of allegiance. This was important. As in a graph, an axis of actual adherence had to be correlated against one of demanded adherence: not every component of Catholicism had equal importance to identify a Catholic and draw the line between orthodoxy and heresy. Specific practices, specific beliefs, might take centuries to become entrenched as 'universal' components; until then they could be legitimately debated, differently understood and licitly doubted (as was 'transubstantiation', long after 1215).[35] That uncertainty, and evolutions which moved some doctrines from 'optional' to 'mandatory', was implicitly acknowledged in the concept of error, a category of flawed belief which was not heresy. 'Error', as 'contrary to the truth and shared determination of the learned',[36] did not contradict proclaimed and acknowledged truth; it challenged an ecclesial consensus which was not dogmatic and therefore might not be right.

The ambiguity which the notion of error brings into the discussion is compounded when calibrating demanded and actual adherence against each other. Where, then, does opinion fit as 'less than faith'? Is it sufficiently distinguishable from faith to count as 'doubt'? At what point on the highly delicate spectrum of belief does orthodoxy shade into doubt and dissent? The question resonates with modern scholarly anxieties about where boundaries lie, and the insecure overlap between present assumptions and medieval experiences. In current work on fifteenth-century English Lollardy, scholars increasingly accept (and expand) a 'grey area' between heresy and orthodoxy. Explicitly between, inherently unstable, it remains neither one nor the other, yet shades into both.[37] This grey area is

---

[34] Alister E. McGrath, *The Intellectual Origins of the European Reformation*, 2nd edn (Oxford, 2004), 17–23, 67–115.

[35] Gary Macy, 'The Dogma of Transubstantiation in the Middle Ages', *JEH* 45 (1994), 11–41.

[36] *Registrum Johannis Trefnant, Episcopi Herefordensis, A.D. MCCCLXXXIX–MCCCCIV*, ed. William W. Capes, CYS 20 (London, 1916), 394.

[37] See Jill C. Havens, 'Shading the Grey Area: Determining Heresy in Middle English Texts', in *Text and Controversy from Wyclif to Bale: Essays in Honour of Anne Hudson*, ed. Helen Barr and Ann M. Hutchison, Medieval Church Studies 4 (Turnhout, 2005), 337–52;

visible through texts, yet existed in lives, as individuals believed on and at the borderlines of the acceptable, possibly wavering repeatedly across it during a lifetime.[38]

Ideally, the practised and experienced faith would be stable and firm; but instability was more likely, and impacts on the interpretation of devotional experience. Yet the divisions which occur when moving away from a stable faith are not those encountered when doubting on the road to faith. John Acton again identifies the problem. Questioning in search of security can be done pertinaciously and rashly, with a mind already to some extent made up. That is heresy. Yet if the questioning is done with no decided goal, motivated only by scruples of conscience, the outcome is more a punishment than a fault, a weakness of personal imagination rather than sin. Such doubting scrupulosity had to be curbed and crushed, yet was not actually deviance, not heresy.[39]

However, the doubts generated by scrupulosity could be as corrosive of individual faith as any heresy. The precise background to the obscure encounter between Archbishop Alexander Neville of York and Agnes Mawson when they talked on the north Yorkshire moors in 1375 is unknown; but she was in spiritual turmoil, feared a loss of faith and needed guidance. They talked, and Neville thought that he had resolved her doubts and uncertainties. He also appealed for help, granting an indulgence to all who prayed to reinforce her faith.[40] This vignette of a bishop firmly engaging in the cure of souls, resolving doubts and reinforcing Catholicism, is matched by Margery Kempe's talks with other bishops, described in her *Book*.[41] It was presumably matched at parish level as priests talked with their parishioners; probably also in discussions between parishioners, engaged in mutual consolation and enhancement of their faith via the Spiritual Works

---

Matti Peikola, *Congregation of the Elect: Patterns of Self-Fashioning in English Lollard Writings*, Anglicana Turkuensia 21 (Turku, 2000), 23–37. See also Stephen Kelly and Ryan Perry, 'Devotional Cosmopolitanism in Fifteenth-Century England', in Vincent Gillespie and Kantik Ghosh, eds, *After Arundel: Religious Writing in Fifteenth-Century England* (Turnhout, 2011), 363–80, at 375–9 (note especially 376 n. 40).

[38] See John A. F. Thomson, 'Knightly Piety and the Margins of Lollardy', in Margaret Aston and Colin Richmond, eds, *Lollardy and the Gentry in the Later Middle Ages* (Stroud and New York, 1997), 95–111; Kelly and Perry, 'Devotional Cosmopolitanism', 364–5.

[39] Athona, 4 ('Resistendum').

[40] York, Borthwick Institute for Archives, Reg. 12, fols 39^r–^{v}.

[41] *The Book of Margery Kempe*, ed. Sanford B. Meech and Hope E. Allen, EETS os 212 (Oxford, 1940), 33–4, 36–7 (*The Book of Margery Kempe*, transl. Barry A. Windeatt [Harmondsworth, 1987], 69–70, 72–3).

of Mercy.[42] The evidence is limited, but suggests that such doubt-resolving discussion was not uncommon, with debates attempting to bring alleged heretics back into the fold part of the same process.[43]

Potentially, scrupulosity might be the most extreme and paradoxical form of doubt, soul-destroying not by eroding faith in God, but by destroying the believer's self-confidence, undermining hitherto firm adherence to the faith. As anxiety over one's own fitness for salvation, exposing the raw nerve of uncertainty otherwise obscured by hope (a state less certain than belief), scrupulosity could get carried away with itself. On the deathbed it could generate despair, a refusal to accept any possibility of divine mercy: self-damning, and therefore to be taken seriously. Hence the deathbed's communal character, as set out in fifteenth-century *ars moriendi* literature, with friends and neighbours clustered around to coax the soul through to purgatory, reassuring of divine mercy and urging trust in God.[44] Hence also the horror of Albert ter Achter's deathbed in Deventer in 1492. A member of a *devotio moderna* community, despite his exemplary life he fell into ranting despair in his last days, and could ultimately be consoled only with great difficulty and a vision of his own merciful judgement by the Virgin and Christ. Even so, it was unclear whether he finally died fit to be saved. All a witness could comment was this: 'His death, most horrible in its external appearance and without any precedent that we can recall was, we sincerely hope, not injurious to him.'[45]

Like anxiety about salvation, scrupulosity could strike at any time. Institutional responses encouraged mechanisms to eliminate it, but perhaps increased it. Conformist rigour among observant regulars was reinforced by ever-increasing regulation and minute prescription.[46] This in turn provoked anxiety about whether those rules were

---

[42] Robert N. Swanson, 'Pastoral Care, Pastoral Cares, Pastoral Carers: Configuring the *Cura pastoralis*', in Peter Clarke and Sarah James, eds, *Pastoral Care in Medieval England: Interdisciplinary Approaches* (forthcoming).

[43] For example, Anne Hudson, ed., *Two Wycliffite Texts: The Sermon of William Taylor, 1406; The Testimony of William Thorpe, 1407*, EETS os 301 (Oxford, 1993), 24–93.

[44] Carl Horstman, ed., *Yorkshire Writers: Richard Rolle of Hampole and his Followers*, 2 vols (London, 1895–6), 2: 409–10, 412–14, 417–20; Robert N. Swanson, ed., *Catholic England: Faith, Religion, and Observance before the Reformation* (Manchester, 1993), 129–31, 134–7, 142–7.

[45] John van Engen, 'The Practices of *Devotio moderna*', in Miri Rubin, ed., *Medieval Christianity in Practice* (Princeton, NJ, and Oxford, 2009), 256–62, quotation at 259; note the caution and uncertainty inherent in 'sincerely hope'.

[46] James D. Mixson, *Poverty's Proprietors: Ownership and Mortal Sin at the Origins of the Observant Movement* (Leiden and Boston, MA, 2009), 202–13.

being sufficiently observed. It was not faith per se that was undermined, but the assurance of salvation that should have accompanied it. It was perhaps no accident that the birth of the Reformation is ascribed to an overly scrupulous Augustinian friar, seeking a way out of this terrifying impasse.

Unavoidable Doubt?

On the road to salvation, doubt-resolving decisions were choices, of routes and paths, of guides and guidance, occasionally matters of reasoned (or even inspired) guesswork. Making an accumulation of binary choices – yes / no, accept / reject – each Christian sought to progress through to faith and to certainty. Those choices were also decisions about the credibility of the Church's definitions and prescriptions for the faith, accepting or rejecting its claims to authority. The end result could be a fatal one, heresy, the term itself acknowledging the power and perils of choice. It was far easier, far safer, from the Church's point of view, for the flock to misbelieve the details but accept its authority, to be heretical without being formally heretics because they wanted to believe as the Church believed. Even if of dubious faith they then still counted among the *fideles*; such permitted wrong-headedness did not entail infidelity.[47]

Ultimately, theological faith was something earth-bound, perhaps quintessentially human. It was not theological knowledge, which would be achieved only after death; therein lay its main limitation. As the end of a progression from doubt and uncertainty, arguably faith could never entirely eradicate questions and uncertainty. Before entry into the afterlife, the strongest hope could be destroyed by a nagging final uncertainty – as Albert ter Achter discovered on his deathbed. Hugh of St Victor said that faith went beyond and eradicated doubt,[48] but he was manifestly wrong, at least at face value. Durand of St Pourçain or Porcien (d. 1332/4) was more on the right path. For him 'knowledge cannot have doubt mixed within it in any way; faith, however, can have doubt mixed within it in some way'.[49] Perhaps faith needed doubt to prove itself.

[47] Athona, 4 ('Resistendum', continued from 3); Lyndwood, 1 ('Sciat').
[48] PL 176, col. 330 (*On the Sacraments*, transl. Deferrari, 168).
[49] *D. Durandi a Sancto Porciano … in Petri Lombardi Sententias Theologicas commentariorum libri IIII*, 2 vols (Venice, 1571), 2: 255[va]. For context, see Kent Emery Jr, 'Cognitive Theory and the Relation between the Scholastic and Mystical Modes of Theology: Why Denys

As the requirements of the faith became increasingly defined, the diversity tolerable within medieval Catholicism became increasingly limited. Moreover, as uncertainties – or doubts – gave way to differing certitudes, so diversity became rigid divergence. The partisan fifteenth-century philosophical chasm indicated by the statement that 'One cannot dispute with those with whom one disagrees on first principles' easily transferred to theological stances.[50] In the sixteenth century, divergence moved a stage further, to division and Reformation. By that point, moreover, the 'crisis of authority' which pervaded the higher levels of the Church had reached a tipping point with Erasmus's retranslation of the Bible, producing a text critically different at crucial points.[51] The implications were fundamental, although not always followed through: if the Western Church had actually got its Bible wrong, authorized itself on false foundations, where was the authority for its faith? What, indeed, was now 'the faith'?

Ironically, the ambivalent and ambiguous reality which the medieval Church lived with may not have achieved clear expression until after the Reformation. In that doctrinal and spiritual free-for-all the quest for faith remained; but so did the problem of doubt. Doubt, though, could now be openly acknowledged and validated as part of the quest, and dealt with (at least in England) without having to match vernacular and Latin vocabularies. In the early 1630s, responding to doubting Thomas's eventual declaration of faith, the obscure William Austin commented: 'No Faith stronger then [= than] what is gotten after a doubt. For hee that never doubted scarce ever well-beleeved.'[52] He was echoing others, notably William Perkins.[53] A stance only implicit in the pre-Reformation centuries was at last openly formulated.

---

the Carthusian outlawed Durandus of Saint-Pourçain', in Spencer E. Young, ed., *Crossing Boundaries at Medieval Universities* (Leiden and Boston, MA, 2011), 145–74, at 168, cf. 157.

[50] Emery, 'Cognitive Theory', 148; for the dictum's origins, see Kent Emery Jr, 'Denys the Carthusian and the Doxology of Scholastic Theology', in Mark D. Jordan and Kent Emery Jr, eds, Ad litteram: *Authoritative Texts and their Medieval Readers* (Notre Dame, IN, and London, 1992), 327–59, at 334–5, but see 351 n. 39.

[51] McGrath, *Intellectual Origins*, 131–7; Diarmaid MacCulloch, *Reformation: Europe's House Divided, 1490–1700* (London, 2003), 99–101.

[52] William Austin, *Devotionis Augustinianae Flamma, or, Certaine Devout, Godly, and Learned Meditations Written, by the Excellently-Accomplisht Gentleman, William Austin, of Lincolnes-Inne, Esquire* (London, 1635), 178–9 (modified).

[53] William Perkins, *A Treatise Tending vnto a Declaration Whether a Man be in the Estate of Damnation or in the Estate of Grace* (London, 1590), 266.

CONCLUSION

In the pilgrim's progress to salvation, with all its uncertainties and choices, doubt was necessary and unavoidable. In the late Middle Ages, for those who moved outside the Catholic faith and Catholic structures, to be of doubtful faith was to be faithless, at least from the inside looking out. Even for those within, the fortress of faith was not impregnable; doubt and uncertainty, the possibility that the blind were leading the blind into a ditch, was everywhere. While not a truth universally acknowledged, many in the pre-Reformation centuries would perhaps have concurred with Austin and Perkins. Their words merely gave explicit recognition to a longstanding reality, that to be questioning and uncertain about the faith could be a prelude to greater faith, because without the resolution out of doubt there was no resolution into the fullness of faith.

Doubting Witchcraft: Theologians, Jurists, Inquisitors during the Fifteenth and Sixteenth Centuries

Matteo Duni*

Syracuse University Florence

The theory of diabolical witchcraft attracted serious doubts from its first formulation early in the fifteenth century. This essay focuses on the writings of a few lay jurists and lawyers who rejected the witch-hunters' claim that witchcraft was made possible by the Devil's ability to operate physically in the world, and argued instead that such acts as consorting sexually with demons, or being carried through the air to the Sabbat, were visions and dreams produced by the Devil. In this heated debate, both doubters and believers frequently crossed their respective disciplinary boundaries as they sought to prove their point. The essay analyses the works of lawyers who confuted the witch-hunters' interpretation of key biblical passages, using them to demonstrate that witchcraft was physically impossible, and that believing otherwise was unsound from both a legal and a religious point of view. It argues that their specific contribution was notable both for its content, as a particularly radical attack on demonological theories, and in itself, as an explicit challenge to ecclesiastical hegemony in the discourse on metaphysics. It concludes that their doubts had a significant, if belated, impact on the Roman Inquisition's policy vis-à-vis witchcraft.

The title of the first question of the *Malleus maleficarum* (*Hammer of Witches*) introduces a note of doubt: 'Whether claiming that sorcerers exist is such a Catholic proposition that to defend the opposite view steadfastly is altogether heretical'.[1] As is well known, the

* Syracuse University Florence, Piazza Savonarola 15, 50132 Firenze, Italy. E-mail: mduni@syr.edu.

I would like to thank Frances Andrews for her kind invitation to present a paper at the Ecclesiastical History Society Winter Meeting, and the anonymous reviewer and the editors of Studies in Church History for having helped me improve my article with their valuable comments and critiques.

[1] Henricus Institoris and Jacobus Sprenger, *Malleus maleficarum*, ed. and transl. Christopher S. Mackay, 2 vols (Cambridge, 2006), 2: 43. Mackay holds on to the traditional idea of a double authorship of the *Malleus maleficarum*, but recent studies unanimously exclude the possibility that the prominent Dominican reformer Jacob Sprenger had any such role: cf. Richard M. Golden, ed., *Encyclopedia of Witchcraft: The Western Tradition* [hereafter: *EoW*], 4 vols (Santa Barbara, CA, 2006), *s.v.* '*Malleus Maleficarum*'.

Malleus maleficarum (1486) was for a long time the most authoritative and widespread handbook for the prosecution of witchcraft available to judges lay and ecclesiastical. Its author, the German Dominican inquisitor Heinrich Kramer, better known as Institoris (the Latin version of his name) was one of the most notorious witch-hunters of all time.[2] In 1484 Pope Innocent VIII had issued the bull *Summis desiderantes affectibus*, which gave Institoris free rein in the prosecution of witches throughout Germany; this was joined to the *Malleus* as a type of foreword.[3] Papal endorsement and thorough treatment of the topic granted the book a remarkable success, and it went through six editions before the end of the century.

Given such an impressive foundation, why would the book open on such a note of doubt? Why is there such urgency to demonstrate that belief in the existence of *maleficos* (sorcerers or witches) was absolutely orthodox, and that its opposite was heresy? Reading through the book's index one realizes that Question One is not isolated: 'whether it is a Catholic proposition to claim that humans can be begotten by incubus and succubus demons' (Question Three); 'whether a Catholic can in any way hold the view that the origin and increase in the number of sorcerers' works derive from the influences of the heavenly bodies or from the superabundant evil of humans, and not from the filthy acts of incubus and succubus demons' (Question Five).[4] While the examination of conflicting theses and the evaluation of arguments for and against each one were certainly dictated by the scholastic style of debating, the subjects treated, and the sense of urgency in rebutting the objections, indicate clearly that the author was set on dispelling doubts and rejecting scepticism.

As research into the witch-hunt over the last twenty years has shown, the opening of the *Malleus* is actually far from surprising. Indeed, it was only natural and logical that Institoris would design the first part of his ambitious work in such a way. He was adding his voice to a then fifty-year long but still very heated debate on a highly contested topic, namely, the nature and the very possibility of

---

[2] The best and most up-to-date treatment of Institoris's life and works is Tamar Herzig, *Christ Transformed into a Virgin Woman: Lucia Brocadelli, Heinrich Kramer, and the Defense of the Faith* (Rome, 2013). See also *EoW*, *s.n.* 'Kramer (Institoris), Heinrich'.

[3] For the annotated English text of the bull, see Alan C. Kors and Edward Peters, eds, *Witchcraft in Europe 400–1700: A Documentary History*, 2nd edn, rev. Edward Peters (Philadelphia, PA, 2001), 177–80.

[4] Institoris, *Malleus maleficarum*, ed. and transl. Mackay, 2: 73, 91.

diabolical witchcraft. While Institoris and his fellow inquisitors held that witches met with the Devil face to face at the Sabbat, and could interact bodily with demons, a series of prominent ecclesiastics and theologians, but also lay authors from different backgrounds, were sceptical in this regard. Indeed, they believed that the supposed witches had only dreamed or imagined that they had experienced these things, though their dreams might have been provoked by the Devil's manipulation of their imagination. In short, the witch-hunters placed an unprecedented emphasis on the Devil's ability to operate physically in the world, including for example the power to carry witches through the air to the Sabbat, or to consort sexually with them. The opponents of the witch-hunt, to whom I will refer as sceptics or doubters, emphasized instead the Devil's skills at tricking the senses and mental faculties of those who gave in to his temptations. They held to more traditional positions than the demonology of their opponents: in particular, sceptics usually adopted the approach articulated in the influential canon *Episcopi*, which warned against the Devil's wiles but characterized them primarily as deceptions.[5] This article will focus on an aspect that scholars have not previously analysed in depth, namely the important contribution of a few sceptical lay jurists to the early phase of the debate. These jurists drew especially on medicine and theology to reject unqualified belief in witchcraft, thus systematically addressing issues outside their area of expertise. I will argue that such an interdisciplinary approach made their attack on the witch-hunters' theories more radical than that represented by traditional scepticism. I will concentrate on the way lay specialists of law – especially Ulrich Molitor and Gianfrancesco Ponzinibio – discussed problems of metaphysics and offered original interpretations of scriptural passages, countering the inquisitors on their own ground.

Institoris and other fifteenth-century inquisitors described witchcraft as a new and frightening heresy, whose adherents would meet the Devil face to face in the course of secret night-time gatherings. At these meetings they would feast and party, then pay homage to their master by some obscene ritual, often involving the defilement

---

[5] Cf. Walter Stephens, *Demon Lovers: Witchcraft, Sex, and the Crisis of Belief* (Chicago, IL, and London, 2002); Martine Ostorero, *Le Diable au sabbat. Littérature démonologique et sorcellerie (1440–1460)* (Florence, 2011). Many of these issues continued to be debated in the following centuries: cf. Stuart Clark, *Thinking with Demons: The Idea of Witchcraft in Early Modern Europe* (Oxford, 1997), especially 195–213; *EoW*, *s.v.* 'Skepticism'. On *Episcopi*, see below, 215–16.

of things sacred and the killing of innocent babies, and almost invariably sealed by the sexual act with the Devil. Having formally renounced Christianity and thus become the Devil's servants, these heretics, variously referred to as *malefic / maleficae, sortilegae* or *strigae*, would receive from their master the power to harm. They would then cause the illness or death of humans with their spells; they would make women and animals barren, and destroy crops by raising up hailstorms and tempests. Denounced by inquisitors and preachers from the first three decades of the fifteenth century, the crimes of the witches conflated elements drawn from learned magic and necromancy with the supposed features of heretical movements persecuted in previous centuries, especially the Cathars and the Waldensians. Witches were believed physically to meet the Devil, like ritual magicians, but unlike the latter they were not seen as isolated practitioners of black magic, but as members of an organized sect, like heretics; indeed, the meeting of witches was usually referred to using the same terms applied to heretical gatherings: 'sect' (*secta*), 'synagogue' (*synagoga*), 'company' (*societas*). However, witches differed from both types of predecessor for a number of crucial reasons. First of all, their affiliation with the evil one consisted in a total, permanent submission, body and soul, manifested by ritual degradation. Second, such perverted ceremony would normally take place in the course of a physical meeting of numerous witches with the Devil. Third, witches received from the Devil more effective magical powers than those of necromancers, without the need of any training or preparation. Finally, they were believed to reach the place of their meeting flying through the air astride sticks, or animals, but really with the help of demons. The Sabbat and the flight of witches signified a change of scale in beliefs about the practice of heresy: thanks to these features a greater number of humans than ever before were enticed into abandoning Christianity with the irresistible prospect of endless pleasures, which were offered to them in the course of regular mass meetings, thus multiplying the occasions of sin and harm. In sum, witches were renegade Christians set on doing as much harm as possible through the exceptional powers that the Devil had granted them, actively participating in a terrifying conspiracy with the final goal of destroying Christianity and overturning the world.[6]

---

[6] Cf. Hans-Peter Broedel, 'Fifteenth-Century Witch Beliefs', in Brian P. Levack, ed., *The Oxford Handbook of Witchcraft in Early Modern Europe and Colonial America* (Oxford, 2013),

One of the first descriptions to include many of these features is found in a rare account of a trial, that of a certain Matteuccia di Francesco, tried at Todi in Umbria in 1428. Probably inspired by the fiery anti-witchcraft sermons of Bernardino da Siena, the trial ended with a capital sentence. Matteuccia had confessed to having killed numerous babies by sucking their blood, but also to having gone to a great meeting of witches:

> … many times with other witches she went to the walnut tree of Benevento … by anointing herself with an unguent made from the fat of a vulture, the blood of an owl, the blood of suckling babies and other things, by saying: 'Unguent, unguent, take me to the walnut tree of Benevento, over water and over wind, and over any bad weather' … And instantly a demon appeared before her in the shape of a billy-goat, and she turned into a she-cat, and riding on that billy-goat she flew to the said walnut tree … as fast as lightning, and there she found many witches and demons from Hell and the great Lucifer who presided and ordered her and the others to travel around to destroy infants and to do other evils.[7]

While witchcraft trials such as that of Matteuccia and early descriptions of the sect multiplied in the 1420s and 1430s, from the following decade theologians, inquisitors and jurists began trying to make sense of the evidence of the new heresy, working out its physical and metaphysical implications, as well as the legal questions posed by its judicial prosecution. An impressive and steady flow of books, most of them printed not long after their composition, documents the sudden urgency of the theme, whilst at the same time charting the dimensions of the budding witch-hunt. Both the persecutions and the publications were markedly international phenomena: they developed from French-Swiss lands, just as the witch-hunts were spreading from the western part of the Alps – Savoy, Val d'Aosta, Valais, Pays de Vaud and Berne – to Southern and then Northern France, and then to the

---

32–49. One of the first inquisitors to articulate clearly this alarming theory was the French Dominican Nicolas Jacquier (see below, 213) in his tract of 1458, *Flagellum fascinariorum haereticorum* (Frankfurt am Main, 1581), 37–51.

[7] Domenico Mammoli, *Processo alla strega Matteuccia di Francesco (Todi, 20 marzo 1428)* (Spoleto, 2013; first publ. 1969), 26–8. Translations from Latin or Italian are mine, unless otherwise specified.

Germanic lands.[8] But there was also a major input from the Italian peninsula, with writers and hunters concentrated mostly in the regions closer to the Alps, and significant contributions from other areas less affected by the witch-hunt, such as the Iberian peninsula.[9] Most of the works were authored by members of the mendicant orders, with Dominicans leading the way: some were well-known theologians, such as the German reformer Johannes Nider, author of the seminal *Formicarius*.[10] Most were inquisitors, such as the French Jean Vineti and Nicolas Jacquier (both active in the mid-fifteenth century), the German Institoris, or Bernardo Rategno, Silvestro Mazzolini and Bartolomeo Spina, all Italian witch-hunters active during the end of the fifteenth and the early sixteenth centuries.[11] While these authors devoted their books specifically (or predominantly) to witchcraft, an even longer series of ecclesiastics discussed the topic at significant length in one or other part of their work. This group includes very prominent figures, such as the Spanish cardinal and influential canonist Juan de Torquemada, Bishop Alfonso Tostado of Ávila, Cardinal Nicholas of Cusa in his capacity as bishop of Brixen, and Tommaso de Vio, master general of the Dominicans, better known as Cardinal Cajetan.[12]

---

[8] Richard Kieckhefer, 'The First Wave of Trials for Diabolical Witchcraft', in Levack, ed., *Oxford Handbook of Witchcraft*, 159–78.

[9] On early Italian authors, see Ostorero, *Le Diable au sabbat*, 681–94; Astrid Estuardo Flaction, 'Girolamo Visconti, un témoin du débat sur la réalité de la sorcellerie au XVe siècle en Italie du Nord', in Martine Ostorero, Georg Modestin, and Kathrin Utz Tremp, eds, *Chasse aux sorcières et démonologie. Entre discours et pratique (XIVe–XVIIe siècles)* (Florence, 2010), 389–406. On early Italian witch-hunts, see Wolfgang Behringer, *Witches and Witch-Hunts: A Global History* (Cambridge, UK, and Malden, MA, 2004), 72–9; Tamar Herzig, 'Italy', in Levack, ed., *Oxford Handbook of Witchcraft*, 249–67.

[10] On Nider, see Michael Bailey, *Battling Demons: Witchcraft, Heresy and Reform in the Late Middle Ages* (University Park, PA, 2005). A selection from the *Formicarius* (with facing French translation) is in *L'Imaginaire du sabbat. Édition critique des textes les plus anciens (1430 c.–1440 c.)*, ed. Martine Ostorero, Agostino Paravicini Bagliani and Kathrin Utz Tremp (Lausanne, 1999), 99–265.

[11] On Vineti and Jacquier and their works, see Ostorero, *Le Diable au sabbat*, 81–116, 117–64 respectively; *EoW, s.n.* 'Jacquier, Nicolas (ca. 1400–1472)'. On Rategno, see Adriano Prosperi, Vincenzo Lavenia and John Tedeschi, eds, *Dizionario storico dell'Inquisizione* [hereafter: *DSI*], 4 vols (Pisa, 2010), *s.n.* 'Rategno, Bernardo'. On Mazzolini, see Michael Tavuzzi, *Prierias: The Life and Works of Silvestro Mazzolini da Prierio (1456–1527)* (Durham, NC, and London, 1997). On Spina, see *DSI, s.n.* 'Spina, Bartolomeo'; Stephens, *Demon Lovers*, especially 159–64.

[12] On Torquemada, see Ostorero, *Le Diable au sabbat*, 634–7. On Tostado, see *EoW, s.n.* 'Tostado, Alonso'. On Nicholas of Cusa and witches, see Carlo Ginzburg, *Ecstasies: Deciphering the Witches' Sabbat* (Chicago, IL, 1991), 94–5. On De Vio and his opinion of

The problems that witchcraft presented were numerous, and had weighty implications. First of all, to believe that witches could commit the nefarious, extraordinary deeds mentioned above, one had to believe that the Devil and demons in general had, or could acquire, a material body. Thomas Aquinas had described the mechanism whereby demons, pure spirits, could create bodies made of thickened air, and with these could not only appear to humans, but also simulate human bodily operations. As early as 1326, Pope John XXII's bull *Super illius specula* condemned magical practices such as conjuring demons in rings or mirrors as based on actual, face-to-face dealings between magicians and the Devil. In the papal pronouncement the pact with Satan was not described as just a spiritual error, happening only in the mind of the heretic, but as something which had a physical, material dimension.[13] What the evidence from trials such as that of Matteuccia and many others indicated, however, was yet another level in the nature of the contacts between humans and demons. These were no longer thought of as the prerogative of a fairly restricted group such as learned magicians practising necromancy, but had become a matter of appalling routine. Witches would meet the Devil face to face, would be materially transported to the Sabbat on a weekly basis, and would have sex with their accompanying demons more often than they would with their spouses. Inquisitors and theologians of the time, working on a scattered body of information, from the witches' confessions to norms of canon law, folkloric tales and sermons, were gradually creating a new, much more 'realist' demonology than that of traditional scholasticism. Their theories accentuated the Devil's powers of intervention in the natural world, as well as the variety of the methods he would employ to tempt and tease, entice and threaten human beings. In this way, as Martine Ostorero has aptly observed, these theologians were providing the metaphysical foundation for the possibility of witchcraft as it was being discovered in the trials, and at the same time finding confirmation of their theories in the transcripts of the trials.[14]

---

the witches' flight as an illusion, see Vincenzo Lavenia, '"Anticamente di misto foro". Inquisizione, stati e delitti di stregoneria nella prima età moderna', in Giovanna Paolin, ed., *Inquisizioni: percorsi di ricerca* (Trieste, 2001), 35–80, at 41–2.

[13] Cf. Alain Boureau, *Satan the Heretic: The Birth of Demonology in the Medieval West* (Chicago, IL, 2006), 10–12; Ostorero, *Le Diable au sabbat*, 236–7.

[14] Ostorero, *Le Diable au sabbat*, 721–3.

The process of endowing Satan with enhanced faculties was certainly not linear or unopposed. To a large extent, the new demonology generated resistance based on the same foundations. The Devil, as explained by Aquinas, could intervene in the physical world not only through his virtual body, but in more subtle ways: for example, he could alter the balance of humours in the human body, causing madness, or trick the senses, causing someone to see things which were not there, or even intervene in a person's imagination to generate fictitious images of people or events that would appear as perfectly real and present.[15] It was therefore completely orthodox to suspect that at least some aspects of what the witches confessed could be the product of demonic delusion, especially since it was believed that the Devil's level of influence on a person's body would be at its maximum in the case of those who had given themselves over to him completely, as witches did.

Such suspicions, particularly those concentrating on the witches' flight as well as the Sabbat, were not only orthodox but enshrined in canon law. One section of the canon *Episcopi* – a text dating probably from the tenth century – distinguished harmful magic, a concrete and very real threat, from the deluded visions of some 'wicked women' (*sceleratae mulieres*) who gave themselves over to the Devil and then, 'seduced by the illusions and phantasms of the demons', believed themselves to be part of the goddess Diana's retinue and to ride at night for long distances 'upon certain beasts'. *Episcopi* calls the women's claims a 'false opinion': it is just a vision produced by the Devil in the imagination of these 'miserable little women' (*mulierculae*), as the text also refers to them, who are thus deluded into believing that such actions take place truly and corporeally.[16] Although it did not mention the Sabbat specifically, *Episcopi* underscored that, by taking hold of the imagination, the Devil could show humans images of many different events and people, fully persuading them of their reality. In the twelfth century *Episcopi* was included by Gratian in his influential *Decretum*, thereby acquiring a very authoritative status. Thus the only norm of canon law which spoke of beliefs

---

[15] Stephens, *Demon Lovers*, 61–8; Euan Cameron, *Enchanted Europe: Superstition, Reason, & Religion, 1250–1750* (Oxford and New York, 2010), 94–100; Michael Bailey, *Fearful Spirits, Reasoned Follies: The Boundaries of Superstition in Late Medieval Europe* (Ithaca, NY, and London, 2013), especially 205–8.

[16] See the text of *Episcopi* with commentary in Kors and Peters, eds, *Witchcraft in Europe*, 61–3. On its impact on the debate on witchcraft, see *EoW, s.v.* 'Skepticism'.

akin to the witches' ride and meeting interpreted them as nothing more than dreams or mental delusions, and stressed that the main error of the *mulierculae* was to believe that these things were actually happening.[17]

The weight of *Episcopi*'s stance explains why several witchcraft writers from the first generation display a marked uncertainty on these issues. In his *Formicarius* Johannes Nider describes the claims of a 'delirious woman' that she would go through the air with Diana and other women, in a chapter devoted to 'delusory dreams'.[18] Indeed, he ridicules the woman for a pathetic attempt to fly to her meeting with 'Domina Venus' by stepping in a bowl she normally used to make dough. However, in another part of the book he presents the art of sorcerers as including the ability of 'moving through the air from one place to another', adding only a slight note of doubt ('as they believe').[19]

While the theologian and reformer Nider has a hard time reconciling incompatible positions, one of the major canonists of the time, Juan de Torquemada, displays granitic conviction. In his commentary to the *Decretum*, dating from around the early 1450s, Torquemada argues at great length that no aspect of the beliefs described in *Episcopi* can ever exist outside of the imagination of these deluded women. He stresses the inherent absurdity of their tales – they cannot really ride with Diana, since this goddess does not exist – but he goes beyond logic and points out the physical impossibility of certain details. For example, their claim of riding animals for very long distances in the complete silence of the night is rejected because no animal could ever do that without resting a while and without being heard. While admitting the possibility that the Devil may transport bodies from place to place 'as if they flew', he refuses to believe that he would materially carry people, as this would mean attributing to him exceptional powers, which borders on paganism and idolatry.[20]

Torquemada does not seem to feel any anxiety over a spread of witchcraft, and deals with the issue in very traditional terms. But his attitude was increasingly perceived as questionable, if not unacceptable, by significant sectors of the ecclesiastical establishment. In 1453, around the time Torquemada was writing, the French

[17] Stephens, *Demon Lovers*, 127–34.
[18] *L'Imaginaire du sabbat*, 207.
[19] Ibid. 178.
[20] Ostorero, *Le Diable au sabbat*, 634–7.

Benedictine monk Guillaume Adeline, master of theology and preacher, was tried at Evreux by the vice-inquisitor of France for having participated in the *synagogue vaudoise*, or the sect of the witches. Besides the usual list of deeds such as the demonic pact, Adeline confessed to having preached, at the instigation of the Devil, that 'this sect of *vauderie* was only an illusion' (*cette secte de vauderie n'estoit qu'illusion*), further calling it 'imagination and daydreaming' (*faintaisie et songerie*), citing the canon *Episcopi*.[21] Evidently, upholding the standard position of canon law could be considered a dangerous heresy, as he was sentenced to life imprisonment. His trial may have represented a turning point in the growing discussion on the nature of witchcraft: mentioned by several different works in the following decades, the case of the master theologian enrolled in the Devil's army provided strong support to the argument developed by Nicholas Jacquier in his *Flagellum haereticorum fascinariorum* (*The Scourge of the Heretical Witches*, 1458).[22] Jacquier is the first author to focus his attention not merely on the threat posed by witches, but particularly on the more insidious danger coming from those who doubt their existence. Indeed, his 'preface to the reader' is entirely devoted to exposing the 'perverse principles and foolish assertions' of 'many people who – coming out in the most untimely manner – greatly favour and defend the *fascinarii* heretics [i.e. witches], to the serious detriment of the Catholic faith'. These unspecified sceptics, writes Jacquier,

> … affirm that witches are deluded by the Devil's operations only in their dreams, so that eventually in their waking hours they believe that they have gone at night to several places, together and in the company of demons, and that they have worshipped the Devil as if in the demons' synagogue, although all these things do not really happen to the witches in their waking hours, but are only a dreamer's illusion …

This is not all, he continues: the doubters also argue that one should not believe that the Devil has been granted such great power to commit as many evil deeds as the witches confess to having perpetrated. Finally, and more insidiously, the sceptics make up the fable (*fabulantur*) that when witches accuse someone of having been with them

---

[21] Ibid. 650–65.

[22] A short selection from the *Flagellum* (in English translation) is in Kors and Peters, eds, *Witchcraft in Europe*, 169–72.

at the Sabbat, they should not be believed, since it is possible that demons created an image of that person and induced the witches falsely to believe that the person was there with them, so that an innocent may be incriminated.[23]

With remarkable lucidity, Jacquier had summed up the arguments of the sceptics better than any of the sceptics themselves had yet managed to do: firstly, the thesis of the illusory nature of the witches' ride and Sabbat, both only existing in the minds of the supposed heretics; secondly, God's love for humankind as an argument against the possibility that he set the Devil free to afflict humans so atrociously through the works of witches; finally and most notably, the legal consequences of the first two points, namely the worthlessness of the witches' confessions or accusations against their supposed accomplices. Doubting witchcraft, then, meant emphasizing the Devil's powers of delusion, especially his ability to tamper with human senses and imagination, more than his skill at manipulating the elements to create a demonic body. Doubt also stemmed from, or encouraged, an optimistic understanding of God's attitude toward humankind, as opposed to the fear that he would be so angry as to abandon humans into the hands of Satan and his minions. In sum, doubters had a rather restricted conception of the extent to which God permitted demons to carry out their malevolent intentions – that is, limiting them to the spiritual sphere.[24] On these grounds, they would conclude that a court case based just on the words of one or more witches was no case at all.

The fact of the matter, however, was that none of these questions had a clear-cut solution, as one could argue both for one thesis and for its opposite with equally strong reasons. Jacquier seems fully aware of this, as he deals in an orderly way with the conflicting possibilities. Starting with the alternative between reality and illusion, he describes the ways in which the Devil can deceive humans by exploiting physiological processes, inducing certain visions – as in dreams – and making a person believe that they are real. This is exactly what happened to the 'miserable little women' of the canon *Episcopi*, who were 'truly' deluded by Satan; but, Jacquier argues cleverly, today's witches are a completely different story. Demons appear to their 'external senses' using bodies made of 'elementary matter', and thus

---

[23] Jacquier, *Flagellum haereticorum fascinariorum*, [1–3] (unpaginated).
[24] Ostorero, *Le Diable au sabbat*, 329–41.

have physical interactions with them at the *synagoga*, including sexual activity. The reality of all these things can be demonstrated according to two orders of proof. The first comes from Scripture and from the lives of the saints (e.g. St Martin, St Anthony and St Theophilus), which show that demons – and equally angels – can effectively appear to men in plain daylight and even imitate vital functions, as did the angel Raphael, who appeared to Tobias as if he were eating and drinking (Tobit 6: 5). The second order of proof comes from the evidence of the trials, which consists in the countless spells cast by the witches and their material effects. But it also includes the tales of sexual debauchery at the Sabbat, which left the witches physically prostrated for days: a confirmation that incubi and their contacts with humans are absolutely real.[25]

Jacquier, however, finds his strongest argument for the reality of witchcraft by investigating why God would permit it. Situating the issue in the framework of the history of the world, he writes that while in former times heresies were created and led by human beings, now demons lead the practice of witchcraft, something which God allows out of anger at Christians' ever increasing sins. Adopting a strongly eschatological tone, Jacquier states that the very existence of the witches' sect is the proof that the prophecies about the end of times are being fulfilled: as the day of judgement is approaching, Satan is running loose, thus increasing the suffering caused by witchcraft.[26] The author devotes a good third of his work to the question of theodicy, trying to explain that divine permission to Satan – *conditio sine qua non* for witchcraft – is always linked to God's overall ends, which are impenetrable to us but necessarily good; and that it is never unlimited, which explains why the Devil cannot do everything he pleases, such as, for example, exterminating humankind.[27]

Jacquier's lengthy survey of a principally theological issue leads to the third, very thorny legal question raised by the sceptics: since God allows the Devil to deceive humans, what should judges do, when a person accused by a self-confessed witch of having been at the Sabbat protests that the witch actually did not see him or her, but only a mental image created by Satan? Jacquier answers by subtly distinguishing two kinds of divine permission to the Devil: the first, 'general', one

---

[25] Jacquier, *Flagellum haereticorum fascinariorum*, 3–38.

[26] Ibid. 44–6.

[27] Ibid. 74–166 (chs 10–25).

was given once and for all at the moment of creation; but there is a second, which demons need in order to carry out specific tasks, such as creating the image of an innocent person in the imagination of a witch. Of this second type of permission, we cannot know anything unless it is revealed directly by God or manifested by some feature of the image from which its demonic origin would clearly result, as in our case. Now, Jacquier states, the burden of proof is on the shoulders of the accused: only if they can provide judges with un-mistakable signs of such demonic intervention can their defence be admitted in court. By requiring that the defence of those accused of witchcraft meet such an evidently impossible requirement, Jacquier aimed to rule it out as *de facto* inadmissible. However, such intricate subtleties reveal his true concern: the real motive why the doubters' claims must be rejected, he is forced to admit, is that the witches' ac-cusations against their accomplices are the only tool inquisitors have against the diabolical sect. If these testimonies were deemed unreli-able, no other evidence could replace them, and therefore no other solid proof could ever be found of the existence of the Sabbat and of witchcraft itself as a collective crime.[28] Not casually, then, in the last chapter Jacquier argues defensively that even if we concede that witches have been deluded in their sleep, they are anyway guilty of heresy, since they keep the commitments taken with the Devil and continue to abhor Christianity even during their waking hours.[29] This was a clearly disappointing conclusion for a book that had portrayed witches as signs of the imminent end of the world. More importantly, it indirectly manifested the types of problems inquisitors could face in the prosecution of witchcraft, a task they shared with lay judges since it was a *crimen mixti fori* ('crime of mixed jurisdiction'). While in-quisitors could condemn even the simple thoughts and visions of the witches as sinful and heretical, this was not always the case in a secular tribunal, where judges would first and foremost seek to ascertain and punish the actual killings or diseases caused through spells.

Jacquier's book was meant to put the prosecution of witchcraft on solid ground, no matter what objections could be raised. As such, it shows once more that the very existence of the crime could be chal-lenged on many accounts: from the mechanisms of sensation and of mental illusion, to the nature of spiritual beings and how they would

---

[28] Ibid. 171–4.
[29] Ibid. 182–3.

interfere with the physical world, to the vexed question of an omnipotent, infinitely loving God tolerating evil in the form of the Devil's work.[30] Theologians and inquisitors, engaging with all these issues, had necessarily to enter into a conversation (sometimes a confrontation) with specialists in other disciplines, especially jurists and physicians. This is what made the witchcraft debate a major occasion for fruitful exchanges between different fields, and also for notable and frequent overstepping of disciplinary boundaries. For example, when lay jurists wrote on witchcraft, they typically intervened on theological questions, bringing their distinctive heuristic principles to bear on complex, sensitive religious issues.[31]

The Italian law professor Ambrogio Vignati (*c*.1410–80) was one of the first jurists to devote a significant portion of one of his works specifically to witches, and an early example of a non-ecclesiastical author dealing with an issue which up until then had been treated almost exclusively by clerics.[32] The twelfth question of his *Tractatus de haeresi* (*Treatise on Heresy*), written at roughly the same time as Jacquier's book (late 1450s), aims to clarify two points: whether things confessed by witches, such as traversing great spaces in a very short time, speaking and having sex with demons, or being changed into the shape of a cat, are possible or even likely; and whether the deposition of one or more witches accusing someone else of having participated in their crimes provides evidence strong enough to justify the torture of the supposed accomplice in order to elicit a confession.[33] Surprisingly for a professor of canon law, Vignati chooses

---

[30] Stephens, *Demon Lovers*.

[31] Cf. Matteo Duni, 'Le streghe e i dubbi di un giurista: il *De lamiis et excellentia iuris utriusque* di Gianfrancesco Ponzinibio (1511)', in Camilla Hermanin and Luisa Simonutti, eds, *La centralità del dubbio. Un progetto di Antonio Rotondò*, 2 vols, Studi e testi per la storia della tolleranza in Europa nei secoli XVI–XVIII 13 (Florence, 2011), 1: 3–26; idem, 'Law, Nature, Theology, and Witchcraft in Ponzinibio's *De Lamiis* (1511)', in Louise Nyholm Kallestrup and Raisa Maria Toivo, eds, *Contesting Orthodoxy in Medieval and Early Modern Europe* (New York and Basingstoke, forthcoming); Federico Martino, *Il volo notturno delle streghe. Il sabba della modernità* (Napoli, 2011).

[32] See *DSI*, *s.n.* 'Vignati, Ambrogio'. To the best of my knowledge, Vignati's text was preceded only by Claude Tholosan's tract *Ut magorum et maleficiorum errores* (*c*.1436), as far as works by non-ecclesiastical jurists are concerned. On Tholosan, see *L'Imaginaire du sabbat*, 357–60.

[33] Ambrogio Vignati, *Quaestio unica de lamiis seu strigibus, et earum delictis, cum commentariis Francisci Peñae sacrae theologiae et iuris utriusque doctoris*, in *Malleus maleficarum, maleficas et earum haeresim framea conterens, ex variis auctoribus compilatus, & in quatuor tomos iuste distributus* (Lyon, 1669), vol. 1/ii, pt II, 131–62.

to deal with the first point almost without drawing on the canon *Episcopi*, but rather through an ambitious – if cursory – analysis of complex theological, as well as physiological, issues. As a matter of fact, he starts by underlining that demons are incorporeal *substantiae* and do not have organs: thus it would be impossible for human beings to have any bodily contact with them. In particular, he argues that, based on medical science, the supposed sexual encounters of witches with demons cannot be real. Since, as physicians say (*dicunt Physici*), semen is the product of the final digestion, demons, who lack all bodily functions including digestion, cannot have semen, and therefore cannot have sexual intercourse with witches.[34] Vignati does not entirely reject the possibility that demons may actually do some of the things witches confess, always by divine permission; but he argues that such permission would be an extremely rare exception since 'as a rule demons are detained in the dark prison of lower air until Judgement Day', clearly an event that did not seem to him to be so imminent as it had to Jacquier.[35] Vignati buttresses this point with a quotation from Augustine's *De Genesi ad litteram* explaining how God had confined demons in the lower air as if in prison, which in turn echoes Jude 6, on the fallen angels who have been kept by God 'in eternal chains in the nether gloom until the judgment of the great day' (RSV).[36] The rest of his analysis draws frequently on ecclesiastical writers and also on biblical passages: for example, he quotes Matthew 8: 28 on the two Gadarene demoniacs in order to demonstrate that demons cannot really do anything without God's permission.

In the end, Vignati argues that the great might of Satan has been 'restrained by God's merciful omnipotence', underscoring that the

---

[34] '[I]t is evident that demons cannot have sexual intercourse, even in the case that they – by divine permission – take up bodies made of air, for a medical reason: since physicians say that semen is what remains after the final digestion, those who do not transform food cannot emit semen, either': ibid. 136.

[35] 'Furthermore, although we can say that both good and reprobate angels may sometimes take on a body by divine permission, nevertheless as a rule they are detained in the dark prison of lower air, until Judgement Day … Thus, if demons sometimes take on a body in order to do harm, this happens by a special permission': ibid. 137.

[36] Augustinus, *De genesi ad litteram libri XII* 3.10 (PL 34, col. 285). The question was addressed and given its definitive solution by Thomas Aquinas, *Summa Theologiae*, Ia q. 64 a. 4, who argued that those angels trapped in the lower air until Judgement Day had the crucial function of putting humans to the test by tempting them; cf. Cameron, *Enchanted Europe*, 95–6.

power he retains over human beings is mostly spiritual, not corporeal. The first conclusion one could draw from his *quaestio* is thus that the more outlandish features of the witches' sect, such as the Sabbat, the flight or shape-shifting, are highly unlikely, if not outright impossible, since their regular occurrence, as alleged by witch-hunters, would imply that God granted the demons too many 'special permissions'.

Vignati had thus first chosen to draw on metaphysics to argue for the demons' incorporeal nature, and had then turned to natural philosophy and medical science in order to strengthen this point, interestingly leaving to the end the discussion of what pertained more strictly to his expertise, the legal side of the crime. As far as witches' depositions against alleged accomplices go, Vignati writes that they do not provide sufficient proof for torture, since they often relate impossible events – such as shape-shifting – which are the product of demonic illusion. No judge, therefore, can proceed to torture someone on the sole basis of a witch's confession.[37] The jurist's conclusion is as radical as Jacquier's parallel argument against the defence of those whom the witches accused, and explains why the latter had appeared so worried. The prohibition against torturing the witches' supposed accomplices advocated by Vignati would have nipped any witch-hunt in the bud, since these were typically based on the confessions of witches giving names of fellow conspirators who, tortured in due course, would provide many more names still.

The analyses of Vignati and Jacquier seem to echo each other on several points, as both examine the witchcraft question from all sides – although of course from opposing angles. Unfortunately it is impossible to determine whether, in fact, Vignati's *Quaestio* was a reaction to Jacquier's *Flagellum* or vice versa, not least because we do not know exactly when Vignati wrote his work, and neither book was published until the late sixteenth century.[38] Objections such as those raised by the Italian jurist must, however, have been widespread within his profession, as shown in the first major witch-hunt to break

---

[37] Vignati, *Quaestio*, 153–7.

[38] On the sixteenth-century edition of Vignati's work, see Matteo Duni, 'The Editor as Inquisitor: Francisco Peña and the Question of Witchcraft in the Late Sixteenth Century', in *Renaissance Studies in Honor of Joseph Connors*, ed. Machtelt Israëls and Louis A. Waldman, 2 vols, Villa I Tatti 29 (Florence, 2013), 2: 306–12.

out in France, the so-called 'vauderie d'Arras' of 1459–60.[39] On that occasion, the *avocat du roi* – a sort of chief prosecutor – had been reluctant to accept the theologians' opinion on the possibility of the witches' flight: 'it was not possible to go flying through the air on a stick', he had declared, commenting scathingly that those who believed it were more heretical than those who confessed it in court.[40] It was obvious that lay practitioners of law looked at witchcraft from a very different perspective from that of inquisitors, and their doubts could be a major obstacle to the prosecution of the crime.

One such lay practitioner was Ulrich Molitor (*c.*1442–1507), a German lawyer who was a prominent civil servant working for the archduke of Austria, and who authored the first printed book expressing strong doubts about witchcraft.[41] His *De lamiis et pythonicis mulieribus* (1489) was meant to be a refutation of at least some of the theses put forth by Institoris in the *Malleus maleficarum*, published just three years earlier. The issues discussed by Molitor include the possibility of witches harming and killing humans, transforming themselves into animals, flying on a stick to their meeting with the Devil, or having sex with demons and bearing children. Like Vignati, Molitor drew on a very broad range of sources: philosophical and theological works, Scripture, classical literature and hagiography. Particularly interesting is his discussion of the question of the children allegedly born out of the sexual encounters between witches and incubi, especially when compared to his polemical target, the *Malleus maleficarum*. Institoris devoted one question to discussing 'How sorceresses practice carnal acts with incubus demons in the present day, and how they are increased in number as a result of these acts'. He did so in keeping with standard scholastic theory, which held that succubi could steal the semen of men and then use it as incubi to make women pregnant, thus overcoming the lack of reproductive organs.[42] Following the same eschatological perspective adopted by Jacquier, Institoris stressed that, while 'in olden times' women were infested by incubi against their will, now witches 'willingly embrace this most foul and miserable servitude'. He depicted demonic sex as a system thanks

---

[39] Cf. Frank Mercier, *La Vauderie d'Arras. Une Chasse aux sorcières à l'automne du Moyen Âge* (Rennes, 2006).

[40] Ostorero, *Le Diable au sabbat*, 678–9.

[41] *EoW, s.n.* 'Molitor, Ulrich'; *DSI, s.n.* 'Molitor, Ulrich'; Stephens, *Demon Lovers*, 139–40.

[42] Institoris, *Malleus Maleficarum*, ed. and transl. Mackay, 2: 259–62 (Pt II, q. I, ch. 4). Stephens, *Demon Lovers*, 61–9.

to which witches could efficiently increase and multiply, since their progeny would be 'strong in the practice of witchcraft'. To prove this point, Institoris drew on Genesis 6: 4: 'The giants were on the earth in those days, and also afterwards, when the sons of God came in to the daughters of men, and they bore children to them. These were the mighty men that were of old'. Based on the Ordinary Gloss (the medieval, multi-author standard commentary to the Bible),[43] Institoris understands the 'sons of God' as the fallen angels, who lustfully consorted with women, and interprets the fact that giants were born from their union as proof that women had had sex with superhuman beings. Now, if those sexual encounters were fertile, it follows that the witches' dealings with demons could be, too. In his conclusion, Institoris argues that the physical reality of children born from the witches' obscene copulations is a crucial part of the diabolical plan to overthrow Christianity through an increase both of the number of witches and of God's wrath, caused precisely by the proliferation of their evil deeds.

As was his usual practice, Institoris corroborated scriptural passages with courtroom evidence: the 'many sorceresses who were turned over to the secular arm by us for punishment in various dioceses, especially in the town of Regensburg in the diocese of Constance' provided through their 'expert testimony' an additional proof that demonic sexual intercourse was real.[44] This is a reference to one of his witch-hunting campaigns, which in 1485 had aroused strong opposition in Molitor's home town, Constance, and had led the lawyer to write *De lamiis et pythonicis mulieribus*.[45] Interestingly, however, in his book Molitor does not refer to the actual trials, as we might have expected a lawyer to do. He chooses instead to respond to the issues raised by Institoris (without ever mentioning him), firstly by proposing a different reading of the same passage from Genesis referred to by the inquisitor. Rejecting the suggestion of the Gloss, Molitor argues that the children born from the 'sons of God' and the 'daughters of men' were 'powerful and magnificent men' who, although called 'giants' for their extraordinary qualities, were simply human beings.[46]

---

[43] On this, see, in this volume, Frances Andrews, 'Doubting John?', 33.

[44] Institoris, *Malleus Maleficarum*, ed. and transl. Mackay, 2: 260.

[45] Cf. Herzig, *Christ Transformed*, 36–48.

[46] The Gloss, Molitor writes, 'speaks dubiously and is not conclusive' (*opinative loquitur et non concludit*). That is why he proposes a radically different understanding of *gigantes* as 'homines potentes et magnifici, qui propter eorum potentiam et magnanimitatem dicti

Such interpretation entailed a clear rebuttal of the theory that their fathers had been superhuman beings – demons. Even more remarkably, Molitor then brings up the incarnation (which Institoris, significantly, had not discussed) as the only known example of a fertile union between a human being and a spirit:

> No man was ever found to be born from a spirit and a woman, except for the Saviour our Lord Jesus Christ who, thanks to God the Father's compassion, deigned to be conceived in the world, without sexual intercourse, from the Holy Ghost and the most glorious Virgin Mary. Far be it from my thoughts, therefore, that a human being be born, without the intervention of a man, from a spirit and a cursed woman![47]

Molitor is evidently grounding his twofold confutation of the reality of the witches' demonic sexual intercourse not on legal arguments but on a careful reading of the Scriptures. On the one hand, he does not take the mention of 'giants' in Genesis literally, but metaphorically, as allowed also by the Gloss's inconclusive interpretation. On the other hand, he (obviously) takes the incarnation as a literal truth, but reads it in the light of its absolutely exceptional status. The union between the Holy Ghost and the purest of human beings took place once and for all due to God's design to become man, and this exposes, by contrast, the utter absurdity of believing that women deprived of God's grace could copulate regularly with demons and multiply in this way, as witch-hunters claimed. Vignati had suggested that the physical transportation of human beings by demons, although not impossible in principle, as shown by biblical examples, must be considered an extremely rare occurrence because it required a specific divine permission. Now Molitor went one step further, presenting the exceptionality of one of Christianity's fundamental mysteries as a strong reason to doubt the supposed normality of demonic sexual intercourse. Both authors implied – Molitor much more forcefully than Vignati – that since such events had happened on a plane so distant from ordinary experience, they could not be drawn on in the

---

sunt gigantes': *De lamiis et pythonicis mulieribus,* in *Malleus maleficarum, maleficas et earum haeresim framea conterens,* 1/ii, pt I, 41–2.

[47] 'Nec unquam inventus est homo qui ex spiritu et muliere natus sit praeterquam Salvator Dominus noster Iesus Christus, qui summi Dei Patris misericordia dignatus est, sine commistione virili, de Spiritu Sancto ex gloriosissima Virgine Maria in mundum nasci. Absit igitur apud me quod homo sine homine de spiritu et maledicta muliere debeat nasci': ibid. 41.

courtroom to accuse common people of extraordinary deeds. The same line of reasoning would be followed, to more radical conclusions, by another lawyer with strong doubts about witchcraft, Gianfrancesco Ponzinibio, as will be discussed below.

Having decried the idea of children born from women and demons as theologically unacceptable and indeed almost blasphemous, Molitor moves on to critique its physical aspects on the basis of medical arguments, just as Vignati had done, but, again, more incisively. He argues that the whole theory of demonically assisted procreation does not hold water, since demons lack not only testicles, but also the main physiological source of procreation, the 'potency of the heart' (*virtus cordialis*), which regulates the operation of the testicles and the production of semen. Without this 'potency', which the incubus cannot acquire, the mere injection of stolen semen in a woman's womb cannot lead to conception.[48] Both natural science and theology, therefore, suggest a firmly negative answer to Institoris's claim that demonic sexual contact is responsible for the dramatic increase of evil in the world and for God's subsequent anger.

Molitor's tract, however, does not end with a sweeping rejection of the entire witchcraft construct, but with a more moderate position of selective scepticism. While admitting that witches may be guilty of truly worshipping the Devil instead of God, the German lawyer defines their heresy, in traditional terms, as a purely mental act without any material consequences, since he restricts Satan's power to the ability to tempt humans to the spiritual level.[49] Thus all the elements composing the 'new crime' of witchcraft – flight, metamorphosis, demonic sexual intercourse – which inquisitors considered possible and real thanks to the Devil's physical capabilities, are interpreted as the mere products of diabolically induced visions. The implicit but very clear message of the book is thus that the alarm launched by witchhunters is based on a grossly exaggerated evaluation of the witches' actual powers.

The extraordinary success of Molitor's book, which surpassed Institoris's *Malleus maleficarum* in terms of the number of editions (ten) by the end of the fifteenth century, highlights the fact that doubts about witchcraft found a vast audience (and provided a large market

---

[48] Ibid. 42. On the *virtus cordialis* as essential to procreation, Molitor's source (duly acknowledged) is Peter of Abano's *Conciliator controversiarum* (Venice, 1565), 'Differentia' 35, fol. 54ᵛ.

[49] Molitor, *De lamiis et pythonicis mulieribus*, 43–4.

for the publishing industry), doubtless including especially legal professionals such as judges and civil servants.[50] It is only logical, then, that the next major attack on the arguments of the witch-hunters would come from another lawyer, the otherwise obscure governmental official, Gianfrancesco Ponzinibio (b. *c.*1460), from Piacenza.[51] In 1511 he authored *Tractatus utilis et elegans de lamiis et excellentia utriusque iuris* (*A useful and elegant Treatise on Witches and on the Excellence of both Laws*), the first book on witchcraft to be published in Italy which had not been written by a cleric. As he explains in the dedicatory letter, the great increase in witch trials in his home town had persuaded him of the necessity to write 'true and useful things' on a matter which had aroused many controversies.[52] There was a problem, though: witchcraft 'seemed to be a matter for theologians'.[53] Indeed, from the very beginning, Ponzinibio identifies the most important foundation of the belief in the reality of the witches' Sabbat as being a passage from Scripture, thus apparently within the sole scope of theologians: the narrative in the Gospels of the temptations of Christ.

> I take what is written in chap. 40 of Matthew [*sic*, actually Matt. 4: 5, 8]: 'The Devil took him [i.e. Christ] to the holy city, and set him on the pinnacle of the temple', and further: 'The Devil took him to a very high mountain.' Based on this, many argue and maintain that these women can be carried to the Devil's game [i.e. the Sabbat] by the same Devil, since if this principle seems to apply – and it really does – to a bigger thing, then it must apply to a smaller one.[54]

Now, if the Gospels are the foundation of any discourse on witchcraft, then in order to bring his opinion to bear on the matter Ponzinibio must first demonstrate that 'civil and canon laws can

---

[50] The success of *De lamiis et pythonicis mulieribus* was probably due also to the fact that it was the first printed book on witchcraft to include illustrations: see Charles Zika, 'Fears of Flying: Representations of Witchcraft and Sexuality in Early Sixteenth-century Germany', in idem, *Exorcising our Demons: Magic, Witchcraft and Visual Culture in Early Modern Europe* (Leiden and Boston, MA, 2003), 237–68, for an analysis of some of them.

[51] See *DSI*, *s.n.* 'Ponzinibio, Giovanni Francesco'.

[52] Cf. Duni, 'Le streghe e i dubbi di un giurista', 11 and n. 21.

[53] Giovanni Francesco Ponzinibio, *Tractatus utilis et elegans de lamiis et excellentia utriusque iuris*, in *Tractatus duo: unus de sortilegiis D. Pauli Grillandi … Alter de lamiis et excellentia iuris utriusque D. Joannis Francisci Ponzinibii* (Frankfurt on Main, 1592), 234. A short selection from *De lamiis* was published in Joseph Hansen, *Quellen und Untersuchungen zur Geschichte des Hexenwahns und der Hexenverfolgung im Mittelalter* (Bonn, 1901), 313–17.

[54] Ibid.

be adduced and brought forward to interpret the Scriptures and to decide on theological issues', and thus that a lawyer has the right to discuss issues relating to Scripture and faith.[55] To this goal Ponzinibio devotes the first, most ambitious and least studied part of the book.[56] He strives to highlight the excellence of both civil and canon law (*de excellentia utriusque iuris*) over all other branches of knowledge, and to argue that, given the lofty status of their discipline, jurists can apply their learning to, and formulate authoritative conclusions on, problems which lie apparently outside the confines of their field.

Having thus established his (and his profession's) right to intervene on the matter of witchcraft, in the second part of the book, starting from the canon *Episcopi*, he proceeds to argue that the witches' experiences are just dreams or hallucinations. To claim that witchcraft is a fact, as inquisitors do, is extremely far-fetched, because there is really no evidence. All testimonies relating how the witches are able to reach places very far away by flying at amazing speed are suspect or falsehoods, as they speak of events which are 'far from likely' (*longe a verisimili*).[57] It follows that those confessing to participation in the Sabbat are deceived, especially since they happen to be mostly women, or at any rate uncouth country folk: both categories are easy prey for the Devil's tricks, and certainly unreliable witnesses in court. The witches' confessions must not be trusted, not only, however, because they are the product of delusion, but also because they contain things – such as their flight – which are evidently impossible when judged on the basis of law and of natural philosophy ('these things are rejected by law and nature').[58] In other words, such confessions can only shed light on the witches' beliefs, but are invalid as far as any fact happening outside of their minds is concerned. Doubt seems to reach greater heights here. By separating fact from mental construct, Ponzinibio was suggesting that

[55] Ponzinibio, *De lamiis*, 234.

[56] See Duni, 'Le streghe e i dubbi di un giurista'. Lack of space precludes detailed discussion here.

[57] Ponzinibio, *De lamiis*, 266 (partially in Hansen, *Quellen*, 314–15).

[58] '[S]ince such persons are deluded, as it is said [in the canon], we must thus conclude that their confession, too, is erroneous and should not be accepted … as a matter of fact, a confession should include true and possible things … whereas both law and nature reject those things [confessed by the witches]. Hence it cannot be argued, that since those women confessed such things, they must be true; indeed such a confession is far removed from the facts, and whatever is against nature is lacking in its own principles, and therefore is impossible by nature': Ponzinibio, *De lamiis*, 271.

the problem of witchcraft should not be examined on the basis of the standards of proof applied by theologians, who held as true an 'opinion condemned' (*opinio reprobata*) by canon law such as the witches' flight. Indeed, he was explicitly urging inquisitors systematically to seek the assistance of lawyers throughout witchcraft trials, implying that it would help avoid serious mistakes.[59]

Yet how could one possibly doubt the account in the Gospels of the temptations of Christ? If Satan had been capable of carrying the Son of God to the pinnacle of the Temple, why should he not be capable of carrying the witches to the Sabbat? Ponzinibio answers that Christ's flight cannot be taken as a valid precedent because of its wholly exceptional circumstances: Christ being God, his bodily 'transvection' or transportation through the air had been the consequence of direct, specific permission given by him to the Devil. Now, jurisprudence teaches that no rule can be derived from extremely rare events (*ex his quae raro accidunt, non fit lex nec regula*), otherwise, on the basis of the resurrection of Lazarus, we would need a 'law on those raised from the dead'.[60] This consideration enables Ponzinibio to turn the witch-hunters' logic on its head: 'since he [Christ] was transported or carried by the Devil by his own permission, we can infer and affirm that such transvection [i.e. that of witches] in no way can or must be admitted. … Indeed, the argument based on Christ can be reversed, and therefore is ineffective.'[61] The conclusion to be drawn from Matthew 4: 5 is not that witches can fly, but that we could believe in the possibility of their flight only if God's permission for it were evident, as in the narrative of the temptations –and this is obviously impossible.

The line of reasoning is clear and appears to be the one Molitor had also followed with regard to the incarnation, but with one major difference. While Molitor had rejected the idea of demonic procreation by passionately denouncing any similarity with the incarnation as blasphemous, Ponzinibio analyzed the question of Christ's transvection rationally, confuting the inquisitors' claims through explicit recourse to law. He aimed to ground his critique of demonology not on emotional response, but on universally recognized legal

[59] Ibid. 281–2.
[60] Ibid. 274.
[61] '[E]t quia fuit portatus ab ipso diabolo, sive assumptus, ex permissu eius, potest inferri et dici quod si non constat de permissu Dei, nullo modo possit vel debeat concedi talis delatio': ibid. 275–6.

principles. More than any other author before him, the Italian jurist had developed and organized his doubts about witchcraft in connection with the system of law, which he thus made the keystone of his approach.

Ponzinbio, however, still needed to deal with the witch-hunters' final argument: the claim that God, angered by the sins of Christians, would currently grant the Devil an unprecedented degree of freedom to intervene physically in nature, thus enabling witches to perform their amazing deeds. Just as Vignati and Molitor had done, Ponzinibio counters this point by proposing a far more optimistic vision of the relationship between God and humankind. Shifting to eschatology and making reference to Revelation, he writes that the sacrifice of Christ has caused the Devil to be chained in hell, and has deprived him of any capability of operating in the material world, including bodily interaction with witches.[62] Indeed, Satan's limitations are very evident when one considers who, and how many, are the persons tried for witchcraft: overall, a very small number of people, and furthermore of lowly status (thus also unreliable as witnesses). Now, if Satan's powers really were as unrestricted as the inquisitors claim, he would gain a virtually unlimited following among all kinds of people, and would be able to carry an infinite throng to the Sabbat – but this is hardly what one finds in the trials.[63] The truth is that Satan does not have any need of transporting his minions to an actual meeting, since what he really aims for is the full control of their minds so that they may worship him inwardly.[64]

---

[62] 'As a result of the death of God, the Devil has been deprived of power over the world, and has been confined in hell, where he will be chained until the times of the Antichrist': ibid. 274. The reference is to Rev. 20: 1–10, especially vv. 1–2: 'Then I saw an angel coming down from heaven, holding in his hand the key of the bottomless pit and a great chain. And he seized the dragon, that ancient serpent, who is the Devil and Satan, and bound him for a thousand years' (RSV).

[63] 'If the Devil were able to do that [carrying witches], why would he do it only with a few persons, and of lowly status, as he is impartial, being the tempter of the whole world? And again, if he really does it, why does he not do it only with those who would be trustworthy witnesses?': Ponzinibio, *De lamiis*, 275.

[64] '[I]t does not follow [that] 'the Devil goes at great lengths to be worshipped, therefore he transports those people really and bodily to the place of the game [i.e. the Sabbat] so that he may be really worshipped', since he may well be worshipped in their [the witches'] homes actually and truly, and indeed there are some of them who said they worshipped him in their homes at night … he just needs to have men's minds entrapped, so that men may be deceived': ibid. 276.

Once again Ponzinibio, like his fellow jurists, had intervened in a theological question (the Devil's powers), and had based his conclusion on an alternative interpretation of Scripture. Turning to Scripture was indeed what both witchcraft believers and sceptics would do. Theologians and inquisitors, such as Jacquier and Institoris, building on a realist demonology which had been over a century in the making, looked to the Bible for evidence of the physical reality of the Devil's powers, and thus of the witches' deeds. While traditional canonists, such as Torquemada, in keeping with the canon *Episcopi*, responded by upholding the view that all demonic manifestations were first and foremost the product of trickery and illusion, the three lay jurists discussed here also articulated their doubts through an ambitious examination of theological arguments and Scripture passages. With varying levels of sophistication and radicalism, Vignati, Molitor and Ponzinibio read the biblical events discussed by witch-hunters in the light of their exceptional, unique status. While Vignati and Molitor had not taken their arguments to their logical conclusion, Ponzinibio affirmed explicitly that, because of their absolute rarity, phenomena such as the bodily interactions between Christ and the Devil did not constitute a legal precedent for judges dealing with real-life situations. Belonging in a meta-historical dimension not comparable with the world of human experience, the events described in the gospels could not be resorted to in order to prove that witchcraft was ordinarily possible.

What the three jurists would ultimately look to the Scriptures for was not any physical evidence of witchcraft, but an alternative metaphysics. God, they implied, was not angrier with human beings now than he had ever been before. Contrary to what both Jacquier and Institoris maintained, therefore, there was no reason to fear that he would free the Devil to wreak his wickedness upon Christians. These sceptics unanimously argued that the Devil could not enable the witches to perform extraordinary feats, because God would never permit it. They all emphasized the limitations of Satan's powers in the physical world, and that the tempter's main sphere of operations was to be found within a man's, and especially a woman's, soul. While witchcraft existed – and witches must be punished severely, as Molitor expressly stated – it consisted essentially in the heretics' decision to worship the Devil as God; it was thus a purely mental act.

The return to a traditional, pre-fifteenth-century demonology by these writers, was not, however, solely due to a more conservative understanding, such as that expressed in the time-honoured canon *Episcopi*. It was the product of a new approach, which emphasized – more or less explicitly according to the author's background and agenda – the absurdity of any attempt at using the Bible to explain supposedly physical events. Significantly, such 'dematerialized', or markedly spiritualized, reading of the Scriptures (and of witchcraft) appears to have been a prerogative of non-clerical authors. By depriving the witches' crime of any material dimension, they implied that theologians and inquisitors, who had been labouring to prove precisely that such a dimension existed, did not understand witchcraft at all. But since any definition of witchcraft was based to a large extent on biblical passages, the sceptics were ultimately challenging ecclesiastical primacy in the interpretation of the Scriptures.

To return to the first pages of this essay and Institoris's anxiety, it is now clear that the history of the witch-hunt is also the history of the doubts that it raised from the start. Some doubts had their roots in traditional theology and canon law. When evaluated on this basis, new theories describing the Devil as capable of carrying the witches through the air and of copulating with them appeared seriously problematic. Witch-hunters, seeking to solve such problems, looked to Scripture for incontrovertible proofs of the demons' corporality, and to the natural sciences for an explanation of the mechanics of the biblical examples they brought forth. Sceptics had thus necessarily to tackle the same issues and discuss the same evidence in a debate which became markedly interdisciplinary. The legal status of witchcraft as a crime over which both ecclesiastical and secular courts claimed jurisdiction caused the debate to broaden further. The witch-hunt thus provided one of the first occasions for an open, and at times tense, confrontation between theologians (most of them also inquisitors) and a number of lay intellectuals, for the most part jurists and lawyers. I have shown that these latter leaned more or less decidedly towards scepticism, and that they fully accepted the challenge of addressing questions outside their own field. I have argued that the specific contribution of the sceptical law professionals was to propose alternative readings of some significant scriptural passages, or of key theological concepts, in order to reject the notion that witchcraft had a physical dimension. They interpreted biblical narratives in the light of their unique character, emphasizing their moral and spiritual value while at the same time confuting their applicability to concrete courtroom cases. Their original interpretation of theological questions was also significant in itself, as a sign that lay intellectuals could consider it part of their professional duty to intervene aggressively in the area of religious doctrine without any reverence for, and actually in open disagreement with, ecclesiastical experts. The rise of increasingly radical doubts about witchcraft thus marks an important step in the broader process of secularization of the debate on metaphysical questions. It is certainly no coincidence that the Dominican inquisitor and witch-hunter, Bartolomeo Spina, who in 1525 confuted Ponzinibio's book violently and called for its burning, had only a few years earlier attacked the Mantuan philosopher Pietro Pomponazzi (1462–1525) for having argued that the human soul is mortal, and that therefore no eternal rewards or punishments await us in the hereafter.[65] Both Ponzinibio and Pomponazzi de-emphasized the Devil's power in the world, though in very different ways and at very different levels of intellectual sophistication. An inquisitor such as Spina would naturally see such theories as a serious threat to the teachings of the Church and to its cultural authority in contemporary society.

However bold and unconventional these ideas may look to us, they do not seem at first to have had a notable impact on the prosecution of witchcraft. Prompted by the first major waves of witch-hunting in northern Italy and southern Germany, the works of the doubters had no practical effect, and the numbers of trials and executions peaked on both sides of the Alps between the 1480s and the 1530s, that is, precisely in the decades when these works were being written and published. While there are good reasons to believe that Vignati, Molitor and Ponzinibio were not isolated within their profession or social groups, their ideas failed to persuade the majority of judges of their day – whether secular or ecclesiastical – that witches were not a terrible threat to Church and society. If we consider a longer time span

---

[65] On Spina, see n. 11 above. On the complex figure of Pomponazzi and his philosophical controversies, see Antonino Poppi, 'Fate, Fortune, Providence and Human Freedom: Pietro Pomponazzi', in Charles B. Schmitt and Quentin Skinner, eds, *The Cambridge History of Renaissance Philosophy* (Cambridge and New York, 1988), 641–67; *DSI, s.n.* 'Pomponazzi, Pietro'. On Pomponazzi's stance regarding magic and witchcraft, see Paola Zambelli, 'Magia e sistemi. Platonici ed aristotelici di fronte a divinazione, prodigi, stregoneria ed eresia', in eadem, *L'ambigua natura della magia. Filosofi, streghe, riti nel Rinascimento* (Milan, 1991), 211–48; Maurizio Bertolotti, 'Pomponazzi tra streghe e inquisitori. Il *De incantationibus* e il dibattito sulla stregoneria intorno al 1520', in *Pietro Pomponazzi: tradizione e dissenso. Atti del Congresso internazionale di studi su Pietro Pomponazzi, Mantova 23–24 ottobre 2008*, ed. Marco Sgarbi (Florence, 2010), 385–405.

in the history of the witch-hunt, however, we observe a surprisingly early and rapid change in the attitude of inquisitors towards at least some aspects of the witches' crimes. The process began in the mid-1520s, when the Spanish Inquisition issued guidelines instructing local judges not to take the witches' confessions at face value and to doubt unverified assertions of having participated in the Sabbat.[66] These new norms, which stated explicitly that witches were often deluded and admitted that their experiences could be a product of their imagination, gradually came to be adopted by the Holy Office of the Inquisition, established in the Italian peninsula in 1542 as the equivalent of the Spanish Inquisition.[67] From the end of the 1550s, supreme inquisitors, organized in a central board based in Rome and controlling local branches throughout Italy, increasingly regarded the more problematic features of witchcraft – encounters with the Devil and flight – as more often than not the fruit of dreams or illusions. By the early 1580s, the Holy Office would routinely forbid local inquisitors to prosecute those people whom witches affirmed they had seen at the Sabbat. The rationale was spelled out in 1593 in a letter addressed to an unnamed inquisitor:

> We must also pay due attention to the fact that these witches are usually not to be trusted as far as anything they affirm they have seen in those nefarious games of theirs [i.e. the Sabbat] goes. Although they may sometimes testify to having seen and recognized many people … , nevertheless we cannot, and must not, prosecute those they have nominated, since the Devil, in order to keep them as if blinded in the deep abyss of their wickedness, through his tricks and delusions shows them (especially in their dreams) the semblance of many righteous and God-fearing men, making them [i.e. the witches] believe that these people belong to their same sect, or that they take part in the same games. …

---

[66] These were the so-called deliberations of Granada (1526), which had a long-lasting effect on the Spanish Inquisition's policy vis-à-vis witchcraft: see *EoW*, *s.v.* 'Inquisition, Spanish'. See also the text of the deliberations (in English translation) in Lu Ann Homza, ed. and transl., *The Spanish Inquisition, 1478–1614: An Anthology of Sources* (Indianapolis, IN, and Cambridge, 2006), 153–63.

[67] The adoption of the Spanish guidelines was probably due to the mediation of Spanish inquisitors and jurists, such as Diego de Simancas and especially Francisco Peña, who had prominent roles in the Roman Inquisition. The new policy of the Holy Office was detailed in an informal internal document, *Instructio in formandis processibus in causis strigum, sortilegiorum et maleficiorum* ('Instruction on how to conduct a trial in cases of witches, enchantments and spells'), probably written in the 1590s but officially printed only in 1657: see *DSI*, *s.v.* '*Instructio*'. On Peña, see Duni, 'Editor as Inquisitor'.

We usually find that silly women fall into these errors more easily than men … Therefore, if you have no proof other than the witches' testimony, you will not proceed against those they have nominated …[68]

The prosecution of alleged accomplices on the sole basis of witches' words had been denounced as a mistake more than a century before by Vignati, and more aggressively by Ponzinibio in 1511. The jurists had challenged the position of inquisitors such as Jacquier, who, on the contrary, argued that the testimony of witches should be trusted absolutely. Now the Holy Office was endorsing the doubters' point, and almost echoing Ponzinibio's warning not to give credence to 'those women' (as he systematically refers to the witches), who are deluded by the Devil and who may thus be instruments in his design to incriminate 'good and righteous men'.[69] However, the inquisitors' about-face was concealed under an appearance of complete harmony with tradition, as was customary for the Roman curia.[70] The contribution of the sceptics was not acknowledged openly, and it was accepted only as far as its legal aspect went: the prohibition on prosecuting supposed accomplices. While recognizing that witches were almost always deluded, and thus that their testimonies were totally unreliable, the Holy Office never affirmed that their claims to have encountered the Devil at the Sabbat were absolutely impossible. In the aftermath of the Council of Trent, cultural hegemony was reasserted, allowing the Church's leading theologians to put aside the troubling doubts that had been raised by the sceptics a century before. If witches, after all, were just silly women, they could be dealt with leniently and without much ado, leaving the difficult question of the reality of witchcraft for another time, another debate.

---

[68] Vatican City, Archivio della Congregazione per la Dottrina della Fede, Stanza storica, Q 3–d, fols 267^v–268^r, 1 October 1593.

[69] Ponzinibio, *De lamiis*, 281.

[70] On the new policy of the Roman Inquisition towards witchcraft, see John Tedeschi, *The Prosecution of Heresy: Collected Studies on the Inquisition in Early Modern Italy* (Binghampton, NY, 1991); Giovanni Romeo, *Inquisitori, esorcisti e streghe nell'Italia del Cinquecento* (Florence, 1990); Adriano Prosperi, *Tribunali della coscienza. Inquisitori, confessori, missionari* (Turin, 1996), especially 368–99; for a synthesis of the findings of current scholarship, see Matteo Duni, *Under the Devil's Spell: Witches, Sorcerers and the Inquisition in Renaissance Italy* (Florence, 2007), 32–8.

'Dowting of ye Cupp': Disbelief about the Eucharist and a Catholic Miracle in Reformation England

Alexandra Walsham[*]

Trinity College, Cambridge

This essay is inspired by an intriguing late sixteenth-century Catholic liturgical object, the Bosworth Hall burse. It commemorates a vision of the crucified Christ seen by the missionary priest (and later martyr) John Payne in Douai in 1575, which apparently dispelled a moment of doubt about the real presence in the consecrated eucharist. The incident is situated in the context of the heated Catholic and Protestant controversies about the doctrine of transubstantiation in post-Reformation England and against the backdrop of similar medieval miracles designed to counter disbelief, including the Mass of St Gregory and the miracle of Bolsena of 1263. The essay illuminates the persistence and transformation of anxieties about the sacred in the sixteenth century, considers the part they played in private and public crises of faith, and explores the mechanisms by which they were resolved. It also investigates how the memory of Payne's miraculous vision was crystallized in a material object.

The stimulus and starting point for this essay is an intriguing liturgical object known as the Bosworth Hall Burse (Fig. 1). A burse is an embroidered case for storing and carrying the corporal, the white linen cloth upon which the host and chalice are placed during the celebration of the eucharist. Dating from the late sixteenth century and worked in silk in double feather-stitch, it shows a chalice, inside of which appears the naked figure of Christ crucified. Beneath is a stylized image of the vernicle, the famous veil of St Veronica upon which the Saviour's face was believed to have been supernaturally imprinted. On either side are two representations of the Holy Name of Jesus, the sacred monogram IHS. The verses embroidered around the edge of the burse reveal that it commemorates a miracle:

AT GWINS FIRST MASS
JOHN PAINE ONCE WAS
Where dowting of ye cupp,

* Trinity College, Cambridge, CB2 1TQ. E-mail: amw23@cam.ac.uk.

Studies in Church History 52 (2016) 232–249
doi: 10.1017/stc.2015.13

Figure 1. (Colour online) The Bosworth Hall burse, photograph from the Bernard Payne Papers, Ushaw College, Durham, UC/P14/1/24-29. Reproduced by permission of Durham University Library.

> Christ God and man
> Rebukt him than
> and made hime thus geve uppe.[1]

The verses refer to a vision experienced by John Payne when he was a young man in training as a missionary priest at Douai College in 1575. Attending the first mass celebrated by a fellow student, the Welshman Robert Gwyn, at St Nicholas's Church, Payne seems to have experienced a moment of hesitation about the real presence of Christ's blood in the wine. But at the same instant as the chalice was raised by the priest, the Saviour appeared to dispel Payne's disbelief and castigate his lack of faith.[2] After his own ordination, Payne returned to England to succour the faithful, before being arrested in

---

[1] Ethelbert Horne, 'The Bosworth Hall Burse', *Burlington Magazine for Connoisseurs* 43 (1923), 80–1, 85.

[2] On Payne and Gwyn, see Godfrey Anstruther, *The Seminary Priests: A Dictionary of the Secular Clergy of England and Wales 1558–1850*, 1: *Elizabethan 1558–1603* (Ware and Durham, 1968), 266–7, 140–1 respectively; B. C. Foley, 'Bl. John Payne, Seminary Priest and Martyr – 1582', *Essex Recusant* 2 (1960), 48–75; James E. Kelly, 'Conformity, Loyalty and the Jesuit Mission to England of 1580', in Eliane Glaser, ed., *Religious Tolerance in the Atlantic World: Early Modern and Contemporary Perspectives* (Basingstoke, 2014), 149–70, at 152–6. See also n. 7 below.

1581. Betrayed by the turncoat George Elliot and accused of plotting the queen's assassination, he was charged with high treason, tortured, and executed the following year.[3] Once in the possession of Payne's Catholic patrons in England, the Petres of Ingatestone Hall in Essex, some time later the burse was transferred to the private chapel of Bosworth Hall, in Leicestershire, where it was revered as a remnant of the martyr.[4]

This essay explores the context and significance of Payne's spiritual vision, using it as an opportunity to investigate the doubts that accumulated around the eucharist in post-Reformation England. The sacrament of the altar was not merely the focal point of heated disputes between Catholics and Protestants; it also precipitated frictions which hardened into lasting denominational divisions between Lutherans and the Reformed. These doctrinal debates were built on the substantial bedrock of scholastic medieval theology, which had sought to resolve the bewildering puzzles and paradoxes that surrounded this central Christian mystery – to explain the metaphysical status of the bread and wine consecrated during the rite and to clarify the complex epistemological question of how precisely Christ could be said to be present in these material species.[5] The aim here is to illuminate the re-emergence and evolution of anxiety about these thorny issues in the sixteenth century, as well as to contribute to current work that is reassessing what Lucien Febvre called 'the problem of unbelief' by underlining the symbiotic rather than oppositional relationship between faith and doubt in the late medieval and early modern period.[6] It will be suggested that the conflicts and schisms

---

[3] For Payne's activities after his arrival in England and arrest, see J. H. Pollen, ed., 'Father Persons' Memoirs (concluded)', *Miscellanea IV*, Catholic Record Society 4 (London, 1907), 1–161, at 39, 47–9.

[4] The burse came to Bosworth Hall through the Petre family and was in the possession of Mrs David T. Constable Maxwell in the 1970s, who loaned it to the Leicester Museum between 1949 and 1957. In 1977 it was once again at Bosworth Hall: see Durham, Ushaw College, Bernard Payne Papers, UC/P14/1/24–29. I am grateful to James Kelly for his assistance in facilitating access to this material.

[5] See James F. McCue, 'The Doctrine of Transubstantiation from Berengar through Trent: The Point at Issue', *HThR* 61 (1968), 385–430; Gary Macy, *Treasures from the Storeroom: Medieval Religion and the Eucharist* (Collegeville, MN, 1999), especially chs 5, 8; Miri Rubin, *Corpus Christi: The Eucharist in Late Medieval Culture* (Cambridge, 1991), ch. 1.

[6] Lucien Febvre, *The Problem of Unbelief in the Sixteenth Century: The Religion of Rabelais*, transl. Beatrice Gottlieb (Cambridge, MA, and London, 1982). For recent revisionist work, see John H. Arnold, *Belief and Unbelief in Medieval Europe* (London, 2005), 216–30; Alec Ryrie, 'Atheism and Faith in Early Modern Britain' (forthcoming). See also Keith Thomas,

engendered by the Reformation served simultaneously to exacerbate and complicate the uncertainties people experienced as internal struggles converged with the formation of confessional identities.

Born in Peterborough, John Payne appears to have been a convert from Protestantism who entered the Douai seminary in 1574 as a mature student, serving for a period as its bursar.[7] Apart from the burse, the only other evidence of the incident that occurred during the mass celebrated by Robert Gwyn is a Latin letter sent by the exiled theologian Gregory Martin to his Jesuit friend Edmund Campion, then residing in Rome, on 20 December 1575. Celebrating God's mercies to the English College, a new Oxford beyond the seas, he described how after adoring the consecrated host 'there came into [Payne's] mind this thought that if the whole Christ were contained also in the second species of wine it would seem that it could be addressed and saluted in the same words as the first. And while he hesitated rather than doubted he saw most clearly, his eyes piercing to the interior of the chalice then being elevated, the venerable form therein of a naked man'.[8] Payne's confessor regarded this as a miracle in

---

Religion and the Decline of Magic (Harmondsworth, 1973 edn), 198–206; David Wootton, 'Lucien Febvre and the Problem of Unbelief in the Early Modern Period', *Journal of Modern History* 60 (1988), 695–730; idem, 'Unbelief in Early Modern Europe', *History Workshop* 20 (Autumn 1985), 82–100; John Edwards, 'Religious Faith and Doubt in Late Medieval Spain: Soria circa 1450–1500', *P&P* 120 (1988), 3–25; Susan Reynolds, 'Social Mentalities and the Case of Medieval Scepticism', *TRHS* 6th ser. 1 (1991), 21–41.

[7] At his trial Payne described his brother as having been 'a very earnest Protestant': William Allen, *A Briefe Historie of the Glorious Martyrdom of Twelve Reverend Priests: Father Edmund Campion and his Companions* (London, 1908; first publ. 1582), 95.

[8] 'Memoriam fecit mirabilium suorum misericors et miserator Dominus. Quorsum haec? Ecce enim, ut haesitantem multorum parvulorum fidem corroboraret, non reliquit eos sine miraculo. Quod te nullo modo celare debeo, quia sacramentum regis abscondere bonum est, opera autem Dei revelare et confiteri honorificum est. In basilica Sancti Nicolai quae adhaeret templo D. Jacobi, dum quidam ex nostris prima sacra faceret, aderat inter caeteros Anglicanae nostrae societatis oeconomus, vir prudens, gravis, maturus, religiosus; cujus in mentem post primae speciei adorationem cum illa venisset cogitatio, ut si totus Christus in secunda quoque vini specie contineretur iisdem quoque verbis quibus prima compellari et salutari posse videretur, jamque haereret potius quam vacillaret, certissime vidit oculis penetrantibus elevatum calicem venerabilem formam quasi nudi hominis. Attonitus novitiate rei valdeque anxius, postquam confessario suo, Societatis vestrae gravissimo viro, id ita esse sanctissime affirmasset homo minime levis aut superstitosus, jamque ipse Alanus tantum habere momenti ad honorem Dei et nostrorum aedificationem existimasset ut palam pro concione declaraverit, tandem ita coeptum est celebrari hoc miraculum ut illius causa in ea ecclesia publice supplicatio fieret et ad populum sermo exhortatorius. Rident ist qui sancta omnia rident, et nisi quod palpari queat nihil volunt credere ... denique cum Apostolus dicat, Charitas omnia credit; nos quid

support of the Catholic doctrine of the mass, and when William Allen was informed he made it the subject of a public discourse 'for the honour of God and the edification of our men'. Special devotions were accompanied by a sermon of exhortation to the local people as the fame of the miracle spread in Douai and beyond. For Gregory Martin, Payne's vision was just one of the wonderful works the Lord had wrought 'to confirm the hesitating faith of many little ones' in a time of profound religious turmoil. Tellingly, he invoked the text of Matthew 14: 31, Jesus's castigation of the fear that led Peter to sink as he walked towards him on the Sea of Galilee: 'O thou of little faith, wherefore didst thou doubt?'[9]

Nothing is more emblematic of the idiosyncratic character and theological mutability of the English Reformation than the successive reorientations of official teaching about the eucharist that marked the first half of the sixteenth century. Henry VIII condemned the heresy of sacramentarianism and sent several Lollards to the stake for rejecting the real presence. Denial of transubstantiation became orthodox doctrine under his evangelical son Edward VI, whose second Prayer Book of 1552 bore the imprint of the memorialist understanding of this sacrament promoted by the Swiss reformers and reflected the gradual eclipse of Lutheran opinion on this and other issues in England. Under Mary, the idea that the eucharist was a mere symbol and sign of Christ's sacrifice rather than a miraculous re-enactment of it was proscribed and vilified once more. The accession of Elizabeth I did little to clear up the confusion created by the rapid theological reversals of the previous decades. The Thirty-Nine Articles declared transubstantiation 'repugnant to the plain words of Scripture' and the source of many 'superstitions', but the ambiguous wording of the revised liturgy, together with the omission of the black rubric, provided room for a range of views to persist within the newly reinstated Church of England. The Catholic practice of reserving the cup to the priest was, however, firmly repudiated.[10]

---

tentamus Deum ut audiamus, Modicae fidei quare dubitastis?': T. F. Knox, ed., *The First and Second Diaries of the English College, Douai: And an Appendix of the Unpublished Documents* (London, 1878), 311.

[9] Ibid.

[10] See Lucy E. C. Wooding, *Rethinking Catholicism in Reformation England* (Oxford, 2000), 166–76. For the Thirty-Nine Articles and their predecessors, the Forty-Two Articles of 1553, see Gerald Bray, ed., *Documents of the English Reformation* (Cambridge, 1994), 301–2. The black rubric explained that although the eucharist was to be received by

Dismissing the precept that the bread and wine were actually trans-muted into Christ's body and blood as a vain 'dream' and an invented tradition, John Jewel's challenge sermon and *Apology* (1562) initiated a new phase in the ongoing battle about beliefs and practices con-nected with the eucharist.[11] From Louvain, Thomas Harding, John Rastell and Thomas Dorman launched vigorous counterattacks de-fending the doctrines of transubstantiation and the real presence, which had been reaffirmed by the Council of Trent in 1551.[12] Others devoted entire treatises to vindicating the Catholic position, notably Nicholas Sander in his *The Supper of Our Lord* (1566), Thomas Heskyns in *The Parliament of Chryste* (1566) and Robert Pointz in *Testimonies for the Real Presence* (1566).[13] In turn these evoked Protestant ripostes by Alexander Nowell and William Fulke.[14] The sheer volume of ink spilt on this issue in English as well as Latin testifies to the concern of clergy on both sides that lay people might be drawn into a quag-mire of error and uncertainty by their enemies' arguments. Hard-ing hoped that by reading his *Confutation* those 'which stumble and slyde, may fynde wherwith to staye them'; Pointz's book was initially

---

communicants kneeling, this did not signify 'any reall and essencial presence'; the bread and wine remained in 'styll in theyr verye naturall substaunces, and therefore may not be adored, for that were Idolatrye to be abhorred of all faythfull christians'.

[11] John Jewel, *An Apology of the Church of England*, ed. J. E. Booty (Ithaca, NY, 1968), especially 31–4.

[12] Thomas Dorman, *A Proufe of Certeyne Articles in Religion, Denied by M. Juell, Sett Furth in Defence of the Catholyke Beleef therein* (Antwerp, 1564); John Rastell, *A Replie against an Answer (Falselie Intitled) in Defence of the Truth* (Antwerp, 1565); Thomas Harding, *An Answere to Maister Juelles Challenge … Augmented with Certaine Quotations and Addiions* (Antwerp, 1565), especially fols 50ʳ–71ʳ, 126ʳ–130ᵛ, 135ᵛ–141ᵛ, 161ʳ–162ᵛ; *A Confutation of a Book Intituled an Apologie of the Church of England* (Antwerp, 1565), especially fols 91ᵃ–106ᵃ; *A Rejoinder to M. Jewels Replie against the Sacrifice of the Masse* ([Louvain], 1567). For a helpful bibliographical guide to these debates, see Peter Milward, *Religious Controversies of the Elizabethan Age: A Survey of Printed Sources* (Aldershot, 1977), ch. 1. For these controversies in their European context, see Lee Palmer Wandel, *The Eucharist in the Reformation: Incarnation and Liturgy* (Cambridge, 2006), ch. 5.

[13] Nicholas Sander, *The Supper of our Lord Set Foorth according to the Truth of the Gospell and Catholike Faith* (Louvain, 1566); Thomas Heskyns, *The Parliament of Chryste Avouching and Declaring the Enacted and Received Trueth of the Presence of his Bodie and Bloode in the Blessed Sacrament, and of other Articles Concerning the Same* (Antwerp, 1566); Robert Pointz, *Testimonies for the Real Presence of Christes Body and Blood in the Blessed Sacrament of the Aultar Set Foorth at Large* (Louvain, 1566).

[14] Alexander Nowell, *A Confutation as wel of M. Dormans Last Boke entituled A Disproufe. &c. as also of D. Sander his Causes of Transubstantiation* (London, 1567), fols 151ʳ–243ʳ; William Fulke, *D. Heskins, D. Sanders, and M. Rastel, Accounted (among their Faction) Three Pillers, and Archpatriarches of the Popish Synagogue* (London, 1579).

prepared to satisfy the worries of a friend, before being published for the benefit of those 'waveringe, being uncertaine which syde to sticke unto'.[15] Lamenting the 'instability of belief' that marked this tempestuous age, Thomas Butler's translation of Antonio Possevino's *Treatise of the Holy Sacrifice of the Altar* (1570) was intended to prevent the defection of people who might be 'lightly seduced to geve eare to Luther, or his Maister the Divel, or any of their scholars, as Musculus, Calvin, Peter Martyr, Beza, Jewel, Latimer, Bale, Horne, and others of their sect, and new devised Parlamente Religion'.[16] And in his handy manual entitled 'Motives', first printed in 1574, Richard Bristow addressed himself particularly to those that 'stande in doubt betwene God and Baal', seeking to provide them with 'diverse plaine and sure wayes' to discover 'the truthe in this doubtful and dangerous time of Heresie'.[17]

Such books examined the many points of eucharistic theology over which medieval nominalists and realists had squabbled and which were now in renewed dispute. At root, the debate revolved around the interpretation of the critical passages in the New Testament in which Jesus declared to the disciples 'this is my body': it turned in large part on 'the true sense and meaning' of the words he had uttered at the Last Supper, out of which, admitted Pointz, 'ariseth al the strife'. Catholics – and indeed Lutherans – tied themselves in knots insisting that this phrase should be understood literally, by contrast with John 15: 15, in which Jesus says 'I am the true vine', which was to be interpreted metaphorically.[18] Discussing the ancient Aristotelian distinction between accidents and substances, Catholics had no less difficulty explaining why the bread and wine still retained their original appearance and shape after they were transubstantiated. Christ's body was really and corporeally present even though it was not 'outwardly perceptible' to sight. Understanding such transmutations lay beyond the capacity of human reason. The devout Christian

---

[15] Harding, *Confutation*, sig. !2[r]; Pointz, *Testimonies*, sig. A3[v].

[16] Antonio Possevino, *A Treatise of the Holy Sacrifice of the Altar, Called the Masse*, transl. Thomas Butler (Louvain, 1570), sig. A5[v].

[17] Richard Bristow, *A Briefe Treatise of diverse Plaine and Sure Ways to Finde out the Truthe in this Doubtful and Dangerous Time of Heresie in Conteyning Sundry Worthy Motives unto the Catholike Faith, or Considerations to Move a Man to Believe the Catholikes, and not the Heretikes* (Antwerp, 1574), sig.*3[r] and title page.

[18] Pointz, *Testimonies*, fol. 5[v]. See also Harding, *Answere*, fols 126[r]–130[v]; Sander, *Supper*, fols 2[r]–[v], 5[v]–6[v], and bk 4; Heskyns, *Parliament*, bk 2, ch. 14; bk 3, ch. 8; Nowell, *Confutation*, especially fols 151[r], 155[r], 198[r]; Fulke, *D. Heskins*, 291.

would heed the Church Fathers like Chrysostom who had warned 'in this high mysterie, not to trust therefore to our own sensual judgement'.[19] The example of the Capernaites in John 6: 52, who, when Christ claims to be the bread of life, ask how he can give them his raw flesh to eat, was frequently discussed by Catholic writers, who condemned their 'gross imaginations' and 'carnal reasoning'.[20] On the other hand the 'Judaicall questions' many Protestants asked about the real presence betrayed no less lack of faith: 'How can one body of Christ be in a thousand places at once? How can it be dayly eaten and never consumed? How can ther be true flesh and blood seing the same is neither seen, felt, nor tasted … ?'[21] The 'wicked heresie' of 'phantasieng' the Lord's body without blood not only constituted 'a great Sacriledge', it also showed how these 'signe makers, and figure feigners' 'streigned oute a gnate, and swallowe[d] … a Cammell … stumble[d] at a strawe, and leap[t] over a blocke'.[22]

Although their aim was to lead lay people safely through these linguistic and philosophical labyrinths, such texts possibly did less to extinguish than they did to augment the perplexities of their readers. The sceptical questions they listed in order to refute may ironically have served to reanimate these same strands of disbelief. Indeed, some Catholic and Protestant divines began to turn away from the task of producing works of controversy towards devotional tracts because they observed that both the educated and uneducated were 'brought many-times to be more doubtfull therby then [they were] before'.[23] Could books such as these have played a part in persuading John Payne to drift away from conformity to the Church of England and embrace the Catholic faith? And might the disputes about the eucharist which they fuelled help to explain the hesitation he felt during Robert Gwyn's mass in December 1575?

The exact nature of Payne's difficulty is hard to unravel from Gregory Martin's letter, though it appears to be linked with the doctrine

---

[19] Pointz, *Testimonies*, fol. 48^v; Harding, *Answere*, fols 130^v, 158^v–162^v.

[20] See Sander, *Supper*, fols 86^v–87^r; Pointz, *Testimonies*, fols 10^r, 14^v; Heskyns, *Parliament*, sig. Aa1^v. For a Protestant response to this point, see Fulke, *D. Heskins*, 217–22.

[21] Pointz, *Testimonies*, fol. 92^r, and see also fols 14^v, 15^r–16^r. For Protestant emphasis on the evidence of the senses in refuting the real presence, see Nowell, *Confutation*, fol. 183^v; Fulke, *D. Heskins*, 282.

[22] Heskyns, *Parliament*, sigs Rr4^r, T4^v, M5^r.

[23] Robert Persons, *A Review of Ten Publike Disputations* (St Omer, 1604), 20; see also Michael C. Questier, *Conversion, Politics and Religion in England, 1580–1625* (Cambridge, 1996), ch. 2.

of concomitance: the idea that the body of Christ is present whole and undivided in both the bread and the wine. Commonly invoked to justify the Catholic practice of distributing the communion to the laity in only one kind, this meant that communicants obtained full sacramental grace from the host alone.[24] Yet Payne's worry does not seem to be about the legitimacy of the tradition of withholding the cup, but rather about the necessity of two distinct consecrations, an issue that had exercised medieval theologians such as Peter of Poitiers too. It perhaps reflects less a moment of doubt about the real presence than a more arcane concern regarding the compatibility of the ritual procedure and the custom of elevating the host for adoration with what Payne had been taught in his theological training as a priest.[25] Arguably it was a product of the very intensity of his meditative focus on the eucharist itself. In turn his vision might be seen as a mystical gift facilitating an existential transition to a deeper level of faith rather than a miracle sent to stop him from succumbing once again to Protestant error and becoming an apostate. The form it took may owe something to the topos of *nudus nudum Christum sequi,* which first appeared in the homilies of St Jerome and became one of the most popular expressions of the desire to imitate Christ in the later Middle Ages.[26]

The apparition of a figure of the crucified Christ during Gwyn's mass must also be situated against the backdrop of the many miracles vindicating the real presence and transubstantiation that fill the pages of medieval compilations of sermon *exempla* and which supplied the

---

[24] On concomitance, see Caroline Walker Bynum, *Christian Materiality: An Essay on Religion in Late Medieval Europe* (New York, 2011), 208–9, 212–13. For contemporary discussions, see Harding, *Answere,* fols 50^r–71^r; Heskyns, *Parliament,* bk 3, chs 67–8; Fulke, *D. Heskins,* 302–17, especially 309.

[25] For medieval speculations on this point, see Rubin, *Corpus Christi,* 54–8. Eamon Duffy comments that the custom of elevating the host emerged to counteract the view that the consecration of both elements was incomplete until the words of institution had also been said over the chalice: *The Stripping of the Altars: Traditional Religion in England* c.*1400*–c.*1580* (New Haven, CT, and London, 1992), 95–6. See also Bede Camm's comments on the case: Stratton-on-the-Fosse, Downside Abbey, Bede Camm Papers (Files on the English Martyrs: Payne). The rite used was presumably that prescribed by the Tridentine missal, which had been issued in 1572: see Wandel, *Eucharist,* 237–9. I am grateful to Catherine Pickstock, Aidan Bellenger and Charlotte Methuen for their advice on this complex issue.

[26] I owe this suggestion to Dermot Fenlon; Giles Constable, 'Nudus nudum Christum Sequi and Parallel Formulas in the Twelfth Century', in *Continuity and Discontinuity in Church History: Essays Presented to George Huntston Williams on the Occasion of his 68th Birthday,* ed. F. Forrester Church and Timothy George (Leiden, 1979), 83–91.

inspiration for artists, sculptors, woodcarvers and print makers. Co-
inciding with the rise of the cult of Corpus Christi, the period from
*c.*1200 to 1500 saw a proliferation of stories about hosts that bled
or turned into raw flesh and of masses in which a sacred infant or
the crucified Christ appeared. Some of these were vehicles for anti-
Semitism and a number of their locations became centres of thriv-
ing pilgrimages, notably the famous shrine at Wilsnack.[27] As Caroline Walker Bynum has argued, these visions and miraculous trans-
formations of holy matter were a measure both of the vitality of
late medieval devotion and of an underside of unbelief: a contemporary crisis of confidence about the sacred that found expression
both in the rise of 'animated materiality' and in the ambivalent fascination it engendered.[28] What we miscall 'credulity' was constantly
accompanied by suspicion that these phenomena might be diabolical
illusions or examples of human fraudulence. Frequently displayed to
rebuke sceptics and disbelievers, they also illustrate Eamon Duffy's
observation that '[e]ucharistic piety was underscored by the problem
of doubt'.[29] And this doubt, as John Arnold has demonstrated, was
often rooted in a 'nexus of practical experience and quotidian reality'.
It was prompted less by the intellectual heresies of John Wyclif than
by mundane reflection on the physical properties of the eucharist, by
a sense that what looked, smelt, tasted and felt like bread might not
hide a sublime mystery and might indeed just be a wafer made out of
wheaten flour and water.[30]

---

[27] Rubin, *Corpus Christi*, 108–29. On medieval eucharistic miracles, see Jules Corblet,
Histoire dogmatique, liturgique et archéologique du sacrement de l'eucharistie, 2 vols (Paris, 1885),
1: 447–515; Peter Browe, *Die eucharistischen Wunder des Mittelalters* (Breslau, 1938); G. J. C.
Snoek, *Medieval Piety from Relics to the Eucharist* (Leiden, 1995), 310–19. For the story of
'a priest who felt a doubt in saying the canon and beheld raw flesh' in Caesarius of Heisterbach's *Dialogue on Miracles* (*c.*1220–35), see John Shinners, ed., *Medieval Popular Religion:
A Reader* (Peterborough, ON, 1999), 90. See also Charles Zika, 'Hosts, Processions and
Pilgrimages: Controlling the Sacred in Fifteenth-Century Germany', *P&P* 118 (1988),
25–64.

[28] Caroline Walker Bynum, 'The Blood of Christ in the Later Middle Ages', *ChH* 71
(2002), 685–714; eadem, *Wonderful Blood: Theology and Practice in Late Medieval Northern Germany and Beyond* (Philadelphia, PA, 2007), esp. 3–5, 86–90, 138–41; eadem, *Christian Materiality*, especially 139–45, 157–9, 224. On miracles as a mechanism for dispelling doubt,
see also Michael E. Goodich, *Miracles and Wonders: The Development of the Concept of Miracle,
1150–1350* (Aldershot, 2007), ch. 4.

[29] Duffy, *Stripping of the Altars*, 102–7, at 102.

[30] John H. Arnold, 'The Materiality of Unbelief in Late Medieval England', in Sophie
Page, ed., *The Unorthodox Imagination in Late Medieval Britain* (Manchester, 2010), 65–95, at
73.

Payne's vision has two particular medieval parallels. The first is the miracle of Bolsena or Orvieto of 1263, when a priest called Peter of Prague was relieved of his doubts about the real presence by blood which dripped onto the corporal from the host he consecrated.[31] Secondly, it is reminiscent of the cluster of stories about the Mass of St Gregory. An early eighth-century version preserved in Jacobus de Voragine's famous *Golden Legend* tells of the woman who laughed when the famous pope was celebrating the eucharist, saying to her companion that she could not believe that the bread she had baked herself was now the body of Christ, only to be convinced when the host was miraculously transformed into a bleeding finger.[32] In later variants of the tale, the housewife is displaced by a group of deacons, and the finger by a vision of Christ as the Man of Sorrows. One of the best known iconographical tropes of the later Middle Ages, the Mass of St Gregory was depicted in altarpieces, paintings and books of hours. After the advent of the mechanical press it infiltrated the homes of laypeople in the guise of indulgenced prints (Fig. 2). As well as reflecting the privatization of the liturgy, the devout meditation of lay people upon such images embodied the assumption that seeing itself was salvific.

For many contemporaries the Mass of St Gregory was a compelling emblem of the miracle of transubstantiation that occurred every time the eucharist was celebrated.[33] In the wake of the

---

[31] On this miracle, see Bynum, *Wonderful Blood*, 119, 135, 149, 304 n. 87; eadem, *Christian Materiality*, 143, 144, 259, 278, 340 n. 62.

[32] For an eighth-century image of the 'doubting matron', see Michael Heinlen, 'An Early Image of a Mass of St Gregory and Devotion to the Holy Blood at Weingarten Abbey', *Gesta* 37 (1998), 55–62. Jacobus de Voragine, *The Golden Legend*, transl. W. G. Ryan, 2 vols (Princeton, NJ, 1993), 1: 179–80.

[33] On the Mass of St Gregory, see Duffy, *Stripping of the Altars*, 238–9; Rubin, *Corpus Christi*, 308–10. A database relating to the subject can be found at: <http://gregorsmesse.uni-muenster.de>. See also Alan Shestack, *Fifteenth-Century Engravings of Northern Europe from the National Gallery of Art Washington DC* (Washington DC, 1968), nos 213–15. For indulgenced prints of the Mass of St Gregory, see Kathleen Kamerick, *Popular Piety and Art in the Late Middle Ages: Image Worship and Idolatry in England 1350–1500* (New York, 2002), 169–72; Christine Göttler, 'Indulgenced Prints of Saint Gregory's Miraculous Mass', in eadem, *Last Things: Art and the Religious Imagination in the Age of Reform* (Turnhout, 2010), 31–69. For a late medieval stone relief of the Mass of St Gregory, see G. McN. Rushforth, *The Kirham Monument in Paignton Church, Devon: A Study in Mediaeval Iconography and in Particular of the Mass of St Gregory* (Exeter, 1927), especially 21–9 and fig. 1. Caroline Walker Bynum argues that later versions of the image were not designed to explicate the doctrine of transubstantiation or dispel doubt: 'Seeing and Seeing Beyond: The Mass of St Gregory in the Fifteenth Century', in Jeffrey F. Hamburger and Anne-Marie Bouché,

Figure 2. (Colour online) Fifteenth-century print of the Mass of St Gregory by Israhel van Meckenhem, British Museum Department of Prints and Drawings, E, 1.112AN52735001. © The Trustees of the British Museum.

Figure 3. Defaced stone reredos of the Mass of St Gregory, Bishop Oldham's chapel, Exeter Cathedral, 1513. Reproduced by permission of the Dean and Chapter of Exeter Cathedral.

Reformation, it is not surprising that depictions of it, such as the reredos on this theme in Bishop Oldham's chapel in Exeter Cathedral dating from 1513, were the targets of iconoclastic violence: such attacks reveal how it was transformed into a symbol of popish idolatry itself (Fig. 3).[34] The multiple representations of the Mass of St Gregory that circulated on canvas and paper and in stone and wood surely supplied a template to which John Payne (and the creator of the Bosworth Hall burse) retrospectively assimilated the interior vision which he had experienced. They provided a repertoire of mental and physical images that shaped and coloured contemporary perception and cognition. In many sculptures, paintings and pictures, the naked Christ appears surrounded by the instruments of the passion, and, as on the burse, by St Veronica's veil.

eds, *The Mind's Eye: Art and Theological Argument in the Middle Ages* (Princeton, NJ, 2006), 208–40.

[34] Göttler, 'Indulgenced Prints', 69. I am grateful to Olive Millward and Ellie Jones for their assistance in obtaining a photograph of the Bishop Oldham reredos.

As Gregory Martin's letter reveals, Payne's own initial reaction to the startling sight of Christ in the chalice was one in which astonishment was mingled with intense anxiety. It was apparently only after consultation with his Jesuit confessor that he recognized it as an authentic divine vision. This reflects a climate in which apparitions of all kinds were coming under increasingly critical scrutiny. In the wake of philosophical developments that were destabilizing their ontological status, and of religious changes that were undermining people's ability to distinguish truth clearly from falsehood, there was growing concern that many visions were merely 'vanities of the eyes'. They might be optical illusions engendered by that arch-magician and scientist Satan, figments of the imagination created by mental or physical illness, or counterfeit effects wrought by human ingenuity. The doubts and dangers surrounding the medieval discernment of spirits were intensified and complicated by the Reformation and on both sides of the confessional divide individuals were taught to respond to experiences of this kind with caution and trepidation.[35] They could also be liabilities in the polemical wars provoked by the schism of Christendom. As Peter Marshall has shown, Protestantism's preoccupation with detecting Antichrist's lying wonders fused with a current of humanist scepticism about feigned miracles epitomized by Erasmus's *Colloquies* and Sir Thomas More's *Dialogue concerning heresies* (1529), which included the notorious case of the Dominican friars of Berne who had deluded local people with a fabricated vision in support of the Immaculate Conception in 1507. According to the rhetoric of forgery deployed by reformed writers, transubstantiation was simply a piece of juggling and trickery. The priest at Paul's Cross who faked a bleeding host miracle by pricking his finger in 1545 was just one of the damaging scandals that played into the hands of Protestant propagandists.[36]

Mid-sixteenth-century Catholics shared in this mood of unease and distrust, and until the 1560s the champions of the Church of Rome were wary of publicizing miracles lest these expose them to

---

[35] See Stuart Clark, *Vanities of the Eyes: Vision in Early Modern European Culture* (Oxford, 2007); idem, 'The Reformation of the Eyes: Apparitions and Optics in Sixteenth- and Seventeenth-Century Europe', *JRH* 27 (2003), 143–60.

[36] Peter Marshall, 'Forgery and Miracles in the Reign of Henry VIII', *P&P* 178 (2003), 39–73, at 66; *The Complete Works of St Thomas More*, 6/1: *A Dialogue Concerning Heresies*, ed. Thomas M. C. Lawler, Germain Marc' Hadour and Richard C. Marius (New Haven, CT, and London, 1981), bk 1, chs 9–10, 14–15, at pp. 87–8.

fresh volleys of sarcasm and ridicule. Heskyns's *Parliament of Chryste* included a chapter on supernatural interventions that confirmed Catholic teaching on the eucharist, including visions of the infant Jesus and the 'doubting Chrystian' in whose hands the sacrament turned to 'verie bloodie flesh'. He declared: 'Let not the Adversarie by scorning travaill to rejecte this miracle or avoide the force of yt by slander, saing that some papist hath invented yt', and defended it as having been recorded within four hundred years of Christ's death – the period which Protestants themselves heralded as a time of primitive purity. He implored his readers not to be dissuaded when 'Sathans scholers' engaged in 'mocking or skorning' the other miracles reported by Cyprian, Ambrose and Gregory he mentioned in his text. William Fulke, however, dismissed all these stories as 'feigned fables' deliberately devised to buttress the false and invented doctrine of transubstantiation.[37] Bristow's *Motives* and *Demaundes* listed both miracles and visions as marks of the true Church, and recounted the story of the foul black dog that appeared to rebuke a wavering Catholic who agreed to receive the heretical communion, as well as the recent vision experienced by a certain Mr Allington, 'a thing most famously knowne' and endorsed by witnesses. But he too anticipated that some Protestants would retort with 'peevish scoffing' at 'uncertaine' and 'false miracles' culled from the *Legenda aurea* and other 'such apocryphall writings' and observed that 'dreames to certaine seeme ridiculous, and Visions foolish: but verily to suche as had rather to believe against Priests, then to beleeve the Priest'.[38] In concluding his account of Payne's remarkable vision, Gregory Martin displayed similar contempt for Protestant incredulity. Alluding to the case of doubting Thomas in John 20: 24 he said: 'Let those laugh who laugh at everything which is holy, and will not believe in anything they cannot handle'.[39] Catholics knew that miracles had the capacity to backfire against them and to stain the integrity of their embattled faith, but they also embraced them as a powerful weapon in the war against disbelief and heresy.[40]

[37] Heskyns, *Parliament*, bk 3, ch. 42, at sig. Ooo6^r; Fulke, *D. Heskins*, 462–7.
[38] Bristow, *Briefe Treatise*, fols 15^r–39^v, at 16^r, 38^r–39^v; *Demaundes to be Proponed of Catholiques to the Heretikes* (Antwerp [Douai], 1576), fols 29–32, 35–6.
[39] Knox, ed., *First and Second Diaries*, 311.
[40] See my 'Miracles and the Counter-Reformation Mission to England', *HistJ* 46 (2003), 779–815, especially 805–8. For Protestant mockery of a seventeenth-century miracle involving Robert Persons, in which the host received by an English gentlewoman in Rome

Finally, we must return briefly to the Bosworth Hall burse. It remains unclear precisely when and by whom this item was made. The reformers repudiated the traditional paraphernalia of the mass and with the advent of Protestantism many vestments and liturgical items were burnt, defaced, cut up or put to 'profane use'. Stolen from churches by conservatives who preserved them in the hope of a Catholic restoration, some were returned during Mary's reign, before being rescued and hidden again after Elizabeth's accession. Much of this popish 'pelfry', 'trumpery' and 'linen bagidg' was probably shipped overseas, but in other cases it remained in the safe-keeping of church papists and recusants.[41] Nonetheless, the first missionaries found the households in which they said mass ill equipped. Like the itinerant Lancashire priest Edmund Arrowsmith, they resorted to transporting chasubles, altar cloths and chalices around with them in chests resembling those carried by travelling salesmen. But as time progressed, the recusant families with whom they resided as chaplains acquired their own apparatus, as raids on their properties reveal. Pious widows and chaste spinsters dedicated themselves to the art of sacred embroidery. Reminiscent of those made by devout medieval ladies, the vestments manufactured by Catholic women such as Helena Wintour were in some sense forms of prayer: they were designed to provoke meditation or to give thanks for a miraculous intervention.[42] One surviving chalice veil, for instance, commemorates the cure of Roger Bodenham following a visit

---

turned into a piece of 'red flesh', see John Gee, *The Foot out of the Snare* (London, 1624), sigs E4ᵛ–F1ᵛ.

[41] On vestments, see Janet Mayo, *A History of Ecclesiastical Dress* (London, 1984), ch. 5 and p. 75; Pauline Johnstone, *High Fashion in the Church: The Place of Vestments in the History of Art from the Ninth to the Nineteenth Century* (Leeds, 2002), especially chs 4–5. For evidence of the survival, adaptation and destruction of Catholic vestments, see Edward Pecock, *English Church Furniture, Ornaments and Decorations, at the Period of the Reformation: As Exhibited in a List of the Goods Destroyed in Certain Lincolnshire Churches, AD 1566* (London, 1866), especially 30, 33, 36, 39, 40–1, 43, 48, 49, 56–7, 66–7, 71, 77, 80–1, 86, 94, 107–8, 119, 131–2, 144, 147, 159, 165.

[42] See Virginia C. Raguin, 'Liturgical Vestments', in eadem, ed., *Catholic Collecting: Catholic Reflection 1538–1850* (Worcester, MA, 2006), 61–8. For Arrowsmith's chest, now preserved at Stonyhurst College, see Maurice Whitehead, ed., *Held in Trust: 2008 Years of Sacred Culture* (Cirencester, 2008), 70–1, also ibid. 80–3; Sophie Holroyd, '"Rich Embroidered Churchstuffe": The Vestments of Helena Wintour', in Ronald Corthell et al., eds, *Catholic Culture in Early Modern England* (Notre Dame, IN, 2007), 73–116; eadem, 'Embroidered Rhetoric: The Social, Religious and Political Functions of Elite Women's Needlework, *c.*1560–1630', 2 vols (PhD thesis, University of Warwick, 2002), 148–252.

to St Winifred's well in 1606.[43] If the creation of objects of this kind can be described as 'subversive stitchery',[44] their preservation likewise entailed overt defiance of the Protestant regime: corporals and chalice veils were rendered holy by their association with the sacred vessels and consecrated species of the mass, the celebration of which was a capital crime. Items that touched the sacramental body of Christ and were in turn touched by believers could function as powerful evocations of the sacred and surrogates for the eucharist in situations where visits from priests were rare or irregular.

Perhaps the Bosworth Hall burse was the work of Payne's patron at the base he established on his arrival in England in 1576 at Ingatestone Hall: Lady Anne Petre, wife of the well-known church papist Sir John. The IHS monograms it bears are suggestive of the intimate connections of Payne and the Petre family with the Jesuits.[45] Another member of the Society, John Floyd, dedicated his translation of Antonio de Molina's *Treatise of the Holy Sacrifice of the Masse* to Anne's descendant Mary in 1623.[46] In the later seventeenth century William, fourth Lord Petre, commissioned a series of silver chalices for the use of the missionaries of the Jesuit district of the College of the Holy Apostles.[47]

While the precise provenance of the burse remains a mystery, Payne's execution at Chelmsford in 1582 ensured that it became a poignant relic. The doubts he experienced as a novice priest found no place in the public account of his martyrdom prepared by Cardinal William Allen and published as part of his *Brief Historie of Twelve Reverend Priests* later that year; nor in Richard Challoner's influential eighteenth-century *Memoirs of Missionary Priests*. But in both texts there appears to be a tantalizing reference to the item itself: raised from his bed by the lieutenant of the Tower of London to be transported to Essex, he 'desired leave to retorne to his chamber to make himselfe ready and to fetch his purse', but his request was denied and he was

---

[43] Whitehead, ed., *Held in Trust*, 84–5.

[44] Rosina Parker, *The Subversive Stitch: Embroidery and the Making of the Feminine* (London, 1984).

[45] See Kelly, 'Conformity, Loyalty and the Jesuit Mission', 152–6.

[46] Antonio de Molina, *A Treatise of the Holy Sacrifice of the Masse, and Excellencies Therof*, transl. I. R. [John Floyd] ([Saint-Omer], 1623).

[47] Virginia C. Raguin, 'Liturgical Vessels', in eadem, ed., *Catholic Collecting*, 49–59, at 53–4.

led away in his cassock.[48] Kept by the Petre family for hundreds of years, the burse is a compelling memorial of the miraculous vision which resolved a niggling worry and strengthened his faith. It is a material object in which the memory of a mystical inner experience has been captured and crystallized, but also subtly remodelled to fit a familiar mould.

This essay has traced the process by which an opaque and private moment of hesitation became a symbol of the dogmatic certainties that solidified into permanent confessional barriers: of the doctrinal conflicts over transubstantiation and the real presence that divided Wittenberg, Geneva, Rome and Lambeth. It has investigated the theological controversies that surrounded and perhaps helped to stimulate Payne's perplexity and the textual and iconographical precedents that conditioned the form that his vision dispelling it took. Probing the intrinsic connection between doubt and faith in late medieval and early modern society, it has shown how a pre-existing substratum of disbelief about the eucharist resurfaced and was transfigured in the wake of England's contested and plural Reformations.

---

[48] Allen, *Briefe Historie*, 89–97; Richard Challoner, *Memoirs of Missionary Priests* (London, 1924 edn), 39–44. Challoner or the manuscript from which he derived this account appears to have mistranslated 'burse' as 'purse'.

Theological Doubt and Institutional Certainty:
An Anglican Paradox

Rowan Williams*

Magdalene College, Cambridge

Explicating John Donne's 'doubt wisely', this essay argues for the theological and psychological sophistication of Richard Hooker's distinction of wise from unwise doubt and shows why this led him to support compulsory adherence to the Church of England. Framed by consideration of how his ideas were adopted by Thomas Browne's Religio Medici *(1643), it explores Hooker's thinking on what is certain in itself and where we can properly doubt. If true, the revealed character of God and the consequent acknowledgement of God as faithful to his elect, is true by necessity, or definition, and may be held with certainty of adherence: whatever my emotional state, adhering is proof that I have not denied my faith and am therefore sincere in my profession. It is wise to doubt the absolute importance of issues such as the right definition of Christ's presence in the sacrament, the God-given character of any specific Church order, and assumptions about the spiritual state of any other baptized person. We cannot, however, be doubtful about the Church to which allegiance is commanded by law. For Hooker, legal enforcement of conformity is a pastoral good: it enables the unsure to establish a practice likely to offer them some anchorage for fluctuating convictions and 'affections'.*

One of the most familiar stereotypes of modern Anglican Christianity is that it combines doctrinal indifferentism with obstinate defensiveness about the externals, ritual, social or legal, of the Church of England and its offshoots – what Donald MacKinnon devastatingly christened 'ecclesiological fundamentalism' in his little book, *The Stripping of the Altars*.[1] Sometimes this is seen as foreshadowed in the positions of divines and scholars of the Church of England's first independent century. Donne's phrase in his 'Satire iii', 'Doubt wisely',[2] might be prayed in aid; and the first book of Thomas Browne's *Religio Medici* gives some colour to the idea that Anglican identity has more to do with belonging than believing, to use what has become a fashionable

---

* Magdalene College, Cambridge, CB3 0AG. E-mail: jeh34@cam.ac.uk.
[1] London, 1969.
[2] 'Doubt wisely; in strange way | To stand enquiring right, is not to stray.'

Studies in Church History 52 (2016) 250–265
doi: 10.1017/stc.2015.14

contemporary distinction. Over and above what is laid down in the articles of religion, says Browne,

> … as points indifferent, I observe according to the rules of my private reason, or the humour and fashion of my Devotion; neither believing this, because Luther affirmed it, or disproving that, because Calvin hath disavouched it; and I could never divide myself from any man upon the difference of an opinion, or be angry with his judgment for not agreeing with me in that from which perhaps within a few days I should dissent myself. I have no Genius to disputes in religion.[3]

Doubts that arise, he continues, he will either forget or defer considering, on the grounds that reason will with the lapse of time find a 'reasonable truce' between warring opinions. And to enter into active controversy may imperil the certainty I have if I do not happen to possess the kind of dialectical nimbleness that can assure victory in argument: 'A man may be in as just possession of Truth as of a City, and yet be forced to surrender.'[4] Later on, he observes in passing that '[m]any things are true in Divinity, which are neither inducible by reason, nor confirmable by sense; and many things in Philosophy confirmable by sense yet not inducible by reason.'[5] 'Reason' cannot persuade anyone of matters of fact: the phenomena of the world are what they are and can be found out by observation: the point being, apparently, that what we can defensibly assert varies from one area of knowledge to another. If 'Philosophy' – that is, in this context, the systematic observation of the natural world – does not depend on what can be predicted on rational principle, we should not be surprised if there are truths which do not depend on either empirical observation or rational generality. As to empirical observation, it is the kind of thing that justifies me in solemnly swearing that such and such is truly the case; but where what I assert goes beyond what I have seen myself by 'infallible warrant', I should hold back from swearing. I may be entirely convinced that something is the case, but it would be improper for me to take my oath on it, since that would imply that I could support what I assert by direct testimony. As we might put it, the 'grammar' of swearing has to do with direct evidence; and so I cannot take my oath about my spiritual condition

---

[3] Thomas Browne, *Religio Medici* 1.5, 6 (first publ. 1643).
[4] Ibid. 1.6.
[5] Ibid. 1.48.

any more than about the existence of the city of Constantinople. I am not in doubt, but the fact of my being convinced is not evidence.[6] The implication is that we must be very modest about the capacities of argument to resolve controversy; we may regard some proposition as certain (and we may as a matter of fact be right about that), yet be unable to establish it by public dispute. Whatever resolves doubt is not going to be dialectic. In the case of the existence of Constantinople, we can always go there; in the case of religious doctrine, we have no ideological high court but may decide – for a huge variety of reasons – to be loyal to an institutional system that makes broad sense to us and is consistently supported by the general tenor of our experience.

It is important to be clear what Browne does and does not say in this informal analysis. He is not arguing for a general agnosticism in matters of doctrine: he accepts the Articles of Religion and whatever is implied in the authorized liturgy. He does not deny that we may have certain knowledge on matters outside rational demonstration and empirical proof; but he implies that we may not know the grounds of our certainty. He identifies 'infallible' knowing with what we can credibly demonstrate on the basis of first-hand sense experience;[7] but in so defining what we simply cannot be wrong about he does not suggest that this is the sole way of being right. He is not a doctrinal indifferentist, though he is clear that there are 'matters of indifference' outside what the Church has decided to pronounce on. In many ways, he echoes themes that had been more fully developed by Richard Hooker (d. 1600); and it may help to look at some of Hooker's key passages to find further illumination on how certainty and uncertainty, personal conviction and public belonging are negotiated in this context. It is in the Fifth Book of the *Lawes of Ecclesiastical Politie* that we find some of the most notable arguments on the subject, specifically in Hooker's discussion of the sacraments of baptism and holy communion. He distinguishes here between 'demonstrable conclusions' and 'demonstrative principles': the latter are axioms whose certainty is either self-evident or 'evident by the light of some higher knowledge'; 'conclusions' are what can be

[6] Ibid. 1.59.
[7] The relation of this to the epistemology of Locke and those who followed him needs more exploration; but it is important to grasp that Browne is not proposing that sense experience is the sole arbiter of true or justifiable belief.

deduced from prior agreed points.[8]   In Christian teaching, both are present, but what is fundamental is the recognition that the 'principles' of this teaching are to be believed with complete adherence on the grounds of what is believed about God. Once we have settled our trust in God, we may take the basic lines of revealed faith for granted; we trust their source. And these 'basic lines', Hooker implies, are to do with the conviction, the 'acknowledgment', that we are loved by God and invited into the fellowship of his Son, not as a reward for our belief but as the condition for it. Baptism establishes in us the gift of this new life as 'children of the promise'; the eucharist, as he spells out a few chapters later, is our conscious appropriation of what has been given. 'We know by grace what the grace is',[9] and are given the discernment to see something both of our growth in holiness and of the entire dependence of such holiness on the action of Christ upon us through the consuming of his sacramental signs.

Thus in baptism what happens is that we are visibly incorporated into the fellowship of Christ: it is now true to say of us that we are children of the promise, and that truth is certain in itself because God has made it to be the case. Through our participation in the eucharist, we acquire increasing subjective certainty about what has been done. This illustrates the argument advanced by Hooker much earlier in his celebrated sermon *Of the Certaintie and Perpetuitie of Faith in the Elect*: we must distinguish between 'certainty of evidence', where we can appeal to clear proofs of some proposition to establish its truth, and 'certainty of adherence', where we have less evidence but stronger affective reason for holding to a belief. We see a putative state of affairs – a claim about God and God's actions, say – 'not only as true but also as good', and so our will is engaged. Not that we are certain simply because we want to be; but our certainty is a matter of consistently desiring a truth we have glimpsed or sensed which, if it is true, matters more than any truth that can be more evidentially grounded, and it reflects a state of affairs more 'sure' in the sense of being more firmly established in actuality, than any empirical matter of fact.[10]   Hooker, as several scholars have observed, is taking

---

[8] Richard Hooker, *Of the Laws of Ecclesiastical Polity*, 5.63.1 (ed. A. S. McGrade, 3 vols [Oxford, 2013], 2: 195).
[9]   Ibid. 5.67.1 (ed. McGrade, 2: 222).
[10] Richard Hooker, *A Learned Sermon of the Certaintie and Perpetuitie of Faith in the Elect* (*Folger Library Edition of the Works of Richard Hooker*, 5: *Tractates and Sermons*, ed. Laetitia Yeandle and Egil Grislis [Cambridge, MA, and London, 1991], 59–82, at 70–1).

for granted a familiar scholastic distinction between truths that are 'self-evident' (*per se notum*) in themselves, in the sense that if true they are necessarily or 'definitionally' true, and truths that are self-evident *quoad nos*: that is to say, something may be necessarily true in that a subject cannot actually be consistently thought or described in any other way, but we may as a matter of fact be ignorant of that intrinsic quality of the truth in question because we have an imperfect grasp of the subject.[11] And Nigel Voak, in his admirable and ambitious study of Hooker's relation to Reformed theology, notes the parallels with Aquinas's location of the believer's apprehension of revealed truth as combining elements of firmness and clarity that belong to proper and conclusive knowledge with the lack of 'clear vision' that belongs to 'doubt, suspicion or opinion'.[12] We are faced with a somewhat paradoxical situation in which the certainty of adherence, despite its apparent unevenness and fragility, is greater than the certainty of evidence where God is concerned, so that it is perfectly possible that we feel doubt or insecurity while still persisting in faithfulness to what has been given.

Hooker's concern in this remarkable sermon is to challenge the suspicion that '[i]f I were faithful it could not be thus'[13] – that is, to persuade those in spiritual doubt and desolation that they are not reprobate. The lack of 'evidence' for election is no evidence of reprobation: suffering, inner struggle and outer failure do not matter so long as we still long for what we have sought to adhere to.[14] If it is evidence we are looking for, it can be found only in that kind of

---

[11] See, classically, Thomas Aquinas, *Summa theologiae*, I q. 2 a. 1, 'Utrum Deum esse sit per se notum'.

[12] Nigel Voak, *Richard Hooker and Reformed Theology: A Study of Reason, Will, and Grace* (Oxford, 2003), 245, referring to *Summa theologiae*, II–IIae q. 2 a. 1. See also ibid. 71–8 for a very helpful overview of Hooker's formulations on the varieties of certainty.

[13] Hooker, *Learned Sermon*, 75. There is an exemplary reading of the argument of this sermon in Debora K. Shuger, 'Faith and Assurance', in Torrance Kirby, ed., *A Companion to Richard Hooker* (Leiden, 2008), 221–50: on Hooker's echoing of Aquinas (and his divergences or different emphases), see especially ibid. 237–41, and ibid. 248–9 which establish that Hooker's use of the distinction between truths certain in themselves and certain for us is picked up directly by Richard Baxter, who then, however, goes on to make a radically different use of Hooker's themes in the service of a far more 'Lockean' epistemology.

[14] 'Are they not greeved for their unbeliefe? they are. Do they not wish it might and also strive that it may be otherwise? wee know they do. Whenc cometh this, but from a secret love and liking which they have of those things that are believed? No man can love the things which in his own opinion are not … then must it needs be that by desiring to beleeve they prove themselves to be true beleevers': Hooker, *Learned Sermon*, 76.

self-examination that tests whether we truly want the good we have dimly apprehended; which is evidence in a very Pickwickian sense, since it can be submitted to no external tribunal. Yet the discussion in this sermon casts light on what Hooker has to say about the eucharist in the *Lawes*: our fidelity in receiving the sacrament intensifies our consciousness of the grace received, helps us to see that in spite of what we may feel we are actually growing in faith, and reminds us that any such growth is the direct effect of a steady and invincible divine presence in the soul. Communicating provides a new level of – if not exactly evidence – what we could call 'evidential reinforcement'. Thus I am not persuaded that (as Voak and others argue) we have to imagine a major theological shift in Hooker's thought between his defence of the possibility of knowing ourselves to be elected in the early sermons and a later repudiation of such knowledge, with the passage on the eucharist thus having to be regarded as an anomaly.[15] It is true that Hooker has hard words in his Preface to the *Lawes* for those who conclude that they are elect (and others are not) on the grounds of 'the fervent earnestness of their persuasion' or 'earnest affection'.[16] What he is querying here is the assumption that we can be certain of our election because of the strength of our feelings; but this is clearly something different from the consistency of the (grace-supported) will which is being appealed to in the sermon, a consistency which may be unchanged even when strength of feeling is absent. Hooker's pastoral concern in the sermon is for those who cannot believe they are elect because they do not have the right emotions; his theological critique in the *Lawes* is directed against those who link their Christian assurance to states of feeling, who want precisely to propose their inner condition as evidence. This challenge to a vulgarized Calvinism (and Hooker is explicit in associating it with a popular distortion of the Calvinist theology, while deliberately leaving us with the general impression that it is a risk which this theology will inevitably run because it gives too much house-room to non-rational and non-ecclesial accounts of how the Holy Spirit works) is not a rejection of the idea that we can know ourselves elect. It is rather to clarify what sort of knowledge this might be; what kind of certainty is involved.

---

[15] Voak, *Hooker*, 222–51.
[16] Hooker, *Laws*, Preface 3.10–11 (ed. McGrade, 1: 14–15).

The paradox is, as we have seen, that while certainty of adherence is in one way stronger than certainty of evidence, it is also more vulnerable, since it lacks external confirmation and so is open to internal variation. Hence the need to uncouple it decisively from states of 'affection'. Certainty of adherence is inevitably something that grows and declines (or appears to decline in intensity). Whereas certainty of evidence has a clear, undisputable and irreversible maximal point – we cannot be more sure than when we have the evidence of our senses[17] – the assurance of faith is not like that, whether in respect of the existence and character of God or with respect to my own spiritual standing. Thus my knowledge of my own spiritual condition – of my election – is a complex affair when analysed. I cannot have evidential certainty about it in the usual sense; and if I look for evidential certainty in the state of my 'affections', I shall go astray, imagining that positive feelings about this or any related issue constitute proof comparable to the proof of the sense in a dispute over material states of affairs. What is available as evidence is the fact of not having gone back on the decision to be faithful; and this is both weaker and stronger than ordinary evidential certainty. I know my own mind, to the extent of knowing what I want, and knowing therefore when I am grieved and deprived by its lack at the level of feeling. It is not that I am to be convinced of my condition by an appeal to the subjective strength of my conviction, but that the fact of not having decided against what I have committed myself to, the fact of adherence, becomes not so much a ground for certainty but a proof against my reprobation. At the level of evidence, what I need pastorally, in Hooker's eyes, is clear proof that I am not reprobate; and this is provided by the consistency of my graced will – what I go on saying I most desire, even when I feel no warmth or comfort in faith.

Discussions of Hooker's thought on this will somewhat miss the point if they do not begin from his purpose in the sermon on *Certaintie*, which is not to give proof positive of election through evidence but to use the certainty of adherence as proof 'negative', proof that I have not denied my faith and am therefore sincere in my profession even when I feel like a liar. The entire argument is certainly meant to assure believers of their spiritual security, but to do so by way of

---

[17] See Richard Hooker, *Answer to the Supplication*, 9 (*Hooker*, 5: *Tractates and Sermons*, ed. Yeandle and Grislis, 211–58, at 236–7).

minimizing dependence on passing states of mind or heart and emphasizing the fact of a decision to trust the fidelity of God, who keeps promises and does not abandon those whom he has addressed and called.[18] What we are given to reason with in respect of our election is what our regular behaviour signals – not the unevenness of our feelings or the chanciness of our external comfort and success, but the steady disposition to persist. Thus we may 'excavate' a firm certainty of adherence which remains solid even when it feels frail; and to strengthen it we may adduce the evidence of our persistence in desiring. And this provides a bridge to the discussion in *Lawes* Book 5 of the eucharist. As we have seen, participation in the eucharist offers the possibility of discernment about one's own progress in grace; and this needs to be read against the background of what Hooker says in the second sermon on Jude about the sacrament.[19] It is an opportunity to examine oneself in the hope of becoming clearer about one's failings and to seek remedy; the sweetness of the sacrament, the 'taste of Christ Jesus in the heart' which it gives, is connected very clearly to the recognition of absolution and renewed grace. In the light of this, it seems that when in the *Lawes* Hooker describes the eucharist as allowing us to measure our increase in holiness, this is not so much an appeal to the evidential force of our spiritual achievement but a reference to our sustained willingness to turn to Christ for forgiveness and aid, since the eucharist assures us primarily of the character of God in Christ as faithful to what he has declared (as in the meditation recommended to the communicant which closes chapter 67 of Book 5: 'why should any cogitation posesse the minde of a faithfull communicant but this, *O my God thou art true, O my soule thou art happie*?').[20]

---

[18] Cf. Hooker's second sermon on the Epistle of Jude, 3, 16 (*Hooker*, 5: *Tractates and Sermons*, ed. Yeandle and Grislis, 36–58, at 37–8, 45–6), allowing for the marked difference of emphasis between this and the *Certaintie* sermon. On the divergences, see especially Shuger, 'Faith and Assurance', 227–8. She is rightly clear that the one thing Hooker is not doing is directly overturning the Calvinist doctrine of perseverance, but that he is proposing a radically reconfigured approach to assurance: ibid. 229–35. For a helpful though not very searching general treatment, see also Egil Grislis, 'The Assurance of Faith according to Richard Hooker', in A. S. McGrade, ed., *Richard Hooker and the Construction of Christian Community* (Tempe, AZ, 1997), 237–49, especially 239–40.
[19] Hooker, *Laws*, 5.10–11 (ed. McGrade, 2: 42–3); these echoes in what is said about the eucharist represent a significant point of continuity between Hooker's earlier and his more mature thought that merits more exploration.
[20] Ibid. 5.67.12 (ed. McGrade, 2: 343, lines 24–6).

But this point now extends further. In chapter 68 of Book 5, Hooker responds to critics of the current practice of the Church of England, particularly to those who attack the Church's willingness to admit known recusants to holy communion without assurance of their abjuration of popish error and their conversion to 'gospel-like' behaviour. Hooker's reply becomes fully intelligible when read in the light of what we have so far discussed about assurance. How do we know if someone is definitively outside the Church of God? Only if they actively and explicitly repudiate Christ. The word 'Church', says Hooker, is what distinguishes those who call on Christ as Lord for those who do not: that is the 'essence' of its definition, relating to 'the object or matter whereabout the contemplations and actions of the Church are properly conversant'. If we introduce into the definition any other matters, we reproduce the error of Roman Catholics who will not admit any other body to be the Church that does not accept the specific opinions that distinguish them from other Christians; and because '[t]hey define not the Church by that which the Church essentially is but by that wherein they imagine their own more perfect than the rest are', they confuse what may or may not belong to the Church's well-being with what belongs to its essence. Schisms and heresies, so far as they do not touch the central distinguishing mark of the Church, its adherence to Christ, are deplorable but not fatal, not necessarily grounds for final and irreparable rupture. 'That which separates therefore *utterly*, that which cuts off *clean* from the visible Church of Christ is plain Apostasy, *direct* denial'. So the puritan critic of admitting recusants to communion is in fact mirroring the Roman error, confusing the essence of ecclesial identity with 'variable accidents'.[21]

What we can be sure of is that the recusant presenting himself or herself for communion in the established Church is to be given every benefit of the doubt; they are giving us 'the strongest pledge of fidelity that man can demand', given the great sensitivities of conscience that attend the matter of sacramental practice (we should not in conscience be able to attend their mass, as this would implicitly commit us to the specific Roman doctrine of presence and sacrifice and priesthood, which Hooker believes both unnecessary and heretical).[22] They are in any case 'capable' of God's sacramental mysteries

---

[21] Ibid. 5.68.6 (ed. McGrade, 2: 234–6).
[22] Ibid. 5.68.7 (ed. McGrade, 2: 237).

'for anything we hear to the contrary' and are in need of nurture.[23] Whatever fragile beginnings of real faith are present should not be quenched; and if they approach the sacrament in a hypocritical spirit, that is their problem and they will answer to God for it. 'For neither does God thus bind us to dive into men's consciences, nor can their fraud and deceit hurt any man but themselves … In the eye of God they are against Christ that are not truly and sincerely with him, in our eyes they must be received as with Christ that are not to outward show against him.'[24]   Christ leaves us the sacrament 'not only for preservation of strength but for relief of weakness'.[25] So to share the sacrament with those whose subjective state of faith is questionable is a properly compassionate pastoral provision. To wait until they have arrived at standards of 'gospel-like behaviour' as laid down by Hooker's puritan critics is to ask more than the law can rightly require (and exactly who is to determine what sort of tests they will need to pass?).

What is interesting here is that Hooker is applying to others – to 'doubtful' conformists in the Church of England – a variant of the test offered to the believer to apply to himself or herself. What do we know of the spiritual state of the church-papist? Only what the evidence of coming to the sacrament supplies: the decision to be visibly part of the sacramental community. Insofar as that decision rests on a genuine desire to be nourished by Christ's life and strength, it is – for all we know – a sign of authentic evangelical faith which will come to fruition in good time. But we cannot determine, and should not try to determine, the degree of sincere adherence, which is known only to God, and which the individual must test by continuing repentance and self-questioning – just as I myself, as a believer, will not have clear and infallible evidence of my own sincerity and integrity of faith, only the evidence that comes from examining what only I can examine, which is my steady disposition to continue to believe. And the evidence of my adherence to the Church's discipline is relevant to this, even if not decisive in the way that direct sense experience is. 'Institutional certainty' is simply the visible evidence of conformity, evidence understood in the context of a set of arguments and assumptions about what gives us grounds for claiming knowledge: we

---

[23] Ibid. 5.68.9 (ed. McGrade, 2: 238).
[24] Ibid. 5.68.8 (ed. McGrade, 2: 238).
[25] Ibid. 5.68.9 (ed. McGrade, 2: 238).

cannot completely and definitively know even our own hearts (in the sense of being wholly truthful about our feelings), let alone those of others, and our self-knowledge as believers is constantly being tested and (we trust) deepened by our tangible practice. Institutional conformity does not guarantee against hypocrisy but that is not its point: it is a necessary but not sufficient condition for claiming a certainty of adherence. And this is why for Hooker the legal enforcement of conformity is a good and proper matter: it gives opportunity to the struggling and unsure, or even the probably heretical, to establish a practice which is likely to offer them some anchorage for their fluctuating convictions and 'affections'. Building up the community on the basis of members who have appropriate 'affections', whose inner states are used to prove points in controversy and to assess the inner states of others, is destructive not only of a viable community life but of the very essence of a faith that must be 'eccentric', having its focus not in the intensity of its self-consciousness as faith but in its looking towards a faithful God and its constantly rediscovered grounding in a steady desire. It is not that such faith knows nothing of affective states; what Hooker writes about the eucharist provides an emphatic refutation of any such idea. But – as the second sermon on Jude strongly suggests, as does the beginning of chapter 67 of the Fifth Book of the *Lawes* – moments of strong affection and spiritual sweetness are given to strengthen the continuing decision to be faithful. They correspond to those fleeting gifts of consolation which the Spanish mystic John of the Cross (d. 1591), for example, sees as a stimulus to continuing fidelity in darkness.

As Voak has persuasively argued, Hooker is reluctant to grant that the Holy Spirit ever acts in us independently of the activity of reason. I have contended here that even what he writes about the eucharist does not necessarily infringe this or suggest that there is simple 'testimony' from the Spirit in our experience at the Lord's Table. The question is – as indeed Voak grants[26] – about what reason is given to work upon; and I agree that Hooker does not stand so very far from a sophisticated puritan like Perkins in affirming that visible habits of self-denial, penitence and tears may be taken as reliable signs of the Spirit's working.[27] But what matters is that strong devotional feelings

---

[26] See, for example, Voak, *Hooker*, 242–3.

[27] Ibid. 250–1; Voak rightly points out the difference between this and Calvin's systematic scepticism about the possibility of deducing anything about one's spiritual state from an

around the eucharist, for example, are treated as illustrating what is presented to our self-awareness (in contrast to what we unknowingly receive at baptism): that is, they are available for reasoning about, and this is what Hooker does with them. They are not direct communications from the Spirit which can establish norms for the Church (and boundaries for the Church). They are modest confirmations of the authenticity of my resolve to continue as part of the visible Church and my loyalty to its disciplines, and apart from this – apart from the kind of self-probing that the *Certaintie* sermon assists with – they have no real significance.

For Hooker, there is a central area of Christian teaching which has to be regarded as certain: all that has to do with the action of God in Christ and the way in which this comes to govern the life of the community and the individual. We hold this with a certainty of adherence, on the grounds that God has shown himself to us as trustworthy, and we have accordingly chosen to commit our lives to continuing in the fellowship of Jesus. If the Church is the totality of those who call upon the name of the Lord, as he asserts in *Lawes* 5.68.6, we cannot imagine a Church in which the authority of Christ was not so confessed. Beyond this, there are two main areas in which doubtfulness has to be confronted and thought through. The first has to do with disputed doctrinal questions (notably those to do with the eucharist); we may, as Hooker implies, have good reason to deny certain doctrines, such as transubstantiation, but we cannot treat that denial with the same certainty with which we approach the essential definition of the Church; even when disagreement over these arises, this does not justify impenetrable barriers of separation. A 'doubtful' doctrine, one which can reasonably be argued about without this affecting the conviction of what makes the Church distinctively what it is, cannot be deployed as a means of exclusion, and, as we have seen, Hooker argues that his opponents are reproducing the mistakes of the very people they want to exclude. We could, in the light of Hooker's overall scheme, say that 'doubtful' doctrines are those which we may hold or not without affecting our basic adherence to God in Christ. Whether or not I believe in transubstantiation does not materially change what I may be certain of in regard to my election and the unqualified generosity of God in determining this. The second

---

external pattern of conduct. See also W. Brown Patterson, *William Perkins and the Making of a Protestant England* (Oxford, 2014).

area of doubt is over what it is to be a true member of the Body of Christ, a doubt which may apply both to myself and to others whom I observe. As to my own standing, I may – this is the burden of the *Certaintie* sermon – treat this as a matter for certainty of adherence in much the same way as with fundamental doctrine: I have good reason for believing because of my conviction about God's saving work, and this is reinforced by inspection of my actions, though this does not turn certainty of adherence into certainty of evidence. As to the standing of any other, I remain uncertain; but what I can be certain of, in a fairly straightforward evidential sense, is that they are to be accounted members of the visible Church on the grounds of their not having repudiated their dependence on Christ, and therefore not being certainly reprobate.

Legally imposed conformity is thus both a pastoral opportunity for the weak or wavering (they are obliged to perform the actions that go with faith, and they may thereby come to a living faith by having available to them the witness of their own 'growing into' their practice) and a way of recognizing that, if we do not have a Church polity based on detailed confessionalism and detailed official scrutiny of behaviour, we are bound to have a Church that proposes as certain simply its own right to exist as the community of those in this place who acknowledge dependence on the name of Jesus Christ, with the obvious corollary that this assumes the certainty of the divine authority of Jesus Christ, something clearly *per se notum* in itself even if not *quoad nos*. We may be sure that the institution is to be accepted and identified with on this basis; and the nature and consistency of our involvement in its life, especially its sacramental life, assists our positive judgement about our own individual election, while giving no ground for pronouncing about anyone else's.[28] The appeal to a legally sanctioned conformity is not in Hooker's eyes a way of stepping back from seriousness about the demands of discipleship but an

---

[28] To the question of whether Hooker accepted and taught the final perseverance of the elect, which he is commonly supposed not to have endorsed by the time of his later writings, there is no crystal-clear answer. The *Certaintie* sermon is designed not so much to assure people of final perseverance on their part as to persuade them that God is able to guarantee their status and that their own lack of warmth or affective conviction is not evidence against this. On the whole, he writes of election as if it is inamissible; and if he did not believe this, much of both earlier and later work becomes unintelligible. What is distinctive is that he will not tie this to an individual sense of security. Our subjective insecurity is one of the things that drives us to constant self-examination, penitence and dependence – and thus to a more authentic and prayerful living out of our inner status.

absolutely necessary recognition of the importance of not confusing different kinds of knowledge and certainty. He is not some sort of Wittgensteinian *avant la lettre*, or a plain religious voluntarist. He is nonetheless clear about the primacy of practice in assessing genuine faith and about the need for a sustained act of will in keeping faith with the gift given. Hooker is not interested in how anyone might 'come to faith' in the contemporary sense of deciding to adopt a religious worldview, and so it is anachronistic to project modern debates about 'fideism' onto his writing. He undoubtedly believes that faith is a rational stance, an adherence based on the revealed trustworthiness of God in Jesus Christ which we continually 'acknowledge' by our continuation in ecclesial fidelity (and which we upset if we are constantly looking for a superior polity that will deliver us from affective uncertainty and the proximity of those of whose election we are doubtful). He definitely does not see faith as an act of 'raw' will, of arbitrary self-definition. But, in a very Augustinian style, he refuses to separate the rational compulsion of the true from the affective authority of the good; if affections are an unreliable authority in themselves, they are not for that reason to be set aside as motivations for cleaving to what has been revealed, which, if true, is necessarily also attractive.

'Doubt wisely', said Donne; and both Hooker and Browne may be taken as illustrations of what such wise doubt might involve. We are not to doubt that God is good and faithful to those he has called; our emotional chill or confusion is not a reason for doubting this. We are summoned to stake ourselves on this conviction, and this means a continuous refreshing of our will and of our awareness of why this belief answers our most significant desire. The dominical sacraments express in clear material form the fidelity of God to his promises, and thus our own fidelity properly takes the shape of obedient participation in the sacraments; and the eucharist speaks directly to our self-awareness, increasing our consciousness both of sin and of growth in recognition of our need of God and so our growth in the only holiness that matters. None of this provides the sort of evidential certainty that would attach to what our senses directly perceive, but that does not matter: certainty may come in various guises, including some that do not entail constant affective clarity and intensity. What we know is that the revealed character of God and the consequent acknowledgement of God as faithful to his elect are certain in themselves (if true, necessarily or definitionally true); and thus that they may properly be held with certainty of adherence. Doubt in any of these areas would not be 'wise'. However, we can equally properly doubt the absolute importance of finding the right definition of Christ's presence in the sacramental elements; the God-given character of any specific Church order; and our assumptions about the spiritual state of any other baptized person, orthodox or heretic. But if it is wise to be doubtful about these things, we cannot be doubtful about the Church to which our allegiance is commanded by law: conformity establishes the context within which we can be assured of what we should not doubt and be reminded of what we need not be sure of.

Such an argument for conformity is easily dismissed by some as a rationalization of a particular kind of confessional and political hegemony; we have had a fair number of scholars to remind us in the last few decades that Hooker is no unworldly innocent in these matters. But the psychological complexity of his analysis of faith and uncertainty at the very least makes it plain that he is not seeking a glib ready-made justification for the Elizabethan Settlement. He wants to do justice to the felt, the sensed, unevenness of religious conviction and to guard against a tyranny of individual insight exalted to supreme determinative authority and a confessionalism far more severe and exclusive than any dreamt of by the Elizabethan regime. He is of course an apologist for a policy that no modern democrat would find defensible; but what we may miss is that he clearly saw that policy as the most pastorally and humanly effective way of managing the Church's institutional life in what was still largely a society that did not question the need for a religious basis. Furthermore, he provides a solid case for regarding the Church of England of his day as doing better justice to the fundamental principle of the Reformation than those who urged more radical reform. Browne's phrasing reflects Hooker's thought very accurately when he says:

> That which is the cause of my Election, I hold to be the cause of my salvation, which was the mercy and beneplacit of God, before I was, or the foundation of the World … [T]he World was before the Creation, and at an end before it had a beginning; and thus was I dead before I was alive: though my grave be England, my dying place was Paradise: and Eve miscarried me before she conceiv'd of Cain.[29]

---

[29] Browne, *Religio Medici* 59.

Our faith deals with matters resolved not by our successful performances in thought, feeling or action, but with the ultimate self-evident certainty of the divine determination, to which we bear constant but uneven witness in our practice; to be doubtful of the validity of the Church by law established is to introduce uncertainty into the heart of the Reformed gospel; hence the triumphant paradox that 'institutional certainty' is a better guardian of Reformed principle than the search for indubitable criteria of authentic personal election. If the English puritan Thomas Cartwright (d. 1603) and his allies were as unimpressed as we should expect them to be, that should not stop us from recognizing the theological sophistication of Hooker's proposals for distinguishing wise from unwise doubt.

Unbelief, the Senses and the Body in Nicholas Bownde's *The vnbeleefe of S. Thomas* (1608)

Patrick S. McGhee*

University of Cambridge

Doubt and unbelief were central to the ways in which ministers and theologians in post-Reformation England thought and wrote about religion. Far from signalling spiritual failure, grappling with unbelief could be an important stage in developing the faith and religious understanding of the individual believer while establishing a role for physicality and the senses. Nicholas Bownde's The vnbeleefe of S. Thomas the Apostle, laid open for the comfort of all that desire to beleeue *(1608) suggests that unbelief was relational and that belief required not only an acknowledgement of doubt but also extensive exploration of what doubtful and unbelieving experiences involved and how they were to be overcome. Bownde's work demonstrates that this ongoing spiritual conversation could make use of important scriptural examples such as the 'Doubting Thomas' episode in order to elucidate intimate theological problems for contemporary believers. This process suggests that early modern religion can only be properly understood with close reference to the role of doubt, unbelief and spiritual uncertainty in religious discourse because belief itself was predicated on the logical possibility of unbelief.*

The scriptural narrative of Thomas the Apostle (John 20: 24–31) represents a unique crossroads between religious doubt and the sensory experience of religion. Appearing in only one of the four gospels, the episode was referenced in sermons, religious writing and art throughout the early modern period, as it had been in earlier centuries. An early seventeenth-century text by the clergyman Nicholas Bownde (d. 1613), *The vnbeleefe of S. Thomas the Apostle, laid open for the comfort of all that desire to beleeue* (first published in 1608, posthumously republished in 1628), suggests that the 'vnbeleefe' of Thomas had multiple meanings and functions alongside religious doubt in post-Reformation discourse about salvation.[1] With

---

* 3 Ellerbrook Close, Heath Charnock, Adlington, PR6 9NQ. E-mail: pm541@cam.ac.uk.

[1] Nicholas Bownde, *The Vnbeleefe of S. Thomas the Apostle, laid open for the comfort of all that desire to beleeue* (Cambridge, 1608; London, 1628); all references are to the 1608 edition.

Studies in Church History 52 (2016) 266–282   © Ecclesiastical History Society 2016
doi: 10.1017/stc.2015.15

reference first to Bownde's discussion of the senses and subsequently to his perspective on the body, this essay will explore the ways in which grappling with unbelief in this period could, far from signalling spiritual failure, represent an important stage in developing religious understanding and reaffirming assurance.

According to Bownde, unbelief could be a dormant affliction within every individual but also a motivation for a renewal of faith in Christ. The language with which theologians and divines responded to religious doubt and unbelief in early seventeenth-century England reveals the distinctive and changing ways in which a new generation of individuals reconceptualized their faith in this period. The reality of unbelief as both an affliction and a necessary aspect of religion was articulated in prescriptive works of practical divinity that sought to instruct readers in ways of believing and practising their religion.[2] Bownde's text is a useful example of this pastoral literature: it sought to offer comfort to those experiencing the spiritual dilemma of unbelief, not only by referring to theological abstractions but also by a particular focus on physicality, the senses and the body. The work is significant because it examines one of the most important scriptural instances of doubt and unbelief with direct reference to its sensory and physical dimensions. Moreover, the text has implications for scholarly understanding of English Protestant theology as illustrating some of the ways in which the prescriptive aspects of religion were affected by the changing pastoral needs of individuals during the post-Reformation period.

These developments complicate the historiography of the Reformation, which has often argued that Protestantism heralded a theological framework based on faith and Scripture and rejected the ritualistic and sensory culture of late medieval religion.[3] However, explorations of the role of the senses and work on post-Reformation treatments of the Thomas narrative have helped to qualify these assumptions. Broadly, studies of visual religious experience have highlighted that the language of sight was informed by Augustinian precepts of simultaneously tangible and intangible, physical and spiritual

---

[2] Kenneth L. Parker and Eric Josef Carlson, *'Practical Divinity': The Works and Life of Revd Richard Greenham* (Aldershot, 1998), 90–1.

[3] See, for example, Arthur G. Dickens, *Martin Luther and the Reformation* (London, 1967); Quentin Skinner, *The Foundations of Modern Political Thought*, 2: *The Age of Reformation* (Cambridge, 1978).

qualities.[4] More specifically, recent discussions of the 'Doubting Thomas' narrative have aimed to complicate earlier contributions, which either claimed that Thomas did not in fact touch Christ or interpreted any apparent deference to the senses figuratively.[5] It has been suggested by Joe Moshenska, for example, that writers such as Lancelot Andrewes and Thomas Cranmer avoided making sharp distinctions between the imagery and reality of Thomas's touch, instead invoking this passage in order to appeal to the senses.[6] Andrewes went to great lengths in one sermon to explain the particular significance for Thomas of touching Christ, a sensory experience that in John 20: 17 had been denied to Mary Magdalene. Andrewes characterized Mary's desire to touch Christ as a means by which she sought to renew her experience of Christ before the resurrection, and contrasted this attitude with the approach taken by Thomas, whose objective was to believe in the resurrected Christ.[7]

Matthew Milner has argued that the role of touch in the Thomas narrative was useful for Protestant writers such as Cranmer and Richard Greenham (d. 1594) precisely because it could be characterized as an exemplary way of using the senses to attain faith.[8] Indeed, instances in which Thomas was invoked to support the primacy of faith and Scripture while retaining a role for the senses can be found in various contexts, including late medieval theatre, as well as post-Reformation theological exchanges and practical divinity.[9] In addition, a text urging almsgiving, written in 1592 by the clergyman Henry Smith, challenged unbelievers to follow Thomas's example: 'I would aduise those of that opinion to doe as *Thomas Didimus* did by Christs wounds, that ere hee would beleeue, put in his hands & felt. And therefore to all such I say, as will not beleeue it, let them goe thither and feele; then doubtlesse they will find it so, and say it is so.'[10]

---

[4] Stuart Clark, 'Afterword: Angels of Light and Images of Sanctity', in Clare Copeland and Jan Machielsen, eds, *Angels of Light? Sanctity and the Discernment of Spirits in the Early Modern Period* (Leiden, 2013), 279–304, at 281–6.
[5] Glenn W. Most, *Doubting Thomas* (London, 2005), 145–54.
[6] Joe Moshenska, *Feeling Pleasures: The Sense of Touch in Renaissance England* (Oxford, 2014), 81.
[7] Ibid. 75–6.
[8] Matthew Milner, *The Senses and the English Reformation* (Farnham, 2011), 164, 187, 195–7; Parker and Carlson, *'Practical Divinity'*.
[9] Milner, *Senses*, 56–9, 186–7, 195–6.
[10] Henry Smith, *The poore mans teares opened in a sermon* (London, 1592), 4.

Examples such as these demonstrate the multiplicity of interpretations surrounding the Thomas narrative, both as a means to comprehend theology better and as a way of countering unbelief. One of the most extensive discussions of St Thomas in which these themes overlap is Bownde's text, which provides a detailed insight into the ways in which the relationship between doubt and the senses could be constructed in post-Reformation theology. Bownde's text does not condemn Thomas or any other unbeliever, but is intended 'for the comfort of all that desire to beleeue'. While critical of sensory perception as a means to access the spiritual, the work nonetheless acknowledges the place of the senses, materiality and the body in the individual's struggle for faith and true religion. In this way, Bownde's focus on the senses and the body can be understood as intrinsic to his Protestantism. An analysis of Bownde's text therefore reinforces wider historiographical developments in the study of the Reformation which argue that Protestantism was by no means devoid of worldly concerns, nor was it wrapped up in *sola scriptura* and *sola fide*. Scholars such as Alec Ryrie, Tara Hamling and Jonathan Willis have convincingly demonstrated that conforming members of the Church of England engaged with a distinctly physical, material and emotional religious world, not in spite of their Protestantism but directly because of it.[11]

Indeed, Milner's work is largely concerned with reasserting the role of the senses during the course of the Reformation in England in order to stress a degree of continuity with late medieval theology.[12] Similar links between doubt, unbelief and the Thomas narrative have been explored in a medieval context by John Arnold, whose work highlights a fourteenth-century appeal to the doubts of St Thomas in a sermon on the eucharist as one of many indicators that material experience was seen as a basis for doubt and challenges to doctrine.[13] Arnold makes the case for the centrality of discourse in the relationship between prescriptive and lay perspectives on unbelief while also

[11] Alec Ryrie, *Being Protestant in Reformation Britain* (Oxford, 2013), 2–4, 17–26; Tara Hamling, *Decorating the Godly Household: Religious Art in Protestant Britain,* c.*1560*–c.*1660* (New Haven, CT, 2010); Jonathan Willis, *Church Music and Protestantism in Post-Reformation England: Discourses, Sites and Identities* (Farnham, 2010).

[12] Milner, *Senses*, 2–6, 163–5.

[13] John Arnold, 'The Materiality of Unbelief in Late Medieval England', in Sophie Page, ed., *The Unorthodox Imagination in Late Medieval Britain* (Manchester, 2010), 65–95, at 80. See also Susan Reynolds, 'Social Mentalities and the Case of Medieval Scepticism', *TRHS* 6th ser. 1 (1991), 21–41.

stressing the 'quotidian materiality' of medieval challenges to religious doctrine.[14]

This relationship between unbelief and physicality resonates in Bownde's text and defines its place within the wider theological discourse of the post-Reformation period. His work echoed the pastoral approach of his stepfather Richard Greenham, who also employed the language of bodily affliction, comfort and healing in his attempts to assuage the anxiety and melancholy of believers.[15] The notion of the afflicted conscience was a central concern in English Calvinist theology and practical divinity. Scholarship on Reformed theology, such as the contributions of Jean Delumeau and John Stachniewski, has tended to focus on double predestination as the primary source of profound emotional uncertainty about divine judgement and salvation.[16] Indeed, the search for assurance of salvation was the foundation of experimental predestinarianism, which encouraged individuals to look within themselves in order to detect signs of election to heaven.[17] However, more recent work by Leif Dixon has stressed the role of this theological framework in comforting rather than creating anxiety about assurance.[18] The complexities raised by Dixon's research make clear the need to engage further with the ways in which contemporaries not only perceived soteriological doubts and uncertainties but also responded to various forms of more explicit unbelief in aspects of doctrine. An important facet of this engagement has to be the trajectories of English Protestantism across the Long Reformation, as a second generation of Protestant theologians and divines sought to respond pastorally to the newly emerging concerns of their congregations. It is in this context that Bownde's early seventeenth-century work can usefully be placed, with its explicit focus on unbelief, the senses and

---

[14] Arnold, 'Materiality of Unbelief', 85–6.

[15] Parker and Carlson, *'Practical Divinity'*, 90–1; *ODNB, s.n.* 'Greenham, Richard (early 1540s–1594)', online edn (2004), at: <http://www.oxforddnb.com/view/article/11424>, accessed 19 May 2015.

[16] Jean Delumeau, *Sin and Fear: The Emergence of a Western Guilt Culture, 13th–18th Centuries*, transl. Eric Nicholson (New York, 1990; first publ. as *Le Péché et la peur*, Paris, 1983); John Stachniewski, *The Persecutory Imagination: English Puritanism and the Literature of Religious Despair* (Oxford, 1991).

[17] R. T. Kendall, *Calvin and English Calvinism to 1649* (Oxford, 1981), 1–16.

[18] Leif Dixon, *Practical Predestinarians in England, c.1590–1640* (Oxford, 2014), 1–17, 26–32, 35–6.

the body as well as on comforting emotional anxiety and 'affliction' triggered by certain aspects of Protestant theology.

Treatments of the Thomas narrative are also of interest to the historiographical exploration of atheism in the early modern period. Seeking to complicate Lucien Febvre's suggestion that atheism was inconceivable in early modern thought, David Wootton has argued that the absence of strong challenges to Christianity in the sixteenth century need not necessarily eclipse the notion of coherent forms of unbelief.[19] Meanwhile, Michael Hunter has argued that early modern anxiety about the phenomenon may have been a response to the emotional uncertainty and genuine doubts faced by many believers.[20] In a useful volume edited by Wootton and Hunter and published in 1992, which included an extensive historiographical survey, Wootton observed that modern distinctions between 'philosophical atheism' and behavioural forms of irreligion may risk eclipsing other, more nuanced instances of unbelief.[21] And indeed, a close reading of Bownde's text strongly implies that various challenges to orthodox faith in the post-Reformation period, from lingering murmurs of doubt to more explicit unbelief, could be perceived as uniquely linked with physicality and sensory perception. Bownde's writing reflects the idea that unbelief could be remedied through comfort and was as much about the body and the senses as it was about the mind.

Bownde himself has received some attention in theological scholarship: Edward Martin Allen has produced an extensive study of Bownde's works with a focus on sabbatarianism, usefully locating his text on St Thomas in a wider context of practical divinity and tracing the interconnected influences of medicine, theology and the

---

[19] Lucien Febvre, *The Problem of Unbelief in the Sixteenth Century: The Religion of Rabelais*, transl. Beatrice Gottlieb (Cambridge, MA, 1982; first publ. as *Le Problème de l'incroyance au XVIe siècle. La Religion de Rabelais*, Paris, 1942); David Wootton, 'Lucien Febvre and Early Modern Unbelief', *JMH* 60 (1988), 695–730, at 726–7; idem, 'Unbelief in Early Modern Europe', *History Workshop* 20 (1985), 82–100.

[20] Michael Hunter, 'The Problem of "Atheism" in Early Modern England', *TRHS* 5th ser. 35 (1985), 135–57, at 153–4. This idea is also explored in Leif Dixon, 'William Perkins, "Atheisme", and the Crises of England's Long Reformation', *Journal of British Studies* 50 (2011), 790–812.

[21] David Wootton, 'New Histories of Atheism', in Michael Hunter and David Wootton, eds, *Atheism from the Reformation to the Enlightenment* (Oxford, 1992), 24–32. For a detailed analysis of the emergence of atheism and the distinctions between various forms of the phenomenon, see A. C. Kors, 'The Age of Enlightenment', in Stephen Bullivant and Michael Ruse, eds, *The Oxford Handbook of Atheism* (Oxford, 2013), 195–211.

ideas of other religious writers.[22] George Hoffmann has touched on Bownde's work in the context of atheism, but scholarly understanding of doubt stands to benefit from further analysis of the text focusing more directly on the connections it makes between doubt, unbelief, the senses and the body.[23]

A puritan clergyman in the Church of England, Nicholas Bownde had been educated at Cambridge and ordained at Ely in 1580. Bownde was influenced by the pastoral interests of his stepfather, but his father had been a physician and medical knowledge permeates his work on St Thomas, which presents unbelief as a physical ailment to be treated. Indeed, Bownde's *The vnbeleefe of S. Thomas the Apostle* followed earlier works in which he provided pastoral, spiritual and medical guidance in response to the plague, which was rampant in 1603.[24] As Bownde's title makes clear, 'unbelief', rather than 'doubt', is the central term in the text. It is this word that Bownde uses to describe Thomas's refusal to believe that Christ had risen. The mention of Thomas in the title of the treatise is followed by the explanation that his unbelief would be 'laid open for the comfort of all that desire to beleeue'. This title did not leave space for a nuanced acknowledgement that it was often quieter doubts rather than explicit unbelief that troubled believers in the sixteenth and early seventeenth centuries.

From the outset, then, Bownde's work constructs a dichotomy between belief and unbelief that continues to frame the remainder of the text. Nonetheless, Bownde does recognize that the limits of belief were often subtle or surreptitious rather that overt and extreme. Hoffmann has emphasized his assertion that, like Thomas, 'we may be true beleeuers in general, and yet vnbeleeuers in many particulars'.[25] Hoffmann points out that Bownde describes unbelief alongside 'doubting and wauering' in the context of his attempts to assuage the anxieties of believers.[26] Bownde's title addresses 'all that desire to beleeue', implying that there are those who wanted

---

[22] Edward Martin Allen, 'Nicholas Bownde and the Context of Sunday Sabbatarianism' (PhD thesis, Fuller Theological Seminary, 2008).

[23] George Hoffmann, 'Atheism as a Devotional Category', *Republics of Letters* 1 (2010), 44–55.

[24] *ODNB, s.n.* 'Bownd, Nicholas (d. 1613)', online edn (2012), at: <http://www.oxforddnb.com/view/article/3084>, accessed 25 August 2014.

[25] Bownde, *Vnbeleefe*, 25, cited in Hoffmann, 'Atheism', 50.

[26] Bownde, *Vnbeleefe*, 26, cited in Hoffmann, 'Atheism', 50.

to believe, but somehow could not. Moreover, his work both acknowledges that unbelief was to be found within all believers and suggests that pastoral comfort based on Scripture could help restore their faith. In this way, Bownde establishes degrees of belief and unbelief as both antithetical and relational. His language encourages the individual to move across two distinct states, away from forms of unbelief and towards belief; but at the same time true belief is predicated – at least in part – on previous, potential or presently underlying forms of unbelief. Discussion of doubt and emotional anxiety about religion in the early modern period therefore needs also to accommodate the vocabulary of 'unbelief' in order to reflect the conceptual concerns of theologians and divines during the period.

At the beginning of his discourse, Bownde includes the biblical account of Thomas's unbelief and his subsequently renewed belief in full.[27] This passage highlights a number of themes that Bownde revisits later in his work. In particular, the senses pervade the biblical narrative from the outset.[28] The first exclamation made by the disciples to Thomas expresses their joy that they 'haue seene the Lord', underlining the value of sight, which remains a focus of Thomas's doubts as well as his eventual belief.[29] Christ's concluding statement emphasizes the function of sight for Thomas's belief before explaining the blessed nature of those 'that haue not seene, and haue beleeued'.[30] In conjunction with this stress on seeing is a focus on touch, specifically Thomas's demand to 'put my finger into the print of the nayles, and put mine hand into his side'.[31] However, the key emphasis here, both in the scriptural narrative and in Bownde's treatment of the passage, is on the primacy of faith over both sight and touch as the true means of believing in the resurrection of Christ. Yet John's Gospel suggests that sensory perception is the only means by which Thomas is initially prepared to believe in Christ's resurrected presence, and whatever he may prescribe for other believers, Christ

---

[27] Bownde, *Vnbeleefe*, 1–2. I have been unable to identify the Bible translation used by Bownde.

[28] Space precludes discussion of several other important themes which could prove fruitful in further research on the post-Reformation period. For example, the significance of spatiality, temporality, presence and absence in the scriptural text of the Thomas episode has been explored in considerable depth by Most, *Doubting Thomas*, 43–68.

[29] Bownde, *Vnbeleefe*, 1–2.

[30] Ibid.

[31] Ibid.

is apparently willing to let Thomas see, and perhaps even touch, for himself.[32]

The object toward which the senses are being directed is also significant, namely Christ's body and his wounds. John's Gospel reports, as quoted by Bownde, that Christ 'stood in the middes' of the disciples, highlighting not just his presence in the room but his centrality to the scene.[33] Finally, the passage introduces readers to a conceptual relationship between being 'faithful' and 'faithless'. A sense of abrupt antithesis is established when Christ tells Thomas, 'be not faithlesse but faithfull'.[34] However, the use of this language also reflects a sense in which faith is predicated on the logical possibility of unbelief. Alec Ryrie has suggested that this same 'symbiotic' relationship can be argued to have contributed to the formation of perceptions of religious doubt among theologians and religious writers in early modern England.[35] This engagement with unbelief, both in the Bible and in subsequent religious discourse, suggests that the concept was credible and even necessary during the period. The themes of sensory perception and the physical body are central to the narrative of Thomas's doubts and reinforce the idea of unbelief as informed by tangible reality. Bownde drew upon these themes in his writing in order to construct a framework for discussing and dealing with unbelief among contemporaries.

Bownde is acutely aware of the significance of sight and touch in Scripture. While John suggests that the other apostles relied largely on sight, Bownde's text draws attention to Thomas's unique role in introducing touch as a conduit for belief. Bownde celebrates Christ's 'wisdome and goodnes' in reappearing to Thomas, and presents touch as integral to the meaning of Christ's 'second and more sensible apparition: when they should not onely see againe the print of the nailes in his hands, but for Thomas also to put his finger into them'.[36] Bownde's decision to place Thomas's interactions with the resurrected Christ, which in the Gospel of John were based on both sight and touch, in the context of the earlier apostolic experiences

---

[32] For a discussion of conflicting early modern perspectives on whether Thomas did in fact touch Christ in the narrative, see Most, *Doubting Thomas*, 145–54.

[33] Bownde, *Vnbeleefe*, 1.

[34] Ibid.

[35] Alec Ryrie, 'Faith, Doubt, and the Problem of Atheism in Reformation Britain', paper presented to the History of Christianity seminar, Cambridge, 20 November 2013. I am indebted to the author for allowing me to make use of this paper.

[36] Bownde, *Vnbeleefe*, 23.

of the resurrection, which in all four gospels had focused predominantly on sight and word of mouth, reflects the importance of touch for Bownde's analysis of the narrative. However, Bownde also suggests that there was an interactive relationship between Thomas and the divine, in the context of which Thomas demanded that two of his senses be satisfied before he would believe, and Christ appeared willing to oblige him. Bownde goes on to highlight Thomas's unwillingness to believe the words of the many other witnesses to Christ's resurrection, explaining:

> all the rest tell him, what they had seene, namely, not onely Christ in some forme, but so certenly that he spake unto them, and shewed them his hands and his feete, and the print of the nayles in them, so that they could not possibly be deceived in so cleare a matter: yet for all this he not onely not giueth credit unto some one of them seuerally, but not vnto all of them joyntly, beeing so many, and so credible witnesses: and further, is so wilfull and obstinate, and so addicted to his owne senses and feeling, that he tells them plainly, that unles he himselfe see the print of the nayles in his hands, and may put his finger into them; and the print of the speare in his side, and may put his hand into that, he will never beleeue it.[37]

This passage reinforces the integral importance of the senses to Bownde's ideas about how unbelief functioned, and in particular Thomas's prioritizing of his own responses to the external world over the primacy of faith as the necessary component for belief. From this, it can be inferred that Bownde sees the reliance on sensory perception not merely as a symptom of doubt but as a fundamental foundation for unbelief and the cause of Thomas's denial of Christ's resurrection. Bownde also reiterates the phrases concerning Thomas's request to put his finger and hand into the prints of the nails and spear, phrases to which he returns throughout his text.

As with much early modern Protestant writing, this repetition reflects a desire to centre theological ideas and guidance as closely as possible on Scripture. This passage also recalls John's earlier account of the piercing of Christ's side at the crucifixion (19: 34) by making direct reference to the spear. While the wound caused by the spear is referred to again during the scriptural narrative of Thomas's unbelief, Bownde focuses not only on Christ's wounds, but also on the ob-

---

[37] Ibid. 23–4.

jects that made them and on Thomas's interactions with the injuries, in order to reinforce the physicality of Thomas's actions and to describe Christ's body in great detail.[38] This fascination with the body suggests that Bownde perceives the relationship between Thomas's senses and Christ's body as central both to the narrative and also to understanding the nature of contemporary unbelief.

Bownde provides numerous criticisms of a sensory approach to belief, taking Thomas's reliance on the senses to a hypothetical extreme in order to highlight the limitations of the senses for believing. Why, asks Bownde, if the senses were truly important for belief, should the opportunity to see and feel Christ directly not be extended to all believers:

> why may not other be of the same minde too? and so Christ should have remained upon the earth unto this day, and not have ascended into heaven: or els often since he should have descended to shew himselfe to those that should beleeue: if none would beleeue further then they should see and feele. Moreover after that he had thus seen him and felt him himselfe, would he not have thought it strange, if others would not have beleeued him, when he preached unto them the resurrection of Christ? why then doth he make such a straight rule to himselfe?[39]

Bownde also stresses the deceptive nature of the senses, asking: 'Are these two senses such sure judges of the truth, that they cannot be deceived? May not a man thinke, that he seeth and feeleth that, which he doth not? and may he not againe doubt, whether he seeth and feeleth that, which indeede he doth?'[40] He examines biblical examples of sensory deception, such as the misinterpreted miraculous provision of water performed by Elisha (2 Kgs 3: 1–27) and Isaac's confusing his sons Jacob and Esau (Gen. 27: 17–46), before explaining: 'Thus wee see that sight and feeling may easily be deceived: and yet this is the nature of vnbeleefe, to give credit more unto these deceiveable senses, then to many other things, that are most sure and certaine. And many men in matters of faith will almost beleeue nothing, untill such time, as they see and feele them'.[41]

---

[38] See also ibid. 21, 85.
[39] Ibid. 87–8.
[40] Ibid. 88.
[41] Ibid. 90.

Bownde's approach reflects his perception that unbelief is generated by too strong an emphasis on the potentially limited and deceptive senses and too weak an emphasis on faith, and his conviction that the senses are to be rejected in favour of faith in God as the proper means to believe. He underscores the seriousness of the underlying problem by exploring the implications of his argument in the context of divine judgement, stating: 'and therefore when they are taught what in heaven is prepared for them that serve God; what in hell for them that disobey him: they are readie to say, who hath seen them? giving us to understand, that they will not beleeue them, until they either see them, or feele them themselves'.[42]

It is apparent, then, that Bownde sees sensory perception as a source of considerable disruption, potentially undermining an individual's faith and jeopardizing their salvation. Here Thomas's unbelief is used to argue that reliance on the senses in matters of religion could have dramatic spiritual repercussions after death. Bownde sees the senses as a barrier to the individual's search for assurance, a source of distraction from godly behaviour and a sinful diversion from salvation. Those who, like Thomas, experience unbelief rely on the senses in order to believe, but it was this very reliance that limits a true, faith-based engagement with God. Indeed, Bownde argues that the senses caused individuals to ignore the providential 'threatenings' and 'promises' delivered by divine will.[43]

However, dependence on the senses and the resulting unbelief do not inevitably lead to damnation. Bownde's text is aimed at dissuading people from trusting this sensory religion and comforting those afflicted with unbelief precisely by locating the solution to the problem in the context of predestination and divine punishment rather than in human assumptions. 'But also if we will examine our selues, & other men', Bownde argues, the community of believers would find '[t]hat though we had often heard that God was just, and would punish sin, yet we presumed otherwise, and did not believe it, because we escaped a while in our sinnes, and did not see and feele the truth of it in ourselves'.[44] It is only internally through self-examination, or through shared exchanges between the godly, that feeling can be used in order to believe. Such an inward-looking approach will reveal

---

[42] Ibid.
[43] Ibid. 93.
[44] Ibid. 96–7.

the truth of divine justice and punishment, judgement and salvation. Bownde is keen to associate true belief with the non-physical and to contrast spiritual, faith-based belief with the idea that unbelief is intensely physical and orientated around the body. For Bownde, 'there is no condemnation to them, that are in Christ Jesus, which walke not after the flesh, but after the spirit' (Romans 8: 1).[45]

While the focus of the scriptural narrative was on Christ's body, Bownde also suggests that the encounter with Christ was necessary because the wounds of unbelief afflicting the body requires healing through the senses. Bownde quite frequently describes unbelief in medical terms, with Christ's physical demonstration of renewed life serving as medication against the corrupting influence of doubt among the apostles:

> So that Christ in shewing them his hands and feete, that so they might be ridde of those thoughts and doubts, that hindred them from beleeuing; did manifestly shew, that he knew the thoughts of their hearts to be these, that unlesse they saw in his hands and feete the print of the nayles, they would not beleeue that it was he. Christ therefore like a skilful physician of their soules did applie his medicine according to their maladie; and therefore when as at his first apparition he did shew unto them his hands and his feete, he doing all things in wisdom and to some good purpose, did thereby declare, what thoughts of vnbeleefe they were troubled with.[46]

This language is not unique to Bownde. References to Christ as a 'physician of the soul' can be found in the late fourth-century work of Gregory Nazianzus, and subsequently in the writing of Gregory the Great, as well as in the post-Reformation period from the 1570s into the mid-seventeenth century.[47] The metaphor focuses on the spiritual dimension of belief, suggesting the soul rather than the body as the means through which Christ was able to encourage belief among the apostles. Nonetheless, Bownde's use of this simile evokes a strong sense of unbelief as a corporeal state that requires an equally physical remedy. This is very similar to the way that works of practical divinity tried to address anxiety, melancholy and other emotional afflictions

[45] Ibid. 101.
[46] Ibid. 31–2.
[47] Allen, 'Nicholas Bownde', 104 n. 85; David Harley, 'Medical Metaphors in English Moral Theology, 1560–1660', *Journal of the History of Medicine and Allied Sciences* 48 (1993), 396–435, at 400 n. 21.

which, alongside unbelief, were characterized as useful opportunities to reassert godliness and reinforce belief itself.[48]

Elsewhere Bownde refers to other passages of Scripture which describe salvation in terms of physical healing. For instance, he comments on Philippians 3: 20–1: 'Our conuersation is in heaven, from whence also we looke for the Saviour, even the Lord Jesus Christ: who shall chaunge our vile bodie, that it may be fashioned like vnto his glorious bodie, according to the working whereby he is able even to subdue all things vnto himselfe'.[49] While Bownde's text seeks to dissuade believers from placing excessive reliance on their senses in their engagement with faith, he nonetheless acknowledges that Christ's mercy could manifest itself physically in order to confront unbelief. Bownde explains that 'we must take heede, how we yield to our vnbeleef: for it will make vs looke for and desire such things at the hand of God, for the confirming of our faith, as haue no ground either from Scripture, or from reason'.[50] Bownde also acknowledges that 'it pleaseth God of his infinite goodnes to beare with men sometimes this way; and to yield to them, either to the strengthening of their faith, or to the leauing of them without excuse in their vnbeleefe'.[51] His text aimed to comfort those experiencing doubt and unbelief, but he also recognized the expectations of physical and sensory experience among individual believers, as well as the centrality of healing to the experience of God. His work was thus particularly suited to the dual purpose of assuaging spiritual anxiety and rectifying unbelief, both of which were necessary aspects of Reformed religion.

Just as unbelief is a 'maladie' to be healed, so the experience of faith is analogous to good health in the body. In a striking passage, Bownde compares belief in Christ to the physical experience of pregnancy:

> For as the woman that is quickned with child, and feeleth it stirre in her bodie, though shee doe not alwaies feele it stirre alike; and sometimes not at all, and sometimes more weakely then before: yet shee assures her selfe, that the child is living, because shee hath felt it stirre before, & so hopeth that shee shall doe againe. So when Christ is formed in us

[48] Parker and Carlson, *'Practical Divinity'*, 87–96.
[49] As cited in Bownde, *Vnbeleefe*, 160–1.
[50] Ibid. 162.
[51] Ibid. 162–3.

first of all, as the Apostle speaketh, we have the feeling of him stirring and mooving in our hearts by his holy Spirit, dwelling in us: which lively motions though wee feele not strongly mooving in us afterwards, or not at all; yet we doubt not, but that Christ dwelleth in our hearts by faith still, and hope to feele it as sensibly againe in time, as we have done: & so much the more, because Christ beeing formed in us, never dieth: and therefore the remembrance of our former Feelings must comfort us over the want of them for the time present: for they are not alwaies alike in any that have them: it is sufficient that we have had them, therefore if we labour after them, they will returne unto us againe, when it shall please God. And thus much for this, that S. Thomas in this matter of faith addicts himselfe to his owne feeling.[52]

This passage has fascinating implications for scholarly understanding of the ways in which belief and unbelief were perceived in early modern thought. Bownde acknowledges the widespread dilemma faced by Christians: that they cannot always feel the presence of the spirit of Christ. He reasserts the importance of faith over physical feeling, arguing that in spite of the lack of continuous spiritual 'feeling' within believers, once they have experienced faith, 'we doubt not, but that Christ dwelleth in our hearts by faith still'.

Perhaps the most important aspect of this passage lies in its comparison between belief in Christ and belief in the living presence of an unborn child. For Bownde, continuous belief in the presence of Christ is not determined by seeing or touching his body, or by 'feeling' his 'stirring and moouing', any more than belief in the presence of one's unborn child is determined by feeling it kick all the time. Nonetheless, Bownde's language strongly implies that he sees belief and unbelief as closely linked to and comparable with sensations in the body. The pregnant woman in the passage may not feel her child stir at this moment, but 'shee hath felt it stirre before, & so hopeth that shee shall doe againe', just as believers who do not presently feel Christ's presence 'hope to feele it as sensibly againe in time'. He goes on to reinforce these appeals to memory and hope of sensation, implying that 'feelings', whether physical or psychological, are by no means beside the point and could serve as useful reminders of God's power. With this parallel, Bownde is making a direct comparison between the way in which believers engaged with and experienced Christ and the physical experience of pregnancy. Though

[52] Ibid. 155–6.

figurative, the association remains significant because it suggests that faith-based belief was not totally divorced from notions of physical 'feeling' in the minds of early modern religious writers. Moreover, the language of maternity used here recalls Mary, while the unborn child in whom the mother must unwaveringly believe is directly compared with Christ, who in turn is 'formed in us'. In this way, Bownde characterizes belief through faith as an example of fertility and healthy new life while simultaneously approaching unbelief as an affliction in the body. Both are internal and profoundly personal experiences that draw physical feelings and sensory experiences together with spirituality. Unbelief is a malady characterized by the search for sensory confirmation of God, an ill-informed pursuit that Christ was nonetheless able to satisfy and thus remedy among the apostles. However, works of practical divinity such as Bownde's text suggest that this spiritual affliction also lay at the heart of belief itself, because grappling with doubt and unbelief was a necessary aspect of introspective godly religion.

Even as Bownde was stressing the importance of faith over physicality and sensory perception, he was providing his readers with linguistic devices and articulating ideas that firmly located unbelief in a physical context. This raises something of a paradox for scholarly understandings of post-Reformation religion. For Bownde, physicality necessarily informed the process by which Thomas expressed his unbelief and subsequently embraced the truth of Christ's resurrection. Bownde's work reflects the idea that unbelief was an affliction in the souls of the apostles that the medicine of Christ's wounded body had cured, while belief could be illustrated by maternal faith in the unborn child, present but largely invisible in the body and mind of the true Christian. Crucially, Bownde's conception of unbelief was linked to the physical and could not be adequately discussed or dealt with through the conceptual theology of faith alone. Thus both doubt and unbelief joined those anxieties and emotional distresses triggered by belief itself as physical afflictions that required pastoral comfort.

Post-Reformation treatments of the Thomas narrative provide a unique window into these afflictions, allowing scholars better to understand the role of unbelief among both divines and their readers. While it is often difficult to trace the intimate religious concerns of individuals, a number of studies have also sought to suggest the relationships between doubt, unbelief and true belief in self-articulated accounts. Crucially, Bownde's approach to the unbelief of Thomas helps to illuminate the nature of the 'symbiosis' highlighted by Alec Ryrie between belief and unbelief during the post-Reformation period, wherein individuals sought to reconcile their doubtful and irreligious thoughts with the Protestant faith.[53] For Bownde, faith could be strengthened through the honest acknowledgement and pastoral correction of doubtful thoughts and particular instances of unbelief. His writing reaffirms the suggestion that doubt was not always an abstract enemy or the antithetical 'other', but a recurring presence and a component of belief in the minds of individual believers.

Bownde's discussion of Thomas represents a revealing intersection between the unbelief faced by individuals and the changing nature of theology during the period, underlining the importance of materiality as a potential prelude to doubt and unbelief. Bownde's text demonstrates that this approach to unbelief, which sees various forms of irreligion as rooted in the physical and sensory world, can also contribute to historical understanding of Calvinist theology and its relationship to individual believers in the post-Reformation period. Alongside his vociferous emphasis on the importance of faith for belief, Bownde's approach to doubt was not hostile to the senses or the body. Rather, he invoked the narrative of Thomas to address the nature of unbelief in the minds and bodies of his contemporaries and relied upon the language of sensory perception and physicality to conduct a dialogue of spiritual and bodily comfort with the individual.

---

[53] Ryrie, 'Faith, Doubt, and the Problem of Atheism'. The close links between doubt, voluntarism and hostility towards atheism have also been explored by Hoffmann, 'Atheism'.

Proving Stigmata: Antonio Daza, Saint Francis of Assisi and Juana de la Cruz

Cordelia Warr*
University of Manchester

The Franciscan Antonio Daza, a native of Valladolid, published his Historia de las llagas de nuestro seráfico padre San Francesco *in 1617. He intended to demonstrate that the stigmata of Francis of Assisi were miraculous and unique. Daza referred to Juana de la Cruz (d. 1534), a Poor Clare, whom he identified as providing evidence of the veracity of Francis's stigmata in her sermons, which had been collected by one of the nuns in her convent in a manuscript known as* El Conhorte. *Juana's sermons were defended as divinely inspired and thus her defence of the miracle of Francis's stigmata was regarded as based on information received directly from God. Yet Juana herself had, according to another work by Daza, the* Historia, vida y milagros, éxtasis y revelaciones de la bienaventurada virgen Santa Iuana de la Cruz *(first published in 1610) received painful marks on her hands and feet in 1524. This paper will consider the tensions evidenced in Daza's work and his tactics in attempting to demonstrate the unique nature of the stigmata of Francis of Assisi whilst at the same time apparently acknowledging a similar miracle experienced by Juana de la Cruz.*

The reception of the wounds of Christ through miraculous means has always been controversial. After the death of St Francis of Assisi on 3 October 1226 a number of voices were raised doubting the miracle of the stigmata so enthusiastically proclaimed by Brother Elias, vicar general of the Franciscan Order, as unique.[1] With Dominican promotion of Catherine of Siena (d. 1380) as a stigmatic

---

* Art History and Visual Studies, University of Manchester, Oxford Rd, Manchester, M13 9PL. E-mail: cordelia.warr@manchester.ac.uk.
[1] On early reactions to Francis's stigmata, see Jacques Dalarun, Michael F. Cusato and Carla Salvati, *The Stigmata of Francis of Assisi: New Studies: New Perspectives* (Saint Bonaventure, NY, 2006); Cordelia Warr, 'Visualizing Stigmata: Stigmatic Saints and Crises of Representation in Early Modern Italy', in Peter Clarke and Tony Claydon, eds, *Saints and Sanctity*, SCH 47 (Woodbridge, 2011), 228–47. On those who doubted the stigmata, see André Vauchez, 'Les Stigmates de Saint François et leurs détracteurs dans les derniers siècles du moyen âge', *Mélanges d'archéologie et d'histoire de l'École française de Rome: Moyen âge et temps modernes* 80 (1968), 595–625.

Studies in Church History 52 (2016) 283–297   © Ecclesiastical History Society 2016
doi: 10.1017/stc.2015.16

from the end of the fourteenth century, the issue of the singularity of the miracle experienced by Francis came to the fore. Catherine's stigmata, received at the church of Santa Cristina in Pisa in 1375 and rendered invisible at her request,[2] were treated with suspicion by the Franciscans, who insisted that their founder was the only true stigmatic.[3] Four centuries after the stigmatization of St Francis, and despite (or perhaps because of) the fact that an increasing number of holy women were reputed to have received the stigmata during the fifteenth and sixteenth centuries, members of the Franciscan Order still perceived a need to demonstrate that the miracle experienced by their founder was *sui generis*. In 1617 the Spanish Regular Observant Franciscan Antonio Daza (or Daça) (d. 1640) added to the writings which aimed to dispel any doubt on this front with the publication of his *Historia de las llagas de nuestro seráfico padre San Francisco (The History of the Stigmata of our Seraphic Father St Francis)*.[4] During his career Daza held various posts within the order and was in Rome between 1621 and 1625 where he met the Franciscan historiographer Luke Wadding. He published on a number of subjects, including two books promoting the Immaculate Conception and the final instalment of Mark of Lisbon's chronicle of the history of the Franciscan Order, both of which demonstrate his careful search for historical sources.[5] Daza also wrote a life of the sixteenth-century Spanish Franciscan mystic and stigmatic Juana de la Cruz (d. 1534), the *Historia, vida y milagros, éxtasis y revelaciones de la bienaventurada virgen Santa Juana de la Cruz (History, Life and Miracles, Ecstasies and Revelations of the Blessed Virgin Santa Juana de la Cruz)*.[6] This essay considers the *Historia de las*

---

[2] Raymond of Capua, *The Life of Catherine of Siena*, 2.6.195 (transl. and intro. Conleth Kearns [Washington DC, 1994], 186).

[3] Arnold I. Davidson, 'Miracles of Bodily Transformation: Or how Saint Francis received the Stigmata', *Critical Inquiry* 35 (2009), 451–80, at 455–6.

[4] Antonio Daza, *Historia de las llagas de nuestro seráfico padre San Francisco, colegida del Martirologio y Breviario Romano y treynta bulas y dozientos autores y santos* (Valladolid, 1617).

[5] For an introduction to Daza's life, see Benedict Mertens, 'Antonio Daza's "Esercitii Spirituali"', *Studies in Spirituality* 11 (2000), 212–53, at 213–19.

[6] I shall refer to Antonio Daza, *Historia, vida y milagros, éxtasis y revelaciones de la bienaventurada virgen Santa Juana de la Cruz* (Madrid, 1614) throughout this essay. Daza originally published the *vida* in 1610 but later had to revise the work after it was reviewed by the Inquisition. For a brief discussion of the publication of Daza's life of Juana, and the changes required by the Inquisition, which centred not on Juana's stigmata but on the beads which Christ was said to have blessed for Juana, see Stephen Haliczer, *Between Exaltation and Infamy: Female Mystics in the Golden Age of Spain* (Oxford, 2002), 69–70. The different versions of

llagas and the *Historia, vida y milagros* within the context of doubt and proof relating to different stigmatic experiences.

Dominican authors were comfortable with, and indeed actively promoted, the idea of multiple types of stigmatic experience. For the Franciscans, however, that anyone other than Francis claimed to have received stigmata cast doubt on the unique miracle experienced by their founder, a miracle which had been carefully crafted in the years following Francis's death.[7] These opposed reactions reflect contrasting ways of dealing with the doubt engendered by miraculous stigmatization. The model used by the Dominicans was one whereby a prospective saint did and experienced things accepted as 'saintly'. The more often often a particular type of miracle could be said to have occurred, the less doubt it attracted.[8] In the case of stigmata, the Dominicans allayed doubts by arguing for a broad spectrum of stigmatic experiences. The Franciscans, by contrast, focused on a model in which certain aspects of the saint's life were projected as new or unique.[9] The very singularity of the miracle of Francis's stigmata as promoted by the Franciscans engendered doubt, which in turn prompted Franciscan authors to support their claims through glosses on the description of the physical appearance of the stigmata as well as increasing recourse to authoritative sources, even when these were not cited accurately.

By the time that Daza wrote the *Historia de la llagas* it was no longer so easy to say, with Elias, that Francis's stigmata were 'a great joy and a novelty amongst miracles', since a number of holy women had been claimed as stigmatics. Many of these were either Dominican or closely associated with the Dominican order, such as Osanna Andreasi of Mantua (d. 1505), Stefana Quinzani of Soncino (d. 1530) and Lucia Brocardelli of Narni (d. 1544). Dominican authors writing during the sixteenth and seventeenth centuries sometimes made great play of the number of stigmatics they could list, and in

---

the *vida* are also discussed by Inocente García de Andrés, *El Conhorte: Sermones de una mujer. La Santa Juana, 1481–1534*, 2 vols (Madrid, 1999), 1: 28–41.

[7] Chiara Frugoni, *Francesco e l'invenzione delle stimmate* (Turin, 1993), 51–104.

[8] For a discussion of the typology of miracles, see André Vauchez, *Sainthood in the Later Middle Ages*, transl. Jean Birrell (Cambridge, 1997), 466–75.

[9] For a discussion of these types of sanctity, see Aviad Kleinberg, 'Proving Sanctity: Selection and Authentication of Saints in the Later Middle Ages', *Viator* 20 (1989), 183–206, at 187.

particular of the number of stigmatics within or attached to, the order in some way, such as through having a Dominican confessor. Miguel Llot de Ribera (d. 1611) composed a life of Maria Raggi, a Dominican tertiary originally from the island of Chios, who died in Rome in 1600, having received the stigmata in 1585; this included the names of other people who were believed to have borne the stigmata, including Lidwina of Schiedam (d. 1433), Gertrude the Great (d. 1301/1302), Elizabeth of Spalbeek (d. 1304), Stefana Quinzani, Helen of Hungary (d. *c*.1270), Francis of Assisi and Catherine of Siena.[10]

Dominicans such as Tommaso Caffarini (d. 1434) in the fifteenth century and Gregorio Lombardelli (d. 1613) in the seventeenth emphasized a wide-ranging definition of stigmata which extended from wounds which were self-inflicted to those imposed through a supernatural or divine medium.[11] Lombardelli defined eight different types of stigmata: those that a person inflicted on themselves with chains of iron, or with whips, or with any other type of instrument which gave cause to a wound; the second type was that received from the devil; the third that given by a religious superior; the fourth was inflicted by a heretic or enemy of the cross on someone who remained firm in the faith; the fifth that in which a wound or scar appeared miraculously without the recipient seeing God, an angel, a demon or a human being; the sixth was when the Lord, an angel, a saint or God appeared and left a sign by striking the person to whom they had appeared; the seventh type was when God, taking human form, beat someone with some kind of instrument without leaving any external sign, although the person who received the blow felt pain; and the eighth type was when Jesus Christ allowed himself to be seen in various ways in order to place his five wounds in a person's body as he, Christ, had received them.[12] For both Caffarini and Lombardelli it was this last type of stigmata which was the most prestigious, giving greatest evidence of God's favour. Both writers were nonetheless concerned to demonstrate the variety of stigmatic experience, ranging from the

---

[10] Michele Llot de Ribera, *Vita della venerabile sor Maria Raggi da Scio, tradotta della latina alla volgare lingua italiana dal padre F. Paolo Minerva da Bari* (Naples, 1609), 65–7. On Llot de Ribera, see Thomas James Dandelet, *Spanish Rome, 1500–1700* (New Haven, CT, and London, 2001), 178–80.

[11] For Caffarini's discussion of different types of stigmata, see 'Tommaso Caffarini' [Thomas Antonii de Senis], *Libellus de Supplemento. Legende prolixe virginis beate Catherine de Senis*, ed. Iuliana Cavalli and Imelda Foralosso (Rome, 1974), 121–211.

[12] Gregorio Lombardelli, *Sommario della disputa a difesa delle sacre stimate di Santa Caterina da Siena* (Siena, 1601), 63–4.

non-miraculous to the miraculous, and also to show that there was no exclusivity attached to any of the types of stigmata. Lombardelli gave four examples of those who received the most noteworthy, eighth type of stigmata: Francis of Assisi, Walter of Strasbourg (d. before 1260), Helen of Hungary and Catherine of Siena.[13] Three of the four were Dominican: an expansion of those deemed to be stigmatics focused, for the Dominican author, on members of the order to which he belonged.

Franciscan reaction to claims that there were stigmatics other than Francis had habitually consisted of a combination of doubt, disbelief and rejection, such as that expressed by Samuele Cassini (d. after 1510) in his *De le sacre stigmate de Sancto Francesco; como femina non puo hauere stigmata* (*On the Holy Stigmata of Saint Francis; how Women cannot have Stigmata*) (Pavia, 1508).[14] Cassini claimed that God did not give stigmata to women, as he believed that their weaker nature made them unsuitable vessels for the reception of such a miracle.[15] His particular concern probably stemmed from the increasing reports of female stigmatics, far outweighing the number of males. However this was easily countered. The Spanish Dominican Vicente Justiniani (d. 1599) pointed out, in his *Pro Divae Catharinae Senensis imaginibus disputatio*, that there was no room for doubt since 'with God, all things are possible' (Matt. 19: 26) and '[t]here is neither Jew nor Gentile, neither slave nor free, nor is there male and female, for you are all one in Christ Jesus' (Gal. 3: 28).[16]

Against the background of increasing numbers of people claimed as stigmatics, Daza marshalled as much evidence as possible in order to dispel any doubt as to the singularity of the miracle experienced by Francis. The first chapter in the *Historia de las llagas*, 'Of the great favour which God did to the world in giving to our

[13] Ibid. 64. For a discussion of the representation of these stigmatics, see Warr, 'Visualizing Stigmata'; Carolyn Musessig, 'The Stigmata Debate in Theology and Art in the Late Middle Ages', in Celeste Brusati, Karl E. E. Enenkel, and Walter S. Melion, eds, *The Authority of the Word: Reflecting on Image and Text in Northern Europe, 1400–1700* (Leiden, 2012), 481–504, at 487–501.

[14] On Cassini, see *DBI* 21, 487–90.

[15] Romeo de Maio, *Rinascimento senza toga* (Naples, 1999), 108.

[16] Giustinani's work was published as an addition to Johannes Nider, *De Reformatione religiosorum libri tres*, ed. Joannes Boucquet (Antwerp, 1611), 403–65, at 452–3. On Giustiniani, see Alessandra Bartolomei Romagnoli, 'Un trattatello cinquecentesco in difesa delle stimmate di Caterina da Siena', *Archivio italiano per la storia della pietà* 26 (2013), 177–226, at 179–80. Bible quotations are taken from the New International Version.

father Saint Francis his most holy wounds',[17] begins by detailing the pre-eminence of the miracle. According to Daza, during an ecstatic vision the Blessed Amadeus of Portugal (d. 1482), was informed by the archangel Gabriel that God could show no greater favour to Francis than that of giving him his most holy wounds.[18] Daza also observed that St Bonaventure (d. 1274) had called the reception of the stigmata 'a stupendous miracle'; Pope Alexander IV (d. 1261) had referred to it as 'a singular and great miracle' and Cardinal Baronio (d. 1607) as 'an immense miracle'; Cardinal Bellarmino (d. 1641) had insisted on its singularity and called it 'almost the greatest of all God's miracles'; and Roberto Caracciolo of Lecce (d. 1495) had written that 'amongst all the great miracles of the faith the stigmatization held first place'.[19] Daza lists his sources in order of rank within the Church, from archangel, to saint, pope, cardinal and (finally) bishop. He is clear that the miracle of the stigmata, as experienced by Francis, is a miracle of the highest order and also unique, a theme to which he returns throughout the *Historia de las llagas*. Daza also explores other aspects of Francis's stigmata, such as how he received them and their exact appearance, both of which underline the exceptional nature of the miracle. Daza's final chapter deals with the institution of the Feast of the Stigmata. This returns to a subject raised at the beginning of the work: in the section addressed to the vicar general of the order, Antonio de Trejo (d. 1635), Daza recalls the recent decision of Pope Paul V, in 1615, to allow the celebration of the Feast of St Francis's stigmata throughout the Catholic Church. The feast had originally been placed in the Roman Calendar in 1585 but had been suppressed in 1602.[20]

---

[17] Daza, *Historia de las llagas*, fols 1^r–14^v.
[18] '[Q]ue fue merced tan singular la que Dios hizo al Serafico Padre san Francisco en darle sus sacratissimas llagas, que no tiene semejante': ibid., fol. 1^v.
[19] '[U]n milagre estupendo' (St Bonaventure), 'singular y grade milagro' (Pope Alexander IV), 'milagro immenso' (Cardinal Baronio), 'singular maravilla, y casi el mayor de todos los prodigios de Dios' (Cardinal Bellarmino), 'entre los milagros grandes de nuestra Fè, tiene el principal lugar la impression de las llagas de nuestro Padre S. Francisco' (Roberto Caracciolo): ibid., fols 1^v–2^r. For more information on Caracciolo and the stigmata of St Francis, see Carolyn Muessig, 'Roberto Caracciolo's Sermon on the Miracle of the Stigmatization of Saint Francis of Assisi', *Anuario de estudios medievales* 42 (2012), 77–93.
[20] On the history of the Feast of the Stigmata of St Francis, see Regis J. Armstrong, J. A. Wayne Hellmann and William J. Short, eds, *Francis of Assisi: Early Documents*, 3 vols (New York, 1999–2001), 3: 661–4; see also *Calendarium Romanum ex Decreto Sacrosancti Oecumenici Concilii Vaticani II Instauratum* (Rome, 1969), 139.

Daza's main strategy in allaying any possible doubts about the singularity and miraculous nature of Francis's stigmata is to refer to as wide a range of sources as possible. He is careful to include not only Franciscan authors, who might reasonably be expected to have supported this line of argument, but also writers who belonged to other religious orders.[21] So focused is Daza on his aim that he sometimes, apparently wilfully, misreads his sources.[22] One source cited by Daza is *El Libro del Conhorte*, which contained the sermons of Juana de la Cruz (d. 1534). Juana Vázquez Gutiérrez had entered the *beaterio* of Franciscan tertiaries of Santa Maria de la Cruz, just outside the village of Cubas (between Madrid and Toledo), in 1496. She became abbess in 1509.[23] Juana benefited from the protection of Cardinal Cisneros (d. 1517), which provided her with a relatively supportive environment compared to some female Spanish mystics of the later sixteenth and seventeenth centuries who had to deal with the effect of the reaction against the *alumbrados* and the religious climate after the Council of Trent.[24] During a period of thirteen years from 1508 Juana delivered sermons while in a state of visionary ecstasy.[25] They were collected in *El Libro del Conhorte* by her companion Sor María Evangelista.[26] These *sermones*, designated as such in the first manuscript,[27] were attended both by the nuns in Juana's convent, who were the primary recipients, and by supporters such as Cardinal Cisneros.[28] Despite the biblical prohibitions on women teaching (particularly 1

---

[21] Daza gives a long list of those who dealt with Francis's stigmata: *Historia de las llagas*, fols 16ᵛ–24ʳ.

[22] Cordelia Warr, 'Changing Stigmata', in Anne Kirkham and Cordelia Warr, eds, *Wounds in the Middle Ages* (Aldershot, 2014), 43–62, at 46.

[23] For brief details on the life of Juana de la Cruz, see Jessica A. Boon, 'Mother Juana de la Cruz', in *Oxford Bibliographies Online: Renaissance and Reformation*, <http://www.oxfordbibliographies.com/view/document/obo-9780195399301/obo-9780195399301-0197.xml>, accessed 12 January 2015; Ronald E. Surtz, *The Guitar of God: Gender, Power and Authority in the Visionary World of Mother Juana de la Cruz (1481–1534)* (Philadelphia, PA, 1990), 3–8; Elizabeth A. Lehfeldt, *Religious Women in Golden Age Spain* (Aldershot, 2005), 169–72.

[24] Haliczer, *Between Exaltation and Infamy*, 292–3.

[25] Daza, *Historia, vida y milagros*, fols 70ᵛ–76ʳ.

[26] Ibid., fol. 74ᵛ. See also García de Andrés, *El Conhorte*, 1: 69–80; Jessica A. Boon, 'Mother Juana de la Cruz: Marian Visions and Female Preaching', in Hilaire Kallendorf, ed., *A New Companion to Hispanic Mysticism* (Leiden and Boston, MA, 2010), 127–48, at 133–6.

[27] Jessica A. Boon, 'Christ in Heavenly Play: Christology through Mary's Eyes in the *Sermones* of Juana de la Cruz', *Archiv für Reformationsgeschichte* 102 (2011), 243–66, at 245.

[28] Ibid. 243–4.

Tim. 2: 12–13), early saints such as Mary Magdalen and Catherine of Alexandria were reputed to have converted their listeners to
Christianity with the power of their words.[29] Jacobus de Voragine
(d. 1298), author of the widely read *Legenda Aurea* (*Golden Legend*),
justified women's preaching on the basis that it was a gift given by the
Holy Spirit.[30] The legitimization of women's sermons by claiming the
gift of prophecy or divine inspiration was a strategy commonly used
by women and by their male supporters, immediately sidestepping
issues of their ability to understand and explicate the word of God.[31]

Daza, who also refers to Juana's ecstatic utterances as *sermones*, is
clear that they were not composed by Juana herself: rather, God had
struck her dumb and spoke through her, 'sometimes every eight days,
or fifteen days, other times every four days, other times every third
day, other days one time after another, and some days twice, more
or less, as it pleased our Lord'.[32] Mention of Francis's stigmata in
'Juana's' sermons thus represented direct corroboration of the miracle from God. Daza refers to Juana de la Cruz in Chapter 5 of the
Historia de las llagas, which deals with how Jesus himself impressed
his holy wounds on St Francis without any mediation.[33] He quotes
Juana's sermon 58, given on the Feast of St Francis:[34]

> Our Lord Jesus Christ, seeing the most profound humility and obedi-
> ence of the glorious father St Francis, was so attached to him [Fran-
> cis] in that hour that he impressed his most holy wounds in the same
> manner that his majesty received them on the cross, going through
> not only the hands and the feet but also breaking through his side and
> making blood come out, and he [Francis] gave out great cries, … and
> the pain that the Seraphic Father had in that hour was so great, that he

---

[29] On the debates about women and preaching between the thirteenth and fifteenth centuries, see Alcuin Blamires, 'Women and Preaching in Medieval Orthodoxy, Heresy, and
Saints' Lives', *Viator* 26 (1995), 135–52. For female Franciscan preaching, see Bert Roest,
'Female Preaching in the Late Medieval Franciscan Tradition', *FS* 62 (2004), 119–54, especially 150–3 for Juana de la Cruz.

[30] Blamires, 'Women and Preaching', 148.

[31] Gillian T. W. Ahlgren, 'Negotiating Sanctity: Holy Women in Sixteenth-Century Spain',
ChH 64 (1995), 373–88, at 386.

[32] Daza, *Historia, vida y milagros*, fol. 71ᵛ.

[33] Daza, *Historia de las llagas*, fol. 37ʳ–47ᵛ.

[34] García de Andrés, *El Conhorte*, 1: 78–80, notes that *El Conhorte* was written towards the
end of the period of thirteen years from 1508 during which Juana preached. Precise dates
for the individual sermons cannot be ascertained.

fell on the ground as though dead after having received them [the stigmata] …[35]

Juana here forms part of a long list of people, including the Dominicans St Antoninus of Florence (d. 1459) and St Vincent Ferrer (d. 1419) and the Franciscan St Bernardino of Siena (d. 1444), all of whom are brought into play as providing evidence that Christ himself impressed the stigmata on Francis. Daza returns to Juana de la Cruz in Chapter 7 of the *Historia de las llagas*.[36] Here he first explains that God allowed Francis to descend into purgatory each year on the anniversary of his death in virtue of the wounds which Christ had given him.[37] Each year Francis would be able to grant immediate salvation to some members of his order who were in purgatory. Those associated with the order could be recognized through their habit. It is perhaps no surprise, then, that the Franciscan habit was favoured by many as burial clothing. Indeed, in sixteenth-century Madrid it was the most popular form of burial attire.[38] According to Daza, that God had allowed Francis to free his followers from purgatory was the occasion for especial bile and scorn in Erasmus Alber's *Alcoranus Franciscanorum* (*The Franciscan Qur'ān*).[39] Alber (*c*.1500–53), who had studied under Luther at Wittenberg, wrote this satirical work in response to the Franciscan Bartholomew of Pisa's late fourteenth-century *Liber de conformitate vitae Beati Francisci ad vitam domini Iesu* (*Book of the Correspondence of the Life of St Francis to the Life of the Lord Jesus*), which promoted St Francis as a second Christ, and which Alber used as a basis from which to attack Francis and his order.[40] It appeared in numerous editions and languages in the sixteenth and seventeenth centuries.[41] For Protestants such as Alber, the power to free souls was one which should have been exercised only by God.[42] Luther, in his preface to the *Alcoranus*, had pointed out that beliefs such as this

[35] Ibid., fols 39^v–40^r.

[36] Ibid., fols 57^r–64^r.

[37] Ibid., fol. 62^v.

[38] Carlos M. N. Eire, *From Madrid to Purgatory: The Art and Craft of Dying in Sixteenth-Century Spain*, rev. edn (Cambridge, 2002), 105–7.

[39] Daza, *Historia de las llagas*, fol. 63^v.

[40] On the *Liber de conformitate*, see Carolly Erickson, 'Bartholomew of Pisa, Francis exalted: *De Conformitate*', *MedS* 34 (1972), 253–74.

[41] Élisabeth Labrousse, 'Bayle et Saint François', *Revue d'histoire de l'Église de France* 70 (1984), 149–55, at 150–3.

[42] On early Protestant views concerning purgatory, see Jerry L. Walls, *Purgatory: The Logic of Total Transformation* (Oxford, 2012), 35–42.

decreased the importance of Christ so that he became one amongst the prophets, as was the case in Islam.[43] Albers's address to the readers, placed at the end of the *Alcoranus Franciscanorum*, rails against the way in which he perceived Francis to be placed above Christ, noting that, according to the *Liber de conformitate*, 'Christ felt the pains of his wounds for a short time. But Francis suffered the pains of his wounds for a full two years. ... And, to say it briefly, Christ did not do anything which Francis did not also do, and many more times.'[44]

Seeking to allay any doubts regarding Francis's ability to free certain souls from the cleansing torments of purgatory, in Chapter 7 of the *Historia de las llagas* Daza again appeals to *El libro del Conhorte* and, in particular, to Juana's sermon 58, which goes on to describe how, on the day of Francis's death each year, the heavens open and two sets of stairs appear which reach from heaven to purgatory. One set of stairs is the colour of rubies and coral whilst the other is as white as pearls. Red signifies the passion; white the purity of the Virgin. Francis and Christ descend to purgatory on these stairs. Although the two sets of stairs are clearly differentiated, the text implies that Francis and Christ descend using both. Francis greets all those souls who are wearing his habit. Only those who are able to identify both Christ and Francis are freed from the torments of purgatory.[45] A further important aspect of sermon 58 is the repeated return to Christ's wounds and Francis's stigmata: the habit is in the shape of the cross; those who wear the habit imprint on themselves the wounds of the crucified Christ.[46] Moreover, once St Francis has assured Christ that he will obey him as a wife obeys her husband, Christ imprints his wounds on Francis as he himself had received them on the cross.[47] Ronald Surtz argues that both the importance and the singularity of Francis's stigmata are demonstrated when 'the Lord emphasises that while other martyrs suffered at the hands of the infidels, Francis was martyred by God himself when he was given the stigmata'.[48] Daza could use Juana's

[43] Michael J. Heath, 'Islamic Themes in Religious Polemic', *Bibliothèque d'Humanisme et Renaissance* 50 (1988), 289–315, at 291. Luther's short preface is contained in most editions of the *Alcoranus*.

[44] Erasmus Albers, *Alcoranus Franciscanorum* (Frankfurt, 1542), unpaginated.

[45] Daza, *Historia de las llagas*, fol. 64ʳ, provides a considerably abbreviated version of the material provided in the *Libro del Conhorte*; for the full text, see García de Andrés, *El Conhorte*, 2: 1248–9 (§14).

[46] Ibid. 1244 (§5).

[47] Ibid. 1245–6 (§8).

[48] Surtz, *Guitar of God*, 45–6; García de Andrés, *El Conhorte*, 2: 1245 (§7).

sermons to dispel any doubts about the pre-eminence of Francis's miraculous stigmata and stigmatization because of their authority: Christ spoke directly through Juana.[49] He provides evidence of this by noting that, during this period, Juana was able to speak in different languages 'of which she never had any former knowledge, especially in Latin, Arabic and others', here appealing to another common trope when writing about religious women who advised or taught others.[50]

Despite the legitimacy established for her sermons, Juana may seem a curious choice of authority in a work aimed at dispelling doubts about the extraordinary nature of Francis's stigmata, since she herself had received painful marks on her hands and feet in 1524. According to Daza's *vida*, Juana had, from the time in which she first entered the convent of Santa Maria de la Cruz, imposed on herself an extremely harsh discipline which was designed to allow her to ex- perience Christ's pain during the passion. Sometimes she would tie herself, naked, to a pillar leaving her arms free so that she could whip herself until she bled with an iron chain at the end of which she had attached a large iron ball; at other times she knelt and struck herself repeatedly on the breast with a flint so hard that the blood which spurted out reached as far as the walls of the cell. As she did this she circled the cell on her knees.[51] Daza details a number of other ex- tremely painful practices in which Juana engaged as part of her quest to experience Christ's suffering. For example, Juana had driven some nails into a wall so that she could push her hands on to them and hang without her feet touching the ground for up to an hour.[52] Such penitential practices were not uncommon amongst holy women of the period. Luisa de la Ascensiòn (d. 1636) was reported to have punished her body through the wearing of iron chains.[53] Catalina de Jesús y San Francisco (d. 1677) was regularly whipped on the order

---

[49] Boon, 'Mother Juana de la Cruz', 127–8.

[50] Daza, *Historia, vida y milagros*, fol. 72. Umiltà of Faenza (d. 1310) was also credited with being able to speak in Latin despite never having studied the language: see Carolyn Musessig, 'Prophecy and Song: Teaching and Preaching by Medieval Women', in Beverly Mayne Kienzle and Pamela J. Walker, eds, *Women Preachers and Prophets through Two Millennia of Christianity* (Berkeley, CA, 1998), 146–58, at 148.

[51] Daza, *Historia, vida y milagros*, fols 22ʳ–23ʳ.

[52] Ibid., fol. 24ʳ.

[53] Haliczer, *Between Exaltation and Infamy*, 133. On painful penitential practices carried out by male and female Spanish mystics, see Maureen Flynn, 'The Spiritual Uses of Pain in Spanish Mysticism', *Journal of the American Academy of Religion* 64 (1996), 257–78.

of her confessor.[54] However, at the age of forty-three, on Good Friday, Juana received marks on her hand and feet in the places where Christ had been nailed to the cross. Daza recounts that she had been praying, in rapture, with her body set in the shape of a cross. Because she remained in her rapture for longer than was normal the nuns carried her into her cell and left her there so that they could go to the choir for holy office. Whilst they were there Juana entered the choir walking with great difficulty: she was leaning on the walls and allowed only her heels and her toes to touch the ground. The nuns asked to see what had happened and discovered that Juana had the signs of the crucifixion in her hands and feet. Daza describes the marks as being round, the size of a coin, and red, of the colour of fresh roses; they were like this both on the tops and soles of Juana's feet and on the backs and palms of her hands.[55] The marks caused Juana great pain, but a fragrant smell emanated from them. In a reflection of the words spoken by the apostle Thomas (John 20: 25), the nuns saw 'with their eyes and felt with their own hands'. Daza of course intended these words to clear away doubt for the reader of the *vida*. Having carried Juana back to her cell, the nuns asked how she had received the marks. She replied that her guardian angel had taken her to a place where she had seen Jesus crucified. He touched her with his wounds and left her with dreadful pains in her hands and feet, and when the vision was over she found herself in her cell with the marks which could be seen, on Fridays and Saturdays, from then until Ascension Day, when, at the time that the Lord ascended, both the pains and the marks disappeared as though they had never been there. Juana had prayed for the marks to be removed but the Lord replaced them with the pains of the passion in every part of Juana's body to a greater extent than she had ever felt them before.[56]

Daza's account of Juana's reception of the wounds claims that God gave her the 'pains and signs of the most holy wounds' but does not address how her experience should be interpreted in relation to Francis's stigmata.[57] Given that Daza's later publication on the *Historia de*

[54] Jodi Bilinkoff, 'Confession, Gender, Life-writing: Some Cases (mainly) from Spain', in Katharine Jackson Lualdi and Anne T. Thayer, eds, *Penitence in the Age of Reformations* (Aldershot, 2000), 169–183, at 171–2.

[55] '[D]el tamaño de un real de plata, de color de rosas muy frescas, y coloradas; y de la propria figura y color correspondian igualmente en los empyenes y plantas de los pies, y de las manos': Daza, *Historia, vida y milagros*, fol. 77ᵛ.

[56] Ibid., fols 77ʳ–78ᵛ.

[57] Ibid., fols 76ᵛ–77ʳ.

las llagas specifically aims to demonstrate the unique nature of Francis's stigmata and stigmatization, a desire to sidestep direct discussion of the issue is understandable. Responding to the question of Juana's wounds as stigmata in either the *vida* or the *Historia de las llagas* would have opened a Pandora's box of doubts in relation to the Franciscan understanding of the miracle experienced by their founder. Yet Daza appears to have been aware of the debate about different types of stigmata, since he dedicated a chapter of the *Historia de las llagas* to discussing the way in which Jesus gave Francis his wounds, emphasizing the lack of any intermediary, a key part of the definitions of both Caffarini and Lombardelli of the most prestigious, eighth type of stigmata.

Daza avoids the question of whether stigmata could be placed on a spectrum of stigmatic experiences, with self-inflicted marks or wounds at one extreme and Francis of Assisi's miraculously imprinted wounds at the other thus demonstrating God's greatest favour. His approach contrasts with that of Dominican writers such as Caffarini and Lombardelli, discussed above, and Luis de Granada (d. 1588), who, in the 'Prologue' to his *Historia de Sor María de la Visitación*, states that God had honoured two women from Lisbon, María de la Visitación,[58] a member of his own order, and Ana de las Llagas, a member of the third order of St Francis, singling them out with the signs of the passion. María received the wounds of the nails and the lance, and Ana had Christ crucified sculpted over her breast and the name of Jesus on her side, made out of her own flesh.[59] Luis de Granada was concerned to demonstrate that varying types of stigmata could be experienced by a range of holy people, in this case both Dominican and Franciscan. Juana's experience, as described by Daza, had similarities to that of contemporary or near-contemporary Dominican female stigmatics whose stigmata appeared, or became more pronounced or painful, during Holy Week or on Fridays. Francesco Silvestri described Osanna Andreasi's stigmata during Holy Week as sometimes appearing 'rosy as though there was blood underneath the skin'.[60]

---

[58] On María de la Visitación, see Ian MacInnes, 'Stigmata on Trial: The Nun of Portugal and the Politics of the Body', *Viator* 31 (2000), 391–8.
[59] Luis de Granada, *Historia de Sor María de la Visitación* (Barcelona, 2011), 11.
[60] Francesco Silvestri, *La vita e stupea di miraculi della gloriosa vergine Osanna Mantovano del Terzo ordine de'Frati Predicatori* (Milan, 1507), bk 3, ch. 6.

Lucia Brocadelli's stigmata bled on Wednesdays and Fridays.[61] As early as the thirteenth century the Franciscan Margherita Colonna (d. 1280) was recorded as having physical symptoms which would have been recognized as stigmata by Caffarini and Lombardelli.[62] Yet whilst the Dominicans acknowledged and celebrated stigmatics both within and outside their order in order to emphasize the importance of meditation on the passion, the Franciscans could not do the same without opening the door to doubts about the unique nature of Francis's stigmatization and stigmata. Nonetheless, by the early eighteenth century, just over a century after Daza had published the *Historia de las llagas*, the Franciscan Pietro Antonio da Venezia, in his revised and expanded version of the *Leggendario Francescano* authored by his co-religionist Benedetto Mazzara, was able to say, as he recounted the life of the Sicilian Poor Clare Arcangela Tardera (d. 1599), that 'the Lord wanted to give her [Arcangela] another most singular grace and that was to imprint on her the signs of his most holy wounds'. He quickly followed this, however, by noting that Arcangela had not experienced the stigmata in the same way as St Francis had done.[63]

Daza could not – or at least did not – articulate this acceptance of different types of stigmata, but his description of Juana's reception of marks on her hands and feet is a tacit acknowledgement of the legitimacy of stigmatic experiences that differed in type and importance from those of St Francis of Assisi, and evidence that the existence of stigmatics such as Juana need no longer be perceived uniformly by Franciscans as casting doubt on the unique nature of their founder's stigmata. Throughout the *Historia de la llagas*, Daza uses his sources to argue for the singularity of Francis's stigmata, both in relation to the method in which he received them and their physical symptoms during the two years between the stigmatization and the death of the saint. To use Juana's divinely inspired sermons as corroborative evidence is consonant with the ways in which Daza uses other sources.

---

[61] Giacomo Marcianese, *Vita della B. Lucia da Narni dell'Ordine di San Domenico* (Viterbo, 1663), 12–113.

[62] Attilio Cadderi, *Beata Margherita da Colonna (1255–1280). Le due vite scritte dal fratello Giovanni, senatore di Roma e da Stefania, monaca di San Silvestro in Capite* (Palestrina, 2010), 8, 169. Margherita received a wound in her side which bled and which she bore until her death. It is mentioned in both her early *vitae*.

[63] 'Un'altra singolarissima grazia volle concederle il Signore, e fu imprimerle i segni delle sue sagratissime Piaghe, non però nel modo, che l'ebbe il Padre S. Francesco': Benedetto Mazzara and Pietro Antonio di Venezia, *Leggendario Francescano*, 12 vols (Venice, 1721–2), 2: 138–43 (8 February), at 142.

However, to use Juana's stigmata as part of the proof that Francis had received stigmata would have gone against centuries of Franciscan thinking, as doing so might have seemed to contain a tacit acknowledgement that Francis's stigmata were not unique. Yet Daza did dwell on Juana's stigmata in the *vida*, and he did so in spite of the relatively recent examples of faked stigmata by a Poor Clare from Córdoba, Maria Magdalena de la Cruz (d. 1560), and the Portuguese Dominican María de la Visitación, whose fraud had been discovered in 1588.[64] His reasons for this may lie in the papal sanction for the celebration of the Feast of the Stigmatization of St Francis throughout the Church in 1615 and the growing tide of stigmatics. The former implicitly acknowledged the primacy of Francis's stigmata and thus may have allowed some Franciscans to relax their opposition to other types. The latter was symptomatic of the importance of meditation on the passion in the lives of religious women, especially those in Spain.[65] Holy women who received the stigmata in sixteenth- and seventeenth-century Spain also had visions of St Francis.[66] Against this background, it would have been increasingly difficult to deny either that women like Juana could have received physical marks in some or all of the places where Christ was wounded on the cross, or that these marks proved the influence of Francis rather than casting doubt on his stigmata. However, Juana's stigmata as described in the *vida* do not appear to have bled and she did not have the wound in the side. The differences between Juana's (partial) stigmata and those of Francis allowed the Franciscan claim that Francis was the only true stigmatic to stand. Nonetheless, by implicitly acknowledging Juana as a stigmatic, Daza moved closer to an acceptance, shared by some other Franciscans, that the existence of different types of stigmatic experience did not ineluctably cast doubt on the unique nature of Francis's stigmata.

[64] On Maria Magdalena de la Cruz, see Jesús Imirizaldu, *Monjas y beatas embaucadoras* (Madrid, 1977), 41–62.
[65] Haliczer, *Between Exaltation and Infamy*, 216, 267.
[66] Ibid. 216.

Doubt, Anxiety and Protestant Epistolary Counselling: The Letter-Book of Nehemiah Wallington

Lucy Busfield*

St John's College, Oxford

This essay focuses on a surprisingly underexplored manuscript of the London puritan woodturner, Nehemiah Wallington. His 'Coppies of profitable and comfortable letters' anthologizes printed correspondence of martyrs and Reformed clergy alongside Wallington's own pious exchanges with ministers, neighbours and friends. Since Wallington's agonies of doubt about his religious estate are well known to early modern historians, his piety provides a particularly valuable lens through which to explore how clergymen and laypeople attempted to address the pastoral obstacle of religious uncertainty. This remarkable manuscript provides insights into clerical status within puritan spirituality, shedding light on the role of Protestant ministers as physicians of the soul, who conceived of themselves as indispensable experts in the diagnosis and cure of the spiritual afflictions of their lay devotees. Wallington and others, seeking resolutions for their doubts and scruples, affirmed the particular authority of these clergy as pastoral specialists. This essay presents evidence of sustained clericalism within Protestant piety, a tendency which acted in tension with a concurrent trend of spiritual individualism. Furthermore, it advances an argument for the significant role which epistolary counselling played in Protestant pastoral ministry to those afflicted by religious doubt.

The piety of the London Presbyterian woodturner, Nehemiah Wallington (1598–1658), is a natural subject for an investigation of religious doubt. Thanks to seven extant manuscript notebooks which he penned between 1618 and 1654, Wallington has become a favoured exemplar of popular Protestantism for early modern historians.[1] He devoted great energy to documenting his unremitting

* St John's College, St Giles, Oxford, OX1 3JP. E-mail: lucy.busfield@sjc.ox.ac.uk.

I would like to thank Judith Maltby and Sarah Apetrei for their helpful comments on this essay; I also gratefully acknowledge the support of the Arts and Humanities Research Council.

[1] Four are in the British Library: MS Sloane 1457, 'A Memoriall of Gods judgments upon Sabbath breakers, Drunkerds and other vile livers'; MS Sloane 922, 'Coppies of profitable and comfortable letters'; Add. MS 21935, 'A Bundel of Marcys'; Add. MS 40883, 'The groth of a Christian'. The remaining three are: London, Guildhall Library,

pursuit of evidence of his election to salvation, regarding the main-
tenance of this record as an important spiritual obligation. Wallington's frequent bouts of melancholy and despair, which ultimately resulted in multiple suicide attempts, have led historians to depict him
as an archetypal victim of the emotional turmoil which experimental
Calvinism could engender.[2] His notebooks have proved conducive to
conventional explanatory narratives of a Reformation-era shift away
from clerical mediation towards heightened trends of individualism
and subjectivity in Protestant spirituality. The recent historiography
of puritan devotional culture has, however, witnessed an increasing
backlash against traditional interpretations of the rise of spiritual self-
writing as a key trigger in the emergence of the modern individual.
Scholars have underscored the limited manifestation of autonomous
selfhood in spiritual memoirs, as well as the significant communal
dimension of both diary-writing and wider godly religious culture.[3]
Nonetheless, historians continue to regard Wallington's writings as
epitomizing a puritan focus on personal self-scrutiny as the chief
tool by which the believer could interrogate his own experiences and
triumph over his doubts.[4] He has, in short, become a byword for
Calvinist introspection. Yet Wallington's manuscripts also reveal alternative illuminating insights into the importance which early modern Protestants placed on obtaining clerical assistance in resolving
their religious uncertainties.

MS 204, 'Record of Gods Marcys, or a Thankfull Remembrance'; Cheshire, Tatton Park,
MS 68.20, 'A Record of marcys continued or yet God is good to Israel'; Washington DC,
Folger Shakespeare Library, MS V.a.436, 'An Extract of the passages of my life or the
Booke of all my writting [*sic*] books'.

[2] David Booy, 'Introduction', in idem, ed., *The Notebooks of Nehemiah Wallington, 1618–
1654: A Selection* (Aldershot, 2007), 1–28, at 19–20, 24.

[3] See Andrew Cambers, 'Reading, the Godly and Self-Writing in England, circa 1580–
1720', *Journal of British Studies* 46 (2007), 796–825; J. C. Davis, 'Living with the Living God:
Radical Religion and the English Revolution', in Christopher Durston and Judith Maltby,
eds, *Religion in Revolutionary England* (Manchester, 2006), 19–41, at 31–5.

[4] Amongst many, see Kate Narveson, *Bible Readers and Lay Writers in Early Modern England:
Gender and Self-Definition in an Emergent Writing Culture* (Farnham, 2012), 94–5, 97, 104–6,
115–21; James S. Amelang, *The Flight of Icarus: Artisan Autobiography in Early Modern Europe* (Stanford, CA, 1998), 34–5; Susan Doran and Christopher Durston, *Princes, Pastors
and People: The Church and Religion in England, 1500–1700*, 2nd edn (London, 2003), 97–8;
Ian W. Archer, 'Religious Identities', in Suzanne Gossett, ed., *Thomas Middleton in Context* (Cambridge, 2011), 135–43, at 137–8. A strong emphasis on individualism remains
characteristic of broad overview treatments such as Jeffrey L. Forgeng, *Daily Life in Stuart
England* (Westport, CT, 2007), 230–1.

Wallington's writing took a distinctive form in the collating of correspondence, of overwhelmingly religious content, in a duodecimo letter-book of over two hundred folios. British Library manuscript Sloane 922, 'Coppies of profitable and comfortable letters', appropriates this genre in a unique manner. Wallington's own epistolary exchanges with neighbours, friends and ministers are anthologized alongside exemplary manuscript letters which circulated amongst the godly community and excerpts from the printed correspondence of martyrs and clerics such as Edward Dering, Richard Greenham, Joseph Hall and Paul Baynes. This manuscript has, however, received surprisingly modest attention. In his excellent monograph, *Wallington's World*, which initiated a wave of interest in the notebooks, Paul Seaver exploited the considerable biographical potential of Wallington's own letters. David Booy has also made reference to these documents in his overarching exploration of how Wallington constructed an 'image of self' through his writings.[5] However, a paragraph-length outline by James Daybell constitutes the only scholarly discussion of the manuscript as a whole.[6] By exploring the role of Wallington as reader and compiler of key examples from the interesting and under-explored genre of printed religious correspondence, as well as drawing more broadly on the wider devotional context of his letter-book, this essay will offer fresh insights into the way in which early modern clergy and laypeople addressed the pastoral obstacles of religious doubt and uncertainty. Contributing to an already increasingly nuanced understanding of puritan individualism through the illuminating perspective of lay-clerical relations, I will underscore the significant status and authority which Protestant ministers could acquire through their expertise in handling the scruples of the laity. Most notably, this essay will demonstrate the important role which epistolary

---

[5] Paul S. Seaver, *Wallington's World: A Puritan Artisan in Seventeenth-Century London* (London, 1985); Booy, ed., *Notebooks*, 12–14. Booy has even reproduced twelve of Wallington's own letters in his abridged edition of the notebooks.

[6] James Daybell, *The Material Letter in Early Modern England: Manuscript Letters and the Culture and Practices of Letter-writing, 1512–1635* (Basingstoke, 2012), 208–9. This material is reproduced in idem, 'Early Modern Letter-Books, Miscellanies, and the Reading and Reception of Scribally Copied Letters', in Joshua Eckhardt and Daniel Starza Smith, eds, *Manuscript Miscellanies in Early Modern England* (Farnham, 2014), 57–72, at 65–6. The most recent large-scale assessment of Wallington's writings makes no reference to correspondence: Robert M. Oswald, 'Death, Piety and Social Engagement in the Life of the Seventeenth-Century London Artisan, Nehemiah Wallington' (PhD thesis, University of Edinburgh, 2012).

counselling played in Protestant pastoral ministry to those afflicted by religious doubt.

Wallington commenced his letter-book by copying edifying excerpts from the correspondence of Marian martyrs featured in John Foxe's *Acts and Monuments*. Their epistles represent the initial forays into a genre of religious epistolary counselling which was to assume a significant place in both Elizabethan and seventeenth-century England. However, the vast majority of the printed materials on which the collection draws reveal an exclusively clerical model of spiritual direction, reflecting the wider shift which occurred within Protestantism, as it moved away from its more revolutionary origins and settled down into the hierarchical model of the established Elizabethan Church. Representative of Elizabethan epistolary counselling are the passages which Wallington transcribed from the *Certaine godly and verie comfortable letters* of the puritan divine Edward Dering (*c.*1540–76). Posthumously published in Middelburgh in 1590, this text is one of the earliest examples of a single-author printed letter collection in English. It formed the basis of a short study by Patrick Collinson, who characterized Dering as 'the archetype of the puritan divine'.[7] Dering attended Christ's College, Cambridge, and later became preacher of St Andrew's, Norwich, a city lecturer and chaplain to Thomas Howard, duke of Norfolk. He adopted the epistle as an alternative vehicle for his preaching ministry, particularly during the years of ill-health which preceded his untimely death.[8] Amongst Wallington's transcriptions are letters addressed to individuals struggling to maintain an assurance of God's love and of their elect status in the face of many 'crosses' and divine 'chastisments'.[9] In response to a 'case' presented by the gentlewoman Catherine Killigrew, who was faltering under the burden of bodily suffering, Dering offered repeated encouragements to ward off doubt. Evoking a habitual Protestant theme of the trial of the faithful through tribulation, he reassured his troubled correspondent 'that this is the lot of Gods saints to enioy his blessings with afflictions so that the more you bee sorrowfull the more you be sure that the liuing God hath giuen you your portion'.[10]

---

[7] Patrick Collinson, 'A Mirror of Elizabethan Puritanism: The Life and Letters of Godly Master Dering', in idem, ed., *Godly People: Essays on English Protestantism and Puritanism* (London, 1983), 289–324, at 290.
[8] Ibid. 294–8, 316.
[9] Wallington, 'Coppies', fols 27ʳ–30ᵛ, at 27ᵛ, 29ʳ.
[10] Ibid., fol. 29ᵛ.

Dering's wider works reveal a lofty conception of the pre-eminence of the clerical office which sat somewhat awkwardly along-side strict predestinarianism; for Dering, the minister is the one 'by whom the people do beleeue'.[11] Collinson argued that 'few English Protestants have held such a "high" doctrine of the ministry'.[12] However, the notion of the minister's indispensability, as God's very mouthpiece, was an orthodox Reformed understanding,[13] which was regularly evoked amongst puritan proponents of a pastorally sensitive ministry with spiritual counselling at its core. Dering's pastoral correspondence is underpinned by this awareness of his own spiritual authority. Although Jason Yiannikkou has suggested, from his frequent use of the homiletic first-person plural to address his devotees, that Dering's letters reflect an 'intense reciprocity' and 'fellow-feeling', they are certainly not lacking in authoritative pastoral exhortation.[14] In one letter, Dering invoked the apostolic model of St John, who could likewise 'see in the people to whom hee wrote' the marks of God's election.[15] Importantly, this pastoral authority is also conveyed through Wallington's selected transcriptions, which include firm pronouncements of 'the blessed life, which God shall giue vnto you and to all his saints', calculated to soothe his correspondent's anxieties about their own salvation.[16]

Wallington similarly drew on the printed correspondence of Richard Greenham (fl. early 1540s, d. 1594), the Elizabethan minister of Dry Drayton, Cambridgeshire. Greenham has been recognized, both in his own time and amongst modern historians, as an exemplary godly pastor. A graduate of Pembroke College, Cambridge, he is particularly remembered for having established a prototype Protestant seminary in his rectory where students could reside to gain practical pastoral training.[17] He devoted himself to ministering to troubled and doubting laity and was renowned for his 'singular dexteritie

---

[11] Edward Dering, *M. Derings Workes: More at Large then Euer Hath Heere to-fore Been Printed in Any One Volume* (London, 1614), sig. A3ᵛ. Here Dering probably alludes to 1 Cor. 3: 5.

[12] Collinson, 'Mirror', 299.

[13] T. H. L. Parker, *Calvin's Preaching* (Edinburgh, 1992), 41–4.

[14] Jason Yiannikkou, 'Protestantism, Puritanism and Practical Divinity in England, c.1570–1620' (PhD thesis, Cambridge University, 1999), especially 42–3, 48, 51.

[15] Edward Dering, *Certaine Godly and Verie Comfortable Letters, Full of Christian Consolation* (Middelburgh, 1590), sig. C8ʳ.

[16] Wallington, 'Coppies', fol. 28ᵛ.

[17] John H. Primus, *Richard Greenham: Portrait of an Elizabethan Pastor* (Macon, GA, 1998), 12, 24, 42–3.

in comforting afflicted Consciences'.[18] According to his editor and ministerial disciple, Henry Holland, this was a most expert skill, lacking in the majority of Greenham's clerical contemporaries. It was on account of his learned and 'certaine rule of art' that Greenham might be accounted a 'spirituall Physition'. Holland contrasted his practice with the spiritual quackery of the 'blinde Empyrikes' who, relying exclusively on experience, 'gesse vncertainlie' at cures with potentially perilous consequences for the afflicted.[19] Although Greenham's pastoral ministry has been the focus of several scholarly studies, the role of epistolary counselling within it has largely been overlooked. Historical focus has centred chiefly on Manchester, Rylands Library English Manuscript 524, a collection of Greenham's sayings and records of his practical pastoral care and counselling composed by a student during the 1580s.[20] In their study of Greenham, Kenneth Parker and Eric Carlson did not quote at all from his letters, although these provide practical and detailed case studies of Greenham's dealings with doubting laity, as well as being amongst his most popular works.[21]

The passage which Wallington chose to include in his compilation is not a true example of the letter form, but rather a series of 'Short Rules', 'Sent by Mr Richard Greenham to a Gentelwoman troubled in minde for her direction and consolation', and subsequently published in 1612 as a broadsheet.[22] It commences with the comforting reassurance that no sin can be attributed to a believer who 'giue not consent in heart'. Evidently, encouraging the scrupulous with this sentiment was one of Greenham's characteristic pastoral strategies, for Samuel Clarke highlighted it in his short biography of

---

[18] Elizabeth Holland, 'To the High and Mightie Monarch, James', in Richard Greenham, *The Works of the Reuerend and Faithfull Seruant of Iesus Christ M. Richard Greenham* (London, 1612), unpaginated.

[19] Henry Holland, 'Preface to the Reader', in Greenham, *Works*, unpaginated. The word 'empiric' refers here to an unqualified medical practitioner who rebuffs formal learning and theory: OED Online, *s.v.* 'empiric, n. and adj.', online edn (March 2014), at: <http://www.oed.com/view/Entry/61340?redirectedFrom=empiric#eid>, accessed 20 March 2014.

[20] Primus, *Richard Greenham*, 9–11; Kenneth L. Parker and Eric Josef Carlson, *'Practical Divinity': The Works and Life of Revd Richard Greenham* (Aldershot, 1998), 34–5.

[21] The letters were frequently reproduced in partial collections of Greenham's works and other anthologies: Parker and Carlson, *'Practical Divinity'*, 362–6.

[22] Wallington, 'Coppies', fol. 31^r; Richard Greenham, *Short Rules Sent by Maister Richard Greenham* (London, 1612).

the divine.[23] From similar statements, Karen Bruhn has observed a striking flexibility within Greenham's theological system: she notes that he regularly tempered predestination in order to extend much needed solace to godly doubting souls.[24] Greenham followed up this reassurance with further aids to achieving certainty for one overcome by 'feare of falling away', advocating meditation on the Scriptural promise that 'whom God loueth he loueth (to the ende) for euer' as a remedy against doubt. Indeed, Greenham exhorted his correspondent to regard 'your present estate to be none other then the estate of Gods children', declaring 'yet are you sure and secure', for Christ will bring you 'to the shore of saluation, without all perill of perishing'.[25]

Interestingly, however, it is a further letter of Greenham's, addressed to one burdened by relentless doubts about their election, which, despite not having been compiled by Wallington, actually displays the most striking parallels with correspondence that the puritan woodturner later sent to his ministerial acquaintances. Berating his addressee for forgetting former mercies, Greenham strove to provide an 'assurance of the loue of God towards you'.[26] As would subsequently be characteristic of Wallington, this anxious correspondent evidently had recourse to clerical counsellors over a sustained period of time; Greenham highlighted the 'innumerable … excellent Physitions of the soule' who had offered 'great comforts … by word in presence, and by letters in absence'.[27] It was through an assurance of the authority of their counsel that Greenham attempted to assuage his friend's crippling doubt. He noted that, because so 'many of the faithfull and expert seruants of Christ haue examined your estate … & haue found all signes vnto health and saluation … [their] testimonie … must bee *as the voyce of God himselfe*'.[28]

At first sight, an apparently incongruous inclusion is Wallington's transcriptions from the *Epistles* (1608–11) of Joseph Hall (1574–1656), an exemplar of Calvinist episcopacy who would become bishop of Exeter and then of Norwich. Hall was a vocal advocate

[23] Wallington, 'Coppies', fol. 31^r; Samuel Clarke, *The Lives of Thirty-Two English Divines* (London, 1677), 14.

[24] Karen Bruhn, '"Sinne Unfoulded": Time, Election, and Disbelief among the Godly in Late Sixteenth- and Early Seventeenth-Century England', *ChH* 77 (2008), 574–95, at 592–3.

[25] Wallington, 'Coppies', fols 32^v, 31^v, 33^r.

[26] Greenham, *Works*, 871–80, at 877.

[27] Ibid. 876–7.

[28] Ibid. 877–8 (my emphasis).

of theological moderation who is remembered especially for his writings on the practice of meditation and his attempt to integrate a long Catholic devotional heritage into Protestant piety.[29] In his youth, he experimented with various genres, including seeing into print sixty religious epistles in three volumes.[30] His churchmanship sits rather awkwardly with Wallington's own anti-episcopalian sentiments: Wallington's personal letters and various notebooks include numerous references to the 'wicked Bishops', and in one memorable passage he actually commemorated Parliament's 1641 impeachment of a dozen bishops, including Hall, and their imprisonment in the Tower.[31] Nonetheless, Hall's letter collection can be firmly located within an emerging Protestant tradition of spiritual counselling, which took inspiration from the pastoral works of godly Elizabethan divines and paved the way for developments in seventeenth-century casuistry. Although Hall was evidently a prolific letter-writer, as well as the first Englishman to publish an extensive collection of his own correspondence,[32] Peter Lake and Kenneth Fincham are amongst the few scholars to have utilized his *Epistles*, as evidence of his ideological agenda and fierce opposition to papistry, separatism and the anti-Calvinism of William Laud and his associates. However, they passed over Hall's many letters of spiritual counsel, from which Wallington made his selection, dismissing their content as 'general moral nostrums'.[33] Yet these epistles are equally revealing about Hall's confessional colouring, exposing his undoubtedly puritan style of piety. Through them, we see the future bishop in the role of physician of the soul.[34] In the context of Nehemiah Wallington's letter-book, the ease with which the godly could embrace Hall's practical divinity is especially well illuminated.

---

[29] Richard A. McCabe, *Joseph Hall: A Study in Satire and Meditation* (Oxford, 1982), 151.

[30] T. F. Kinloch, *The Life and Works of Joseph Hall, 1574–1656* (London, 1951), 191. It is important to observe that these carefully crafted epistles were very probably composed with publication in mind. Hall presumably always intended them to speak to a wider audience than merely their original addressees: see Frank Livingstone Huntley, *Bishop Joseph Hall, 1574–1656: A Biographical and Critical Study* (Cambridge, 1979), 67.

[31] Wallington, 'Coppies', fols 106^r, 142^r–144^r; idem, 'The groth of a Christian', fol. 24^v; idem, 'A Bundel of Marcys', fols 9^v, 39^v.

[32] Alan Stewart, 'Letters', in Andrew Hadfield, ed., *The Oxford Handbook of English Prose, 1500–1640* (Oxford, 2013), 417–33, at 426.

[33] Kenneth Fincham and Peter Lake, 'Popularity, Prelacy and Puritanism in the 1630s: Joseph Hall explains Himself', *EHR* 111 (1996), 856–81, at 862.

[34] McCabe has suggested that certain letters might owe a debt to the methods of Greenham: *Joseph Hall*, 210.

Of particular interest to Wallington was the counsel which Hall addressed to a 'Mistris A. P.', who had apparently confided to him her fears that she lacked 'true Faith'. Hall's response construed her doubts in positive terms, as a necessary accompaniment to Christian certainty. He reassured his anxious correspondent that 'you belieue whiles you complaine of vnbleefe[.] That man neuer beleeued that neuer doubted … Those doubts are but to make way for assurance'. Hall summed up his counsel in comforting, albeit rather condescending, terms, concluding of her spiritual condition: 'To be happy, and not know it, is littel aboue misrable[.] Such is your state'.[35] Wallington also compiled an epistle which Hall had addressed to his sister, 'Mistris B. Brinsly', in which he praised her anxious 'lamentation' of being unable to 'enough grieue' for her sins. According to Hall's diagnosis, her very doubts about the sufficiency of her sorrow stood as tangible evidence of true penitence.[36] This pastoral trope recurs frequently in epistolary source material; Protestant devotional writers, seeking to draw positive comfort from the doubts which pious self-examination often generated in believers, regularly asserted that such unsettling qualms could never beleaguer the cold formalist numbed by false assurance of salvation. Outside of Wallington's letter-book, this line of reasoning appears in a copy of a 1631 manuscript letter penned by the puritan divine Thomas Gataker (1574–1654), who attempted to dispel a scrupulous correspondent's fears of hypocrisy by discerning numerous signs of their election. Gataker wrote: 'But you doubt, you say, of the sincerity & soundnes of thease yor purposes & desires. Thease very feares & doubtings … thoe infirmities & weakenesses of themselvs, yet they argue a good soul'.[37]

Alongside this theological defence of doubt, many of Hall's letters are concerned with soothing and alleviating the spiritual anxieties of his correspondents. He highlighted personal deathbed instruction as an essential duty of the faithful pastor and expected that ministers would 'priuatly prepare men for death, and arme them against it', composing 'comfortable letters' to 'stir vp their fainting harts'.[38]

---

[35] Wallington, 'Coppies', fol. 44^{r-v}.

[36] Ibid., fols 38^r–39^v, at 38^r.

[37] Cambridge, Cambridge University Library, MS Dd.3.83 (19), 'A letter of Thomas Gataker to a friend concerning his spiritual state', 6, 11.

[38] Joseph Hall, *Epistles, The Second Volume: Conteining Two Decads* (London, 1608), 201–2. Epistolary counsel was especially fitting when contagious disease prevented the minister's personal presence.

Wallington transcribed one such epistle to a 'Master I. B.', which commenced, 'You complaine, that you feare deathe … If you would learne the remidy, knowe the cavse … our feare is from doubt and our doubt is from vnbleefe, and whence is our vnbeleefe, but chiefly from ignorance'. Hall then urged the acquisition of 'true knowledg and true faith' through contemplation of the assured delights of heaven. He concluded his letter with a comforting pledge which echoes the earlier assurances of election given by Dering and Greenham: 'Take but these, and I dare promise you securitie'. This rhetoric reveals the authoritative expertise which Hall assumed to impart pastoral counsel and which can be observed in Wallington's transcriptions from his *Epistles*.[39]

The radical puritan cleric Paul Baynes (*c*.1573–1617) is the final Reformed divine whose letters were anthologized by Wallington. Baynes is a minister of whom few biographical details are known with any certainty, and his works have received little historical attention. Like Dering, he was educated at Christ's College, and he then took up a lectureship at St Andrew the Great, Cambridge, succeeding William Perkins in this role. Baynes was banned from St Andrew's in 1605 on account of his unlicensed preaching, but he was soon back in the pulpit and was only finally suspended from his position during Archbishop Bancroft's 1608 metropolitical visitation.[40] His *Christian Letters* were printed posthumously in 1620 and were amongst his most popular writings, being reproduced in three editions by 1637. The preface to the work claims that some of the letters were also transcribed during Baynes's lifetime, 'full many a time; yea, hundreds of times, or nearer a thousand times, if some godly persons haue not misreckoned', implying a significant manuscript circulation of correspondence.[41] Baynes too was famed for his practical divinity. Samuel Clarke particularly associated his activities as an 'excellent *Casuist*' with the period after he was prohibited from exercising a preaching ministry. But he also identified Baynes's pastoral care of troubled

---

[39] Wallington, 'Coppies', fols 50ʳ–51ᵛ.

[40] Although the details surrounding this event have been variously reported, an article by Andrew Atherstone has cleared up much confusion: 'The Silencing of Paul Baynes and Thomas Taylor, Puritan Lecturers at Cambridge', *Notes and Queries* 54 (2007), 386–9. One letter in the collection makes reference to this 'great businesse', with Baynes reporting that he had been 'warned to preach' at the upcoming '*Metropolitans* visitation': Paul Baynes, *Christian Letters: of Mr. Paul Bayne. Replenished with Diuers Consolations, Exhortations, and Directions* (London, 1620), sig. G2ᵛ.

[41] Ibid., fols A3ᵛ–4ʳ.

and perplexed individuals as a trigger for his suspension, stating that because so 'many doubting Christians repaired to him for satisfaction in cases of Conscience' the bishops accused him of keeping conventicles.[42] In addition, Baynes's letters hint at the copious amount of time he devoted to fulfilling his pastoral duties on an epistolary level.[43]

A key theme of Baynes's collection is the necessity of maintaining faith and assurance in the face of divine afflictions. In one interesting letter, which Wallington copied, Baynes addressed a man weighed down with doubts because of the great sufferings 'visited' upon his wife. He declared: 'if I had sooner knowen of your heauines, I would before this haue written vnto you'. Whilst Baynes recognized that such sorrows had left his friend 'shaken in beleefe', he assured him that afflictions could 'confirm faith' for, amongst great tribulation, 'many precious graces are discerned'.[44] Similar comforts were addressed to others struggling with religious uncertainties in the face of the death of loved ones. Baynes exhorted another grieving correspondent: 'we must looke to Christ that he would not let our faith hope and meekenesse of minde bee shaken'. Wallington, who was himself tragically affected by numerous bereavements, collected three of these epistles together in his letter-book, using manicules[45] to highlight the 'motiues' for patiently bearing grief which Baynes recommended.[46] Throughout his letters, Baynes employed medical imagery to compare healing 'afflictions' with bitter 'potions' and purges. In a phrase which Wallington transcribed, 'the physicke must make vs sicke that that [sic] doth vs any good'.[47] For Baynes, God was the supreme spiritual physician, a frequent designation amongst godly writers. However, 'the Minister of the Gospell', as mediator of God's heavenly physic to the laity, was himself 'a wise Physitian' and healer of souls.[48] In a parallel with Dering, Baynes referred to

---

[42] Clarke, *Lives*, 23–4.

[43] Baynes, *Christian Letters*, sig. F11[r].

[44] Wallington, 'Coppies', fols 64[r]–65[r].

[45] A symbol consisting of a pointing hand ☞, used to identify passages of interest or importance.

[46] Wallington, 'Coppies', fols 58[v]–63[v], especially 60[v]–61[r].

[47] Ibid., fols 54[r], 59[r], 62[r], 63[v], 67[r]–68[v].

[48] Ibid., fols 54[r], 57[r]; see also, for example, Greenham, *Works*, 794; Paul Baynes, *An Entire Commentary vpon the Whole Epistle of the Apostle Paul to the Ephesians* (London, 1643), 394. See David Harley, 'Spiritual Physic, Providence and English Medicine, 1560–1640', in Ole Peter Grell and Andrew Cunningham, eds, *Medicine and the Reformation* (London, 1993), 101–17, at 109–10.

ministers as God's 'blessed instruments to save their [people's] soules', the ultimate channels of grace.[49] It is in this expert, professional capacity that Wallington's letter-book presents Baynes. In one epistle, penned to bolster a troubled correspondent's faith, the puritan cleric pressed for details of his friend's spiritual condition with the warning that, since he could 'easily … procure that which would refresh you seasonably', Baynes's addressee ought not to 'neglect a good meanes which Gods prouidence doth shew you'.[50] In another, Baynes spoke of the need to determine a precise spiritual diagnosis before profitable counsel could be prescribed.[51]

Amongst the works of the clerical dispensers of epistolary counsel featured in Wallington's manuscript, a recurring discourse affirming the dignity of the ministerial office emerges, with clergy encouraging troubled and doubting laity to have recourse to their expertise, and conveying these pastoral ideals through their practical performance of spiritual counselling. Interestingly, these sources appear to support Rosemary O'Day's assertion that, deprived of their elevated sacramental status and seeking 'a new raison d'être', the post-Reformation English clergy placed particular emphasis on their commitment to the exercise of their duties of pastoral care and oversight.[52] Wallington's reading of this printed advice literature shaped his own approach to spiritual direction. As the final section of this essay will demonstrate, Wallington seems largely to have internalized these contemporary models of pious practice, so that his own experience of epistolary counselling served to affirm rather than undermine ministerial authority.

James Daybell has recently concluded that despite his lay status 'Wallington's own correspondence represents him in the role of spiritual counsellor'.[53] In addition to engaging in some essentially reciprocal edificatory correspondence with several godly companions,[54] it is certainly true that Wallington penned several letters, dating from the 1640s, in which he fiercely rebuked neighbours and relations for

---

[49] Paul Baynes, *A Commentarie vpon the First and Second Chapters of Saint Paul to the Colossians* (London, 1635), 143.

[50] Wallington, 'Coppies', fol. 54[v].

[51] Ibid., fols 57[v]–58[r]; see also Baynes, *Christian Letters*, sig. B8[r–v].

[52] Rosemary O'Day, *The English Clergy: The Emergence and Consolidation of a Profession, 1558–1642* (Leicester, 1979), 126.

[53] Daybell, *Material Letter*, 208.

[54] See, for instance, Wallington, 'Coppies', fols 107[r], 121[r], 139[r–v], 144[v]–145[r].

their transgressions. Thus, Wallington addressed an old friend, Master Wade, 'louingly reprouing him for his sinnefull life' and reflecting on the divine retribution awaiting those who indulge in the 'sinnes of Drvnkennesse and Hordome'. He wrote also to his 'Cozen Iohn Wallington' that 'I here intend to deale plainly and louingly with you shewing you your woefull and miserable condition that you are in'.[55] As Paul Seaver has noted, these letters display a conviction of the necessity of reproving fellow believers, although Wallington did feel the need to accompany these interventions with repeated justifications of his authority to reprimand. He frequently employed the biblical command of Leviticus 19: 17: 'Thou shalt not hate thy Brother in thine heart But thou shalt plainly rebuke thy Neigh[b]our and suffer him not to sinne'.[56] Nonetheless, it is also true that most of these letters were composed either subsequent to, or around the time of, Wallington's election as a ruling elder for St Leonard Eastcheap in the fourth London Classis in 1646. It therefore seems fair to assume that this appointment heightened his already existing sense of his religious obligation to admonish and correct sinners.

Most significantly, though, Wallington's own letters display an ideal of fraternal admonition which fundamentally differed from the paternal, pastoral model of detailed consideration of intricate cases of conscience, which Wallington encountered through his reading of epistolary advice literature. The main body of his letters of reproof often constituted little more than extensive quotations from Scripture, copied out for his addressees' easy reference, followed up with recommendations to read various printed texts and sermons.[57] A few brief references in his notebooks do reveal Wallington in the role of spiritual counsellor to the doubt-ridden and disturbed. During the 1640s Wallington twice mentions that he had been called on to advise godly women who were troubled in conscience. This was presumably as a result of his significant personal experience in battling with doubt and despair, a qualification which ministers recognized as particularly fitting an individual to assist others. Despite his high sense of the clerical office, even Richard Greenham acknowledged that the most effective comforts might be those proffered by a believer who had suffered similarly.[58] Wallington reported of the first occasion: 'I

---

[55] Ibid., fols 148[r–v], 160[r]–162[v].

[56] Ibid., fols 134[v], 148[r], 155[r], 160[r]; Seaver, *Wallington's World*, 145–6.

[57] For example, Wallington, 'Coppies', fol. 137[v].

[58] Greenham, *Works*, 871.

could not fasten any comfort on her, but the other woman th[t] I went vnto I myselfe did reciue good by' and of the other, he stated, 'I did the best I could', again noting that 'I receiued much comfort from her'. In 1654 he reported that he had successfully related 'such counsell as I Received of the Lord' to two afflicted believers. However, it does not appear that he actively sought out opportunities to assume this authoritative role, and he seems rather to have valued these experiences primarily for the potential they presented for mutual spiritual growth.[59]

By contrast, when plagued with doubts and insecurities for which he sought resolution, it was to ministers of the gospel that this scrupulous artisan turned. Seaver notes that the clergy were 'in an obvious sense the technical experts', to whom Wallington looked for aid. Furthermore, Booy observes the importance which 'ministerial guidance' exerted over Wallington's writing throughout his various notebooks. Yet Seaver also asserts that Wallington's godly community were not a 'priest-ridden people', playing down the striking degree of deference towards pastors and dependence on their guidance which frequently emerges from Wallington's letter-book.[60] Amongst his personal correspondence are several letters which Wallington exchanged with his brother-in-law, Livewell Rampaigne, rector of Broxholme in Lincolnshire, between 1625 and 1632. One such, 'concerning consoling [*sic*] and Instructings', conveys the strong impression that Rampaigne was intimately acquainted with Wallington's turbulent religious state. From his position of trust and respect, he berated his brother-in-law for giving free rein to creeping doubts about his election, repeatedly warning him against dwelling excessively on grief, sorrows and knowledge of his 'corrvptions', 'least you be ouerwhelmed and swollowed vp of it'.[61] Rampaigne hoped to quieten Wallington's anxious qualms that he had fallen out of divine favour, urging him to reflect rather on the many 'causes of comfort the Lord reacheth out to you' and 'from them conclude a continuance of his kindnes'.[62] These letters strongly suggest that Wallington was the instigator of their pious conference. He applied to his brother-in-law in a way analogous to that of the spiritual patients recorded in the epistles of Hall, Baynes and others, voicing a 'complaint' or 'grieuance'

---

[59] Wallington, 'The groth of a Christian', fols 169[r], 172[r–v]; Booy, ed., *Notebooks*, 336.
[60] Seaver, *Wallington's World*, 187–8; Booy, ed., *Notebooks*, 17–20.
[61] Wallington, 'Coppies', fol. 75[r–v], cf. 79[r], 82[r]–83[r].
[62] Ibid., fol. 83[r–v].

against his own religious behaviour, and, in return, expecting Rampaigne to supply lists of 'rvles' for his consolation and direction. For his part, Rampaigne sometimes failed to offer prompt responses, complaining of the many other duties which consumed his time. At one point he even had, rather remorsefully, to thank Wallington 'for putting me in minde of my great and weaighty charge'.[63]

Such evidence sits awkwardly alongside Kate Narveson's recent portrayal of Wallington's confident spiritual self-sufficiency and her assertion that he did 'not need a minister to explain how to regard and respond to any particular occasion'.[64] Further revealing exchanges, dating from 1638 to 1643, also survive between Wallington and the curate in his own parish, Henry Roborough. In one letter, prompted by the lesson of Malachi 2: 7, 'that the prest lips shall presarue knowledg and thou shalt seeke it at his mouth', Wallington made 'bould to write my mind vnto you desiering you to helpe me in this my temptations'.[65] Through this letter, Wallington bared his soul to his pastor, pouring out a personal and particular confession. He justified his address by evoking a gendered image, that of a woman in time of spiritual trial having recourse to her husband as the one set in loving authority over her. Tormented by the potential consequences of having broken a vow of spiritual 'reformation' made during a life-threatening sickness almost fifteen years previously, as well as overcome by fear that he might have profaned the sacrament by receiving it not 'with cherefulnes and delight' but out of 'costom, or for feare to offend my Father', Wallington besought Roborough: 'I pray you do not bauke with me in anything but deale as a faithfull dispenser of the truth'.[66] In a later letter, doubting the authenticity of his own faith, Wallington frantically sought confirmation of 'whither my trouble and sorrow were a right trouble and sorrow and my ioy a true and right ioy'. Labelling Roborough 'a skilfull phis[i]tion for my soule', the only occasion on which he employed this precise terminology of spiritual direction, Wallington implored: 'take some paines to studdy and finde out … whether my graces and comforts be of the right stampt or no'.[67] Paul Seaver has remarked of this letter that Wallington 'somehow believed Roborough could correctly diagnose'

[63] Ibid., fols 80ᵛ, 76ʳ.
[64] Narveson, *Bible Readers*, 119.
[65] Wallington, 'Coppies', fol. 118ʳ.
[66] Ibid., fols 118ʳ–119ᵛ.
[67] Ibid., fols 122ʳ–123ʳ.

his spiritual condition.[68] From a holistic examination of his letter-book, such a request appears entirely unsurprising, corresponding to the kind of aid to intricate emotional self-scrutiny which Baynes, Hall and others were regularly called upon by perplexed and doubting laity to provide.[69]

Wallington's remarkable text provides a window onto the wider genre of spiritual letter-writing and its importance in relation to Protestant practical divinity. The role of epistolarity in post-Reformation pastoral ministry offers significant scope for further historical investigation. As Gary Schneider has recently noted, the study of religion and letter-writing in the early modern period is a rich field of enquiry which is only now beginning to receive the historical attention it merits.[70] Further research is also required into the phenomenon of spiritual direction within English Protestantism; a thorough investigation of the role and status of the 'physician of the soul' offers potential for a re-evaluation of conventional understandings of the nature of contemporary lay-clerical relations.

As a contribution to these broader enquiries, this essay has offered a fresh perspective on the experience of religious doubt at the level of the individual believer and the ways in which both clergy and laity attempted to overcome it. A reassessment of the piety of Nehemiah Wallington, as the archetypal Calvinist 'doubter' and the archetypal godly 'individual conscience', has uncovered a significant and far-reaching counter-narrative of puritan religious experience. For many in a post-Reformation age, agonies of doubt could not be combated merely through introspection and personal self-examination, charting a lone course of spiritual progress through to a final assurance of salvation. An alternative tendency to regard the resolution of salvation anxieties as hinging on expert interpretation of signs and evidence is prevalent in the source material. Scrutiny of the printed letters and wider works of prominent exponents of spiritual counselling has uncovered a recurring discourse of the authoritative expertise of the Protestant clergy, who regarded themselves as spiritual physicians, adept at diagnosing and curing lay devotees. Whilst

---

[68] Seaver, *Wallington's World*, 105.
[69] See the analogous epistolary request from Hall's sister and Baynes's offer to diagnose a correspondent in this way: Wallington, 'Coppies', fols 38ʳ–39ᵛ, 57ᵛ–58ʳ.
[70] Gary Schneider, 'Introduction', in Anne Dunan-Page and Clotilde Prunier, eds, *Debating the Faith: Religion and Letter Writing in Great Britain, 1550–1800* (Dordrecht, 2013), 1–15, at 11–12.

Rosemary O'Day's contention that the period following the Reformation witnessed a professionalization of the clergy has not met with universal acceptance, the writings of these pastors certainly suggest their desire for the clerical office to be viewed in these terms.[71] Moreover, Wallington and other godly laity, seeking practical instruction in their uncertainties and scruples, affirmed the particular authority of ministers as the spiritual experts on whom the welfare of souls primarily rested.

---

[71] O'Day, *The English Clergy*; eadem, *The Professions in Early Modern England, 1450–1800: Servants of the Commonweal* (Harlow, 2000), 50–110. See critiques in Michael Hawkins, 'Ambiguity and Contradiction in the "rise of professionalism": The English Clergy, 1570–1730', in *The First Modern Society: Essays on English History in Honour of Lawrence Stone*, ed. A. L. Beier, David Cannadine and James M. Rosenheim (Cambridge, 1989), 241–69; John Morgan, *Godly Learning: Puritan Attitudes towards Reason, Learning and Education, 1560–1640* (Cambridge, 1988), 79–81.

Polemicist as Pastor: Daniel Featley's Anti-Catholic Polemic and Countering Lay Doubt in England during the early 1620s

Greg Salazar*

Selwyn College, Cambridge

In the months immediately before the collapse of the Spanish Match in 1623, an important debate took place between the Protestant controversialist Daniel Featley and John Percy (alias Fisher), the notorious Jesuit polemicist. The accounts of the debate alleged that the meeting was originally intended to be a small, informal, private conference to provide satisfaction to Humphrey Lynde's ageing cousin, Edward Buggs, concerning some doubts he was having about the legitimacy of the Protestant faith. Nevertheless, it is argued that Protestants used this conference to showcase a strong stance against Rome at a crucial moment when Catholicism was beginning to intrude further into England, and deliberately subverted royal policy by engaging Catholics in debate and publishing anti-Catholic polemical works. This was done to increase other Protestants' confidence that their Church was the true Church and Catholicism was a counterfeit version of Christianity. Ultimately, this episode demonstrates how Protestants' pastoral concerns about lay conversion could go hand in hand with their polemical activities and gives us a window into the particular mechanisms that Protestants employed as they struggled against the tide of political and ecclesiastical circumstances which threatened to diminish their influence in the 1620s.

In June 1623, a conference took place between England's foremost anti-Catholic polemicist, Daniel Featley, and the notorious Jesuit polemicist, John Percy (alias Fisher). In Featley's accounts of the debate, *The Fisher Catched in His Owne Net* (1623) and *Romish Fisher Caught and Held in His Owne Net* (1624), he alleged that the meeting was originally intended to be a small, informal, private conference to satisfy Edward Buggs, the ageing cousin of Featley's fellow controversialist Humphrey Lynde.[1] Buggs, having had several

---

* Tyndale House, 36 Selwyn Gardens, Cambridge, CB3 9BA. E-mail: gas43@cam.ac.uk.

[1] For the publications surrounding the conference, see Daniel Featley, *The Fisher Catched in His Owne Net* (London, 1623); idem, *The Romish Fisher Caught and Held in His Owne Net* (London, 1624); idem, *An Appendix to Fisher's Net* (London, 1624); A. C. [John Percy], *An*

Studies in Church History 52 (2016) 315–330
doi: 10.1017/stc.2015.18

© Ecclesiastical History Society 2016

encounters with Percy, was now having serious doubts about whether the Protestant Church was the true Church.[2] His situation was not uncommon: Percy had extensive experience as a Catholic apologist in England and was influential in the conversions of several prominent Londoners, including the countess of Buckingham. Indeed, the fact that Percy converted a member of the court of James VI/I illustrates his significance. The king and others had attempted to counter her doubts, not merely through offering a bribe (reportedly the huge amount of £2,000) but even by arranging a secret three-day conference at which Percy debated against the two anti-Calvinists Francis White and William Laud, and even against the king himself.[3] In spite of these endeavours the countess eventually converted to Catholicism.[4]

Answer to a Pamphlet Intitled: The Fisher Catched in His Owne Net (Saint-Omer, 1623); idem, *A Reply to D. White and D. Featley* (Saint-Omer, 1625); L. D. [John Sweet], *A Defense of the Appendix* (Saint-Omer, 1624); Edward Weston, *The Repaire of Honour, Falsely Impeached by Featlye a Minister* (Bruges [imprint false, printed at Saint-Omer], 1624); Henry Rogers, *An Answer to Mr. Fisher the Iesuite, His Five Propositions Concerning Luther* (London, 1623). See also Peter Milward, *Religious Controversies of the Jacobean Age: A Survey of Printed Sources* (London, 1978), 220–4; Joshua Rodda, '"Dayes of Gall and Wormwood": Public Religious Disputation in England, 1558–1626' (PhD thesis, University of Nottingham, 2012), 222–36, published as *Public Religious Disputation in England, 1558–1626* (Farnham, 2014).

[2] Buggs probably encountered Percy because his London residence was in 'Drurie lane', which Questier notes was a notorious hotbed of Catholicism: Featley, *The Fisher Catched*, sig. A2ʳ; Michael Questier, *Catholicism and Community in Early Modern England: Politics, Aristocratic Patronage and Religion, c.1550–1640* (Cambridge, 2006), 396.

[3] An account of this conference is in London, LPL, MS 1372, 'King James I meets John Percy, S. J. (25 May, 1622)', fols 58ᵛ–61ᵛ, which Timothy Wadkins transcribed and published: 'King James I meets John Percy, S. J. (25 May, 1622): An unpublished Manuscript from the Religious Controversies surrounding the Countess of Buckingham's Conversion', *Recusant History* 19 (1988), 146–54. For the various other accounts of this conference, see Francis White, *A Replie to Jesuit Fishers Answer* (London, 1624); Robert Baillie, *An Answere to Mr. Fishers Relation of a Third Conference Between a Certaine B. (as he stiles him) and Himselfe* (London, 1624); William Laud, *A Relation of the Conference Betweene William Lawd … and Mr. Fisher the Iesuite by the Command of King James* (London, 1639); A. C. [John Percy], *True Relations of Sundry Conferences had Between Certaine Protestant Doctours and a Iesuite Called M. Fisher* (Saint-Omer, 1626); I. F. [John Fisher], *The Answere Unto the Nine Points of Controversy, Proposed by Our Late Soueraygne* (Saint-Omer, 1625); A. C., *Reply to White and Featley*. See also Timothy Wadkins, 'The Percy-"Fisher" Controversies and the Ecclesiastical Politics of Jacobean Anti-Catholicism, 1622–1625', *ChH* 57 (1988), 153–69; idem, 'Theological and Religious Culture in Early Stuart England: The Percy/Fisher Controversies, 1605–41' (PhD thesis, Graduate Theological Union, 1988), 25–70; Rodda, 'Dayes of Gall and Wormwood', 198–212. According to Milward, Laud was actually the author of the Baillie account: *Religious Controversies*, 224.

[4] Wadkins notes that after her formal conversion the countess was 'banished from court' and 'Percy continued to live on parole in her home for the next ten years': 'The Percy-

Percy's primary tactic, which he used on both Buggs and the countess, was to argue that the Protestant Church – unlike the Catholic Church – could not produce a list of credible names of those who subscribed to the Protestant faith before Luther. Although Percy had formerly been in and out of London's Gatehouse and New Prisons, he was released shortly before 1622 on account of the increased toleration given to Catholics as a result of the Spanish Match negotiations.[5] Central to these negotiations was James's scheme to secure a political alliance between England and Catholic Spain through a marriage union between his son Charles and the Catholic infanta. During the period of negotiation, it became clear that, if the match were to be successful, the English would have to heed the demand of the Spanish for greater toleration for English Catholics.[6]

Fortunately for Buggs, Featley had gained considerable experience in confronting lay doubt and debating with Catholics during his tenure as an embassy chaplain to the English ambassador Sir Thomas Edmondes in Paris. There, between 1611 and 1613, he debated with the Catholic apologists 'D. Stevens', Richard Smith and Christopher Bagshaw, and apparently had remarkable success. In the first debate, a Scottish Catholic was converted to Protestantism, while in each of the two later debates, both of which were similarly prompted by wavering Protestant laypeople in need of credible replies to Catholic assaults on the Protestant faith, Featley managed to 'save the day' by assuaging the Protestants' doubts.[7] Moreover, since Featley was

---

"Fisher" Controversies', 158. See also Questier, *Catholicism and Community*, 395; Arthur Marotti, *Religious Ideology and Cultural Fantasy: Catholic and Anti-Catholic Discourse in Early Modern England* (Notre Dame, IN, 2005), 54; Caroline Hibbard, *Charles I and the Popish Plot* (Chapel Hill, NC, 1983), 66; *ODNB, s.n.* 'Villiers, Mary (*c*.1570–1632)'.

[5] *ODNB, s.n.* 'Percy, John [alias Fisher] (1559–1642)'. On Percy's evangelistic activity in prisons, see Peter Lake with Michael Questier, *Antichrist's Lewd Hat: Protestants, Papists and Players in Post-Reformation England* (New Haven, CT, 2002), 206; Wadkins, 'The Percy-"Fisher" Controversies', 155. On the increased tolerance of English Catholics in the early 1620s, see Questier, *Catholicism and Community*, 394–5.

[6] See Michael Questier, 'Introduction' to idem, ed., *Stuart Dynastic Policy and Religious Politics 1621–1625*, Camden 5th ser. 34 (Cambridge, 2009), 1–130, at 6; Thomas Cogswell, *The Blessed Revolution: English Politics and the Coming of War, 1621–1624* (Cambridge, 1989), 13, 15–16; idem, 'England and the Spanish Match', in Richard Cust and Ann Hughes, eds, *Conflict in Early Stuart England: Studies in Religion and Politics 1603–1642* (London, 1989), 107–33, at 111. See also W. B. Patterson, *King James VI and I and the Reunion of Christendom* (Cambridge, 1997), 315.

[7] For Featley's first conference, see Daniel Featley, *Transubstantiation Exploded* (London, 1638), sigs B8^v–B11^v; for his second, with 'D. Stevens' and subsequently Christopher Bagshaw, see ibid., sigs L7^r–N5^v; for his final debate, against Richard Smith, see Daniel

not only a trusted friend of Lynde but widely acknowledged as 'the leading anti-Catholic spokesman of the day' and a defender of the established Church and monarchy, he was the ideal person to alleviate Buggs's doubts.[8]

The debate itself, which took place in Lynde's house on Sheer Lane on Friday, 27 June 1623, is portrayed as rather uneventful, with each side jockeying to avoid deliberating according to the other's terms.[9] By examining the published accounts of this episode, this essay will explore lay doubt through the lens of a disputation between two leading apologists, one Catholic, the other Protestant. As we shall see, in this instance doubt about the nature of the true Church was a significant factor prompting conversion between Protestantism and Catholicism. Moreover, Featley and his contemporaries seemed to recognize that the early 1620s were witnessing a marked increase in the presence of doubt among the laity as to whether Protestantism was the genuine expression of Christianity. They appear to have associated this phenomenon with the prospect of the Spanish Match, and to perceive this increase in doubt as a sign of the growing dominance of Catholicism in England. I will argue that Featley and his Protestant cohort employed several tactics in order to counter this increased doubt among the laity. These strategies ultimately aided them in taking a strong stance against Rome in a large public forum at a crucial moment, when Catholicism was beginning to intrude further into England, and were designed to engender confidence in the Protestant laity that their Church was indeed the true Church. Through analysing an incident in which Protestant ministers went to great lengths to combat ideologies and political circumstances that were perceived to be generating doubts and endangering the souls of

---

Featley, *The Summe and Substance of a Disputation Between M. Dan. Featley, Opponent, and D. Smith … at Paris. Sept. 4. 1612* (London, 1630), appended to idem, *The Grand Sacrilege of the Church of Rome* (London, 1630), sigs Rr3[r]–Vv3[v]; idem, *Transubstantiation Exploded*; Myrth Waferer, *An Apologie for Daniel Featley* (London, 1634), especially sigs O2[r]–[v]. For Catholic replies, see S. E. [Edmund Lechmere], *The Conference Mentioned by Doctour Featly in the End of His Sacrilege* (Douai, 1632), especially sigs. A2[r]–[v]; L. I. [John Lechmere], *The Relection of a Conference Touching the Reall Presence* (Douai, 1635), especially sigs Oo3[r]–[v]. See also Hugh Adlington, 'Chaplains to Embassies: Daniel Featley, anti-Catholic Controversialist Abroad', in idem, Tom Lockwood and Gillian Wright, eds, *Chaplains in Early Modern England: Patronage, Literature and Religion* (Manchester, 2013), 83–102.

[8] Wadkins, 'The Percy-"Fisher" Controversies', 164.

[9] Featley, *Romish Fisher Caught*, sig. *3[r].

their laypeople, this essay will contribute to our historical understanding of conversion.

In addition, this analysis will shed light on several of the wider themes of early Stuart political and religious history. In his study *Conversion, Politics and Religion*, Michael Questier focused on the more inward, personal and experiential reasons for conversion, and argued that polemical discourse was not the sole reason, but that shifts in allegiance were actually 'the culminations of a range of experiences as wide as the number of causes which unsettled the minds of contemporaries in religion'.[10] What follows will build on Questier's work by exploring the specific ideologies that generated lay doubt and will demonstrate how, in this instance, the political and ecclesiastical circumstances of the early 1620s could affect lay conversion.

Throughout, it is important to remember that knowledge of the details of this debate has been transmitted through several highly stylized polemical publications. These works were published during the politically charged period of the early 1620s and the truthfulness of each side's account was strongly contested by their opponents. For this reason, it will be necessary to explore how the Protestant account of this debate made its way into print and to assess its credibility.[11] Since the episode explored here is an isolated case study, the focus will be on drawing conclusions about its nature and purpose. More general conclusions about the dynamics of lay doubt and the connections between doubt and conversion must be set aside for another occasion.

COUNTERING LAY DOUBT IN EARLY STUART ENGLAND

Doubt was a considerable pastoral issue for early Stuart Protestants. Anthony Milton has noted that during this period the Catholic appeal to a concrete historical record, rather than the Protestant appeals to arguments of doctrine, 'seemed to offer the clearest guide to the troubled layman'. Accordingly, Catholic polemicists 'increasingly focused upon the issue of the Protestants' ancestry' because 'the visible continuity of an institutional church became the more necessary if men's

---

[10] Michael Questier, *Conversion, Politics and Religion in England, 1580–1625* (Cambridge, 1996), 39.

[11] Space precludes examination of how the Catholic account made its way into print, or of the credibility of that account.

salvation and their access to a properly validated divine authority were to be assured'. As a result, many Protestant ministers began to articulate their views about the problems they were having with laypeople in their parishes and some laypeople even left the faith.[12]

Doubts were perceived to have eternal implications. Questier has pointed out that in early Stuart England opinions about which Church was counterfeit and which was authentic were significant, since individuals gave their allegiance to the Church that 'professed the true religion, the only certain path to salvation'. As we have noted, the presence of doubt among the laity was also becoming a significant pastoral issue, and it functioned as a litmus test of whether Catholicism was gaining an upper hand, especially if – as with the countess of Buckingham – the layperson was a high-profile individual. Moreover, since many believed that the genuine Church 'must continually increase', a decrease in Protestant members through conversion might produce further doubts as to whether their Church was the true Church.[13]

Doubts could creep in through either private or public conferences with Catholics, as well as through reading anti-Protestant polemical tracts. Protestants therefore chose to counter lay doubt by similarly combating Catholics through conferences and publication.[14] Canon 66 of the 1603 Canons of the Church of England presented conferences with recusants as a pastoral duty,[15] and Featley referred to this canon in his explanation of why he took part in such events, explaining that he had a pastoral duty to protect the flock under his care from harmful ideologies that might prompt doubts and ultimately lead lay members away from the true Church. He could not 'suffer Wolves to enter into our Folds, and worry our dearest Lambs, bought at the high price of our Redeemer's Blood, and that before our eyes, and not open our mouthes for their rescue'.[16] Believing that Percy was labouring 'to keep those in the dungeon, whom [he held] in captivity' by '[forbidding his] Captives to read our Relations',

---

[12] Anthony Milton, *Catholic and Reformed: The Roman and Protestant Churches in English Protestant Thought, 1600–1640* (Cambridge, 1995), 270–1.

[13] Questier, *Conversion, Politics and Religion*, 12, 9.

[14] Ibid. 13–14.

[15] Gerald Bray, ed., *The Anglican Canons 1529–1947*, CERS 6 (Woodbridge, 1998), 357; cf. Richard Montagu, 'Concerning Recusancie of Communion with the Church of England', ed. Anthony Milton and Alexandra Walsham, in Stephen Taylor, ed., *From Cranmer to Davidson: A Church of England Miscellany*, CERS 7 (Woodbridge, 1999), 69–101, at 73.

[16] Featley, *Appendix to Fisher's Net*, sig. H3*[r].

Featley toiled even more to set these prisoners free. This disputation, therefore, was for Featley not merely an academic undertaking; he was driven by a deep pastoral concern for the souls of those under his care, and laboured that many might 'see a glimpse of light' and 'look after more'.[17] He believed that disputation with Catholics and the publication of anti-Catholic polemic would aid in resolving the doubts of the laity.

Accordingly, Featley's most common device in countering lay doubt was to demonstrate that Roman Catholicism was a counterfeit version of Christianity.[18] Central to his argument was the attempt to prove the incompatibility of the doctrines established at the Council of Trent with the Scriptures and the early Church. In the course of the debate, therefore, Featley listed fifteen doctrines that he believed to have been established at Trent, but which were contrary to the Scriptures and the Church's teaching throughout history. These included 'that there is a treasury of Saints merits', the necessity of the Latin mass, 'that Pope's pardons are requisite or useful to release soules out of Purgatory', dependence on the pope for 'all ecclesiastical power', and the pope's authority to canonize saints.[19] In his efforts to debunk Catholicism, Featley also appealed to many of the same scriptural texts and the same apocalyptic rhetoric used by other early Stuart Protestants to prove that the papacy was the Antichrist.[20] Clearly, Featley's method was designed to convince any who might doubt the credibility of Protestantism by not only focusing on Catholicism's fraudulent claims but also drawing out the stark contrast between a truthful Protestant Church and a deceitful and counterfeit Catholic adversary.

---

[17] Ibid., sig. Dd3ᵛ.

[18] Featley could also employ a more ambiguous form of anti-Catholicism that incorporated more inclusive language, yet was still far removed from the moderate positions of White and Laud: see ibid., sigs D3ᵛ, Ff1ᵛ, Gg3ᵛ, L3∗ʳ, Ii4ᵛ–Kk1ʳ; Anthony Milton, 'A Qualified Intolerance: The Limits and Ambiguities of Early Stuart Anti-Catholicism', in Arthur F. Marotti, ed., *Catholicism and Anti-Catholicism in Early Modern English Texts* (New York, 1999), 85–115, at 86–7, 89, 90, 110; idem, *Catholic and Reformed*, 176–9; Montagu, 'Concerning Recusancie', ed. Walsham and Milton, 75–6.

[19] Featley, *Fisher Catched*, sigs B2ʳ–ᵛ. For his critique of the pope's ability to canonize the saints, see idem, *Appendix to the Fisher's Net*, sig. L4∗ᵛ; for other critiques, see ibid., sig. Ii3ʳ.

[20] Ibid., sigs Gg3ᵛ–Hh2ᵛ, N4∗4ʳ; cf. Anthony Milton, 'The Church of England, Rome, and the True Church: The Demise of a Jacobean Consensus', in Kenneth Fincham, ed., *The Early Stuart Church, 1603–1642* (Basingstoke, 1993), 187–210, at 194; idem, *Catholic and Reformed*.

THE STRUGGLE OVER THE TRUE CHURCH IN HISTORY

Featley also combated lay doubt by countering the notion that the Protestant Church was obliged to produce a catalogue of names to prove that it was a true Church. Percy argued that the Scriptures clearly decreed that the Church must be visible and continuous at all times in history. This is why the Catholic Church had already produced their own historical catalogue of committed adherents to the Catholic faith throughout its sixteen centuries, since that record was 'the easiest and readyest way, to discerne this true visible Church of Christ, from all Hereticall Conventicles'.[21] Featley countered Percy's claims, arguing that 'divine and infallible faith is not built upon the deduction out of humane history' since 'the names of all Professors are not nor ever were upon Record' and 'all ancient Records are not now extant'.[22] By analysing his question, Featley undercut the root of Percy's query by showing that it was grounded on a false supposition. The doubts that resulted from Percy's heckling were unwarranted, since his reasoning was faulty.[23] Instead, the wavering layperson could have confidence in their Protestant Church: the Protestant faith alone was consistent with the Scriptures and the early Church.[24]

By carefully analysing Featley's approach, one can note a number of remarkable features of his strategy. First, it is clear that Featley rejected the response to Percy's 'where was the Protestant Church before Luther?' given by some of his fellow Protestants. In tracing their pre-Reformation Protestant heritage, these Protestants cited the most significant clergy – 'Schoolmen, abbots, and even popes' – who held 'Protestant' views, but who remained within the Catholic Church. By contrast, Featley aligned himself with the 'Foxeian' tradition that located its Protestant line in 'the medieval heretical sects: the Waldensians, Albigensians, Lollards, Hussites and others' – those

---

[21] A. C., *Answer to a Pamphlet*, sig. G4ᵛ; Percy, *Reply to White and Featley*, sigs B1ᵛ, L2ʳ. The Catholic works Percy lists as including catalogues are John Percy, *A Reply Made Unto Mr. Anthony Wotton and Mr. Iohn White Ministers* (Saint-Omer, 1612), sigs Ii3ʳ–Kk3ᵛ; S. N., *Appendix to the Antidote* (Saint-Omer, 1621). For a list of other Protestant authors who responded in print to Percy, see Wadkins, 'The Percy-"Fisher" Controversies', 166.

[22] Featley, *Appendix to the Fisher's Net*, sigs S1∗ᵛ, S3∗ʳ.

[23] Ibid., sig. S2∗ᵛ.

[24] Ibid., sig. A4ᵛ; cf. idem, *Fisher Catched*, sigs A4ᵛ–B1ʳ. Featley also published a complete catalogue that he supposedly received from his 'friend' at Oxford: *Appendix to the Fisher's Net*, sigs F4ʳ–G1ᵛ.

who had been persecuted by the erring Catholic church and may not have been even mentioned in any official record.[25] Featley flatly denied that he 'ought to prove the Visibility of the Protestant Church, by having recourse merely to the corrupt Popish Church'. Though 'that way [was] perhaps beaten by some' it seemed to him 'a slipperie & dirty way'. He did not need 'to seek the golden purity of faith, amidst the dung, and drosse of Romish superstitions, and deprivations in later ages'. Instead, he cited Abbot, Ussher, Simon Voious, Illiricus, Wolssius, Lydius and Crispin as those 'worthies' who 'have shewne mee a more excellent way'.[26]

That Featley sided with the Foxeian tradition and sidestepped Percy's demands reveals that the lack of an explicit Protestant history, particularly for the centuries leading up to Luther, was a serious point of vulnerability for Protestantism in general.[27] As a result, Featley expended significant effort to make sure that the focus of his contributions remained on the flaws within the Catholic faith rather than the weaknesses within Protestantism. At one point of climax Percy's supporters interrupted the quarrel by shouting 'names, names, names', to which Featley replied: 'What, will nothing content you but a Buttery booke? You shall have a Buttery Booke of names, if you will stay a while'.[28] At the conclusion, Featley finally consented to give a list of names, although he did so only for the first two centuries of the early Church, then saying that he would not continue until Percy confirmed that these were the names of legitimate Protestants.[29] His objective was to maintain control over the direction of the debate, for in this way he was able to minimize the flaws in his own position and accentuate the reasons why one should doubt not only the validity of Percy's questions, but also, and especially, Catholicism's claim to be the true Church. This carefully devised strategy seems to have been crafted with the intention of dissolving the doubts of wavering Protestants and giving them

[25] For these two groups, see Milton, *Catholic and Reformed*, 281–95.

[26] Featley, *An Appendix to Fisher's Net*, sigs K3*[r]–[v]. Nonetheless, it is important to remember that Featley was not wholly 'Foxeian' since in his catalogues he drew on clerics whom many Foxeians would have opposed. Also, the non-Foxeian, Simon Birckbek, notes in his preface 'to the reader' that Featley 'gave mee the right hand of Fellowship, encouraging me to go on with my Catalogue': Simon Birckbek, *The Protestants Evidence* (London, 1635), 'To the Reader'; see Milton, *Catholic and Reformed*, 284–5.

[27] Featley, *Romish Fisher Caught*, sig. F2[v]; idem, *Appendix to Fisher's Net*, sig. V2*[v].

[28] Featley, *Fisher Catched*, sig. B4[r].

[29] Ibid., sigs D1[r]–D2[r].

confidence that their faith was indeed authentic and that their salvation was secure.

PROTESTANT SUBVERSION IN THE 1620S

By examining closely the details of how Protestants organized this conference and how Protestant accounts of the debate were published, one can detect a consistent pattern of risk-taking and strategic manoeuvring from the Protestant side. These tactics allowed the Protestants to subvert royal policies and to continue publishing antipapal polemical works and engaging Catholics in debate. These two tools in particular were utilized to counter doubt and their subversion tactics shielded them from the consequences of being discovered by the authorities. In the early 1620s, James VI/I went to significant lengths to silence anti-Catholic polemic. The 1620 and 1621 proclamations, 'against excess of lavish and licentious speech of matters of state', and the 'directions on preaching' promulgated in August 1622 were designed to ensure that all forms of anti-popery were removed from publications and preaching, on the ground that they called his foreign policy into question.[30] Some ministers, including Joseph Hall, were temporarily imprisoned for disobeying the king's orders, and after these proclamations were issued Cogswell has found that 'very little even implicit criticism of royal policy slipped into print'.[31] James's regulations were stringent policies indeed, and by comparison, asserts Cogswell, 'Archbishop Laud never restricted the activities of his clergy as drastically as James I did with the 1622 Directions'.[32] It appears that these Directions were intended to hinder Protestants from publishing anti-Catholic polemic and engaging in anti-Catholic conferences, the two weapons they used to counter doubt. The fact that the conference between Featley and Percy was held at all, and that any account of the event was published, gives us a clear indication of how resolute Protestants were in their mission to counter doubts in Protestant England.

---

[30] For the 1620 and 1621 proclamations, see J. F. Larkin and P. L. Hughes, eds, *Stuart Royal Proclamations*, 2 vols (Oxford, 1973), 1: 495–6, 519–21. The 4 August 1622 'directions on preaching' are printed in Thomas Fuller, *The Church History of Britain* (London, 1655), sigs Oooo3^r–^{v}; cf. Cogswell, *Blessed Revolution*, 20, 32.

[31] Cogswell, *Blessed Revolution*, 34. For Hall's imprisonment, see ibid. 44–5; for other imprisonments, see Alexandra Walsham, '"The Fatall Vesper": Providentialism and Anti-Popery in Late Jacobean London', *P&P* 144 (1994), 36–87, at 80.

[32] Cogswell, *Blessed Revolution*, 51.

All accounts agree that the meeting was originally framed as a private conference following dinner at Humphrey Lynde's house. However, when the Jesuits arrived they were shocked to find Lynde's house filled with a large crowd drawn from London's elite society, which included (among others) the earl of Warwick.[33] When Percy and his assistant protested to Lynde of 'the inequalitie of that Audience', both Lynde and Featley replied that they 'could not helpe it'[34] since they 'did not expect' such a crowd.[35] While it is possible that a massive crowd of London's Protestant elite had happened to hear about the conference at Lynde's house, it is much more likely that the Protestants overplayed the extent to which they were innocent of publicizing the debate or helpless to turn the crowd away. Instead, the presence of the large crowd at a supposedly private debate may also have been engineered to counter lay doubt. The fact that the Catholics were overwhelmingly outnumbered, and clearly on hostile territory, might reassure the hesitant layperson and further confirm the superiority of Protestantism. Simply surveying the sheer strength in the number of observable Protestant adherents present might be enough. This plan was foolproof: since the crowd had not been formally invited, Lynde certainly could not be accused of organizing an event that went against the king's orders. Moreover, the fact that Featley's assistant was Francis White, a noted moderate polemicist, would help to shield those present. The group would also be protected by the presence of the earl of Warwick, who, according to Featley, was there to act as a mediator and 'seasonably [interpose]' if 'the Disputants or standers-by grew into any heat or distemper'.[36]

Despite James's regulations, several of the Protestants involved in the Sheer Lane conference seem additionally to have made deliberate plans to continue publishing anti-Catholic literature. Featley claimed that his initial account of the conference, *The Fisher Catched in His Owne Net* (1623), was licensed and published without his

---

[33] Wadkins, 'The Percy-"Fisher" Controversies', 164; *ODNB*, *s.n.* 'Percy, John [alias Fisher]'; Featley, *Appendix to the Fisher's Net*, sig. Bb2ᵛ; cf. L. D., *Defense of the Appendix*, sig. B4ʳ.

[34] A. C., *Answer to a Pamphlet*, sig. B4ᵛ.

[35] Featley, *Fisher Catched*, sig. A3ᵛ. For Featley's reply to this accusation, see *Appendix to the Fisher's Net*, sig. Bb2ᵛ.

[36] Featley, *Romish Fisher Caught*, sig. *3ʳ.

knowledge.[37] While this scenario also is not impossible, it is suspect, since Featley was an ecclesiastical licenser (an official authorizer of manuscripts for publication), and keenly alert to James's publication policies.[38] Moreover, the work was only later attributed to Featley, and was his only anti-Catholic work to be published anonymously.

Featley never confessed to publishing anti-Catholic literature anonymously in defiance of James's policies; nor did he specify in print that publication of this conference was motivated by a desire to assuage the doubts of troubled Protestants. Nevertheless, there is some evidence that this is at least a credible possibility. It may be significant that a manuscript account of the conference exists in the Bodleian Library that is virtually identical to *The Fisher Caught*. Although the hand is somewhat different from the majority of Featley's other writings, it does bear a striking resemblance to that used in at least one letter attributed to him.[39] If this manuscript is Featley's original account, it is notable that his name is absent, so that it may have been intended to be anonymous from its inception. The manuscript (like the later printed work) was probably crafted on the basis of the three sources he allegedly used to write his later relation of the conference, *The Romish Fisher Caught and Held in His Owne Net*: his memory, the testimony of those 'who were present at the Conference' and 'especially' the 'Notes as were taken in the Conference'.[40]

---

[37] Ibid., sig. *3ᵛ. On the plausibility of Featley's claim that the account was published without his knowledge, see Arnold Hunt, *The Art of Hearing: English Preachers and their Audiences, 1590–1640* (Cambridge, 2010), 138–41.

[38] For the list of works Featley licensed, see Edward Arber, ed., *A Transcript of the Registers of the Company of Stationers of London, 1554–1640*, 5 vols (London, 1875–94), 3: 283b – 4: 185 (21 July 1617 – 1 October 1629). On Featley's licensing activities, see Anthony Milton, 'Licensing, Censorship, and Religious Orthodoxy in Early Stuart England', *HistJ* 41 (1998), 625–51; Arnold Hunt, 'Licensing and Religious Censorship in Early Modern England', in Andrew Hadfield, ed., *Literature and Censorship in Renaissance England* (Basingstoke, 2001), 127–46; Peter Lake, *The Boxmaker's Revenge: 'Orthodoxy', 'Heterodoxy' and the Politics of the Parish in Early Stuart London* (Stanford, CA, 2001); Cyndia Susan Clegg, *Press Censorship in Jacobean England* (Cambridge, 2001); eadem, *Press Censorship in Caroline England* (Cambridge, 2008); S. Mutchow Towers, *Control of Religious Printing in Early Stuart England* (Woodbridge, 2003); Sheila Lambert, 'Richard Montagu, Arminianism and Censorship', *P&P* 124 (1989), 36–68.

[39] For the manuscript account, see Oxford, Bodl., Rawlinson MS D.817, 'The occasion and office of the late conference had betweene Dr White and Dr Ffeatley, w[i]th Mr Ffisher and Mr Sweete Jesuits', fols 156ʳ–169ᵛ. This hand looks similar to a letter attributed to Featley in Rawlinson MS D.47, fols 20ᵛ–22ʳ.

[40] Featley, *Romish Fisher Caught*, sig. *3ʳ.

Before publishing his accounts, Featley was clearly aware that James was displeased that the conference had taken place. The bishop of Durham, Richard Neile, who as a noted anti-Calvinist was no doubt delighted to relay the news, apparently informed Featley that James demanded 'that the truth of the late Conference be certified to his Maiestie', 'further meetings staid', and 'all future meetings … forbidden'.[41] It was Neile, not George Abbot, archbishop of Canterbury, who was the one chosen to relay James's message to Featley. This is surprising, not least because Featley was Abbot's chaplain, and is a strong indication of Abbot's marginalization. Despite printing his work anonymously, Featley came dangerously close to being censured by James, but was rescued by the formal collapse of the Spanish Match in 1624, which prompted James to lift the ban on the publication of anti-papal polemical literature and participation in anti-Catholic debate.[42]

The Sheer Lane conference and subsequent publications are striking illustrations of the fact that Featley went to significant lengths to rescue wavering laypeople by continuing to publish anti-Catholic polemic and to engage in anti-Catholic debate. This pattern of risk-taking and strategic manoeuvring was directly linked to his mission to counter lay doubt. The early 1620s were an anxious time for English Protestants. Given the prospect of the Spanish Match and the fact that a number of the Protestant laity had already defected to the Catholic faith, Protestant ministers were worried about their fate, and with good reason. They knew that with the match would come further toleration of Catholics, and Catholicism in England would continue to increase.[43]

Featley was aware that he was already losing his influence at court and with it his capacity to confront lay doubt by contending in these important battles for the souls of those defecting to Rome. Several historians have noted that Featley would have been the obvious choice for the role of responding to the countess's doubts in the 1622 conference. Despite this – and also despite the fact that he had already begun drafting both a treatise (presumably in preparation for the conference) entitled 'The trial by fayth by the tutchstone of truth; for the Countesse of Bucking[ham]' and a letter to her – he

---

[41] Featley, *Fisher Catched*, sig. D2^v.
[42] Featley, *Romish Fisher Caught*, sig. ¶4^v.
[43] Cogswell, 'England and the Spanish Match', 115.

was denied the opportunity. That Featley was passed over and White and Laud were chosen instead is significant, for the views of White and Laud were characteristic of a more moderate position that would counteract Catholicism's claims without anathematizing Rome's status as a true Church and thereby calling James's developing foreign relations policy into question.[44] Featley's marginalization from the debate concerning the countess of Buckingham was seen by Protestants as an indication of whether or not they would be given future opportunities to contend against their Catholic adversaries.

The fact that Featley and his Protestant cohort were losing their potential to influence doubting Protestants motivated them to take active steps to defy the encroachments of Catholicism, and to alleviate doubts in the 'sheep' under their care by boldly publishing anti-Catholic polemic, despite the associated risks. The publication of anti-papal propaganda and practice of anti-Catholic debate were essential and indispensable tools for this mission. Anti-popery could attract wavering laypeople during emotionally heightened times, suggests Lake, since 'it incorporated deeply held beliefs and values and it helped to dramatize and exorcise the fears and anxieties produced when those values came under threat'.[45] This was especially true during periods like the 1620s, 'when men groped for the reassuring certainties and simplicities of extreme confessional regulation'.[46] Although we can never be certain when exactly Featley and the organizers of the conference decided to capitalize on this opportunity, it nevertheless gave them the chance to engender vital assurance in a wavering Protestant populace, and to prevent the laity from being thrust further towards the precipice of converting to the religion of the Antichrist.

Following the conference, Featley claimed that Buggs approached Lynde to thank him for arranging the meeting and to '[assure] him that he was well resolved now of his Religion'.[47] Despite Percy's scepticism regarding this claim, Lynde too gave his final confirmation of this report in a letter published at the end of Featley's *Appendix to the*

[44] For Featley's unfinished treatise and letter to the countess, see Rawlinson MS D.47, fols 1ʳ–4ᵛ, 15ʳ. On the appointment of Laud and White instead of Featley, and the shifts at court, see Wadkins, 'The Percy-"Fisher" Controversies', 164; Milton, *Catholic and Reformed*.
[45] Peter Lake, 'Anti-Popery and the Structure of Prejudice', in Cust and Hughes, eds, *Conflict in Early Stuart England*, 72–106, at 97.
[46] Milton, 'Qualified Intolerance', 110.
[47] Featley, *Fisher Catched*, sig. D2ᵛ.

Fisher's Net. There we learn that Buggs had a son who had defected to Rome. Nevertheless, on account of Featley's labours, Buggs boldly avowed that he was now so convinced in his faith that even 'if his sonne would not leave his religion, and the priests company, he would leave him'.[48] It is difficult to assess how seriously we can take these claims, since they are reported in a propagandist tract. Buggs may have been snatched from the enemy's hand, but even had his doubts remained, the Protestants wanted it to appear as if they had been resolved. By presenting the outcome of the debate in this way Featley and his contemporaries attempted to assure other wavering laypeople that their doubts could likewise be resolved. Indeed, portraying one's own side as victorious seems to have been a consistent feature of these stylized publications from both Protestants and Catholics. It was through the medium of these and other similar works that Catholic and Protestant apologists hoped to have an impact beyond the select few who attended the debate and to attract further converts to their respective Churches. In the end, in the Protestants' public portrayal of the debate the outcome was clear: Featley had succeeded in forging bonds of faith and confidence which were even more enduring than family ties.

CONCLUSION

The episode explored in this essay sheds light on wider debates and themes relevant to early Stuart political and religious history. In particular, this essay has built on Questier's work by demonstrating how the political and ecclesiastical circumstances of the 1620s appear to have been a factor in shaping the encounter between Featley, Buggs and Percy. Featley and his Protestant cohort appear to have linked the amplified presence of doubt among the laity with the proposed Spanish Match, and to have interpreted this upsurge as a warning that Catholicism was beginning to infiltrate England. As such, they were not passive bystanders, but seem to have gone to great lengths to develop strategies and mechanisms to defy the political shifts that increasingly marginalized them in the early 1620s. By exploring the nature of these Protestants' steadfast commitment to countering lay

---

[48] Featley, *Appendix to the Fisher's Net*, sig. Bb4ᵛ. For Percy's scepticism, see A. C., *Answer to a Pamphlet*, sig. F4ʳ. For Featley's response to Percy's doubts, see Featley, *Appendix to the Fisher's Net*, sigs Oo1ᵛ–Oo2ᵛ. Featley published as a part of his *Appendix to the Fisher's Net* a short treatise by Lynde, which defended Featley: ibid., sig. Bb4ᵛ.

doubt, this study has shed light on early Stuart Protestantism more generally by demonstrating that even those Calvinist conformists, like Featley, who were celebrated as activists and defenders of the established Church and the monarchy, could in some circumstances employ subversive tactics which were strikingly similar to the manoeuvres normally ascribed to more radical early Stuart Protestants.

Additionally, by investigating the theme of conversion, we have observed how on this occasion doubt over the nature of the true Church could be a significant factor in an individual's defection to a different faith. This has confirmed Anthony Milton's arguments by demonstrating that there could be a strong correlation between one's denominational commitment and the perceived eternal consequences of conversion: Buggs' salvation was perceived to be dependent on whether or not he was a part of the true Church. Accordingly, this study has shown that the disputants were not merely involved in an academic exercise, but were concerned to play a pivotal pastoral role in shaping laypersons' perceived eternal destiny.

Ultimately, while this essay is only a case study, it has explored the various strategies that pastors employed to shepherd the sheep under their care, especially when various ideologies generated doubts that endangered the flock. Moreover, it has shown that when a 'private' conference was made public through publication, these works were likely to be tailored in order to present their respective party as victorious in order to win further converts. Perhaps, as additional studies are conducted and we gain a firmer grasp of these complex and intricate questions, we will better understand the ideologies, experiences and contexts that ultimately conspired to generate both doubt and conversion within the early Stuart Church in England.

'Perhaps he cannot know': John Wesley's Use of Doubt as a Principle of his 'Catholic Spirit'

Kelly Diehl Yates*
University of Manchester

John Wesley published his sermon 'Catholic Spirit' in 1750, after he and his preachers had experienced persecution by Church leaders. Wesley stressed that persecution stemmed from lack of tolerance, and one of the reasons for this was the absence of liberty of thinking in the Church. In order for liberty of thinking to be practised, one had to be able to doubt one's own opinions, thereby accepting the limitations of one's knowledge. Most of this sermon, now lauded for its ecumenical brilliance, asserts that such acceptance provides space for tolerance. This tolerance leads to Christian unity. In addition to exploring the sermon, this essay addresses An Answer to the Rev. Mr. Church's Remarks on the Rev. Mr. John Wesley's Last Journal *(1745),* Letter to a Roman Catholic *(1749) and Wesley's correspondence with Gilbert Boyce (1750). The argument thus provides an example of how doubt contributed to the Methodist emphasis on tolerance.*

'My first desire (and prayer to God) is that I may live at peace with all men', declared John Wesley (1703–91), Church of England priest and a founder of the Methodist movement, in 1745.[1] Wesley may have yearned for peace, but he often found himself embroiled in controversy, especially in the first thirty years of his ministry.[2] This may be one of the reasons he wrote much of his corpus in

---

* 6729 NW 39th St, Bethany, OK 73008, USA. E-mail: kelly-yates@outlook.com.

  I would like to express my appreciation to Geordan Hammond for his helpful comments on this essay, and to Hunter Cummings and Timothy Crutcher for their insights on an earlier draft.

[1] John Wesley, *An Answer to the Rev. Mr. Church's Remarks on the Rev. Mr. John Wesley's Last Journal* (1745), in *The Works of John Wesley*, ed. Frank Baker et al. (Oxford / Nashville, TN, 1976–), 9: 81–122, at 81.

[2] See Josiah Henry Barr, *Early Methodists under Persecution* (New York, 1916); David Hempton, *Methodism: Empire of Spirit* (New Haven, CT, 2005), 1–92; Albert Lyles, *Methodism Mocked: The Satiric Reaction to Methodism in the Eighteenth Century* (London, 1960); Brett C. McInelly, *Textual Warfare and the Making of Methodism* (Oxford, 2014). For a list of works by opponents, see Clive D. Field, 'Anti-Methodist Publications in the Eighteenth Century: A Revised Bibliography', *Bulletin of the John Rylands University Library of Manchester* 73 (1991), 159–280.

Studies in Church History 52 (2016) 331–346   © Ecclesiastical History Society 2016
doi: 10.1017/stc.2015.19

pragmatic response to his opponents, even though he claimed he hated writing 'controversially'.[3] His 1750 sermon, 'Catholic Spirit', was no exception, as the strife he encountered immediately before writing it was probably what provoked its inception.[4] Not only was he at odds with Calvinists who opposed his Arminianism, but he had recently experienced riots instigated by Roman Catholics against him and his preachers in Ireland.[5] Wesley wrote *Letter to a Roman Catholic* at about the same time as 'Catholic Spirit', as he sought to convince Roman Catholics in Ireland to end their violence against the Methodists.[6] The question Wesley wished to answer in the two works was one that many Anglicans had been attempting to answer since the Glorious Revolution of 1688/9: 'How shall we form our beliefs on fundamental matters of religion and morality so as to live together in social harmony, when we can no longer appeal to a shared and unified tradition?'[7] This enquiry stems from an underlying philosophical problem, which is as old as humanity itself: 'Is it possible for people to live together in peace and harmony?'

This essay will examine the arguments for creating religious coexistence that emerged from John Wesley's writings on relations with Catholicism. In 'Catholic Spirit', Wesley argued that through

---

[3] For Wesley's writings as response to controversy, see Albert Outler, 'The Place of Wesley in Christian Tradition', in Kenneth Rowe, ed., *The Place of Wesley in the Christian Tradition: Essays delivered at Drew University in Celebration of the Commencement of the Oxford Edition of the Works of John Wesley*, 2nd edn (Lanham, MD, 1980), 15–32; Isabel Rivers, *Reason, Grace and Sentiment: A Study of the Language of Religion and Ethics in England 1660–1780*, 2 vols (Cambridge, 2005), 1: 206. For instance, Wesley wrote *Principles of a Methodist* in 1740 in response to Josiah Tucker (1713–99), who had published an essay documenting what he called 'inconsistencies' in Methodism in *A Brief History of the Principles of Methodism* (Oxford, 1742): Rupert E. Davies, 'An Introductory Comment to *Principles of a Methodist*', in *Works*, ed. Baker et al., 9: 47. For Wesley's hatred of controversy, see ibid. 21: 134 (*Journal*, 13 January 1758).

[4] John Wesley, 'Catholic Spirit', in *Works*, ed. Baker et al., 2: 81–96. The sermon first appeared in Wesley's *Sermons on Several Occasions*, 3 vols (London, 1750), 3: 181–7, and later as a separate publication, *Catholick Spirit: A Sermon on 2 Kings x. 15* (London, 1755).

[5] For the Calvinist-Arminian controversy as influencing the writing of 'Catholic Spirit', see James L. Schwenk, *Catholic Spirit: Wesley, Whitefield, and the Quest for Evangelical Unity in Eighteenth-Century British Methodism* (Lanham, MD, 2008), 29–48. For early Methodist work in Ireland and subsequent persecution, see C. H. Crookshank, *History of Methodism in Ireland*, 3 vols (Belfast, 1885); Samuel J. Rogel, *John Wesley in Ireland 1747–89*, 2 vols (Lampeter, 1993); Dudley Levistone Cooney, *The Methodists in Ireland* (Dublin, 2004).

[6] John Wesley, *Letter to a Roman Catholic* (Dublin, 1750), and a total of three editions in Wesley's lifetime: *The Works of the Rev. John Wesley, M.A.*, ed. Thomas Jackson, 14 vols (London, 1872; first publ. 1829–31), 10: 80.

[7] Nicholas Wolterstorff, *John Locke and the Ethics of Belief* (Cambridge, 1996), x.

'doubting one's opinions' it was possible to express liberty of conscience and so pave the way for religious tolerance. He expressed a similar approach in another tract to be examined here, *Letter to a Roman Catholic*. Doubt therefore became for Wesley a means by which it was possible to reach an accommodation with those who held differing religious beliefs.

In the generation immediately preceding Wesley, British empiricist philosophers attempted to answer the question of how to live in harmony, seeing their task as a vital one. They were confronting questions raised about the treatment of Dissenters and Jews, and trying to keep Britain from revolution.[8] Thomas Hobbes (1588–1679), Francis Bacon (1561–1626) and John Locke (1632–1704) all took up this enterprise, giving slightly different resolutions.[9] It is in two of John Locke's treatises, *An Essay concerning Human Understanding* and (the first) *Letter concerning Toleration*, that we may find the closest parallel to Wesley's 'Catholic Spirit'.[10] Wesley drew indirectly from Locke regarding the limits of human understanding, which included acknowledgement that one's own opinions could be incorrect, or that doubting one's opinions may lead to admitting that the opinions of another person or Church might be correct. Together, these themes could lead to what Locke called 'toleration', which may be seen as a synonym for Wesley's 'Catholic Spirit'.

Wesley read Locke's *Essay* in 1725, a month after he had been ordained deacon at Christ Church, Oxford.[11] Although he was to write an evaluation of it in 1781, this did not address 'doubt' or 'opinions', although he did say that Locke's work contained 'many

---

[8] For the treatment of Jews in late seventeenth-century England, see David S. Katz, *The Jews in the History of England 1485–1850* (Oxford, 1994), 145–89.

[9] For an overview of British empiricism, see Stephen Priest, *The British Empiricists*, 2nd edn (New York, 2007), 1–10. For Locke and the Jews, see Nabil Matar, 'John Locke and the Jews', *JEH* 44 (1993), 45–62.

[10] For Locke and toleration, see John Marshall, *John Locke, Toleration and Early Enlightenment Culture* (Cambridge, 2006). For Locke and Wesley, see James E. Pedlar, 'Sensing the Spirit: Wesley's Use of Empiricism and his Use of the Language of Spiritual Sensation', *Asbury Journal* 67 (2012), 85–104.

[11] Richard Paul Heitzenrater, 'John Wesley and the Oxford Methodists' (PhD dissertation, Duke University, 1972), 58, 511; according to Heitzenrater, Wesley not only read *An Essay concerning Human Understanding*, but also owned a copy. It was included in the curriculum of the school he founded, Kingswood: John Wesley, 'A Short Account of the School in Kingswood, Near Bristol' (1768), in *Works*, ed. Jackson, 13: 283–9, at 288.

excellent truths'.[12] Whilst Wesley used principles from Locke, he was not aiming for a purely epistemological approach to opinion, doubt or tolerance. Instead he used themes from Locke's writings to explore how Methodism could survive alongside other Christian traditions. This essay is not an attempt to prove that Wesley had either of Locke's works in view while penning 'Catholic Spirit'. It accepts that, as Henry D. Rack has argued, in philosophical terms Wesley was an 'empiricist disciple of Locke even though with some important limitations'.[13] Timothy J. Crutcher is also correct in arguing that Wesley was influenced by Aristotle; however, this need not lead to denying that Locke influenced Wesley.[14] This essay argues instead that 'Catholic Spirit' evokes the essential nature of the toleration that was so eloquently expressed in Locke's work and in the Glorious Revolution: the hope that Christians, by doubting their own opinions in humility, could live side by side without violence.

'Catholic Spirit' has been described as an influential document in the promotion of Christian tolerance. David Butler, for instance, called it 'the best example in the Wesleyan corpus of his early understanding of toleration', and Herbert McGonigle described it as a call for Christians to put aside unkind criticism, judgements and strife.[15] Jean Orcibal suggested that even by the end of the twentieth century, 'Catholic Spirit' had not been given the recognition it deserved:

> It is in no way to detract from the founder of Methodism to state that [Wesley's] immense efforts to reveal to Anglo-Saxon Protestantism the spiritual riches of other Christian traditions were preceded and made

[12] John Wesley, *Remarks upon Mr. Locke's Essay concerning Human Understanding* (1781), in *Works*, ed. Jackson, 13: 455–64.

[13] See Henry D. Rack, *Reasonable Enthusiast: John Wesley and the Rise of Methodism*, 3rd edn (London, 2002), 33; idem, 'A Man of Reason and Religion? Wesley and the Enlightenment', *Wesley & Methodist Studies* 1 (2009), 1–17. Richard E. Brantley, *Locke, Wesley and the Method of English Romanticism* (Gainesville, FL, 1984), aligned Wesley directly with Locke. Rack agrees that Wesley was influenced by Locke, but disagrees with Brantley about the extent of this influence, arguing that Brantley conveniently avoided Wesley's appeal to spiritual senses, which was not Lockean: Henry D. Rack, 'Methodism and Romanticism', *Proceedings of the Wesley Historical Society* 45 (1985), 63–5, at 64.

[14] Timothy J. Crutcher, *The Crucible of Life: The Role of Experience in John Wesley's Theological Method* (Lexington, KY, 2010), 16.

[15] David Butler, *Methodists and Papists: John Wesley and the Catholic Church in the Eighteenth Century* (London, 1995), 50; Herbert McGonigle, 'John Wesley: Exemplar of Catholic Spirit', in *Ecumenism and History: Studies in Honour of John H. Y. Briggs*, ed. Anthony R. Cross (London, 2002), 50–68, at 55.

possible by the unwearied and generous activity of an author whose literary mission has not yet been granted the recognition it deserves in the history of ecumenism.[16]

In order to grasp the meaning of 'Catholic Spirit', Wesley's main argument must be understood. The relevant paragraph, located about a quarter of the way into the message, states that:

> … although every man necessarily believes that every particular opinion which he holds is true (for to believe any opinion is not true, is the same thing as not to hold it); yet can no man be assured that his own opinions, taken together, are true. Nay, every thinking man is assured they are not, seeing *humanum est errare et nescire*: 'To be ignorant of many things, and to mistake in some, is the necessary condition of humanity.' This, therefore, he is sensible, is his own case. He knows, in the general, that he himself is mistaken; although in what particulars he mistakes, he does not, perhaps he cannot know.[17]

To put it simply, Wesley is saying that every person has opinions and believes them strongly, but has no guarantee that his or her system of opinions is true. This lack of assurance and certainty is equivalent to doubt. A thoughtful person will acknowledge that he or she has opinions and is consequently obliged to admit that others also have opinions. In order to admit that another person has different opinions, he or she must doubt the veracity of all their own opinions. This doubt is not a doubt of one's faith, or about whether or not a person has 'assurance of salvation', or doubt of the existence of God. It is doubt of one's own capacity for perceiving knowledge.

Of individual Christian groups, at least before 1777, Wesley remarked that their distinctives could often be defined only as opinions.[18] In 1745 he had said of the Moravians, from whom he had

---

[16] Jean Orcibal, 'The Theological Originality of John Wesley and Continental Spirituality', transl. R. J. A. Sharp, in Rupert Davies, A. Raymond George and Gordon Rupp, eds, *A History of the Methodist Church in Great Britain*, 4 vols (London, 1965–88), 1: 83–111.

[17] *Works*, ed. Baker et al., 2: 84.

[18] See ibid. 3: 579–92, a sermon preached at the laying of the foundation stone of his New Chapel in London on 21 April 1777, in which he described the Calvinist separation from his movement, beginning with the protest of George Whitefield (1714–70) when Wesley published the sermon 'Free Grace' (1739; ibid. 542–63). He asserted: 'None of these have any manner of connection with the original Methodists. They are branches broken off from the tree; if they break from the Church also, we are not accountable for it': ibid. 591. Rowland Hill (1744–1833), a Dissenting minister, wasted no time in publishing a

learned so much and with whom he nonetheless disagreed theolog-ically: 'I am still afraid their whole Church is tainted with Quietism, universal salvation, and antinomianism – I speak (as I said elsewhere) of antinomian opinions, abstracted from practice, good or bad. But I should rejoice if there lay no other objection against them than that of erroneous opinions'.[19] Also in 1745, he began Part II of *A Farther Appeal to Men of Reason and Religion* with a reflection on the same theme: 'It is not my present design to touch on any particular opin-ions, whether they are right or wrong; nor on any of those smaller points of practice which are variously held by men of different per-suasions'.[20] In this case, then, he distinguishes the opinions from the argument, so as to minimize their importance.

In the same way, Locke, in his 'Epistle to the Reader' introduc-ing *An Essay concerning Human Understanding*, admitted concerning his own work: 'For though it be certain, that there is nothing in this Treatise of the Truth whereof I am not fully persuaded; yet I con-sider myself as liable to Mistakes as I can think thee; and know, that this book must stand or fall with thee, not by any Opinion I have of it, but thy own.'[21] Locke here illustrated what Wesley would ar-gue sixty years later: doubting one's own opinions leads to humility, which leads in turn to tolerance. However, whilst Locke admitted in humility that he was capable of mistakes, Wesley did not often do the same. This became evident as Wesley and his preachers were caught up in successive conflicts, from the second Jacobite rising to local riots.

Wesley did later admit that he had changed, writing that he had stepped back from his more rigid assertions concerning the Church. He addressed this issue further in his reply to the Anglican bishop of Exeter, George Lavington (1684–1762), who had authored a scathing

---

scathing attack on Wesley for this sermon in *The Imposture Detected, and the Dead Vindicated in a Letter to a Friend, Containing Some Gentle Strictures on the False and Libellous Harangue Lately Delivered by Mr. John Wesley, upon his Laying his First Stone of his New Dissenting House, near the City Road* (London, 1777). Hill accused Wesley of deism, of 'Popish Pelagianism', of allowing women to preach, and of Dissent, and quoted from the 1770 Methodist *Conference Minutes* in which the doctrine of predestination was officially denounced.

[19] *Works*, ed. Baker et al., 9: 85. On Wesley and antinomianism, see W. Stephen Gunter, *The Limits of Love Divine* (Nashville, TN, 1989).

[20] John Wesley, *A Farther Appeal to Men of Reason and Religion*, Part II, in *Works*, ed. Baker et al., 11: 203–71, at 203.

[21] John Locke, *An Essay Concerning Human Understanding* (1689), ed. Peter H. Nidditch (Oxford, 1975), 7.

attack on Wesley in *The Enthusiasm of Methodists and Papists Compar'd.*[22] Lavington declared: 'We may see in John Wesley that he was once a strict Churchman, but gradually put on a more catholic spirit, tending at length to Roman Catholicism.'[23] To this, Wesley replied: 'This is half true (which is something uncommon with you) and half false. It is true for thirty years past I have "gradually put on a more catholic spirit", finding more and more tenderness for those who differed from me either in opinions or *modes of worship*.'[24] Moreover, Wesley exclaimed, 'not only do you not believe yourself; you do not believe the conclusion which you make as if you would prove'.[25] This appears to be an astute recommendation to Lavington that he should doubt his own opinions. Yet, even in sharp debate, Wesley assured Lavington: 'you are at liberty to enjoy this argument also; and let it prove what it can prove',[26] thereby assuring him of his 'liberty of conscience'.

Liberty of conscience was a key issue for Wesley. He used the phrases 'liberty of conscience' and 'liberty of thought / thinking' interchangeably. Most eighteenth-century Anglicans believed that liberty of conscience was comprised of at least two components: the preservation of an established Church and freedom of worship secured by law for Protestant Dissenters (excluding Unitarians).[27] Liberty of conscience was a principle that allowed people freedom to choose their own religion (provided that it was Protestant and Trinitarian) and freedom to worship God according to their own conscience; Jews and Roman Catholics were not granted the same rights

---

[22] Lavington was bishop of Exeter from 1746 to 1762: *ODNB*, *s.n.* 'Lavington, George (1684–1762)', online edn (May 2009), at: <http://www.oxforddnb.com/view/article/16136>, accessed 11 February 2015. There had been rioting against the Methodists before Lavington arrived in Exeter, according to John Cennick, *An Account of a Late Riot at Exeter* (London, 1745); see also Colin Haydon, 'Bishop George Lavington of Exeter (1684–1762) and *The Enthusiasm of Methodists and Papists Compar'd*', *Southern History* 37 (2015), 60–85.

[23] George Lavington, *The Enthusiasm of Methodists and Papists Compar'd*, Part II (London, 1750).

[24] John Wesley, *A Second Letter to the Author of* Enthusiasm of Methodists and Papists Compar'd (London, 1751), in *Works*, ed. Baker et al., 11: 387–429, at 422–3.

[25] Ibid. 426.

[26] Ibid. 410.

[27] John C. English, 'John Wesley and the Rights of Conscience', *Journal of Church and State* 37 (1995), 351–63, at 352. Freedom of worship did not extend to Roman Catholics, who were under the limits of penal law until the Roman Catholic Relief Act of 1791 (31 Geo. III. c. 32).

as Protestants.[28] Wesley asserted that liberty of conscience was a right 'by the law of God and nature as well as that of England'.[29] Regarding religious liberty, Wesley argued for natural right, as in his *Thoughts upon Liberty*, where he asserted that religious liberty was the right to choose our own religion, 'to worship God according to our own conscience, according to the best light we have'.[30]

Wesley did not believe that Roman Catholicism at the time allowed for liberty of conscience, as he assumed that belief in papal supremacy did not allow for this. He declared outright that he believed the 'fundamental doctrine of popery' to be the 'universality of the Roman Church and the supremacy of the Bishop of Rome'.[31] This doctrine had been articulated in *Unam Sanctam* (1302): 'furthermore, we declare, we proclaim, we define that it is absolutely necessary for salvation that every human creature be subject to the Roman Pontiff'.[32] Wesley reprinted this declaration in his abridgement of John Williams's *Catechism*, changing 'the Roman Pontiff' to the 'Pope of Rome', and replying that Christ alone is the head of the Church.[33] In *The Advantage of the Members of the Church of England over those of the Church of Rome* (1753), Wesley addressed the importance of liberty of

[28] Jews had been expelled from England by Edward I in 1290. They were readmitted to England in 1655/6, but were not granted citizenship until the Jewish Naturalization Act of 1753 (26 Geo. II. c. 26), which was repealed in 1754: David Feldman, 'Conceiving Difference: Religion, Race, and the Jews in England *c*.1750–1900', *History Workshop Journal* 76 (Autumn 2013), 160–81, at 167. It was not until the Jewish Relief Act of 1858 (21 & 22 Vic., cap. 49), which allowed Jews to sit in Parliament, that all restrictions against Jews were lifted.

[29] *The Letters of the Rev. John Wesley, A.M.*, ed. John Telford, 8 vols (London, 1931), 4: 151–2 (John Wesley to the Earl of Dartmouth, 10 April 1761).

[30] John Wesley, *Thoughts upon Liberty*, in *Works*, ed. Jackson, 11: 34–46, at 37–8; see also Theodore R. Weber, *Politics in the Order of Salvation: Transforming Wesleyan Political Ethics* (Nashville, TN, 2001), 322.

[31] *Letters*, ed. Telford, 3: 246 (John Wesley to 'A Gentleman at Bristol', 6 January 1758).

[32] *CICan.* 1: 1245. The Council of Trent (1545–63), though it addresses justification, does not address the issue of those who are justified being subject to papal authority: see Norman P. Tanner, ed., *Decrees of the Ecumenical Councils*, 2 vols (London, 1990), 2: 671–80.

[33] [John Wesley], *A Roman Catechism faithfully drawn out of the allowed Writings of the Church of Rome with a Reply thereto* (1756), in *Works*, ed. Jackson, 10: 86–128, at 87. This document is an abridgement of a tract by John Williams, later bishop of Chichester, *A Catechism representing the Doctrines and Practices of the Church of Rome with an Answer thereunto* (London, 1683); see also Butler, *Methodists and Papists*, 94–9. Wesley affirmed that he had published *A Roman Catechism. Works*, ed. Baker et al., 22: 167 (*Journal*, 20 December 1768). A copy in the John Rylands Library, Manchester, states that it was 'reprinted' in 1756 but lacks any ascription of authorship; however, it can be assumed that this is the document to which Wesley referred, though it is obviously a reprint of Williams's work.

conscience, asserting that this liberty had been restored to Protestants in the Reformation.[34]

Much later, Wesley reacted to the Catholic Relief Act of 1778 by publishing his *Letter to the Printer of the* Public Advertiser (1780). Here Wesley seems to limit liberty nearly to the point of conscience alone for Roman Catholics.[35] He feared that giving them more freedom would threaten his ideas of liberty, because his understanding was that they were shackled by their allegiance to a foreign power, the pope.[36] He did not believe that a Catholic could be trusted even if they did take an oath to the government because the pope had the power to overturn any oath a Catholic swore.[37] This letter seems at first to contradict what Wesley had written thirty years previously in *Letter to a Roman Catholic*. Nevertheless, while he sought to preserve English liberty, which he believed could be threatened by Roman Catholics, Wesley did not proscribe them from worshipping God in the way that they chose.

Although it appears there was no Roman Catholic response to 'Catholic Spirit', there was a later, broader critique of the Methodists. In 1760, Richard Challoner (1691–1781), vicar apostolic of the London district, wrote that Wesley and his followers, along with other Protestants, were not part of the true Church of God.[38] Challoner's assumption was that salvation is only guaranteed to those who belong to the true Church of God, which he defined as the Roman Catholic Church. It had been this sort of thinking that Wesley had sought to counter in 'Catholic Spirit'.

Wesley had commented on Challoner's earlier publication, *The Grounds of the Old Religion*, in his *Journal* during 1743, criticizing Challoner's claim that 'the Scripture is not the sole rule of faith; at least if not interpreted by private judgment, because private judgment has no

---

[34] John Wesley, *The Advantage of the Members of the Church of England over those of the Church of Rome* (1753), in *Works*, ed. Jackson, 10: 133–9, at 139.

[35] Catholic Relief Act (18 Geo. III, c. 60); *Letters*, ed. Telford, 6: 370–3 (John Wesley to the printer of the *Public Advertiser*, 12 January 1780).

[36] Weber, *Politics*, 330–1.

[37] *Letters*, ed. Telford, 6: 370–3.

[38] Richard Challoner, *A Caveat against the Methodists: Shewing how unsafe it is for any Christian to join himself to their Society, or to adhere to their Teachers* (London, 1760), 17–18. This went through six editions: Oliver A. Beckerlegge, ed., *John Wesley's Writings on Roman Catholicism* (London, 2003), 19. On Challoner, see James Barnard, *The Life of the Venerable and Right Reverend Richard Challoner, D.D., Bishop of Debra* (Dublin, 1793); Eamon Duffy, *Challoner and his Church* (London, 1981).

place in matters of religion'. Wesley responded: 'Why, at this moment you are appealing to *my* private judgment, because private judgment; and you cannot possibly avoid it. The foundation of *your* as well as *my* religion must necessarily rest here.' He continued: 'First you must judge for yourself whether you are implicitly to follow the church or no. And also which is the true church. Else it is not possible to move one step forward.'[39] In appealing to private judgement, one must doubt one's own opinions. This assertion of the importance of private judgement is indicative of the value Wesley attributed to liberty of conscience.

Wesley defined 'opinion' in a letter he wrote fifteen years after publishing 'Catholic Spirit'. Answering John Newton's request that Wesley clarify the difference between 'essential' and 'opinion', Wesley answered, 'Whatever is "compatible with a love to Christ and a work of grace" I term an opinion.' Specifically regarding his theological disputes with Calvinists, he designated election and final perseverance as opinions, which, he explained, was why he had not expelled preachers from his connexion who had Calvinist leanings. Nonetheless, some preachers had left of their own accord because 'they did not hold our doctrine'.[40] These preachers considered 'Particular Election' and 'Final Perseverance' as essential, but Wesley did not.

Unfortunately, Wesley did not give his definition of 'essential' in this letter to Newton. Wesley's *Letter to a Roman Catholic* comprises a list of beliefs shared by both Protestants and Catholics which Ted Campbell has suggested could be viewed as defining Wesley's 'essentials'. These include: the existence of one God, Christ's incarnation and atonement, his crucifixion and resurrection, the work of the Holy Spirit, forgiveness of sin, and the reality of heaven and hell. From this, Campbell concludes that Wesley would label any religious statements other than these as opinions.[41]

Herbert McGonigle pointed out that there are connections between 'Catholic Spirit', and *Letter to a Roman Catholic,* in that they were written within months of each other whilst Wesley was in Ireland facing opposition to the Methodist movement, and both address the issue of how Christians with different opinions can live and work

---

[39] *Works*, ed. Baker et al., 19: 320 (*Journal*, 25 March 1743).

[40] *Letters*, ed. Telford, 4: 297 (John Wesley to John Newton, 14 May 1765).

[41] Ted A. Campbell, 'The Shape of Wesleyan Thought: The Question of John Wesley's Essential Doctrines', *Asbury Theological Journal* 59 (2004), 27–48, at 30–1.

together in tolerance.[42] Several scholars have explored the similarities. Thomas Oden called the *Letter to a Roman Catholic* 'a model of what is meant by the Catholic Spirit'.[43] Albert Outler described it as 'an olive branch to the Roman Catholics', and declared it an appeal to the 'potential community of faith and love between Roman Catholics and those commonly called Protestant'.[44]

Randy Maddox, on the other hand, in an attempt to clarify Wesley's use of the word 'opinion', contrasted it with his use of the word 'doctrine'. In this reading, doctrines, according to Wesley, were 'authoritative Christian teachings of religion *in their own right*'.[45] These included Scripture, the Church Fathers, the Thirty-Nine Articles, and the Anglican Homilies. 'Opinions', in contrast, were an individual's *personal understanding or interpretation* of those doctrines.[46] Maddox observed that 'such a distinction between opinions and doctrines was essentially a theological expression of the emerging Enlightenment conviction of a disjunction between one's knowledge or ideas (opinions) and their objects (doctrines)'.[47] He traced this conviction to Locke's *Essay concerning Human Understanding*.[48] The central proposition of Wesley's conviction 'was not that some ideas were less certain than others, but that all human ideas and judgements were fallible',[49] and that, therefore, they must forever remain open since further evidence might cause them to change.[50] Wesley articulated it this way: 'although every man necessarily believes that every particular opinion he holds is true (for to believe any opinion is not true is the same thing as not to hold it), yet no man can be assured that all his opinions taken together can be true'.[51] Locke dealt with 'opinions' in a similar way in *A Letter concerning Toleration*:

---

[42] McGonigle, 'John Wesley', 65.

[43] Thomas C. Oden, *John Wesley's Teachings*, 2 vols (Grand Rapids, MI, 2012), 1: 126.

[44] Albert Outler, ed., *John Wesley* (London, 1964), 92.

[45] Randy Maddox, 'Opinions, Religion, and "Catholic Spirit": John Wesley on Theological Integrity', *Methodist History* 47 (1992), 63–87, at 65.

[46] See *Letters*, ed. Telford, 3: 157–8, 167 (John Wesley to William Dodd, 5 February, 12 March 1756).

[47] Maddox, 'Opinions', 81 n. J. C. D Clark, *English Society, 1660–1832: Ideology, Social Structure and Political Practice during the Ancien Regime*, 2nd edn (Cambridge, 2000), 9, argues that 'Enlightenment' is no longer a useful term of historical explanation.

[48] Locke, *Essay* 2.8.7 (ed. Nidditch, 134).

[49] Maddox, 'Opinions', 65.

[50] Ibid. 81 n.

[51] *Works*, ed. Baker et al., 2: 84.

We must, therefore, seek another cause of those evils that are charged upon religion, and if we consider right, we shall find it to consist wholly in the subject that I am treating of. It is not the diversity of opinions (which cannot be avoided), but the refusal of toleration to those that are of different opinions (which might have been granted), that has produced all the bustles and wars that have been in the Christian world upon account of religion.[52]

Locke lamented further that a person who refused to tolerate others was 'cruel and implacable towards those that differ from him in opinion, be he indulgent to such iniquities and immoralities as are unbecoming the name of a Christian … let such a one talk never so much of the Church, he plainly demonstrates by his actions that it is another kingdom he aims at and not the advancement of the kingdom of God'.[53] Intolerance of others, therefore, according to Locke, had no place in the behaviour of a Christian. Wesley agreed. In his *Letter to a Roman Catholic* he declared,

Does your tender love to all men – not only the good, but also the evil and unthankful – approve you the child of your Father which is in heaven? Otherwise, whatever you believe and whatever you practice, you are of your father the devil. Are you ready to lay down your life for your brethren? And do you do unto all as you would they should do unto you? If not, do not deceive your own soul: you are but an heathen still.[54]

Once again he appealed to opinions: 'Now, can nothing be done, even allowing us on both sides to retain our own opinions, for the softening our hearts towards each other, the giving a check to this flood of unkindness, and restoring at least some small degree of love among our neighbours and countrymen?'[55] He acknowledged the extensive history of strife between Roman Catholics and Protestants, and confessed that fault lay on both sides. Instead of asking Catholics to convert he appealed to them to practise their own religion, which taught love of their neighbour, and to doubt that their particular brand of Christianity was the only one. Wesley then listed

[52] John Locke, *A Letter concerning Toleration*, 3rd edn (Boston, 1743), 24–5. Locke did not extend toleration to atheists or Roman Catholics.
[53] Ibid. 10.
[54] *Works*, ed. Jackson, 10: 80.
[55] Ibid.

rhetorical questions to which he knew Catholics had to answer 'yes' about the shared practices between them and Protestants, for example: 'Do you hurt nobody, by word or deed? Are you true and just in all your dealings? Do you take care to pay whatever you owe?'[56] He concluded:

> O brethren, let us not still fall out by the way! I hope to see you in heaven. And if I practice the religion above described, you dare not say I shall go to hell. You cannot think so. None can persuade you to it. Your own conscience tells you the contrary. Then, if we cannot as yet think alike in all things, at least we may love alike.[57]

In the eighteenth century, each side of the Catholic-Protestant debate often declared that the other was heading for hell. Challoner, for example, in his *Caveat*, argued that their beliefs would result only in the judgement of God.[58] On the other side, the Anglican bishop George Lavington argued that the Methodists taught 'popish doctrine', for which there was no escape from the 'damnation of hell'.[59] Instead, Wesley here asked his Catholic readers to suspend that certainty, and by doing so to doubt that they were the only ones who would be in heaven. Locke had been concerned with the same issue:

> For every church is orthodox to itself, to others, erroneous or heretical. For whatsoever any church believes, it believes to be true and the contrary thereunto those things it pronounces to be error. So that the controversy between these churches about the truth of their doctrines and the purity of their worship is on both sides equal; nor is there any judge, either at Constantinople or elsewhere upon earth, by whose sentence it can be determined.[60]

If there is no judge that can determine whether what one Church believes is correct over against another Church's doctrine, then even a Church must doubt some opinions. Wesley adopted the same point of view.

---

[56] Ibid. 84.

[57] Ibid. 81.

[58] Challoner, *Caveat*, 5.

[59] George Lavington, *The Enthusiasm of Methodists and Papists Compar'd*, Part I (London, 1749), 13.

[60] Locke, *Toleration*, 25.

In the *Letter to a Roman Catholic*, Wesley tried to reason with Catholics and to persuade them to acknowledge that their shared heritage with Protestants could be a bridge across the great divide of schism. Outler is right to understand the historical background to *Letter to a Roman Catholic* as the Methodist movement's first attempts at preaching and founding societies in Ireland. He views it as a letter to a presumably friendly Irish Catholic, and suggests that nothing 'like this little essay in ecumenical theology appears anywhere else in Wesley's writings, but it is consistent with his essential beliefs and heterogeneous opinions; it is also a fair sample of what he actually meant by "catholic spirit"'.[61] For Outler, 'Wesley's point, here and elsewhere, is that religious reality lies deeper than religious conceptuality – as evidenced by those simple but true believers whose "opinions" may be incompetent and those impeccably orthodox persons whose hearts nevertheless remain estranged from God.'[62]

Wesley's method in 'Catholic Spirit' may seem practical, but problems of applying it arose when he encountered Christians who disagreed with his definition of essentials and opinions.[63] Gilbert Boyce (1712–1800), for instance, pastor of the General Baptist church in Coningsby, Lincolnshire, argued that believers' baptism was an essential, but Wesley argued it was not: an apparently irreconcilable difference.[64] The solution to the problem of applying the method of 'Catholic Spirit' may, nonetheless, lie in a letter from Wesley to Boyce. Wesley engaged Boyce in a civil and calm exchange, explaining that he 'held nothing to be (strictly speaking) necessary to salvation but the mind which was in Christ'. If he were to hold to believer's baptism as necessary for salvation, then he would have to conclude that every Quaker was not a Christian, and this Wesley was not willing to do. Wesley therefore qualified believer's baptism as an 'outward mode of worship', remarking: 'I do not conceive that unity in the outward modes of worship is so necessary among the children of God that they cannot be children of God without it – although I once was.'[65] Wesley had made the same point in 'Catholic Spirit'.[66]

[61] Ibid. 493.
[62] Ibid. 92.
[63] *Works*, ed. Jackson, 10: 133–9.
[64] See *Works*, ed. Baker et al., 26: 418–26, for the correspondence between them during 1750.
[65] Ibid. 425.
[66] Ibid. 2: 86.

Never in the correspondence did he claim that Boyce's salvation was at risk due to his different beliefs, but he knew that he was unlikely to convince Boyce to change his mind, so he conceded that the debate was finished. His work, he wrote, was not the making of Baptists or Anglicans but the making of Christians.[67] He allowed Boyce to keep his own opinion, for he did not insist that Boyce agree.

This essay has argued that Wesley's idea of 'doubting one's opinions' led to an emphasis on liberty of conscience, which informed his 'Catholic Spirit'. Locke's epistemic doubt, upon which Wesley drew – which may be expressed as 'I do not know whether or not I know' – became a key element of this 'Catholic Spirit'. Although Wesley defined 'opinion' in his letter to Newton, scholars such as Maddox and Campbell have attempted to clarify what he meant. In his *Letter to a Roman Catholic*, Wesley articulated beliefs that Catholics and Protestants shared, and these may be seen as 'essentials', which he considered vital to faith.

The Anglican Lavington correctly accused Wesley of having formerly been rigid in his beliefs, but Wesley not only argued that he had changed, he slyly encouraged Lavington to doubt his opinions and assured him of his own liberty of conscience. In remarking on the Catholic Challoner's writings, Wesley argued that Challoner was not allowing for liberty of conscience, which was one of Wesley's main issues with Catholicism. In Baptist pastor Gilbert Boyce, Wesley encountered the conflict caused by differing definitions of opinions and essentials. Although he had once been rigid about 'outward modes of worship' as essentials, he had 'gradually put on a more catholic spirit'.

Wesley never employed this idea of doubt in a way that would lead to a lack of assurance of faith or lack of trust in God. As a Protestant, he did not ask Roman Catholics to deny transubstantiation. As an Arminian, he did not expect Calvinists to put aside predestination or the Moravians their quietism to attain salvation.[68] All of these, Wesley concluded, were opinions, and opinions could be doubted. In

---

[67] Ibid. 26: 426.

[68] Wesley did argue that Calvinists should give up predestination, which he called 'blasphemy': *Works*, ed. Baker et al., 3: 542–63. However, he did not say that those who believed in predestination were not a part of the Church. See also *A Dialogue between a Predestinarian and his Friend*, 2nd edn (London, 1741), which ran to five editions in Wesley's lifetime: *Works*, ed. Baker et al., 13: 227–38. In *Predestination Calmly Considered* (London, 1752), which ran to seven editions in Wesley's lifetime, Wesley pleaded: 'If we serve God, our agreement is far better than our difference. Therefore, as far as may be, setting aside

a 'Catholic Spirit', all Christians were asked to humbly doubt the truth of their own opinions, for by doubting they allowed others liberty of conscience.

---

that difference, let us unite in destroying the works of the devil, in bringing all we can from the power of darkness into the kingdom of God's dear son': ibid. 13: 258–320, at 319–20 . Finally, he asserted that no one could doubt that Calvinists had true religion, but held wrong opinions: 'On the Trinity' (1775), ibid. 2: 374–86, at 376.

'The extirpation of Athanasianism': The Considerable Doubts of Francis Stone (1738–1813)

Colin Haydon*

University of Winchester

This essay examines the doubts of Francis Stone, rector of Cold Norton, Essex – doubts which brought him notoriety and ruin. In 1806, Stone preached a sermon, four editions of which appeared by 1809, expressing doubts about Anglican doctrine and the Thirty-Nine Articles. He maintained that Christ, though God's 'great messenger', was merely human, and that the Virgin Birth was a myth. Moreover, he also doubted the 'Athanasian trinity in unity' and the doctrine of the atonement. Stone's doubts were far from new. He had expressed various concerns forcibly in print and had played a major part in the raising of the anti-subscription Feathers Tavern petition. He was determined to teach only 'that, which … [might] be concluded and proved by the Scripture'. But the storm provoked by the sermon was terrible. In 1808, Stone was arraigned before the bishop of London's consistory court. There he declared that the Church of England had no authority to override his conscience. Nevertheless, the court rejected his arguments and deprived him of his living; when he appealed to the Court of Arches, it upheld the sentence. Stone's doubts produced an important test case and a powerful warning for Anglican clerics holding heterodox opinions (and, indeed, liberal churchmen wanting just 'free' and 'candid' theological debate) in the conservative 1800s. Moreover, the issues Stone raised foreshadowed controversies which erupted long after his death.

Following the English Reformation, popery was often likened to a dragon or hydra; but by the early eighteenth century Church of England divines seemed satisfied that, doctrinally, gifted polemicists such as Edward Stillingfleet had slain it. Moreover, by the 1730s Dissent was in disarray and appeared in decline. Yet within the bosom of the established Church lay a serpent which, though largely slumbering, periodically uncoiled: a serpent of doubt about the Church's own doctrines and, principally, its adherence to the doctrine of the Trinity.

* Department of History, Faculty of Humanities and Social Sciences, University of Winchester, Winchester, SO22 4NR. E-mail: Colin.Haydon@winchester.ac.uk.
 I am grateful to Grayson Ditchfield and Anthony Mansfield for their help when I was preparing this essay.

Studies in Church History 52 (2016) 347–363   © Ecclesiastical History Society 2016
doi: 10.1017/stc.2015.20

The Scriptures themselves gave no direct sanction to Trinitarian belief. The one possible warrant in the King James Bible, 1 John 5: 7, had been rejected as a spurious interpolation by such intellectual colossi as Richard Bentley (notably in his 1717 praelection as Regius Professor of Divinity at Cambridge), Edward Gibbon and Richard Porson.[1] Trinitarianism could appear a suspicious and unjustifiable reconciling of Christian theology and Greek philosophy. The most unequivocal statement of the doctrine was the Athanasian Creed (whose date and authorship were, and remain, the subject of scholarly debate).[2] Besides its dogmatic assertion of 'the Unity in Trinity, and the Trinity in Unity', the Creed contained anathemas insisting that, without belief in 'the Catholick Faith', including Trinitarianism, a soul 'shall perish everlastingly', in 'everlasting fire'. The Athanasian Creed was an integral part of the Church of England's doctrine and liturgy: the eighth of the Thirty-Nine Articles proclaimed that it and the Nicene and Apostles' Creeds 'ought thoroughly to be received and believed: for they may be proved by most certain warrants of holy Scripture', and in 1662 the Book of Common Prayer decreed that the Athanasian Creed should be said at morning prayer on thirteen days each year, including Christmas Day, Epiphany, Easter Sunday, Ascension Day, Whit Sunday and, naturally, Trinity Sunday. Subscription to the Thirty-Nine Articles and their Trinitarianism was required for matriculation at Oxford and graduation at Cambridge, and, for the clergy, upon nomination to a benefice. Unitarianism was outlawed under the Blasphemy Act of 1698 and 'any person … deny[ing] in his Preaching or Writing the Doctrine of the Blessed Trinity' was ineligible for the benefits of the 1689 Toleration Act.[3]

Eighteenth-century Dissenters were beset by grave theological doubts, and Arianism and Socinianism split Dissenting ministers and congregations.[4] The divisions were spotlighted at Salters' Hall in 1719 by London ministers' debates on adherence to Trinitarianism; within a century, most Presbyterians and many General Baptists had

---

[1] *ODNB, s.nn.* 'Bentley, Richard (1662–1742)'; 'Porson, Richard (1759–1808)'.
[2] J. N. D. Kelly, *The Athanasian Creed* (London, 1964).
[3] 9 Will. III c. 35, §1; 1 Will. & Mar. c. 18, §14.
[4] Arianism – from the Alexandrian priest Arius (d. 336) – represented Christ as a subordinate deity to the Father but upheld the former's pre-existence and the doctrine of the atonement. Socinians – from the Sienese Fausto Sozzini or Faustus Socinus (1539–1604) – denied Christ's divinity, his pre-existence and the atonement.

embraced Unitarianism.[5] But doubts about Trinitarian doctrine, with, particularly, their obvious implications for belief in Christ's divinity, had the potential to create discord among Anglicans too. The open anti-Trinitarianism of William Whiston, the successor as Lucasian Professor of Mathematics at Cambridge to Newton (whose own radical and heretical theology had been largely kept veiled),[6] cost him his chair in 1710. In 1714, Convocation threatened to prosecute the illustrious Samuel Clarke, rector of St James's, Piccadilly, for the publication of his neo-Arian *The Scripture-Doctrine of the Trinity* (1712). Ninety years later, it was a minor clergyman's considerable anti-Trinitarian doubts which produced first a *cause célèbre* and then a test case for the Church of England's authorities.

JEWISH PROPHECY: STONE'S SERMON OF 1806

On 8 July 1806, Francis Stone, rector of Cold Norton in Essex, preached a sermon, which he later published, at nearby Danbury. The occasion was the visitation of the archdeacon of Essex, William Gretton, and the sermon, spluttered the Pittite cleric Edward Nares, proved 'most extraordinary … entirely in abuse of the Creeds, and articles of the establish'd Church'.[7] The sermon was lucidly argued, learned (though not ostentatiously so), eloquent – and explosive. Its premise was that Christian Scripture concerning Christ should match Old Testament prophecies perfectly: when it did not, either the former was spurious or the latter misapplied. Using this touchstone, Stone concluded that Christ, although God's 'great messenger',[8] was just a man (the prophecies had foretold nothing more), and that the Virgin Birth was a myth and the first two chapters of Matthew's Gospel forgeries.[9] How, Stone asked, was 'plain, pure, primitive christianity … absorbed in the monstrous figments and incredible errors of men'?[10] For him, and those like him, the answer was clear: through 'the interpolations and misinterpretations of … [genuine Christian Scripture] by the perverse disputing Christian sophists of

[5] Michael R. Watts, *The Dissenters: From the Reformation to the French Revolution* (Oxford, 1978), 375–6.
[6] *ODNB, s.n.* 'Newton, Sir Isaac (1642–1727)'.
[7] Oxford, Merton College Archive, E.2.42, Autobiography of Edward Nares, 54.
[8] Francis Stone, *Jewish Prophecy, the Sole Criterion to Distinguish between Genuine and Spurious Christian Scripture*, 4th edn (London, 1809), 49.
[9] Ibid. 25–9.
[10] Ibid. 32.

the Platonic school of Alexandria'.[11]   By aligning Plato's doctrines (necessarily corrupted) and Christian theology, those sophists had concocted the Arian Trinity, which soon 'swell[ed] … into that monster of error and absurdity, the Athanasian trinity in unity' ('that most senseless doctrine of human invention').[12]   Furthermore, Stone assailed the doctrine of the atonement as a 'disgusting impossibility'.[13] It was necessary, he maintained, for the Church to renounce these errors which constituted the principal barriers to Christianity's acceptance by pagans, deists, Jews and Mahometans;[14] for, after their various conversions '"shall the earth be full of the knowledge of the Lord, as the waters cover the sea"', and 'the beautiful economy of the several divine dispensations, the patriarchal, the Mosaic, and the Christian, be completely developed'.[15]

THE DEVELOPMENT OF STONE'S THEOLOGY AND THE RESPONSE TO THE SERMON OF 1806

Commenting on Stone's behaviour in a letter of December 1807, Hannah Lindsey, writing for her husband, the great Unitarian Theophilus Lindsey, described Stone as 'a conscientious (tho' too hasty man)'.[16] Too hasty? Stone was an old man when he preached his sermon: as he said in it, 'it is improbable, that, at my advanced period of life, an eligible opportunity similar to the present, should [again] occur, to bear my public testimony against … corruptions of Christian doctrine'.[17]   But, as he reminded those present, he had proclaimed his anti-Trinitarianism – though less fully and forcefully – over thirty-five years before.[18] In 1768, two years after the publication of Francis Blackburne's *Confessional*, which attacked compulsory subscription to the Thirty-Nine Articles, Stone had published, anonymously, *A Short and Seasonable Application to the Public, In Behalf of a Respectful Address to the Parliament, to Procure a Legal*

---

[11] Ibid. 39.

[12] Ibid. 41, 38.

[13] Ibid. 46.

[14] '[T]he Mahometan', Stone contended, 'entertains more rational and consistent ideas of the unity of the Supreme Being than many Christians': ibid. 56.

[15] Ibid.

[16] Theophilus Lindsey, *The Letters of Theophilus Lindsey (1723–1808)*, ed. G. M. Ditchfield, 2 vols, CERS 15, 19 (Woodbridge, 2007, 2012), 2: 637.

[17] Stone, *Jewish Prophecy*, 32.

[18] Ibid. 48.

Redress of Notorious, Religious Grievances. In it, he maintained that the Athanasian Creed was unsupported by Scripture and that it, together with Athanasian forms of worship, defiled the Church's liturgy.[19] Moreover, he asserted, subscription to the Thirty-Nine Articles was a burden to the scrupulous, and one which grew ever heavier as rational explanations of the Scriptures dispelled error.[20] Stone advocated replacing subscription to the articles with a simple assent to the Scriptures, with a renunciation of popery and Jacobitism.[21] He urged 'unitarian believers of weight, whether laity or clergy' to petition Parliament to this end, and wanted a society, to include Dissenters, formed in London for 'the extirpation of Athanasianism'.[22] Indeed, a clerical society was established at the Feathers Tavern in the Strand in 1771, and a petition to Parliament produced for the abolition of compulsory subscription. Stone became the society's chairman and was one of the few Oxford graduates to support the petition strongly; in addition, he apparently secured the signatures of many Essex clergymen: they comprised thirty-one of some two hundred clerical signatories.[23] The House of Commons rejected the petition in February 1772 by 217 to 71,[24] and thereafter nine signatories seceded from the Church; Lindsey left his living in 1773, and his friend John Disney did likewise in 1782. Yet Stone kept his benefice. That was not dishonourable: he wanted to remove, *from within*, 'every gross church-corruption in doctrine, discipline, and worship',[25] the stance of Blackburne himself.[26] Thus, in the debate over the visitation sermon, Stone provocatively described himself as a 'Unitarian Christian Minister in the Church of

---

[19] Tyro-Theologus [Francis Stone], *A Short and Seasonable Application to the Public, in Behalf of a Respectful Address to the Parliament, to Procure a Legal Redress of Notorious, Religious Grievances* (London, 1768), 6–9.

[20] Ibid. 12.

[21] Ibid. 11, 13–14, 16.

[22] Ibid. 8, 21.

[23] For an incomplete list of the signatories, see V. M. H., 'List of Petitioning Clergy, 1772', *Monthly Repository* 13 (1818), 15–18.

[24] It was reintroduced in 1774, and rejected without a division: G. M. Ditchfield, 'The Subscription Issue in British Parliamentary Politics 1772–79', *Parliamentary History* 7 (1988), 45–80.

[25] Tyro-Theologus, *Short and Seasonable Application*, 22. As a correspondent later wrote to the *Monthly Repository*, Stone had 'many more opportunities, by preaching in a Trinitarian church, of making converts to Unitarianism, than if he preached to Unitarians themselves': C. G., 'Defence of Mr. Stone: To the Editor of the Monthly Repository', *Monthly Repository* 2 (1807), 20–1, at 20.

[26] Blackburne accordingly regretted the secessions of Disney and Lindsey, who were his sons-in-law.

England'.[27] But was that a chimera, the term an oxymoron? Could Stone be permitted to retain his living?

Besides the *Short and Seasonable Application*, Stone presented his ideas more fully in 1783 in *A Call to the Jews: By a Friend to the Jews*. Although again published anonymously – Stone did not affirm his authorship until 1806[28] – Lindsey and his circle easily identified the writer.[29] The work detailed Stone's considerable doubts about key orthodox – not only for the established Church – doctrines. The book cast doubt on 'the absurd hypothesis of the miraculous conception of Christ Jesus, in the womb of a virgin': the Old Testament had not prophesied that, and the Gospels of St Matthew and St Luke contained differing accounts of the journeyings of Mary and Joseph at Christ's birth.[30] Christ was Joseph's son, an 'absolutely good man', exceptional because he lived a 'literally sinless life'.[31] Stone ridiculed 'that incomprehensible arch-mystery of human invention, the Athanasian trinity in unity': God was not 'a fanciful *tripartite* Divinity', 'three divine beings jumbled together'.[32] It was vital to dispel 'the thick black mist, raised by *human* systems of *divinity*', and to expunge the 'absurd dogma of the Christian Platonists'.[33] Interpolations and forgeries in the Scriptures had to be exposed and rejected.[34] Once this had been done, the Jews, recognizing that the uncorrupted Christian Scriptures entirely accorded with the Old Testament prophecies, would convert to Christianity. Stone, displaying a bizarre egotism or megalomania,[35] even declared his willingness to lead them back to Israel, a fantasy which he seemingly shared with the asinine Lord George Gordon.[36]

---

[27] Stone, *Jewish Prophecy*, v.

[28] *Morning Chronicle*, 2 September 1806.

[29] Lindsey, *Letters*, ed. Ditchfield, 1: 384.

[30] [Francis Stone], *A Call to the Jews: By a Friend to the Jews* (London, 1783), 37, 44–5, 60, 99–100.

[31] Ibid. 20, 65, 238.

[32] Ibid. 9, 98, 133.

[33] Ibid. 15, 59.

[34] Ibid. 40–1, 123, 125.

[35] For other examples, see below, 371. Stone believed that Providence had made him an instrument for the Jews' conversion: *Call to the Jews*, 235.

[36] Ibid. 169, 234–5; Robert Watson, *The Life of Lord George Gordon* (London, 1795), 79; Marsha Keith Schuchard, 'Lord George Gordon and Cabalistic Freemasonry: Beating Jacobite Swords into Jacobin Ploughshares', in Martin Mulsow and Richard H. Popkin, eds, *Secret Conversions to Judaism in Early Modern Europe* (Leiden, 2004), 183–232; Iain McCalman, 'New Jerusalems: Prophecy, Dissent and Radical Culture in England 1786–1830',

By comparison with Stone's 1806 sermon, this earlier publication remained relatively unknown; but the storm raised by the sermon was ferocious. The *Orthodox Churchman's Magazine and Review* was appalled by it: Stone, this 'miserable Revolter', 'this nauseous gangrene', 'this hoary veteran in blasphemy and heresy', was both 'impudent and dishonest'.[37] His sermon was a 'superlatively heretical and blasphemous composition', poisonous and contagious, and seemed 'to strike at the very fundamental articles of our Religion'.[38] The 'shameless outrageousness of the offence' merited exemplary punishment.[39] Edward Nares soon produced a response, and, although he endeavoured to refute Stone's theology carefully and sustainedly, he could not resist invective. The sermon inspired in him 'extreme disgust'; its derision of orthodox doctrine was wanton, insolent and weak; and its language was sometimes 'barbarously low and vulgar'.[40] One wonders if Stone, though highly intelligent and gifted, had failed to anticipate the furore because he had so long associated with heterodox clerics. Educated at the Charterhouse, for most of his years there its master was the Arian Nicholas Mann.[41] After a period at University College, Oxford, Stone became curate to his uncle, Henry Taylor, Arian

---

in Knud Haakonssen, ed., *Enlightenment and Religion: Rational Dissent in Eighteenth-Century Britain* (Cambridge, 1996), 312–35.

[37] 'Review of New Publications', Review of Stone, *Jewish Prophecy*, *Orthodox Churchman's Magazine and Review* 11 (1806), 296–306, at 300; Jonathan Drapier, 'On the State of the Church', ibid. 370–3, at 371; Clericus, 'On Stone's Visitation Sermon', ibid. 428–33, at 432.

[38] Ibid. 431; Observator, 'To the Editor of the Orthodox Churchman's Magazine', and 'To the Worshipful the Archdeacon of Essex', ibid. 12 (1807), 28–33, at 28, 29; Clericus, 'On Stone's Visitation Sermon', ibid. 120–5, at 121.

[39] 'To the Archdeacon', 28. Other periodicals were more sympathetic. The *Critical Review*, championing freedom of theological discussion, praised Stone for his 'truly christian frankness and intrepidity', and claimed that he had 'evinced a freedom of research, and a boldness of inference, which the ministers of the establishment have seldom manifested in any of their publications': 'Monthly Catalogue, Religion', *Critical Review* 3rd ser. 11 (1807), 93–4. The *Monthly Review* was astonished by, but gingerly admired, his courage: 'The magnanimity of the preacher of this discourse is more striking than his worldly prudence. Such a visitation sermon has, we believe, been rarely delivered': 'Monthly Catalogue, Single Sermons', *Monthly Review* 53 (1807), 333–4, at 333.

[40] Edward Nares, *A Letter to the Rev. Francis Stone, M.A.* (London, 1807), 2, 44, 66.

[41] *ODNB*, *s.n.* 'Mann, Nicholas (*bap.* 1680?, *d.* 1753)'. Mann anonymously attacked the Athanasian Creed in *Critical Notes on Some Passages of Scripture* (London, 1747), 87–92, emphasizing, like Stone, that it alienated pagans, Jews and Mahometans: ibid. 92. Stone, perhaps nostalgically envisaging the Charterhouse's mastership as a heterodox refuge, applied for it in 1804: *Morning Post*, 1 December 1804.

controversialist and rector of Crawley, Hampshire.[42] Appointed curate of Worth in Sussex two years later, he enjoyed close friendships with two nearby Arian clergymen, John Bristed and William Hopkins.[43] By 1783, he was associated with Theophilus Lindsey's Essex Street Unitarian congregation.[44] Yet, given his 1806 discourse's occasion and provocative wording, it is difficult to believe that Stone did not intend to shock and anger his hearers and subsequent readers. During the sermon, Archdeacon Gretton confessed himself '*so surprized and shocked* that *had he not considered it his Duty to stay … he would have left the Church*'.[45] Another clergyman, 'being extremely disgusted', stormed out.[46] One warning Stone ignored was the case of Edward Evanson, vicar of Tewkesbury, whose heterodox opinions, as he knew, strongly resembled his own, and who, having openly proclaimed them, felt pressured into resigning his living in 1778.[47] Nares ominously argued that 'any Jew, Turk, infidel, or heretic, might as safely and as reasonably minister in the Church of England' as Stone.[48]

REAPING THE WHIRLWIND: STONE AND THE CHURCH COURTS

On 10 April 1807, Stone received a citation, summoning him to the bishop of London's consistory court.[49] He was charged, under twenty-one heads, with preaching and publishing doctrines that were directly contrary or repugnant to the 'Articles of Religion as by Law

---

[42] F. Stone, 'Brief Account of the Rev. Henry Taylor', *Monthly Repository* 8 (1813), 285–7, at 287; *ODNB, s.n.* 'Taylor, Henry (1711–1785)'. Taylor notoriously trumpeted his heterodoxy in the 1770s in *The Apology of Benjamin Ben Mordecai*. For Gibbon, he was 'Taylor the Arian': *Miscellaneous Works of Edward Gibbon, Esquire*, ed. John, Lord Sheffield, 2 vols (London, 1796), 1: 154. Taylor provided testimonials when Stone sought ordination both as deacon and priest: Winchester, Hampshire Record Office, 21M65/E1/4/807, 825.

[43] *ODNB, s.n.* 'Stone, Francis (*bap.* 1738, *d.* 1813)'.

[44] Lindsey, *Letters*, ed. Ditchfield, 1: 384.

[45] London, LPL, Microfiche 10854–86, Records of the Court of Arches, Process Books, D2002, Stone v. Bishop (1808), 1446–7.

[46] Ibid. 1038–9.

[47] Lindsey, *Letters*, ed. Ditchfield, 1: 384; G. M. Ditchfield, 'Varieties of Heterodoxy: The Career of Edward Evanson (1731–1805)', in Robert D. Cornwall and William Gibson, eds, *Religion, Politics and Dissent 1660–1832* (Farnham, 2010), 111–26.

[48] Nares, *Letter*, 68.

[49] Francis Stone, *A Letter to the Right Rev. Dr. Beilby Porteus, Lord Bishop of London* (London, 1807), 4.

established'.[50] His case was heard in May 1808, when he defended his stance fiercely. He also published an open letter to the bishop, Beilby Porteus, avowedly seeking 'the greatest publicity possible' because the prosecution wanted the proceedings conducted in 'the greatest privacy', 'in a small private parlour'.[51] In his *Letter*, like a skilled tactician determined not to quit secure ground, he reminded Porteus that he had promised at ordination to teach only 'that, which … [he was] persuaded … [might] be concluded and proved by the Scripture' – a fact, he added, that could not 'be too often repeated'.[52] Since subscription predated ordination, the latter rescinded acceptance of the Thirty-Nine Articles.[53] Following ordination, he was obliged to 'drive away all erroneous and strange doctrines', and the Church, he declared, had no authority to impose human interpretations of the Scriptures or override his conscience.[54] Moreover, he maintained, the sixth of the Thirty-Nine Articles, with its stress on the principle of *sola scriptura*, entirely supported his stance.[55] Stone restated such arguments in a tauntingly titled pamphlet, *An Unitarian Christian Minister's Plea for Adherence to the Church of England* (1808). Bravely, to his enemies' fury, he republished the visitation sermon, writing 'a most obnoxious preface' for the second edition.[56] By 1809, four editions had appeared. His efforts availed him nothing. The evidence against him was solid, the offences proved, and his arguments dismissed. When Stone last attended the court, it found that he 'still … persist[ed] in and … [had] not revoked his … Error'.[57] He was accordingly condemned,

---

[50] London, LMA, DL/C/191, Consistory Court of London, Allegations, Libels and Sentence Book, May 1807 – December 1817, fols 25ʳ–38ʳ.

[51] Stone, *Jewish Prophecy*, viii.

[52] Stone, *Letter*, 6, 10.

[53] Ibid. 9. However, seemingly inconsistently, Stone stated that, to secure advancement in the Church, he would resubscribe: Francis Stone, *An Unitarian Christian Minister's Plea for Adherence to the Church of England* (London, 1808), 41. By contrast, Blackburne had resolved not to resubscribe, thereby precluding his promotion.

[54] Stone, *Letter*, 6, 7, 10, 22–3, 40.

[55] 'Holy Scripture containeth all things necessary to salvation; so that whatsoever is *not* read therein; nor may be proved thereby, is not to be *required* of any man, that it should be *believed* as an Article of the *faith*, or be thought requisite or necessary to salvation': ibid. 28–9 (Stone's italics). Stone's rejection of some biblical passages qualified the principle, however.

[56] Clericus, 'On the Second Edition of Stone's Sermon: To the Editor of the Orthodox Churchman's Magazine', *Orthodox Churchman's Magazine and Review* 12 (1807), 359–65, at 359.

[57] Libels and Sentence Book, May 1807 – December 1817, fol. 41ᵛ.

and Bishop Porteus deprived him of his living, worth £300 per annum.[58]

Stone now appealed to the Court of Arches, which re-examined his case minutely: the manuscript records run to 1,844 pages.[59] The theology of the sermon was anatomized and the statements of some who were at Danbury demonstrate the discourse's impact: after time had lapsed, witnesses could well remember the most disturbing assertions.[60] Other depositions proved that Stone had published the sermon.[61] Unsurprisingly, the Court of Arches upheld the consistory court's sentence. Lastly, Stone sent a petition to George III, but was told in June 1809 that the king 'was not Pleased to give any Commands respecting it'.[62]

After the Deprivation

Stone was now a sad, if somewhat perplexing, figure. He had apparently written his memoirs, but failed to publish them.[63] Few (excepting Unitarians) were, it seems, interested, and he probably failed to raise the necessary subscription. He was ruined financially and, from Michaelmas 1810, was confined as a debtor within the rules of King's Bench prison. After his first wife's death and 'when rather advanced in life', he had married his cook, who had borne him 'numerous … children'.[64] By the *annus horribilis* 1808, he had nine – two more had not survived – and another was born subsequently, though he listed only eight in his will, made in February 1813.[65] Humiliatingly, his

---

[58] Ibid., fols 42^r–^{v}. On the day of the sentence, Stone wrote to Sir William Scott, the consistory court's judge. He had not appreciated, he stated, his preaching's violation of 13 Eliz. I c. 12, the 1571 Act for the Ministers of the Church to Be of Sound Religion, which, *inter alia*, enjoined the clergy's conformity to the Thirty-Nine Articles (§§1, 2). He therefore undertook 'not to offend again in like manner'. However, he reiterated his conviction that his ordination promises sanctioned him to preach as he had: Process Books, D2002, Stone v. Bishop (1808), 1823–5. That raised inconvenient questions about the respective jurisdictions of Church and state, and presumably ensured the compromise's rejection.

[59] Process Books, D2002, Stone v. Bishop (1808).

[60] Ibid. 1084, 1131–2, 1369. One noted that Stone spoke of one doctrine he attacked 'in the most contemptuous manner': ibid. 1359.

[61] Ibid. 1656–99.

[62] London, BL, Add. MS 38321, Liverpool Papers 132, fol. 85^r.

[63] *Morning Chronicle*, 12 April 1809; *DNB*, *s.n.* 'Stone, Francis (1738?–1813)'.

[64] BL, Add. MS 36527, J. Hunter, Notices of Contemporaries 1827–36, fol. 89^r.

[65] Stone, *Unitarian Christian Minister's Plea*, 40; *ODNB*, *s.n.* 'Stone'; Kew, The National Archives, PROB 11/1554/127, Will of Francis Stone, 15 February 1813.

son-in-law, an army captain, was now the mainstay of the whole fam-ily.[66] 'The family is in deep distress', wrote one sympathizer, and 'the poor old man is incapable of doing any thing to extricate them out of their difficulties.'[67] The Unitarians were dismayed by the 'persecu-tion', whose sole object, Lindsey thought, was to beggar a wretched man; and they raised a subscription giving Stone £100 a year, al-though he remained a member of the Church of England.[68] Even Nares – who was, admittedly, prone to self-deception – expressed pity, saying he had meant Stone no harm.[69] Stone died in November 1813.

POLITICS AND PERSONALITY

Stone's 1806 sermon was the antithesis of a tract for the times. For most of the eighteenth century, Latitudinarians in the Church of England, heirs and continuators of Locke and Tillotson, ques-tioned constricting dogma and old, perhaps obsolete, theological for-mulae; often the Athanasian Creed was a target. They interpreted antiquated articles of religion liberally, hoping for doctrinal and liturgical reform grounded on painstaking biblical study and ratio-nal argument; and shunned sacerdotalism and surviving vestiges of 'superstition' in the Church. Among them were bishops, including Benjamin Hoadly, Edmund Law, Jonathan Shipley and Richard Wat-son, and powerful theologians, such as Francis Blackburne and William Paley.[70] Yet from the 1780s, the appeal of Latitudinarian thinking was diminishing, and the advancement of Latitudinarian clerics checked. The French Revolution powerfully promoted con-servatism in the Church. Stone's sermon was studded with Latitu-dinarian vocabulary: 'plain sense', 'dispassionate', 'impartial', 'can-dour', 'superstitious error', 'truly rational', 'a free, dispassionate, impartial investigation':[71] wording which, as Nancy Uhlar Murray

---

[66] Hunter, Notices, fol. 89ʳ.

[67] Northallerton, North Yorkshire County Record Office [hereafter: NYCRO], Wyvill of Constable Burton Records, ZFW 7/2/215/9. I owe this and the other references to this collection to Grayson Ditchfield.

[68] Lindsey, *Letters*, ed. Ditchfield, 2: 637; NYCRO, ZFW 7/2/215/7, 19; 7/2/243/1; *ODNB, s.n.* 'Stone'. After Stone's death, provision was made for his widow and children: *Monthly Repository* 9 (1814), 133.

[69] Autobiography of Nares, 56.

[70] B. W. Young, *Religion and Enlightenment in Eighteenth-Century England* (Oxford, 1998).

[71] Stone, *Jewish Prophecy*, 22, 23, 25, 42, 47–8, 50.

demonstrated, had largely disappeared by 1806 from the writings of those liberal churchmen who had welcomed the Revolution in 1789.[72] Furthermore, Stone's politics were comparably suspect in the 1790s and 1800s. Stone was a long-standing Whig. Following George II's death, he had composed a poem praising the late king, the duke of Cumberland and 'the Glories of the Brunswic [*sic*] Line'.[73] His Whiggism shaded into radicalism. In 1776, he published *A New, Easy, and Expeditious Method of Discharging the National Debt*, advocating the appropriation of the Church's property (for the state's use); the removal of bishops from the House of Lords and, indeed, the abolition of bishops and other ecclesiastical dignitaries; and the introduction of a standard clerical stipend (£200 per annum).[74] In 1789, he published his *Political Reformation, on a Large Scale*, proposing the separation of the executive and legislature; universal male suffrage (excluding civil and judicial office-holders); Catholic emancipation; the creation of new constituencies, all with roughly equal populations; annual Parliaments; the payment of MPs; provisions for combating corruption; and much else besides.[75] He also wanted the abolition of the slave trade and slavery.[76] Also in 1789, Stone praised the French Revolution as 'a glorious struggle for … [the French nation's] recovery of the natural equal rights of men',[77] and in 1792 he produced a lengthy and forceful riposte to Edmund Burke's *Reflections on the Revolution in France*.[78] Small wonder that some of his enemies thought him a clerical Tom Paine.[79]

---

[72] Nancy Uhlar Murray, 'The Influence of the French Revolution on the Church of England and its Rivals 1789–1802' (DPhil thesis, University of Oxford, 1975), 80.

[73] BL, Add. MS 37683, P. A. Taylor Papers 2, fol. 45ʳ. On Cumberland's victory at Culloden, Stone wrote: 'The impious Rage of foul Rebellion quell'd; | And the hideous Hydra-headed Monster slew, | With all her viperous Brood; dire Foes to Freedom's Reign': ibid., fol. 40ʳ.

[74] Francis Stone, *A New, Easy, and Expeditious Method of Discharging the National Debt* (London, 1776), 21–6. Stone wanted the 'entire subversion of the constitution in church, as it now stands, established by law': ibid. 23. He had long disliked and distrusted bishops: Tyro-Theologus, *Short and Seasonable Application*, 18–19.

[75] Francis Stone, *Political Reformation, on a Large Scale* (London, 1789), 1–53.

[76] Francis Stone, *Thoughts in Favour of the Abolition of the Slave Trade, and the Emancipation of the Negroes* (London, 1792).

[77] Stone, *Political Reformation*, 63.

[78] Francis Stone, *An Examination of the Right Hon. Edmund Burke's* Reflections on the Revolution in France (London, 1792).

[79] *Orthodox Churchman's Magazine and Review* 11 (1806), 301, 431. On the wider links between religious heterodoxy and political radicalism, see J. C. D. Clark, *English Society, 1660–1832: Ideology, Structure and Political Practice during the Ancien Regime*, 2nd edn

Stone's fate was not only determined by the times but also by his goading personality. Doubts about doctrine and pride in his powerful intellect combined to spawn an utter conviction of his rightness and a liking for combat. 'I glory in exposing … [nonsense] to contempt and ridicule', he declared in his 1806 sermon, and he likened the Feathers Tavern petitioners to the Marian martyrs.[80] Later, he would claim that his 'Christian fortitude' was equal to St Paul's 'apostolic boldness' and Luther's 'intrepid spirit'.[81] Arrogance begat dislike. An exasperated reviewer of *Political Reformation* ridiculed his pretensions and hinted at his eccentricity.[82] A 'very vain old man', *The British Critic* snorted.[83] Stone's difficult personality was long-standing. As a young curate in Hampshire, he had exhibited an 'insolent', near-ungovernable temper; a 'most provokingly haughty' and contemptuous demeanour when riled; a 'self-conceited' manner; 'Weakness, Obstinacy, & Perverseness of Conduct, as Never Met in one Character'.[84] In a society lubricated by patronage, such traits were highly damaging. There was also an alienating theatricality about his behaviour, smacking of the fraudulent. When the consistory court's sentence was pronounced, Stone 'cast up his eyes to Heaven, and exclaimed, "God's will be done"'.[85] For a period after losing his living, he went to Bath, where he met Joseph Hunter, the Presbyterian minister and antiquary. Hunter recorded that Stone was not well received among the Dissenters, who felt he lacked the 'Sobriety of Mind' of Disney and Lindsey.[86] Disney, indeed, called Stone a scaramouch, and Hunter observed that 'there was about him something to justify' this, adding that there 'was nothing of the gravity of the Confessor

---

(Cambridge, 2000), 318–422; A. M. C. Waterman, 'The Nexus between Theology and Political Doctrine in Church and Dissent', in Haakonssen, ed., *Enlightenment and Religion*, 193–218.

[80] Stone, *Jewish Prophecy*, 46, 48.

[81] Ibid. ix. Stone believed that 'the affection of modesty is more disgusting than the display of vanity'(!): *Political Reformation*, 60.

[82] 'The length of title, and the name of the author, forbid our entering into a close examination of the plan. We fear Mr. S. is not the Hercules who can cleanse the Augean stable, which has baffled the wisdom of the legislature, and the wisest patriots': 'Review of New Publications', *Gentleman's Magazine* 59 (1789), 341.

[83] 'British Catalogue: Divinity', Review of Stone, *Jewish Prophecy*, *British Critic* 29 (1807), 211–12, at 211.

[84] Peter Alfred Taylor, ed., *Some Account of the Taylor Family* (London, 1875), 294, 295.

[85] *Aberdeen Journal*, 1 June 1808.

[86] Hunter, Notices, fol. 89^r.

about him'.[87]   Even his intellectual claims excited suspicion. When Stone told Hunter that he was a Fellow of the Society of Antiquaries, the latter was, it seems, inclined to disbelieve him.[88] But it was true; and, only a year before his death, Stone published a collection of documents in the Society's periodical, *Archaeologia*.[89]

CONCLUSIONS

If an increasingly conservative era and Stone's problematical personality wrought his ruin, that ruin was none the less avoidable. Stone insisted that, from his ordination, he was 'absolutely required ... to lay before the people mine Unitarian Christian principles', and never to withhold them 'from the lower classes of the community'.[90] But that was hogwash. Others sharing his doubts, including William Hopkins, unobtrusively adapted the Church's services to their beliefs, omitting those parts they rejected;[91] had Stone done likewise, prosecution would have been improbable. Besides, he was non-resident: instituted to Cold Norton in May 1765, his visitation return the next year states that he did not live there for reasons of health.[92]   He resided in London, and in 1783 Lindsey noted 'he never does any duty now as Minister of the Ch. of E.'[93] In his stead, Stone employed curates (a strategy which Christopher Wyvill, who signed the

---

[87] Ibid. The *Monthly Review* criticized Stone's *Thoughts in Favour of the Abolition of the Slave Trade* for some levity on the subject: 'Monthly Catalogue, Slave Trade', *Monthly Review* 8 (1792), 447.

[88] Hunter, Notices, fol. 89ʳ.

[89] *A List of the Society of Antiquaries of London, April 24, MDCCXCIII* [London, 1793], 6, col. 2; Francis Stone, 'Copies of an Original Letter ... Communicated by the Rev. Francis Stone, F.A.S.', *Archaeologia* 16 (1812), 181–93.

[90] Stone, *Letter*, 21; idem, *Unitarian Christian Minister's Plea*, 50–1.

[91] F. Stone, 'A Brief Account of the Rev. W. Hopkins', *Monthly Repository* 8 (1813), 425–7, at 426. William Chambers, rector of Achurch, Northamptonshire, did this, as did Disney before his secession: *ODNB, s.nn.* 'Chambers, William (1724?–1777)'; 'Disney, John (1746–1816)'.

[92] LPL, MS Film 31, Diocese of London, Visitation Returns 1766, fol. 349ᵛ. This was repeated in the 1790 visitation return: LPL, MS Film 37, Diocese of London, Visitation Returns 1790, No. 58/2. The explanation for non-residence was a common one: Viviane Barrie-Curien, *Clergé et pastorale en Angleterre au XVIIIᵉ siècle. Le Diocèse de Londres* (Paris, 1992), 266–9.

[93] Lindsey, *Letters*, ed. Ditchfield, 1: 384. In the proceedings against Stone, one of Cold Norton's churchwardens testified that the rector preached in the parish church 'about four times a year', and an Essex clergyman observed that he 'hardly ever' attended archidiaconal visitations: Process Books, D2002, Stone v. Bishop (1808), 1343, 1749.

Feathers Tavern petition, also adopted),[94] and they presumably conformed to the liturgy. His unprovoked challenge to his ecclesiastical superiors in 1806, and his subsequent refusal to retract satisfactorily, were principled but foolhardy. Thomas Belsham, from 1805 minister at the Essex Street chapel, disapproved of Stone's 'whole conduct', and repeatedly castigated his imprudence: in his eyes, Stone had 'solicited & provoked' the 'persecution'.[95]

Stone's test case demonstrated that an uncompromising and vocal 'Unitarian Christian Minister' was intolerable within the Church of England. That said, for the established Church, Stone's memory – especially given his family's suffering – was an embarrassment. And Stone's doubts about the authenticity of some Scripture passages also alienated or alarmed those heterodox Dissenters who upheld the Bible's authenticity and scrupulously sought to validate their Unitarianism from the Scriptures.[96] Stone was best forgotten.[97] Revealingly, when the *Oxford Dictionary of National Biography* was produced, his 1897 *Dictionary of National Biography* entry was merely revised: his career, it was deemed, failed to merit extensive re-examination.[98]

Yet the manifold doubts which Stone expressed soon resurfaced after his death. Most broadly, his doubts about the authenticity of parts of the gospels anticipated the 'higher criticism' which emerged later in the nineteenth century, and that higher criticism proved destructive of the Bible-based Unitarianism of men like Lindsey. Within the Church of England, Stone's concerns were given voice by new generations of theologians. One of great distinction in the 1830s was Renn Dickson Hampden, Fellow of Oriel, Bampton Lecturer in 1832 and, from 1836, Oxford's Regius Professor of Divinity: how different from a maverick Essex rector. 'The Apostles' Creed', contended Hampden, 'states nothing but facts. The transition is immense from this to the scholastic speculations involved in the Nicene

---

[94] *ODNB*, *s.n.* 'Wyvill, Christopher (1738–1822)'.

[95] NYCRO, ZFW 7/2/215/7, 19; 7/2/243/1.

[96] See Lindsey's criticisms of *Call to the Jews*: Lindsey, *Letters*, ed. Ditchfield, 1: 383. Stone directly attacked Arianism and Socinianism, besides Athanasianism, in the work: *Call to the Jews*, 21, 105, 107, 248.

[97] William Turner, for example, did not include Stone in his *Lives of Eminent Unitarians*, 2 vols (London, 1840–3), although he included Edward Evanson.

[98] Sufficient sources survive to make possible the writing of a full biography of Stone; and certainly his *ODNB* entry needs further revision.

and Athanasian Creeds.'[99] Dogmatic statements were human deductions from Scripture, not (necessarily) Christian truths. Hampden's doubts, like Stone's, were productive of clear reasoning. Regarding the Church's Articles and 'in particular … the Nicene and Athanasian Creeds, as they stand in our Ritual, or are adopted into our Articles', Hampden argued, if 'it be admitted that the notions on which their several expressions are founded, are both unphilosophical and unscriptural; it must be remembered, that they do not impress those notions on the Faith of the Christian, as matters of affirmative belief'.[100] Accordingly, he advocated the abolition of Oxford's subscription at matriculation.

In 1865, a general 'assent' was substituted for clerical subscription to the Thirty-Nine Articles.[101] Then came the full Victorian controversy over the Athanasian Creed. The Royal Commission on Ritual, appointed in 1867, issued its final report in 1870 and recommended the creed's retention. By contrast, Archbishop Tait wished to discontinue its use and Dean Stanley to relax it: stances deplored in turn by E. B. Pusey and Canon Liddon. Its place in the Church's worship was hotly debated in Convocation: if it were not to be omitted, should it be retranslated, or its anathemas' force moderated by some explanatory formula? However, the Lower House rejected any change, and none was effected, although a declaration on the creed's content was constructed. Partial adjustment came in the Revised 1928 Prayer Book, with a new translation, permission for the omission of the anathemas and the making of the recitation optional.[102] In the twentieth century, the Church of England silently but overwhelmingly abandoned the use of the Athanasian Creed.[103]

In the mid-1930s, the influential Dick Sheppard, then a canon of St Paul's, threatened to throw himself from the Whispering Gallery during the saying of the Athanasian Creed.[104] He did not follow that imprudent course, but, in his lifetime, the creed was plainly withering on the vine. Had Francis Stone appreciated that *quieta non movere* was

[99] R. D. Hampden, *The Scholastic Philosophy considered in its Relation to Christian Theology*, 2nd edn (London, 1837), 544 n. H.

[100] Ibid. 378.

[101] A less rigid form was introduced in 1975.

[102] R. C. D. Jasper, *Prayer Book Revision in England 1800–1900* (London, 1954), 103–14.

[103] Kelly, *Athanasian Creed*, 49.

[104] Arthur Burns, 'From 1830 to the Present', in Derek Keene, Arthur Burns and Andrew Saint, eds, *St Paul's: The Cathedral Church of London, 604–2004* (New Haven, CT, 2004), 84–110, at 97.

sometimes a wise strategy, not necessarily dishonourable, the likelihood would have been a satisfactory old age with his young family, and the avoidance of a snap petrifaction of Anglican doctrine which halted, albeit temporarily, fundamental thinking in the Church: the very opposite of his intended achievement.[105] Piecemeal modifications, omissions, compromises, fudges were the most viable, if imperfect, salves for the (ultimately irresolvable) doctrinal doubts which so vexed Stone. But, as Lindsey observed, he was 'too hasty' a man for those.

---

[105] Sadly, he here resembled Luther less than K. B. McFarlane's Wycliffe, who 'did little or nothing to inspire [the English Reformation] and in effect everything possible to delay' it: *John Wycliffe and the Beginnings of English Nonconformity* (London, 1952), 186. Ironically, in the year of Stone's death, Parliament formally legalized Unitarianism by the Doctrine of the Trinity Act, 53 Geo. III c. 160 (an attempt to do so in 1792 had failed). Stone's plans for reform of the Church prefigured some debated in the 1830s (although they more strikingly resemble the ecclesiastical reforms implemented in France in 1789 and 1790). Parts of his political and social vision were gradually realized.

Christian Doubt and Hope in Early Socialism

Philip Lockley*

Durham University

*The diverse forms of socialism which emerged in the nineteenth century had a com-
plex relationship with both Christian beliefs and the Churches. Socialist movements are commonly remembered as anti-religious and anti-clerical. Doubt, forged
in the familiar nineteenth-century 'crisis of faith', shaped not only Marxism, but
also Owenism, the earlier social theories of Robert Owen. Church historians have
long pointed to another narrative of socialism and religion in the Victorian era:
the rise of Christian Socialism after 1848, led by F. D. Maurice, J. M. Ludlow,
Charles Kingsley and others. Here, they recall a response to doubt with faith, and
an answer to anti-clericalism with a new vision for the Churches' social role. Yet
socialism before 1848 had a more contested interaction with Christianity than this
history assumes. By exploring the specific nature of Christian doubt among early
Owenite socialists, then following how this doubt was answered by contemporary
Christian supporters of Owen, this essay uncovers an alternative, noteworthy response to doubting Christianity – the nature of Christian hope in early socialism.*

Socialism has been associated with doubting Christianity since its origins in the nineteenth century. Even before the central prophets of
communism, Karl Marx and Friedrich Engels, were ever influenced
by the sceptical works of David Friedrich Strauss and Ludwig Feuer-
bach, or developed their view of religion as 'the opium of the people',
earlier forms of socialism were allied with doubt and opposition to
religion.[1] In Britain and America, the first 'socialists' were followers of Robert Owen, the Welsh-born cotton-master and social theo-
rist who presented a panacea for emerging industrial capitalism in a
future communitarian and cooperative society.[2] Owen was among

* St John's College, Durham University, 3 South Bailey, Durham, DH1 3RJ. E-mail:
pjlockley@gmail.com.

This essay was researched, written and presented as a paper while the author was a British
Academy Postdoctoral Fellow and Junior Research Fellow of Trinity College, Oxford.

[1] On Marxism and modern theology, see Gareth Stedman Jones, 'Religion and the Origins
of Socialism', in Ira Katznelson and Gareth Stedman Jones, eds, *Religion and the Political
Imagination* (Cambridge, 2010), 171–89.
[2] The major studies of Owenism include J. F. C. Harrison, *Robert Owen and the Owenites
in Britain and America: The Quest for the New Moral World* (London, 1969); Barbara Taylor,

Studies in Church History 52 (2016) 364–380   © Ecclesiastical History Society 2016
doi: 10.1017/stc.2015.21

the most prominent freethinkers of his age, openly declaring all exist-ing religions to be erroneous. The movements Owen initiated either took their cue from this assertion, or were perceived to do so in the public mind. In Cincinnati in 1829, Owen held an infamous debate on the evidence for Christianity with the co-founder of the Disciples of Christ, Alexander Campbell.[3] American Owenism soon evolved into an urban campaign for secularism. In Britain, Owenites likewise developed this country's earliest institutions of doubt, a network of Halls of Science promoting freethought, and in 1840, the first na-tional campaign against socialism was initiated by an outraged bishop of Exeter. A decade later, as Owenism disintegrated, ex-Owenites founded the National Secular Society.[4]

Church historians of the English-speaking world have long opted to narrate another story of socialism and Christianity in the nine-teenth century, commonly beginning as Owenism ended and reach-ing well into the twentieth century. The tradition labelled Christian Socialism is dated in Britain from 1848, and the initiative of Frederick Denison Maurice, John Ludlow and Charles Kingsley.[5] It was revived by Maurice's Anglo-Catholic followers in the 1870s, then spread into Free Church denominations, before being taken across the urbaniz-ing British and American empires of the Edwardian era.[6] In some places it combined with the parallel Social Gospel movement; in time it influenced William Temple and others to make the Christian case for welfare democracy in the wake of the First World War.[7]

Fondly remembered by socially conscious Churches today, the Christian Socialist tradition seemingly offers a compelling counter to the tendency to socialist doubt, namely faith. A faith in humanity forged by a theology of the incarnation threads through the tradition

---

Eve and the New Jerusalem (London, 1983); Gregory Claeys, *Citizens and Saints: Politics and Anti-politics in Early British Socialism* (Cambridge, 1989); Edward Royle, *Robert Owen and the Commencement of the Millennium* (Manchester, 1998). A more recent collection of essays is Noel Thompson and Chris Williams, eds, *Robert Owen and his Legacy* (Cardiff, 2011).

[3] *Debate on the Evidences of Christianity ... between Robert Owen, of New Lanark, Scotland, and Alexander Campbell, of Bethany, Virginia* (London, 1839).

[4] Edward Royle, *Victorian Infidels: The Origins of the British Secularist Movement, 1791–1866* (Manchester, 1974).

[5] Edward Norman, *The Victorian Christian Socialists* (Cambridge, 1987).

[6] Peter d'Alroy Jones, *The Christian Socialist Revival, 1877–1914* (Princeton, NJ, 1968); Paul T. Phillips, *A Kingdom on Earth: Anglo-American Social Christianity, 1880–1940* (University Park, PA, 1996).

[7] Matthew Grimley, *Citizenship, Community, and the Church of England* (Oxford, 2004).

up to Temple.[8] Faith in the Church as both an institution engaged with present society and a symbolic revealing of the divine society stands at the core of Maurice's theology.[9] Faith in the Kingdom of God above and beyond a materialist reading of history likewise characterizes the common theology of this entire tradition.

Maurice, Ludlow and Kingsley coined the term 'Christian socialist' to be deliberately provocative – to place side by side two terms already widely considered contradictory.[10] Despite the fact that the *Communist Manifesto* also appeared in 1848, the oxymoronic character of 'Christian Socialism' was widely assumed, in a British context, on the basis not of Marxist but of Owenite doubt. Church historians have rarely concerned themselves with the distinction between these two traditions of socialist doubt, nor have they adequately explored the ambiguous and contested relationship with Christianity which characterized the pre-Marx, pre-Maurice socialisms of the 1820s, 1830s and 1840s.[11] The intellectual and political bases of doubt and opposition to Christianity among Owenites shared some similarities with Marxists, but differed in other ways. There were, notably, also many Christian Owenites, a phenomenon frequently forgotten by scholars in thrall to the Maurice tradition. Through an exploration of the specific nature of Christian doubt among early Owenite socialists, and how it was answered by contemporary Christian Owenites, this essay ultimately uncovers an alternative, noteworthy response to doubting Christianity – the nature of Christian hope in early socialism.

Socialist Doubts

Early socialist doubts in Britain and America followed a pattern set by the career and convictions of Robert Owen himself. Born in Newtown in mid-Wales in 1771 to an artisan family of limited means, Owen grew up in a context of customary affiliation to the established Church of Wales, with some contact with Calvinistic Methodism.[12] Religion probably exercised Owen from an early age, although his later autobiography dubiously foreshadowed a celebrated

---

[8] John Atherton, ed., *Social Christianity* (London, 1994).

[9] Jeremy Morris, *F. D. Maurice and the Crisis of Christian Authority* (Oxford, 2005).

[10] Alec R. Vidler, *The Church in an Age of Revolution* (Harmondsworth, 1971), 97.

[11] Several Christian Owenites are briefly discussed in Gilbert Binyon, *The Christian Socialist Movement in England* (London, 1931), 40–51.

[12] Robert Davis and Frank O'Hagan, *Robert Owen* (London, 2010), 11.

freethinking future by suggesting that at the age of eight he was already disturbed by the comparative claims and disagreements between world religions, and that he had rejected all religion by the time he was ten.[13] More likely, as Robert Davis has argued, Owen's suspicion of orthodox religion stemmed from his move during his late teens to Manchester.[14] Admitted to the Manchester Literary and Philosophical Society in 1793, and thereafter an active member, Owen now moved in a climate of rational criticism of revealed religion extending out of eighteenth-century Arianism and Unitarianism.[15] Here, Owen encountered the ideas of William Godwin, Voltaire and other sceptical *philosophes*. By the time he secured control of New Lanark mills in southern Scotland in 1799, Owen was a classic Enlightenment deist, dismissing all beliefs contrary to reason.

At New Lanark, Owen carried out his celebrated experiments in improving workers' circumstances to improve their characters, the test case for his developing theory of environmental determinism, that humans do good or bad entirely because of circumstances. Owen promoted temperance, cleanliness and order in his factory village; he excluded physical punishment from the workplace, ensured the quality and value of goods in the company store, and provided education for young children. As a result, crime, ill-health and absenteeism at New Lanark fell, and profits rose. Owen subsequently employed artful self-publicity to project lessons from his experiments as a wider social solution: his 'new view of society'.[16] Religion was rarely mentioned in Owen's essays published under this title, yet, as Robert Davis has pointed out, the 'moral psychology' of the work was 'profoundly irreconcilable with orthodox Christianity'.[17]

By insisting that circumstances form human character, Owen implicitly denied the principle of free will, or individual responsibility for good or evil behaviour. In turn, this contradicted the

---

[13] Robert Owen, *The Life of Robert Owen, Written by Himself*, 2 vols (London, 1857), 1: 3–5, 16.

[14] Robert A. Davis, 'Robert Owen and Religion', in Thompson and Williams, eds, *Owen and his Legacy*, 91–112, at 92–3.

[15] E. M. Fraser, 'Robert Owen in Manchester, 1787–1800', *Transactions of the Manchester Literary and Philosophical Society* 82 (1937–8), 29–41. Until 1799, the Literary and Philosophical Society met in an outpost of rational dissent, Cross Street Chapel, the later stronghold of Manchester Unitarianism: Michael Watts, *The Dissenters: From the Reformation to the French Revolution* (Oxford, 1978), 477.

[16] Robert Owen, *A New View of Society* (London, 1813).

[17] Davis, 'Robert Owen and Religion', 95.

conventional Christian understanding of sin as purposeful disobedience, whether conceived as original sin constraining the extent of human perfectibility in a fallen world, or the sins said to originate in the individual's will and responsible action. The broader logic of Owen's principle 'that character is universally formed *for*, and not *by*, the individual' was that by changing people's circumstances – principally their poverty, but also their education and physical treatment – you could change the character of all humanity.[18] Owen's successive proposals for self-supporting communities, a rational school system and cooperative initiatives all developed from this dictum, so at odds with orthodox Christian teachings regarding the fallen yet autonomous human person, with the capacity to adopt an ethic of behaviour for themselves.

Owen avoided questions over his orthodoxy for some time, gaining considerable support for his plans among the English and Scottish aristocracy and Church figures, including, apparently, Charles Manners-Sutton, archbishop of Canterbury.[19] However, growing impatient with opposition to his plans, in a public speech in London during August 1817 Owen identified religion as both the principal obstruction to his success and the ultimate cause of human misery.[20] Religion was the reason, Owen declared, 'so many countless millions … through each successive generation, have been the victims of ignorance, of superstition, of mental degradation, and of wretchedness'.[21] All existing religions 'forced on the minds of men, deep, dangerous, and lamentable principles of disunion, division, and separation'; all religions appeared to Owen 'united with much – yes, very much – error'.[22]

---

[18] Owen's 'doctrine of circumstances' was likely influenced by William Godwin's idea of 'necessity', which understood human actions to be determined or necessary within a set of circumstances, leaving no room for a separate power of will, although Owen never explicitly acknowledged this: William Godwin, *Enquiry Concerning Political Justice*, 2 vols (London, 1793), 1: 283–317.

[19] According to the *ODNB*, Manners-Sutton 'briefly flirted with Robert Owen's plan': *ODNB, s.n.* 'Sutton, Charles Manners- (1755–1828)', online edn (2006), at: <http://www.oxforddnb.com/view/article/17964>, accessed 12 August 2014.

[20] Robert Owen, 'Address Delivered at the City of London Tavern, August 21 1817', in idem, *A New View of Society and Other Writings*, ed. Gregory Claeys (London, 1991), 191–203.

[21] Ibid. 199.

[22] Ibid. 199–200.

Owen would look back on this speech as a turning point in his life.[23] He believed that he had stood up and pronounced 'truth', and in subsequent writings he adopted a triumphalist tone: now was 'the Dominion of FAITH ceased; its reign of terror, or disunion, of separation, and of irrationality … broken to pieces'.[24] The coming society concerning which Owen would prophesy for the rest of his life was now linked explicitly to the removal of 'irrational' elements of religion, the divisive influence of religious sectarianism and the broader hindrance caused by religious doctrines to the realization of socialism. Coupled with Owen's prior denial of human responsibility for sin, these form four principal doubts discernible among many early socialists who followed Owen into disbelief.

One such Owenite was the Newman brother most people have never heard of: Charles Newman, the middle brother between John Henry and Francis. Charles was first influenced by Robert Owen's ideas in the early 1820s, while John was securing his Oriel College fellowship and Francis – the subsequent Brethren missionary, then Unitarian classicist – was just beginning a brilliant student career.[25] Charles did not attend university himself, though he was not lacking in intellectual gifts. He worked as a clerk, and then as a tutor for periods, but showed signs of mental instability, and mostly lived off his brothers. Charles's career is not well known, partly because he lived much of it in seclusion, partly because his brothers wanted it that way. John declared Charles's life 'aimless, profitless, forlorn'; Francis considered it 'wasted … better left in silence'.[26]

Evidence for Charles's views may nonetheless be pieced together from John's letters and writings.[27] As Frank Turner has noted, '[t]hroughout John Newman's life he measured much of his own

[23] Owen, *Life of Robert Owen*, 1: 160–2; W. H. Oliver, 'Owen in 1817: The Millennialist Moment', in Sidney Pollard and John Salt, eds, *Robert Owen: Prophet of the Poor* (London, 1971), 166–87.

[24] Ibid. 177.

[25] On Francis Newman, see David Hempton, *Evangelical Disenchantment* (New Haven, CT, 2008), 41–69.

[26] Martin J. Svaglic, 'Charles Newman and his Brothers', *Proceedings of the Modern Language Association* 71 (1956), 370–85, at 370; see also Seán O'Faoláin, *Newman's Way* (New York, 1952), 74–8. A recent but slanted study of Charles and 'the idea of socialism' appears in Edward Short, *Newman and his Family* (London, 2013), 115–39.

[27] Nowhere near the same quantity of evidence exists for Charles's life and thought as for John and Francis, not least because John bought up letters and burned them for fear of blackmail: Svaglic, 'Charles Newman', 370.

religious thought against that of his younger siblings', in *Grammar of Assent* even narrating a case of 'three Protestants, one [who] becomes a Catholic, a second a Unitarian, and a third an unbeliever'.[28] From 1823 to 1825, John debated Charles's 'irreligion' in their correspondence, with Charles arguing principally from the 'absurdity' of beliefs regarding everlasting punishment, and people's obsession with sinfulness. The idea of punishing sin made no sense if sin was caused by circumstances. 'Man is not so bad', Charles insisted to John; 'your way of asking for grace is very round-about; so much machinery'.[29] In 1825, Charles attacked the Christian response to social problems: 'I think Mr Owen for practical motives to action … beats St Paul hollow'.[30]

John Newman varied his stance on his younger brother's beliefs, which he found 'truly lamentable'.[31] In 1833 he refused to recommend Charles for a teaching post on account of his views, but relented the following year, composing a recommendation in which he pointed out that Charles was 'not a believer in Christianity, but he had promised me he would neither directly or indirectly introduce the subject'.[32] For a brief period around 1837, Charles 'returned to the Church' (in John's words), but by 1841 John was writing that Charles was 'going in his old way' and had 'given up religion. He is very intimate with the Socialists and now does not shrink from the name'.[33] In December Charles wrote unapologetically to John, explaining that 'conventional society, or very religious society is no society to me'; he could no longer bear to live 'among persons who do not aim at least among themselves at justice as a means toward well being in this

---

[28] Frank M. Turner, *John Henry Newman: The Challenge to Evangelical Religion* (New Haven, CT, 2002), 111. J. H. Newman, *An Essay in Aid of a Grammar of Assent* (London, 1870), 238.

[29] John Newman, Journal entry, 9 August 1823, quoted in Svaglic, 'Charles Newman', 375.

[30] Charles Newman to John Newman, 23 February 1825, in *The Letters and Diaries of John Henry Newman*, 1: *Ealing, Trinity, Oriel, February 1801 to December 1826*, ed. Ian Ker and Thomas Gornall (Oxford, 1978), 212.

[31] Svaglic, 'Charles Newman', 376.

[32] John Newman, 'Memorandum on Charles Newman', in *The Letters and Diaries of John Henry Newman*, 4: *The Oxford Movement, July 1833 to December 1834*, ed. Ian Ker and Thomas Gornall (Oxford, 1980), 131–6, at 134.

[33] Maisie Ward, *Young Mr Newman* (New York, 1948), 360; John Newman to Thomas Mozley, 5 March 1841, in *Letters and Diaries*, 8: *Tract 90 and the Jerusalem Bishopric, January 1841 – April 1842*, ed. Gerard Tracey (Oxford, 1999), 55.

life for themselves and others'.[34] For Charles, then, the believer in human goodness in improved circumstances, Christianity was to be rejected for obstructing the socialism which sought justice in this life, and not the doubted next.[35]

I turn now to consider more briefly two rather different Owenite unbelievers. Emma Martin and Frances Wright were lecturers for the socialist and secularist cause on the two sides of the Atlantic. Emma Martin became a Particular Baptist at seventeen, after a middle-class upbringing in the Church of England in Bristol.[36] Keenly involved in chapel life, yet unhappily married, Martin developed her literary and public speaking skills to question the contemporary status of women from the perspective of Christian Dissent. In 1839, Martin went to hear the Owenite lecturer Alexander Campbell (not the Disciples of Christ leader) condemn the 'evils of our present social system', and was elated to hear him emphasize 'the degraded condition of women'.[37] Yet when Campbell subsequently attacked Christianity and dismissed its compatibility with socialism, Martin was shocked, and immediately challenged Campbell to debate the claims and social system of Christianity. In the course of her preparations and the debates themselves, Martin discovered her own doubts overwhelming. Seeking to read the Bible 'rationally' presented her with 'inaccuracies and inconsistencies' difficult to defend.[38] Very publicly, Martin switched sides, and became one of the Owenites' most formidable and notorious advocates.[39] Key elements of the early socialist vision were the emancipation of women from loveless marriages and domestic restrictions, which Owen's plan for life in community and the overturning of property

---

[34] Charles Newman to John Newman, 3 December 1841, in *Letters and Diaries*, 8, ed. Tracey, 362. Charles had 'often wished I could find some religious party of similar aim', but seemingly never did.

[35] Charles was later an ally of the leading socialist freethinker George Jacob Holyoake. His articles for Holyoake's *Reasoner* were republished posthumously as *Essays in Rationalism* (London, 1891).

[36] *ODNB*, *s.n.* 'Martin, Emma (1811/12–1851)', online edn (2004), at: <http://www.oxforddnb.com/view/article/45460>, accessed 13 June 2014; Laura Schwartz, *Infidel Feminism: Secularism, Religion and Women's Emancipation, England 1830–1914* (Manchester, 2013).

[37] Emma Martin, *A Few Reasons for Renouncing Christianity, and Professing and Disseminating Infidel Opinions* (London, 1840), 4–5.

[38] Schwartz, *Infidel Feminism*, 81.

[39] Martin's career is discussed extensively in Schwartz, *Infidel Feminism*.

law (and with it, conventions of women as property) would achieve.[40] For Emma Martin, 'irrational' biblical Christianity's underpinning of conventional women's roles made it an obstacle to socialism, so necessitating its removal.

Frances Wright was born in Dundee, but achieved fame in the American Owenite movement, founding a model community for freed slaves in Tennessee, then establishing the first secularist Hall of Science in New York City in 1829.[41] A full decade before Martin, Wright came to much the same view of Christianity as upholding patriarchy and sexual conservatism and opposing socialism. In an infamous series of *Popular Lectures*, circulated widely in the United States, she advocated free rational enquiry 'as a means of obtaining just knowledge', turning this Enlightenment approach – after Owen – to critique the truth claims of revealed religion, and to condemn the social divisions and waste it caused.[42] Wright declared to the American Churches:

> … you are now engaged in the pursuit of what is *not* knowledge. … you are now paying … towards the support of a system of error, which, from the earliest date of human tradition, has filled the earth with crime and deluged its bosom with blood, … [which] fills your country with discord, and impedes its progress in virtue, by lengthening the term of its ignorance.[43]

For Wright, 'idle speculations in matters of faith' were the origin of so much 'positive misery', of 'disputes and dissentions', 'unjust actions' and 'uncharitable feelings'.[44] Wright saw 'free enquiry' as leading to her own deist beliefs and open freedom of opinion in socialist community.

For a range of early socialists, then, doubts about Christianity spanned these four issues identified in Owen's thought: first, the denial of human responsibility for sin, then views of Christianity as divisive, as a hindrance to the coming of socialism and as 'irrational'. After Owen articulated these views openly from 1817, he lost substantial support for his reform proposals, especially among an outraged Christian establishment. For decades after, Owen's 'infidel'

---

[40] The classic study of Owenism and early feminism is Taylor, *Eve and the New Jerusalem*.
[41] Ibid. 65–70; C. M. Eckhardt, *Fanny Wright: Rebel in America* (Cambridge, MA, 1984).
[42] Frances Wright, *Course of Popular Lectures* (New York, 1829), 85–105.
[43] Ibid. 101.
[44] Ibid. 102.

views branded him suspect in most church circles, a distrust which came to a head in 1840 when the arch-Tory bishop of Exeter, Henry Phillpotts, was apoplectic at Owen's presentation to the young Queen Victoria, leading him to denounce the socialist menace to the House of Lords.[45]

CHRISTIAN OWENITES

Despite this history, a significant proportion of Owen's supporters in Britain and America in the 1820s and 1830s were Christians. Many looked beyond Owen's personal beliefs and reputation, and recognized something in his social system's communal or cooperative principles which squared with their persisting Christianity. Mapping the views of these diverse Christian Owenites on either side of the Atlantic reveals how each of the issues exercising Owenite doubts generated alternative Christian answers.

Beginning with Owen's environmental determinism and the denial of human responsibility for sin, several innovative responses were formulated. Some suggested that the Bible might endorse Owen's view of the power of circumstances to shape humanity. The most common proof text was Proverbs 22: 6: 'Train up a child in the way he should go: and when he is old he will not depart from it'.[46] Others pointed to Job 10: 8–9 and Lamentations 4: 2 as 'passages in Scripture favouring this view of man', and describing human beings as being 'like clay in the potter's hand'.[47]

Some sympathizers, such as the Quaker, William Allen, endorsed attempts to frame Owen's doctrine as referring only to 'the worldly character, not the religious'. Allen's *Philanthropist* journal declared it no 'interference with religion, to say that the worldly qualities of man's nature are operated upon by worldly circumstances'. By this, the fallen human capacity to sin – the 'worldly qualities of man's nature' – was distinguished from a person's religious identity, their being a Christian in such circumstances. It was pointed out that Christian adherence equipped the human person with an impulse to overcome or avoid sin, yet the familiar refrain in the Lord's Prayer, 'lead us not into temptation', demonstrated that orthodox Christianity still presupposed a 'dependence of conduct upon situation'. Christians do

---

[45] On this episode, see Royle, *Victorian Infidels*, 65–9; Harrison, *Robert Owen*, 216–19.

[46] *The Economist*, no. 7 (10 March 1821), 108.

[47] John Minter Morgan, *Hampden in the Nineteenth Century* (London, 1834), 17.

not pray for God to 'prevent them from sinning … but to remove from them such circumstances as would work upon their nature to make them sin'.[48] The journal thus acknowledged a 'truth' in Owen's principles, yet adjusted this to the concept of 'circumstances of temptation', and the persisting need for people still to convert to Christianity. For Allen, changing circumstances was indeed a way of changing humanity, in the sense that such changes offered a means to aiding future human improvement by making it easier to be a better Christian.

Elements of Allen's argument were echoed by the Anglican philanthropist, John Minter Morgan, perhaps the leading Christian advocate for Owenism after 1817. Morgan composed, among other works, the admirably perspicuous *Mr. Owen's proposed Villages for the Poor shown to be highly favourable to Christianity*.[49] Morgan's writings in this period sought to make Owen's environmental determinism more palatable to Christians by insisting that sinful behaviour was promoted in conditions of human 'error', and that humans themselves had created many of these 'evil' conditions: 'they are our own errors alone that have impeded the amelioration of mankind'.[50] Morgan looked at contemporary British society and was shocked by the domestic cultures of 'intemperance, brutality, ill-nature', and 'dissipating … amusements'.[51] Owen's social plans offered 'a better system' under which so many circumstances conducive to sin would be expelled. After such a 'withdrawment of the mind from temptation', Morgan contended, 'our holy religion will have free course; since those obstacles which at present impede its progress will be … diminished'.[52] As they would surely promote 'the more extended practice of genuine Christianity', Owen's social proposals were therefore worthy of all Christians' support.[53]

---

[48] 'A New View of Society … Essays first and second', *The Philanthropist* 3 (1813), 93–118, at 115.

[49] Christianus [John Minter Morgan], *Mr. Owen's proposed Villages for the Poor shown to be highly favourable to Christianity* (London, 1819). Morgan remains an understudied figure, although I intend to correct this in a future article on 'The Church of England and Early Socialism'. Until then, the most extensive study remains W. H. G. Armytage, *Heavens Below* (London, 1961), 130–44, 209–23.

[50] Philanthropos [John Minter Morgan], *Remarks on the Practicability of Mr Robert Owen's Plan to Improve the Condition of the Lower Classes* (London, 1818), 38–9.

[51] [Morgan], *Owen's proposed Villages*, 9–10.

[52] Ibid. 10–12.

[53] [Morgan], *Remarks*, 39.

Many early supporters of Owen's cooperative trading recognized his theory as an antidote to divisive competitive capitalism, and cast this as a more harmful social division than religion. Cooperation was often viewed as exemplifying explicitly Christian 'friendship and brotherly love', with one contributor to the *Co-operative Magazine* resenting Owen's 'religio-phobia' because 'the Christian religion most expressly commands and most continually inculcates, as the first thing necessary, the practice of our System'.[54] At a mass meeting of the Sheffield Co-operators in May 1832, the Revd Christopher Blencow Dunn, curate of Cumberworth, near Huddersfield, proposed cooperation as a remedy for 'all the moral, political and commercial abuses and disorders' of the present.[55] Secretary of the relief committee in Denby Dale – a region of the Yorkshire West Riding woollens industry desperately affected by falling piece-rates and an erratic trade cycle – Dunn described the 'beneficial effects' cooperation had already produced. 'It has united in the bonds of brotherly love thousands of industrious fellow citizens', Dunn asserted; 'it has raised the laborious and useful classes in their own estimation, as well as in the estimation of others'. Conscious of Owen's reputation, Dunn stressed 'the morality of our doctrines. There is nothing in cooperation which is at all disgraceful, demoralizing, or illegal'. Dunn knew of 'no institution' beside cooperation 'which, in its nature, is so essentially religious, being a practical development of the whole system of pure and primitive Christianity. It anticipates the establishment of a condition of social equality, in which there will exist a community of interests, a community of happiness, and a community of wealth.'[56]

Dunn's suggestion that cooperation and shared property were an outworking and completion of Christianity was echoed in responses to Owen's community plans, providing a counter to the view that Christianity delayed socialism. One writer in *The Economist* – 'a periodical paper explanatory of the New System of Society projected by Robert Owen' – eagerly declared: 'the earthly triumph of Christianity would be the establishment of the new system of society'.[57] In the United States, Owen's earliest publicists were mostly Quakers, whose Owen-inspired 'New York Society for Promoting Communities'

---

[54] *Brighton Co-operator*, 1 November 1828; *Co-operative Magazine*, December 1827, 534.
[55] *Sheffield Courant and Advertiser*, 18 May 1832.
[56] Ibid.
[57] *The Economist*, no. 42 (10 November 1821), 256.

declared its object: 'to convince the pious of all denominations, …
to institute and establish in every religious congregation, a system of
social, and equal, and inclusive rights … and privileges to all real and
personal property'.[58] The New York Society likewise evoked Old
Testament prophecy and a coming millennium: 'we have reasons to
believe, that by a growth in the virtues of social love and affection,
each shall be enabled to love one another as one's own self, and thus
introduce that gospel state of "peace on earth and good will to men;"
"every man seeking not his own, but his neighbour's wealth"'.[59]

A leading figure in the Society for Promoting Communities was
Dr Cornelius Blatchly, a physician struck by growing social distress in New York City, whose earlier work on the *Causes of Popular
Poverty* (1817) had contrasted contemporary property ownership in
the United States, which produced an 'excess of riches in the hands
of the few', with the biblical model of land 'for general use and benefit and not for individual aggrandizement'.[60] For Blatchly – like other
Christian sympathizers with early socialism – the truly Christian approach to property was represented by the Jerusalem church holding
'all things in common' in Acts 2 and 4.[61] The future of Christianity would see the 'restoration' of such 'pure and perfect communities', and thus a realizing of the divine intention for human society so
quickly forfeited by the early Church.[62]

Back in Britain, Morgan's analysis of references to 'the plan of a
Community of Goods' in New Testament writings, led him to conclude 'that it was either itself a Divine suggestion, or at least considered by the apostles and the first converts as a necessary consequence
of the doctrines that had been revealed to them'.[63] The subsequent
demise of this 'plan of life' from the Church was no indication that
it had been found 'impracticable'; rather its 'departure affords no
better argument against the primitive practice, than is presented by
any other corruption of Christianity against its genuine doctrines'.[64]

[58] Cornelius Blatchly, *An Essay on Common Wealths* (New York, 1822), 1–3.
[59] Ibid. 3.
[60] Cornelius Blatchly, 'Some Causes of Popular Poverty', appended to [Thomas Brana-
gan], *The Pleasures of Contemplation* (Philadelphia, PA, 1817), 176–206, at 199–201.
[61] Acts 2: 44–5; 4: 32.
[62] Blatchly, *Essay on Common Wealths*.
[63] [John Minter Morgan], 'An Inquiry respecting Private Property and the Authority and
Perpetuity of the Apostolic Institution of a Community of Goods', *Monthly Repository* 16
(1821), 88–101, at 91.
[64] Ibid. 89.

James Smith, a former Church of Scotland minister, likewise declared 'community of goods ... the true Christianity', explaining to an Owenite audience that the passages in Acts were 'the prophetic glance which the founders of Christianity themselves gave of the future destiny of the church'.[65] 'If priests and legislators knew their own interests', Smith insisted, 'they would establish the social system of communities at once. If they understood Christianity, they would see that they are nothing but the Christian millennium about to be fulfilled'.[66]

Millennial beliefs were just one of a variety of recognizably Romantic forms of religion common among Christian Owenites, which represented a distinct response to Owen's 'Enlightenment' dismissal of revealed religion.[67] James Smith became the leading Owenite of this trend, producing *The Shepherd* (1834–8), a journal discussing prophecy, millennialism and how socialism could be sympathetic to spiritual experience.[68] From this period of the 1830s, mysticism and the soul's experience attracted increasing attention as an alternative to materialism, with doubts voiced about the absolute influence of physical circumstances. It was for the socialist to choose to lead a moral life, a choice which concerned their own individuality and recognized the character of the soul as subject to the work of God. 'Circumstances may deform, but cannot form the character', a work on religion and Owenism now declared:

> ... circumstances are to the individual, what the soil and the atmosphere are to a plant; they may facilitate or obstruct the expansion of his powers and the unfolding of his character, but the energy that triumphs over all circumstances, and gives maturity to the noblest sentiments, comes from a deeper source.[69]

---

[65] James Smith, 'Lecture on a Christian Community', in Gregory Claeys, ed., *Owenite Socialism: Pamphlets and Correspondence 1832–1837*, 10 vols (London, 2005), 4: 200.

[66] Ibid. 199.

[67] David Bebbington has identified the increased interest in apocalypticism and the millennium in early nineteenth-century Evangelicalism as 'a symptom of Romanticism': *Evangelicalism in Modern Britain: A History from the 1730s to the 1980s* (London, 1989), 80–5. On the use of millennial rhetoric by Owen and secular Owenites, see especially Harrison, *Robert Owen*, 92–139.

[68] On Smith's *Shepherd* and his principle of 'practical mysticism', see Philip Lockley, *Visionary Religion and Radicalism in Early Industrial England* (Oxford, 2013), 240–52.

[69] John Minter Morgan, *Colloquies on Religion, and Religious Education* (London, 1837), 10.

Among the Owenites attracted to the varieties of 'sacred socialism' which emerged was Alexander Campbell, the once-sceptical lecturer.[70] Campbell adopted the mystical communitarianism of James
Pierrepont Greaves, whose Surrey 'Concordium' set the path of socialism back towards the monastery.[71] A regime of uncooked, vege-
tarian food, cold baths and celibacy sought to purify both body and
soul from sin and make moral beings for a harmonious future.

Related ideas circulated within contemporary Transcendentalism
in New England, as the philosopher Amos Bronson Alcott also cri-
tiqued Owen's materialist doctrine of circumstances with a theory of
'spiritual circumstances' in his own community experiments.[72] Alcott
and other Transcendentalists shared an interest in Coleridge's ideal-
ism and Romantic concepts of organic development with the 'sacred
socialists', and the two groups were closely aligned through friendships and correspondence networks.[73] For Alcott, whose early interests centred on educating children to be open to God, it was clear that
'wisdom and happiness' could be determined by environment, but it
was unwarranted to assert that circumstances had 'the transcendent
importance which they receive in the theory of Mr Owen'.[74] To grant
such power to circumstances was a 'one-eyed philosophy', one of
the 'half-visaged theories of materialism'. Only when combined with
God-given free will to 'form and modify institutions' for a better future would an awareness of the influence of circumstances allow human beings to meliorate their own and others' 'outward condition'.[75]
Alcott's own interest in living in an ascetic community stemmed from
this belief in overcoming the unhappy effects of 'external nature', an
intention which Alcott equated with 'the purpose of Heaven' and the
next stage in the intended development of humanity, when:

> … the faded image of Humanity is to be restored, and Man to reappear
> in his original brightness. It is to mould anew our Institutions, our

[70] W. H. Marwick, *The Life of Alexander Campbell* (Glasgow, 1964).
[71] See Jackie Latham, *Search for the New Eden* (London, 1999).
[72] Richard Francis, 'Circumstances and Salvation: the ideology of the Fruitlands Utopia',
American Quarterly 25 (1973), 202–34; see also Anne Rose, *Transcendentalism as a Social Movement, 1830–1850* (New Haven, CT, 1981).
[73] Alcott visited the Surrey Concordium, and several English sacred socialists joined Alcott's Fruitlands community in Massachusetts: see especially Latham, *Search*, 187–221;
Richard Francis, *Fruitlands* (New Haven, CT, 2010).
[74] Cambridge, MA, Harvard University, Houghton Library, A. Bronson Alcott, MS Journals 7, fol. 29 (23 April 1834), quoted in Francis, 'Circumstances and Salvation', 206.
[75] Ibid. 206–7.

Manners, our Men. It is to restore Nature to its rightful use, purify Life; hallow the functions of the Human Body, and regenerate Philosophy, Literature, Art, Society. The Divine Idea of Man is to be formed in the common consciousness of this age.[76]

CONCLUSION

As is clear from Alcott's reflections on what 'is to be', from the preceding discussion of socialists preparing their souls and bodies for forthcoming harmony, and from all the ideas of fulfilling the Christian millennium, restoring the early Church's 'pure and perfect communities', anticipating conditions of social equality and happiness and planning society to facilitate the overcoming of sin, these Christian early socialists were commonly concerned with the future: an imagined, better future. Of course, all socialisms are ultimately about imagined futures. They are envisaged from within the present and project forward in time to when current conditions of injustice and inequality will be no more, or when marginal existing experiments in communal or cooperative living will be made universal.[77] In this way, socialisms, however doubtful over doctrines, retain an obvious point of prospective interaction and overlap with future-thinking in Christian eschatology, or, as some would term it, theologies of hope.[78] The socialist tendency to doubt Christianity is perhaps paradoxically accompanied by an inherent hopefulness about the future which is open to recognition and reclamation by Christians.

It was with hope that early nineteenth-century Christians sympathetic to Owenite socialism most commonly answered or avoided the doubts of their fellow socialists. Owen's determinist views of circumstances and sin were sometimes squared with a biblical perspective, yet also reshaped into the prayerful hope of realizing social circumstances which led 'not into temptation'. During the 1820s and 1830s, Christians living with the early effects of capitalist competition recognized this economic order as the greater cause of social division, and cast their Christianity on the side of the hope of future social unity. Looking towards a fulfilment of Christianity's communal ethic, in a

---

[76] A. Bronson Alcott, *The Doctrine and Discipline of Human Culture* (Boston, MA, 1836), 4.

[77] On socialism and imagined futures, see Philip Lockley, 'Transatlantic Reputations: Protestant Communalism and Early Socialism', in idem, ed., *Protestant Communalism in the Trans-Atlantic World, 1650–1850* (Basingstoke, forthcoming 2016), ch. 7.

[78] Jürgen Moltmann, *Theology of Hope*, transl. James W. Leitch (London, 1967).

millennial age or an evocation of the primitive Church, they considered their religion a hopeful direction, not an obstruction to socialism. Furthermore, significant numbers of socialists were left unpersuaded by the Enlightenment rationalist accounts of human existence offered by Owen or Frances Wright: religious experience remained a palpable factor in their lives. Several developed a more Romantic social ethics, taking account of a divine immanence and involvement in the world, and placed their hope in grounding individual choice and character in the soul and their God-given free will.

Thus, in contrast to the familiar Christian Socialist tradition of conventional ecclesiastical history, which so consistently proffered 'faith' as the counter to socialist doubt, Christians engaged by an earlier socialism claimed the alternative antonym of hope from within the dynamic of socialism itself, and turned it to their own Christian purpose – the purpose of imagining a more Christian future.

'Isaiah's Call to England': Doubts about Prophecy in Nineteenth-Century Britain

Gareth Atkins*

Magdalene College, Cambridge

Prophetic thought in nineteenth-century Britain has often been presented as divided between those mostly evangelical constituencies who 'believed' in its literal fulfilment in the past, present or future and those who 'doubted' such interpretations. This essay seeks to question that division by tracking the uses of one set of prophetic passages, those concerning the 'Ships of Tarshish' mentioned in Isaiah 60: 9 and elsewhere. It examines their appropriation from the late eighteenth century onwards by those seeking prophetic-providential justification for the British maritime empire. Next it shows how such such ideas fuelled missionary expansion in the years after 1815, suggesting that by mid-century that there was a growing spectrum of ways in which such passages were used by religious commentators. The final section shows how biblical critics seeking to bolster the integrity of the Bible as a text reconstructed the geographical and economic settings for these passages, establishing their historical veracity as they did so but in the process undermining their supernaturally predictive status. Thus one way of bolstering 'faith' – the study of prophetic fulfilments – was rendered doubtful by another. By the end of our period Tyre and Tarshish retained much of their homiletic punch as metaphors for the sin brought by trade and luxury, but those who saw them as literal proxies for Britain were in the minority.

In January 1860, the Bolton clergyman Walter Chamberlain completed his latest book. In 424 closely wrought pages, *Isaiah's Call to England* sought to expose how 'Isa[iah] xviii is an unfulfilled prophecy, foretelling the ingathering of all Israel to Zion; … and that, for such purpose of ingathering, Isaiah hails a people friendly to Israel, and to be renowned for their ships and maritime power.' That power, Chamberlain revealed triumphantly, was 'ENGLAND'.[1] If this was not immediately obvious from the passage, which talked in vague terms of woe to a land beyond the rivers of Ethiopia, and of

* Magdalene College, Cambridge, CB3 0AG. E-mail: ga240@cam.ac.uk.

[1] Walter Chamberlain, *Isaiah's Call to England: Being an Exposition of Isaiah the Eighteenth* (London, 1860), iv–v.

Studies in Church History 52 (2016) 381–397 © Ecclesiastical History Society 2016
doi: 10.1017/stc.2015.22

vessels of bulrushes sent to a scattered people, Chamberlain maintained that this was because commentators had wrongly assumed Isaiah 18 to be ancient history. In applying it to events as yet unfulfilled, Chamberlain starts with tame exposition, but begins before long to pull exegetical rabbits out of the hat: the apparent 'woe' in verse one of the chapter is in fact Isaiah's favourable 'ho!'; the lions on the English and Scottish arms match references culled from Ezekiel; and the events Isaiah foretold are imminent, to take place between 1864 and 1914.[2] Layers of ancient Scripture are stripped back to reveal modern visions: a prophesied highway translates into a railway from the Euphrates to the Mediterranean, while in the most bizarre passage, 'vessels of bulrushes' become, through a process of philological scrutiny, 'steam-packet boats'.[3] Even Chamberlain realized that this was a bit much – 'I have halted here a little while just to give the reader time to laugh' – but he believed it all the same.[4] He concludes with a seventeen-point prognostication concerning the likely steps towards Israel's restoration, encompassing the machinations of France under Napoleon III, the collapse of the Ottoman empire, a Russian invasion of the Middle East and, lastly, the preservation of England – 'TARSHISH' – as fulcrum of the divine plan.[5]

One way of dealing with *Isaiah's Call to England* is to pigeonhole it as a throwback to the chiliastic jeremiads that had proliferated between 1820 and 1840 and still littered the publishing landscape.[6] While historicist premillennialists like Chamberlain continued to treat the apocalyptic books of the Bible and current events as mutually reinforcing interpretative keys, others were doubtful about the utility of this method. The ecclesiastical tattler W. J. Conybeare was one of them, his famous *Edinburgh Review* article of 1855 on 'Church Parties' lampooning those obsessed with 'the Red Dragon', 'Gog and Magog', the ten lost tribes of Israel and the location of Armageddon.[7] Yet Chamberlain was by no means the outré fanatic Conybeare had in mind. 'Should any one suspect me of being a dreamer or an enthusiast', he remarked drily, they ought to try

---

[2] Ibid. 333, 341–4; 357–9.
[3] Ibid. 423, 203–29.
[4] Ibid. 227.
[5] Ibid. 422–4.
[6] Boyd Hilton, *A Mad, Bad, and Dangerous People? England, 1783–1846* (Oxford, 2006), 397–406.
[7] [W. J. Conybeare], 'Church Parties', *Edinburgh Review* 98 (1853), 273–342, at 297.

moving to Bolton, where 'the cooling sedative of six months' residence in a manufacturing town' would soon put paid to flights of fancy.[8] Nor was Chamberlain uneducated. A graduate of Corpus Christi, Cambridge,[9] his career was punctuated by publications not just on prophecy but on questions that were of more general concern to Anglican clergymen. He wrote in 1863 against Bishop Colenso's critical account of the Pentateuch, for example, and fought Irish disestablishment later in the decade.[10] If the apocalyptic writing and painting that had so thrilled audiences in earlier decades no longer appealed to such a broad audience, prophetic books and periodicals still found a ready readership, in evangelical circles especially.[11] The *Quarterly Journal of Prophecy*, edited by the Free Church of Scotland minister Horatius Bonar, was among several publications that noticed *Isaiah's Call* favourably.[12] Only two years later, in 1862, one of the classics of the genre, Edward Bishop Elliott's *Horae Apocalypticae*, went into its fifth edition.[13] Recent scholarship suggests that apocalyptic language continued to appeal to politicians, preachers and activists for much of the nineteenth century.[14]

Nevertheless, Chamberlain was speaking to an intellectual subculture that, while still viable, was coming to look old-fashioned. There were a variety of reasons for this. As W. H. Oliver suggested, in what remains the best survey of the subject, 'few parts of the Bible were as vulnerable to modern critical scholarship as those dwelt upon by prophetical exegetes': the books of Daniel and Revelation, and (to a lesser extent) Isaiah, Jeremiah and Ezekiel.[15] Just as important as

---

[8] Chamberlain, *Isaiah*, x.

[9] J. and J. A. Venn, *Alumni Cantabrigienses,* 2: *From 1752 to 1900*, 6 vols (Cambridge, 1940–54), 2: 3.

[10] Walter Chamberlain, *A Plain Reply to Bishop Colenso* (London, 1863).

[11] See, for example, Martin Spence, *Heaven on Earth: Reimagining Time and Eternity in Nineteenth-Century British Evangelicalism* (Eugene, OR, 2015).

[12] *Quarterly Journal of Prophecy* 12 (1860), 395–7; see also *London Review and Weekly Journal of Politics, Literature, Art, and Society*, 4 October 1862, iv.

[13] Elliott, like Chamberlain, was a learned man, a one-time fellow of Trinity College, Cambridge, who ended his days as incumbent of St Mark's, Kemptown, in well-heeled Brighton: see J. Bateman, *The Life of the Rev. Henry Venn Elliott* (London, 1868).

[14] Crawford Gribben and Timothy C. F. Stunt, 'Introduction' to eidem, eds, *Prisoners of Hope? Aspects of Evangelical Millennialism in Britain and Ireland, 1800–1880* (Carlisle, 2004), 1–17; see also Ralph Brown, 'Victorian Anglican Evangelicalism: The Radical Legacy of Edward Irving', *JEH* 58 (2007), 675–704.

[15] W. H. Oliver, *Prophets and Millennialists: The Uses of Biblical Prophecy in England from the 1790s to the 1840s* (Auckland, 1978), 239–40.

higher criticism was a growing sense among liberal thinkers inside and outside the Churches that the historicity of the Bible was less important than the eternal truths it contained. Instead of warping recent history and ancient texts to fit one another, maintained Thomas Arnold of Rugby, commentators would be better employed in applying the timeless moral lessons articulated by biblical prophets to present-day ills.[16] And there was also the problem of dates. For those who had followed Elliott in predicting on the basis of the 'Year-Day Theory' that the millennium would take place in 1866, the non-event necessitated an embarrassing climbdown.[17] 'Recent events have fully confirmed the belief that the 1260 years of Papal Supremacy were to close', insisted the Revd Samuel Minton of Eaton Chapel. 'But the discovery of a strange, though very general, oversight in the application of Daniel's supplemental period of 75 years, has revealed the truth that the overthrow of Papal rule, is not the overthrow of the Papacy itself.'[18] While many simply altered their calculations, for hostile observers it served to underline the futility of the exercise *tout court*.

What follows charts the rise and fall of the providentialist readings of Britain's maritime empire that Chamberlain found so seductive. Tempting though it is to assume that the sidelining of such ideas took place against an increasingly secular backdrop, it should already be clear that changing conceptions of the Bible, prophecy and Providence necessitated a constantly shifting reassessment of what belief and doubt meant, and how they fitted together. To say one 'believed' in a prophetic passage in around 1800 was different from saying the same thing in 1850 or 1900, and this essay seeks to examine why. Prophetic topoi did not trace a course of linear decline; nor were they the preserve of evangelical literalists, as readers of much of the existing work on the subject might conclude. We cannot assume that there was ever general agreement as to what prophecies meant and that people then 'doubted' that meaning. Rather, the potency of prophecy was dependent on 'current affairs' and a host of other

---

[16] Arthur Penrhyn Stanley, *The Life and Correspondence of Thomas Arnold*, 2 vols (London, 1844), 1: 65, 177–80.
[17] The erstwhile Brethren leader Benjamin Wills Newton was especially scornful of Elliott's argument: see Benjamin Wills Newton, *Aids to Prophetic Enquiry*, 3rd edn (London, 1881), 241 n.
[18] Samuel Minton, *The Merchants of Tarshish, or, England, America, and Russia in the Last War* (London, 1868), iv.

scholarly and cultural influences that rendered them applicable and doubtful by turns, and that altered how such passages were to be read, understood and applied. This essay reflects on how inherited strands of prophetic thought did not fray entirely in the nineteenth century but were repeatedly respun for new purposes. In doing so, it emphasizes how countering one form of doubt could leave the way open for new uncertainties in other areas. Protestant scholars continued, as they always had done, to deploy discoveries about the texts, biblical geography and linguistics in order to underline the Bible's coherence and bolster its authority. As we will see, however, those tools were two-edged, encouraging the sort of historical contextualization that made Scripture appear chronologically remote and culturally strange, and rendering hitherto accepted typological and prophetic readings inadmissible or just plain wrong.[19]

THE BIBLE AND BRITISH NAVAL POWER

Chamberlain was far from being the first to associate Old Testament passages with British maritime ventures. Ever since the early modern period, Protestants had used scriptural passages pertaining to Israel to frame interpretations of military victories and defeats, sudden deaths, harvests, famines and extreme weather, interpretations which continued to echo in the nineteenth century.[20] They saw in the defeat of the Spanish Armada parallels with the Israelite escape through the Red Sea ('God blew and they were scattered'), while from 1690 until its pruning in 1859 the Book of Common Prayer enshrined memories of another Protestant wind in its service for 5 November, which, as well as commemorating the Gunpowder Plot, celebrated William of Orange's landing at Torbay in 1688.[21] The eighteenth century added further layers of naval-providential rhetoric. 'The Wrecks of

---

[19] See Michael Ledger-Lomas, 'Conder and Sons: Dissent and the Oriental Bible in Nineteenth-Century Britain', in idem and Scott Mandelbrote, eds, *Dissent and the Bible in Britain, c.1650–1950* (Oxford, 2013), 205–22.

[20] The recent literature on this is vast. Highlights include Alexandra Walsham, *Providence in Early Modern England* (Oxford, 1999), 281–325; Pasi Ihalainen, *Protestant Nations Redefined: Changing Perceptions of National Identity in the Rhetoric of the English, Dutch and Swedish Churches, 1685–1772* (Leiden, 2005); John Coffey, *Exodus and Liberation: Deliverance Politics from John Calvin to Martin Luther King Jr.* (Oxford, 2014), 25–78. None of this should imply that providentialism was the preserve of Protestants; see, for instance, Marjorie Reeves's seminal study, *The Influence of Prophecy in the Later Middle Ages: a Study in Joachimism* (Oxford, 1969).

[21] Coffey, *Exodus and Liberation*, 36–7.

our Navies and Fleets Preach to us, that 'tis in vain we pretend to be Wall'd about by the Ocean, and ride Masters of the Sea', Daniel Defoe had written after the Great Storm of 1703, warning that God was punishing Britain by the obliteration of her ships and commerce.[22] Annual 'storm sermons', endowed to impress the message on future generations, were still being preached in the 1780s, while Defoe continued to be read long after that.[23] In the 1790s the ex-slaver turned clergyman John Newton glumly likened Britain to her Old Testament counterpart both in her divinely conferred advantages and in her flagrant disregard for the obligations this entailed, embodied most glaringly, Newton thought, in the triangular trade.[24] Abolition (1807) and emancipation (1833) would thus provide Victorian sermonizers with a satisfying narrative of national redemption. Typology and prophetic fulfilment were part of an apologetic edifice developed to show both the applicability of the Bible and the continuing intervention of the Almighty in human affairs.[25]

Yet if posing as a 'new Israel' had worked well for embattled states like sixteenth-century England, such language had less to offer for a global power whose sway depended on naval hegemony. Scriptural references to maritime trade supplied a rich alternative vocabulary for those keen to celebrate commercial success or to condemn its demoralizing effects.[26]

> Since the first dominion of men was asserted over the ocean, three thrones, of mark beyond all others, have been set upon its sands: the thrones of Tyre, Venice, and England. Of the First of these great powers only the memory remains; of the Second, the ruin; the Third, which inherits their greatness, if it forget their example, may be led through prouder eminence to less pitied destruction.[27]

These sermonic cadences were those of John Ruskin in the celebrated opening to *Stones of Venice* (3 vols, 1851–3), but his message would have been recognizable to many a seventeenth- and

---

[22] Daniel Defoe, *The Lay-Man's Sermon upon the Late Storm* (London, 1704), 6.

[23] E.g. Samuel Stennett, *A Sermon in Commemoration of the Great Storm of Wind* (London, 1788).

[24] J. H. Pratt, ed., *Eclectic Notes: or, Notes of Discussions on Religious Topics at the Meetings of the Eclectic Society, London, during the Years 1798–1814*, 2nd edn (London, 1865), 330.

[25] Paul J. Korshin, *Typologies in England, 1650–1820* (Princeton, NJ, 1982).

[26] Walsham, *Providence*, 299.

[27] John Ruskin, *The Stones of Venice: The Foundations* (London, 1851), 1.

eighteenth-century congregation. It was not just a poignant image. Commentators had long sought to counter doubts about the inspiration of the Bible by demonstrating the accuracy of the prophecies it contained, and the recorded facts of Tyre's destruction by Nebuchadnezzar and its fall to Alexander the Great in the great siege of 332 BC made this a straightforward but resonant example of how Old Testament predictions had been fulfilled. Travellers' morbid accounts of the ruins were read both literally, as confirmatory evidence, and figuratively, as warnings to modern nations tempted to pursue profit at the expense of virtue.[28]

Rhetorically useful in a different way was Tarshish, with which Tyre was often associated. The prophet Jonah sought to flee there, explains Father Mapple in *Moby Dick*, because it was modern-day Cadiz, 'as far by water, from Joppa, as Jonah could possibly have sailed in those ancient days, when the Atlantic was an almost unknown sea'.[29] Mapple was certainly up-to-date with modern scholarship; but although the French geographer Samuel Bochart had convincingly identified Tarshish with Strabo's Tartessus, in southwestern Spain, as long ago as 1646, this did not prevent its typological appropriation.[30] It appears twenty-one times in the King James Bible, but aside from obscure references in genealogy and geography, what really excited prophetic commentators was the relationship of Tarshish with Israel. It crops up repeatedly as a source of wealth, most significantly in 1 Kings 10: 22, in connection with the legendary golden age of Solomon: 'once in three years came the navy of Tharshish [*sic*], bringing gold, and silver, ivory, and apes, and peacocks'.[31] Yet there was also a sense in which Tarshish was associated with prophecies unfulfilled. Could it be that it referred to shores beyond those of Spain? George Horne's much reprinted *Commentary on the Psalms* (1776) offered a multi-layered reading of the appearance of Tarshish in Psalm 72, encompassing the treasures of Solomon; the queen of Sheba; the gifts of the Magi, 'the first-fruits of the Gentiles';

---

[28] Thomas Newton, *Dissertations on the Prophecies*, 3 vols (London, 1766), 1: 314–51, extensively cited travellers' accounts by Richard Pococke, Thomas Shaw and Henry Maundrell; Thomas Hartwell Horne's *Landcape Illustrations of the Bible*, 2 vols (London, 1836; unpaginated), supplemented these with accounts from modern travellers, including William Jowett and James Silk Buckingham.

[29] Herman Melville, *Moby-Dick; or, The Whale* (New York, 1851), 46 (ch. 9).

[30] For Bochart, see Zur Shalev, *Sacred Words and Worlds: Geography, Religion, and Scholarship, 1550–1700* (Leiden, 2012), 141–204.

[31] And in variations elsewhere: see 2 Chron. 9: 21.

and 'lastly, the accession of the nations to the faith' – 'even these "isles of the Gentiles"', he ventured.[32] Isaiah, which Horne cross-referenced, provided the most tantalizing passages of all. Isaiah 60: 9 evokes a future time when from the 'isles', the 'ships of Tarshish' will 'bring thy sons from afar', restoring the exiles of Israel to the Promised Land, while Isaiah 66: 19 prophesies how 'the isles afar off' would declare God's glory among the Gentiles. If Chamberlain was unusual in his focus on Isaiah 18, the quotation of Isaiah 60: 9 on his title page placed him among numerous others who had considered the verse's implications.

The idea that Britain's destiny and the fate of the Jews were peculiarly intertwined was not, then, a new one.[33] But in the 1790s shadowy aspirations came to look like concrete certainties.[34] The outbreak of revolution in 1789, the execution of Louis XVI in 1793, the expulsion of Pope Pius VI from the papal states in 1798 and the invasion of Egypt by Napoleon the same year each prompted commentators to revise their eschatological timetables.[35] French defeats in the Middle East at the hands of Nelson and Sidney Smith, in particular, sparked an orgy of prophetic speculation about Britain's place in the divine plan, not just from wild-eyed enthusiasts but also from cultured high churchmen like the bishop of Rochester, Samuel Horsley, and from the respectable evangelical commentators G. S. Faber, James Bicheno and James Hatley Frere.[36] 'Is it an improbable conjecture', asked Henry Kett, '… that *this maritime, commercial, Protestant* kingdom should take the lead in executing the Divine will?'[37] Ralph Wedgwood was more bullish, his discovery that 'Brit' was the Hebrew word for 'covenant' acting as springboard for the extravagant theory that Scripture prophecies did not in fact refer to the Jews at all: '*the British Empire is the peculiar possession of Messiah, and his promised Naval*

---

[32] George Horne, *A Commentary on the Book of Psalms*, new edn (London, 1849), 283.

[33] See Donald M. Lewis, *The Origins of Christian Zionism* (Cambridge, 2009), 25–48, for a useful summary of seventeenth-century puritan interest in the subject.

[34] Mayir Verete, 'The Restoration of the Jews in English Protestant Thought 1790–1840', *Middle Eastern Studies* 8 (1972), 3–50; Nabil Matar, 'The Controversy over the Restoration of the Jews', *Durham University Journal* 87 (1990), 29–44.

[35] Stuart Semmel, *Napoleon and the British* (New Haven, CT, 2004), 72–106.

[36] C. D. A. Leighton, 'Antichrist's Revolution: Some Anglican Apocalypticists in the Age of the French Wars', *JRH* 24 (2002), 125–42.

[37] Henry Kett, *History the Interpreter of Prophecy*, 2 vols, 4th edn (London, 1801), 2: 291–2 n.

Dominion.[38] Frere, likewise, thought that to oppose Britain was to oppose 'the Israelitish Nation', the new chosen people of God, an idea given added credence by Napoleon's attempts to align himself with Catholicism and Islam.[39] Others were more pessimistic. Bicheno coupled Bonaparte's success with his overtures to the Jews, warning that this showed France, not Britain, to be Tarshish and that to oppose her was to risk being crushed under the inexorable wheels of Providence.[40] The Unitarian Ebenezer Aldred went further, mocking loyalist attempts to read Jacobins into the book of Revelation and inverting Protestant typology to argue that not Rome but Britain was the whore of Babylon. His language deliberately echoed the denunciations of Isaiah and Ezekiel: 'we make gold our God, commerce our God, our navy our God'.[41] Yet even this frenzy of predictive writing was not as certain as it seemed. Each new event prompted scholars and savants to elaborate further their roadmaps of the route to Armageddon, drawing caustic commentary from sceptics.

PROPHECY AND PROVIDENTIAL OPTIMISM IN POST-WAR BRITAIN

Doubt cannot have been further from the minds of patriotic sermonizers in the aftermath of Waterloo.[42] The victory seemed to vindicate claims about Britain's special providential status, fostering a consensus that British philanthropy, wafted around the world on maritime trade routes, now had a special part to play in the global spread of Christianity. Thus the missionary publicist Edward Bickersteth cited the 'vessels of bulrushes' in Isaiah 18 in equating maritime power with the despatch of 'Christian ambassadors to all the inhabitants of the world'; the Methodist scholar Adam Clarke wondered whether the angel of Revelation 14: 6 might in fact be the British and Foreign Bible Society; and two of the most ambitious works, Alexander Keith's *Signs of the Times* (1832) and Elliott's *Horae Apocalypticae* (1844), interpreted British naval victories as the second vial poured

[38] Ralph Wedgwood, *The Book of Remembrance* (London, 1814), 46.
[39] James Hatley Frere, *A Combined View of the Prophecies of Daniel, Esdras and St John*, 2nd edn (London, 1815), 114.
[40] James Bicheno, *The Restoration of the Jews, the Crisis of all Nations*, 2nd edn (London, 1807), 227–35.
[41] 'Eben-Ezer' [Ebenezer Aldred], *The Little Book* (London, 1811), 69.
[42] 'Sermons in Aid of the Waterloo Subscription', *Critical Review* 5th ser. 2 (1815), 523–8; see also 'Art. VII', *Monthly Repository* 11 (1816), 216–17.

out in Revelation 16: 3, the turning of the waters into blood denoting extensive casualty lists and the deaths of 'every living creature' being tenuously applied to the cessation of trade brought about by British wartime blockades.[43]

Although ingenious manipulation of Scripture texts was not always married to self-awareness, it emphasizes how demonstrations of the predictive precision of the Bible could be used to buttress believers against doubt, and illustrates the intense interest among evangelicals both in the conversion and the restoration of the Jews.[44] Enthusiasts were predictably thrilled by the installation of Michael Solomon Alexander, a Jew by birth, as first Anglican-Lutheran bishop of Jerusalem in 1841. Here too the participation of Britain's vaunted navy was a key piece in the symbolic jigsaw. 'Wonderfully surprised', gushed the future earl of Shaftesbury in his diary. 'Received yesterday a short note from Peel, stating that "orders would be given for an Admiralty steamboat to carry out the Bishop to Syria"!' '"Surely the Isles shall wait for thee and the ships of Tarshish first, to bring thy sons from afar and thy daughters from the ends of the earth"', he marvelled.[45] 'He will go out and disembark under the British flag', reported Bickersteth joyfully. 'Hail to the ships of Tarshish! We have here sanctified our national standard.'[46] The prophetic writer William Cuninghame of Lainshaw went so far as to maintain that the ship assigned, the unfortunately named *HMS Devastation*, was literally that prophesied in Isaiah 60, 'devastation', he claimed, being equivalent to the Hebrew word Tarshish: 'to reduce' or 'to be reduced to poverty'.[47]

Linguistic contortions aside, reactions to the new bishopric serve also to emphasize the perils of hitching one's prophetic cart too closely to current affairs. If wars and rumours of wars in the 1790s

---

[43] Edward Bickersteth, *A Scripture Help* (London, 1825), 240–1; Adam Clarke, *The New Testament of Our Lord and Saviour Jesus Christ*, 2 vols (New York, 1831), 2: 1048; Alexander Keith, *Signs of the Times*, 2 vols, 2nd edn (Edinburgh, 1832), 2: 120–9; Edward Bishop Elliott, *Horae Apocalypticae*, 3 vols, 3rd edn (London, 1847), 3: 329–30.

[44] W. T. Gidney, *The History of the London Society for Promoting Christianity amongst the Jews, from 1809 to 1908* (London 1908), 51–200; Lewis, *Christian Zionism*, 67–106.

[45] Edwin Hodder, *The Life and Work of the Seventh Earl of Shaftesbury*, 2 vols (London, 1886), 1: 378. He was conflating Isa. 43: 6 and 60: 9.

[46] T. R. Birks, *Memoir of the Rev. Edward Bickersteth*, 2 vols, 2nd edn (London, 1852), 2: 182–3.

[47] William Cuninghame, *The Political Destiny of the Earth, as revealed in the Bible*, 3rd edn (London, 1842), xii.

and 1800s had encouraged prophetic commentators to construct ever more detailed timelines, the long-running boom in such works gave hostile commentators plenty of ammunition. As mentioned earlier, even the most painstaking apocalyptic number-crunchers might be sent back to the drawing board, as in 1866. There was a growing division between the mostly evangelical constituencies who looked for the literal fulfilment of prophecy, and those who did not, although the line between them was not always clear. British geopolitical interest in the decaying Ottoman empire continued to provide reassuring portents for 'Christian Zionists' right up until the First World War, but it also attracted scriptural and quasi-scriptural language from those who did not believe in the predictive potency of Scripture.[48] This division was further problematized by a growing ambivalence at mid-century about the part Britain was destined to play in global evangelization. For although 'Commerce and Christianity' provided mid-Victorian missionaries with a catchy slogan, booming trade was not matched by mass conversions. 'We know not how long it may please God to uphold the mighty fabric of the British Empire', mused the bishop of Llandaff, Alfred Ollivant, in an 1850 sermon before the University of Cambridge. Christ's promise to be with his disciples, he pointed out, was 'inseparably connected' with the fulfilment of the Great Commission, a burden that some, he averred, were reluctant to take up.[49] Britain's privileged status, Ollivant warned, was provisional.

It may be significant that Ollivant avoided referring to the literal fulfilment of Old Testament prophecy, which was becoming a niche interest. A very different brand of providentialism was in evidence in the annual sermons given before the Master and Brethren of Trinity House, effectively the British lighthouse authority. This was a set-piece occasion, the sermon being in the gift of the Master, who was usually a high-ranking politician, and the polished offerings published as a result evince a gradual shift away from earlier certainties among establishment thinkers.[50] To trace the series through its heyday in

---

[48] Britain's acquisition of Cyprus ('Kittim') particularly excited E. J. Hytche, 'The Ships of Tarshish', *The Prophetic News and Israel's Watchman*, April 1881, 89–91. Americans who disapproved of the British empire dwelt with gloomy relish on the vengence promised to *all* nations, predicting divine leniency for their own land alone because of its favourable treatment of Jewish immigrants: George N. H. Peters, *The Theocratic Kingdom*, 3 vols (New York, 1884), 2: 778–80.

[49] Alfred Ollivant, *The Duty of a Christian Nation to her Colonies and Foreign Dependencies* (Cambridge, 1850), 27.

[50] For accounts of the spectacle, see *Illustrated London News*, 17 June 1843; 5 June 1847.

the 1820s, 1830s and 1840s is to find preachers playing safe, extolling the corporation's protection of British seafarers but steering clear of direct prophetic application in favour of moral and metaphorical parallels drawn from the usual maritime-themed texts. The Claphamite evangelical, C. R. Sumner, hit a familiar-sounding note in 1824, warning how 'the navies that were of old [had] perished' and that the commerce of Tyre and Tarshish had failed to preserve them: 'if we would secure to our own maritime eminence a more abiding inheritance, we must range ourselves on the side of the Lord'.[51] Nevertheless, this was a far cry from the full-blown prophetic mode. Perhaps in the optimistic early 1820s the Old Testament was less relevant for those, like Sumner, who held that missions were effectively writing new chapters in the book of Acts. Others, such as the up-and-coming high churchman Richard Mant (1818) and the Cambridge scientist William Whewell (1835) avoided even veiled references to catastrophic judgements, opting instead to outline the 'great machinery' of trade, enterprise and civilization benevolently ushering humanity towards more perfect knowledge of God.[52]

Contextualizing Prophetic Passages

If Trinity House preachers offered broad brushstrokes rather than detailed blueprints, it was partly because it was becoming harder to read Britain into the Bible. The emphasis was shifting, from using current events to defend the predictive accuracy of prophetic passages to using past events to reinforce the integrity and historicity of the Bible as a whole. Even among evangelicals there were those such as Samuel Lee, Regius Professor of Hebrew at Cambridge, who maintained that Old Testament prophecies concerning Israel had already been fulfilled.[53] One did not have to be learned to appreciate the point: readers of the evangelistic *Sailor's Magazine and Naval Journal* in 1837 were informed that 'Ships of Tarshish' was a generic phrase for large, sea-going merchant ships.[54] E. B. Pusey was making much the same point in a Bible commentary of 1860 when he

---

[51] Charles Richard Sumner, *The Duties of a Maritime Power* (London, 1824), 21.

[52] Richard Mant, *The Sovereignty of God in the Natural World, and the Agency of Man, Practically Considered* (London, 1818), William Whewell, *A Sermon Preached on Trinity Monday … 1835* (London, 1835), 17–18.

[53] Samuel Lee, *An Inquiry into the Nature, Progress, and End of Prophecy* (London, 1849).

[54] 'Ships of Tarshish', *Naval Journal and Sailor's Magazine* 10 (1837–8), 346–7.

equated 'Tarshish-ships' with 'the East-Indiamen which some of us remember': it was a label, not a place of origin.[55] It was possible, of course, for inherited providentialist interpretations to coexist with scholarly ideas. After all, if Mediterranean seafarers were capable of getting to Tartessus, they were surely also capable of visiting Britain. 'We know that the Phoenicians did come to the British Isles for tin, why not Jews also? The islands were well known to Herodotus.'[56] The idea that the products of Cornish mines might have adorned the Solomonic Temple remained seductive.[57] So too did the recurring Protestant fantasy that Paul had visited Britain to impart Christianity direct from the fountainhead, which theory avoided embarrassing concessions about the role of papal missionaries in her conversion.[58] When the Oxford philologist Max Müller asked in an 1867 essay 'Are there Jews in Cornwall?', his answer – no – prompted a lengthy and learned reply from the Cornish clergyman-scholar Dr John Bannister.[59] By the later nineteenth century, however, such ideas were becoming the preserve of writers on the wilder fringes of evangelicalism, and of British Israelites, whose racially tinged ideas drew eclectically on evangelical philosemitism, antiquarian texts and cod linguistics to argue that the British were literally descended from the ten lost tribes.[60]

The eclipse of prophetic literalism bespoke changing priorities among the British clerical scholarly establishment. In the decade after *Essays and Reviews* (1860), the main concern was to defend the historical truth and textual integrity of the Bible against German 'higher critics' such as De Wette and Wellhausen, whose questioning of traditional assumptions about authorship, canonicity, textual integrity and supernatural inspiration were regarded with suspicion. Prophecy was still useful in countering doubt, but not for what it said about the future. Instead it was the scientific recording by archaeologists of predictions long fulfilled – the fall of Jerusalem, say, or the destruction of Babylon – that provided extra-biblical evidence to support

[55] E. B. Pusey, *The Minor Prophets* (London, 1860), 267.
[56] Gidney, *London Society*, 16.
[57] Edward S. Creasy, *History of England from the Earliest to the Present Time*, 5 vols (London, 1869), 1: 18.
[58] See Michael Wheeler, *The Old Enemies* (Cambridge, 2006), 51–76.
[59] F. Max Müller, 'Are there Jews in Cornwall?', in idem, *Chips from a German Workshop*, 4 vols (London, 1867–75), 4: 299–329; John Bannister, *Jews in Cornwall* (Truro, 1867).
[60] See John Wilson, *Our Israelitish Origin* (London, 1840), for one of the earliest developed statements of this position.

beleaguered advocates of the Bible's historical accuracy. William Smith's *Dictionary of the Bible* (3 vols, 1860–3) was a case in point. Its mostly Anglican contributors sought to use archaeology, travel literature and natural science to throw new light on Middle Eastern life, languages, flora and fauna, and in so doing to show that it was a creation of its times and culture. Facts were what mattered. Thus entries for 'Metals', 'Ship', 'Solomon' and 'Tarshish' elucidated the place of Tarshish in Israel's economy and diplomacy, but gave no hint that it was or ever had been linked with Britain, save possibly via Phoenician tin merchants.[61] Believers could thus guard against doubt by reassuring themselves that the biblical books were backed up by other forms of evidence.

This did not prevent speculation about the location of Tarshish; but the arguments adduced drew not on recent events but on philology and ancient geography. In 1859 the statesman and littérateur George Cornewall Lewis rehearsed in *Notes and Queries* the argument from classical literature for its being in Spain, but by the time his friend Edward Twisleton came to write the *Bible Dictionary* entry, another scholar-cum-civil servant, Sir James Edward Tennent, was championing a fresh theory.[62] Tarshish, he argued, was not one place but two. Most Old Testament references were to a source of silver and lead in the extreme west of the ancient world – Tartessus – while those in Chronicles must refer to another, accessible through Ezion-Geber – Idumea – on the Red Sea, and thus far to the east. The peacocks were the clincher: while the gold of 2 Chronicles 9 could have been procured from Ophir, and ivory and apes from Africa, 'the peacock is an Indian and not an African bird', its Hebrew name supposedly having Tamil roots.[63] The 'great oriental mart' on which the fleets of Hiram and Solomon descended triennially, Tennent concluded triumphantly, was Point de Galle in Ceylon.[64] His findings serve to underline a growing scholarly fascination with the Phoenicians as vectors for, and bridges between, Hebraic and Homeric

---

[61] William Aldis Wright, 'Metals', in William Smith, ed., *Dictionary of the Bible*, 3 vols (London, 1860–3), 2: 341–3; John Saul Howson, 'Ship', ibid. 2: 1282–7; Edward Hayes Plumptre, 'Solomon', ibid. 2: 1342–54; Edward Twisleton, 'Tarshish', ibid. 2: 1438–41.

[62] James Edward Tennent, 'Tarshish', in *Encyclopaedia Britannica*, 22 vols (Edinburgh, 1853–60), 21: 26–8; see also William Houghton, 'Peacocks', in Smith, ed., *Dictionary*, 2: 763–4.

[63] Twisleton, 'Tarshish', 1441.

[64] Tennent, 'Tarshish', 28.

mythologies.[65] Tarshish continued to attract attention, then, but not as a coded reference to or metaphor for Britain.

Yet seeing Tarshish for what it really was diminished its significance: it became an interesting if obscure fragment in a wider civilizational mosaic of which biblical history itself was increasingly only a part. When Matthew Arnold set forth *The Great Prophecy of Israel's Restoration arranged and edited for Young Learners* (1872) his intention was to make 'Hebrew literature in its perfection', namely Isaiah chapters 40–66 (as Deutero-Isaiah was then defined), accessible to young readers alongside the best of the Roman and Greek authors. Carefully sidestepping the question of whether or not they foretold the future, Arnold, like his father, held that the grandeur of the prophets lay in their unflinching moral courage and imagination.[66] His Isaiah still foresaw a time when the 'the isles shall wait for his law': but only because Arnold thought it sounded better than 'sea-coasts', which was the more accurate translation.[67] Deutero-Isaiah was read by Arnold as one among many beautiful and thus morally elevating ancient expressions of the universal 'human spirit'. There was no sense in which it foretold the future, or could be used to corroborate events in the present: it was simply a beautiful ancient poem.[68] Late Victorian schoolchildren looking for references to Tarshish, Tyre and Ophir would find them in Rider Haggard's 1885 adventure novel *King Solomon's Mines*, but this was designed to give a sense of the exotic rather than to bolster belief.

Conclusion

Like much current work on nineteenth-century religion, this essay has sought to nuance received assumptions about the direction of cultural and intellectual travel. On the one hand it shares the scepticism of recent work towards the now tired paradigm of 'faith and doubt' that takes George Eliot, Arthur Hugh Clough and Thomas Hardy as reference points on a gradual but inevitable slide towards

---

[65] See, for instance, Ernest Renan, *Mission de Phénicie* (Paris, 1864); William Ewart Gladstone, *Juventus Mundi: The Gods and Men of the Heroic Age*, 2nd edn (London, 1870), especially 119–50; George Rawlinson, *History of Phoenicia* (London, 1889).
[66] Matthew Arnold, *The Great Prophecy of Israel's Restoration*, 4th edn (London, 1875), xxix.
[67] Ibid. xxvii.
[68] Ibid. xxxv–xxxvi.

secularization.[69] On the other it has used a particular set of texts to argue that, although prophecy and providential language retained rhetorical and homiletic purchase, by the end of the century even ardent believers did not believe that they could be applied in the ways that they had been a hundred years before. This has important implications for how we see the place of 'doubt' in nineteenth-century thought. Serious cases of doubt could indeed prove fatal to belief, but it is clear that in others shifting ideas about received aspects of Christianity did not lead to systemic collapse. As the previous section underlined, new discoveries in geography, natural science and biblical studies did not so much undermine faith as reshape its foundations. As threats to the Bible shifted, so too did the majority of interpreters in how they read significant passages.

This raises important issues for the study of prophecy. For here, too, unhelpful binary distinctions in the secondary literature between the mostly evangelical constituencies who 'believed' in the literal fulfilment of Scripture predictions and those who 'doubted' them has obscured the extent to which prophetic ideas and passages could infuse people's thinking in more subtle, more provisional ways. Such passages could soften into emblems or they could harden again into something more concrete: witness how General Allenby's entry into 'Jerusalem the Blessed' in December 1917, for example, prompted renewed adventist activity among British evangelicals in particular.[70] If this essay leaves us with a disjuncture, it is between those who saw prophecy and its current or past fulfilment as apologetically useful, and those who did not. By that measure, both Chamberlain and the more up-to-date scholars who participated in Smith's *Bible Dictionary* were engaging in similarly apologetic endeavours, endeavours that higher criticism would expose as futile by showing prophetic texts to be subject to processes of composition, editing and redaction. Just as telling was the issue raised by Matthew Arnold and others: why would one need or want to confirm the archaeological veracity of a text whose content was moral or spiritual? Whether 'true' or not, biblical portrayals of Rome, Jerusalem and Babylon continued to provide

[69] For a good recent summary, see Kirstie Blair, *Form and Faith in Victorian Religion and Poetry* (Oxford, 2012), 1–20; see also, in this volume, eadem, 'Reforming the Religious Sonnet: Poetry, Doubt and the Church in the Nineteenth and Twentieth Centuries', 427–51.
[70] D. W. Bebbington, 'The Advent Hope in British Evangelicalism since 1800', *Scottish Journal of Religious Studies* 9 (1988), 103–14.

poets and sermonizers with some of their most resonant metaphors of glory, power, luxury, commerce and corruption. Kipling was no orthodox believer, but his 'Recessional', printed in *The Times* as a would-be lay sermon against complacency commenting on Victoria's Silver Jubilee celebrations in 1897, was soaked in familiar scriptural-prophetic phraseology:

> Far-called, our navies melt away;
> On dune and headland sinks the fire:
> Lo, all our pomp of yesterday
> Is one with Nineveh and Tyre!
> Judge of the Nations, spare us yet,
> Lest we forget – lest we forget![71]

If the imagery was close to that of Chamberlain, the beliefs that animated it were worlds away. Ultimately, then, this essay has identified a growing dichotomy in ideas about how prophecy was to be used. For those who imbibed modern scholarship, prophecy bore witness to the contexts in which it was written: it demonstrated the veracity of the Bible as a set of Near Eastern texts. For those like Kipling it provided ringing words. But as the twentieth century dawned there remained a significant subculture that saw prophetic passages as a prophylactic against doubt in a very different sense, as a code waiting to be unscrambled by faithful exegetes alert to the unfolding of events. Given that parts of the internet are populated with people still convinced that Britain (or America) really is Tarshish, that subculture continues to resonate with some even today.[72]

---

[71] *The Times*, 17 July 1897, 13. It was later sung to the tune MELITA ('Eternal Father, Strong to Save'), which had strong maritime connections.
[72] See, for example, 'Is America in Bible Prophecy?', at: <https://www.raptureready.com/featured/ice/AmericaInBibleProphecy.html>, last accessed 8 August 2015.

'Telling lies on behalf of the Bible': S. R. Gardiner's Doubts about Catholic Apostolic Teaching

Tim Grass*

Spurgeon's College, London

The reasons for the historian Samuel Rawson Gardiner's departure from the Catholic Apostolic Church in the mid-1860s are speculated upon but not generally known. This essay makes use of letters, hitherto in family hands and unknown to researchers, from Gardiner and his wife Isabella to her brother Martin Irving in order to trace the growth of Gardiner's doubts and his alienation from the Catholic Apostolic Church. In particular, the letters show how Gardiner felt the Church was mishandling the intellectual challenges exercising contemporary churchmen. The aim is to shed light on an aspect of Gardiner's biography which has not previously been explained adequately, and so to illuminate the response of one conservative religious movement – the Catholic Apostolic Church – towards the challenges presented by developments in the disciplines of geology and Biblical studies. It is argued that for Gardiner doubt was a necessary function of the quest for truth.

The reasons for the departure of the historian Samuel Rawson Gardiner (1829–1902) from the Catholic Apostolic Church in the mid-1860s are not generally known, primarily because scholars have not had access to relevant personal correspondence. Many who have written about Gardiner do not comment on his move. Of the minority who do, J. S. A. Adamson asserts that Gardiner abandoned the Catholic Apostolic Church in favour of 'Darwin-inspired evolutionism in sociology, positivism in philosophy and liberalism in politics'.[1] Timothy Lang's *The Victorians and the Stuart Heritage* (1995) places considerable emphasis on Gardiner's Catholic Apostolic upbringing and offers the fullest discussion of his departure from that Church, but

* 1 Thornhill Close, Ramsey, Isle of Man, IM8 3LA. E-mail: tgrass.work@gmail.com.
 I am grateful to †Elizabeth Martin and her son †Graham for granting me generous access to the letters on which this essay is based. Thanks are also due to the editors and peer reviewer of Studies in Church History, and to David Bebbington, Manfred Henke and Timothy Larsen for their assistance.
[1] J. S. A. Adamson, 'Eminent Victorians: S. R. Gardiner and the Liberal as Hero', *HistJ* 33 (1990), 641–57, at 642.

in the absence of evidence Lang has to speculate about the causes of Gardiner's defection. He sees these as including the death of Gardiner's father in 1863, the perceived irrelevance of Catholic Apostolic apocalypticism in the settled climate of the 1850s and 1860s (an awareness strengthened by Gardiner's developing study of the English Civil War period and his observation that apocalypticism was a recurrent feature in English history rather than a divinely inspired response to contemporary workings of Providence), the incompatibility of a literal reading of Scripture with historical method, and (most importantly, according to Lang) the hindrance presented to his career prospects by his Catholic Apostolic membership and ministry.[2] The most recent work on Gardiner, Mark Nixon's *Samuel Rawson Gardiner and the Idea of History* (2011), whilst fairly conversant with the religious background, offers no explanation of Gardiner's doubts or his move to Anglicanism.[3]

This essay uses letters from Gardiner and his wife Isabella (1834–78), daughter of Edward Irving (on whom more below), to Isabella's brother Martin (1831–1912), in order to trace the growth of his doubts about Catholic Apostolic thinking and his consequent alienation from the movement, to some extent correcting Lang's interpretation and filling out Nixon's portrait. These letters are in family hands and have not previously been used by researchers.[4] Lang's frustration that 'Gardiner never mentioned … what Irvingism meant to him' and the *ODNB*'s assertion that he 'never explained his defection' can now to some extent be overcome.[5] Although the process by which he came to doubt and then reject the Catholic Apostolic Church's teaching was essentially complete by 1865, he had published relatively little up to that point which would provide insights into his change of outlook. This correspondence therefore increases greatly the evidence available concerning the process.

---

[2] Timothy Lang, *The Victorians and the Stuart Heritage: Interpretations of a Discordant Past* (Cambridge, 1995), 146–7.
[3] Mark Nixon, *Samuel Rawson Gardiner and the Idea of History* (Woodbridge, 2010).
[4] An unpublished family history refers to further letters covering the periods 1850–5 and 1875–85: London, Society of Genealogists, Michael Gardiner, 'The Gardiners Volume One' (typescript, 1992), 189. However, these appear to have gone missing; I have also been unable to locate the extensive correspondence, said by the same author to exist, concerning Gardiner's not being allowed to proceed to the degree of MA at Oxford: ibid. 190.
[5] Lang, *Victorians*, 148; *ODNB*, *s.n.* 'Gardiner, Samuel Rawson (1829–1902)'.

Gardiner was born at Whitchurch, Hampshire, in 1829, his father being a former East India Company judge, Rawson Boddam Gardiner (1787–1863).[6] Gardiner *père* was an early adherent of Edward Irving (1792–1834), minister of the National Scotch Church in London's Regent Square, whose preaching about biblical prophecy, advocacy of the doctrine that Christ took fallen human nature in the incarnation, and encouragement of the charismatic gifts of tongues, prophecy and healing scandalized the sermon-tasting metropolis.[7] After Irving's eviction from Regent Square in 1832 he formed a new congregation, the first of what was to become the Catholic Apostolic Church.[8] His deposition from the Church of Scotland ministry for heresy followed in 1833, and he died in December 1834. July 1835 saw the separation of twelve apostles to lead the new Church. All Christendom was called to accept their authority and their message as presented in *Testimonies* to the heads of Church and state, and to receive the grace available through them in order to prepare for the imminent return of Christ and avoid impending divine judgement.[9]   By 1836, there were at least two dozen congregations in various parts of England and Scotland, and the following year Rawson Gardiner became the 'angel' (roughly equivalent to a bishop in the Ignatian sense, but subject to the apostles) of the congregations at Everton and Lymington in Hampshire.[10]   Samuel (known in the family as Sam) thus grew up at the heart of the new movement. His

[6]   Gardiner, 'Gardiners Volume One', 138–9.

[7]   Among many biographies of Irving, see Mrs M. O. W. Oliphant, *The Life of Edward Irving*, 2 vols (London, 1862); H. C. Whitley, *Blinded Eagle* (London, 1955); Tim Grass, *The Lord's Watchman: A Life of Edward Irving* (Milton Keynes and Eugene, OR, 2011).

[8]   On the Catholic Apostolic Church's history, see Edward Miller, *The History and Doctrines of Irvingism, or of the so-called Catholic and Apostolic Church*, 2 vols (London, 1878); Plato E. Shaw, *The Catholic Apostolic Church, sometimes called Irvingite: A Historical Study* (New York, 1946); R. A. Davenport, *Albury Apostles: The Story of the Body known as the Catholic Apostolic Church (sometimes called 'The Irvingites')* (London, 1970); Columba Graham Flegg, *'Gathered under Apostles': A Study of the Catholic Apostolic Church* (Oxford, 1992). None has much to say about the denomination's response to nineteenth-century intellectual developments. I am currently working on a new history, *The Lord's Work: A History of the Catholic Apostolic Church* (forthcoming).

[9]   The *Testimonies* were first issued between 1836 and 1838, and set out the apostles' assessment of the state and prospects of Christendom, calling upon the baptized to flee the judgement to come. One was addressed to William IV, one to the bishops of the Church of England, and another, the fullest and most often cited subsequently, to the heads of Church and state throughout Christendom. This last was the so-called *Great Testimony*.

[10]   H. B. Copinger, 'Annals: The Lord's Work by Apostles in the Nineteenth and Twentieth Centuries' (typescript, *c.*1951), 70.

younger brother Charles Baring Gardiner (1833–1912) would also become an angel.[11] Sam, however, never rose higher than the rank of deacon.[12]

Sam Gardiner received what Lang calls 'an Anglican education' at Winchester, evidence that his father did not see Anglican and Catholic Apostolic allegiance as incompatible.[13]   In 1847 he went up to Christ Church, Oxford, proceeding to his BA in 1851. He had been awarded a studentship in 1850, but was unable to retain it because in 1851 he became a Catholic Apostolic deacon and thus closed the door on his being ordained in the Church of England, a condition of the award's continuance.[14]   Gardiner would have become a full member of the Catholic Apostolic Church on receiving the rite of sealing by the laying on of an apostle's hands, which for those brought up in the movement was administered on reaching the age of twenty.[15] He was therefore probably already a member when granted his studentship; it was not membership but ministry in the Catholic Apostolic Church which was to cause him to resign it. What happened was that he was called to the diaconate by prophecy on 24 July 1851, it being indicated that the diaconate was a stepping stone to higher ministry,[16] and on 27 October he was admitted as a deacon in the church at Paddington in London.[17] Four days later the resignation of his studentship was recorded.[18]

[11] Charles served as a deacon until his ordination as priest in 1865: Isabella Gardiner to Martin Irving, 26 February 1865. In 1882 he became angel of the church at Brighton: Seraphim Newman-Norton, *A Biographical Index of those associated with the Lord's Work* (London, [1972]), 44. He appears to have ministered there until his death.

[12] The Catholic Apostolic diaconate was regarded as a permanent office in its own right, although some deacons were in time ordained as priests.

[13] Lang, *Victorians*, 149.

[14] C. H. Firth, 'Dr. S. R. Gardiner', *PBA* 1 (1903–4), 294–301, at 294; *ODNB*; Lang, *Victorians*, 148. Subscription to the Thirty-Nine Articles, then still required of those proceeding to degrees at Oxford, was not the issue here: Catholic Apostolics would have had no problem with that.

[15] [John Bate Cardale], *Readings upon the Liturgy and other Divine Offices of the Church*, 2 vols (London, 1879, 1878 respectively), 2: 429, 435. The rite was first administered in 1847.

[16] 'There was an indication of the mind of the Lord in the word spoken to S. R. G. that He would use him to preach the Gospel first to the poor & then to the rich also _ intimating that He would use him first in a lower then in a higher sphere': 'Southampton Record of Events', undated ms book held with the letters.

[17] Ibid.

[18] Oxford, Christ Church, Dean and Chapter records, D&C, i.b.10, fol. 136ᵛ, 31 October 1851: 'D[ominu]s Gardiner having tendered to the Dean by letter his resignation of his Student[']s place, it is declared vacant from this day'. I am grateful to the librarian, Judith

From 26 January 1852 until about 1866, Gardiner served as a deacon-evangelist,[19] and was sent on preaching missions or took up temporary residence in places such as Lymington, Newport (Isle of Wight) and Bath. His primary responsibility appears to have been preaching to outsiders, seeking to present the claims of the new movement and to awaken hearers to inquire about the Lord's work by apostles, as well as distributing copies of apologetic literature such as the *Testimonies* to interested clergy and lay people.[20] Given the Church's readiness to have him preach evangelist sermons at Gordon Square, where the denomination's flagship church was opened in 1853, it would seem that the apostles had high hopes for his future ministry.

By the mid-1840s the family were living at 22 Gordon Street in Bloomsbury, close to Gordon Square.[21] In 1856, Sam married Isabella and the couple also settled at 22 Gordon Street, presumably sharing the house with Sam's father (his mother had died in 1853). Later that year his first published work appeared: a translation of *Christian Family Life* by Heinrich W. J. Thiersch (1817–85) of Marburg in Germany. Thiersch, the son of a noted classicist, had given up a promising academic career as professor of theology at Marburg in 1849 to enter the Catholic Apostolic ministry; he shared Gardiner's interest in seventeenth-century English history, and Nicholas Tyacke thinks that he may 'possibly have influenced Gardiner's own historical studies'.[22] The two first met in May 1856 when Thiersch was staying with Gardiner's father for a meeting and correcting the translation

---

Curthoys, for providing me with a copy and transcription of this source. Nixon uses the verb 'expelled' to describe what happened to Gardiner: *Gardiner*, 83. This is too strong, but he may perhaps have been asked to resign. Removal of his name from the college's books meant that he did not proceed to the degree of MA until 1884: Oxford, All Souls' College, Anson, S. R. Gardiner to William Anson, 19 November 1884.

[19] Southampton Record; Lang, *Victorians*, 145.

[20] E.g. Isabella Gardiner to Martin Irving, 3 June 1856, 11 October 1857.

[21] Gardiner, 'Gardiners Volume One', 143. Lang, on the basis of Post Office directories for Southampton and London, has the family moving in 1853: *Victorians*, 146.

[22] Nicholas Tyacke, 'An Unnoticed Work by Samuel Rawson Gardiner', *Bulletin of the Institute of Historical Research* 47 (1974), 244–5, at 245. On Thiersch, see Paul Wigand, *Heinrich W. J. Thierschs Leben (zum Teil von ihm Selbst erzählt)* (Basel, 1888); R.-F. Edel, *Auf dem Weg zur Vollendung der Kirche Jesu Christi: Die oekumenische Sendung der katholisch-apostolischen Gemeinden an die Gesamtkirche Jesu Christi dargestellt in Leben und Wirken des Prof. Dr. Heinrich W. J. Thiersch*, Oekumenische Texte und Studien 18, 2nd edn (Marburg an der Lahn, 1971), although neither appears to mention Gardiner.

of his book.[23] They became friends, Thiersch meeting or staying with Gardiner on several occasions when visiting England, and the Gardiners staying with Thiersch and his family when on holiday in Germany in 1867.[24]

Intellectually speaking, Gardiner was head and shoulders above anyone else in the Catholic Apostolic Church in England. As early as 1856 Isabella confided her concerns to her brother, then en route to Australia to take up an appointment as professor of classics at the newly founded University of Melbourne.[25] In Martin's absence, she felt that Sam had nobody to talk to about his reading, although the Church authorities were of the opinion that delivering the *Testimony* to clergy and talking to them about the work would help him.[26] Thiersch would have been his equal, but the two could not often meet. Gardiner's doubts, then, began with his intellectual isolation as a Catholic Apostolic member and minister. He lacked an intellectually supportive community which could reinforce his belief system.

Gardiner's developing sense of intellectual frustration with the Catholic Apostolic Church was fuelled by a conviction that when its ministers did speak about contemporary currents of thought, they did not know what they were talking about; this would have threatened the credibility of his own ministry as a deacon-evangelist. In 1856, he wrote:

> Mr. Taplin has come across Comte's positive philosophy in some shape or another, & has been teaching against it … I wish he would leave it alone, for he does not seem to understand what he is attacking. Amongst other things he accuses the universities of being the seats of this philosophy. I only know I never came across a Comtist, when I was at Oxford.[27]

Moreover, Catholic Apostolic scholarship tended to look backwards, the liturgical researches of the chief apostle, John Bate Cardale (1802– 77), being a prime example. At this point there were few if any

[23] Isabella Gardiner to Martin Irving, 18 May 1856.

[24] Isabella Gardiner to Martin Irving, 26 September 1867.

[25] Martin Irving proceeded to the degree of MA in 1856, although J. A. Froude later suggested that filial piety had kept him from taking a fellowship at Oxford: cited in John S. Martin, *Martin Howy Irving: Professor, Headmaster, Public Servant* (Melbourne, 2006), 49.

[26] Isabella Gardiner to Martin Irving, [June 1856] and 16 December 1858.

[27] S. R. Gardiner to Martin Irving, 23 November [1856]. Edward Taplin (1800–62) was the 'Pillar of Prophets', the chief representative of that ministry in the Catholic Apostolic Church.

members able to wrestle with the issues presented by contemporary developments in various sciences, and more often than not ministers were content to continue advocating a pre-critical approach to Scripture, calling on eighteenth-century writers in support. The apostle John Tudor (1784–1861), for instance, rejected the understanding of geological stratification as an entirely natural process occurring over a long period of time and argued for a literal six-day creation and for the importance of Noah's flood as an act of God.[28] Nevertheless, at this stage Gardiner seems to have been confident about the compatibility of his religious allegiance with a commitment to careful historiography; when a prospective employer expressed the fear that he would be 'sectarian' in his approach to modern history, he rejected the charge as 'gammon', telling his brother-in-law: 'if anybody can be unsectarian, we can; or at least, next door to the infidels'.[29]

There is a two-year gap in the correspondence from early 1859 to early 1861; thereafter Gardiner continued writing to Irving about Church affairs, but there are no further references to his preaching, and it appears that he was becoming less active in ministry. This may mean that the Church was losing confidence in his ministry, or that he was asking too many awkward questions, or simply that he was increasingly busy with the demands of his vocation as a historian (which was becoming his main source of income) and his growing family. But he was not yet expressing doubts openly, even to Martin. In 1861 he dismissed two controversial books: 'I haven't read Essays & Reviews, & I haven't read the Gorilla book. Am not I ignorant? I haven't time to read very much except Reviews & Magazines.'[30] In February 1863 he quoted a couple of limericks about J. W. Colenso,

---

[28] [John Owen Tudor], *On the Reconciliation of Geological Phenomena with Divine Revelation* (London, 1856); cf. idem, *Sacred Geology; or, The Scriptural Account of the World's Creation maintained* (London, 1847), xiv–xvii.

[29] S. R. Gardiner to Martin Irving, 3 January 1858. The Catholic Apostolic Church claimed that it alone could rise above all sectarian distinctions, because it was led by apostles, who were intended to head up the whole Christian Church on earth. It therefore accepted no name which would mark it out as a subset of the company of the baptized.

[30] S. R. Gardiner to Martin Irving, 15 September 1861. The 'Gorilla book' is not identifiable from the letter, but it may have been Paul du Chaillu, *Explorations and Adventures in Equatorial Africa* (London, 1861), which became a best-seller thanks to the interest excited by the author's collection of gorilla bones and skins which he had exhibited in London that February: see Jochen Petzold, '"How like us is that ugly brute, the ape!" Darwin's "Ape Theory" and its Traces in Victorian Children's Magazines', in Barbara Schaff, Eckart Voigts and Monika Pietrzak-Franger, eds, *Reflecting on Darwin* (Farnham, 2014) 57–71, at 59–60. I owe this reference to Frances Andrews.

the Anglican bishop of Natal whose work on the Pentateuch had caused such a furore, in order to fill up a short letter, doing so in a way which implies that he did not feel there was any serious challenge to be met in the bishop's writings.[31]

Two months later, however, when his father was dying, Sam concluded a letter by informing Martin: 'I can't go on writing about other things which I want to say, in the midst of this trouble.'[32] What the 'other things' were appears from his letter informing Irving of Rawson Gardiner's death; it is conceivable that his father's passing allowed him to express thoughts which hitherto he had kept to himself. The letter contains a fuller expression of his concerns regarding the way in which the Catholic Apostolic Church was meeting the intellectual challenges of the day. Dr Augustus Bayford, who had defended G. C. Gorham before the Court of Arches in his legal battle with Bishop Phillpotts of Exeter,[33] had undertaken at short notice to deliver a course of lectures against *Essays and Reviews*. Sam was unimpressed: 'he told us that we ought to be prepared to deny boldly any conclusions whatever to which Geology[,] Ethnology &c. might lead us, not because we knew anything about the matter but because though they were logically faultless they didn't agree with Genesis. In other words our business is to tell lies on behalf of the Bible.'[34] A month later he returned to the last allegation: 'I haven't read Colenso because he is an ass & I haven't time to read asses' books. I have read Lyell. All I can say is that it is no use trying to please God by telling lies which is the line that nine tenths of the good people at Gordon Square take.' Even those ministers who were not guilty of this stopped short of serious engagement with the issues, Cardale the chief apostle included.[35]

About this time Martin evidently commented on Colenso's ideas in a letter, for Isabella felt it necessary to account for her husband's lack of response by explaining to him: 'To tell you the truth I think

---

[31] S. R. Gardiner to Martin Irving, 19 February 1863.

[32] S. R. Gardiner to Martin Irving, 27 April 1863.

[33] A. F. Bayford, *The Argument of Dr Bayford on behalf of the Rev. G. C. Gorham in the Court of Arches*, 2nd edn (London, 1849).

[34] S. R. Gardiner to Martin Irving, 25 May 1863.

[35] S. R. Gardiner to Martin Irving, 25 June 1863. He was probably referring to a lecture by Charles Lyell to the British Association for the Advancement of Science in 1859 arguing for belief in an 'old earth', or to Lyell's 1863 book *The Geological Evidence of the Antiquity of Man*: see James C. Livingston, *Religious Thought in the Victorian Age: Challenges and Presuppositions* (New York and London, 2007), 155–6.

he feels too much about the whole matter, to know exactly how to write to you about it. We have had many trying teachings & sermons about it all here.'[36] At this stage, however, Sam appears to have been questioning rather than rejecting Catholic Apostolic belief, and seeking to understand the issues presented by contemporary challenges to orthodox Christian thought. His doubts appear to have been provoked as much by the perceived inadequacy of Catholic Apostolic responses to contemporary scientific writers as by the writers themselves. Although he was reading various journals, his letters do not mention many scientific authors in a manner which indicates serious first-hand engagement with their books. A month later, in response to Martin's inquiry as to whether he would be asked to go to Melbourne as a minister, he confessed: 'There are several things I want to understand myself, before I can be asked to teach other people.'[37]

However, by March 1865 Gardiner had taken a further step away from his religious roots, ceasing to worship in the Catholic Apostolic Church. His conviction that his brother-in-law would value the quest for truth more highly than allegiance to a particular theological system enabled him to share his doubts freely with him. Among the issues he mentioned were the inadequacy of the movement's response to new scientific challenges. Its approach might have been appropriate when the issues under discussion concerned intra-Christian disputes, but the challenges now concerned the credibility of Christianity itself rather than that of one Christian group over against another.

> … after much and anxious thought I have come to the conclusion that it is impossible for me any longer to continue taking part in the worship to which I have been accustomed from my childhood. As long as the religious questions under discussion around [*sic*] were merely sectarian disputes I felt, and I suppose we all felt that we were standing on a ground which gave us larger views, and fuller faith. But I feel that it is very different now. New questions are arising of a very different character, and what ever may be the true answers to them it is impossible for any one who watches what is going on around to imagine that they will be found at Gordon Square. There is nothing there but recurrence to old formulas. Whether we accept Dr Bayford's doctrine that it is the

---

[36] Isabella Gardiner to Martin Irving, 26 September 1863.
[37] S. R. Gardiner to Martin Irving, 25 October 1863.

duty of a Christian to assert, in spite of any evidence however conclusive, the falsehood of scientific proof when it clashes with our accepted system; or whether we hold with Mr Groser[38] that science is no doubt true, but that we had better shut our eyes to any difficulty it presents, I don't see that there is much chance of being of any use whatever to ourselves or those around us.

And besides this, the more I look into the history of the world, the more the presence of God becomes revealed not in a pattern organization, or in a complete theological system, but as showing itself in the blessing which crowns the work of men who from various sides and with partial success grasp by turns some portion of the Divine order which is not wholly revealed to any.

Again and again I have longed to be able to talk over my thoughts with you; because I know that you would think first of what was true, and not as too many others do of what was true according to a certain system. I don't think I can say any more. But you will know how much trouble and sorrow this has caused in many ways.[39]

Isabella's comment on reading this over was that her husband's care for her, and his 'simplicity & uprightness' remained unchanged; God knew his heart, and she trusted God with her future, although 'it looks different now from what it did' when they married.[40] Given such hints as the prophecy at his admission to the diaconate marking him out for a higher sphere of service, it is probable that the Church authorities had envisaged his eventual call to the priesthood.[41] She may well have anticipated, then, that her husband would become a full-time minister. Now she had to come to terms with the realization that this was never going to happen; yet she referred in the same letter to Sam's conducting family prayers, and on Sunday evenings

[38] Groser, formerly a Baptist minister, was an early convert to the movement. The Gardiners were friends with him, and Sam had earlier expressed appreciation of his preaching: Gardiner to Martin Irving, 1 November 1856. Groser continued to dine with them until at least 1870.

[39] S. R. Gardiner to Martin Irving, 27 March 1865.

[40] Isabella Gardiner to Martin Irving, 26 March 1865.

[41] It had been suggested in 1857 that he offer himself as a candidate for ordination to the priesthood, but he refused, feeling that whilst he was a bad deacon he would make a worse priest: S. R. Gardiner to Martin Irving, 9 September [1857].

the couple were reading together, from the latest volume of Edward Irving's sermons, those on 'Social Religion'.[42]

Sam's final statement regarding his changing views came in a letter of August 1865, written from Pontresina in Switzerland. Thanking Martin for his 'very, very kind letter', which was probably a reply to his earlier confession, he explained that it was difficult to know how to put his doubts into words; for one thing, so much was 'the product of feeling rather than of reasoning'. Gardiner was evidently not a rationalist pure and simple. The two principles guiding his thinking were, firstly, that

> Every where the good is partial & subject to continual change of form according to the wants of the age. Everywhere definite organization and definite logical forms put forward as a universal panacea are the sure precursors of decay & death. How then can I tell men that to submit to certain definite ordinances, & to accept certain beliefs upon the word of certain men is the way to a universal restoration?

Secondly, he had come to disbelieve the phenomenon of charismatic prophecy, which occupied a central place in Catholic Apostolic worship. Once again, he stressed that it was not a rational issue, but 'a matter of feeling and spiritual perception' (appropriately, given that prophecy was itself regarded as a matter of 'spiritual perception'). Furthermore, Martin had said that 'questions about geology & science should not trouble us', but whilst Sam admitted that religious teachers should not be expected to 'know everything correctly', he complained that Bayford had been 'allowed without contradiction to put forth opinions which could only lead to a universal scepticism', insisting, for instance, that belief in a six-day creation was non-negotiable.[43] The problem, as Gardiner saw it, was not so much what Bayford had asserted, but the fact that he had been allowed to do so without any alternative opinion being offered. And such teaching was not refuted but 'eagerly received by many'.

The beauty of the Catholic Apostolic liturgy was widely deployed as an apologetic argument in favour of the movement's divine origin; Gardiner had done so himself and Irving had advanced the same

---

[42] Edward Irving, *Collected Writings*, ed. Gavin Carlyle, 5 vols (London, 1865), 3: 217–340.
[43] However, Groser warned against excessive dogmatism in this matter, and appears to have regarded the six days as long periods: *Sermons preached in the Catholic Apostolic Church, Gordon Square* (London, 1871), 78–9, 84.

argument in a letter to him. Now, however, whilst Gardiner could accept, in Plato's terms, that whatever was beautiful must in some sense be true, he could not accept that it must be the truth without any admixture of error. Like all apprehensions of truth in this world, it was partial and liable to be superseded. As Gardiner read his father-in-law's published works, he readily acknowledged the good in them which had come from God, but denied that such blessing had, or must, come through supernatural intervention. Rather, it was Irving's personal qualities as a Christian which God had used. Such an argument struck at the heart of what Edward Irving had stood for regarding charismatic manifestations, and hence at the basis for the Catholic Apostolic Church's separate existence.

It would appear that Gardiner had shared his doubts with others, for he went on:

> It has been said to me, & you will perhaps say the same. 'If you admit all this, why not remain where you were?' My answer to this is, Because it is dishonest. Unless I believe more than this I cannot by my presence even at the services tell men that more than this is true. Every time I went to Church latterly I felt as if I were in a manner telling a lie to God & man.

It was his commitment to truth which led Sam to act and think as he did. That commitment, and his conviction that human perception of truth in this life must inevitably be partial, made it impossible for him to accept any longer the Catholic Apostolic approach to questions of truth. Martin may have suggested that the Church's teachings could be interpreted in terms of metaphor, story or ideal, but Sam would have seen that this could never be acceptable to the Catholic Apostolic apostles. He was not, however, adopting a positivist view in which facts were everything, for, as Nixon points out, he occasionally made use of a story about a historical figure which, whilst not demonstrably true in the sense that it actually happened, nevertheless offered a true insight into the subject's character.[44] Moreover, his later historical writing would bear out his belief in the need for imagination on the part of a historian seeking to step inside the past.[45]

Gardiner did not regard himself as having abandoned Christian faith: 'In God[']s protecting guidance, in the assurance that he will

[44] Nixon, *Gardiner*, 121–3.
[45] Cf. ibid. 29.

lead us all in his ways sooner or later my faith is as strong as ever it was.'[46] To the extent that he retained a teleological understanding of personal history, then, he was still shaped by the perspective advocated by his father-in-law more than three decades earlier, which the Catholic Apostolic Church had adopted as its own. But as far as the Christian Church's relationship to society was concerned, he had turned that perspective on its head: whereas Edward Irving and the Catholic Apostolics thought in terms of the Church's decay from apostolic perfection into final apostasy, the faithful being rescued by divine intervention, Gardiner seems to have inclined to the idea of progress towards a fuller apprehension of truth, and increasingly to see his Church's dogmatic pronouncements as hindrances to that progress. His change of outlook reflected a wider trend: the apocalypticism which had been a prominent feature of the social milieu of the 1830s was no longer so attractive by the middle of the century, having to a large extent given way to notions of progress and achievement. Gardiner's belief in progress was not new; in 1858 he had expressed approval of Hegel's *Philosophy of History* because it argued that progress was measured by 'freedom to submit to the law of truth', whereas submission to tyranny or the arbitrary exercise of power represented decline.[47] One wonders whether he saw the Catholic Apostolic ministry as guilty of these failings.

Gardiner's complete disengagement from the Catholic Apostolic Church took a while longer, because it did not rush to strike members off its registers. As late as 1870 he continued to have quite extensive social contact with its ministers and people. But by 1871, when he applied for the professorship of modern history at King's College, London, a character reference was provided by the Anglican vicar of All Saints, Gordon Square, stating that Gardiner had been a regular communicant for several years.[48] Nonetheless, it was only in 1872 that Gardiner was formally declared by the Catholic Apostolics to be lapsed.[49] This was supposed to take place only after protracted attempts at reclamation had been made, but we have no

---

[46] S. R. Gardiner to Martin Irving, 12 August 1865.

[47] S. R. Gardiner to Martin Irving, 8 August 1858.

[48] London, King's College London, Secretary's in-correspondence, KA/IC/G50, Arthur Godson to the Council of King's College, 20 November 1871. Lang thinks that he continued as a communicant Anglican until his death: *Victorians*, 141; cf. *ODNB*.

[49] Lang, *Victorians*, 146, citing information provided by the Catholic Apostolic Trustees. The Church's extensive archives are inaccessible to researchers.

evidence of any such action in his case.[50] Perhaps other ministers – even Christopher Heath (1802–76), the angel, who would have been a family friend – were afraid of his intellectual standing, a final instance of the intellectual isolation of which he, and Isabella on his behalf, was all too conscious.

In conclusion, then, Gardiner's doubts and ultimate departure from the Catholic Apostolic Church owed much to the habits of mind which governed his work as a historian, but the issues for him were not the same as those put forward by Lang. Lang could not be certain whether Gardiner left the Catholic Apostolic Church for religious reasons or career ones; the letters examined here demonstrate clearly that the former was the case. This was the man whose honesty compelled him to take a course of action which would estrange him from the circle within which he had been brought up, and whose wife testified to his continuing 'simplicity & uprightness'.[51] What mattered most to him was pursuing the truth, wherever that might lead, and in the course of that pursuit he was convinced that all apprehension of truth in this life was partial at best: no ideology or system of religious dogma could fully encapsulate it. As such he could not accept something as true simply on the authority of another, as the Catholic Apostolic Church expected the utterances of its higher ministers to be accepted; nor could he be as assertive and categorical as they were. Commitment to seeking the truth required him to doubt the word of its ministers. Gardiner was convinced that his Church was being economical with the truth. He would have shared Thiersch's opinion: 'It is lying which works the death of souls.'[52]

It is therefore appropriate to reverse the *ODNB*'s assertion that Gardiner's 'religious experience had an impact on his approach to history': it was his approach to history, and to truth in general, seeking to get at the facts of the matter and to use them in constructing a historiographical narrative, which shaped his religious experience. This way of thinking may, incidentally, also have dictated his approach to the question of Irish Home Rule in the 1880s: Nixon has suggested that '[i]t is a serious possibility that Gardiner's political views regarding Ireland resulted from his historical study of seventeenth-century

---

[50] *General Rubrics; or, Rules for the Celebration of the Divine Offices, etc.* (London, 1852), Appendix I; cf. *Book of Regulations* (London, 1878), §635.
[51] Isabella Gardiner to Martin Irving, 26 March 1865.
[52] Heinrich W. J. Thiersch, *Christian Family Life*, transl. S. R. Gardiner, 2nd edn (London, 1880), 160.

Ireland.'[53] Further research might usefully explore whether a similar outlook was manifest in the thinking of other historians who came to doubt orthodox Christianity (such as Froude and Seeley), as well as comparing this with the outlook of those historians who retained (or returned to) mainstream belief (such as Acton, Döllinger and Lightfoot).[54] Such an investigation would need to reach back into the eighteenth century, for as Butterfield notes regarding the new German historical school which emerged from the 1760s, many of its chief luminaries had intended to become clergy but 'had been converted to history by their theological studies'.[55] Much more work has been done on the manifestations of doubt among the scientific community than on its appearance in historians. Gardiner is a promising subject for inquiry: he could no more tell lies on behalf of the Bible than he could on behalf of any of the historical figures whom he admired. Doubt, for him, was a function of his commitment to the quest for truth.

[53] Nixon, *Gardiner*, 13.
[54] Timothy Larsen to the author, e-mail, 31 December 2014.
[55] Herbert Butterfield, *Man on his Past: The Study of the History of Historical Scholarship* (Cambridge, 1955, repr. 1969), 36.

Reforming the Religious Sonnet: Poetry, Doubt and the Church in the Nineteenth and Twentieth Centuries

Kirstie Blair*

University of Stirling

This essay examines the tradition of 'doubting' poetics through an assessment of selected nineteenth- and twentieth-century sonnets. Through considering recent work on Victorian literature and culture, it argues for the importance of the poetics of faith in this period, and assesses the presence of nineteenth-century Christian, and particularly Anglican, forms and concepts in the genre of the sonnet. Analysing later twentieth-century sonnets by Geoffrey Hill and Carol Ann Duffy, it suggests that the sonnet remains vitally linked to the literature of faith and that these sonnets have vital links to their Victorian predecessors.

Of all periods in British history that might be regarded as the 'age of doubt', a brief survey of twentieth-century works of literary criticism and history suggests that the Victorian era is the top contender. 'Faith', in the titles of Victorian literature seminars and university courses, is inevitably succeeded by 'doubt', and the most popular summary of the state of religion in Victorian Britain would tend to describe belief crumbling under the onslaught of Darwinism, geology, biblical criticism and the relentless progress of knowledge, inevitably leading to the scepticism and secularism of the twentieth century. Perhaps the best-known text of Victorian doubt is Matthew Arnold's poem 'Dover Beach', with its famous invocation of the withdrawal of faith:

> The Sea of Faith
> Was once, too, at the full, and round earth's shore
> Lay like the folds of a bright girdle furled.
> But now I only hear
> Its melancholy, long, withdrawing roar,
> Retreating, to the breath

* Division of Literature and Languages, University of Stirling, Stirling, FK9 4LA. E-mail: kirstie.blair@stir.ac.uk.

Studies in Church History 52 (2016) 413–436   © Ecclesiastical History Society 2016
doi: 10.1017/stc.2015.24

Of the night-wind, down the vast edges drear
And naked shingles of the world.[1]

As has been often noted, Arnold's metaphor reflects new scientific, and particularly geological, advances; the eternal process by which the cliffs of Dover are worn down and the oceans advance or recede. The poem is 'often seen as one of the representative poems of its age' precisely because it 'registers a deep sense of spiritual alienation'.[2] But 'Dover Beach' not only represents the lens through which generations of twentieth-century students and their teachers have regarded Victorian faith, it also indicates the central role that *poetry* has played in this perception. Many key themes and genres covered on introductory undergraduate or graduate courses in Victorian literature – gender and sexuality, imperialism and race, realism, sensation, decadence and so forth – are taught primarily through works of fiction. Religion is one of the few topics that undergraduate students of Victorian literature and culture today would strongly associate with poetry: Alfred Tennyson, Arnold, Arthur Hugh Clough, Christina Rossetti, Gerard Manley Hopkins and others. As I have argued elsewhere, this is entirely justifiable given that Victorian writers themselves attached enormous importance to poetry and poetics as ways of expressing, supporting and developing attitudes towards faith and unbelief.[3]

What this essay seeks to do is offer a reassessment of the role of 'doubting' poetics, through a consideration of one key genre, the sonnet. After a brief discussion of the state of the field in Victorian studies in relation to recent reconsiderations of the literature of doubt, I will turn to the sonnet as a form that was widely deployed in the nineteenth century to indicate adherence to faith in general, and to the Church in particular. The sonnet was by no means exclusively used by Anglican and Anglo-Catholic writers, but in this period it proved especially amenable for writers from the burgeoning high church movement.[4] The formal constraints of the

---

[1] Matthew Arnold, 'Dover Beach', lines 21–8, in idem, *The Complete Poems*, ed. Kenneth Allott, 2nd edn (London, 1979), 242.

[2] Daniel Brown, 'Victorian Poetry and Science', in Joseph Bristow, ed., *The Cambridge Companion to Victorian Poetry* (Cambridge, 2000), 137–58, at 144.

[3] See Kirstie Blair, *Form and Faith in Victorian Poetry and Religion* (Oxford, 2012).

[4] I include a brief discussion of the Anglo-Catholic sonnet in *Form and Faith*, ch. 6. For a good discussion of the religious sonnet in this period, see Joseph Phelan, *The Nineteenth-*

sonnet and its consequent reliance on regular and predictable metres and rhyme-schemes gave writers an opportunity to meld form and content in reflections on the value of the regular, predictable, familiar and formally delimited aspects of worship in the Anglican and Roman Catholic traditions. If poetry in general made a substantial contribution to ecclesiastical history in the long nineteenth century, the sonnet in particular lent itself to ideological movements such as Tractarianism or Anglo-Catholic ritualism. I will argue here that far from vanishing in the twentieth century, these aspects of the sonnet remain key to interpreting major sonnets by diverse twentieth-century poets, using examples by Geoffrey Hill and Carol Ann Duffy to suggest that the religious sonnet retains considerable force in late twentieth-century literature. By paying close attention to the form and language of twentieth-century sonnets, we can see the allusions to a Victorian literature of faith that underlie apparently secular works, showing how a contemporary poetics of doubt, a poetics that often rejects church-going and questions the function of Christianity in modern society, remains haunted by Victorian religion.

I

The agonized but resigned pessimism of 'Dover Beach' was accepted as the standard attitude of leading Victorian thinkers by the majority of twentieth-century scholars. Lance St John Butler's 1990 study of Victorian literature, *Victorian Doubt*, for instance, argued:

> It seems that early in the nineteenth century a major shift in consciousness took place such that no *enfant de siècle*, as de Musset called his generation in 1836, could seriously write in the old way, and the new way was to write in a language and a manner shot through with doubt even when the intention was to assert freedom from doubt.[5]

Butler's account is implicitly dismissive of religious literature (which constituted, of course, a massive percentage of all literature published in the Victorian period) as reactionary and behind the times. No true

---

Century Sonnet (London, 2006). Phelan offers a detailed discussion of arguably the most important self-reflexive sonnet of the long nineteenth century, Wordsworth's 'Nuns fret not at their narrow convent room'.

[5] Lance St John Butler, *Victorian Doubt* (Hemel Hempstead, 1990), 10. For a more nuanced account of Victorian doubt from the same period, see Elisabeth Jay, *Faith and Doubt in Victorian Britain* (London, 1986).

Victorian could evade doubt, he suggests, whether they wanted to or not, and thus no form of literature reliant on belief could be 'serious', in the sense of adequately representing its period.

This is in itself a serious charge, and one very much open to contestation. In the last two decades, there has been a perceptible shift away from such assumptions, towards a more complex and contested view of the dominance of 'doubt' in Victorian culture. Timothy Larsen's *Crisis of Doubt: Honest Faith in Nineteenth-Century England* and his subsequent monographs represent a key recent indication of this shift.[6] Larsen's convincing argument uses a set of case studies of famous 'doubters' to show that their trajectory was not simply from faith to loss of belief, but often the reverse, in that many returned to Christianity in later life. Larsen rightly laments the tendency of scholars to present the loss of faith as inevitable for any right-thinking Victorian: 'In some instances, the theme of "honest doubt" has been so presented as to leave the impression that Victorians who were keeping up with their reading and had the wit to understand it would inevitably have lost their faith if they had the courage to face the truth.'[7]

As he notes, it is 'the field of English or literary studies' that has been 'a major contributor to this distortion'.[8] Reading these words a few years after the publication of Larsen's monograph, however, I questioned his use of the present tense. As a literary critic working in the field of Victorian literature and religion since the early 2000s, I had witnessed – and in a small way contributed to – the marked movement in my field towards a greater concentration on the literature of faith. By the time I wrote my own work on the subject, I was able to draw on the important new insights produced by studies such as F. E. Gray's *Christian and Lyric Tradition in Victorian Women's Poetry* (2010); Cynthia Scheinberg's *Women's Poetry and Religion in Victorian England* (2002); Charles LaPorte's *Victorian Poets and the Changing Bible* (2011) and Emma Mason and Mark Knight's quietly revolutionary introduction, *Nineteenth-Century Religion and Literature* (2006).

This in itself represents a small sample of new work on Victorian religious poetics. When it comes to the two writers whose work has attracted most critical attention, Christina Rossetti and Gerard

---

[6] See Timothy Larsen, *A People of One Book: The Bible and the Victorians* (Oxford, 2011); idem, *The Slain God: Anthropologists and the Christian Faith* (Oxford, 2014).

[7] Timothy Larsen, *Crisis of Doubt: Honest Faith in Nineteenth-Century England* (Oxford, 2006), vii.

[8] Ibid. 5.

Manley Hopkins, the last two decades have seen an extensive re-assessment of their religious poetics.[9] Indeed, it could plausibly be argued that we owe much of this new discussion of the poetry of faith to the re-emergence of Rossetti from the 1980s onwards as one of the major Victorian poets. Two of the general studies cited above, plus Mason's *Women Poets of the Nineteenth Century* (2006) – groundbreaking in its primary focus on religion – concentrate on women's poetry, and the rediscovery of the literature of faith has thus been substantially aided by the drive to recover and reassess Victorian women's writing. This is also true in recent work on 'minor' religious novelists, with a new and substantial body of emerging criticism on writers such as Charlotte Yonge and her contemporaries.[10]

Yet if these scholarly works indicate the renewed energy devoted to the literature of faith, it is by no means certain that they have, as yet, altered the popular perception of the Victorian period as an era of 'doubt'. Following A. N. Wilson's *God's Funeral* (1999), which argued that 'the nineteenth century had created a climate for itself … in which God had become unknowable', Christopher Lane's *The Age of Doubt* (2011) similarly sets out to defend nineteenth-century doubt in the light of a perceived rise in religious fundamentalism at the end of the twentieth century.[11] Lane's explicitly polemical book, also aimed at a popular as well as an academic audience, sets out to defend secularism and unbelief in the face of the rise of the Christian right in the United States: 'This book advances an argument on behalf of doubt itself. It dwells on the advantages of religious and philosophic

[9] On Rossetti, see, for example, Diane D'Amico, *Christina Rossetti: Faith, Gender and Time* (Baton Rouge, LA, 1999); Lynda Palazzo, *Christina Rossetti's Feminist Theology* (London, 2002); Mary Arseneau, *Recovering Christina Rossetti: Female Community and Incarnational Poetics* (London, 2006); Dinah Roe, *Christina Rossetti's Faithful Imagination: The Devotional Poetry and Prose* (London, 2006); Karen Dieleman, *Religious Imaginaries: The Liturgical and Poetic Practices of Elizabeth Barrett Browning, Christina Rossetti, and Adelaide Procter* (Athens, OH, 2012); Elizabeth Ludlow, *Christina Rossetti and the Bible: Waiting with the Saints* (London, 2014). See also Emma Mason's forthcoming *Christina Rossetti: Green Grace* (Oxford, forthcoming 2017). Few publications on Hopkins do not discuss his religious convictions: see, for example, Bernadette Waterman Ward, *World as Word: Philosophical Theology in Gerard Manley Hopkins* (Washington DC, 2002); Jill Muller, *Gerard Manley Hopkins and Victorian Catholicism: A Heart in Hiding* (New York, 2003); Duc Dau, *Touching God: Hopkins and Love* (London and New York, 2013). For recent reconsiderations, see also the essays in *Religion and Literature* 45/2 (Summer 2013), in the section on Hopkins edited by Martin Dubois.

[10] See, for example, Tamara S. Wagner, ed., *Charlotte Yonge: Rereading Domestic Religious Fiction* (New York, 2011).

[11] A. N. Wilson, *God's Funeral* (London, 1999), 12.

uncertainty as a creative stimulant and assesses the benefits of scepticism in a world that still tries to rid us of that quality.'[12] In this endeavour, Lane returns to a vision of Victorian intellectual and cultural life as premised on the loss of faith, directly agreeing with Butler's argument that 'doubt became something positive' in this period, and espousing the standard view that religious doubt was exciting and radical, since it 'ultimately involved questioning the fabric of British social and cultural life'.[13] Like Butler and Wilson, he implies that leading intellectuals of the period inevitably became doubters – or if they did not, then this in itself is an indication that they were not at the forefront of intellectual developments.

Lane's work confirms that 'English or literary studies' (his disciplinary field) remains heavily invested in a faith-and-doubt paradigm. What has not, perhaps, been adequately explored is the fact that this is as much due to aesthetic perceptions as to political and ideological convictions. When Lane makes appeal to the 'major poetic statements on doubt – from Alfred, Lord Tennyson's *In Memoriam* (1850) to Gerard Manley Hopkins' *Wreck of the Deutschland* (1875) and Thomas Hardy's "God's Funeral" (*c.*1908)' – to back up his arguments, he is calling upon some of the most innovative and exciting literary works of the period.[14] In contrast, nineteenth-century Christian verse can often seem bland and uninteresting. Take these stanzas from John Keble's 'Morning', for example, some of the best-known lines from arguably the best-known collection of poetry in the Victorian period:

> New every morning is the love
> Our wakening and uprising prove;
> Through sleep and darkness safely brought,
> Restored to life, and power, and thought.
>
> New mercies, each returning day,
> Hover around us while we pray;
> New perils past, new sins forgiven,
> New thoughts of God, new hopes of heaven.

---

[12] Christopher Lane, *The Age of Doubt: Tracing the Roots of our Religious Uncertainty* (Princeton, NJ, 2011), 5.
[13] Butler, *Victorian Doubt*, 2; Lane, *Age of Doubt*, 3.
[14] Lane, *Age of Doubt*, 67.

If on our daily course our mind
Be set to hallow all we find,
New treasures still, of countless price,
God will provide for sacrifice.[15]

Keble's poem is formally regular and entirely predictable, using a standard four-line stanza and iambic tetrameter with firm rhyming couplets. He speaks in an authoritative and universalized voice of standard comforting platitudes – or, at least, ideas that were to become platitudes as *The Christian Year* established itself as one of the most widely read works of the period. Compare this to a typical Hopkins stanza from 'The Wreck of the Deutschland':

    Thou mastering me
      God! giver of breath and bread;
   World's strand, sway of the sea;
     Lord of living and dead;
  Thou hast bound bones & veins in me, fastened me flesh,
  And after it almost unmade, what with dread,
   Thy doing: and dost thou touch me afresh?
Over again I feel thy finger and find thee.[16]

Even on a cursory glance, and without reading Hopkins's lines, it is clear that his poem represents a startling break from the norm in its layout on the page, its varied line-lengths and lack of clear pattern. Hopkins, in sharp contrast to Keble, speaks from a confessional first-person perspective, directly sharing his doubts and agonies with the reader, and embodying his questioning through the jagged and broken structures of the poem. One of these extracts is utterly conventional and conservative, one is radical. One unquestioningly accepts faith, one appears to call every certainty into question. Critics have devoted thousands of pages to analysing 'The Wreck of the Deutschland', and will continue to do so, while Keble's poem has rarely attracted any serious analysis. If 'Morning' is typical of the literature of

---

[15] John Keble, 'Morning', lines 21–32, from *The Christian Year*, 3rd edn (Oxford, 1829). 'Morning' is the opening poem of the collection. It is one of relatively few poems in the *Christian Year* that also became well known as hymns.
[16] Gerard Manley Hopkins, 'The Wreck of the Deutschland', lines 1–8, in *Gerard Manley Hopkins: The Major Works*, ed. Catherine Phillips (Oxford, 2002), 110.

faith, why would we, as literary critics invested in the close reading of poetry, ever choose to study or teach it over Hopkins?

Yet to perceive Keble and Hopkins as aesthetically opposed, rather than as belonging to the same spectrum, is profoundly problematic, in ways that hint at the syllogism that sometimes seems to haunt studies of literary doubt: doubt equals experimentation and novelty; this poem is experimental and innovative; therefore it is part of the literature of doubt. In fact, of the three major poetic works Lane cites in passing as key examples of doubt, only Hardy's poem – written more than half a century after Tennyson's – unquestionably fits into this mode. Tennyson was unequivocally a Christian. *In Memoriam* circles around some of the most unsettling issues for Victorian orthodox Christians; it raises them and agonizes over them; and it expresses the poet's vexed relationship to secure belief in the light of the loss of someone dearly loved. But it begins, and ends, with expressions of faith. So does 'The Wreck of the Deutschland'. Like countless religious poets, including Tennyson, Hopkins considers how a pointless and horrific tragedy leads to questions about God's justice and goodness. Those questions are, however, answered within the poem. Moreover, formally speaking, a stanza like that cited above is misleading, because it initially appears far less ordered and structured than on closer examination it is. It has a strong rhyme-scheme (ababcbca), where the last rhyme circles back to the first, and makes use of Hopkins' experimental alliterative stress-patterns, which he himself did not see as a break with tradition but as a return to a neglected aspect of English verse.[17] It is entirely possible to argue that Hopkins sees himself as obeying rules as strict as, if not stricter than, the conventions deployed by Keble. Both he and Tennyson are in the tradition of George Herbert, John Donne, John Milton and many other religious poets writing in English, whose poems frequently express the poet's doubts and fears before coming, in their conclusions, to a renewed sense of faith. 'The Wreck of the Deutschland' is a work of faith that examines how doubts are resolved; it is not therefore a 'major poetic statement on doubt'.[18]

---

[17] A considerable amount of recent Hopkins criticism has been devoted to reassessments of his prosodic theory and practice and how these relate to his religious beliefs and affiliations: see, for example, *Hopkins Quarterly* 38/1–2 (Winter-Spring 2011), a special issue edited by Meredith Martin, on 'Hopkins's Prosody'.

[18] Lane, *Age of Doubt*, 67.

Moreover, privileging poetry such as Hopkins's over the 'standard' religious poems of the period is also misleading because it gives an inaccurate picture of the reading habits of most literate middle-class Victorians. 'The Wreck of the Deutschland' was published in the Jesuit periodical *The Month*, but it did not meet with approval and its circulation was extremely limited. Most of Hopkins's poetry was not published in his lifetime. In contrast, Keble's poetry, whether or not we like it, had a profound impact on the literary and religious cultures of his period, including on Hardy and Hopkins. Studies of the literature of doubt draw our attention to some of the most aesthetically important works written in the Victorian period, yet these are not always the texts that were most read and most widely circulated. Anyone who examines *popular* literature from the long nineteenth century is immediately faced with the fact that the vast proportion of it is Christian, pious and conventional. 'Doubting' poets and other writers were well aware how inescapable this culture was, and indeed often made little effort to escape it. For Hardy, for instance, God might be dead, but religion was not. His poems consistently return to imagery of faith and ritual even at their most despairing. As the crowd in 'God's Funeral' affirms:

> How sweet it was in years far hied
> To start the wheels of day with trustful prayer,
> To lie down liegely at the eventide
> And feel a blest assurance he was there![19]

Quite possibly in an allusion to Keble's entirely assured 'Morning', Hardy's imagined doubters long for the trust that they cannot feel. Butler argued that the language and style of Victorian literature was 'shot through with doubt', but it is just as accurate to assert that even the most doubting works of literature from this period are shot through with faith, embodied here, and in a great many other poems, by a sense of (ecclesiastical) ritual and tradition.

II

In the remainder of this essay, I will examine a small sample of nineteenth and twentieth-century sonnets, in order to suggest that this

---

[19] 'God's Funeral', in *The Complete Poetical Works of Thomas Hardy*, ed. Samuel Hynes, 4 vols (Oxford, 1984), 2: 36.

remains true into the twentieth century and that like the hymns in Hardy's ghost-poem, 'The Dead Quire', the forms and language of faith may have 'waned', yet they also 'linger', 'like the notes afar | Of banded seraphim'.[20] While many poetic genres could be used in such a discussion, the sonnet is particularly apt because of its long tradition of use in English religious poetry, especially in the seventeenth-century sonnets of Donne, Herbert and Milton. In addition, religious thinkers and literary critics have conceived of the sonnet as a form particularly significant for religious purposes, due to its formal constraints. Keble, in his lectures as Oxford's Professor of Poetry, argued that the sonnet, 'one of the most favourite forms in the present day', was popular despite its 'extremely narrow limits' and 'restraints' because '[t]he fact that it was unusually stringent enabled it to soothe and compose [poets'] deepest emotions and longings without violating a true reserve.'[21] Keble's poetic theory, and indeed his adherence to the Church of England, were premised on the importance of 'soothing' in religion, and this is one of many instances in which he advocates strictness of form, in poetics as in religious practice, for its ability simultaneously to express and to conceal emotion. The sonnet, he suggests, is ideal for these purposes. Along similar lines, C. S. Lewis, discussing sixteenth-century sonnet writers, argued that the impersonality created by the sonnet's formal structure meant that:

> A good sonnet … was like a good public prayer: the test is whether the congregation can 'join' and make it their own, not whether it provides interesting materials for the spiritual biography of the compiler. … The whole body of sonnet sequences is much more like an erotic liturgy than a series of erotic confidences.[22]

Both Keble and Lewis perceive the sonnet in liturgical terms, as a poetic form premised on repetitive, rhythmic structures with which the reader is expected to be familiar, and as a 'public' rather than a deeply personal form, one that may express the poet's feelings, yet inevitably does so with restraint and reserve.

[20] Ibid. 1: 310.
[21] John Keble, *Keble's Lectures on Poetry, 1832–41*, transl. E. K. Francis, 2 vols (Oxford, 1912), 2: 99, 101.
[22] C. S. Lewis, *English Literature of the Sixteenth Century, excluding Drama* (Oxford, 1954), 490–1.

This perception is borne out by the vast number of sonnets, and sonnet sequences, published on Church themes in the nineteenth century. Perhaps because the sonnet was also a form with relatively easy rules to learn, and because writing sonnets was in effect a standard exercise in middle- or upper-class Victorian education, virtually every Anglican clergyman seemed to try his hand at sonneteering in praise of the Church of England. The model here was William Wordsworth's *Ecclesiastical Sonnets* (first published in 1822 as *Ecclesiastical Sketches*, and revised and expanded in succeeding decades), a lengthy sequence reflecting Wordsworth's increasingly high church views through a review of the history of Anglicanism in England and beyond. Poets in the Tractarian or high church tradition could also be inspired by Isaac Williams's sonnet sequences, particularly his book-length sonnet sequence *The Altar; or Meditations in Verse on the Great Christian Sacrifice* (1847), a work worth revisiting if only for its importance as a potential influence on the greatest writer of religious sonnets in the period, Christina Rossetti, who was a keen admirer of Williams's writings. Ecclesiastical sonnets were a substantial if now largely forgotten part of the lively reassessment of the Church of England's past, present and future that was ongoing throughout the Victorian period.

Anglican sonnet-writers tended to use the traditional structures of the sonnet as a way of arguing for the significance of the traditional structures of the Church. Richard Mant, bishop of Down, Connor and Dromore from 1842, supplies a typical example in 'The Apostles' Liturgy', sonnet XXIII in his sequence 'Musings on the Church and her Services', appended to one of his prose works:

> If, by the rule Apostolick, to plead
> For all that God holds good, and deprecate
> What He holds evil; if with our estate
> Our brother man's to blend, and intercede
> For friend and foe, but chief that we may lead
> In peace, and rul'd by God's crown'd delegate,
> Lives pure and holy; if to dedicate
> Thanks for past good with pray'r for present need;
> Be welcome worship: *then content with thee,*
> *My country's Church, I join the voice to raise,*
> *Collect, and psalm inspir'd, and litany,*

And hymn of glory. Ever-varying phrase
God seeks not; pleas'd, when from corruption free,
And cloth'd with truth, his Church her homage pays.[23]

In the italicized passage, Mant proclaims the value of the liturgy in supporting morality, communal feeling, and 'lives pure and holy' under the king. What is notable here is that Mant particularly defends the use of repetition in worship – '[e]ver-varying phrase | God seeks not' – and the significance of participating in a repetitive tradition with others – 'I join the voice'. The poem sees Church services as a key component of national feeling, 'my country's Church'. The Church may have been under threat in the 1830s, as Mant's warning about corruption suggests, but its liturgy was still divinely sanctioned. Choosing a sonnet sequence to express these ideas enabled Mant to connect this repetitive and tightly structured poetic format to his argument about the value of repetition.

To take another instance, from the Anglo-Catholic (later Roman Catholic) poet Aubrey De Vere. In 'Prayer II', again part of an ecclesiastical sonnet sequence, De Vere uses the sonnet to argue once more for the importance of 'rightful worship':

Then what is prayer? Peruse that Gospel word:
Mark, learn, examine; it shall teach thee well.
That Word 'which was with God, and was God, Lord
Of life, the light of men!' in parable
Familiarly expounded; oracle
Pronouncing weal or woe; in precepts heard
With tears by the renouncing infidel;
In those meek orisons, whose pure accord
The human with the divine nature blends
So subtly that at once we recognize
Man's best emotions and the will of God.
With these sure guides, so studied that our ends
Be truth, not argument, our hearts shall rise
To heaven, in rightful worship, understood.[24]

---

[23] Richard Mant, *The Happiness of the Blessed* (Philadelphia, PA, 1833), 155 (italics added).
[24] Aubrey De Vere, XIV: 'Prayer II', in *A Song of Faith* (London, 1842), 136.

De Vere's final line specifically references Herbert's famous sonnet, 'Prayer (I)', which concludes:

> Church-bells beyond the stars heard, the soul's blood,
> The land of spices, something understood.[25]

But where Herbert's poem ends in glorious mystery, deliberately refusing to define what is 'understood' and how, De Vere responds to this by implying that understanding occurs through the act of 'rightful' (i.e. Anglican) worship. De Vere is not speaking about personal, informal prayer, but about the precepts and orisons of the Church, the only 'sure guides' to faith. As in Mant's sonnet, the poem argues for the importance of adhering to set forms of worship by using a set form itself.

III

Mant and De Vere are typical of hundreds of Anglican sonnet-writers in the Victorian period. Their sonnets, like Wordsworth's, reflect upon the persistence of a national religious and literary tradition and emphasize the ability of poetry to soothe and manage emotion, as a form both expressive and restrictive. What happens to this particular genre of religious verse after 'God's Funeral', at a point in the twentieth century when it cannot be assumed that readers are familiar with Church services or ritual, and that may, suggests David Jones, have seen 'the severing of the link between the English language and Christian iconography'?[26] There are no doubt many sonnets by lesser known Christian poets in the first half of the twentieth century, but the major 'modernist' poems we might most associate with reimaginings of Anglican and Roman Catholic forms, such as T. S. Eliot's *Ash Wednesday* (1930) or David Jones's *The Anathemata* (1952), do not deploy this form. W. H. Auden, who was deeply influenced by the Church of England and its liturgy and returned to churchgoing in later life, was a leading writer of sonnets, and the links between his use

---

[25] George Herbert, 'Prayer (I)', lines 13–14, in *The Complete English Poems*, ed. John Tobin (London, 2004), 46.

[26] David Jones, cited in Michael Symmons Roberts, 'Contemporary Poetry and Belief', in Peter Robinson, ed., *The Oxford Handbook of Contemporary British and Irish Poetry* (Oxford, 2013), 694–706, at 695.

of the form and his faith would repay detailed consideration.[27] John Betjeman, perhaps surprisingly, did not use the sonnet in his Anglican poetics, though another of the great mid- to late-century British religious poets, R. S. Thomas, did.[28] Although it is not overtly concerned with Church history and rituals, Thomas's outstanding sonnet, 'The Other', in which the speaker meditates on prayer while listening to the waves breaking against the shore, is arguably a vital reworking of Arnold's 'Dover Beach' and thus a twentieth-century reconsideration of Victorian doubt.[29]

Within the British poetic tradition, however, the twentieth-century sonnets which resonate most with the Victorian genre described above (and which might indeed be described as neo-Victorian in their intensive engagement with the culture of this period) are Geoffrey Hill's, particularly his sequence 'An Apology for the Revival of Christian Architecture in England'.[30] The religious sonnet does not disappear in the period prior to this sequence, from the turn of the century to the 1970s, but with Hill's poem its relationship to these Victorian predecessors comes sharply back to attention. Hill, one of Britain's most respected living poets, is known for his engagement with religious history and culture. The purpose of my discussion is not to assess his own beliefs or affiliations, about which he has been famously cagey. While a great many of his poems heavily reference the Anglican tradition in which he grew up, he declared in a 2011 interview that his status as an 'Anglican' poet was not of his making: 'There was a brief period when the Church of England took me up after I published *Tenebrae* but subsequent books have once more put a distance between us, to our mutual relief I believe.'[31] Hill's comments on his religious poetics often appear to locate his work in the grand

---

[27] Auden's sonnet sequences, such as 'The Quest', do not, however, reference the history and ritual of the Church in the same way as those discussed here. On Auden's religion and his poetics, see Arthur Kirsch, *Auden and Christianity* (New Haven, CT, 2005).

[28] On Betjeman's Anglican poetics, see Kevin J. Gardner, *Betjeman and the Anglican Imagination* (London, 2010).

[29] R. S. Thomas, 'The Other', first published in *Destinations* (1985), in his *Collected Poems* (London, 1993), 457.

[30] On Hill as neo-Victorian, see David Wheatley, '"Dispatched Dark Regions Far Afield and Farther": Contemporary Poetry and Victorianism', in Matthew Bevis, ed., *The Oxford Handbook to Victorian Poetry* (Oxford, 2013), 291–308.

[31] Interview with Jessica Campbell, *Oxford Student*, 26 May 2011, cited in Kathryn Murphy, 'Geoffrey Hill and Confession', in John Lyon and Peter McDonald, eds, *Geoffrey Hill: Essays on his Later Work* (Oxford, 2012), 127–42, at 135.

tradition of 'doubting' poets such as Hardy, with whom he has a clear affinity:

> If critics accuse me of evasiveness or the vice of nostalgia, or say that *I* seem incapable of grasping true religious experience, I would answer that the grasp of true religious experience is a privilege reserved for very few, and that one is trying to make lyrical poetry out of a much more common situation – the sense of *not* being able to grasp true religious experience.[32]

Yet, like Hardy, Hill has written many poems in which allusions to the Church and to ecclesiastical history, not least *formal* allusions, emphasize the doubtful survival of religion in the face of the poet's or his society's troubled relationship to 'true religious experience'.

'An Apology for the Revival of Christian Architecture in England' is perhaps the most notable of Hill's poems in relation to specifically Victorian religious and poetic experiences. First published as three sonnets in 1973, in a collection in homage to George Barker, the sequence was later revised and published in 1978, in *Tenebrae*, as a sequence of thirteen sonnets. The title repeats that of Augustus Pugin's architectural and theological treatise of 1843, part of Pugin's very successful campaign to revive medieval Gothic architecture, a cause taken up by the young men of Cambridge, in the Cambridge Camden Society, and in part by the Oxford Movement.[33] Hill originally incorporated an epigraph to the sequence from Benjamin Disraeli's religio-political novel *Sybil* (1845), indicating the link between the architectural revival and the political culture of Young England, with its passion for perceived medieval ideals of chivalry and community. As Hugh Haughton has noted, Hill's reprisal of Pugin's title 'might even tempt the modern reader into classifying its author as a deviously nostalgic revivalist of outmoded poetic and theological architecture': the 'architecture' referenced here is the architecture of the ecclesiastical sonnet sequence itself.[34] Hill's complex, ambiguous sonnets are consciously restrained, deliberately reserved about the poet's attitude

---

[32] Cited in Christopher Ricks, '*Tenebrae* and at-one-ment', in Peter Robinson, ed., *Geoffrey Hill: Essays on his Work* (Milton Keynes, 1985), 62–85, at 65.

[33] See James F. White, *The Cambridge Movement: The Ecclesiologists and the Gothic Revival* (Cambridge, 1962).

[34] Hugh Haughton, '"How fit a title …": Title and Authority in the Work of Geoffrey Hill', in Robinson, ed., *Geoffrey Hill*, 129–48, at 129.

towards the past, even when considering such vexed issues as British imperialism, in sonnets 5 and 6, 'A Short History of British India'. For this reason, 'An Apology' was the prime exhibit in a bitter critical debate about whether Hill's poetics should be seen as conservative and reactionary, and continues to attract intelligent commentary about his particular relationships to nostalgia and England's national past.[35]

The purpose of my reading here is not to enter into these debates, but to note briefly the affinity of Hill's work with the religious sonnet tradition that I have described. In the octet of 'Loss and Gain', for example, seventh in the sequence, he writes:

> Pitched high above the shallows of the sea
> lone bells in gritty belfries do not ring
> but coil a far and inward echoing
> out of the air that thrums. Enduringly,
>
> fuchsia-hedges fend between cliff and sky;
> brown stumps of headstones tamp into the ling
> the ruined and the ruinously strong.
> Platonic England grasps its tenantry[36]

Like each poem in the sequence, this has a strong (conventional) rhyme-scheme, though with more doubtful half-rhymes on 'sky / tenantry' and 'ling / strong', which could introduce a note of slight uncertainty. Beneath the enjambment and run-on sentences, a standard iambic pentameter beat is apparent. 'Pitched' implies both musical pitch and the height of a cliff-top steeple, with a potential recollection of the receding waves of 'Dover Beach' in 'shallows of the sea'. Church bells are one of the most constant sounds in Victorian religious verse, and one of the staple reminders of faith in the

---

[35] See Tom Paulin, 'The Case for Geoffrey Hill', *London Review of Books* 7 (4 April 1985), 13–14, and subsequent letters by Craig Raine, Martin Dodsworth, John Lucas and Eric Griffiths in response: 2 and 23 May, 6 and 20 June, 18 July, 1 August, 5 September, 3 October, 7 November, 15 December 1985; *London Review of Books* 8, 6 February 1986. These letters constitute a significant debate about the function of this sonnet sequence, and can be accessed by non-subscribers at: <http://www.lrb.co.uk/v07/n06/tom-paulin/the-case-for-geoffrey-hill>, accessed 21 October 2014. Andrew Michael Roberts includes a good discussion of 'An Apology', mentioning the *London Review of Books* dispute, in *Geoffrey Hill* (Tavistock, 2004), especially 50–8.

[36] Geoffrey Hill, 'Loss and Gain', lines 1–8, in idem, *Broken Hierarchies: Poems 1952–2012*, ed. Kenneth Haynes (Oxford, 2013), 128.

literature of unbelief. Here, the church bell is not part of a communal peal but alone; the grittiness of the belfry suggests a floor unswept, uncared for, and the bell is silenced. Yet the presence of these church bells charges the atmosphere, as their echoes (including memories of their literary use) electrify the air. 'Enduringly', its placement at the line-end meaning that it at first seems to follow on from 'thrums', instead stretches out over a blank space, a gap on the page, rendering this endurance more tentative. Surviving graves are 'stumps', suggesting that the words of commemoration they might have held are lost, yet they are fiercely rooted in the particular English soil, indicated by the dialect term 'ling' for heather. In 'ruinously strong', Hill suggests the power retained by such indicators of an apparently silenced Christian past. Not, of course, in entirely positive terms. If its effects continue to be 'ruinous', who or what is being ruined? The Coleridgean 'Platonic England', referenced in another epigraph to 'An Apology', is an imagined world that has not necessarily lost its grip on the England of the 1970s. Its tenants are the forgotten dead, but what 'Loss and Gain' suggests is that they might also include the poet.

In this poem, the Church and its history, embodied in the buildings that mark the English landscape, are inescapably present, although the poem presents itself as in an uneasy alliance with this tradition, in sharp contrast to the security of Victorian ecclesiastical sonnets. *Loss and Gain* is the title of John Henry Newman's mid-Victorian novel about a young man's painful conversion to Roman Catholicism, and the loss referred to there is the loss of the safety and familiarity of the Church of England. The allusion to Newman is particularly significant in the light of the strong connections between 'An Apology' and Geoffrey Hill's essay 'Redeeming the Time', from *The Lords of Limit*, which influentially argues that converts from Anglicanism to Roman Catholicism, such as Newman or Hopkins, experienced a loss of the 'familiar rhythms' of the Church.[37] Hill's sonnet sequence, published in the same year that 'Redeeming the Time' first appeared, reflects on whether twentieth-century Britain has also experienced this loss, and whether it might be seen as gain. But the formal and linguistic patterning of this poem suggest that even if the belfries are empty and silent and the buildings and gravestones of the Church decaying, it is impossible, for an English poet of Hill's background and education,

---

[37] Geoffrey Hill, 'Redeeming the Time', in idem, *The Lords of Limit* (London, 1984), 84–103, especially 89.

to escape the familiar rhythms of religious *poetry*. The vexed acceptance of these, and of their own inheritance (including the rhythms of the King James Bible and the Book of Common Prayer), represents both a loss of freedom and independence, and a valued heritage.

'Idylls of the King', the eleventh poem in Hill's sequence, takes its title from Tennyson's Arthurian epic of the same name, dedicated in its final version to the memory of Prince Albert and usually read as an effort to bolster British national and imperial pride. But the poem opens with a half-echo of the famous opening of a far less optimistic Tennyson poem, 'Tithonus', 'The woods decay, the woods decay and fall':[38]

> The pigeon purrs in the wood; the wood has gone;
> Dark leaves that flick to silver in the gust,
> And the marsh-orchids and the heron's nest,
> Goldgrimy shafts and pillars of the sun. (lines 1–4)

The poem seems to refer to the decay and fall of a natural setting, a place imbued with a sense of the holy, as the 'shafts and pillars' falling through the trees, and hinting at Church architecture, suggest. Like all the sonnets in the sequence, this keeps to a standard Petrarchan sonnet-structure while playing with half-rhymes and introducing what seems like a stanzaic structure, rather than fourteen lines in one block, so that the octet is divided into two four-line units and the sestet into two three-line units:

> 'O clap your hands' so that the dove takes flight,
> Bursts through the leaves with an untidy sound,
> Plunges its wings into the green twilight
>
> Above this long-sought and forsaken ground,
> The half-built ruins of the new estate,
> Warheads of mushrooms round the filter-pond. (lines 9–14)

The disconcerting lack of a final harmony in the dissonance between 'ground' and 'pond' is a particularly notable effect here, especially as it succeeds the deceptively firm rhymes of 'flight / twilight' and

---

[38] Tennyson, 'Tithonus', line 1, in *The Poems of Tennyson*, 3 vols, ed. Christopher Ricks (London, 1969), 2: 605.

'sound / ground'. Hill's rhymes, like his rhythms, mimic the gestures towards set forms that the sonnets adhere to but never fully embrace. 'O clap your hands', as critics have noted, is a direct quotation from the opening of Psalm 47 (KJV):

> O clap your hands, all ye people; shout unto God with a voice of triumph.
> For the LORD most high is terrible, he is a great King over all the earth.
> He shall subdue the people under us, and the nations under our feet.
> He shall choose our inheritance for us …

The 'King' of the title is thus implicitly both Tennyson's national hero, Arthur, and the powerful God of the Old Testament. What is at stake in this allusion? Hill's quotation marks, which are unusual in his many unsigned intertextual references, may signal that it is not so much an allusion to the prose of Psalm 47 as to Church music. 'O clap your hands' is the title of two famous anthems, by the sixteenth-century composer Orlando Gibbons and the late nineteenth / early twentieth-century Ralph Vaughan Williams. Hill, who sang in a church choir for much of his childhood, would undoubtedly be aware of this, and so the allusion draws into this sonnet about survivals of the past an echo of a communal voice, a moment of worship. But this then sends the metre of the poem into disorder. 'Bursts through the leaves with an untidy sound' is deliberately untidy, and resists falling into any even metrical pattern, while 'twilight', an uneasy word in terms of where the stress in English speech might fall, does not reach an expected full stop or provide a firm metrical close to these three lines. At this micro-level of form, the poem highlights the absence of familiar rhythms. The new estate may be a literal housing estate, and it is possible to read this sonnet in this light as resistant to a new soulless architecture and antithetical to modernity, as epitomized also by the 'mushrooms' that, in conjunction with 'warheads', recall the real presence of nuclear threat in the period in which Hill composed these poems. 'New estate', however, is also a reference to man's estate, always part ruined and part in progress, torn between an allegiance to history and to new developments. In this poem, and the whole sequence, gestures towards God and the language of the Bible and Church suggest moments of connection to the past that then fracture and dissipate.

There are no clear answers to the questions that Hill's sonnets raise, either about the poet's own investment in the past or about these investments on a national scale. The poems negotiate uneasily between a sense of forsakenness, and a feeling of being trapped by an inheritance neither chosen nor necessarily wanted. What is clear, however, is that Hill's sonnets continually, if obliquely, allude to the function of the sonnet as a vehicle for engaging with ecclesiastical 'history'. In part they revise this function, chronicling ruin and absence; in part, they are indicative of its survival. As Rowan Williams has observed with great perception in his consideration of Hill's later volumes, the poems they contain are 'not in any usual sense "religious poetry" – but poetry in which faith and loss are bound together; not a poetry about loss of faith, the deserted Arnoldian beach, but a poetry in which the language of faith is finally the only language appropriate for speaking honestly of loss'.[39]

This assessment might equally well apply to the final sonnet I want to consider, Carol Ann Duffy's 'Prayer'. No two poets could seem more antithetical than Duffy, the current poet laureate, whose work is very widely taught in schools across the UK and who has a firm commitment to broadening the remit and appeal of poetry; and Hill, whose consciously difficult poems deliberately eschew accessibility, and whose work is much discussed in the academy but relatively little known outside it. In fact, in early 2012 newspapers gleefully reported that Hill had dismissed Duffy's attitude towards popular poetics and heavily criticized one of her poems in a lecture at Oxford.[40] Unlike Hill, Duffy's poetry has very seldom attracted commentary on its religious themes. Yet this particular sonnet speaks strikingly to the English tradition identified in this essay, and deserves to be considered as a substantive negotiation with the poetry of faith and doubt. Duffy, more avowedly a sceptical and secular poet than Hill, grew up in the Roman Catholic Church and has acknowledged that she retains its influence:

> I think, now, I retain some of the motifs of all that and none of the feelings; faith, guilt, whatever. I do envy people who have a religious

---

[39] Rowan Williams, 'The Standing of Poetry: Geoffrey Hill's Quartet', in Lyon and McDonald, eds, *Geoffrey Hill*, 55–69, at 58.

[40] Alison Flood, 'Carol Ann Duffy is "wrong" about poetry, says Geoffrey Hill', *The Guardian*, 31 January 2012, online at: <http://www.theguardian.com/books/2012/jan/31/carol-ann-duffy-oxford-professory-poetry>, accessed 21 October 2014. Hill did also take this occasion to praise as well as critique Duffy's use of language.

faith – I can recall the comfort, the sense of a safety net. I still enjoy the sensuality of aspects of the Catholic religion and a lot of the imagery.[41]

Duffy positions herself here as a doubter, in the sense that, like every famous Victorian doubter, she is envious of those who still manage to believe. Several of her poems draw on 'aspects of the Catholic religion', among which the most notable – and the most steeped in religious allusion – is 'Prayer'.

Printed as the closing poem in Duffy's seminal 1993 collection, *Mean Time*, and thus on an end page by itself, 'Prayer' is a striking use of the sonnet form to engage with faith and its absence. Opening, 'Some days, although we cannot pray, a prayer | utters itself', the sonnet continues:

> Some nights, although we are faithless, the truth
> enters our hearts, that small familiar pain;
> then a man will stand stock-still, hearing his youth
> in the distant Latin chanting of a train.
>
> Pray for us now. Grade I piano scales
> console the lodger looking out across
> a Midlands town.[42]

Critical response to this poem has seen it as offering, as Deryn Rees-Jones puts it, 'some kind of secular consolation' in place of Christian consolation, or commented on its 'startlingly secular use' of 'specifically religious terms'.[43] Anna Smail, in a recent discussion, reads the poem in terms of its depiction of isolation, noting: 'As a mode of address, prayer is inherently problematic – a form of communication that typically persists without hope of reciprocation. Duffy's poem

---

[41] In an interview from 1991, cited in Deryn Rees-Jones, *Carol Ann Duffy*, 3rd edn (Tavistock, 2010), 46.

[42] Duffy, 'Prayer', lines 5–11, in eadem, *Selected Poems* (Harmondsworth, 1994), 127. A complete text of the poem is quoted in William Crawley's blog, *Will and Testament*, 'Carol Ann Duffy's "Prayer"', 2 May 2009, online at: <http://www.bbc.co.uk/blogs/legacy/ni/2009/05/carol_ann_duffys_prayer.html>, accessed 27 March 2015.

[43] Rees-Jones, *Carol Ann Duffy*, 48; Jane Thomas, '"The chant of magic words repeatedly": Gender as Linguistic Act in the Poetry of Carol Ann Duffy', in Angelica Michelis and Antony Rowland, eds, *The Poetry of Carol Ann Duffy: 'Choosing Tough Words'* (Manchester, 2003), 121–42, at 140.

further removes the possibility for dialogue by redefining prayer as a random instant of personal recognition and relief.'[44]

This is, however, a problematic way of seeing prayer in the context of faith: prayers may not be, technically, answered, but they are nonetheless received and assumed to be heard in the context of a reciprocal relationship. Duffy's sonnet, far from defining prayer as a 'random instant', connects it firmly to familiar rhythms, known, felt and viscerally affective. It is, of course, not possible for any poet in English to title a sonnet 'Prayer' without an immediate recollection of George Herbert, and Duffy's 'Prayer' is similarly engaged in an intense consideration of what constitutes prayer, what it is and what it might do for us, a consideration that, very much like Herbert and his nineteenth-century successors, always understands that a measured poem can in itself approximate a form of prayer.

'Prayer' quotes directly from the Roman Catholic liturgy in the phrase 'Pray for us now', words which are addressed to Mary in the 'Hail Mary': 'Pray for us sinners, now and in the hour of our death'. In the first twelve lines, Duffy's sonnet engages with ritual and repetition through this allusion, through its references to repetitive musical practice (the piano scales of a beginner), and through the 'distant Latin chanting of a train' which recalls communal traditional or pre-Vatican II Catholic worship. To combine the imagery of the mass with the (Victorian) industrial technology of the train, in a line which mimics the train's mechanical rhythm in its consonance and the regularity of its beat, in itself recalls Robert Browning's meditation on the rhythms of faith and the rhythms of train travel in his long poem on faith and unbelief, 'Christmas-Eve' (1855).[45] Duffy's poem positions these rhythms as a powerful nostalgic force, in juxtaposition to the grief of ageing, loss and death. It is particularly significant that the phrase 'and in the hour of our death' is an unspoken presence in line 9, haunted by the missing conclusion to one of the Catholic Church's best-known prayers. The symbolic significance of the lodger in a 'Midlands town', as day turns to night, may be to suggest temporariness and liminality as wider concerns in human existence, as well as to provide a suggestion of a bleak industrial, rather than natural, setting.

---

[44] Anna Smail, 'Audience and Awkwardness: Personal Poetry in Britain and New Zealand', in Robinson, ed., *Contemporary British and Irish Poetry*, 596–616, at 610–11.

[45] In *The Poems of Robert Browning*, ed. John Pettigrew and Thomas J. Collins, 2 vols (Harmondsworth, 1981), 1: 469.

Inasmuch as 'Prayer' offers 'secular' consolation, it does so through these rhythms, and most powerfully through the closing invocation of the shipping forecast, traditionally the last programme of the day before Radio 4 switches to the World Service:

Darkness outside. Inside, the radio's prayer –
Rockall. Malin. Dogger. Finisterre. (lines 13–14)

Yet in the light of the substantial tradition of religious sonnets that reflect upon rhythmic ritual and communal worship, and position their own formal commitments as part of this tradition, the question of the secular in this poem is vexed. The shipping forecast is designed to provide the latest weather information to those in peril on the sea, but for most listeners it serves as a reference to the dangers faced by others while they remain safely at home, secure from the 'darkness outside'. That is, the language of the broadcast, in popular culture, is emptied of direct and literal meaning and becomes instead the repetition of words that are soothing because of their familiarity from repeated listenings to this 'service'.

Rockall, Malin, Dogger and Finisterre (now renamed Fitzroy) are locations covered by the shipping forecast. Recalling Wordsworth and others' strong sense of the religious sonnet as directed to and about an imagined national as well as religious community, I would suggest that these references are likely to be familiar to British people of a certain age and perhaps class, and impregnable to readers from other traditions. The shipping forecast, Radio 4 and the BBC are British cultural possessions that help to define a sense of national community; the 'we' of Duffy's poem. Borrowing but expanding upon Smail's definition above, a radio broadcast such as the shipping forecast is also a form of prayer: it cannot expect direct reciprocation or dialogue, but it is assumed that someone is listening and responding. The individual listener, in turn, knows that he or she is part of a community engaged in the same ritual behaviour, consisting of listening to a variable but primarily set pattern of words, at a specific time each day. The poem, I think, questions whether this is in itself an act of prayer, of faith. There is a profound ambiguity about the unspecified 'truth' that 'enters our hearts' in the poem: language that borrows from the standard tropes of religious conversion. While I do not wish to propose a full counter-reading of the poem which would argue that it espouses religious belief, the conjunction of 'truth' with the phrase '*although* we are faithless' opens up potential for such a reading, as Duffy's sonnet flirts with the possibility of an unsought solicitation from the divine.

'Prayer' and the sonnets from Hill's 'An Apology for the Revival of Christian Architecture in England' are religious sonnets, part of the ecclesiastical sonnet tradition, not because of the poets' faith but in spite of their doubt. In one sense, the faith that they hold is faith in this literary tradition, as much as faith in God. There remains a great deal to say about how Christian poetics in Britain have developed in the twentieth and early twenty-first centuries, and how writers such as Duffy and Hill reflect upon their place in this tradition. What I suggest here, through analysis of one genre only, is that the concerns with faith and doubt which we tend to read as 'Victorian' do not disappear from more recent literature, and that placing the emphasis on doubt, in readings of twentieth-century as much as Victorian literature, does not always do justice to a literary work.

Doubt, our modern Crown of Thorns

Charles M. Stang*

Harvard Divinity School

This essay uses T. E. Lawrence's characterization of doubt as 'our modern crown of thorns', as an entrée into thinking through the coincidence of doubt and faith in the four canonical gospels. However much each of the gospels may wish to induce faith, it leaves its readers with the distinct impression that doubt, understood differently in each, cannot be fully dispelled. The gospels thereby testify to a lively, ancient appreciation for the irrepressibility of doubt. This essay then turns to the problem of scepticism in modern philosophy. In his work on Ludwig Wittgenstein, the American philosopher Stanley Cavell suggests that scepticism is a 'condition' of knowledge, both in the sense of something from which we suffer as if from a chronic illness, and in the sense of that which makes knowledge possible at all. The reader is invited to think of the dialectics of doubt and faith in a similar way, of doubt as the very condition of faith.

Let us ever more quickly
carry to the others
the certainty of doubt
Anna Kamienska, 'Emmaus'

But what then am I? A thinking thing. – And what is that? Something
that doubts …
René Descartes, *Meditations on First Philosophy*

I suspect I was invited to reflect on this theme because of something I wrote on the figure of 'Doubting Thomas' from the Gospel
of John.[1] I will have more to say about the apostle Thomas and his

* Harvard Divinity School, 45 Francis Avenue, Cambridge, MA 02138, USA. E-mail:
cstang@hds.harvard.edu.
  I wish to thank Michael Ennis for his indispensable research assistance at the very beginning and end of my writing this essay. I should also like to thank the editors of Studies
in Church History and the anonymous reviewers for their keen and critical comments,
which I have tried to answer and incorporate.
[1] Charles M. Stang, 'Doubting Thomas, Restaged: Between Athens and Berlin', *Harvard
Divinity Bulletin*, Winter/Spring 2013, 41–50.

Studies in Church History 52 (2016) 437–455   © Ecclesiastical History Society 2016
doi: 10.1017/stc.2015.25

legacy later, but I would like to begin with another Thomas, another doubting Thomas. Perhaps some readers will already have recognized the allusion in my title to Thomas Edward or T. E. Lawrence, better known to the world as 'Lawrence of Arabia'. After having allegedly lost the first draft of his monumental memoir and confession, *Seven Pillars of Wisdom*, at Reading Station in November 1919, he rewrote it at a feverish pitch over the course of the next three months at a flat on 14 Barton Street in Westminster.[2] In an early chapter of the final version, Lawrence says of the Arabs whose revolt against Ottoman rule he was helping to orchestrate that they 'despise[d] doubt, our modern crown of thorns'.[3] We may wonder whether Lawrence, as a representative of the British empire in what is arguably its last expansionist paroxysms, is not rather projecting onto the Arabs his own culture's failure to see the grey amidst the black and white, what he goes on to call the 'hesitating retinue of finer shades'.[4]

Be that as it may, I wish to use Lawrence's phrase as our entrée into doubt, its perils and its promises, ancient and modern. His words will carry us back to the four canonical gospels, and their different handling of that event about which Christ's disciples, then and now, have had the greatest doubts, namely the resurrection. We shall witness, and have occasion to question, the irrepressibility of doubt in the four gospels, the urgency with which doubt is felt and then quickly resolved, even banished – or allegedly so, since doubt seems never to let faith relax into certainty. Having brought this tension in the gospels to the fore, I will suggest that we step forward in time, and sideways in discipline, to consider an adjacent conversation in philosophy about the threat scepticism poses to our knowledge of the world and of ourselves – a classical 'problem' in the history of modern philosophy, at least since Descartes. Here I will have occasion to pay homage to one of my own teachers, Stanley Cavell, whose reframing of scepticism from a 'problem' to something more like a 'condition' will, I hope, raise anew the question of whether and how doubt really

---

[2] The so-called 'Oxford Text', completed in 1922, and recently made available in *Seven Pillars of Wisdom: The Complete 1922 Text*, ed. Jeremy Wilson (Salisbury, 2003).
[3] The so-called 'Subscribers' Edition', published as a private edition in 1926 by the George Doran Publishing Company, and then again more widely by Jonathan Cape in 1935: *Seven Pillars of Wisdom: A Triumph* (London, 1935), 38.
[4] Ibid.

poses a threat to faith. With that, we will return to Lawrence, that very modern – more precisely, modernist – apostle of doubt.

I am conscious of, even somewhat sensitive to, the fact that I am not playing the role of a historian, although contributing to a volume published by an esteemed society of ecclesiastical historians. In her 'Outline of [a] Presidential Theme', however, Frances Andrews lists a number of possible areas of discussion, at least two of which I see this essay as reflecting: first, the study of the Bible and its problematic passages; second, how doubt relates to scepticism.[5] If my inquiry into these two areas seems insufficiently historical, I find some consolation in Herodotus and the fact that his inaugural use of the term 'history' meant just that – an inquiry.[6]

So then, let us first inquire into the title: 'doubt, our modern crown of thorns'. What does it mean that Lawrence equates doubt with that crown of thorns the Roman tormentors mockingly placed on the head of Christ during his passion? To say that the crown is *ours* puts us in Christ's place in that passion, and suggests that our doubt is part of our drama of suffering and salvation. That the crown is *one of thorns* means that it is an instrument of mockery and torture, and thus suggests that doubt inflicts us with wounds.

The irony of this episode from the passion, of course, is that Christ does deserve a crown, but not the crown the Romans think he is claiming for himself as King of the Jews (INRI), and so not the crown they place on his brow in mockery of that claim.[7] In this regard the crown can serve as a synecdoche for the entire passion and crucifixion. For the Romans, the passion and crucifixion are merely the everyday execution of a troublemaker, which gives free licence for cruelty. For the canonical gospels, the passion and crucifixion are the very glory of Christ, the suffering and death to be overcome in resurrection.[8] And so, while the Romans may have placed the crown

---

[5] <http://www.history.ac.uk/ehsoc/event/2014–15-conferences-doubting-christianity-church-and-doubt>, accessed 27 July 2015.

[6] *Historia* from *historeō*, meaning 'to inquire': see Seth Benardete, *Herodotean Inquiries* (The Hague, 1969). I should also acknowledge that I have quite intentionally not buttressed my inquiry into doubt with notes and citations from the vast deposit of secondary literature on New Testament resurrection narratives or on the problem of scepticism in modern philosophy.

[7] The acronym title 'INRI' appears only in the Gospel of John; Jesus is crowned with thorns in the Gospels of Matthew, Luke and John, but not in the Gospel of Mark.

[8] I recognize that each of the four canonical gospels has a different interpretation of the passion, crucifixion, glorification and resurrection of Christ. When I write, 'For the

on Christ's head, it was not really theirs to give: it was always first and foremost Christ's own crown; it was, as it were, always already out of their hands.

By figuring doubt as our modern crown of thorns, Lawrence suggests, first, the coincidence of faith and doubt, and that such a coincidence is both our greatest torment and our greatest glory; and second, that this coincidence of faith and doubt is peculiarly modern. One way to test both suggestions is to revisit the ancient Christian gospels, and the heightened anxiety around faith and doubt that Christ's resurrection prompts.

* * *

I turn now to examine what we might call the dialectics of doubt and faith in each of the canonical gospels, beginning with the earliest of the four, the Gospel of Mark.[9] Many New Testament scholars will tell you that Mark's original narrative ends abruptly in the sixteenth chapter without any appearance from a risen Jesus.[10] Instead we read that on the first day of the week, three women go to Jesus's grave to anoint his body. They find instead an open tomb, and inside a young man 'dressed in a white robe' (16: 5). They are 'amazed', we read, and so he says to them, 'Do not be amazed; you seek Jesus of Nazareth, who was crucified. He has risen, he is not here; see the place where they laid him. But go, tell his disciples and Peter that he is going before you to Galilee; there you will see him, as he told you' (16: 6–7). The women flee the scene and, in fear and trembling, do not tell of what they saw.

A reader might very well have doubts about this narrative, first and foremost because it fails to explain how the story was ever circulated: it effectively calls itself into question by saying that the women 'said nothing to any one' (16: 8). Even if we were to glide over that gap, we are faced with precious little evidence of a resurrection, only a pair of testimonies. No one has in fact seen Jesus risen from the dead; an anonymous young man has told three women that Jesus has, and

---

canonical gospels', I might be accused of obscuring those differences. But here I am taking up a retrospective, harmonizing perspective on the four different narratives – the sort of harmonizing perspective I think Lawrence is also taking up.

[9] Unless otherwise noted, quotations from the New Testament follow the Revised Standard Version.

[10] For a judicious summary, see Joel Marcus, *Mark 8–16* (New Haven, CT, 2009), 1088–98.

they have told no one. Did they even believe him? Why should we? Sensing how deeply unsatisfactory this ending was, that the gospel read as if unfinished, two ancient readers chose to append their own endings to the narrative. The first, and shorter, version does little more than close the narrative gap by explaining that the three women did after all tell 'Peter and those with him all that they had been told'.

It is in the longer version (16: 9–20), however, that we must take an active interest, for here we see the persistence, the irrepressibility, of doubt. In a rather spare narrative, we read that the risen Jesus does in fact appear to Mary Magdalene, and that she does in fact tell the other disciples straight away. But they do not believe her, just as we might be inclined to doubt the young man's single testimony. The drama is heightened when Jesus next appears 'in another form' not to a single woman, but to two of his male disciples. They too straight away tell of what they saw, but again their fellows do not believe them. The tension surrounding doubt or 'unbelief' (*apistia*) is now mounting: how are the disciples, never mind we readers, ever to find faith? Jesus appears now a third time, this time to the eleven disciples (including the two who saw him before, but not including Mary). We read that 'he upbraided them for their unbelief and hardness of heart, because they had not believed those who saw him after he had risen' (16: 14). To reinforce his point, Jesus goes on to promise a reward and issue a threat: 'He who believes and is baptized will be saved; but he who does not believe will be condemned' (16: 16). This third and final appearance, together with the promise of salvation and the threat of condemnation, seems to do the trick: there is no further mention of the disciples' doubting. But neither is there any explicit mention of their all coming to believe, although this is what the author of this longer ending seems to imply in the final verse: 'And they went forth and preached everywhere, while the Lord worked with them and confirmed the message by the signs that attended it. Amen' (16: 20).

With this 'Amen' the author has sought to bring closure to this narrative and the unsettling persistence of doubt. But has he? His silence on whether or not the disciples believe that Jesus is risen from the dead is a crack through which doubt can slip back in. That crack widens as we wonder how it is that a third appearance should decisively resolve the matter. Everything we have read in this longer version suggests that those to whom Jesus appears believe instantly in what they see: that he is risen from the dead. But everything we have read also suggests that the natural reaction of those to whom he has not appeared, but who only hear (or, by extension, read) about his appearance from such witnesses, is to doubt. So how does either the final appearance to the eleven or their faith presume to resolve the lingering doubt for others, for us? How can their faith spill over to those others of us who were not witnesses? Is Jesus's promise of salvation and threat of condemnation supposed to secure the faith of those of us who are destined only to hear, or to read, about his appearances and his words?

Glenn Most's book *Doubting Thomas* was immensely helpful to me in my first attempt to write on that apostle, and has again proved helpful as I now return to doubt. He says of this longer version in the Gospel of Mark:

> the very excessiveness of the means of conviction that the interpola-tor's Jesus is compelled to deploy – his repeated appearances, his angry rebuke of the doubters, and his explicit linkage between disbelief and damnation – suggests just how virulent the malady of skepticism is that he must combat … For the doubt [the longer version] introduces seeps beyond its apparent intended function and goes on to infect a story that must be cleansed of it repeatedly, and by ever more drastic means.[11]

The Gospel of Matthew adorns Mark's rather spare narrative with dazzling details. The women are met at the tomb not by an anony-mous young man, but by an 'angel of the Lord' whose 'appearance was like lightning, and his raiment white as snow' (28: 2, 3). Having received much the same message as they did in Mark's Gospel, the women straight away run to tell the disciples. But before they can deliver their message to the doubtful disciples, they are stopped in their tracks by the risen Jesus himself, whose feet they take hold of and whom they worship. In Matthew's narrative, the women are not said to doubt the angel's words – how could they, for those words are straight away confirmed. Nor are the disciples said to doubt the women's testimony, as they did in Mark and as they will do again in Luke. The disciples' doubt seems to have been successfully ban-ished from the narrative, and the slow spread of faith secured. We

---

[11] Glenn Most, *Doubting Thomas* (Cambridge, MA, 2005), 18. I have found Most's readings of all four gospels fresh and insightful, and his influence can be seen in my own approach in this essay.

go on to read, however: 'Now the eleven disciples went to Galilee, to the mountain to which Jesus had directed them. And when they saw him they worshipped him; but some doubted' (28: 16–17). 'But some doubted.' Mind you, these eleven men now see the risen Jesus before them, back from the grave. This sort of 'autopsy' or 'seeing for oneself' was, for Mark's Gospel, always sufficient to secure the witnesses' faith. But now even the authority of autopsy begins to waver, for them certainly, and by extension for us. Matthew does not tell us who doubted, or why, what exactly they doubted, or whether or not they were ever convinced – only that they doubted. And so Matthew's narrative, which prior to this had seemed to succeed so well in banishing the disciples' doubt, reintroduces doubt – without explanation or resolution – in its very final verses.

Glenn Most remarks that 'the words "but some doubted" tear open a wound of disbelief in the body of a text whose sole aim is to induce belief in its readers'.[12] The obvious question, then, is 'why?' Why would the author of this gospel choose to reintroduce doubt at just this moment, seeming to sabotage his own efforts to banish it from the narrative? Most speculates that the most plausible answer is that the author had to do so, in other words, that there was a tradition, a memory, that some of Jesus' disciples had in fact doubted, even when seeing him risen from the dead.[13] According to Most, then, the author was obliged to include that tradition or risk jeopardizing his own credibility. In other words, in order that he might make his narrative believable, he had to put belief once again at risk from doubt.

This is, indeed, a plausible and insightful interpretation. But I wonder if we might do well to question the assumption that the 'sole aim' of the text in hand, Matthew's Gospel, 'is to induce belief in its readers'.[14] I would question that assumption by pressing gently on two embedded assumptions. First, the easier of the two: can we really say that any text, or for that matter any author, has a sole aim? Is this how a text or an author in fact intends, so singly? Second, what exactly do we mean when we say 'induce belief'? If we mean that to induce belief is to establish it in someone in such a way that it is certain, secure – as it were, without a shadow of a doubt – then it is hard to say that

---

[12] Ibid. 26.
[13] Ibid. 26–7.
[14] Ibid. 26.

this is the 'sole aim' of this text, since it quite obviously and explicitly reintroduces the shadow of doubt in its final verses. It would seem to me that in order to understand why the Gospel of Matthew includes the phrase 'but some doubted', we will have to jettison one or both of these prior assumptions. Perhaps the text does not have a sole aim, in which case it can be said to be at cross-purposes with itself: inducing belief, on the one hand, and undermining belief, on the other. Or perhaps the aim is singular, but singularly ambivalent, in which case to induce belief is not to banish doubt, but rather to acknowledge doubt's persistent purchase, even (perhaps especially) its inexplicable purchase, that the shadow or spectre of doubt arises for reasons we cannot finally know. To pinpoint doubt – who doubted, what they doubted, why they doubted – would then run the risk of participating in the fantasy that we could locate doubt, contain it, even excise it. Rather than a wound that tears open the body of this text, then, I would suggest that with the phrase 'but some doubted', doubt falls like a shadow over the whole of the narrative. But it is up to us to decide in any circumstance whether shadows are the source of an unknown threat or rather a refuge. Can shadow be shade?

A different shadow of doubt falls over our third gospel, Luke's. When the three women tell the eleven disciples of their experience at the tomb, they are again met with doubt: infamously in the verse, 'these words seemed to them an idle tale, and they did not believe them' (24: 11). Following the pattern of Mark's Gospel, Jesus next appears to two of the disciples, this time on the road to Emmaus. 'Their eyes were kept from recognizing him' (24: 16), we are told, until such time as he had heard their version of recent events, rebuked them for their foolishness, interpreted the Scriptures concerning recent events (including himself), and finally blessed and broken bread with them. Just as the scales fall from their eyes and they recognize him, but before he could eat any of the bread, he vanishes. The two hurry back to Jerusalem to tell the others.

From Mark's narrative we expect their fellows to meet them and their story with incredulity, but Jesus in fact intrudes into the narrative before the other disciples have had a chance to voice any doubts. Jesus appears before them, but in contrast to Mark and in complement to Matthew, the disciples have questions, doubts even, about who or what they are seeing. They are 'troubled' because they seem to think that Jesus is a ghost (*pneuma*), not a person brought back to life and with a body. Jesus tries to persuade them, saying: 'See my hands and my feet, that it is myself; handle me, and see; for a spirit (*pneuma*) has not flesh and bones as you see that I have' (24: 37–9). Note that the disciples do not accept Jesus's invitation to touch his body: this will be crucial for understanding Doubting Thomas in the Gospel of John. Instead, we read, 'they still disbelieved out of joy, and wondered' (24: 41). Here the shadow of doubt has a different opacity than it has in either Mark or Matthew: doubt follows not on despair, but on joy. What does it mean to doubt out of joy? We have seen how the gospel characters regularly doubt each other's testimony, and doubt whether the man they are seeing is in fact who he appears to be. In both cases the doubt seems oriented outward, towards either the witness whose testimony one is weighing or the appearance whose reality one is discerning. But to doubt out of joy is to doubt oneself, that is, to doubt one's own desires and their role in constructing one's testimony and perceptions. It is not another person's words or the external world that is called into question with this kind of doubt, but rather that complicated storm of desires I harbour within myself, that mix of desires frustrated or fulfilled that might cloud my judgement. In this case I am the object of my own doubt. This is the last mention of doubt in Luke: as in Matthew, it is never explicitly dispelled. Certainly the narrative ends triumphantly, with the disciples 'return[ing] to Jerusalem with great joy, … continually in the temple blessing God' (24: 52–3). But if we read the gospel closely, that great joy is tinged with doubt, that blessing of God with a questioning of oneself. By way of anticipation of Cavell, and in the words of Emerson, I ask: is that such an unhandsome condition?[15]

We have come now to our fourth and final gospel, John's, where the tension between faith and irrepressible doubt plays out in an exchange – unique to this gospel – between the risen Jesus and the apostle Thomas, who was also (so we are told) 'called the Twin' (20: 24). We catch up with the narrative just after Jesus's appearance to Mary Magdalene, who does not at first recognize him but mistakes him for the gardener. Only when he calls by her name do the scales fall from her eyes, and she bursts out, 'Rabboni!' Jesus quickly tells her, 'Do not touch me' – famously *noli me tangere* in Latin – 'for I have not yet ascended to the Father' (20: 16–17). How different from Matthew's Gospel, where Mary Magdalene and Mary the mother of Jesus not only touch Jesus, but 'take hold' (*ekratēsan*) of his feet; and

[15] See footnote 27.

how different, at first glance, from Jesus's invitation to Thomas, soon to come, to touch him.

The scene shifts from a single woman in a garden tomb to a group of men huddled in a dark room. Into this room Jesus suddenly comes, greeting the disciples, 'Peace be with you', and breathing the Spirit over them, and with it the right to retain or forgive sins (20: 19). And 'when he had said this, he showed them his hands and his side' (20: 20).[16] For reasons we are never told, Thomas is away at that hour. When he returns, his fellows share the unbelievable good news that they 'have seen the Lord' (20: 25). He replies, however, with a defiant conditional: 'Unless I see in his hands the print of the nails, and place my finger in the mark of the nails, and place my hand in his side, I will not believe' (20: 25). As in the Gospels of Mark and Matthew, the appearance of the risen Jesus seems sufficient to secure the belief of witnesses: none of those who were present have any doubts. But Thomas doubts, and in an entirely new register: he demands not only 'autopsy', that he see for himself, but that he confirm with his fingers that Jesus has a body bearing the wounds of his passion.

Jesus had shown the disciples his hands and his side (20: 20), and presumably the wounds therein. They must have told Thomas of these exact wounds, for he demands to see them: the wound in his side from the spear (19: 34), and the holes in his hands from the nails (19: 18), but not the holes in his feet, or the wounds from his scourging (19: 1), or even the wounds from the crown of thorns (19: 2). First, why are these particular wounds (the hands and the side) the grounds for belief, why this the condition to defeat his doubts? In other words, what is the relationship of faith (or doubt) to wounds, these wounds? Second, why does Thomas insist not only on seeing the wounds, but touching them? Touching seems a natural enough

---

[16] Compare with Luke 24: 38–43: 'And he said to them, "Why are you troubled, and why do questionings rise in your hearts? See my hands and my feet, that it is I myself; handle me, and see; for a spirit has not flesh and bones as you see that I have." And while they still disbelieved for joy, and wondered, he said to them, "Have you anything here to eat?" They gave him a piece of broiled fish, and he took it and ate before them.' The question here is whether the risen Jesus is showing his hands and feet so as to show the wounds from his crucifixion (but curiously, not the side wound), or whether he is offering up his body as proof of his corporeality. François Bovon favours the former interpretation: 'In the episode of the doubting Thomas, the fourth evangelist dots the "*i*". By looking and touching, the disciple wants to find the print of the nails (John 20: 25). Without explicitly saying so, Luke wants to achieve the same result. The feet and hands must bear the marks that reveal an identity': Bovon , *Luke*, 3: *A Commentary on the Gospel of Luke 19: 28 – 24: 53* (Minneapolis, MN, 2012), 391.

reaction when I am reunited with someone I thought I had lost, as Mary and Mary grasp Jesus's feet in Matthew's Gospel. But why does Thomas seem to want not only to touch the wounds, but through them to reach inside Jesus? In other words, what is the relationship of faith (or doubt) to touch, especially when Jesus has just told Mary, who has already believed, 'do not touch me'? And what is at stake for faith (or doubt) that the touch reach inside its object?

John's Gospel does not directly address these questions about the relationship of faith (or doubt) to wounds and touch. But it may be said to address these questions indirectly by raising and directly addressing others. The narrative skips ahead eight days, and finds the disciples still huddled in that dark room, but this time with Thomas present. The doors shut, Jesus nevertheless appears in their midst, addressing them all first, 'Peace be with you', before turning to Thomas. To the Twin he says, "'Put your finger here, and see my hands; and put out your hand, and place it in my side; do not be faithless, but believing." Thomas answered him, "My Lord and my God!"' (20: 27–8). There is so much to say about this brief exchange, but let me begin with what I will not say, at least not here. I will not rehearse what I have argued elsewhere – which, perhaps alone among the things I have written, I regard as indisputable – namely that the gospel is very clear that Thomas does not touch Jesus, as he is invited to do.[17] Why the exegetical tradition – both in text and image – has largely understood Thomas as having touched Jesus's wounds is a fascinating question, but one I will not take up now.[18]

One thread of my reading of this episode from John's Gospel, however, I must repeat here, as it bears directly on the dialectics of doubt and faith. The question is this: why, upon hearing Jesus's invitation to touch him, does Thomas immediately drop his defiant conditional and acclaim him 'My Lord and my God'? Here is how I answered that question in my last attempt to make sense of doubting Thomas:

> When Jesus appears to Thomas the week after he appeared to the others, he preemptively and freely offers Thomas precisely what Thomas had earlier insisted he would demand of his Lord. But the point is that

---

[17] See Stang, 'Doubting Thomas, Restaged', 42–4; also Most, *Doubting Thomas*, 51–73.
[18] Most addresses this question in the second half of his book, although he does not give due consideration to the Reformers' fairly consistent refusal of the patristic and thereafter Roman Catholic interpretation that Thomas did in fact touch Jesus.

it is precisely the *invitation* to touch him – not the act of touching him – that elicits Thomas's faithful acclamation, 'My Lord and my God!' Or, to be even more precise, it is the fact that his Lord's invitation includes the demand Thomas uttered privately, if defiantly, to his fellows behind closed doors a week before. Thus, the Gospel of John turns on its head Thomas's insistence that certain conditions be met before he recognizes Jesus: for it is Jesus who first recognizes Thomas and, moreover, recognizes him by knowing and naming his most ardent desire. Only by realizing that this episode is about Jesus's prior recognition of Thomas can we appreciate how it forms a diptych with Jesus's appearance to Mary in the garden. In both episodes, a human can only recognize a God if that God first recognizes him or her. If, indeed, this is the point of John's narrative, as I believe it is, then Thomas cannot have touched his risen Lord. When Jesus recognizes Thomas's ardent desire and defiant condition, when he names them in the free offer of his open body, the recognition and offer together fulfill a different desire Thomas had not known he had – namely, a desire to be known – and annul his defiant condition by rendering its satisfaction irrelevant.[19]

I stand by this reading; I do not wish to amend it here so much as put my weight on a different part of it. Thomas's acclamation is the only place in the New Testament where Jesus is called 'God', and to it he adds the possessive 'my': 'my God'. What could explain this startling acclamation if not the inversion I mentioned already, that the divine act at work here is not so much that a man has come back to life but that he has known his disciple's deepest desire, a desire hid most especially from the disciple himself, namely a desire to be known? In other words, to be fully known by another is to feel and so to exclaim the intimate presence of the divine.[20] It is the reach of the risen Jesus into Thomas that explains the exclamation, my God, that is, the God who knows my desires, who knows me. This, of course, only compounds the inversion, because whereas earlier Thomas demanded that he reach inside Jesus through his open wounds, he now discovers that he himself has already been breached, his desires already reached, and in their having been reached, reformed.

Jesus then asks a question: 'Have you believed because you have seen me?' Had he asked it of the other disciples, their answer would

[19] Stang, 'Doubting Thomas, Restaged', 43.
[20] This is in fact a pattern already well established in the Gospel of John, chs 1 and 4, in Jesus's exchanges with Nathanael and the Samaritan woman, respectively.

be 'yes'. But he does not ask it of them, only of Thomas. And Thomas's answer must be 'no, that is not why I have believed', because Thomas has believed, has overcome his doubts, not by any 'autopsy', not by seeing for himself, but by being completely seen and known by someone else.[21] Jesus's final line, 'Blessed are those who have not seen and yet believe' (20: 29), is often understood to signal to the readers of this gospel that they are blessed if they believe without seeing, that is, if their faith in the risen Jesus is not conditioned on seeing him. This serves as something of a rebuke to the other disciples, and suggests that the readers stand at something of an advantage: they can believe without seeing. But what might make readers believe? What might silence their natural doubts? This verse suggests that the gospel wishes the reader to be so convinced by its own narrative that it induces faith without sight, never mind touch.[22] I wonder, though, if a reader of this gospel might draw a different lesson from this narrative. If Thomas believes because he is known, because he is known from within, because his very own desires are known, then might a reader reasonably expect that this is the proper condition for belief? Might a reader expect to be known in just the way Thomas was, named in just the way Mary was? If this is right, then the reader waits on the fulfilment of this condition, waits to be known and named, and so waits on faith. I would suggest, then, that while John's Gospel does not leave the reader's faith undone by doubt, it does leave the reader waiting on faith, weighing his doubts, waiting for those doubts to be named and known, reached and reformed. It puts the reader in Thomas's place for those eight long days in darkness, waiting defiantly with his desires and demands, waiting to have them rendered irrelevant.

---

[21] Some translations treat this as a statement rather than a question. There is no way to be certain either way from the Greek itself, without the interrogative particle *ara* or the existence of a question mark (which was not introduced into the manuscript tradition until much later). The predominant tradition treats it as a question, based largely on medieval manuscripts. My interpretation requires that we understand it as a question, because the only answer that makes sense, from Thomas's perspective at least, is 'no': he has believed not because he has seen and known, but because he has been seen and known. For a discussion of this verse as a statement or a question, see C. K. Barrett, *The Gospel according to St John: An Introduction with Commentary and Notes on the Greek Text* (London, 1955), 573.

[22] As it more or less states in the next two verses: 'Now Jesus did many other signs in the presence of the disciples, which are not written in this book; but these are written that you may believe that Jesus is the Christ, the Son of God, and that believing you may have life in his name' (20: 30–1).

My reading of the gospels is that however much they may wish to induce faith in their readers, they leave their readers with an understanding of faith dappled with doubt, and doubt of different kinds. The Gospel of Mark: is doubt a threat that cannot be fully protected against, and thus a source of anxiety? And how do we, can we, should we live with this anxiety? The Gospel of Matthew: is doubt a shadow that falls over us, with no obvious whence or whither? And do we, can we, should we experience this shadow as shade? The Gospel of Luke: is doubt less about an external object and more about our own desires, frustrated and fulfilled, and their role in shaping our faith? And do we, can we, should we doubt out of joy, bless God while questioning ourselves? Finally, the Gospel of John: is doubt a defiant conditional we place between faith and ourselves? And how do we, can we, should we live waiting for that doubt to be named and known, reached and so reformed? These are the questions that make up the dialectics of faith and doubt in the four gospels. They seem ample evidence of a lively, ancient appreciation for the irrepressibility of doubt, for the coincidence of faith and doubt.

∗ ∗ ∗

As promised, I propose that we now step forward in time, and sideways in discipline, in order to consider this ancient dialectic of faith and doubt from the perspective of a perennial problem in modern philosophy, namely the problem of scepticism. Ever since Descartes sat by a warm fire and began to doubt systematically the existence of everything around him, including himself, modern philosophers have been much agitated by scepticism's challenge to our knowledge of the external world, and our knowledge of what is often called 'other minds'.[23] To put it simply, the problem has not been solved. I wish to invoke a teacher of mine, Stanley Cavell, a name that may not be well known among contemporary ecclesiastical historians. Cavell is an American philosopher who has spent nearly his entire career at Harvard University, and under whom I studied as an undergraduate.

One of Cavell's singular contributions is his insistence that scepticism is not a problem admitting of a solution as much as a chronic condition requiring care. I do not think he would regard this as his own contribution per se, but rather that of the early

---

[23] See the first of Descartes' six *Meditationes de prima philosophia*, first published in 1641.

twentieth-century Viennese philosopher, Ludwig Wittgenstein, especially the later Wittgenstein of the *Philosophical Investigations*. Vexed by philosophy's inability to answer the sceptic's question, some early twentieth-century philosophers responded by arguing that the question itself was meaningless, that the sceptic's calling knowledge into radical doubt is merely a perversion of language, nearly beyond recognition. By attending to how language actually works, these 'ordinary language philosophers' sought to cut the sceptic's question off at the pass, to refuse it the purchase it claimed to have. Rather than argue for or against scepticism, they thought it deserved no such hearing at court. One of Cavell's own teachers, J. L. Austin, was among those who regarded scepticism as resulting from confusion in language.

Wittgenstein is sometimes thought to have believed the same, that scepticism arises out of philosophy's misuse of our words. And so if we would but use our words properly, such questions would not arise. For this reason some credit (or debit) Wittgenstein with ending philosophy. But Cavell reads Wittgenstein differently, that on the contrary there is a deep 'truth of skepticism': its truth is, in Cavell's words, 'an experience or sense that one may know *nothing* about the real world'.[24] This is not a doubt about this or that, but instead a profound sense of alienation from one's own words, and from one's own world: I do not know it, I do not even know myself. If such scepticism results from confusion, from misuse of our words, from the gap between saying and meaning, then, Cavell insists, it is an entirely 'natural' result of our being the sorts of 'creature[s] complicated or burdened enough to possess language at all'.[25] What we call 'philosophy' is then the acute articulation of this natural result, of this chronic condition of being language users. By putting this experience of alienation (from words) into words, philosophy diagnoses our condition, names it. Philosophy does not err by diagnosing our condition, but by misdiagnosing it as something that can be cured, as if our alienation were truly alien rather than constitutive. When Wittgenstein says in the *Philosophical Investigations* that we 'bring words back from their metaphysical to their everyday use', Cavell takes him to mean that we return scepticism from being a metaphysical problem allegedly begging solution to it being an everyday condition, by which

---

[24] Stanley Cavell, *The Claim of Reason: Wittgenstein, Skepticism, Morality, and Tragedy* (New York, 1979), 7, 140.
[25] Ibid.

is meant not an experience we have every day, but an experience to which we are open because of what we do every day: we live.[26]

I am reminded of a line from one of Cavell's favourite plays, Samuel Beckett's *Endgame*: 'You're on earth; there's no cure for that!'[27] This is Cavell's understanding of scepticism: there is no 'cure', no 'escape', no answer to scepticism; instead, there is a 'response', even a 'therapy'.[28] The problem with some ordinary language philosophy, in this view, is that it fails to let the severity of the sceptic's situation take hold, and thus in effect denies the condition both in symptom and in root; the problem with traditional philosophy, in this view, is that while it recognizes the severity of the sceptic's situation, by looking for a cure it fails to recognize it as a chronic condition requiring care, or therapy. Cavell understood Wittgenstein to be one of philosophy's great therapists, and his *Philosophical Investigations* a text designed to diagnose and treat someone gifted with the affliction of language.

Why have I cited Cavell and his contribution in this discussion of the dialectics of doubt and faith? Just as doubt is traditionally understood as inimical to faith, as threatening it, so scepticism is traditionally understood as a threat to our knowledge of the world. With Wittgenstein's help, Cavell invites us to consider whether instead scepticism might be a condition of knowledge, a 'condition' both in the sense of something from which we suffer as if from a chronic illness, and in the sense of that which makes knowledge possible at all. In other words, knowledge is constituted by its 'vulnerability' to scepticism.[29] To pretend otherwise, to disown scepticism, is in fact, for Cavell, to disown knowledge, and so to disown ourselves as those creatures conditioned to know, that is, to share a language in which we strive (and fail) to mean what we say.[30]

---

[26] 'When philosophers use a word—"knowledge", "being", "object", "I", "proposition", "name"—and try to grasp the essence of the thing, one must always ask oneself: is the word ever actually used in this way in the language-game which is its original home?— What we do is to bring words back from their metaphysical to their everyday use': Ludwig Wittgenstein, *Philosophical Investigations*, transl. G. E. M. Anscombe (2nd edn, Oxford, 1958), §116.

[27] As cited in Stanley Cavell, *Must we Mean what we Say?* (Cambridge, 1976), xx.

[28] Ibid.

[29] Ibid. xxi.

[30] I have borrowed this phrase from Cavell's book on Shakespeare and scepticism, *Disowning Knowledge: In Six Plays of Shakespeare* (Cambridge, 1987).

What if we were to view doubt and faith along similar lines? What would it mean to treat doubt not as an illness to be cured, a cancer to be cut out, but as a condition of faith, as both a chronic condition needing ongoing care and the very condition that makes faith possible at all? What would it mean to understand faith as constituted (rather than threatened) by its vulnerability to doubt? What strikes me is that these are questions pressed upon me, made urgent, both by ancient gospels and their diverse witness to a tense dialectic of doubt and faith, doubt's irrepressible purchase on faith, and by very modern debates about scepticism and the conditions of knowledge. Ralph Waldo Emerson once wrote: 'I take the evanescence and lubricity of all objects, which lets them slip through our fingers when we clutch hardest, to be the most unhandsome part of our condition.' Cavell entitled his book on Emerson, for which this quotation is the epigraph, *Conditions Handsome and Unhandsome.*[31] In doing so he questions just how unhandsome this condition is: if unhandsome to clutch and so let slip, then perhaps handsome to let go and so hold fast. I can imagine Doubting Thomas saying something like that.

* * *

Let us return to our ancient apostle: we could say that in the Gospel of John the character of Doubting Thomas shifts the problem of doubt from a problem of our knowing something to a problem of our being known by something. One of the dangers in such a reading, however, is the temptation to see Thomas as having solved once and for all the problem of doubt, at least for himself, when he is known in that moment and acclaims the risen Jesus 'my Lord and my God'. If we readers are put in the place of Thomas, and so left waiting to be known, we wait on a moment of being known, such that we can dispel our defiant doubt, and attain an unblemished faith. But what is this moment of being known and the attendant, instantaneous acclamation within an entire lifetime? Is it enough to have been known once? Do we not change? Do our desires and demands not shift under us, within us, from moment to moment, from day to day, from year to year? What good is it if I was once known, if I am now unknown?

---

[31] The quote is from Emerson's essay 'Experience', and serves as the epigraph to Cavell's 1988 Carus Lectures, *Conditions Handsome and Unhandsome: The Constitution of Emersonian Perfectionism* (Chicago, IL, 1990).

The gospel does not narrate Thomas's life, whether and how his faith continues to be constituted by a vulnerability to doubt. Here is where Cavell's handling of scepticism as a condition seems urgently pertinent. For Cavell, following Wittgenstein, the very condition of knowledge is scepticism. There are inalienable moments of alienation from knowledge, and the issue at hand is not so much how we solve the problem as how we live from moment to moment, such that our life is open and responsive to scepticism. Our challenge is not to secure our certain knowledge, but to be faithful to the condition of our knowledge, responsive to our vulnerability, such that when the question of scepticism comes we do not deny its purchase or existence, but acknowledge it and work to lead it home. If Cavell is right, then Thomas and (more importantly) we readers of John's Gospel are waiting on the dissolution of doubt, on a moment of being known that is crowned with a pious acclamation. But that moment is not invulnerable, which is to say it is open, open to the future, when we will have changed, and when we once again wish to be named and known, reached and reformed.

Speaking of ancient Thomas, we should return in closing to his modern twin. I suggested earlier that T. E. Lawrence's phrase – 'doubt, our modern crown of thorns' – invites us to ponder the relationship of doubt and faith, of doubt as both our greatest torment and our greatest glory: a condition handsome and unhandsome. In an earlier version of *Seven Pillars of Wisdom*, the so-called Oxford Text, the line read differently: 'doubt, that modern crown of thorns which some western thinkers wore with such a grace'.[32] Following his ancient apostolic namesake, and anticipating Wittgenstein and Cavell, Lawrence could be said to define faith as a life crowned with doubt, worn gracefully. To disown doubt, then, is faithless and disgraceful. Whereas John's Gospel does not narrate the life of Doubting Thomas, Lawrence narrates his own, one of doubt-riddled faith: from *Seven Pillars of Wisdom*'s tortured exploration of his doubts about everything, chiefly himself, to his later memoirs of enlisted life in the service, entitled *The Mint*, where Lawrence attempts to find a faith in fraternity. Few people know that when Lawrence died, untimely, from a motorcycle accident, he was planning a new book, something that would incorporate *The Mint* but reframe it, retitle it: a *Confession*

[32] Lawrence, *Seven Pillars of Wisdom*, ed. Wilson, 18.

of Faith. We have some hints as to what this projected book would have looked like. The final sentence of the book it was meant to incorporate reads: 'I can't write "Finis" to this book, while I am still serving. I hope, sometimes, that I will never write it.'[33] Whatever faith was for Lawrence, then, and whatever its relationship to doubt, it was something to which he hoped we would never write, 'Finis' ('conclusion' or 'end'). To that I say, 'Amen'.

---

[33] T. E. Lawrence, *'The Mint' and later Writings about Service Life* (Salisbury, 2009), xxx.

New to Cambridge in 2016

Studies in Church History

Published for the Ecclesiastical History Society, Cambridge

STUDIES IN
CHURCH HISTORY

VOLUME 48

THE CHURCH
AND LITERATURE

EDITED BY PETER CLARKE
and CHARLOTTE METHUEN

For the Ecclesiastical History Society
BOYDELL & BREWER

Editors
Charlotte Methuen, *University of Glasgow, UK*
Andrew Spicer, *Oxford Brookes University, UK*

Studies in Church History is an annually published series comprising papers and communications delivered at the Ecclesiastical History Society's conferences. Each volume presents important new work, by established as well as new scholars, on a particular theme. Volumes are available to members of the society at a reduced price.

Studies in Church History
is available online at:
http://journals.cambridge.org/stc

**To subscribe contact
Customer Services**

in Cambridge:
Phone +44 (0)1223 326070
Fax +44 (0)1223 325150
Email journals@cambridge.org

in New York:
Phone +1 (845) 353 7500
Fax +1 (845) 353 4141
Email
subscriptions_newyork@cambridge.org

Free email alerts
Keep up-to-date with new
material – sign up at
journals.cambridge.org/stc-alerts

For free online content visit:
http://journals.cambridge.org/stc